Tammy Fox

Red Hat® Enterprise Linux® 5 Administration

UNLEASHED

800 East 96th Street, Indianapolis, Indiana 46240 USA

Red Hat Enterprise Linux 5 Administration Unleashed

ISBN-10: 0-672-32892-5

ISBN-13: 978-0-6723-2892-3

Library of Congress Catalog Card Number: 2005910113

Printed in the United States of America

First Printing: April 2007

10 09 08 07 4 3 2 1

Trademarks

Warning and Disclaimer

Bulk Sales

Sams Publishing offers excellent discounts on this book when ordered in quantity for bulk purchases or special sales. For more information, please contact

U.S. Corporate and Government Sales
1-800-382-3419
corpsales@pearsontechgroup.com

For sales outside of the U.S., please contact

International Sales
international@pearsoned.com

Acquisitions Editor
Mark Taber

Development Editor
Songlin Qiu

Managing Editor
Patrick Kanouse

Senior Project Editor
San Dee Phillips

Copy Editor
Katherin Bidwell

Indexer
Ken Johnson

Proofreader
Paula Lowell

Technical Editor
Brock Organ

Publishing Coordinator
Vanessa Evans

Book Designer
Gary Adair

Page Layout
TnT Design, Inc.

Contents at a Glance

Table of Contents

About the Author

Tammy Fox has been using Linux for programming, writing, system administration, and all day-to-day computer tasks for more than 10 years. From 2000 until 2005, she worked for Red Hat as a technical writer, team lead, programmer, build script maintainer, magazine editor, and marketing project manager. During her time in documentation, she created a new manual, the *Red Hat Linux Customization Guide*, which eventually became the *Red Hat Enterprise Linux System Administration Guide*. She also wrote and contributed to the Red Hat configuration tools, including writing Red Hat Logviewer. Before joining Red Hat, Tammy co-wrote and taught Linux integration and performance classes for a leading computer manufacturer. She has also been a computer consultant for leading computer communication companies.

Tammy has founded three efforts to continue the education of Linux users. She is the founding editor of *Red Hat Magazine*, which continues to be an online publication. She is also the founding leader of the Fedora Docs Project, acting as the organizer, a writer, and an editor. And she continues to provide free online content for new Linux users with her website www.linuxheadquarters.com, which was established with her husband in 2000.

Dedication

To my family.

For my husband, Brent, who has always supported my dreams and reminded me to dream big.

For my children who never cease to amaze me and remind me everyday what life is about.

Acknowledgments

This book would not have been possible without the people at Pearson. Thanks to Linda Harrison, my original acquisitions editor, and to Mark Taber for taking over half way through the book. Thanks to Songlin Qiu for reading multiple revisions of my book as the development editor. Thanks to Brock Organ for providing excellent technical editing skills to my book to make it even better.

Thanks to Red Hat for allowing me to work at such a remarkable company. I will always feel like I was part of something that changed the computer industry for the better. Special thanks to all the wonderful people I worked with at Red Hat. I had the privilege of working with some exceptional people, who are passionate about what they do. The Red Hat culture inspired me to always challenge myself and never accept the status quo.

Finally, thanks to the worldwide open source community: all the users, developers, testers, advocates, and supporters. Linux continues to improve because of everyone's efforts.

We Want to Hear from You!

As the reader of this book, *you* are our most important critic and commentator. We value your opinion and want to know what we're doing right, what we could do better, what areas you'd like to see us publish in, and any other words of wisdom you're willing to pass our way.

You can email or write me directly to let me know what you did or didn't like about this book—as well as what we can do to make our books stronger.

Please note that I cannot help you with technical problems related to the topic of this book, and that due to the high volume of mail I receive, I might not be able to reply to every message.

When you write, please be sure to include this book's title and author as well as your name and phone or email address. I will carefully review your comments and share them with the author and editors who worked on the book.

Email: opensource@samspublishing.com

Mail: Mark Taber
Associate Publisher
Sams Publishing
800 East 96th Street
Indianapolis, IN 46240 USA

Reader Services

Visit our website and register this book at www.samspublishing.com/register for convenient access to any updates, downloads, or errata that might be available for this book.

Foreword

Red Hat Enterprise Linux 5 is more a platform of technologies than an operating system. With this release, Red Hat has focused on integrating a range of open source technologies to deliver true server and storage virtualization.

The challenge for the intermediate-to-advanced Linux user now is learning how to harness the power of virtualization. Whether your goal is to learn about server consolidation, hardware abstraction, or resource management, Tammy has provided a concise step-by-step guide in Appendix B, "Creating Virtual Machines." This includes how to use the new graphical utility, Virt-Manager, for administering all aspects of the virtualized system or libvirt and virsh, the new library and command-line utility, to implement your own management tools.

Security remains a cornerstone of Red Hat offerings, and Tammy has done a great job of explaining the background and history of the Linux Audit System and Security Enhanced Linux (SELinux). You will notice how Tammy has used the theory to bring a better understanding to the day-to-day commands that you need to ensure you stay on top of system security.

Software management of Red Hat Enterprise Linux has also evolved with the introduction of yum. You may already be familiar with yum from your use of Fedora or other Linux distributions, but of great value in this book is Tammy's excellent overview of this new utility and importantly how to use yum and its new functionality with your Red Hat Network subscriptions.

For me though I think the real benefit of Tammy's new book is that being part of the Unleashed series it builds upon a solid foundation of comprehensive information built up over the years, covering everything from installation to backups.

Tammy's fresh approach to presenting information in a concise, easy to follow way makes it a great technical library asset for the general user and system administrator alike. Having had the pleasure of working with Tammy for a number of years at Red Hat, it was an honor to have the opportunity of writing this foreword for her new book. Tammy's experience both with Red Hat Enterprise Linux and technical writing means that you are making a great decision purchasing this book.

Paul Gampe

Vice President, Engineering Services and Operations

Red Hat, Inc.

Introduction

So you've decided to buy my book (or you are at least intrigued enough to read the introduction). This book is a comprehensive guide to Red Hat Enterprise Linux 5, specifically geared at system administrators.

Read on to find out what Red Hat Enterprise Linux is, why this book is different than all the other Linux books out there, who the target audience is, and what type of information can be found in it.

I hope reading this book helps you understand Linux administration more. If it allows you to be better informed of the Linux technology before making an important decision, helps you develop a solution to an administrative problem, or serves as a reference for your day-to-day tasks, I have accomplished my goal in writing this book—providing concise, easy-to-read technical content that educates administrators and empowers them to do their job with ease and confidence. Use this book to explore all the possible administrative solutions available in Red Hat Enterprise Linux 5 and determine which ones are best for you and your organization, whether your organization consists of just you or thousands of users.

What Is Red Hat Enterprise Linux?

Starting in 2001, Red Hat, Inc. began offering Red Hat Enterprise Linux in addition to their original consumer operating system, Red Hat Linux. In 2003, Red Hat started the Fedora Project to release the Fedora Core operating system instead of Red Hat Linux.

The Fedora Project progresses at a rapid rate, releasing a new version of Fedora every four to six months. This allows new technologies to be tested by millions of users, which in turn decreases the amount of time it takes for these technologies to stabilize into production-ready software. Each release of Red Hat Enterprise Linux is based on a Fedora operating system release. The kernel and all of the other software in Red Hat Enterprise Linux are specifically configured and tested for enterprise-level usage.

Both Red Hat Enterprise Linux and Fedora are based on open source software developed by the open source community, some of whom are members of the Red Hat engineering team. The term *open source* means that the programming code is freely available to anyone and that anyone can submit code to an existing open source project as long as the code stays open source. New projects or programs can be created based on a different open source project or program. Open source developers live all over the world, and they collaborate on projects every day together.

Key Features of This Book

Unlike most Linux books, this book gives and discusses examples for administering one or thousands of systems at the same time. It provides guidelines for writing procedures and policies such as backup procedures and user management policies so that they are scalable for future growth. It also provides details about the new features of Red Hat Enterprise Linux 5 including Virtualization for setting up virtual machines in which multiple operating systems are run on the same physical hardware, Security-Enhanced Linux and ExecShield for protecting against common forms of intrusion, and Kdump for capturing kernel dump information for further analysis.

64-bit processors are quickly becoming the new standard in computing power. This book recognizes this shift and provides specific instructions for 32-bit and 64-bit processors, including a chapter dedicated to how Red Hat Enterprise Linux supports 64-bit, multi-core, and Hyper-Threading Technology processors.

This book is written in a concise writing style to allow the reader to find the information he is looking for as quickly as possible. This is especially important when an administrator needs to recover from a system failure. Step-by-step procedures are given whenever possible so the reader can read it once and then quickly bookmark the reference content so they can go back to it time and time again.

For potential Red Hat Enterprise Linux customers, this book demonstrates why Red Hat Enterprise Linux is an enterprise operating system. For existing Red Hat Enterprise Linux subscribers, it offers insight into the new technologies available since version 4. For the seasoned administrator, it helps develop a deeper insight into system optimization and task automation.

After reading this book, the reader will have a deeper knowledge of what tools and resources are available for Red Hat Enterprise Linux 5. For example, many of the system performance monitoring and tuning tools are not well documented or not documented at all because of their recent arrival to Red Hat's enterprise operating system. They will serve as invaluable tools for a Linux administrator.

Who Should Read This Book

This book is dedicated to helping administrators who manage networks of all sizes. The core audience is Linux system administrators for small-to-medium businesses all the way up to large corporations. The concepts explained in this book can be scaled for a few hundred or a few thousand systems . Other intended readers include decision makers interested in an overview of Red Hat's enterprise offerings and anyone curious about what Linux can do.

Use this book as a concise reference for all the administration tools available in Red Hat Enterprise Linux. Knowing what tools and resources are available is half the battle of becoming an efficient, flexible system administrator. This book saves administrators time by giving them the foundation they need to learn more details about a particular concept or application as well as assists them in delivering their IT solutions.

How This Book Is Organized

This book is divided into six parts:

Part I: Installation and Configuration

Part II: Operating System Core Concepts

Part III: System Administration

Part IV: Network Services

Part V: Monitoring and Tuning

Part VI: Security

Part I, "Installation and Configuration," discusses how to install Red Hat Enterprise Linux 5 on a single system or multiple systems at the same time using a set of preselected installation options in a kickstart script. After installation, this part guides you through post-installation configuration from logging in to the system to adding boot parameters. The part ends with a chapter on updating your systems with the latest, most secure software sets.

Before detailing system administration practices, important operating system concepts must be understood or reviewed. The concepts in the Part II, "Operating System Core Concepts," will prove beneficial to you as you read and study the remainder of this book.

Part III, "System Administration," is dedicated to common administrative tasks and how to perform them as efficiently as possible. After guiding you through user and group creation, deletion, and maintenance, it outlines best practices to consider when starting your user database. For large organizations such as enterprise-level companies, starting with solid, scalable rules for user names, home directory locations, and more will prove useful as the organization expands and as users come and go. Backup and administration scripts must be written and customized for your needs, and this part discusses backup concepts, the Amanda backup program in Red Hat Enterprise Linux, the basics of writing scripts, and how to automate the execution of scripts on Linux.

Network services are what differentiate server and client systems. Part IV, "Network Services," teaches administrators how to configure network services for tasks such as user authentication and file sharing. Each chapter in this part is organized in a similar format so you can quickly find the information you are looking for.

System administrators are constantly monitoring multiple systems and learning new ways to tune their systems to accommodate their users. Discovering problems before the system goes down is key to avoiding downtime. Part V, "Monitoring and Tuning," explores the multitude of Linux utilities available for monitoring and tuning. This part is divided into three chapters, or three subcategories of monitoring and tuning applications: system resources, the kernel, and applications.

Finally, Part VI, "Security," introduces a relatively new security-prevention feature in Red Hat Enterprise Linux called Security-Enhanced Linux, or SELinux for short. The part includes information for configuring a firewall using IPTables as well as a chapter on the Linux Auditing System for logging specific actions such as system calls.

This book also includes four appendixes: "Installing Proprietary Kernel Modules," "Creating Virtual Machines," "Preventing Security Breaches with ExecShield," and "Troubleshooting." If you find yourself having to use a kernel module not provided with Red Hat Enterprise Linux, read Appendix A for how it is recognized by the operating system and some tips when using it. The last appendix is organized into the same six parts mentioned earlier. It is designed to help you find answers to questions should you get stuck along the way. It also includes a few helpful hints about commands that didn't fit in the rest of the book.

Conventions Used in This Book

Every book uses a slightly different method for formatting text so that the reader can better understand it. In a technical book like this one, it is especially important because commands must be typed verbatim and you need to be able to follow the examples to fully understand the concepts.

- When commands are shown, the command prompt is omitted to eliminate confusion. When a command is given, type everything shown. For example, type the following command to view the current kernel version:

  ```
  uname -r
  ```

- In commands or sample output, pointy brackets are used around the parts of the command or output that should be replaced by user-specific data such as an IP address or user name:

  ```
  ssh <ipaddr>
  ```

- All code, computer output, commands, and filenames are typeset in a special `monospace` font.
- Throughout the book, short paragraphs of text are highlighted for emphasis. These callouts can be in one of three forms:

NOTE

Notes are used to provide small bits of extra information such as books or websites with additional information.

TIP

A tip can be an alternate way of performing an action or a way to improve on a particular process.

CAUTION

Read cautions carefully. They highlight important information crucial to the success of the action being described or provide warnings about actions that might cause problems.

Feedback and Corrections

Despite the number of times I tested each procedure and command in this book, I'm sure there are parts that can be improved or just plain errors. For a list of corrections, supplemental material, or to submit feedback and corrections, go to the author's website for this book:

http://www.linuxheadquarters.com/rhel5adminbook/

Updates and additional information regarding the book can also be found on the publisher's website:

http://www.samspublishing.com/

PART I

Installation and Configuration

IN THIS PART

CHAPTER 1

Installing Red Hat Enterprise Linux

IN THIS CHAPTER

- Choosing an Installation Method
- Creating the Installation Source
- Starting the Installation
- Performing the Installation
- Installing with Kickstart
- Installing with PXE
- Performing an Upgrade
- Red Hat Network Provisioning

The Red Hat Enterprise Linux installation program is quite versatile. It can scale from an interactive program used to install the operating system on individual systems to a scripted, non-interactive program for simultaneous installation on multiple systems. The installation process can even be customized and scheduled via Red Hat Network. All these installation methods can retrieve the installation software from a central installation source. This chapter describes the different installation methods so that an administrator can decide which method is best for his organization and his users' needs. It details how to make the installation files available to the systems to be installed depending on the installation method. Then, it provides a guide through the installation program. If an automated, non-interactive installation is desired, this chapter provides a reference for the kickstart method. If the system to be installed includes a network interface card with PXE support, consider using PXE to start the installation instead of a CD as discussed at the end of the chapter.

Choosing an Installation Method

One of the many strengths of the Red Hat Enterprise Linux installation program is that the installation files can be retrieved in a variety of ways. For example, if you are only installing one or two systems, performing a traditional CD-ROM installation is probably easiest because it requires minimal setup time. However, if you are installing tens or hundreds of systems on the same network, the time it takes to set up a centralized installation source with the necessary files will ultimately save the administrator time and allow the administrator to scale his efforts. The installation

CDs do not have to be swapped out of each machine as they are needed. To perform simultaneous installs on all the systems, all the systems can be booted using PXE instead of burning a set of CDs for each system, and they can all be installed from one set of installation files shared over the network.

Keep in mind that you do not have to standardize on just one installation method. A combination of methods might work best for you.

The following installation methods are available:

- CD-ROM

  Installing from a set of installation CDs is the most direct method. Insert the media into the system, make sure the BIOS is configured to boot off the CD, and boot the system. The administrator is stepped through the process from keyboard and language selection to choosing which software sets to install.

- Hard Drive

  Installing from the hard drive requires the ISO images of the installation CDs to be on a hard drive partition accessible by the installation program (formatted as ext2, ext3, or vfat). It also requires a boot CD created from the `boot.iso` image found on the first installation CD. Refer to the "Creating the Installation Source" section for details on creating a boot disc.

- Network Install (via NFS, FTP, or HTTP)

  This method also requires a boot CD created from the `boot.iso` image or PXE boot. After booting, select the preferred network installation method (NFS, FTP, or HTTP). The installation source must be available to the system using the selected network protocol. Refer to the "Creating the Installation Source" section for details on setting up the installation source.

- Kickstart

  Kickstart is the name of the Red Hat scripted installation method. A kickstart-formatted script is written, the installation program is started with a boot CD or via PXE and then given the location of the kickstart file. Refer to the "Installing with Kickstart" section for details.

- PXE

  PXE, or Pre-Execution Environment, is available on some Network Interface Cards (NICs) and can be used to perform a network installation by connecting to a network file server and booting from files retrieved over the network instead of from local media such as a CD. Refer to the "Starting the Installation" section for details.

- Red Hat Network Provisioning

  This method requires an additional subscription to the RHN Provisioning module and an RHN Satellite Server. The web interface to the RHN Satellite Server includes a Kickstart Profile creation wizard, which can be used to create and store a customized kickstart file. Then the clients are installed from this kickstart file. Refer to the "Red Hat Network Provisioning"" section for a brief synopsis. Refer to the "Installing with Kickstart" section for further information on kickstart installations.

Creating the Installation Source

Because each Red Hat Enterprise Linux subscription comes with access to Red Hat Network, the files necessary to install the operating system can be downloaded from RHN. Each installation CD is archived into one file called an *ISO image*. These ISO image files can be used to create the installation source, depending on which installation method is used. Table 1.1 summarizes the installation sources per installation method.

TABLE 1.1 Location of Installation Source per Method

Installation Method	Installation Sources
CD-ROM	Installation CDs created from CD ISO images
Hard drive	ISOs on ext2, ext3, or vfat partition
NFS	ISOs available via NFS
FTP	Loopback mounted ISOs available via FTP
HTTP	Loopback mounted ISOs available via HTTP

This section discusses creating each of these installation sources.

Creating the Installation CDs

The ISO images for the installation CDs can be downloaded from Red Hat Network and then burned onto the media. An ISO image is a file, usually with the `.iso` extension, which contains files properly formatted so they can be written to a CD-R or CD-RW, including making the disc bootable if necessary.

Go to http://rhn.redhat.com/ and log in to your account. Click **Channels** from the horizontal navigation menu on the top, and then click **Download Software** from the vertical menu on the left. The software channels most relevant to your systems are shown by default. Select the name of the channel to download the ISO images for it. If you don't see the correct channel, click **All** from the vertical navigation menu on the left to view a list of all available channels.

The download software page provides links to the installation and source CDs for the initial release of the Red Hat Enterprise Linux version and variant you selected as well as links to download the installation and source CDs for all update releases available. Each update release contains all the files necessary to perform a complete installation, so you do not need to download each update release. To use the latest, most secure version of the software channel selected, download the install disc images for the latest update release. You do not need to download the source discs unless you need access to the source RPMs (the actual source code) used to create the software to be installed.

TIP

This page also provides a link to a page with instructions for properly downloading the ISO image files with `curl` or `wget`. Read it carefully before downloading the ISO files. Download times will vary and depend on the speed of your Internet connection.

In the table containing the links to the ISO images, notice the third column. This long string of numbers and letters is called a *checksum*, which can be used to verify that the ISO file you downloaded hasn't been corrupted. If the column contains MD5 checksums, check the MD5 checksum of an ISO file after downloading it with the following command, replacing `<iso>` with the filename of the ISO image downloaded (repeat for each ISO file):

```
md5sum <iso>
```

If the column contains SHA1 checksums, check the SHA1 checksum of an ISO file after downloading it with the following command, replacing `<iso>` with the filename of the ISO image downloaded (repeat for each ISO file):

```
sha1sum <iso>
```

When the utility is finished computing the checksum, it is displayed at the command line. Compare it to the checksum listed on the RHN page. If they match exactly, the download was successful in retrieving the entire file without corruption. If they do not match exactly, remove the ISO file and download it again until the MD5 checksum returned matches the checksum on the RHN page exactly.

Creating a Boot Disc

Network installations, including kickstart installations, can be started with a boot CD created from the `boot.iso` image found in the `images/` directory on the first installation CD. Instead of creating the first installation CD to access this file, the files from the ISO image of the disc can be loopback mounted so the `boot.iso` file can be retrieved and used to create a boot disc.

When an ISO image is loopback mounted, the files from the image are listed in a dedicated directory as they would appear on the disc if the image was written to disc. The files do not actually exist as separate files in this directory on the filesystem. When they are accessed, the files are read from the ISO image. If they are copied to the filesystem, each file copied will actually exist on the filesystem.

To loopback mount an ISO image, use the following steps:

1. Create an empty directory to mount the image into, such as `/tmp/rhel/`.
2. Mount the image into this new directory (if the image is not in the current directory, provide its full path so it can be found):

   ```
   mount -o loop <image-name>.iso /tmp/rhel/
   ```

3. The `/tmp/rhel/` directory now contains a list of all the files from the image. Copy the `boot.iso` image file over to the filesystem:

```
cp /tmp/rhel/images/boot.iso /tmp
```

4. Unmount the ISO image:

```
umount /tmp/rhel/
```

Create the boot disc from `boot.iso` by browsing for it in the Nautilus file browser, right-clicking on it, and selecting **Write to Disc...** from the menu. Alternatively, use the `cdrecord` command to write the image to disc if the graphical desktop is not available.

TIP

If you already have the first installation CD created, you can issue the command `linux askmethod` at the `boot:` prompt after booting from the CD instead of booting from a boot disc.

Using the ISO Files

All the installation types except for the CD-ROM installation method can use ISO image files as the installation source. The ISO files can be used in the following ways:

- ISO files in a directory on the hard drive for the hard drive installation method or available via NFS for the NFS installation method
- ISO files loopback mounted and then made available with FTP or HTTP

TIP

Before using the ISO files for installation, be sure to verify their checksums as described in the "Creating the Installation CDs" section earlier in this chapter.

For a network installation, set up the NFS, FTP, or HTTP server, depending on which installation method you want to use. Don't forget to make it accessible by all the clients on which you are installing Red Hat Enterprise Linux. Refer to Part IV, "Network Services," for details on setting up these network services.

The same network server can provide different variants or versions of the same operating system. When doing so, place each set of ISO images in their own directory. Use descriptive directory names such as `RHEL5Server` or `RHEL5U2Client` so you can quickly determine which OS variant and version they contain.

For hard drive installations, transfer all the ISO images into an ext2 or vfat partition on one of the hard drives in the system on which you are about to install. This partition cannot be formatted during installation because the installation program must access these ISO files during the entire installation. Be sure you have enough hard drive space for the installation after dedicating the partition to storing the ISO image files.

For an NFS installation, copy all the ISO image files into the shared directory on the NFS server. For an FTP or HTTP installation, use the following steps to share the contents of each ISO image in its own directory on the FTP or HTTP server:

1. In the shared directory on the FTP or HTTP server, for each ISO image, create a subdirectory called `discX`, where `X` is the number of the ISO image starting with the number `1`.
2. For each ISO image, loopback mount it into its corresponding `discX` directory with the command:

```
mount -o loop <name>.iso /shared/directory/discX
```

Now the installation program can access all the installation files from the network server. Next, start the installation with the instructions from the "Starting the Installation" section later in this chapter.

Instead of burning a set of installation CDs and then creating the installation source, you can loopback mount the ISO images as described in the "Creating a Boot Disc" section and copy the files.

Adding Updates to Installation Media or Source

Sometimes updates or bug fixes to the Red Hat installation program are released, similar to the way updates are released for the packages that make up the OS. Since the code for the installation program is on the installation media or in the shared directory containing the installation source, you need a way to use this updated code for the installation program, which are essential updated Python files. The updates are distributed as an update image, which is usually named `updates.img`. If an update image is available for your version of Red Hat Enterprise Linux and it is necessary to install the OS on your system, provide the image to the installation program using one the following locations:

- Floppy disk. After starting the installation, type **`linux updates`** at the `boot:` prompt.
- `images/` directory of installation tree or first installation CD, with the filename `updates.img`. If the image is found, the updates in it are automatically used for installation. This requires all the files from the ISO for disc 1 to be copied to the `disc1/` directory on the network share instead of just loopback mounting it so that the `images/` directory can be created.
- FTP or HTTP server, with the filename `updates.img`. After starting the installation, type **`linux updates=ftp://<path>`** or **`linux updates=http://<path>`** where `<path>` is the directory containing the updates image.

Starting the Installation

Each installation method is started a bit differently because some require more information to find the installation files. For example, in the CD installation method, all the files are on the CDs, with the first one already mounted and accessible by the installation program. However, for a network installation, the network protocol to use and the location of the installation files on the network server must be provided.

Starting a CD Installation

To start a CD installation, insert the first installation CD, make sure the BIOS is configured to boot off the CD-ROM device, and start the computer. Before the welcome screen appears, you are prompted to run the mediacheck program to verify each installation CD. Even if you verified the checksums of each ISO before creating CDs from the ISOs, it is highly recommended that the mediacheck be performed to make sure an error did not occur while you were creating the CDs from the ISO images.

After the welcome screen, select the language to use for the installation as shown in Figure 1.1. The same language is used as the default language for the installed system.

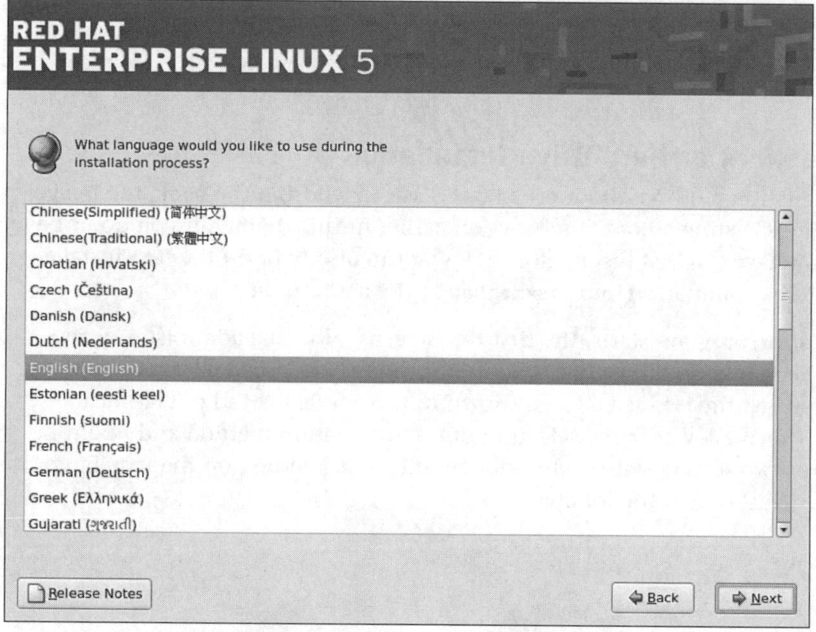

FIGURE 1.1 Language Selection

After the language selection, select the keyboard layout as shown in Figure 1.2 to use for installation. As with language selection, this preference is also used as the default value for the installed system.

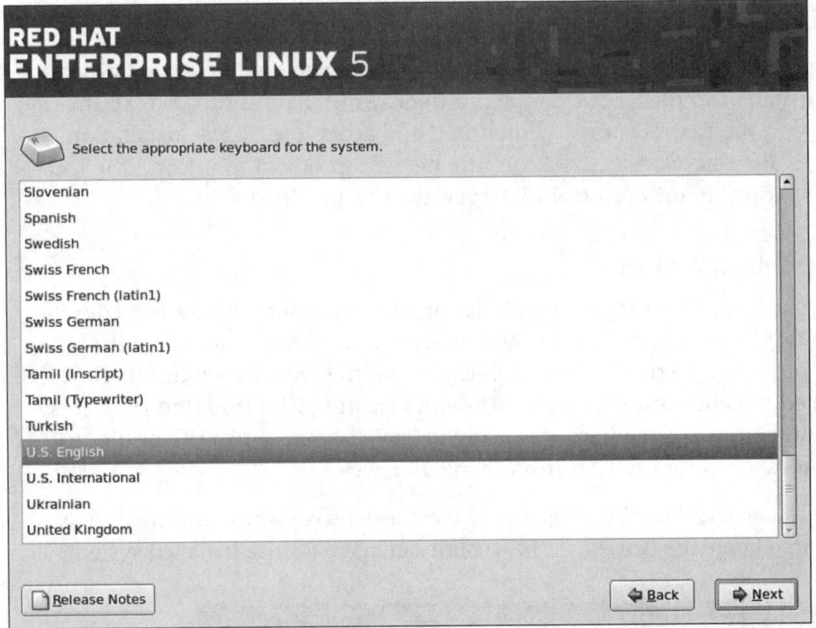

FIGURE 1.2 Keyboard Selection

Starting a Network or Hard Drive Installation

For all other installation methods, boot off a boot disc created from the `boot.iso` image as described in the "Creating a Boot Disc" section earlier in this chapter. If you don't have a boot CD but you have the first installation CD, you can also boot off the first installation CD and type the command **`linux askmethod`** at the `boot:` prompt.

When the installation program starts, the first two screens allow the administrator to select the language and keyboard layout to use as previously described for a CD-ROM installation except that the two screens are shown in text-mode instead of graphical mode. The third screen allows for the selection of the installation method and might be followed by one or two screens with additional questions, depending on the installation method selected. Select one of the following:

- Local CDROM
- Hard drive
- NFS image
- FTP
- HTTP

If **Local CDROM** is selected and the first installation CD is already inserted, the installation is as described in the "Performing the Installation" section. If **Local CDROM** is selected and a boot CD was used to start the program, the first installation CD must be inserted when prompted to continue.

If **Hard drive** is selected, the partition containing the installation ISOs must be selected from the list, and the directory containing the ISOs must be provided. If **NFS image**, **FTP**, or **HTTP** is selected, the server name and shared directory containing the ISO images or the installation source must be given. If **FTP** is selected, it is assumed that the server accepts anonymous connections for the share. If a username/password combination is necessary, select the **Use non-anonymous FTP** option.

After selecting the installation method and providing the necessary information, the welcome screen is shown. To finish the installation, follow the instructions in the "Performing the Installation" section.

Starting a Kickstart or PXE Installation

To start a kickstart installation, read the "Installing with Kickstart" section later in this chapter to learn how to create a kickstart file, make it available to the systems to be installed, and start the kickstart installation.

To start a PXE installation, read the "Installing with PXE" section later in this chapter for instructions on configuring the PXE server and starting the network installation.

Performing the Installation

After starting the installation as described in the previous section, the administrator is prompted for an installation number as demonstrated in Figure 1.3. This number is provided when the Red Hat Enterprise Linux subscription is purchased and is used by RHN to control customer subscription entitlements. It also unlocks specific software groups (if appropriate) within the installation media so that they can be installed during the installation process This unlocks specific software groups so that they can be installed. For example, an installation number might cause the installation of the software necessary for creating virtual machines with Virtualization or the clustering filesystem.

The installation program then searches for existing installations. If one is found, the following two options are displayed:

- Install Red Hat Enterprise Linux
- Upgrade an existing installation

If you choose to upgrade an existing installation, also select the root partition of the existing installation to upgrade. Refer to the "Performing an Upgrade" section later in this chapter for more details on upgrades. The rest of this section pertains to installing Red Hat Enterprise Linux.

Partitioning is one of the most important decisions you will make during the installation process (see Figure 1.4 for the start of the partitioning process). Decisions such as which software packages to install and the root password can be changed after installation, but changing the way a filesystem is partitioned is much harder to modify after installation. Refer to the "Deciding on a Partitioning Method and Type" section later in this chapter for details.

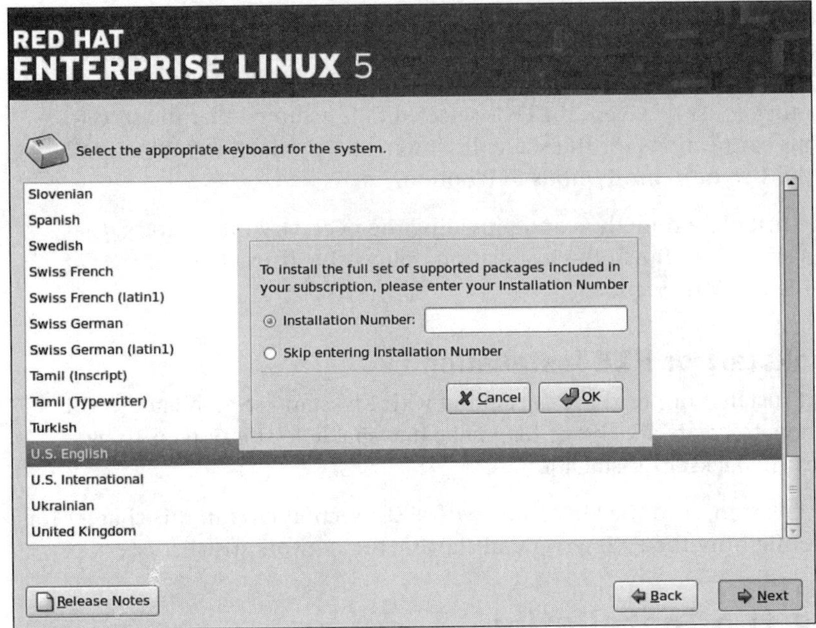
RED HAT
ENTERPRISE LINUX 5
Select the appropriate keyboard for the system.
Slovenian
Spanish
Swedish
Swiss French
Swiss French (latin1)
Swiss German
Swiss German (latin1)
Tamil (Inscript)
Tamil (Typewriter)
Turkish
U.S. English
U.S. International
Ukrainian
United Kingdom
To install the full set of supported packages included in your subscription, please enter your Installation Number
Installation Number:
Skip entering Installation Number
Cancel
OK
Release Notes
Back
Next

FIGURE 1.3 Providing an Installation Number

RED HAT
ENTERPRISE LINUX 5
Installation requires partitioning of your hard drive.
By default, a partitioning layout is chosen which is
reasonable for most users. You can either choose
to use this or create your own.
Remove linux partitions on selected drives and create default layout.
Select the drive(s) to use for this installation.
sda 286181 MB ATA Maxtor 6L300S0
Advanced storage configuration
Review and modify partitioning layout
Release Notes
Back
Next

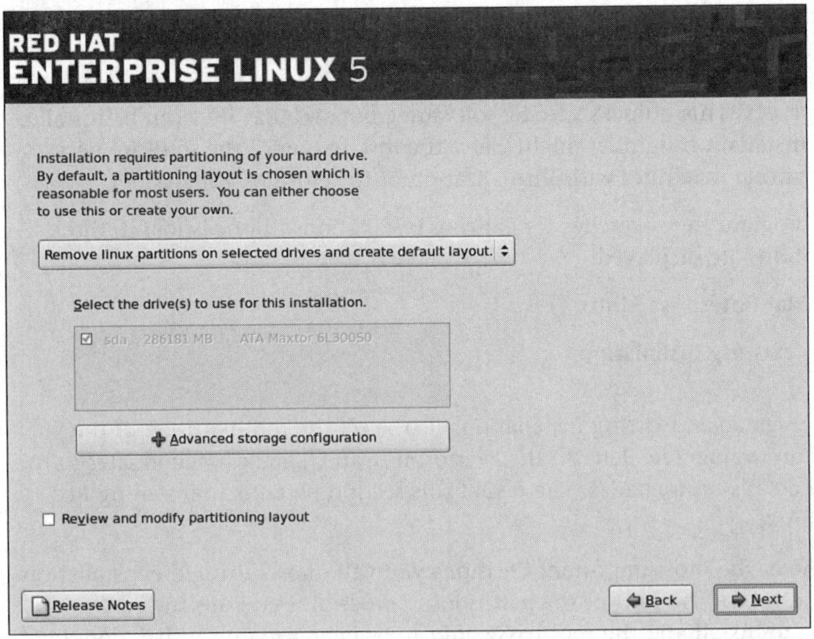

FIGURE 1.4 Selecting a Partitioning Scheme

A boot loader must be installed to boot into the operating system. The GRUB boot loader is installed by default (see Figure 1.5). Options such as enabling a boot loader password can be selected. Because GRUB is only used for x86 and x86_64 systems, this screen will vary for other architectures.

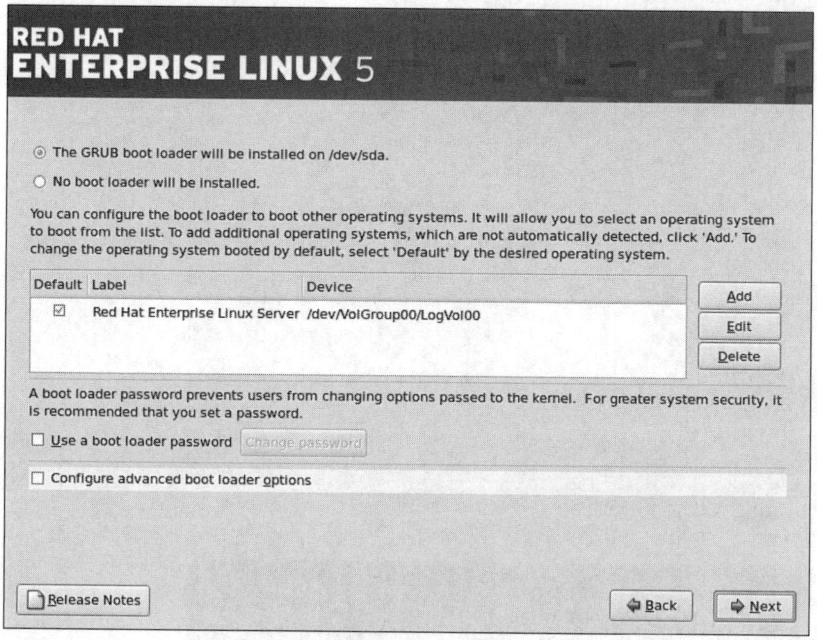

FIGURE 1.5 Configuring the GRUB Boot Loader

Network devices are detected and configured to use DHCP and are active at boot time as shown on the **Network Devices** screen in Figure 1.6. Uncheck the **Active at Boot** option next to a network device if you do not want it to retrieve an IP address at boot. If your network does not use DHCP, you can select to configure an IP address and network settings for each device on this screen.

For the **Time Zone** screen, click on the map to select a time zone. On the **Root password** screen, enter a root password for the system and then type it again to confirm it. If they do not match, you are prompted to enter them again.

Certain software sets are installed by default, varying slightly with each variant of Red Hat Enterprise Linux such as including the DHCP server with Red Hat Enterprise Linux Server. Some additional software sets such as Software Development and Web Server can be selected during installation. These additional software sets also vary depending on the installation number and the Red Hat Enterprise Linux variant being installed.

Also, select to **Customize later** or **Customize now**. If **Customize later** is chosen, no further options are presented. If **Customize now** is selected, the screen shown in Figure 1.7 is displayed showing a list of software groups in the top-left box.

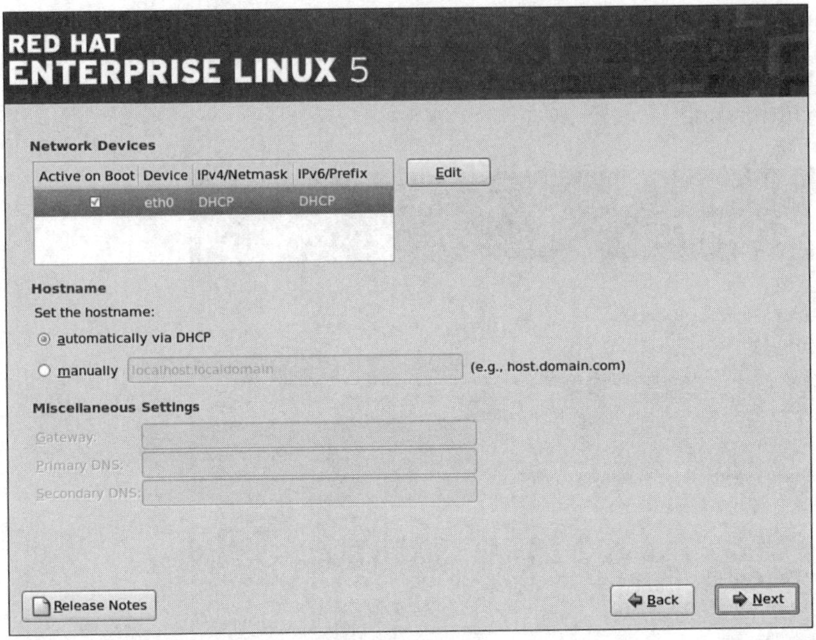

FIGURE 1.6 Activating Network Devices

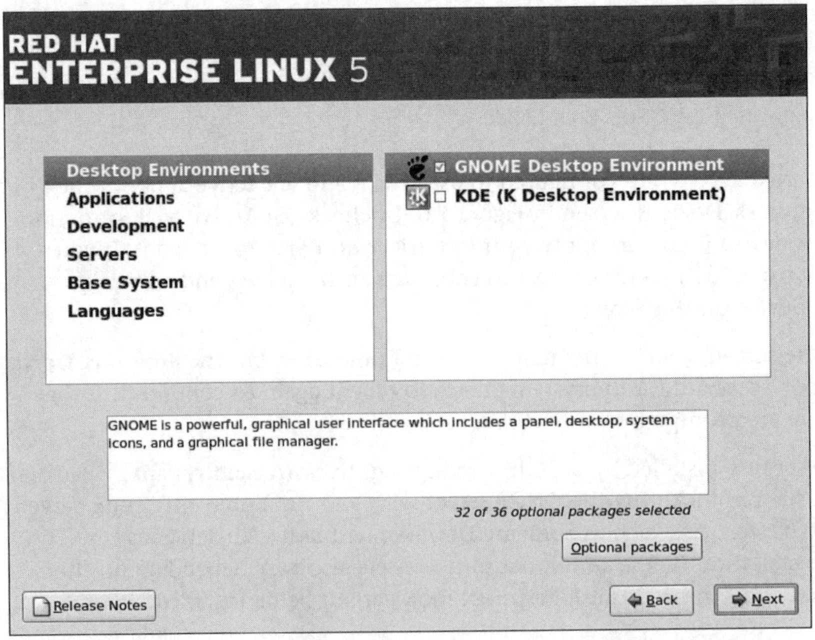

FIGURE 1.7 Customizing Software

As a software group is selected on the left, software sets are displayed on the right with check boxes next to each name. Click the check box next to the software sets to install in addition to the software selected by default. As software sets on the right are selected, a brief description is shown on the bottom of the screen. If the software set selected contains optional packages, the **Optional packages** button on the bottom right of the screen is active and can be clicked to further customize the individual software packages installed for the software set.

The software groups shown on the left side vary slightly depending on the installation number entered at the beginning of the process. For example, if an installation number to include virtualization is used, the **Virtualization** software group is shown in Figure 1.8.

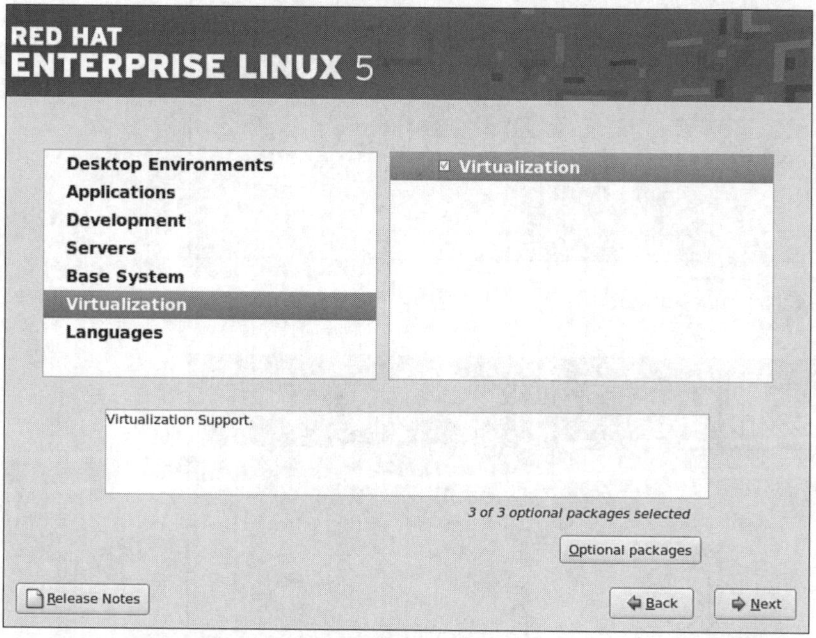

FIGURE 1.8 Virtualization Software Group

After additional software is selected, the installation program checks for software dependencies. A software dependency is an RPM package that must be installed for the RPM package you selected to work properly. As the software is installed, the progress is shown as a time estimate and a progress bar (see Figure 1.9). If you are performing a CD installation, a popup window is displayed when the next CD is needed.

When all the necessary files are installed and all post-installation actions such as writing the bootloader are complete, Figure 1.10 is displayed. After the system is rebooted, the Setup Agent is automatically started. Refer to Chapter 2, "Post-Installation Configuration," for details on the Setup Agent.

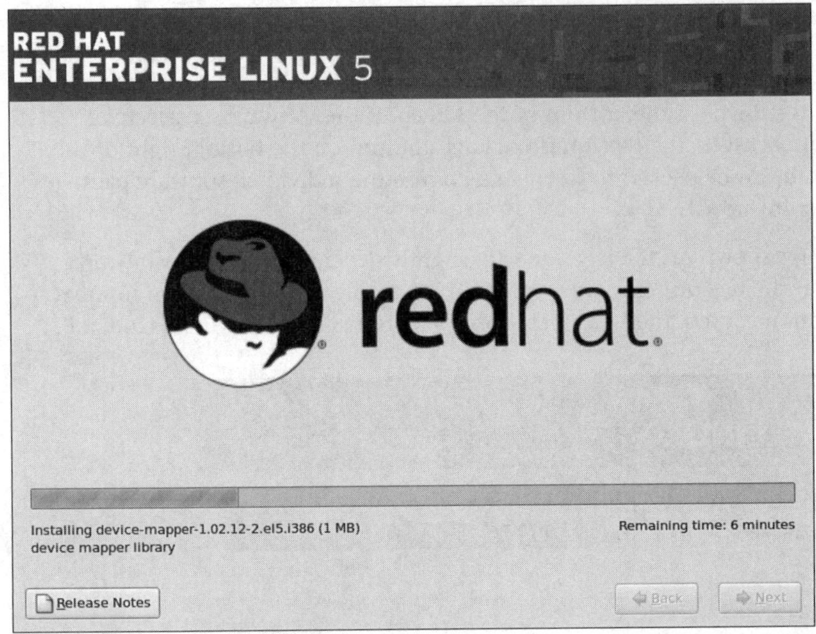

FIGURE 1.9 Installing the Software

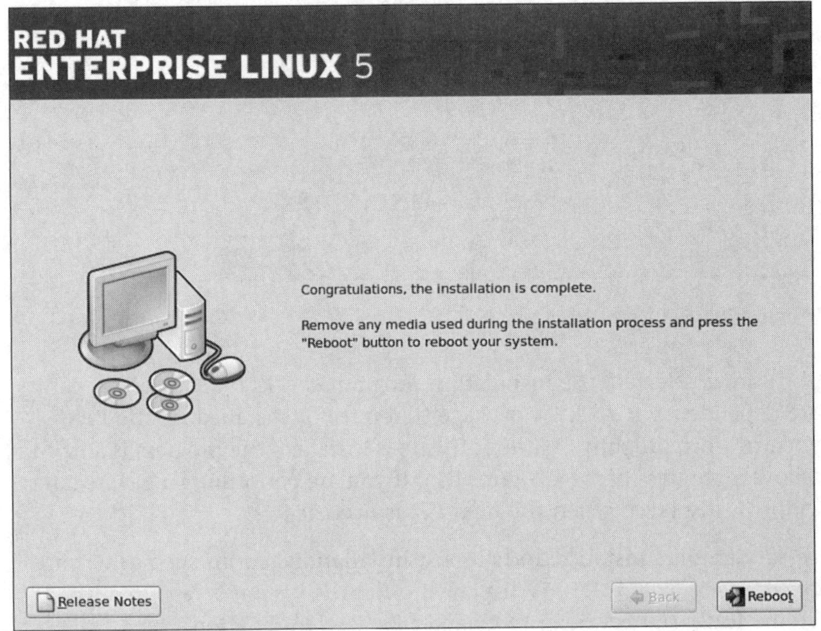

FIGURE 1.10 Installation Complete

NOTE

As noted on the last screen of the installation program, a log of the installation is saved in the `/root/install.log` file and a basic kickstart file is created based on the installation in the `/root/anaconda-ks.cfg` file. Both of these files are in plain text format and can be read by the root user after the system is rebooted.

Deciding on a Partitioning Method and Type

As shown in Figure 1.4, use the pull-down menu to choose one of the following partitioning schemes so the filesystem can be partitioned and formatted:

- Remove Linux partitions on selected drives and create default layout (default)
- Remove all partitions on selected drives and create default layout
- Use free space on selected drives and create default layout
- Create custom layout

If the option you selected creates a default layout, you can select the option to **Review and modify partitioning layout**. Figure 1.11 shows the review and modify partitioning screen. This is the same interface used when creating a custom layout. If the option you selected requires partitions to be deleted, you will be asked to confirm their deletion before continuing.

A root partition (/) is required at a minimum. For x86 and x86_64 systems, it is also recommended that a swap partition and `/boot` partition be created. For x86 and x86_64 systems, the default partitioning layout creates a root partition (`/`), swap partition, and `/boot` partition. LVM is used by default except for the `/boot` partition, which cannot be part of a logical volume group. The default partitions required and created for other architectures might be different. For example, on Itanium systems, a `/boot/efi` partition is recommended instead of a `/boot` partition. If a `/boot/efi` partition is created, it must be the first primary partition.

Most administrators will need to either create a custom layout or create the default layout and then modify it to fit the needs of the system. For example, creating a separate `/tmp` partition prevents a program from creating temporary files that fill up the entire filesystem. Unless the users' home directories are going to be mounted from a different server, creating a separate `/home` directory is beneficial and is even more flexible if the separate partition is on a separate hard drive. It allows the administrator to limit the total amount of disk space used for home directories and gives the administrator the flexibility to replace the hard drive with the `/home` partition with a larger drive or a network drive with minimal reconfiguration. Should the system fail while users still need access to their data, the hard drive containing the `/home` partition can be quickly moved to a backup system already installed with the OS (assuming the failure is not with the physical hardware associated with the `/home` partition).

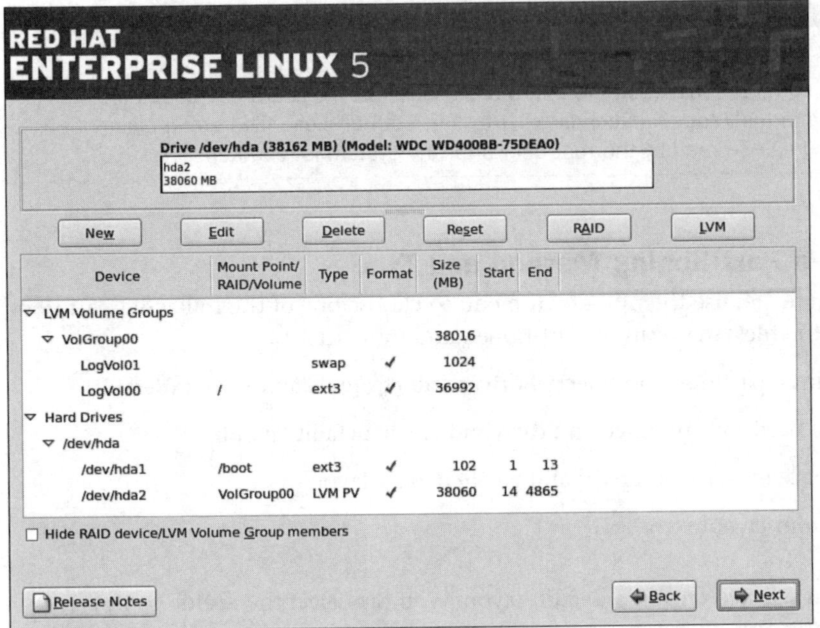

FIGURE 1.11 Reviewing and Modifying Partitioning

As previously mentioned, by default, LVM is used to partition the filesystem. However, standard disk partitions and software RAID are also available during installation. The following subsections describe how to use these different partitioning methods during installation. Chapter 7, "Managing Storage," describes how to set up and maintain them after installation.

Setting Up Basic Partitions During Installation

To use standard disk partitions, complete the following steps for each partition as demonstrated in Figure 1.12:

1. Click **New**.
2. Enter a mount point such as `/` or `/boot`.
3. Select **swap** as the filesystem type if the partition is to be used as swap space. Select **ext3** for all other Linux partitions.
4. Select the allowable drives if multiple drives exist. Basic partitions cannot span over more than one physical drive. If more than one drive is selected, the partition will be created on one of the selected drives depending on the free disk space available on the selected drives and the desired size of the partition.
5. The partition size can be set as a fixed size, a variable size up to a specific size depending on the amount of free disk space, or the total amount of free disk space available on one of the allowable drives selected.

6. Optionally, select whether to force the partition to be a primary partition. This is necessary for some partitions such as `/boot/efi` on Itanium systems.
7. Click **OK** to return to the partition list.

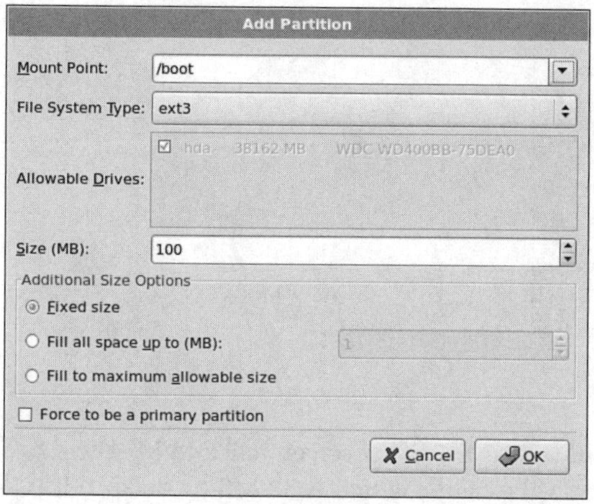

FIGURE 1.12 Creating a Standard Disk Partition

Setting Up LVM During Installation

LVM, or Logical Volume Manager, is a storage management solution that allows administrators to divide hard drive space into *physical volumes* (*PV*), which can then be combined into *logical volume groups* (*VG*), which are then divided into *logical volumes* (*LV*) on which the filesystem and mount point are created. Refer to Chapter 7 for a more detailed explanation.

To partition with LVM during installation either allow the installation program to create the default layout or create a custom layout.

TIP

Instead of creating logical volumes from scratch, you can allow the installation program to create the default layout and then modify it to your specifications.

To create the LVM layout from scratch, use the following steps:

1. Create a standard disk partition for the `/boot` partition because it can't be within a LVM (or a `/boot/efi` partition for an Itanium system) as described in the previous section "Setting Up Basic Partitions During Installation."
2. Create the physical volumes (PVs). A PV must be created for each physical hard drive you want to use for logical volumes. Click **New** again, except this time select **physical volume (LVM)** as the filesystem type as shown in Figure 1.13. Click **OK** to return to the partition list. Repeat this step for each PV needed.

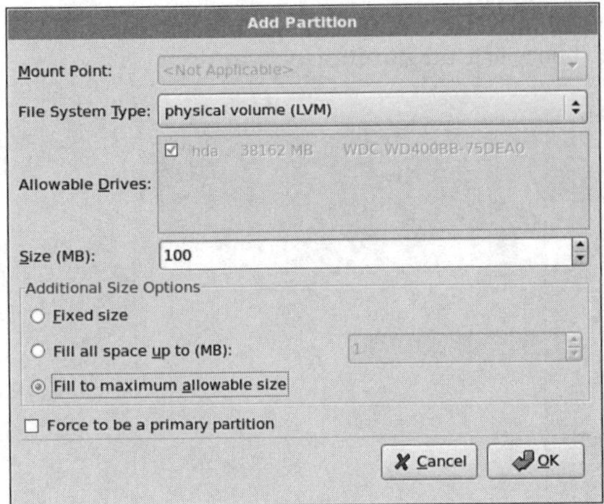

FIGURE 1.13 Creating a Physical Volume

3. Create the volume groups (VGs). From the partition list screen, click **LVM**. The size of the VG is set by the number of physical extents, which is 32 MB by default. It is not recommended you modify the physical extent size. As shown in Figure 1.14, a unique name is given to the VG. Modify the name if you want to use a different naming convention. Select the physical volumes to include in the VG. The total size for the VG might not be equal to the summation of the PV sizes because a small amount of disk space is used as overhead. Click **OK** to return to the partition list. Repeat this step for each VG needed. Otherwise, continue to the next step.

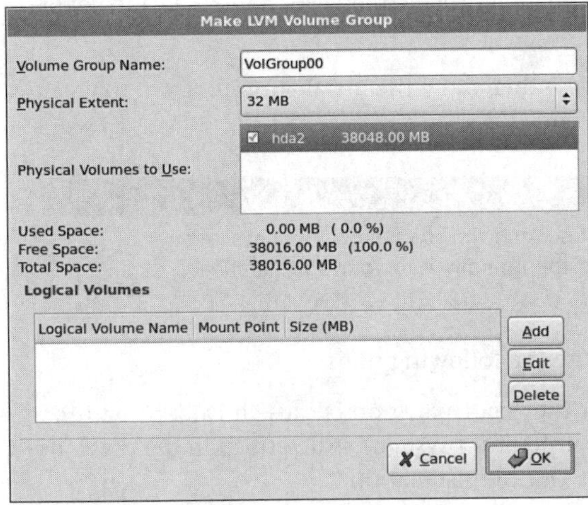

FIGURE 1.14 Creating a Volume Group

4. Create logical volumes (LVs) inside the volume groups. An LV must be created for the root (`/`) mount point and for the swap space. Additional LVs such as `/home` and `/tmp` are optional. To create a logical volume, from the partition list, select the VG in which to create it, and click **Edit**. (Or keep the dialog window open after creating the volume group.) Click **Add** in the **Logical Volumes** section at the bottom of the dialog window. As shown in Figure 1.15, the mount point, filesystem type, LV name, size, and whether the LV should be formatted must be specified. Click **OK** to return to the volume group dialog and repeat this step for each LV needed. Then click **OK** to return to the partition list in the main window of the installation program.

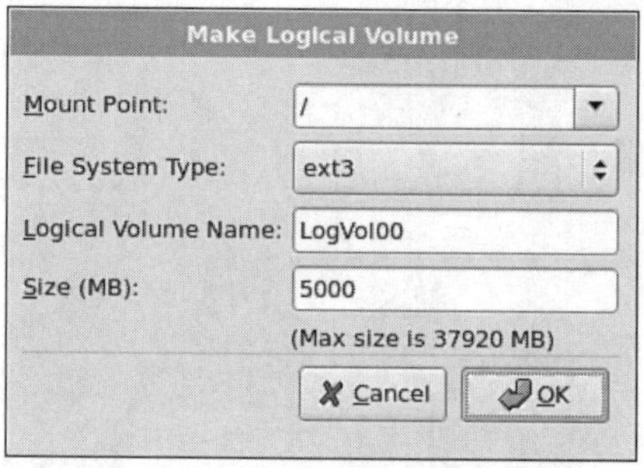

Make Logical Volume

Mount Point: /

File System Type: ext3

Logical Volume Name: LogVol00

Size (MB): 5000

(Max size is 37920 MB)

Cancel OK

FIGURE 1.15 Creating a Logical Volume

After LVM is set up, the main window with the partition list should look similar to Figure 1.16.

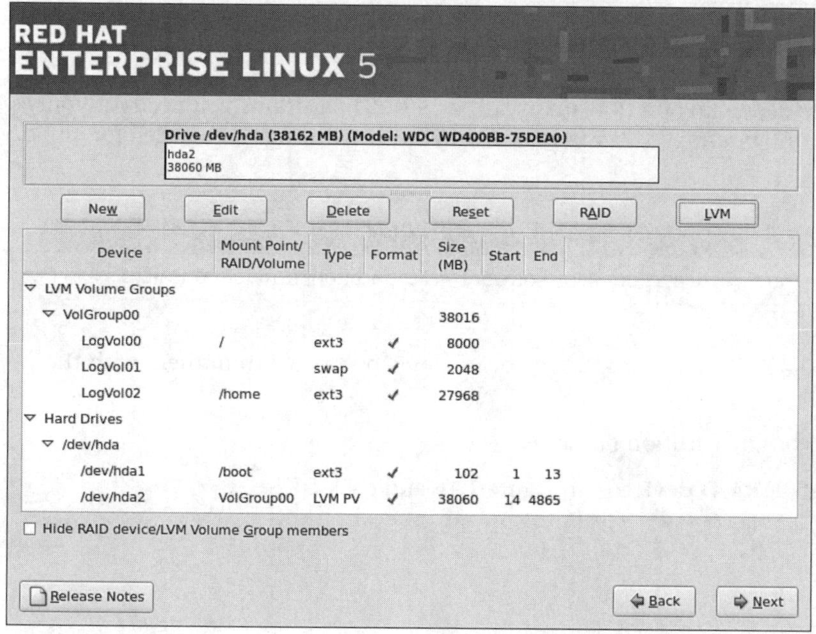

FIGURE 1.16 LVM Configuration

Setting Up Software RAID During Installation

Refer to the "Understanding RAID" section of Chapter 7 for an explanation of software RAID. Then use the following steps to create a RAID partition:

1. Click the **RAID** button.
2. Select **Create a software RAID partition** and click **OK**.
3. The **Add Partition** dialog used to create a standard disk partition appears. As shown in Figure 1.17, select **software RAID** as the filesystem type, select the allowable drives, and set its size. Click **OK**.

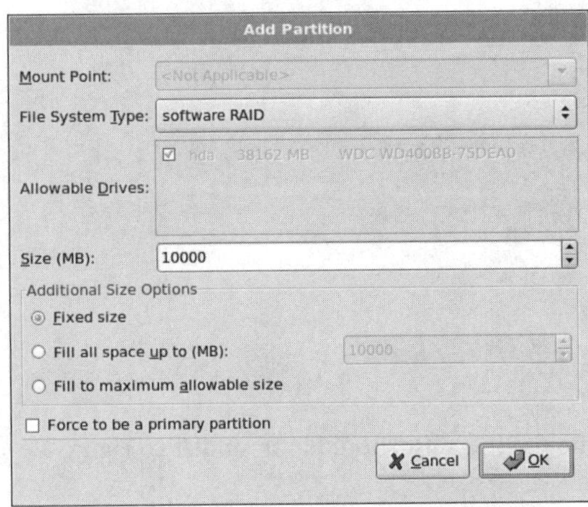

FIGURE 1.17 Adding a Software RAID Partition

Repeat these steps depending on how many software RAID partitions you need for your particular RAID configuration. At least two software RAID partitions are needed for any of the RAID levels.

NOTE

If the `/boot` or `/boot/efi` partition is a software RAID partition, it must be RAID 1.

After setting up the RAID partitions, RAID devices must be created from them with the following steps:

1. Click **RAID** on the partition list screen.
2. Select **Create a RAID device** as in Figure 1.18 and click OK.

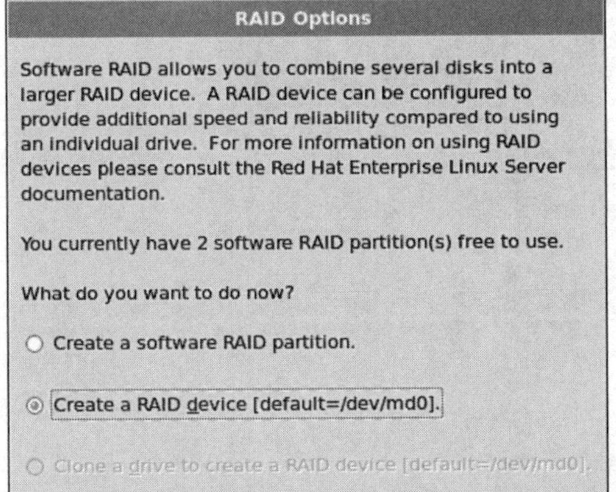

FIGURE 1.18 Creating a RAID Device

3. In the dialog shown in Figure 1.19, give the name of the mount point, and select **ext3** or **swap** as the filesystem type. Select the RAID device name, where md0 is the first RAID device, md1 is the second, and so on. Select the desired RAID level (refer to Chapter 7 for an explanation of the levels), and select the RAID members from the list of RAID partitions created earlier. If RAID 1 or 5 is selected, also select the number of spare partitions to create.

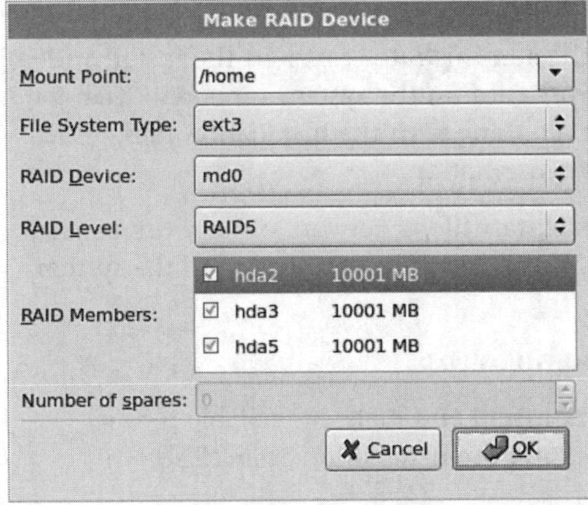

FIGURE 1.19 RAID Device Specifications

Repeat these steps until all the desired RAID devices are created. All mount points for the system do not have to be RAID devices. For example, Figure 1.20 shows all the partitions as standard disk partitions except for the `/home` partition because it contains data that changes frequently and would most benefit from RAID.

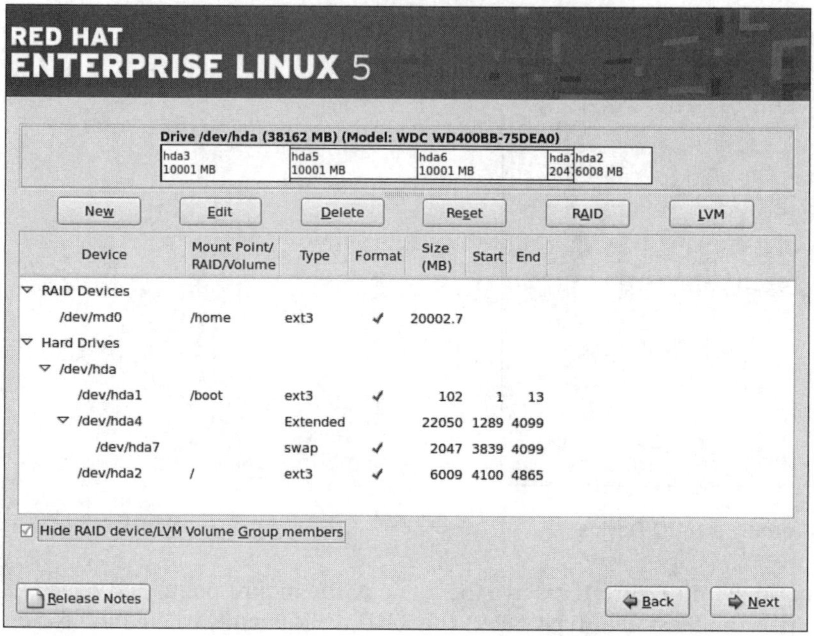

FIGURE 1.20 RAID Example

Installing with Kickstart

A kickstart installation is started from a kickstart file containing the answers to all the questions in the installation program so that the administrator can start the install and then walk away until it is finished. If the network card on the system supports PXE boot, the kickstart file can even be on a different server along with the installation files, allowing for an easy, automated, and non-interactive installation.

Although a CD installation is possible with a kickstart file, a network or hard drive installation is more convenient, otherwise the administrator will have to return to the system to change CDs.

To perform a kickstart installation, use the following steps:

1. Create an installation tree for the network install and make it available to the systems being installed. Refer to the "Creating the Installation Source" section earlier in this chapter for details.
2. Create the kickstart file.
3. Create a boot CD (unless you are using PXE).
4. Copy the kickstart file to the boot CD or make it available over the network.
5. Start the kickstart installation.

Creating the Kickstart File

A kickstart file is a plain text file with each kickstart directive on a separate line. A simple text editor should be used to write or modify the file. Do not use a program that automatically line wraps because each directive must be on its own line. If a long line is wrapped, the installation program might read it incorrectly and cause the installation to fail. Lines that begin with the pound sign (#) are comments.

The directives listed in the kickstart file must be grouped as follows:

- Command section
- `%package` section
- `%pre` and `%post` sections

TIP

If you have already performed an installation, a kickstart file based on the installation is written to `/root/anaconda-ks.cfg`. You can start with this sample file and modify it as needed.

Command Section

The command section consists of directives to answer all the questions from the interactive version of the installation program. They can be listed in any order as long as they all appear before the `%package`, `%pre`, and `%post` sections. This section groups them in categories to make it easier to determine which directives are suitable for your needs.

Notice that some commands are required. If any required directives are missing from the kickstart file, the automated installation will pause on the screen for which no information was provided in the kickstart file. To continue the installation, the administrator must complete the instructions for the screen and click **Next**.

This section divides the kickstart commands into categories based on their usage: installation, basic setup, partitioning, and additional. Some directives such as the `install` directive require related directives to be listed on separate lines. If a directive is followed by an equals sign (=), a value must follow it. Also notice that some directives are required.

Installation Commands

For all kickstart files, either the install or upgrade directive is required. The other installation commands are optional.

- `install`

  Install Red Hat Enterprise Linux as opposed to performing an upgrade. If this command is specified, one of the following installation methods must also be listed on a separate line:

  `cdrom`

  The first CD-ROM drive contains the installation media.

```
harddrive --partition=<partition> --dir=<dir>
```

The installation CD ISOs or source is located on a hard drive partition in the system, which is formatted as ext2, ext3, or vfat. The partition and directory containing the installation source or ISOs must be specified as options to the command.

```
nfs --server=<server> --dir=<dir>
```

The installation files are located on an NFS share accessible by the system. The hostname or IP address of the server and the directory on the NFS server containing the installation tree must be listed. If a hostname is listed, the system being installed must be able to resolve it to an IP address. NFS options can also be provided with the --opts=<options> argument to the nfs command.

```
url --url=<url>
```

The installation tree or installation ISOs are located on an FTP or HTTP server accessible by the system being installed. The <url> can be in either of the following forms:

```
http://server.example.com/install/tree/dir/

ftp://<username>:<password>@server.example.com/install/tree/dir/
```

- upgrade

  Upgrade the existing system instead of performing a full installation.

- autostep

  Show each installation screen as kickstart automatically performs the steps from the screen. Useful for debugging.

- interactive

  Similar to autostep except that each screen is populated with the values from the kickstart file and shown for verification or modification. To continue, the administrator must click **Next** for each screen after reviewing it.

- key

  Provide the installation number for the system. Use key --skip if you do not want to enter an installation number.

- cmdline

  Use the non-interactive command-line installation mode. Useful for S/390 systems with the x3270 console.

- text

  Force the installation to be performed in text-mode. Network, hard drive, and CD-ROM installations are performed in graphical mode unless the text command is listed.

Basic Setup Commands

- `authconfig` (required)

  Execute the `authconfig` utility from the installation program to configure system authentication. Refer to the `authconfig` man page for options.

- `bootloader` (required)

  Describe how the boot loader (GRUB for x86 and x86_64 systems) is installed and configured.

  `--append=`

  Used to provide kernel boot options. Separate two or more kernel parameters with spaces.

  `--driveorder=`

  Hard drive boot order from the BIOS. Separate each drive such as `sda` or `hda` with commas.

  `--location=`

  Where to write the boot record. Must be one of following: `mbr` (default), `partition` (install on the first sector of the partition on which the kernel is installed), or `none` (do not install).

  `--password=`

  If using GRUB, use to set up a boot loader password to restrict access to the GRUB shell.

  `--md5pass=`

  If using GRUB, the same as `--password=` except the password provided is already encrypted. Useful if unauthorized users have access to the kickstart file.

  `--lba32=`

  Force lba32 mode.

  `--upgrade=`

  Upgrade boot loader while keeping existing boot entries in `grub.conf`. Can only be used when performing an upgrade of Red Hat Enterprise Linux.

- `keyboard` (required)

  Set the keyboard type used after installation. Must be one of the following for x86, x86_64, and Itanium (additional layouts might exist for other architectures):

`be-latin1, bg, br-abnt2, cf, cz-lat2, cz-us-qwertz, de, de-latin1, de-latin1-nodeadkeys, dk, dk-latin1, dvorak, es, et, fi, fi-latin1, fr, fr-latin0, fr-latin1, fr-pc, fr_CH, fr_CH-latin1, gr, hu, hu101, is-latin1, it, it-ibm, it2, jp106, la-latin1, mk-utf, no, no-latin1, pl, pt-latin1, ro_win, ru, ru-cp1251, ru-ms, ru1, ru2, ru_win, se-latin1, sg, sg-latin1, sk-qwerty, slovene, speakup, speakup-lt, sv-latin1, sg, sg-latin1, sk-querty, slovene, trq, ua, uk, us, us-acentos`

The keyboard types are also listed in the `/usr/lib/python2.4/site-packages/rhpl/keyboard_models.py` file from the `rhpl` package.

- `lang <lang>` (required)

  Set the default language for the installed system. The file `/usr/share/system-config-language/locale-list` from the `system-config-language` package contains a list of valid languages. Each line in this file lists a different language. Use the value of the first column such as `en_US.UTF-8` for `<lang>`.

- `monitor`

  If this command is not used, the installation program probes for the monitor. Use this command to manually configure the monitor attached to the system or force the installation program not to probe the monitor with the following options:

  `--hsync=`

  Horizontal sync rate.

  `--monitor=`

  Monitor name from the `/usr/share/hwdata/MonitorsDB` file from the `hwdata` package (the second value from the semicolon-separated list of values for each monitor). This value is ignored if `--hsync=` and `--vsync=` are also specified.

  `--noprobe=`

  Don't probe for the monitor.

  `--vsync=`

  Vertical sync rate.

- `network`

  If the installation method chosen is not a network install, networking is not configured for the system. If a network install is chosen, it is performed over the first Ethernet device (eth0) using DHCP with the installed system being configured to use DHCP as well. If a different type of networking protocol is required for the network install, use this command to configure it. The installed system will use these settings as well. Options include

`--bootproto=`

Boot protocol to use. Must be one of `dhcp`, `bootp`, or `static`. If `static` is chosen, all network configuration must be listed as well with the `--ip=`, `--netmask=`, `--gateway=`, and `--nameserver=` options.

`--device=`

Specify the Ethernet device to use such as `eth0`.

`--ip=`

IP address to use with a static configuration.

`--gateway=`

Gateway to use with a static configuration.

`--nameserver=`

Primary nameserver to use with a static configuration.

`--nodns=`

Don't configure a DNS server.

`--netmask=`

Netmask to use for a static configuration.

`--hostname=`

Hostname for the system.

`--ethtool=`

Used to configure network settings passed to the `ethtool` utility.

`--essid=`

Network ID to use for the wireless network.

`--wepkey=`

WEP key to use for the wireless network.

`--onboot=`

If set to `yes`, the network device is enabled at boot time.

`--class=`

DHCP class to use.

- `iscsi`

  The Internet SCSI (ISCSI) protocol provides SCSI over TCP/IP networks for data transfer. It is a lower cost alternative to a Fibre Channel storage area network (SAN).

  `--ipaddr=`

  IP address of remote connection.

  `--target=`

  Remote disk to connect to.

  `--port=`

  Port used to connect to target.

  `--user=`

  Username for remote connection, if required.

  `--password=`

  Password for remote connection, if required.

- `iscsiname`

  ISCSI initiator name. Must be a unique, per-host identifier used with ISCSI.

- `rootpw` (required)

  Root password for the installed system. To specify an encrypted password, use the `--isencrypted` option before specifying the encrypted password.

- `timezone` (required)

  Time zone for the installed system.

Partitioning Commands

- `autopart`

  Create default partitions (a root (`/`) partition, swap partition, and `/boot` partition). The sizes of these partitions can be modified with the `part` directive.

- `clearpart`

  Remove specific partitions or partition types before creating new partitions. If this command is used, the `--onpart` command can't be used on a logical partition.

  `--all`

  All partitions are removed.

  `--drives=`

  All the partitions on the drives listed, such as `hda` or `sdc`, are removed.

--initlabel

Initialize the disk label to the default for the system's architecture. Useful when installing to a new hard drive that has not been initialized.

--linux

Only existing Linux partitions are removed.

--none (default)

No partitions are removed.

- volgroup <name> <partition> <options>

  Create an LVM group. The following <options> are available:

  --noformat

  Do not format. Useful for retaining an existing volume group.

  --useexisting

  Use existing volume group. The LVM group is formatted by default unless --noformat is also specified.

  --pesize

  Size of physical extents.

NOTE

Create the partition with the partition directive before creating a logical volume group with volgroup. After creating the LVM group, use the logvol directive to create a logical volume.

Refer to Chapter 7 for details about LVM and LVM configuration.

- logvol <mountpoint> -vgname=<name> --size=<size> --name=<name> <options>

  Create logical volume after creating a logical group with volgroup. The following <options> are available:

  --noformat

  Do not format. Useful for existing logical volume.

  --useexisting

  Use existing logical volume. Reformatted unless --noformat is also specified.

  --fstype=

  Filesystem type. Must be one of ext2, ext3, swap, or vfat.

`--fsoptions=`

Mounting options to use for the filesystem. They are copied to `/etc/fstab`.

`--bytes-per-inode=`

Size of inodes for the filesystem on the logical volume. Ignored if the filesystem specified does not support this feature.

`--grow`

Allow size of logical volume to increase if space is available. If a maximum size is provided with `--maxsize=`, logical volume will not be bigger than this maximum size.

`--maxsize=`

If `--grow` is used to allow the size of the logical volume to increase, this option should be set to the maximum size the logical volume is allowed to grow, in megabytes.

`--recommended`

Let the installation program automatically calculate the size of the logical volume depending on free space available.

`--percent`

Size of the logical volume as a percentage of the free space available.

- `partition` (required for installs)

Create a filesystem partition. Formatted by default unless `--noformat` and `--onpart` are specified. Only applicable to installations, not upgrades.

The following options are available:

`<mntpoint>`

Mount point for the partition. Valid formats for the mount point are as follows:

Directory path such as `/`, `/tmp`, or `/home`

`swap` to specify a swap partition

`raid.<id>` for software RAID

`pv.<id>` for LVM

`--size=`

Minimum size for the partition, in megabytes.

`--grow`

Allow size of partition to increase if space is available. If a maximum size is provided with `--maxsize=`, logical volume will not be bigger than this maximum size.

`--maxsize=`

If `--grow` is used to allow the size of the partition to increase, this option should be set to the maximum size the partition is allowed to grow, in megabytes.

`--noformat`

Do not format partition. Use with `--onpart` directive.

`--onpart=`

Existing partition such as `sda1` on which to place the partition. Use `--noformat` if you don't want the existing partition to be formatted during installation.

`--ondisk`

Hard drive such as `sda` on which to create the partition.

`--asprimary`

Create partition as a primary partition or fail.

`--fstype=`

Filesystem type. Must be one of `ext2`, `ext3`, `swap`, or `vfat`.

`--fsoptions=`

Mounting options to use for the filesystem. They are copied to `/etc/fstab`.

`--bytes-per-inode=`

Size of inodes for the filesystem on the partition. Ignored if the filesystem specified does not support this feature.

`--label=`

Filesystem label to use for the partition.

`--start=`

If `--ondisk=` is used, this directive can be used to provide a starting cylinder for the partition. The ending cylinder must be listed with the `--end=` directive, and the partition size must be provided with `--size=`.

`--end=`

Ending cylinder for partition if `--start=` is used.

`--recommended`

Let the installation program automatically calculate the size of the partition depending on free space available.

`--onbiosdisk`

Create the partition on a specific hard drive as determined by the BIOS.

- `raid`

  Create a software RAID device with the following options:

  `<mntpoint>`

  Mount point for the RAID filesystem. RAID level must be 1 for the `/boot` partition or the partition containing the `/boot` directory such as the `/` partition.

  `--level=`

  RAID level. Must be `0`, `1`, or `5`.

  `--device=`

  RAID device name to use from `md0` to `md7`.

  `--fstype=`

  Filesystem type. Must be one of `ext2`, `ext3`, `swap`, or `vfat`.

  `--fsoptions=`

  Mounting options to use for the filesystem. They are copied to `/etc/fstab`.

  `--bytes-per-inode=`

  Size of inodes for the filesystem. Ignored if the filesystem specified does not support this feature.

  `--spares=`

  Number of spare drives for the RAID array.

  `--noformat`

  Do not format. Use with `--useexisting`.

  `--useexisting`

  Use an existing RAID device. Formatted unless `--noformat` is also specified.

- `dmraid`

  Rename an IDE RAID device.

  `--name=`

  New device name.

  `--dev=`

  Device to rename.

- `multipath`

  Multipath is a kernel feature that allows a device to be configured with multiple spare devices in case of device failure. Use the following syntax:

  ```
  multipath --name=<name> --device=<devicelist> --rule=<rule>
  ```

1

- `zfcp`

  On IBM System z systems, the `zfcp` driver can be used to support Fibre Channel Protocol (FCP) devices. All zFCP devices must be configured manually (not automatically configured during installation). All of the following arguments are required.

  `--devnum=`

  Specify the 16-bit device number.

  `--fcplun=`

  Specify the 64-bit FCP LUN.

  `--scsiid=`

  Specify the SCSI ID number.

  `--scsilun=`

  Specify the SCSI LUN.

  `--wwpn=`

  Specify the 64-bit World Wide Port Number (WWPN).

- `ignoredisk`

  Ignore the listed disks when partitioning, formatting, and clearing.

  `--drives=[list]`

  The list should be a comma-separated list of drive names.

Additional Commands

- `device`

  If the installation program does not properly probe one or more PCI devices, use this directive to configure them with the following required parameters:

  `<type>`

  Either `scsi` or `eth`.

  `<modulename>`

  Kernel module to use for the device.

  `--opts=`

  Kernel module options. To list more than one option, separate them by a space and place all the options inside one set of quotation marks.

- `driverdisk`

  Location of driver disk to use for installation. Can either be on a hard drive partition on the system or an FTP, HTTP, or NFS server accessible by the system being installed. To list a hard drive partition containing the contents of the driver disk, where `<fstype>` is either `ext2` or `vfat`:

  ```
  driverdisk <partition> --type=<fstype>
  ```

  To list a network location, where `<proto>` is `ftp`, `http`, or `nfs`:

  ```
  driverdisk -source=<proto>://path/to/driverdisk
  ```

- `firewall`

  Firewall settings to use. Can be modified with `system-config-securitylevel` after installation. One of `--enabled` or `–disabled` must be used if this directive is listed. Optionally use the following parameters:

  `--trust=`

  Devices such as `eth0` from which to allow all incoming traffic. To list multiple devices, reuse the `--trust` parameter such as `--trust=eth0 --trust=eth1`.

  `--ssh`

  Allow incoming SSH connections.

  `--telnet`

  Allow incoming Telnet connections.

  `--smtp`

  Allow incoming SMTP connections.

  `--http`

  Allow incoming HTTP connections.

  `--ftp`

  Allow incoming FTP connections.

  `--port=`

  Allow incoming traffic from a specific port in the port:protocol format such as `2049:tcp`. Separate multiple port/protocol combinations with commas.

- `firstboot`

  If `--enable` is specified, the Setup Agent is started the first time the system boots after installation. If `--disable` is specified, the Setup Agent is not started at first boot. If `--enable --reconfig` is used with the `firstboot` directive, the Setup Agent is started at first boot in reconfiguration mode.

- `reboot`

  Reboot when the installation is finished. If not specified, the system waits for a key response before rebooting.

- `repo` (experimental)

  Additional yum repository in which to locate RPM packages for installation. Specify one repository per line in the kickstart file. Specify the repository ID with the `--name=` option. Use either `--baseurl=` to provide the URL for the repository or `--mirrorlist=` to provide the URL for a mirror list.

- `selinux`

  Configure Security-Enhanced Linux (SELinux) for the installed system. Set to one of the following:

  `--disabled`

  Disable SELinux.

  `--enforcing`

  Enforce the default SELinux policy.

  `--permissive`

  Enable SELinux in permissive mode, only logging events that should be denied but not enforcing them.

NOTE

If not set, SELinux will be enforced by default. Refer to Chapter 23, "Protecting Against Intruders with Security-Enhanced Linux," for more information about SELinux.

- `services`

  Enable or disable specific services for the installed system. The disabled list is processed before the enabled list. Specify services to disable with `--disabled=<list>`, where `<list>` is a comma-separated list. Use `--enabled=<list>` to configure which services to start at boot time.

- `skipx`

  Do not configure the X Window System on the installed system.

- `user`

  Create a new user on the installed system with the following parameters:

  `--name= (required)`

  Username.

`--groups=`

The user is automatically added to a user private group with the same name as the username. To add the user to additional user groups, specify them in a comma-separated list.

`--homedir=`

Home directory for the user if you do not want to use the default value `/home/<username>`.

`--password=`

Password for the user. If not specified, the account is locked.

`--isencrypted`

Use if the password provided with `--password` is already encrypted.

`--shell=`

Login shell. Defaults to bash if not specified.

`--uid=`

UID for the user. If not specified, the next available non-system UID is used.

- `vnc`

  Start the VNC server so that the graphical version of the installation program can be displayed remotely. If no arguments are provided, the VNC server is started, and the command to connect a remote client is displayed. Optionally, include the following arguments on the same line in the kickstart file:

  `--host=`

  After starting the VNC server, connect it to the VNC viewer on this host.

  `--port=`

  Port on which the remote VNC viewer is listening.

  `--password=`

  Password that must be correctly given to connect to the VNC server running the installation program. If this option is not used, a password is not configured.

- `xconfig`

  Set up the X Window System if it is to be installed on the system. The following options are available and should be listed on the same line:

`--driver=`

Video card driver to use.

`--videoram=`

Amount of RAM on the video card.

`--defaultdesktop=`

Set the default desktop to either `GNOME` or `KDE`. The desktop chosen must also be installed in the `%packages` section.

`--startxonboot`

If used, the login screen is set to the graphical login screen and users are provided with the default graphical desktop after successful login.

`--resolution=`

Default resolution for the screen. Must be compatible with the video card and monitor combination. Possible values are `640x480`, `800x600`, `1024x768`, `1152x864`, `1280x1024`, `1400x1050`, and `1600x1200`.

`--depth=`

Default color depth. Must be compatible with the video card and monitor combination. Possible values are `8`, `16`, `24`, and `32`.

- `zerombr`

  If set to `yes`, all invalid partition tables found are initialized.

- `logging`

  Customize installation logging.

  `--host=`

  Write log messages to a remote host, which has syslogd running and accepts remote logging.

  `--port=`

  Specify a port to use for remote logging.

  `--level=`

  All log messages are written to the log file. Use this option to configure what messages appear on tty3 during installation. Set to `debug`, `info`, `warning`, `error`, or `critical`.

- `%include`

  Use to provide the path to another file containing kickstart commands. The contents of the additional file are read as if they were located in the kickstart file in place of the `%include` line.

Package Section

The installation program installs a certain list of packages by default and allows for limited selection of additional software sets as described in the "Performing the Installation" section. The `%package` section of the kickstart file allows the administrator to list additional packages or package groups.

Under the `%package` line, package group names are preceded by the `@` symbol and a space. Individual package names are listed by themselves, one per line. If the individual package name is preceded by a minus sign (`-`), the package is not installed.

A list of package groups and the individual packages in each group are listed in the `<variant>/repodata/comps-<name>.xml` file on the first installation CD. Replace `<variant>` with `Server`, `Client`, or another directory name associated with an additional software entitlement such as `VT` for virtualization. Replace `<name>` with the rest of the filename used such as `rhel5-server-core` for the `Server/repodata/` directory.

In the `comps` file, under the `<group>` level, the value of the `<name>` or the `<id>` field can be used as the package group name in the kickstart file. The default and optional packages in the group are under the `<packagelist>` tag.

The Core and Base package groups are always installed and do not have to be listed in the `%packages` section. Listing 1.1 shows an example `%package` section.

LISTING 1.1 Example `%package` Section

```
%packages
@ DNS Name Server
@ FTP Server
dhcp
```

In Red Hat Enterprise Linux 4 and lower, language support in addition to the default language listed with the `--lang` directive in the command section was added with the `--langsupport` directive. Additional language support is now added in the `%package` section with a package group name such as `Croatian Support` as listed in the `comps.xml` file.

If the `--ignoremissing` parameter is used on the `%packages` line, packages or package groups listed but not found are ignored and the installation will continue without them. If this parameter is not used, the installation program will pause and prompt whether or not to continue, requiring user interaction before continuing or aborting.

Preinstallation Section

Optionally, a script can be provided and run immediately after the kickstart file is parsed and before the installation begins. The network is available, but DNS lookup is not.

The section must begin with the `%pre` line. The following parameters can be specified after `%pre` on the same line:

`--interpreter <interpreter>`

Use a specific scripting language such as `/usr/bin/python` to process the script.

`--erroronfail`

If the script fails, pause the installation and display an error dialog showing the location of the failure in the script.

Post-installation Section

Optionally, a script can be run immediately after the installation is complete and before the system is rebooted. After installation, the network is available. However, DNS servers are not available unless a primary nameserver was specified when configuring a static IP address. If DHCP was used, DNS lookup is not available and IP addresses must be used.

The section must begin with the `%post` line. The following parameters can be specified after `%post` on the same line:

`--nochroot`

Don't run the post-installation script in the change root environment. By default, the post-installation script is run in a change root environment where the `/mnt/sysimage` directory is treated as the root filesystem. Thus, by default, certain operations such as copied files from the installation media will not work unless the `--nochroot` option is used.

`--interpreter <interpreter>`

Use a specific scripting language such as `/usr/bin/python` to process the script.

`--erroronfail`

If the script fails, pause the installation program and display an error dialog showing the location of the failure in the script.

Making the Kickstart File Accessible

The kickstart file must be copied to a location accessible by the installation program. These locations include the following:

- Hard drive partition
- Floppy disk
- HTTP, FTP, or NFS share
- Boot CD

The first three locations are self-explanatory. For example, after setting up an HTTP, FTP, or NFS server, place the kickstart file in a directory shared by the network protocol. However, placing the file on the boot CD created from the `boot.iso` file needs further details. This section also explains how to provide an NFS server location via DHCP.

On the Boot CD

As described in the previous section "Making a Boot Disc," a boot CD can be created from the `images/boot.iso` file on the first installation CD. However, after the boot CD is made from this image, it is read-only, and files cannot be added to it after the CD is created.

The kickstart file must be named `ks.cfg` and must be located in the top-level directory of the CD. To add this file before creating the CD, loopback mount the `boot.iso` image, copy the contents to a different directory, add the `ks.cfg` file to the directory, and then use `mkisofs` to create a new ISO image:

1. Create two empty directories such as `/tmp/bootiso/` and `/tmp/bootisoks/`. The first one will be used to loopback mount the `boot.iso` image, and the second one will be used to create the boot CD with a kickstart file on it.
2. After retrieving the `boot.iso` image from the first installation CD as described in the "Creating a Boot Disc" section earlier in this chapter, use the `su -` command to become the root user, and loopback mount the image into the directory just created:

   ```
   mount -o loop boot.iso /tmp/bootiso/
   ```

3. Type **`exit`** to return to using your normal user account instead of a root shell.
4. Recursively copy the contents of the CD into the second new directory:

   ```
   cp -r /tmp/bootiso/* /tmp/bootisoks/
   ```

5. Change into the directory that now contains the files for the new boot disc:

   ```
   cd /tmp/bootisoks
   ```

6. Change the file permissions of the `isolinux/` directory so you have write access to them:

   ```
   chmod u+w isolinux/*
   ```

7. Copy the kickstart file into this directory, making sure it is named `ks.cfg` on the boot ISO (provide the proper path to the kickstart file):

   ```
   cp <kickstart-file> isolinux/ks.cfg
   ```

8. Create a new ISO image of the boot CD with the kickstart file on it. The command should be issued as one command without the backslash (\). The backslash is used in the following command because the command is too long to fit on one printed line:

   ```
   mkisofs -o bootks.iso -b isolinux.bin -c boot.cat -no-emul-boot \
   -boot-load-size 4 -boot-info-table -R -J -v -T isolinux/
   ```

9. Write the `bootks.iso` image to a CD by either right-clicking on the file in the Nautilus file manager and selecting **Write to Disc...** or using the `cdrecord` utility.

Use this boot CD to start the kickstart installation as described in the "Starting the Kickstart Installation" section later in this chapter.

Over NFS as Defined by the DHCP Server

Instead of having to type the NFS server name and location of the kickstart file on the NFS server each time you start a kickstart installation, you can configure the DHCP server to send this information to the system being installed, as long as it is configured to retrieve its network information via DHCP and the DHCP server supports this feature (Red Hat Enterprise Linux as a DHCP server supports this feature). The DHCP and NFS servers used for kickstart installations can be the same physical system, but they do not have to be.

After setting up the NFS server and making the installation tree available on it, create a directory such as `/kickstart` on the NFS to store the kickstart files for the systems you want to install. Copy the kickstart files to this directory and make sure it is configured as a shared directory via NFS.

Assuming your DHCP server is a Red Hat Enterprise Linux server, on the DHCP server, use the following lines in `dhcpd.conf` to define the NFS server sharing the kickstart files:

```
filename "/shares/kickstart/";
next-server nfs.example.com;
```

If the filename listed in the DHCP server configuration file ends in a slash (/), it is assumed to be a directory, and the installation program looks for the file `<ip-address>-kickstart`, where `<ip-address>` is the IP address of the system being installed as assigned by the DHCP server. If the NFS server is not defined with `next-server`, the installation program assumes the NFS server has the same IP address as the DHCP server. If a path or filename is not specified with `filename`, the installation program assumes the kickstart file is in the `/kickstart` directory on the NFS server with the filename `<ip-address>-kickstart`.

Starting the Kickstart Installation

To start a kickstart installation by PXE booting, refer to the "Installing with PXE" section for details.

Otherwise, to start a kickstart installation, make sure the system's BIOS is configured to boot off the CD-ROM drive, and boot from a boot CD created with `boot.iso` or the first installation CD. Booting off the first installation CD is only required if you are performing a CD-ROM installation. After booting from the CD, a specially formatted command must be issued at the `boot:` prompt. This command varies depending on the location of the kickstart file:

- CD-ROM

  If the kickstart file is located on the boot CD as previously described in the "Making the Kickstart File Accessible" section, use the following command at the `boot:` prompt:

  ```
  linux ks=cdrom:/ks.cfg
  ```

- NFS server

  If the kickstart file is on an NFS server, use the following command at the `boot:` prompt, replacing `<server>` with the hostname or IP address of the NFS server and `<filename>` with the filename of the kickstart file or the path of the directory containing the kickstart file:

  ```
  linux ks=nfs:<server>:/<filename>
  ```

  If the filename listed in the DHCP server configuration file ends in a slash (/), it is assumed to be a directory, and the installation program looks for the file `<ip-address>-kickstart`, where `<ip-address>` is the IP address of the system being installed as assigned by the DHCP server.

- HTTP server

  If the kickstart file is on an HTTP server, use the following command at the `boot:` prompt, replacing `<server>` with the hostname or IP address of the HTTP server and `<filename>` with the filename of the kickstart file or the path of the directory containing the kickstart file:

  ```
  linux ks=http://<server>/<filename>
  ```

- Floppy disk

  If the kickstart file is on a floppy disk, the disk must be formatted as an ext2 or vfat filesystem. If the file is named `ks.cfg` at the root level of the disk (not in a directory), the installation can be started with the following command at the `boot:` prompt:

  ```
  linux ks=floppy
  ```

  If the file is on a floppy disk formatted as an ext2 of vfat filesystem but not on the root directory of the disk, the path to the file as well as the filename can be specified as follows:

  ```
  linux ks=floppy:/<filename>
  ```

- Hard drive

  If the kickstart file is on an ext2 or vfat partition of the hard drive in the system to be installed, use the following command at the `boot:` prompt, replacing `<device>` with the hard drive device name such as `sda1` and `<file>` with the filename of the kickstart file including the full path.

  ```
  linux ks=hd:<device>:/<file>
  ```

- NFS server defined by DHCP

  As described in the previous section "Making the Kickstart File Accessible," the DHCP server can send information about the kickstart file located on an NFS server to the system to be installed. If this configuration is used, use the following command at the `boot:` prompt:

  ```
  linux ks
  ```

NOTE

All of these boot commands assume that the network connection started should use the first Ethernet device (eth0). To use an alternate Ethernet device, append a space and the following to the end of any of the boot commands, replacing `<device>` with the Ethernet device name such as eth1 for the second Ethernet card:

```
ksdevice=<device>
```

Installing with PXE

Some NICs include the ability to boot using a Pre-Execution Environment (PXE). It works by sending out a broadcast request for a DHCP server on the network. If the DHCP server is configured to send the client the IP address or hostname of a tftp server and the location on that tftp server of the files needed to start the Red Hat Enterprise Linux installation, the client can start a network installation without having to boot from local media such as a CD.

This method can also be used with kickstart to perform an automated network installation; it allows the administrator to boot multiple systems and then walk away while the client received first the PXE boot information and then the kickstart file to perform the installation.

To perform a network installation using PXE boot, use the following steps:

1. Create an installation tree for the network install and make it available to the systems being installed. Refer to the "Creating the Installation Source" section earlier in this chapter for details.
2. Configure the tftp server.
3. Configure the DHCP server.
4. Boot the system to start the installation.

Configuring the tftp Server

Information such as the IP address or hostname of the network server sharing the installation tree to use must be retrieved by the client to be installed. The tftp service is used for this purpose. The server running this xinetd service can be the same system used as the NFS, FTP, or HTTP server exporting the installation tree.

The tftp server is not installed by default. Use Red Hat Network as described in Chapter 3, "Operating System Updates," to install the `tftp-server` package, which provides the tftp server. You also need the `syslinux` package if it is not already installed.

The following information must be set for the tftp server:

- *Operating system identifier*: One unique word that describes which installation tree the PXE server points the client to.

  This is used for a unique directory name.

- *Protocol for installations*: Protocol used to export the installation tree on the server. Must be one of NFS, HTTP, or FTP. If non-anonymous FTP is required, uncheck the Anonymous FTP option and enter the username and password for the FTP server.

- *Kickstart location* (optional): If also performing a kickstart installation, the location of the kickstart file. The location can be a local file on the PXE server or a URL such as `http://server.example.com/ksfiles/ks.cfg`.

- *Network server IP address*: IP address or hostname of the NFS, FTP, or HTTP server exporting the installation tree. If a hostname is used, the server must be able to resolve it to a valid IP address.

- *Installation tree location*: Directory on the network server containing the installation tree. Must contain the `images/pxeboot/` directory.

Setting Up the tftp Server Files

First, set up the `/tftpboot/linux-install/<os-ident>/` directory and populate it with the files necessary to start the installation program via PXE (all commands must be executed by the root user):

1. The `/tftpboot/` directory is created by the `tftp-server` package. Create the `/tftpboot/linux-install/` directory.

2. Copy the `/usr/lib/syslinux/pxelinux.0` file installed by the `syslinux` package into the newly created `/tftpboot/linux-install/` directory:

   ```
   cp /usr/lib/syslinux/pxelinux.0 /tftpboot/linux-install/
   ```

3. Create the `/tftpboot/linux-install/msg/` directory.

4. Copy all the .msg files from the `isolinux/` directory in the installation tree or from the first installation CD in the newly created `/tftpboot/linux-install/msg/` directory.

Now, you should have the following files:

```
/tftpboot/linux-install/msgs/boot.msg
/tftpboot/linux-install/msgs/expert.msg
/tftpboot/linux-install/msgs/general.msg
/tftpboot/linux-install/msgs/param.msg
/tftpboot/linux-install/msgs/rescue.msg
/tftpboot/linux-install/msgs/snake.msg
/tftpboot/linux-install/pxelinux.0
```

Use the following steps to configure the files specific to the Red Hat Enterprise Linux version and variant to be installed:

TIP

The same PXE server can be used to offer multiple versions and variants of Red Hat Enterprise Linux if the files for each are located in different `/tftpboot/linux-install/<os-ident>/` directories.

1. Create the `/tftpboot/linux-install/<os-ident>/` directory where `<os-ident>` is a unique identifier for the version and variant of Red Hat Enterprise Linux to install via PXE. For example, `RHEL5Server` could be used for Red Hat Enterprise Linux Server 5.
2. Copy the `initrd.img` and `vmlinuz` files from the `images/pxeboot/` directory of the installation tree or the first installation CD into the `/tftpboot/linux-install/<os-ident>/` directory.
3. If performing a kickstart installation, copy the kickstart file in the `/tftpboot/linux-install/<os-ident>/` directory as well with the `ks.cfg` filename.

Use the following steps to configure the files specific to the systems connecting to the PXE server for installation:

1. Create the `/tftpboot/linux-install/pxelinux.cfg/` directory on the PXE server.
2. The `/tftpboot/linux-install/pxelinux.cfg/` directory should contain a file for each system to be installed, where the filename is the IP address or hostname of the system to be installed. If the system to be installed does not have a configuration file based on its IP address, the configuration information in the file named `default` is used. An example file for the `pxelinux.cfg/` directory is in Listing 1.2. In Listing 1.2, replace `<os-ident>` with the directory name created for Red Hat Enterprise Linux version and variant to install on the system, and replace `<method>` with the network installation method to use for the installation such as `nfs:<server>:/<dir>`.

LISTING 1.2 Example pxelinux.cfg/ File

```
default local
timeout 100
prompt 1
display msgs/boot.msg
F1 msgs/boot.msg
F2 msgs/general.msg
F3 msgs/expert.msg
F4 msgs/param.msg
F5 msgs/rescue.msg
F7 msgs/snake.msg

label local
  localboot 1

label 0
  localboot 1


label 1
  kernel <os-ident>/vmlinuz
  append initrd=<os-ident>/initrd.img ramdisk_size=6878 \
  method=<method> ip=dhcp
```

Enabling and Starting the tftp Service

After configuring the `tftp` server and which clients are allowed to connect to it, to PXE boot a network installation of Red Hat Enterprise Linux, enable the service at boot time and start it. The `tftp` service is controlled by `xinetd`, so enable `tftp` and `xinetd` with the following commands as the root user:

```
chkconfig -level 345 xinetd on
chkconfig -level 345 tftp on
```

If xinetd is already running, restart it as the root user:

```
service xinetd restart
```

If it is not already running, start it as the root user:

```
service xinetd start
```

Configuring the DHCP Server

If you do not already have a DHCP server setup on your network, consult Chapter 14, "Granting Network Connectivity with DHCP," for details. The lines in Listing 1.3 must be in the `dhcpd.conf` file to enable PXE booting. Replace `<server-ipaddress>` with the IP address or hostname of the PXE server.

LISTING 1.3 Enabling PXE Booting on the DHCP Server

```
allow booting;
allow bootp;
class "pxeclients" {
   match if substring(option vendor-class-identifier, 0, 9) = "PXEClient";
   next-server <server-ipaddress>
   filename "linux-install/pxelinux.0";
}
```

Starting the PXE Network Installation

To start the PXE installation, configure the client to boot via PXE. This step varies per system, so consult your motherboard or network card documentation for details. Then, boot the system and wait for the first installation screen to appear. Follow the steps in the "Performing the Installation" section earlier in this chapter to finish the installation. If performing a kickstart installation, wait for the installation to complete and reboot the system.

Performing an Upgrade

If the system already has an older version of Red Hat Enterprise Linux installed, it can be upgraded, preserving the data on the system while upgrading the packages to the latest versions.

To perform an upgrade, either choose **Upgrade an existing installation** during the interactive installation or use the `upgrade` directive in the kickstart file.

CAUTION

Even if you are not reformatting partitions with data that needs to be preserved, it is important that you back up all data before performing the upgrade in case an error occurs.

When performing an upgrade, the steps are similar to those described in the "Performing the Installation" section earlier in this chapter. However, some screens are omitted because their operations are not permitted for upgrades. For example, the system cannot be repartitioned because it would cause data loss.

An upgrade is achieved by using the upgrade option to RPM as discussed in Chapter 5, "Working with RPM Software." Refer to Chapter 5 to learn more about how configuration files are preserved if a package is upgraded.

Red Hat Network Provisioning

Red Hat Enterprise Linux subscribers who have opted to set up a RHN Satellite Server can also subscribe to the RHN Provisioning module, which allows clients to retrieve a kickstart file from the Satellite Server.

After setting up the Satellite Server, connect to its web interface from any system on the network. From the top horizontal menu, select **Systems, Kickstart**, **System Details, Provisioning** to access the kickstart profile creation wizard.

If the system to be installed has a NIC with PXE, you can use PXE booting to start the installation as described in the "Installing with PXE" section with the location of the kickstart file being on the satellite server using the HTTP protocol.

Summary

As you now know, installation can range from a simple sequence of questions to a complex list of directives with optional preinstallation and post-installation scripts. It can also be scheduled and automated with Red Hat Network. The Red Hat Enterprise Linux installation program can be adapted to fit your needs as an administrator, depending on how many systems you need to install and how often you install or reinstall.

CHAPTER 2

Post-Installation Configuration

IN THIS CHAPTER

- Red Hat Setup Agent
- Logging In for the First Time
- Network Configuration
- Printer Configuration
- Adding Boot Parameters

Chapter 1, "Installing Red Hat Enterprise Linux," detailed the Red Hat Enterprise Linux installation process. A customized software set was installed based on the system's hardware and a series of questions answered by the installer. However, before the system is up and running, it is necessary to answer a few more questions with the Red Hat Setup Agent. This chapter also discusses common configuration changes usually made shortly after installation.

Red Hat Setup Agent

The Red Hat Setup Agent guides you through some important post-installation configuration tasks, including setting up a basic firewall, deciding whether to enable SELinux, registering your system for Red Hat Network so it can receive updates, and adding users.

After installing Red Hat Enterprise Linux and rebooting, the Setup Agent welcome screen appears (see Figure 2.1). The list on the left side of the screen shows the tasks the Setup Agent will guide you through. Click Forward to continue.

NOTE

The screenshots for the Red Hat Setup Agent shown in this chapter are for the graphical version. This version is shown if you have selected to use the graphical login screen (the default). If you configured your system to use a text-based login screen, which is the default if you do not install a graphical desktop, the Red Hat Setup Agent appears in text-mode. The questions are the same, but the interface will look slightly different.

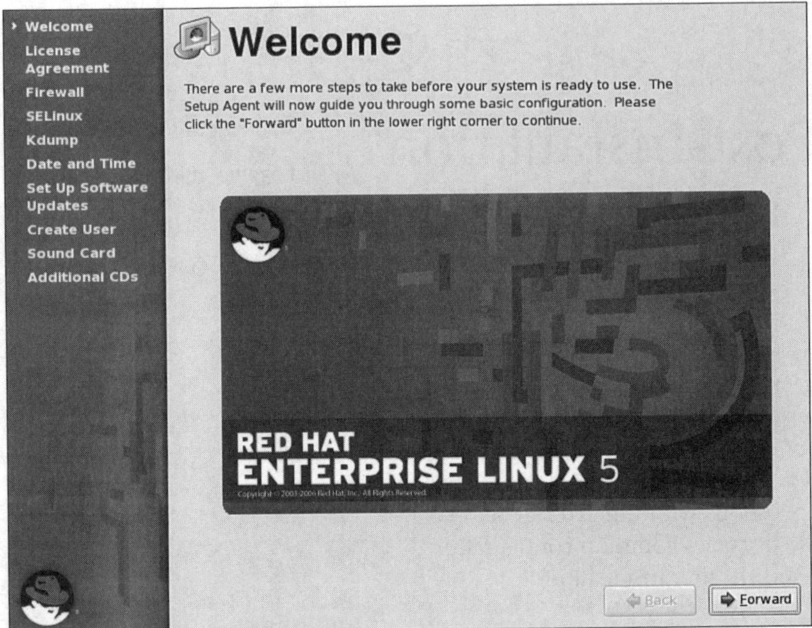

FIGURE 2.1 Welcome to the Setup Agent

The first task is to read the License Agreement, which explains that the software can be copied, modified, and redistributed with the exception of a few image files such as the Red Hat logo. You must agree to the license before continuing to use Red Hat Enterprise Linux.

The next step is to determine whether or not to enable the built-in firewall (see Figure 2.2). If you prefer to configure a custom firewall using IPTables (refer to Chapter 24, "Configuring a Firewall") you can either disable the built-in firewall or enable it for now and then disable it later after configuring IPTables.

To modify the firewall settings later, start the Security Level Configuration Tool by selecting the **System** menu from the top panel of the desktop and selecting **Administration, Security Level and Firewall** or by executing the `system-config-securitylevel` command. If you are not root when you run the tool, you will be prompted to enter the root password before continuing.

Security-Enhanced Linux, or SELinux, allows administrators to add an additional layer of security to Linux. Instead of relying on users to secure their files with file permissions and software distributors to make the default file permissions of critical system files secure, SELinux only allows processes access to files they absolutely need to function. For details on SELinux, refer to Chapter 23, "Protecting Against Intruders with Security-Enhanced Linux." Select one of three SELinux modes (see Figure 2.3):

- **Enforcing**: Configure SELinux for the system using the default targeted policy
- **Permissive**: Only warn about services protected by SELinux
- **Disabled**: Turn off SELinux

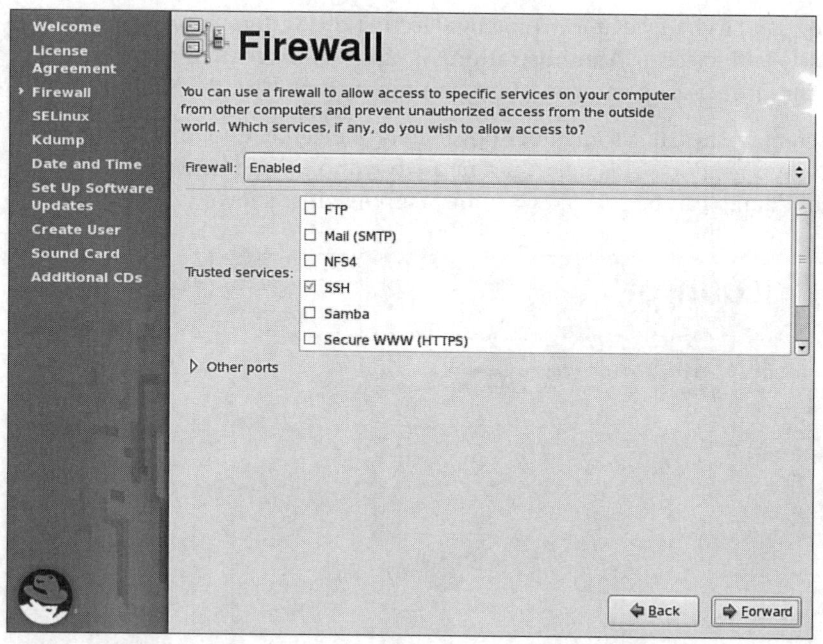

FIGURE 2.2 Enabling a Basic Firewall

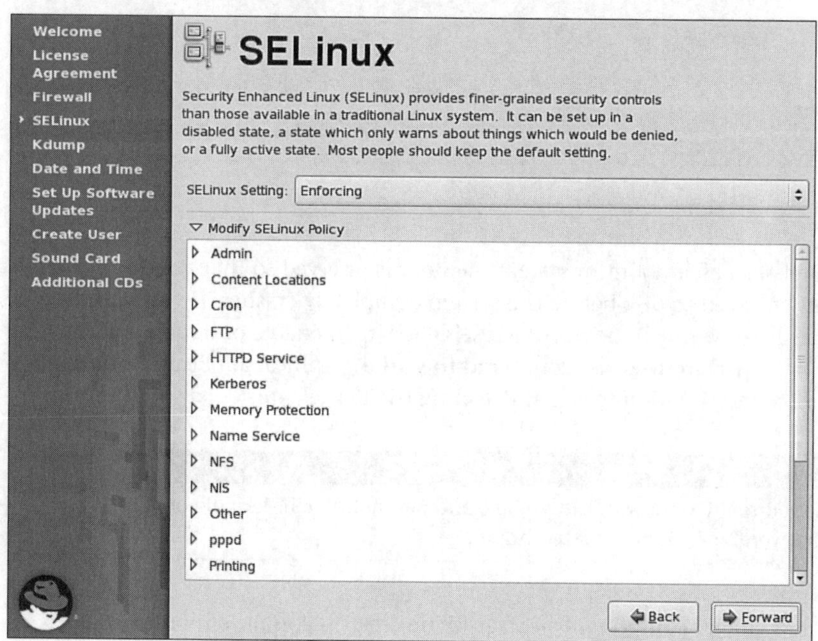

FIGURE 2.3 Security-Enhanced Linux

The SELinux mode can be changed at any time by selecting the **System** menu from the top panel of the desktop and selecting **Administration**, **SELinux Management** or by executing the `system-config-selinux` command. After starting the tool, click the **SELinux** tab.

When a Linux system crashes, it is sometimes possible for the kernel to output a snapshot, or *dump*, of the system memory. This dump can be analyzed to try and determine the cause of the crash. Kdump can be enabled with the Setup Agent as shown in Figure 2.4.

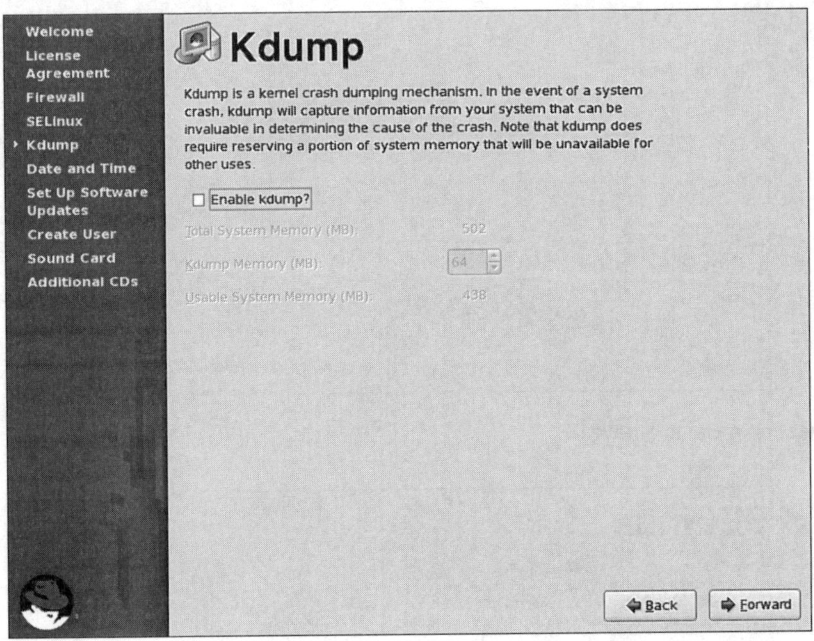

FIGURE 2.4 Enabling Kdump

If Kdump is enabled, a small amount of system memory is reserved so that the dump can be written to it and then saved to disk before the system completely crashes. If you select to enable Kdump, specify how much memory to reserve for it. To enable or disable Kdump later, execute the `system-config-kdump` command to start a graphical application for configuring it. Refer to Chapter 21, "Monitoring and Tuning the Kernel," for details on Kdump.

CAUTION

Kdump does not currently work with the Visualization kernel. If your kernel version ends with the keyword `xen`, do not enable Kdump.

The system time is a crucial component of a server or desktop computer whenever files are shared or synchronized. The Date and Time screen in Figure 2.5 can be used to set the correct date and time and optionally configure a Network Time Protocol (NTP) server that synchronizes the system's time with a time server. For more information about NTP, refer to Chapter 19, "Explaining Other Common Network Services."

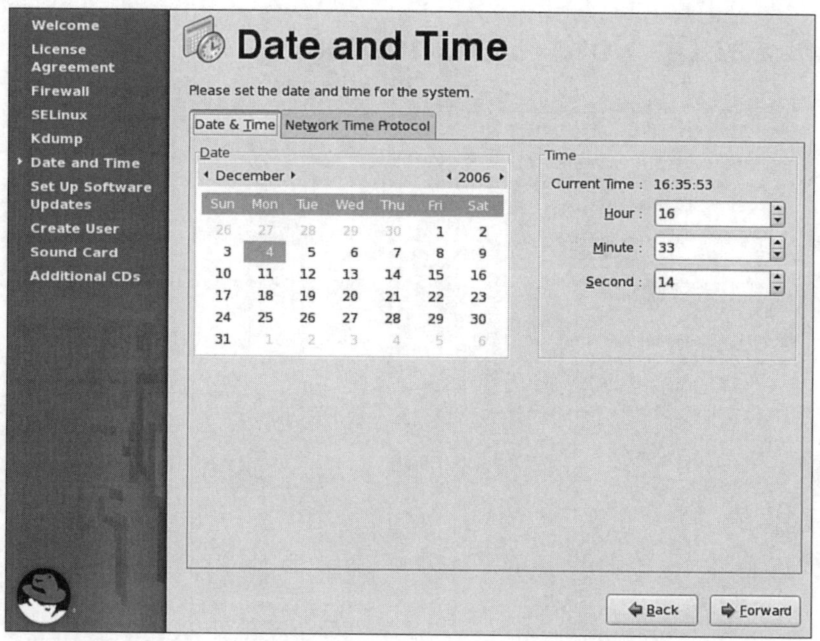

FIGURE 2.5 Setting the Date and Time

The Red Hat Network (RHN) activation process begins next, as shown in the screen in Figure 2.6. Parts of the RHN service including software updates are included with each Red Hat Enterprise Linux subscription. RHN notifies administrators of updates, permits updates to be applied immediately or scheduled, allows additional software to be installed, and more. Refer to Chapter 3, "Operating System Updates," for details.

To activate the RHN subscription for the system, select **Yes, I'd like to register now** and click **Forward**.

TIP

If you choose not to activate your subscription or register the system with RHN, you can do so later by going to http://www.redhat.com/apps/activate/ and executing the command rhn_register as root.

Next, you need to choose which server to connect to for receiving software updates (see Figure 2.7). Most users will connect to Red Hat Network. Only select the other option if you have an RHN Satellite or RHN Proxy Server setup on your network.

If you don't have a Red Hat login, click **Create a New Account** on the next screen. Otherwise, enter your existing Red Hat login and password to continue. If you already have a login, it is extremely important to use it for every system registration so that all your systems are associated with the same account and can be grouped for services or mirroring later.

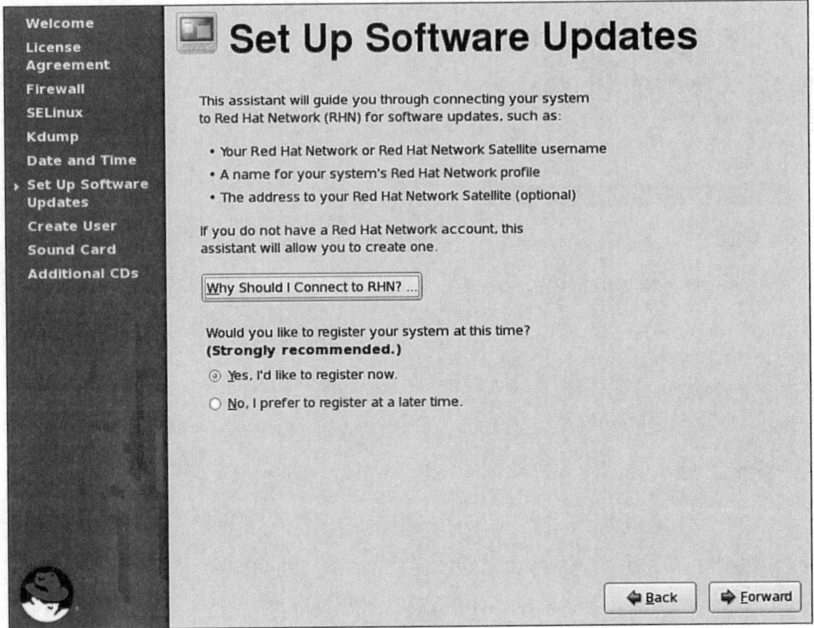

FIGURE 2.6 Setting Up Software Updates

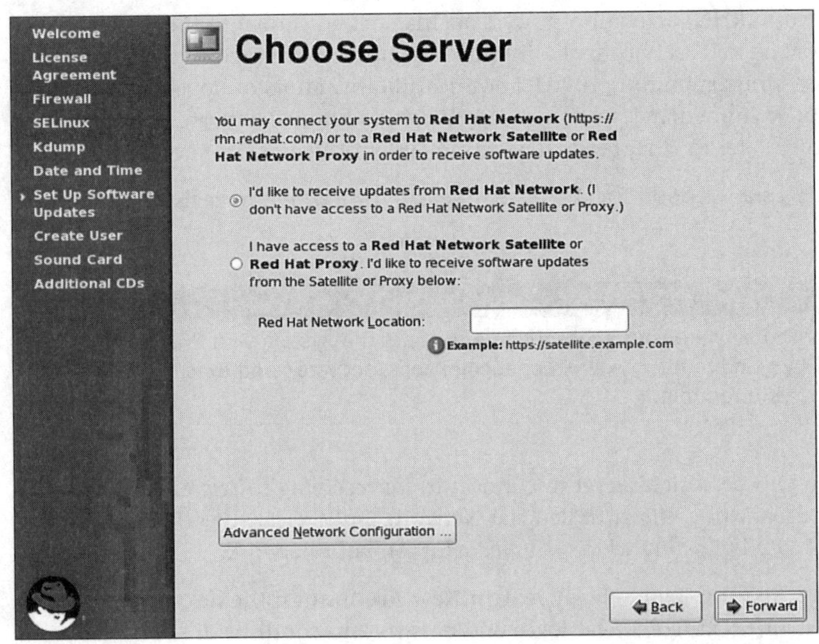

FIGURE 2.7 Connecting to RHN

After you have entered a valid username and password combination or created a new login, information for the system profile is requested (see Figure 2.8). The default system name is the fully qualified hostname, but it can be changed to a more descriptive name such as *Primary Backup System* or *Web Server #3*. By default, hardware and software information is also saved in the system's Red Hat Network profile. If you choose not to include the package list as part of the RHN profile, Red Hat Network will not be able to notify you when updates are available for the system because it doesn't know what packages are already installed. The next two Setup Agent screens provide a summary of your RHN subscription and inform you that an icon will appear on the graphical desktop panel when updates are available.

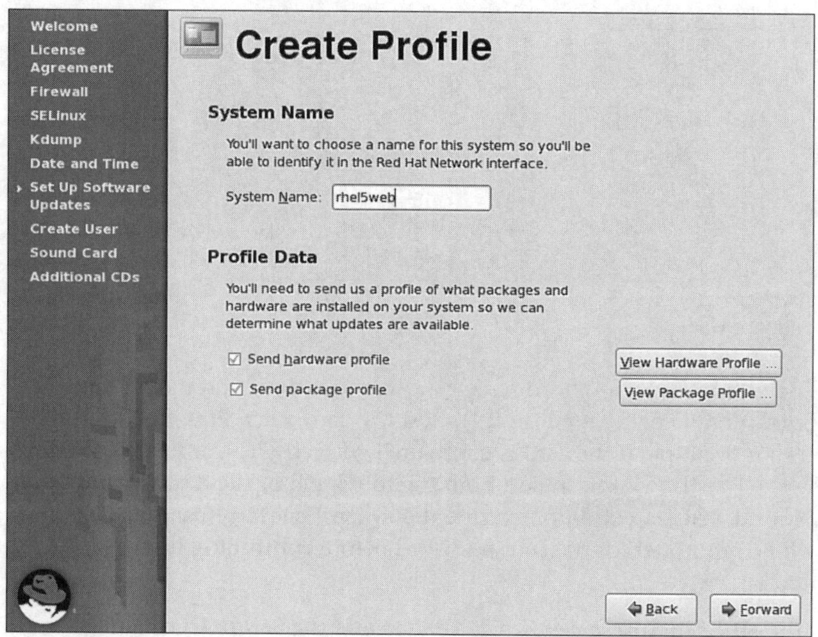

FIGURE 2.8 Creating an RHN System Profile

When installing the operating system, you set up a root password for the administrative account. You should not log in as the root user for normal day-to-day activities. The root account should only be used to perform administrative tasks because certain files are only accessible by the root user. This is for security and also to protect the files from accidentally being deleted, modified, moved, or damaged. The Create User screen in Figure 2.9 allows you to create a non-root user account for everyday use. To add additional users later, select the **System** menu from the top panel of the desktop and select **Administration, Users and Groups** or execute the `system-config-users` command. If your network uses network authentication such as Kerberos or NIS instead, click **Use Network Login**. For more information on network authentication, refer to Chapter 12, "Identity Management."

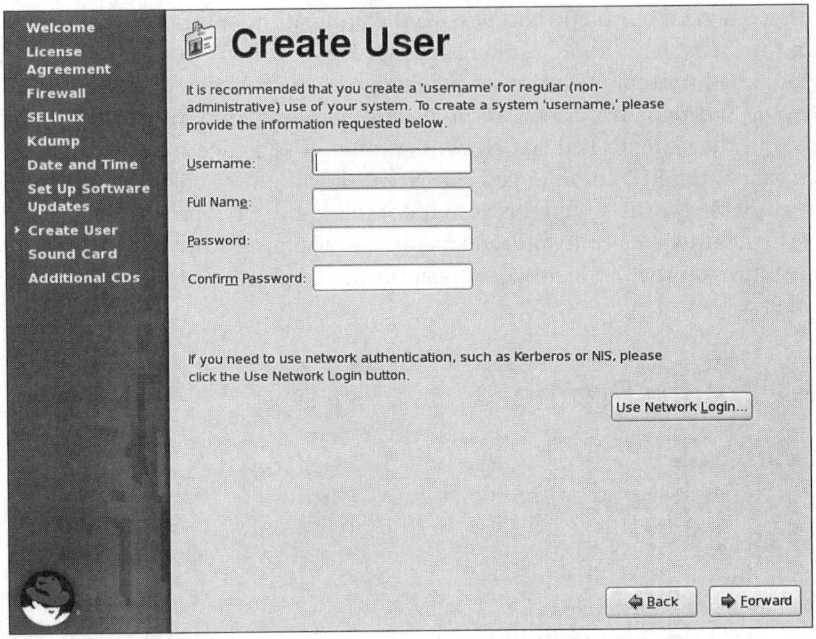

FIGURE 2.9 Creating a User

If a sound card is detected, the Sound Card screen shows the vendor and model number along with the kernel module being used for it. To test the card, click **Play test sound**. You should hear a sound sample if the card is configured correctly. To configure or test the sound card later, select the **System** menu from the top panel of the desktop and select **Administration**, **Soundcard Detection** or execute the `system-config-soundcard` command. You will be prompted for the root password before continuing if you start the application as a non-root user.

The last screen is the **Finish Setup** screen. Click **Next** to exit the Setup Agent and go to the login screen.

Logging In for the First Time

After going through the Setup Agent, the graphical login screen appears if you installed the graphical desktop. If you chose not to install the graphical desktop, a text-based login prompt appears.

At the login screen or prompt, type the username you configured on the Create User screen of the Setup Agent or any non-root user authenticated with a network service such as Kerberos or NIS, press Enter, and type the password for the user.

Upon successful authentication, the graphical desktop as shown in Figure 2.10 appears if the graphical desktop was installed, or a command prompt appears if the graphics subsystem was not installed.

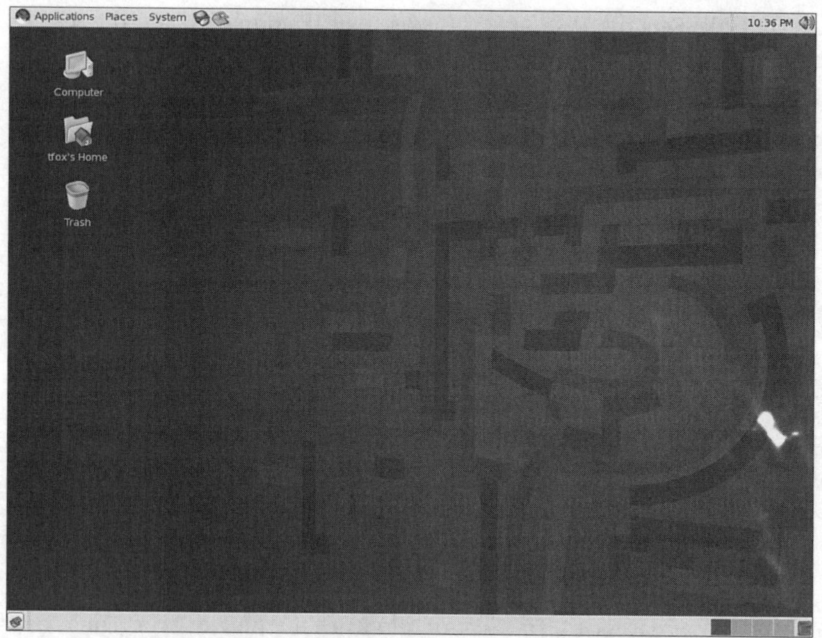

FIGURE 2.10 Default Graphical Desktop

Network Configuration

If an Ethernet card was present during installation, the installation program allowed you to configure the device. This section explains how to modify the configuration after installation. Even if you don't need to modify the network settings, you can use the information in this section to verify the settings are correct.

NOTE

Because some servers do not have graphical desktops installed, this section discusses network configuration from the command line by modifying configuration files. If you have a graphical desktop and want to use a graphical application, go to the **System** menu on the top panel and select **Administration, Network**.

Network Configuration Files

The following configuration files exist for network configuration:

- `/etc/modprobe.conf` file: Assigns a kernel module to each network device.
- `/etc/sysconfig/network` file: Sets the hostname and whether the networking is enabled. IPv6 is enabled or disabled in this file.
- `/etc/hosts` files: Lists hosts and their IP addresses for hostnames that can't be resolved by the DNS servers such as systems on the local network.

- `/etc/resolv.conf` file: Sets the DNS servers (using their IP addresses) and the search domain. The values of the DNS servers are often added when the network is activated because the data can be provided by DHCP or a similar service.
- `/etc/sysconfig/network-scripts/` directory: Contains scripts to start and stop a network device and a specialized configuration file for each device.
- `/etc/rc.d/init.d/network` file: Initialization script that starts and stops the network.

CAUTION

If the Graphical Network Configuration Tool from the Administration, Network menu item of the System menu has ever been run on the system, an `/etc/sysconfig/networking/` directory will exist. The files in this directory are only used by the graphical tool and are not referenced by any of the network scripts. If changes are made to these files, they will not be applied to the actual network configuration files used.

Some of the network configuration files such as the `ifup` and `ifdown` scripts in `/etc/sysconfig/network-scripts/` do not need to be modified in most cases and should not be modified unless absolutely necessary. This section discusses the network configuration files that may be modified to change the network settings and how to enable the changes.

Listing 2.1 shows an example of a `/etc/modprobe.conf` file. The first line assigns the e100 kernel module to the eth0 network device. If the network card is supported, the module is automatically configured during installation or by Kudzu the first time the system is booted with the new card. Refer to Chapter 6, "Analyzing Hardware," for more detailed information about how Kudzu works, how to add module parameters to the `/etc/modprobe.conf` file, or how to change which kernel module is used for each device.

LISTING 2.1 /etc/modprobe.conf

```
alias eth0 e100
alias scsi_hostadapter sata_sil
alias scsi_hostadapter1 ata_piix
```

The `/etc/sysconfig/network` file usually contains the content shown in Listing 2.2. If the `NETWORKING` option is set to `yes`, the networking subsystem is enabled but not necessarily started at boot time. The value of the `HOSTNAME` option is the hostname for the system. If one is not set, the default hostname is localhost. Refer to the file `/usr/share/doc/initscripts-<version>/sysconfig.txt` for additional options for this file.

LISTING 2.2 /etc/sysconfig/network

```
NETWORKING=yes
HOSTNAME=smallville
```

The /etc/hosts file lists IP addresses and hostnames that should resolve to the IP addresses as shown in Listing 2.3. The first one listed, 127.0.0.1, is referred to as the loopback interface and should never be removed. If some hostnames can not be resolved by the DNS servers, list them with their IP addresses after the loopback device. For example, if your network only consists of a handful of systems, it might be easier to list them in the /etc/hosts file on each local system than set up a DNS server on the local network for name resolution.

CAUTION

Be careful when listing hostnames that can be resolved by the DNS servers and those that are not under your control. If the IP address of the hostname changes, you will not be able to connect to the host because any IP addresses listed in /etc/hosts have precedence over any IP addresses resolved through the DNS servers.

LISTING 2.3 /etc/hosts

```
# Do not remove the following line, or various programs
# that require network functionality will fail.
127.0.0.1               localhost.localdomain localhost
192.168.0.1             metropolis
192.168.0.2             lois
182.168.0.3             clarkkent
```

A typical /etc/resolv.conf is shown in Listing 2.4. Each nameserver line represents a DNS server, and the search line specifies domain names to try if only the first part of a hostname is used. For example, if just the name smallville is used as a hostname, smallville.example.com and then smallville.example.org will be tried if the /etc/resolv.conf file in Listing 2.4 is on the system.

LISTING 2.4 /etc/resolv.conf

```
nameserver 192.168.0.254
nameserver 192.168.10.254
search example.com example.org
```

In the /etc/sysconfig/network-scripts/ directory, each network device has its own configuration file with the filename ifcfg-<devicename> such as ifcfg-eth0 for the first Ethernet device.

If the device uses DHCP to retrieve network settings, a typical /etc/sysconfig/network-scripts/ifcfg-eth0 file contains the lines from Listing 2.5. If the device is configured for a static IP address, the interface configuration file looks similar to Listing 2.6.

LISTING 2.5 Ethernet Interface Configuration File for DHCP

```
DEVICE=eth0
BOOTPROTO=dhcp
ONBOOT=yes
```

LISTING 2.6 Ethernet Interface Configuration File for Static IP

```
DEVICE=eth0
BOOTPROTO=none
ONBOOT=yes
NETWORK=192.168.1.0
NETMASK=255.255.255.0
IPADDR=192.168.1.15
USERCTL=no
```

If the ONBOOT option is set to yes, the device is activated at boot time using the network initialization script.

Other device names include lo for the local loopback device, pppX for dialup interfaces, and irlanX for infrared devices where X is the device number starting with 0. Refer to the file /usr/share/doc/initscripts-<version>/sysconfig.txt for additional options for the files in this directory.

Starting and Stopping the Network

If an Ethernet device is found during installation and configured, the network is configured to start automatically at boot time unless you unchecked the **Activate on boot** option for the device. To disable it at boot time after installation, use the chkconfig network off command. To enable it at boot time, use the chkconfig network on command.

The /etc/hosts and /etc/resolv.conf are referenced each time they are used, so modifications to them take place immediately. If the hostname is modified in /etc/sysconfig/network, the change does not occur until the next reboot. To immediately change the hostname, execute the command hostname <newhostname> as the root user at a shell prompt, replacing <newhostname> with the new hostname for the system.

If you modify network settings in /etc/sysconfig/network-scripts/, the changes do not take place until the network is restarted or the individual device is shut down and brought back up. To restart the entire network (the loopback device and all network devices), use the command service network restart as root. To shut an individual device down and bring it back up, as root, execute the command ifdown <devicename> and then ifup <devicename>, where <devicename> is the name of the device such as eth0.

To stop all the network devices, use the service network stop command as root. To start the network, use the command service network start as root.

CAUTION

If administering the system remotely, it is better to use `service network restart` if you need to restart the network since stopping the network will prevent you from accessing your system remotely to bring the network back up.

Printer Configuration

One common task not covered by the installation program or the Setup Agent is configuring a printer. Red Hat Enterprise Linux uses the Common UNIX Printing System, also known as *CUPS*. CUPS uses the *Internet Printing Protocol* (IPP) to allow local printing and print sharing. The `/etc/cups/` directory stores all the configuration files for printing. However, these files can be easily managed with the Printer Configuration Tool in Red Hat Enterprise Linux.

NOTE

If you need to share the printer with other computers on the network, use this section to configure the printer and then refer to the "Creating a Network Printer with CUPS" section of Chapter 19, "Explaining Other Common Network Services," for details.

To start the Printer Configuration Tool, go to the System menu on the top panel and select **Administration**, **Printing** or execute the command `system-config-printer`. If you are not root, you will be prompted for the root password.

If no printers are available for the system, only the Server Settings view is available for selection. If local printers are configured, a Local Printers menu is available.

CUPS is the default printing system used by Red Hat Enterprise Linux, and one of its many advantages is that it uses IPP to broadcast shared printers on the network so that other systems can browse for them, select one as the default printer, and print to it without any further configuration. If any printers are broadcast on your network, they will appear in a Remote Printers menu. Figure 2.11 shows a system with both local and remote printers. If a list isn't already expanded, click on the triangle icon to the left of it.

TIP

The log files for the CUPS printing system are located in the `/var/log/cups/` directory. Refer to this directory for access and error logs.

Adding a Printer

If the printer you want to connect to is in the list of remote printers, select it from the list, click **Make Default Printer** from the Settings tab, and click **Apply**. The selected printer becomes the default printer for the system, and all print jobs are sent to it by default.

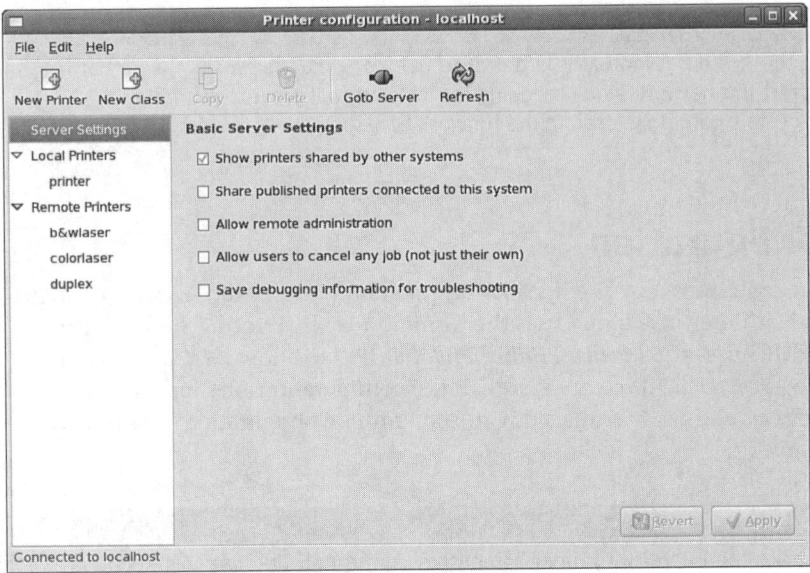

FIGURE 2.11 Local and Remote Printer Lists

If the printer you want to connect to is not already listed (such as a locally connected printer), click **New Printer** on the toolbar. In the dialog window that appears (see Figure 2.12), accept the default queue name or change it to a short, descriptive name that begins with a letter and does not contain spaces. Optionally, give the print queue a short description and location.

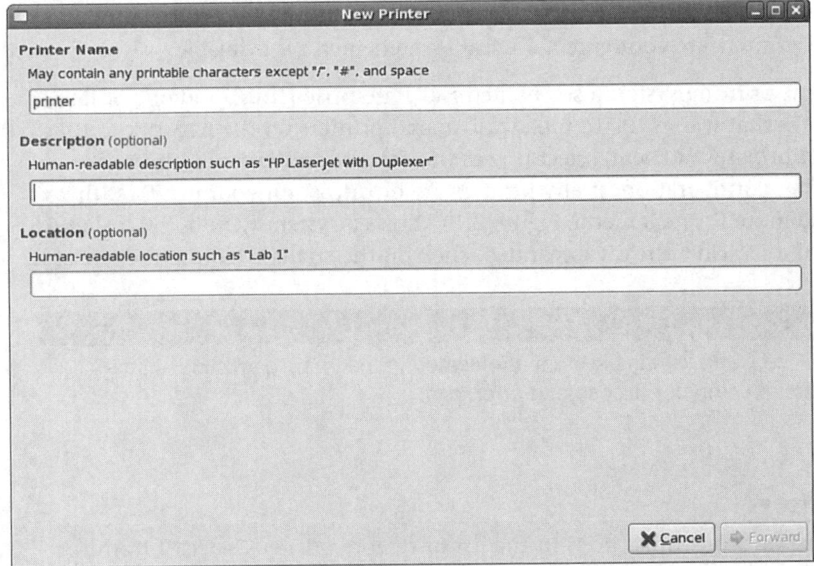

FIGURE 2.12 Entering a Queue Name

In the next window as shown in Figure 2.13, select the connection type.

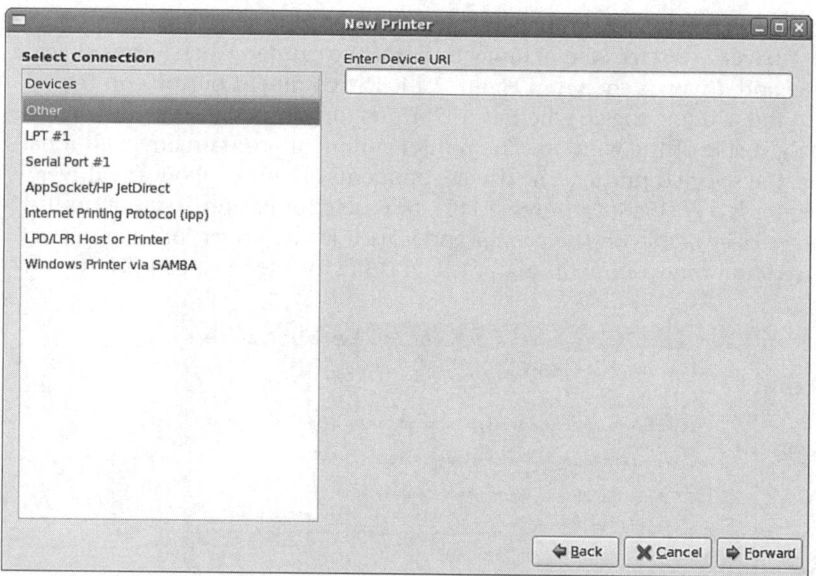

FIGURE 2.13 Selecting a Connection Type

The connection types listed vary per system because the port types vary from system to system. Some systems might have a USB port but not a parallel port. Some systems might have the opposite: a parallel port but no USB port for a printer to connect to. Other than local ports, the Printer Configuration Tool can be used to add the following types of remote printers (all networked printers must allow the system to connect to it via port 631, and all systems trying to connect to a shared printer must be allowed to send and accept connections on port 631):

- **AppSocket/HP JetDirect**: Printer available on the network using HP JetDirect. Provide the hostname as a fully qualified domain name or an IP address of the printer along with the port used to connect to it (default port is 9100).
- **Internet Printing Protocol** (ipp): Printer available on the network using the Internet Printing Protocol (IPP) such as one shared by another Red Hat Enterprise Linux system. Provide the hostname as a fully qualified domain name or an IP address. Also provide the printer name as defined on the print server.
- **LPD/LPR Host or Printer**: Printer available on the network using LPD. Older versions of Linux used LPD. Provide the hostname as a fully qualified domain name or an IP address. Also provide the printer name as defined on the print server.
- **Windows Printer via SAMBA**: Printer available on the network using Samba (SMB) such as a printer connected to and shared by a Microsoft Windows computer. The networked is scanned for Samba shares, and any Samba-shared printers can be found in the list. Click the triangle beside each workgroup or computer name in the list to expand the list. Select the printer or enter its hostname and printer name in the field starting with smb://. If a username and password are required for authentication, supply them as well.

After selecting the connection type and possibly providing additional information for the connection, click **Forward** to select the manufacturer for the printer. Click **Forward** again to select the model and driver as shown in Figure 2.14. The comment buttons on the bottom left side of the window toggle whether the printer, driver, and PPD comments are displayed on the right side of the window. The printer comments contain any additional information about the selected printer. The driver comments are notes about the driver selected. If the printer is a PostScript printer, a PPD, or PostScript Printer Description file, it describes the features available on the printer and is used as the driver for the printer. The PPD comments show any comments about the PPD file for the selected print driver.

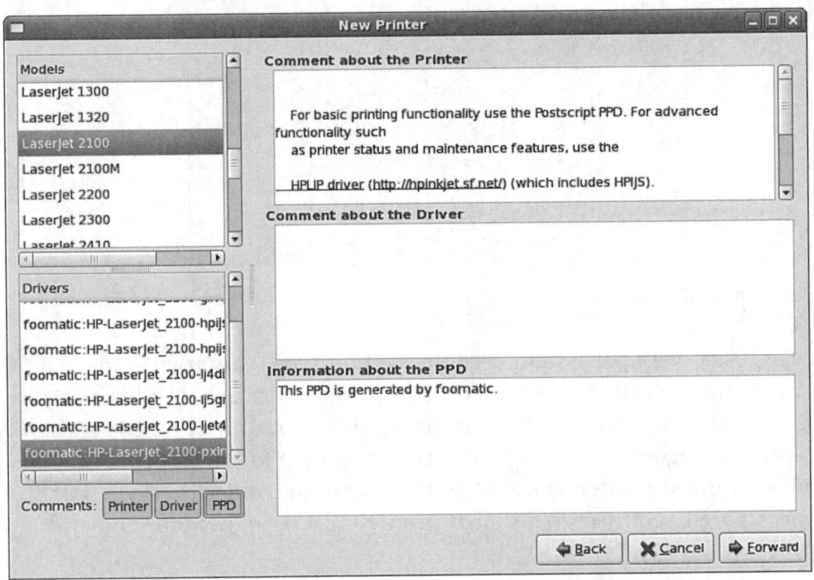

FIGURE 2.14 Selecting a Printer Model and Driver

To finish, click **Forward** and click **Apply** to confirm the printer creation. The main window for the Printer Configuration Tool should now show the new printer in the list. The printer is now ready to accept print jobs. Select it from the list to set advanced options shown in Figure 2.15 such as the default page size, toner density, and whether or not to use a starting or ending banner for each print job.

To print a test page to verify that the printer is configured properly, select the printer from the list on the left, and click **Print Test Page** on the Settings tab.

Adding a Printer Class

A printer class is a group of printers available to the system. The group can consist of both local and remote printers. If a printer class is set as the default printer or is selected as the print queue when printing, the first available printer in the class is sent the print job. One major advantage of using a printer class instead of an individual printer is not having to set a new default printer if the default printer goes offline because of failure or maintenance. It also saves users time by preventing them from sending a print job to a printer already in heavy use. Instead, their print job is sent to a printer that can process it faster.

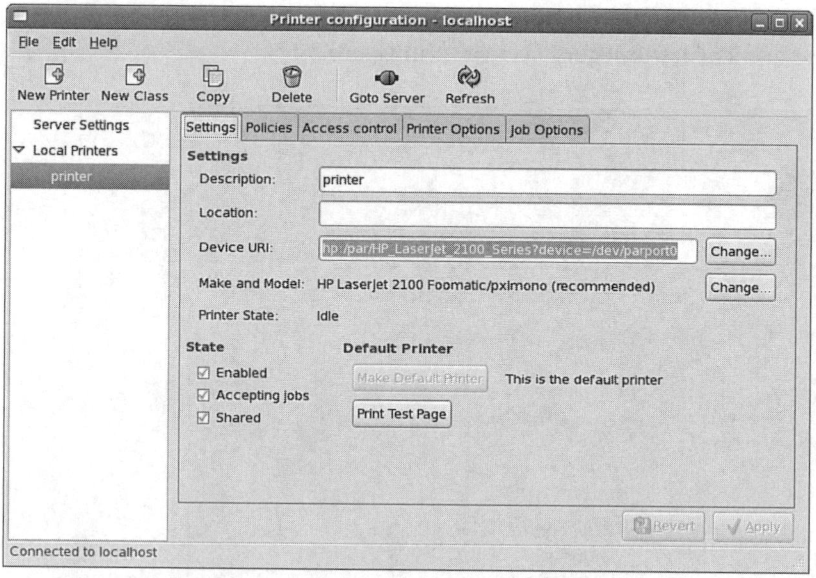

FIGURE 2.15 Advanced Printer Options

To configure a printer class, click **New Class** on the toolbar. Give the printer class a unique name, an optional description, and an optional location. After clicking **Forward**, move one or more configured printers from the Others list to the Members of this Class list as demonstrated in Figure 2.16. Click **Forward** to continue.

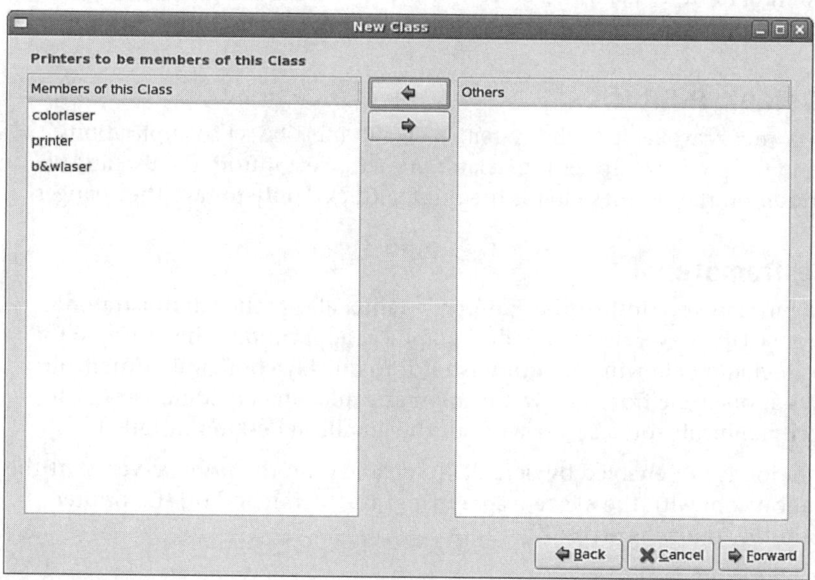

FIGURE 2.16 Selecting Printers for the Class

Click **Apply** to confirm the class creation; the new printer class appears on the main window under the Printer Class category (as shown in Figure 2.17).

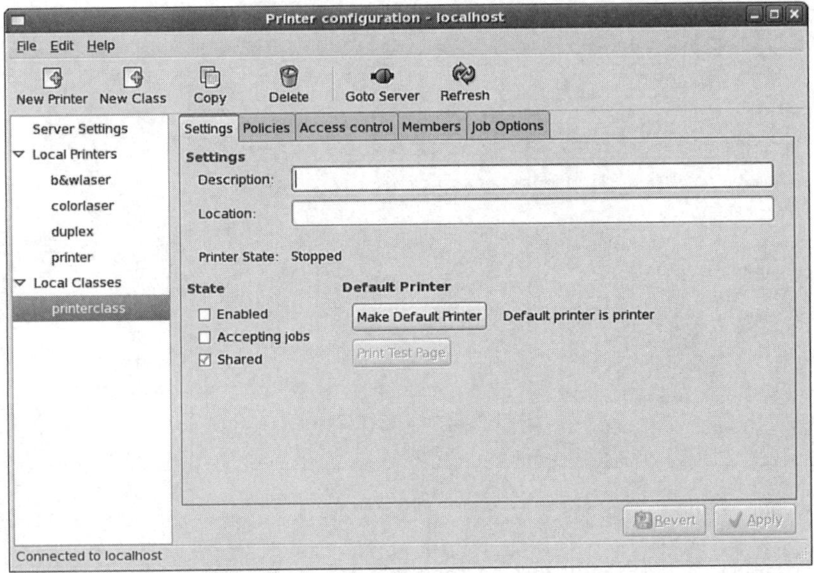

FIGURE 2.17 Printer Class Added

The advanced settings for the printer class are similar to those for an individual printer. You can enable sharing for it, make it the default printer (where the first available from the group is given the print job), and limit the usage to specific users.

Setting the Default Printer

If more than one printer is available to the system, a default must be set so applications know where to send the print job. To set the default printer, select it from the list, and click **Make Default Printer** on the Settings tab for the printer. Click **Apply** to save the changes.

Administering Remotely

The Printer Configuration Tool in Red Hat Enterprise Linux allows the administrator to connect to a remote CUPS server using the local graphical application. This is useful for a variety of reasons including allowing an administrator to quickly configure printers on multiple machines at one time from one workstation and allowing an administrator to configure a printer graphically on a server without the graphical desktop installed.

Remote administration is not enabled by default. To enable it on the print server, start the Printer Configuration Tool with the `system-config-printer` command on the printer server, and perform the following steps:

1. Select **Server Settings.**
2. Select **Allow remote administration.**
3. Click **Apply.**

If the print server does not have the software necessary to run the graphical Printer Configuration Tool, the `/etc/cups/cupsd.conf` file can be edited directly. Make a backup copy of the file before editing it. Remove the lines from Listing 2.7, and add the following lines from Listing 2.8. Also modify the `Allow` lines in the `Location` sections to read `Allow @LOCAL` instead of `Allow localhost` as shown in Listing 2.9. To apply the changes, restart the CUPS service with the `service cups restart` command as root.

LISTING 2.7 Remove to Allow Remote Administration

```
# Only listen for connections from the local machine.
Listen localhost:631
```

LISTING 2.8 Add to Allow Remote Administration

```
# Allow remote access
Port 631
Listen /var/run/cups/cups.sock
```

LISTING 2.9 Modify to Allow Remote Administration

```
<Location />
  # Allow remote administration...
  Order allow,deny
  Allow @LOCAL
</Location>
<Location /admin>
  Encryption Required
  # Allow remote administration...
  Order allow,deny
  Allow @LOCAL
</Location>
<Location /admin/conf>
  AuthType Basic
  Require user @SYSTEM
  # Allow remote access to the configuration files...
  Order allow,deny
  Allow @LOCAL
</Location>
```

After enabling remote administration on the print server, start the Printer Configuration Tool on a different system and click **Goto Server** on the toolbar. In the dialog shown in Figure 2.18, enter the hostname or IP address of the CUPS server and the username to use for authentication. The default username is root, which will work for most cases.

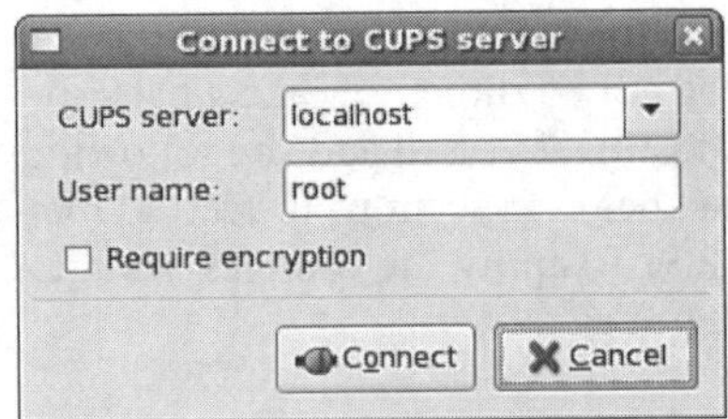

FIGURE 2.18 Connect to Remote Server

Enter the root password when prompted. After successful authentication, the printers and printer classes displayed are for the remote server. The title of the window also changes to reflect the IP address or hostname of the print server being managed.

Adding Boot Parameters

To boot a computer into an operating system, a *boot loader* is needed. When the computer is booted, the boot loader starts the kernel that then starts the rest of the operating system. Different architectures use different boot loaders as shown in Table 2.1.

TABLE 2.1 Boot Loaders for Each Architecture

Architecture	Boot Loader	Boot Loader Configuration File
x86	GRUB	`/etc/grub.conf`
AMD® AMD64	GRUB	`/etc/grub.conf`
Intel® Itanium™	ELILO	`/boot/efi/EFI/redhat/elilo.conf`
IBM® eServer™ iSeries™ (pre-POWER5)	OS/400	`/boot/vmlinitrd-<kernel-version>`
IBM® eServer™ iSeries™ (POWER5)	YABOOT	`/etc/yaboot.conf`
IBM® eServer™ System z	z/IPL	`/etc/zipl.conf`

Sometimes, boot parameters are needed for a system to boot or run properly. For example:

- `noht`: Disable Hyper-Threading
- `noapic`: Disable Advanced Programmable Interrupt Controller (APIC) available on select motherboards
- `acpi=off`: Disable advanced configuration and power interface (acpi)

GRUB

For x86, x86_64, and AMD64 systems, the GRUB boot loader configuration file is `/etc/grub.conf`. Each installed kernel contains a title section, which includes a line that begins with `kernel`. Add boot parameters to the end of the `kernel` line. Listing 2.10 shows the `noht` parameter added.

LISTING 2.10 GRUB Configuration File

```
default=0
timeout=5
splashimage=(hd0,0)/boot/grub/splash.xpm.gz
hiddenmenu
title Red Hat Enterprise Linux (2.6.16-1.2096)
        root (hd0,0)
        kernel /boot/vmlinuz-2.6.16-1.2096 ro root=LABEL=/ rhgb quiet noht
        initrd /boot/initrd-2.6.16-1.2096.img
```

ELILO

In the /boot/efi/EFI/redhat/elilo.conf file on an Itanium system, the boot parameters are added to the end of the append line. Listing 2.11 shows the 3 parameter added to boot the system into runlevel 3.

LISTING 2.11 ELILO Configuration File

```
prompt
timeout=20
default=linux
relocatable
image=vmlinuz-2.6.9-34.EL
        label=linux
        initrd=initrd-2.6.9-34.EL.img
        read-only
        append="rhgb quiet root=LABEL=/ 3"
```

OS/400

For pre-POWER5 iSeries systems, the /boot/vmlinitrd-<kernel-version> file is installed with each kernel. To add boot parameters, determine the default side with the cat /proc/iSeries/mf/side command, and then execute the following command where <options> are the boot parameter options to add (command divided into two lines with the \ character for readability):

```
dd if=/boot/vmlinitrd-<kernel-version> \
of=/proc/iSeries/mf/<side>/vmlinux bs=8k <options>
```

YABOOT

The YABOOT configuration file /etc/yaboot.conf contains an image section for each installed kernel. The boot parameters are added to the end of the append line. Listing 2.12 shows the 3 parameter added.

LISTING 2.12 YABOOT Configuration File

```
boot=/dev/sda1
init-message=Welcome to Red Hat Enterprise Linux!
Hit <TAB> for boot options

partition=2
timeout=30
install=/usr/lib/yaboot/yaboot
delay=10
nonvram

image=/vmlinux--2.6.9-5.EL
        label=linux
        read-only
        initrd=/initrd--2.6.9-5.EL.img
        append="root=LABEL=/ 3"
```

z/IPL

The z/IPL configuration file `/etc/zipl.conf` contains a section for each installed kernel. The boot parameters are added to the end of the `parameters` line. Listing 2.13 shows the `3` parameter added.

LISTING 2.13 z/IPL Configuration File

```
[defaultboot]
default=linux
target=/boot/
[linux]
        image=/boot/vmlinuz-2.6.9-5.EL
        ramdisk=/boot/initrd-2.6.9-5.EL.img
        parameters="root=LABEL=/ 3"
```

After making changes to the `/etc/zipl.conf` file, you must execute the `/sbin/zipl` command to enable the changes.

Summary

After installation, the Setup Agent guides you through the configuration and customization of the system. A few of the crucial tasks include determining a security level, deciding whether to enable SELinux, and activating your Red Hat Network account so you can receive software updates. After logging in for the first time, tweak the network configuration if necessary. If you need to print from the system, configure a printer using the Printer Configuration Tool. Verify the proper kernel was installed and customize if necessary, and, finally, add boot parameters if needed.

CHAPTER 3

Operating System Updates

IN THIS CHAPTER

- Navigating Through the RHN Website
- Assigning Users for the RHN Website
- Subscribing to RHN Channels
- Performing Actions on Individual Systems from the RHN Website
- Using System Groups on the RHN Website
- Retrieving Software from RHN with YUM

This chapter focuses on software updates and software installation. Two methods are discussed to download and install or update software from Red Hat Network servers: the Red Hat Network website and YUM (both the command-line utility and two graphical programs).

Chapter 2, "Post-Installation Configuration," guided you through the Setup Agent, including registering your Red Hat Enterprise Linux system with Red Hat Network (RHN). Every Red Hat Enterprise Linux subscription includes access to the Red Hat Network Update module for software updates.

If you did not register your system with RHN during the Setup Agent, go to https://www.redhat.com/apps/activate/ to activate your subscription if it hasn't already been activated. Then, run the `rhn_register` command on the system. If you aren't logged in as the root user, you will be prompted for the root password before continuing. If you have more than one system to register, be sure you use the same login (the one associated with your RHN entitlements) to register all of them. The systems cannot be managed, provisioned, or monitored together as a group if a different login is used for each one. Additional logins can be created for the organization and allowed access to specific systems or system groups.

To receive updates via RHN, each registered system must be entitled to a valid subscription. Each Red Hat Enterprise Linux subscription includes an RHN entitlement. If the login used has available entitlements, the system is automatically entitled when it is registered. If there are no available entitlements associated with the account when a system is registered, you must purchase an additional entitlement for the system and associated it with the newly registered system before receiving updates.

NOTE

Go to http://rhn.redhat.com/ for details on each RHN module and to read more comprehensive documentation on all of their features.

Navigating Through the RHN Website

After registering the system with RHN, go to https://rhn.redhat.com/ and log in. After you log in, the main RHN page appears.

NOTE

The RHN website is constantly updated and modified based on user feedback and to improve its usability. The instructions in this chapter for the RHN website might differ from the current layout of the website.

After logging in to the RHN website, you will see two menus: a vertical menu and horizontal menu. The vertical menu changes depending on which view is selected from the horizontal menu.

The views available from the horizontal menu include:

- **Your RHN**: Link to return to the main RHN page.
- **Systems**: List of systems and system groups, including whether updates are needed. Access to the System Set Manager for scheduling errata, installing or removing packages, managing groups, and assigning channels.
- **Errata**: View of all errata or a customized list of errata relevant to your registered systems.
- **Channels**: Index of software channels (one base channel per Red Hat Enterprise Linux release and child channels for software add-ons such as Red Hat Global File System), packages in each channel, and how many registered systems are associated with each channel. Every system must be associated with a base channel and can be associated with one or more child channels, from which the software updates are retrieved. The Channels view also provides access to download ISO images, which can be used to create installation CDs of the software.
- **Schedule**: Table of scheduled actions that have not yet taken place, actions that failed to complete, actions that have been completed, and actions that have been archived.
- **Users**: List of users for the organization and their roles. Each user's roles determine which RHN actions they are allowed to perform. (Only Organization Administrators can see this link as explained in the following section "Assigning Users for the RHN Website.")
- **Help**: Access to online documentation including a quick start guide, FAQs, reference guide, and best practices guide.

The following views are available from the vertical menu when Your RHN is the view selected from the horizontal menu:

- **Your RHN**: The most crucial information about the systems registered with RHN such as the systems with the most software updates available and the most relevant security errata issued.
- **Your Account:** Form to change the personal information associated with the account such as the password and email address.
- **Your Preferences**: Options for the user to elect whether or not to receive email notifications and customize how data is displayed.
- **Locale Preferences**: Options to select time zone and language preference.
- **Subscription Management**: Interface for renewing, purchasing, and managing Red Hat Enterprise Linux subscriptions as well as applying RHN entitlements to registered systems if necessary.

Assigning Users for the RHN Website

Most organizations have more than one administrator with each administrator being responsible for specific systems. RHN also allows more than one user to view and manage each system. Each user is assigned one or more roles. Some roles might not be available, depending on which RHN modules you have subscribed to. More than one user can exist for each role. The possible user roles are as follows:

- **User**: Also referred to as a System Group User. Default user role with access to any global channels to which anyone can subscribe. Can be given access to system groups and software channels.
- **Activation Key Administrator**: Allowed to create, modify, and delete activation keys for the organization.
- **Configuration Administrator**: Allowed to manage system configurations for the organization using the RHN website or the Red Hat Network Configuration Manager. Must be subscribed to the Provisioning Module for this user role to exist.
- **Monitoring Administrator**: Only available for the RHN Satellite Server Monitoring module. Allowed to schedule probes and manage the monitoring functionality.
- **Organization Administrator**: Highest level of user roles. Can perform any action from the other user roles. A login with this user role should be used to register systems so the OrgAdmin can create additional users for the organization.

Only Organization Administrators (OrgAdmins) see the **Users** link in the horizontal menu, and only OrgAdmins can add or disable users. Click **Users** in the horizontal menu to view a list of active users.

Click the **create new user** link in the upper-right corner of the page to create new users. After a user has been created, click on the username from the list of active users to assign roles and grant users access to systems and system groups.

Subscribing to RHN Channels

When a system is registered with RHN, software and hardware information is gathered so that relevant errata updates can be determined for it. The software information includes the Red Hat Enterprise Linux release and the system architecture. From this data, the system is associated with a *base channel* such as Red Hat Enterprise Linux (v. 5 for 32-bit x86). Each base channel contains all the latest software, including software updates, for the release version and architecture. A base channel can have child channels associated with it. A *child channel* contains software that can be installed on any system with the OS release and architecture from the base channel.

A system can only be associated with one base channel, but it can be subscribed to one or more child channels. By using the RHN website or YUM, systems can only receive updates or package installations from channels to which they are subscribed. For example, a system subscribed to the Red Hat Enterprise Linux (v. 5 for 32-bit x86) base channel can also be subscribed to the RHEL Virtualization (v. 5 for 32-bit x86) child channel.

Channel subscriptions for systems are managed through the RHN website. To subscribe a system to one or more child channels or change the parent channel, log in to the RHN website at rhn.redhat.com, and select **Systems** from the horizontal menu. Click on the name of the system to show a more detailed view of it. Under the Subscribed Channels header, click **Alter Channel Subscriptions**. All child channels available for subscription are shown. Select which ones to subscribe to, and click **Change Subscriptions**. To change the parent channel, select a new channel from the pull-down menu, and click **Modify Base Channel**.

Performing Actions on Individual Systems from the RHN Website

To perform an action on an individual system using the RHN website, log in, and click **System** on the horizontal menu. From the individual system view, many actions can be performed including the following:

- Update software
- Install software
- Modify channel subscription
- Edit system properties such as entitlement and description
- View pending actions for the system

For example, using the RHN website, an administrator can quickly view a list of updates for a specific system registered with RHN and apply one or more of these updates to an individual system. After selecting **Systems** from the horizontal menu, another horizontal menu appears on the page under the name of the system. Click **Software** from the secondary horizontal menu. Then, click on the **Errata** menu item that appears below that to view a list of relevant errata. Select the errata you want to apply (there might be more than one page of errata), and click **Apply Errata**. Review the errata updates selected. To add the errata update action to the list of pending actions for the system, click **Confirm**.

On the confirmation page, notice that three times are shown: the last system check-in time, the current RHN time, and the expected next check-in time. When actions are performed using the RHN website, they are actually scheduled to happen the next time the system checks in with RHN. A system registered with RHN should have the RHN daemon (`rhnsd`) running on it. The daemon periodically connects the RHN servers and asks whether any actions have been scheduled for it. Having the system contact the RHN servers for actions prevents a non-RHN server from trying to contact your system and masquerade as a real RHN server. To determine whether the RHN daemon is running, execute the `service rhnsd status` command. If it is not running, start it with the `service rhnsd start` command as the root user. To make sure it is started every time the system boots, execute the `chkconfig rhnsd on` command as the root user.

TIP

If you want to apply all available errata to a system, there is a quicker way. Click **Systems** on the horizontal menu, click on the name of system, and click the **update now** link. A list of all errata available for the selected system is shown. Click **Confirm** to apply them all. The next time the system checks in with the RHN daemon, all relevant errata will be applied to the system. The **update now** link is only shown when updates are available.

To install new software on an individual system, from the individual system view, click the **Software** link in the secondary horizontal menu under the system name. Click the **Install New Packages** option from the list of actions. Select one or more packages to be installed. The list can be filtered by name, or you can skip to packages that begin with a specific letter. After selecting all the packages to be installed, click **Install Selected Packages**. Finally, click **Confirm** to schedule the installation action.

Using System Groups on the RHN Website

Systems can be grouped for two main reasons: to allow actions to be performed on the group as a whole, and to grant users access to the systems within a defined group instead of having to grant them access to individual systems. This section describes how to perform these two actions as well as how to perform actions on a system group.

Performing Actions on a System Group

It is also possible to perform actions such as software updates and package installation to multiple systems at the same time either using a defined system group or selecting certain systems from the system list and performing a one-time action using the System Set Manager (SSM).

First, select which systems to update with one of the following methods:

- *Select specific systems for one-time use*: Select **Systems** from the horizontal menu. Select the systems you want to work with using the check boxes in the first column of the list, and click **Update List**. After the update list action is finished, the page view does not change. Click **System Set Manager** from the vertical menu to perform a one-time action on these selected systems.
- *Use a predefined system group*: To create a system group that can be used repeatedly, select **Systems** from the horizontal menu, and then select **System Groups** from the vertical menu. Click the **create new group** link in the upper-left corner of the page. To perform an action on a system group, select **Systems** from the horizontal menu, **System Groups** from the vertical menu, and then click **Use Group** under the **Use in SSM** column for the desired system group.

From the **System Set Manager**, the following actions can be performed:

- List the systems you have selected to work with
- Schedule software updates (errata) relevant to selected systems
- Upgrade, install, remove, and verify packages
- Create and manage groups
- Manage software channels
- Provision systems (requires subscription to RHN Provisioning Module)
- Update hardware and software profiles
- Add and remove additional RHN entitlements
- Delete systems from RHN profile
- Reboot selected systems

For example, to apply software updates, click the **Schedule errata updates** link. A list of errata that can be applied to one or more systems from those you just selected or the system group selected is shown. Select the errata to apply (there might be multiple pages of errata), and click **Apply Errata**. On the next page, make sure all the errata you want to apply are listed. Select to either schedule action as soon as possible or schedule it for no longer than a specific time. Finally, click **Schedule Updates** to finish.

TIP

To check on the status of the action, click the **Schedule** link in the horizontal menu.

To install software via the RHN website on a set of systems, select **Install** from the list of **System Set Manager** actions. If the selected systems or the system group has more than one parent channel, select the channel containing the software to be installed. Select the software packages to install from the list. Use the quick alphabet letter links to skip to packages that begin with that letter or use the **Filter by Name** feature to narrow down the list of packages displayed. After selecting all the packages to install, click **Install Packages**. Verify the packages to be installed and the system on which to install them. Select a time to install the packages: as soon as possible or no longer than a specific time. Click **Schedule Updates** to complete the action. Alternatively, if you click **Run Remote Command**, you can schedule a custom script to run before or after the package update if Remote Command execution is enabled on the system. Use extreme caution when using this feature, especially if executing the script as the root user.

NOTE

Administrators can only schedule software to be installed from a base or child channel to which the system is subscribed.

Granting Users Access to Specific Systems

To add users to your RHN account, follow the instructions in the "Assigning Users to the RHN Website" section earlier in this chapter. Next, create system groups as described earlier in this section based on the administrative groups for your organization. For example, if one set of administrators is responsible for all web servers and another team manages all internal servers, you might want to create a system group of web servers and a system group of internal servers.

Select **Systems** from the horizontal menu, and then select **System Groups** from the vertical menu to view a list of all defined system groups. For each system group, use the following steps to assign which RHN users can perform actions on them via the RHN website:

1. Click on the name of the system group to show the detailed view of it.
2. Click the **Edit group administrators** link in the Admins section.
3. Select the desired RHN users.
4. Click **Update**.

Retrieving Software from RHN with YUM

Although software maintenance for systems can be done via the RHN website, sometimes it is necessary or preferred to perform the same actions from the local system needing the updates or additional software. Previous versions of Red Hat Enterprise Linux used the Update Agent (`up2date`) program to download and install software from RHN. The Update Agent could be run from the command line or as a graphical program. As of Red Hat Enterprise Linux 5, the YUM utility has replaced the Update Agent. YUM can install or upgrade software by using either the command-line version (executed with the `yum` command) or one of two graphical programs:

- **Pirut**: For adding and removing software.
- **Pup**: Package updater that only shows software updates available from RHN.

Before you can use YUM to install or upgrade software, remember you must set it up to connect to RHN. Either register the system with RHN directly after installation with the Setup Agent (as described in Chapter 2) or at any time by executing the `rhn_register` command. Root access is required, so you will be prompted for the root password if you run the program as a non-root user.

This following sections explain what YUM is, how to use the `yum` command-line utility, and how to use the two graphical interfaces to YUM included with Red Hat Enterprise Linux.

NOTE

Although the RHN website might differ from the instructions in this chapter, the YUM utility should be the same as the one described in this chapter.

What Is YUM?

YUM stands for *Yellow dog Updater, Modified* because it is based on YUP, the *Yellow dog Updater*. Where does the name *Yellow dog* come from? Yellow Dog is a version of Linux for the Power Architecture hardware and is RPM-based, just like Red Hat Enterprise Linux and Fedora. YUP, and later YUM, were written by the Linux community as a way to maintain an RPM-based system. Fedora Core can be updated with the YUM utility, and, now Red Hat Enterprise Linux can be as well starting with Red Hat Enterprise Linux 5.

Some of the advantages of YUM include

- Automatic resolution of software dependencies. If a package installation or upgrade request is made and requires the installation or upgrade of additional packages, YUM can list these dependencies and prompt the user to install or upgrade them as long as they are in a repository YUM is configured to use.
- Command-line and graphical versions. The command-line version can be run on a system with a minimal number of software packages. It also allows administrators to write scripts to automate software maintenance actions, which can be scheduled at times convenient for everyone. The graphical versions offer ease-of-use and a user-friendly graphical interface to software management.
- Multiple software locations at one time. YUM can be configured to look for software packages in more than one location at a time. The user doesn't have to remember to provide a location each time he performs an action. Software dependencies can sometimes be resolved even if the additional packages are not in the same location as the requested package.

- Ability to specify particular software versions or architectures. Software locations accessible by YUM can contain multiple versions of the same RPM package and different builds for different architectures such as one for i686 and one for x86_64. When performing software management actions, optionally, a certain version or build for a certain architecture can be requested.

YUM downloads software from *repositories* located over the network, either on the local network or over the Internet. The files, including the RPM package files, in these repositories are organized in a specific way so that they can be found by the YUM client.

For Red Hat Enterprise Linux, the repository is Red Hat Network. After registering the system with RHN, the system is configured to use the RHN repository, so no further configuration is required.

Because the RPM database has to be manipulated and most packages require files to be installed in locations only available to root, most of the `yum` commands must be run as the root user.

Managing Software with YUM

This section discusses common actions performed with YUM, using both the command line and graphical versions.

The first time YUM is run as the root user to connect to the RHN repository, whether it is run from the command line or a graphical application, the package headers are downloaded and stored in cache. On all subsequent connections to RHN, only changes to package headers are downloaded to cache.

Installing Software

Installing a software package is pretty straightforward:

```
yum install <pkgname>
```

Replace `<pkgname>` with the name of one or more packages. If more than one package is given, separate them with spaces. If just the package name such as `nfs-utils` is given, the latest version of the package build for the architecture of the system is installed. To specify a particular version of a package:

```
yum install <pkgname>-<version>
```

To specify a particular architecture for the package to be installed:

```
yum install <pkgname>.arch
```

These can even be combined. For example, the following installs version 2.3.4-1 of the example package for the x86_64 architecture:

```
yum install example-2.3.4-1.x86_64
```

TIP

The -y option can be used with yum to assume the answer "yes" to any questions asked, such as whether to install package dependencies. For example:

```
yum -y install httpd
```

When a yum command is executed, the progress of the transaction is displayed so that you watch the progress. Listing 3.1 shows the progress of the command `yum -y install httpd`. As you can see, it finds the `httpd` package, downloads the header for it, determines its software dependencies, lists the packages to be installed, and finally installs them. Before completing and returning to the command prompt, it lists the packages installed, the additional packages installed to resolve dependencies, and that the transaction is complete.

LISTING 3.1 Example YUM Transaction

```
Loading "installonlyn" plugin
Loading "rhnplugin" plugin
Setting up Install Process
Setting up repositories
rhel-x86_64-server-5   100% |=========================| 950 B    00:00
Reading repository metadata in from local files
primary.xml.gz            100% |=========================| 634 kB    00:01
################################################## 2088/2088
Parsing package install arguments
Resolving Dependencies
--> Populating transaction set with selected packages. Please wait.
---> Downloading header for httpd to pack into transaction set.
httpd-2.2.3-5.el5.x86_64.rp 100% |=========================| 53 kB    00:00
---> Package httpd. x86_64 0:2.2.3-5.el5 set to be updated
--> Running transaction check
--> Processing Dependency: libapr-1.so.0 for package: httpd
--> Processing Dependency: libaprutil-1.so.0 for package: httpd
--> Restarting Dependency Resolution with new changes.
--> Populating transaction set with selected packages. Please wait.
---> Downloading header for apr to pack into transaction set.
apr-1.2.7-10.x86_64.rpm     100% |=========================| 10 kB    00:00
---> Package apr.x86_64 0:1.2.7-10 set to be updated
---> Downloading header for apr-util to pack into transaction set.
apr-util-1.2.7-3.x86_64.rpm 100% |=========================| 7.2 kB    00:00
---> Package apr-util.x86_64 0:1.2.7-3 set to be updated
--> Running transaction check
--> Processing Dependency: libpq.so.4 for package: apr-util
--> Restarting Dependency Resolution with new changes.
--> Populating transaction set with selected packages. Please wait.
---> Downloading header for postgresql-libs to pack into transaction set.
```

LISTING 3.1 Continued

```
postgresql-libs-8.1.4-1.1 100% |=========================|  15 kB    00:00
---> Package postgresql-libs.x86_64 0:8.1.4-1.1 set to be updated
--> Running transaction check

Dependencies Resolved

=============================================================================
 Package                Arch       Version          Repository        Size
=============================================================================
Installing:
 httpd                  x86_64      2.2.3-5.el5       rhel-x86_64-server-5  1.1 M
Installing for dependencies:
 apr                    x86_64      1.2.7-10          rhel-x86_64-server-5  123 k
 apr-util               x86_64      1.2.7-3           rhel-x86_64-server-5   75 k
 postgresql-libs        x86_64      8.1.4-1.1         rhel-x86_64-server-5  195 k

Transaction Summary
=============================================================================
Install      4 Package(s)
Update       0 Package(s)
Remove       0 Package(s)

Total download size: 1.4 M
Downloading Packages:
(1/4): postgresql-libs-8. 100% |=========================| 195 kB    00:00
(2/4): apr-1.2.7-10.x86_64. 100% |=========================| 123 kB    00:00
(3/4): httpd-2.2.3-5.el5. 100% |=========================| 1.1 MB    00:02
(4/4): apr-util-1.2.7-3.i 100% |=========================|  75 kB    00:00
Running Transaction Test
Finished Transaction Test
Transaction Test Succeeded
Running Transaction
  Installing: apr                          ######################### [1/4]
  Installing: postgresql-libs              ######################### [2/4]
  Installing: apr-util                     ######################### [3/4]
  Installing: httpd                        ######################### [4/4]

Installed: httpd.x86_64 0:2.2.3-5.el5
Dependency Installed: apr.x86_64 0:1.2.7-10 apr-util.x86_64 0:1.2.7-3 postgresql-
libs.x86_64 0:8.1.4-1.1
Complete!
```

To install RPM packages using a graphical program, select **Add/Remove Software** from the **Applications** menu on the top panel of the desktop. If you are not the root user, you are prompted to enter the root password before continuing. Figure 3.1 shows the interface. The Package Manager program can also be started by executing the `pirut` command. This application is provided by the `pirut` RPM package, which is installed on a Red Hat Enterprise Linux system by default.

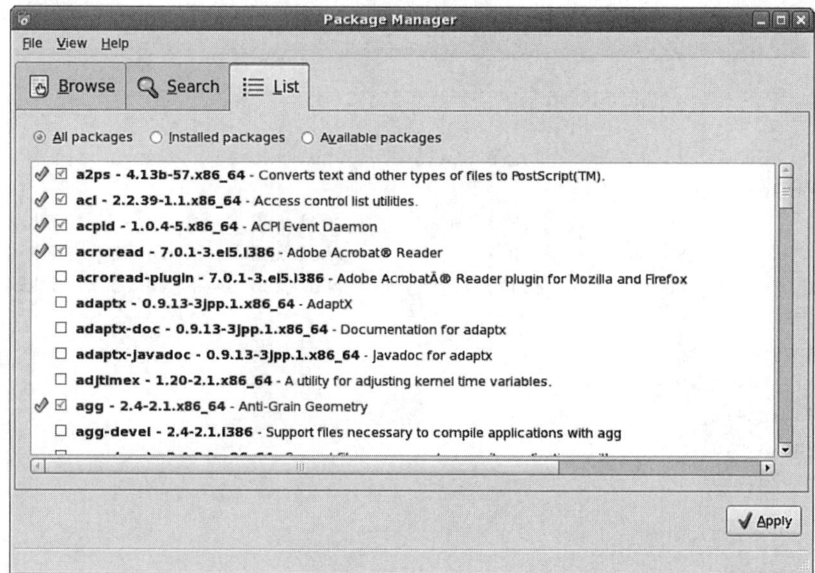

FIGURE 3.1 Installing Software

The application consists of three tabs, which provide different functions:

- **Browse**: Browse packages by software sets. This is the same interface used during installation.
- **Search**: Search for a package by its name. Filter results by already installed packages or available packages.
- **List**: List all packages in the RHN channels to which the system is subscribed, list all installed packages, or list all packages available for installation on the system. Packages with a check mark beside them are already installed or are packages selected for installation.

To install a package with the Package Manager, use one of the three tabs to find the package to install, and click the check box beside it so that a check mark appears in it. For example, on the **Search** tab, select the **Available packages** option, enter a package name to find, and click **Search**. To view a brief description of a package found, select it from the list, and click the triangle icon beside **Package Details** as shown in Figure 3.2.

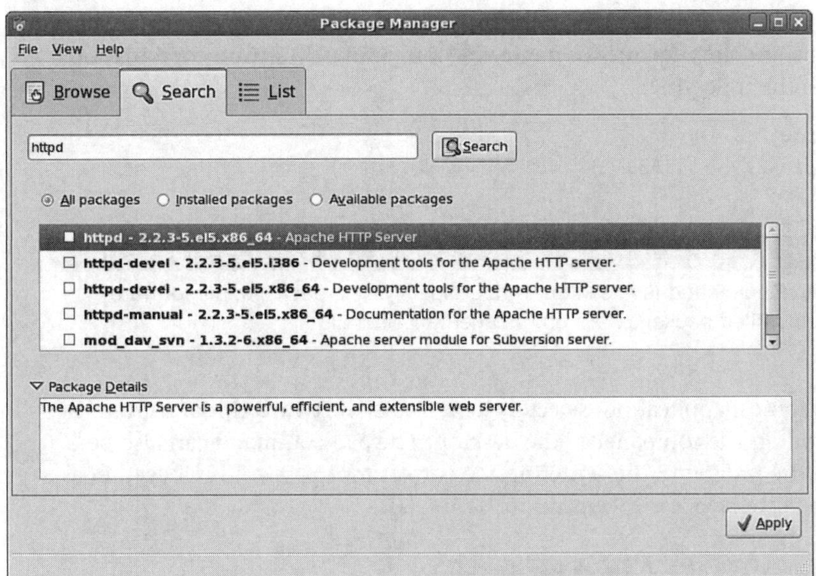

FIGURE 3.2 Viewing Package Details

After selecting which packages to install, click **Apply**. A dialog appears to confirm which package to install. Click **Continue**. If additional packages need to be installed to resolve dependencies, the dialog displays dependencies added. Click **Continue** to accept the installation of these packages as well. A progress bar shows the status of the installation, and a completion message is shown when finished.

Updating Software

There are several ways to determine whether software updates are available for your Red Hat Enterprise Linux system:

- Log in to the RHN website and view the errata list for the system as described earlier in this chapter.
- Receive email notifications from RHN if you elected to receive them.
- See the RHN applet (`puplet`) appear.
- Use the `yum check-update` command.
- Use the Software Updater (`pup`).

When executed, the `yum check-update` command queries the RHN repository and checks for any software updates for the RPM packages currently installed. If any are found, they are listed in alphabetical order along with the package versions available for updating.

Updating an already installed package via the command line is similar to installing:

```
yum update <pkgname>
```

As with yum install <pkgname>, you can replace <pkgname> with just the name, name and version, name and architecture, or name, version, and architecture combination. Examples include the following:

```
yum update example-2.3.4-1
yum update example-2.3.4-1.i686
```

TIP

If the yum update command is executed without specifying a package, all software updates for all installed packages are downloaded and installed.

If you prefer a graphical application, select **System Tools, Software Updater** from the Applications menu on the top panel of the desktop. The pup command can also be executed to start the program. After entering the correct root password if logged in as a non-root user, the interface is displayed as in Figure 3.3.

FIGURE 3.3 Viewing Software Updates

As you can see, the interface is simple and easy to use. The program contacts RHN and displays a list of packages that have updates available for it. By default, all available software updates are selected as indicated by the check marks beside them. Unselect any updates you don't want to apply, and click **Apply updates** to update all the selected software packages.

Removing Software

To remove one or more RPM packages from a system, use the following command as the root user:

```
yum remove <pkgname>
```

As with the install and update commands, <pkgname> can be a one package name or multiple package names separated by spaces. Package versions and architectures can be specified as in the following examples:

```
yum remove example-2.3.4-1
yum remove example-2.3.4-1.i686
```

Packages can be removed with the `rpm -e <pkgname>` command as later discussed in Chapter 5, "Working with RPM Software"; however, deleting packages with YUM has the big advantage of resolving software dependencies for you. For example, Listing 3.2 shows the results of the `yum remove httpd` command. As you can see, many other packages depend on the `httpd` package and must be removed at the same time.

LISTING 3.2 Removing Software with the yum Command

```
Loading "rhnplugin" plugin
Loading "installonlyn" plugin
Setting up Remove Process
Resolving Dependencies
--> Populating transaction set with selected packages. Please wait.
---> Package httpd.x86_64 0:2.2.3-5.el5 set to be erased
--> Running transaction check
Setting up repositories
rhel-x86_64-server-5      100% |=========================| 950 B    00:00
Reading repository metadata in from local files
--> Processing Dependency: webserver for package: webalizer
--> Processing Dependency: httpd = 2.2.3-5.el5 for package: httpd-manual
--> Processing Dependency: httpd >= 2.0.40 for package: mod_python
--> Processing Dependency: httpd-mmn = 20051115 for package: mod_perl
--> Processing Dependency: httpd-mmn = 20051115 for package: php
--> Processing Dependency: httpd-mmn = 20051115 for package: mod_python
--> Processing Dependency: httpd-mmn = 20051115 for package: mod_ssl
--> Processing Dependency: httpd = 0:2.2.3-5.el5 for package: mod_ssl
--> Restarting Dependency Resolution with new changes.
--> Populating transaction set with selected packages. Please wait.
---> Package mod_python.x86_64 0:3.2.8-3.1 set to be erased
---> Package php.x86_64 0:5.1.6-3 set to be erased
---> Package mod_ssl.x86_64 1:2.2.3-5.el5 set to be erased
---> Package httpd-manual.x86_64 0:2.2.3-5.el5 set to be erased
---> Package webalizer.x86_64 0:2.01_10-30.1 set to be erased
---> Package mod_perl.x86_64 0:2.0.2-6.1 set to be erased
--> Running transaction check
--> Processing Dependency: php = 5.1.6-3 for package: php-ldap
--> Restarting Dependency Resolution with new changes.
--> Populating transaction set with selected packages. Please wait.
---> Package php-ldap.x86_64 0:5.1.6-3 set to be erased
```

LISTING 3.2 Continued

```
--> Running transaction check

Dependencies Resolved

=============================================================================
 Package                 Arch       Version          Repository        Size
=============================================================================
Removing:
 httpd                   x86_64     2.2.3-5.el5      installed         2.9 M
Removing for dependencies:
 httpd-manual            x86_64     2.2.3-5.el5      installed         3.4 M
 mod_perl                x86_64     2.0.2-6.1        installed         6.7 M
 mod_python              x86_64     3.2.8-3.1        installed         1.2 M
 mod_ssl                 x86_64     1:2.2.3-5.el5    installed         175 k
 php                     x86_64     5.1.6-3          installed         3.3 M
 php-ldap                x86_64     5.1.6-3          installed          45 k
 webalizer               x86_64     2.01_10-30.1     installed         259 k

Transaction Summary
=============================================================================
Install      0 Package(s)
Update       0 Package(s)
Remove       8 Package(s)

Is this ok [y/N]: y
Downloading Packages:
Running Transaction Test
Finished Transaction Test
Transaction Test Succeeded
Running Transaction
  Removing    : mod_ssl                     ######################### [1/8]
  Removing    : php-ldap                    ######################### [2/8]
  Removing    : mod_python                  ######################### [3/8]
  Removing    : php                         ######################### [4/8]
  Removing    : httpd                       ######################### [5/8]
  Removing    : httpd-manual                ######################### [6/8]
  Removing    : webalizer                   ######################### [7/8]
  Removing    : mod_perl                    ######################### [8/8]

Removed: httpd.x86_64 0:2.2.3-5.el5
Dependency Removed: httpd-manual.x86_64 0:2.2.3-5.el5 mod_perl.x86_64 0:2.0.2-6.1
mod_python.x86_64 0:3.2.8-3.1 mod_ssl.x86_64 1:2.2.3-5.el5 php.x86_64 0:5.1.6-3
php-ldap.x86_64 0:5.1.6-3 webalizer.x86_64 0:2.01_10-30.1
Complete!
```

CAUTION

Although the `-y` option to `yum` can be used with `yum remove <pkgname>`, it is not recommended. As shown in Listing 3.2, removing one package might mean needing to remove more packages that depend on it. If you use the `-y` option to answer yes to all questions, you are agreeing to remove all the packages that depend on the one you want to remove without knowing what those packages are. You might depend on one of those packages. Read the list of additional packages to remove carefully before answering yes.

The Package Manager graphical program as previously described in the "Installing Software" section can also be used to remove one or more packages and their dependencies. Start it as previously described and use the **Search** or **List** tabs to find the packages to delete. Instead of clicking the check box beside the package to install it, click the check box beside the packages to remove the check mark. Click **Apply** to start the package removal process.

Confirm the list of packages to remove by clicking **Continue**. If additional packages need to be deleted as software dependencies, they are listed next. Click **Continue** to agree to their removal as well. When the package removal is complete, a message is displayed.

Performing More Actions

The command-line version of YUM can perform additional actions useful when managing RPM on a system. Read the `yum` man page invoked with the `man yum` command for a complete list. The following are a few highlights:

```
yum deplist <pkgname>
yum list available
yum list updates
```

The `yum deplist <pkgname>` command displays the software dependencies for the package listed. The `yum list available` outputs a list of packages that are available for installation on the system. The `yum list updates` shows all the software updates available for but not yet installed on the system.

Summary

Software maintenance is crucial to system administration, but it doesn't have to be labor intensive or tedious. Every Red Hat Enterprise Linux subscription includes the ability to be notified of and retrieve updates from Red Hat Network, so why not take advantage of its many features including email notifications of newly released software updates and the ability to schedule package updates, installations, and removals? These actions can be performed via the RHN website or YUM. YUM can be used from the command line or from one of two graphical programs. The RHN website offers the flexibility of scheduling actions. The `yum` command-line utility allows administrators to manage software on a minimally installed system or using scripts that require non-interactive commands. The graphical YUM programs provide a customized list of software updates specific to your system for quick and easy maintenance.

PART II

Operating System Core Concepts

IN THIS PART

CHAPTER 4

Understanding Linux Concepts

IN THIS CHAPTER

So far, this book has covered installing Red Hat Enterprise Linux and post-installation essentials. Before continuing, it is important to establish a firm background in a few basic UNIX and Linux topics such as navigating the desktop, knowing how the filesystem is structured, being able to use the command line, and understanding file permissions. If you are already familiar with this information, skim through it quickly as a review and continue. If you are new to a UNIX-based operating system, this chapter can serve as an overview of Linux concepts.

Learning the Desktop

Unless you customized the installation and only installed the programs absolutely necessary for the system to function in its desired capacity, you most likely installed the software necessary to use the graphical desktop environment. If so, after the system boots, the graphical login screen appears as discussed in Chapter 2, "Post-Installation Configuration."

As you can see, it consists of the actual desktop area, a few icons on the desktop, and two panels. The top panel contains the menus, icons to common desktop applications such as a web browser, the system time, and a volume control icon.

The menus on the top panel are divided into three categories:

- **Applications**: Contains the majority of the program menu items, which are also divided into categories such as Internet and System Tools to make it easier to find the program you need.

- **Places**: Allows the user to open a graphical file browser (by selecting **Home Folder**, **Desktop**, or **Computer**), go directly to bookmarked folders, connect to network shares as discussed in Part IV, "Network Services," search the filesystem, or quickly access recently opened documents.
- **System**: Provides menu items to set preferences, perform administration tasks, view available documentation, lock the screen so others can't access it while you are away from your computer, log out of the graphical desktop, and suspend or shut-down the computer.

TIP

Mouse over the system time on the top panel to display the date, or click on it to view a calendar.

From left to right, the bottom panel includes a button to minimize all the windows and show the desktop area, a list of open application windows, a workspace switcher, and the trash icon.

To bring a different application window forward on the desktop, click on its title in the list of open windows on the bottom panel. You can also switch between open windows by using the key combination Alt+Tab.

To the left of the Trash icon, there are four small squares. These are miniature representations of desktop *workspaces*. Each workspace has the same desktop background, icons on the desktop, and panels. The difference is that each workspace contains different application windows. At first, this might seem unnecessary to the user, but users can develop their own methods of using the workspaces to organize how they use their computers. For example, if you usually work on more than one project at a time or throughout the day, you can use a workspace for each project you are working on. When you are working on one project, you can concentrate on the applications for it without having to close all the windows for a different project. When you are ready to return to a different project, just switch workspaces. The necessary applications for the different project are open on a different workspace waiting for you to return to them. Or, you can sort application windows by type. You can use one workspace for your online communications by having it contain your email and instant messenger clients. You can reserve one workspace for your office communication needs such as word processing or spreadsheet programs. Yet another workspace can be used only for web browsing.

As an administrator, if you are monitoring several systems at the same time, you can have all the monitoring applications for each system on a separate workspace and switch back and forth between them. That way, when you are looking at the monitoring tools, you don't have to constantly think about which system you are analyzing.

By default, the desktop is configured to have four workspaces, but this can be customized by right-clicking on the workspace switcher (the squares) and selecting **Preferences**. As shown in Figure 4.1, you can even label the workspaces. To switch between workspaces, click on the square that represents it on the bottom panel.

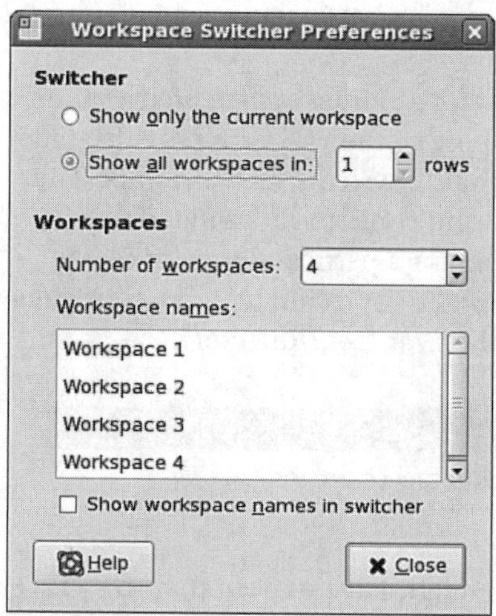

FIGURE 4.1 Customizing the Desktop Workspaces

On the far right side of the bottom panel is the **Trash** icon. Drag files or folders to it from the desktop or the file browser to delete them. They are not truly deleted until the trash is emptied. To empty the Trash and permanently remove the files in it, right-click on the **Trash** icon, and select **Empty Trash**. You must confirm the deletion of the files before they are really deleted. After they are deleted with the **Empty Trash** function, they cannot be retrieved. If files are still in the trash, click on the **Trash** icon to retrieve them. A window will open displaying the contents of the Trash. Drag the file or folder to another graphical file browser window or the desktop to restore it.

To further customize the desktop, play around with the preferences by going to the **System** menu on the top panel and selecting programs from the **Preferences** menu. For example, Figure 4.2 shows the program to customize the keyboard shortcuts for the graphical desktop.

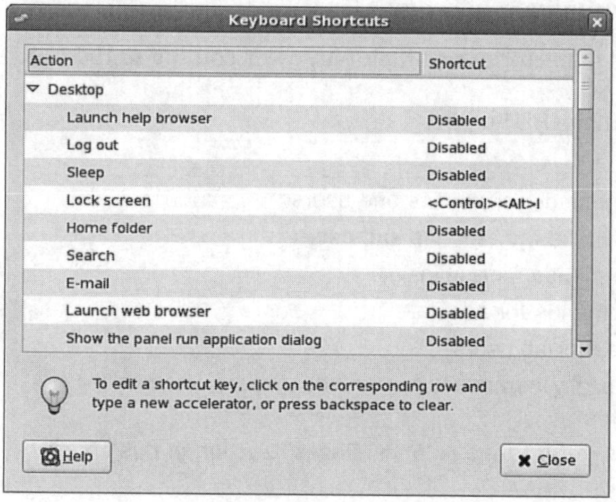

FIGURE 4.2 Customizing the Keyboard Shortcuts

Filesystem Hierarchy System

The location of the files and directories in a Red Hat Enterprise Linux system are based on the *Filesystem Hierarchy System* (FHS) guidelines. The purpose of the FHS is to provide guidelines for file and directory locations for UNIX-based operating systems such as Linux. The major advantages of using the FHS are the predictability and consistency of file locations. Instead of an administrator searching the entire filesystem for a particular type of file, he can know that it will be in one of a few established locations. For example, most configuration files are in the `/etc/` directory, and log files are in the `/var/log/` directory.

TIP

For more information on the FHS, refer to http://www.pathname.com/fhs/.

If you have ever browsed around a Linux filesystem, you might have noticed that the `/bin/`, `/usr/bin/`, `/sbin/`, and the `/usr/sbin/` directories contain commands but that only the commands in `/bin/` and `/usr/bin/` are in your `PATH` by default. (When you execute a command, it must be in one of the directories in your `PATH` environment variable or you will receive the `command not found` error message even if the command exists on the system. Refer to the "Shell Basics" section later in this chapter for details.) This is because, according to the FHS, `/bin/` contains essential user commands that can be used by administrators and users, and `/usr/bin/` contains most user commands. On the other hand, `/sbin/` should only contain essential system administration commands, and `/usr/sbin/` contains additional administration utilities. Usually, the commands in the `/sbin/` and `/usr/sbin/` directories can only be executed by root. The FHS guidelines for these directories makes it easy to find commands and separate them by who is allowed to execute them.

An administrator is constantly monitoring log files for error messages, connections by unauthorized users, disk usage, and more. Because the FHS defines the `/var/log/` directory as the location for log files, it is easy for an administrator to find the log files she is looking for because they are all in one common directory.

Table 4.1 describes some commonly used directories and their purpose according to the FHS.

TABLE 4.1 Common Directories and Their FHS Purpose

Directory	FHS Purpose
`/bin/`	Essential commands for admins and users
`/usr/bin/`	Common commands for admins and users
`/sbin/`	Essential commands for admins
`/usr/sbin/`	Common commands for admins
`/tmp/`	Temporary files for all users
`/usr/local/`	Location for locally-installed software independent of operating system updates
`/usr/share/man/`	Manual pages (refer to the "Manual Pages" section in this chapter for details)
`/usr/src/`	Source code

TABLE 4.1 Continued

/var/	Variable data files such as spool files and log files
/var/log/	Log files, can include subdirectories
/etc/	Configuration files, can include subdirectories
/proc/	Kernel virtual filesystem
/dev/	Device files

Shell Basics

Even though Red Hat Enterprise Linux provides a graphical desktop and graphical applications for most administration tasks, it is wise to know the basics of the command line, also known as the *shell prompt*. For example, you will need to know how to use the shell prompt if you are accessing a system remotely without X forwarding, working with a system that does not have a graphical desktop installed, trying to diagnose a problem with the X Window System, or booting into rescue mode without a graphical desktop.

There are two ways to start a shell prompt. If the X Window System is not installed, the system defaults to a black screen with a login prompt. After you log in, you are at a shell prompt. If you have a graphical desktop installed, log into the system at the graphical login screen, and then start a shell prompt by clicking on the **Applications** menu on the top panel and selecting **Accessories**, **Terminal**. A terminal window as shown in Figure 4.3 will appear.

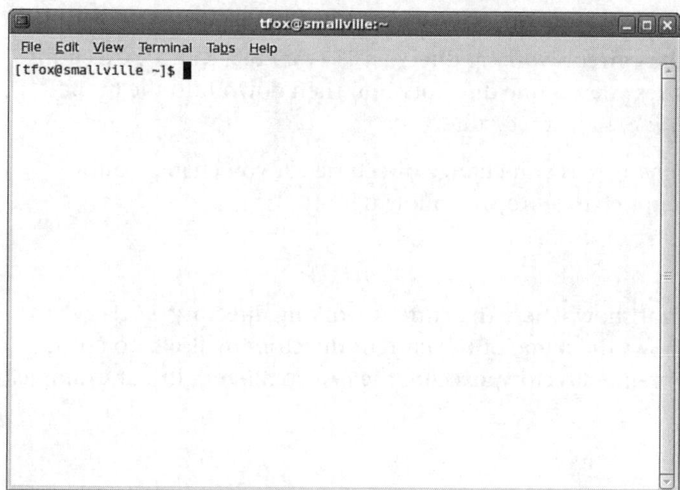

FIGURE 4.3 Starting a Terminal

Once in the terminal window or after logging in at the text-based login prompt, *commands* can be executed to navigate around the filesystem, read files, start applications, and perform administrative tasks.

Navigating the Filesystem

Now that you understand a bit about how the filesystem is organized and how to invoke a shell prompt, you need to know how to navigate through it using the command line.

By default, the prompt looks like the following:

```
[tfox@smallville ~]$
```

The first word before the `@` symbol is the username of the person currently logged in, and the word after the `@` symbol is the hostname of the system. The part that follows the space after the hostname is referred to as the *current working directory*. In this case, the ~ symbol means that the current working directory is the home directory of the user. When you start a terminal, the default directory is your home directory.

To change to a different directory, use the `cd <directory>` command. The `<directory>` can either be the *full path* to the directory or a directory *relative* to the current directory. The full path is the path through the filesystem to the desired directory starting with the root directory (/) such as `/home/tfox/` for my home directory or `/var/log/` for the log files directory. Specifying a directory relative to the current working directory means that you don't begin the directory with the root directory. Instead, you begin it with a directory inside the current working directory such as `documents/` for the `/home/tfox/documents/` directory if you are already in the `/home/tfox/` directory. If the directory doesn't begin with a forward slash for the root directory, the current working directory is assumed for the beginning of the path. When specifying a relative directory, you can specify more than one level deep such as `documents/project1/`.

When giving a relative directory, you can also specify up one or more directories with the `..` notation. For example, if the current working directory is `/var/log/samba/`, executing the command `cd ../httpd` takes you up one directory and then down into the `httpd` directory, placing you in the `/var/log/httpd/` directory.

Notice that the shell prompt changes as you change directories. If you change to the `documents/` directory, the prompt changes to the following:

```
[tfox@smallville documents]$
```

Notice that the prompt does not show where the current working directory is relative to the entire filesystem. It just shows the name of the current directory by itself. To output the full path to the current working directory, execute the `pwd` command. In our example, the `pwd` command displays:

```
/home/tfox/documents
```

To create a directory, use the `mkdir <directory>` command. Again, the `<directory>` can be relative to the current directory or it can be the full path. For example, to create a directory named `project1/` in the `/home/tfox/documents/` directory either change into the `/home/tfox/documents/` directory and then execute the `mkdir project1` command, or execute the `mkdir /home/tfox/documents/project1/` command from any directory.

To remove a directory, invoke the rmdir <directory> command, where <directory> is a directory within the current directory or the full path to the directory. If any files are still in the directory , the error message Directory not empty will be displayed, and the directory will not be deleted. This prevents users from removing a directory that still contains files.

TIP

To force the removal of a directory with all the files and subdirectories within that directory, use the rm -rf <directory> command. This command does not ask you to confirm the deletion, and there is no way to reverse the removal of the files and directories. Use extreme caution with this command. Double-check the directory specified before pressing Enter to execute the removal.

To remove a file, use the rm <file> command. If only the filename is specified, it must be in the current working directory. Alternatively, the full path to the file and the filename can be specified such as the rm /home/tfox/status.odt command.

To view the contents of a current directory, execute the ls command, or use the ls <directory> command to view the contents of <directory>. As with the other commands discussed, <directory> can be relative to the current working directory or the full path to a directory. The ls command accepts the * wildcard character. For example, to list all the OpenOffice.org text documents, use the ls *.odt command, or the ls status* to find all files whose filename begins with status. Multiple wildcards can be used such as ls *status* to list all files that have status somewhere in their name.

To copy a file from one location to another, use the cp <from> <to>, where <from> is the file to copy and <to> is the directory or filename to copy it to. If the <to> specified is a directory, the file is copied to that directory using the same filename. The directory can be the full path to a location or a directory relative to the current working directory. If a filename is specified for <to>, the original file is copied to another file with the specified name. If a path followed by a filename is used, the file is copied to another file with the new name in the specified directory. For example, the cp status.txt reports/status01.txt will copy the status.txt file from the current working directory to the reports/ directory relative to the current working directory as the new filename status01.txt. The reports/ directory must exist, or the error message cp: cannot create regular file `reports/status01.txt': No such file or directory is displayed, and the file is not copied.

When a file is moved, the file no longer exists in the original location. The mv <from> <to> command is similar to the cp command. The only difference is that the original <from> file will no longer exist after the move operation.

Multiple files can be specified as the <from> for both the cp and mv commands, and both commands accept the * wildcard. For example, the mv *.txt textfiles/ command moves all files that end in .txt to the textfiles/ directory in the current working directory. Or, multiple files can be specified using their filenames. For example, cp chap1.odt chap2.odt chap3.odt backup/ copies the chap1.odt, chap2.odt, and chap3.odt files to the backup/ directory.

Helpful Hints

The default shell called the *bash shell* offers many useful shortcuts that can speed up your operations on the command line. For example, instead of typing the entire command, you can type the first few characters of it and press the Tab key. If no other command begins with the characters you have typed, the command will be completed for you. If no results are displayed after pressing the Tab key once, press it again. If there is no command that begins with the character you typed, the cursor will not move and no results will be displayed. If there is more than one command that begins with the characters you typed, pressing the Tab key twice will display them. If there are too many commands that begin with the characters, you will see a message telling you how many completions exist and ask you to confirm whether you want them displayed such as the following example:

```
Display all 112 possibilities? (y or n)
```

Press the Y key to display all the results, or press the N key to go back to the prompt and type a few more characters to the desired command. Using *tab completion* takes some practice and getting used to, but it will quickly increase the speed at which you will be able to use the command line.

TIP

Because it sometimes takes pressing the Tab key twice to return results, it is a good habit to always press the Tab key twice when using tab completion to speed up the results.

When you type commands at a shell prompt, they are saved as part of your *command history* so you can reference them later. Type the command `history` at a shell prompt to see the results. If you have ever forgotten a recently used command or forgotten which command line arguments you used for a particular command, you can see how this might be useful. If you know all or part of the command you are searching for, use the following command:

```
history | grep 'part of the command'
```

The `grep` command stands for *get repetitions*. It can also be used when displaying the contents of files as discussed in the "Reading Text Files" section later in this chapter.

Alternately, press the Ctrl and R keys simultaneously. Pressing multiple keys at the same time is usually written with a plus sign between the keys such as Ctrl+R. This will change the prompt to read `(reverse-i-search)`':` while still providing a cursor to type. Start typing any part of the previous command you want to recall and you will start seeing results. If the command displayed is not the one you are searching for, keep typing. The results change as you type and completions are found.

At a shell prompt, you can also press the up arrow to start listing your command history starting with the most recently executed ones. After you have initiated the history scrolling, press the down arrow to go in the opposite direction. Keep in mind that not every command you have ever typed is saved. If you cannot find the command you are looking for, it may not be in your command history anymore.

TIP

If the terminal screen is starting to look cluttered or you just want what is on the screen to go away, type the command `clear` to clear the screen and place the prompt at the top of the screen.

If you are familiar with the Emacs editor (refer to the "Editing Text Files" section later in this chapter), you might know a few of its shortcuts to delete a word, jump to the beginning of a line, and jump to the end of a line. These shortcuts are also available on the command line courtesy of the bash shell. To delete the word in front of the cursor, press Alt+D. To move the cursor to the beginning of the line, press Ctrl+A. Press Ctrl+E to move the cursor to the end of the line. To clear the line from the cursor back to the prompt, press Ctrl+U.

These shortcuts can be used in conjunction with the up and down arrows to scroll through your command history or the Ctrl+R shortcut to perform a reverse lookup. Why is this useful? If you mistyped a long command and don't want to retype the entire command, just press the up arrow, and use the editing shortcuts to find the typing error, remove it, and replace it with the correct characters. After you have a little practice with it, it will be faster than retyping the entire command. This method is also useful if you are experimenting with different command-line arguments to the same command. Try one argument, then press the up arrow to try a different argument without having to retype everything.

Finding Files

There are two invaluable commands that can be used to find files on the filesystem: `locate` and `find`.

The `locate` command is the easier of the two to use. Just type the command followed by part or all of the filename you are searching for such as `locate .odt` to find all OpenOffice.org text files or `locate compare` to find all filenames that contain the word *compare*. Notice that no wildcard characters are used. It is assumed that what you type may only be part of the filename you are looking for.

The only catch to this command is that it relies on the generation of a database file so it can quickly display results. The `locate` command is provided by the `mlocate` package, which also provides the cron script `/etc/cron.daily/mlocate.cron` to automatically generate this database daily. If you are looking for a file created that same day, it might not appear in the `locate` results if the database hasn't been updated since the file was created.

The `find` command is a bit more complicated to use and takes longer to produce results because it does not rely on a database to produce results. Because it takes longer, it is possible to specify a specific directory to look in. The basic syntax is as follows:

```
find <directory> -name <filename>
```

Replace `<directory>` with the directory to start looking in. It will look recursively through the directory, meaning that it will look in any subdirectories, subdirectories of the subdirectories, and so on. Replace `<filename>` with the filename for which you are searching. To search in the current directory and below, replace `<directory>` with a dot (.) character such as:

```
find . -name guidelines.txt
```

Finding Commands

If you know a command exists on the system but keep getting the error message `command not found`, check to make sure you are typing the command correctly. Otherwise, it might not be in your `PATH` environment variable. To view the value of your `PATH`, execute the command `echo $PATH` from the command line. As you can see, your `PATH` is a list of directories. When you execute a command without providing its full path, it must be in one of the directories listed in your `PATH`. Otherwise, the `command not found` error is displayed. You can provide the full path to the command if you know it, such as `/sbin/lspci` to execute the command to list the PCI devices. If you use the command often, but it is not in your `PATH`, you can add the directory to your `PATH`.

To add a directory to your path, modify the `.bashrc` file in your home directory. Refer to the "Editing Text Files" section later in this chapter if you don't know how to modify a text file. For example, to add the `/usr/sbin/` and `/sbin/` directories to your `PATH`, add the following line to the `.bashrc` file in your home directory:

```
export PATH=:$PATH:/usr/sbin:/sbin
```

It is not recommended that you add the dot (.) character to your path so that it includes whatever the current working directory is. Although this might be tempting when writing and testing your own scripts, it is a security risk because an authorized or nonauthorized user can place a different version of common commands in a directory you are likely to be in while executing them such as the `/tmp/` directory, which is writable by all users. For example, if someone places a different version of the command `ls` in the `/tmp/` directory and (which represents the current working directory) is listed before `/bin` in your `PATH`, you will be executing a different version of `ls`, which could contain code to do something harmful to your data or the system. If you need to execute a command in the current working directory, precede it by `./` such as `./test.pl` or provide its full path when executing it.

TIP

To verify which command you are executing, type the command `which <command>`. If a match to the command is found in the directories from your `PATH`, the full path to the command is displayed.

Reading Text Files

Sometimes you want to quickly read a text file such as a configuration file without having to open a text editor. This is possible with the `less`, `more`, and `cat` command-line utilities.

All three have the same basic syntax but work differently and have different command-line options. To use them in their default modes, type the command followed by the text file to read such as `less output.txt`, `more /var/log/messages`, or `cat /etc/sysconfig/network`.

With the `less` command, the Page Up and Page Down keys can be used to scroll up and down the contents of the file. The `more` command only allows you to scroll down the file using the spacebar to advance. The `cat` command outputs the contents of the file to the command line and then exits, so if the file is longer than the number of lines in your terminal, you will only see the last part of the file.

The `cat` command can also be used in conjunction with the `grep` command that was previously discussed with the `history` command. For example, to view only the kernel messages in the system log file, use the following command:

```
cat /var/log/messages | grep kernel
```

Because only root can view this file, you need to be logged in as the root user to view the contents. Are you already logged in as a user? Read the later section "Becoming the Root User" to find out how to perform administrative tasks while logged in as a user.

For information on text editors that can read and modify text files, refer to the "Editing Text Files" section in this chapter.

TIP

If you are unsure of the type of a particular file, use the `file <filename>` command to find out. If the file type is recognized, the file type will be displayed.

Starting Applications

Starting an application from the command line is as easy as knowing the name of the command, typing it, and pressing the Enter key. For example, to start the application for configuring the X Window System, type the command `system-config-display` and press Enter. If the command is executed from a terminal window within a graphical environment, the graphical version of the application is started as shown in Figure 4.4.

If the application requires the root password to continue, a dialog window appears so that the correct root password can be used to authenticate the administrator. A few tools have both graphical and text-based versions. However, if you are in a non-graphical environment and try to start a program that only has a graphical version, an error message such as `cannot open display` or `requires a currently running X server` will be displayed.

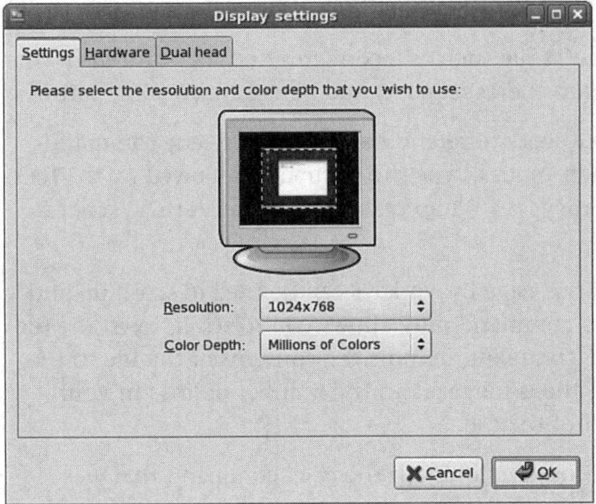

FIGURE 4.4 Graphical Version of the Display Configuration Tool

Becoming the Root User

As you learned in Chapter 2 it is important to log in with your user account instead of as the root user when performing day-to-day tasks. Some of the graphical administration tools will prompt you for the root password if you try to run them as a regular user. But, what if you are logged in as a user and need to perform an operation only the root user can do? It would be time consuming to close all your open windows, log out of the graphical desktop, log back in as root, execute root-only commands, log out again, and then log back in with your user account.

Instead, you can temporarily start a terminal session as root. From a shell prompt, execute the following command to temporarily become the root user:

```
su -
```

Notice the space and then a hyphen after the `su` command. These are extremely important parts of the command. Without it, you have root privileges but you don't inherit any of the environment variables of the root user, including the important `PATH` variable previously discussed. Without the proper `PATH` that includes `/sbin/` and `/usr/sbin/`, it will appear as if many administrative commands don't exist. After executing the `su -` command, you will be prompted to enter the root password before being granted access. If the correct root password is entered, you will notice that the prompt changes to show that the root user is the currently logged-in user.

When you no longer need to be root, type the `exit` command and then press **Enter** to return to your user shell.

Manual Pages

One great feature of Linux and other UNIX-based operating systems is the inclusion of manual pages, also known as *man pages* for most commands. They can be read from a graphical or nongraphical environment and do not require a network connection like documentation available over the Internet.

Man pages are divided into eight sections:

1. Commands
2. System Calls
3. Library Calls
4. Special Files
5. File Formats and Conventions
6. Games
7. Conventions and Miscellaneous
8. System Management Commands

To read the man page for a command, execute `man <command>` from a shell prompt. If a man page exists for the command, it will be displayed. Use the Page Up and Page Down keys to scroll through the text. To find a word or phrase in a man page, press the forward slash key (/) followed by the word or phrase you are looking for. After you press the forward slash, the colon at the bottom of the screen changes to a forward slash. As you type what you are searching for, it appears after the slash at the bottom of the screen. Press Enter to start searching. Press the N key to jump to the next instance of the word or phrase.

Sometimes, there are multiple man pages for the same command. For example, there are two man pages for man pages. When you execute the command `man man`, the page from section one, "Commands," is shown explaining the basics of how to use the command. There is also another man page for man in section 7, "Conventions and Miscellaneous," which describes how to write man pages. To view the man page for a topic in a specific section, include the section in the command such as `man 7 man` or `man 8 useradd`.

If you prefer to read the man pages in a graphical environment, select the **System** menu from the top panel and then select the **Help** menu item to start the graphical help program. Select **Manual Pages** from the list on the left side. The list of man page topics to choose from is slightly different than the man page sections previously discussed, but you should still be able to find the pages you are looking for such as the one shown in Figure 4.5.

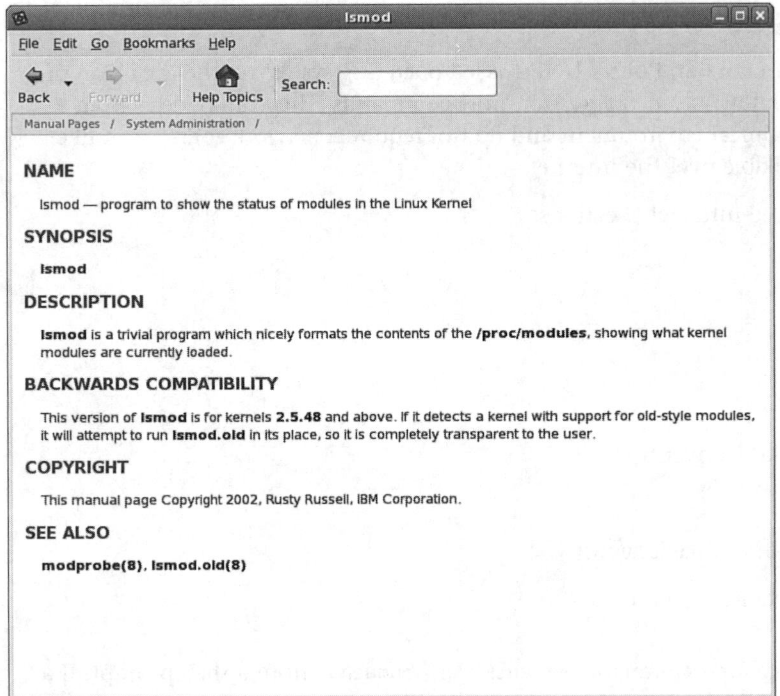

FIGURE 4.5 Graphical View of Man Pages

Editing Text Files

What if you want to make some quick notes without having to open a graphical word processor program? Do you need to make a simple edit to a configuration file? Do you need to edit a file from a remote terminal with limited bandwidth or with X forwarding disabled? Sounds like you need a simple nongraphical text editor.

There are too many text editors for Red Hat Enterprise Linux to discuss all of them in this brief chapter. Instead, this section discusses the two most popular ones: Vi and Emacs. They are both very different to use, and users of each are often very hesitant to use the other because of these differences. Ultimately, you must choose one that you feel the most comfortable with. Also consider that some systems might not have both installed, so it is a good idea to at least be familiar with the basics of both such as how to open a file, perform basic modifications, save the file, and exit. If you are in a critical situation in which you only have a text environment in rescue mode, knowing the text editor available might mean the difference between fixing the system quickly and struggling through it. In minimal environments such as rescue mode, Vi is often available more than Emacs because it requires less disk space and system resources.

Vi Editor

The Vi editor is text based, so it must be run in a terminal. To use it, you must have the `vim-minimal` RPM package installed. If it is not installed, install it as described in Chapter 3, "Operating System Updates."

To open a file in Vi, type `vi <file>` at the shell prompt. If the file does not exist, it will be created with the filename you provided the first time you saved it. Remember, you can always give the full path to the file if you are not in the directory that contains the file. Also remember that you can only modify files you have write permission to. Vi will let you open files you have only read access to but will deny the save operation if you do not have write access. For more information on read and write permissions, refer to the "File Permissions" section later in this chapter.

As shown in Figure 4.6, the Vi editor is very basic. By default, you are not even allowed to input characters.

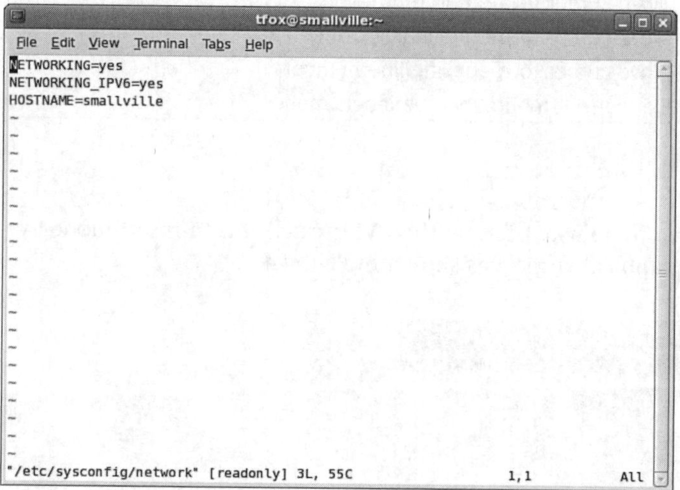

FIGURE 4.6 The Vi Editor

To start making changes to the file or start typing content into a new file, change to insert mode by pressing the I key. You will notice that the status at the bottom of the screen changes to `-- INSERT --`. Next, start typing. Vi does not have automatic word wrap, so you must press Enter to move the cursor to the next line. When you are finished typing the contents of the file, press the Esc key to exit insert mode. To save a file, exit insert mode, type `:w` (the `w` is for write), and press Enter. If you have permission to save the file, it will be saved. If you started Vi without specifying a filename, type `:w`, press the spacebar to add a space, type the desired filename, and press Enter to save the file.

To exit Vi, type `:q` (for quit), and press Enter. To exit without saving the file, follow the `:q` command by an exclamation point (`!`).

Common Vi operations are provided in Table 4.2. For even more instructions on using the Vi editor, pick up an inexpensive book on the editor or read some of the numerous Vi tutorials on the Web.

TABLE 4.2 Common Vi Commands

Command	Description
:w	Save the file
:w <filename>	Save the file with a different filename
:q	Quit Vi
:q!	Quit Vi without saving any changes
/<search item>	Search for a phrase, word, or group of words
n	Repeat last search
a	Start insert mode after cursor
A	Start insert mode at the end of the line
dd	While not in insert mode, cut the current line into the buffer
p	While not in insert mode, paste the last cut line from the buffer
x	While not in insert mode, delete the character at the cursor
$	Move cursor to the end of the line
0	Move cursor to the beginning of the line
:<linenum>	Move cursor to a specific line number
ESC	Exit current mode such as insert mode

Emacs Editor

The Emacs editor is considered more user-friendly than Vi because it is in insert mode by default and is available in a graphical version as shown in Figure 4.7.

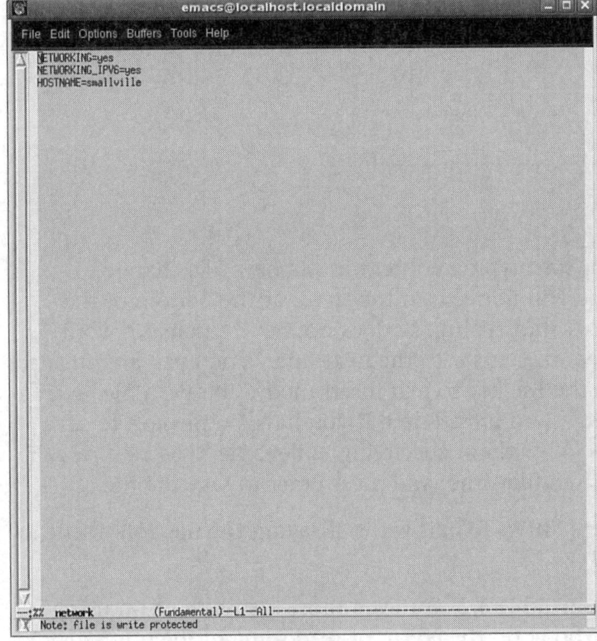

FIGURE 4.7 The Emacs Editor

A text version is also available for use at the command line as shown in Figure 4.8.

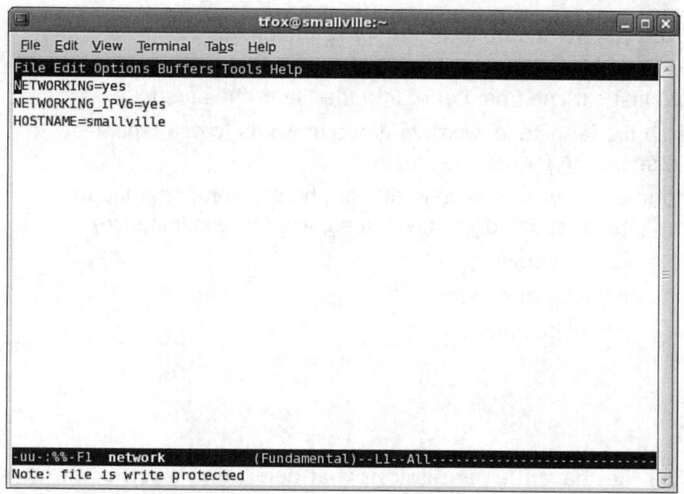

FIGURE 4.8 The Text-Based Version of the Emacs Editor

The `emacs` RPM package must be installed to use this editor. If it is not installed, install it as described in Chapter 3. To begin, type the `emacs` command. Just like Vi, the `emacs` command can optionally be followed by a space and a filename. If the file exists, it will be opened in the editor. If it doesn't exist, it will be created the first time the file is saved.

To force the editor to start in text-based mode, execute the `emacs -nw` command for "no window."

Most Emacs commands are key combinations. After typing the contents of the file, press Ctrl+X, Ctrl+S to save the file. Press Ctrl+X, Ctrl+C to quit Emacs. To open a file, use the Ctrl+X, Ctrl+F key combo, enter the filename at the prompt at the bottom of the editor, and press Enter. If a file is already open in the editor, the new file will be opened at the same time. To switch between open files, use the Ctrl+X, B key combo. Either press Enter to switch to the "buffer" listed at the bottom of the editor or press Tab to see a list of available open files.

Common Emacs operations are provided in Table 4.3. For even more instructions on using the editor, pick up an inexpensive book on the editor or read some of the numerous tutorials on the Web.

TABLE 4.3 Common Emacs Commands

Command	Description
Ctrl+X, Ctrl+S	Save the file
Ctrl+X, Ctrl+W	Save the file with a different filename
Ctrl+X, Ctrl+C	Exit Emacs
Ctrl+X, Ctrl+F	Open a file
Ctrl+X, b	Switch buffers
Ctrl+A	Move cursor to beginning of the line
Ctrl+E	Move cursor to end of the line

4

TABLE 4.3 Continued

Command	Description
Ctrl+K	Cut the current line from the cursor to the end of the line into the buffer
Ctrl+Y	Paste last cut line from buffer into the file at the cursor
Ctrl+S	Search file for phrase, word, or group of words (press repeatedly to keep searching for next instance)
Ctrl+R	Perform a backward search in file for phrase, word, or group of words (press repeatedly to keep searching for next instance)
ESC D	Delete word at cursor
Ctrl+D	Delete character at cursor
Ctrl+G	Cancel current command

File Permissions

In Red Hat Enterprise Linux, all files have file permissions that determine whether a user is allowed to read, write, or execute them. When you issue the command `ls -l`, the first column of information contains these file permissions. Within this first column are places for 10 letters or hyphens. The first space is either a hyphen, the letter `d`, or the letter `l`. A hyphen means it is a file. If it is the letter `d`, the file is actually a directory. If it is the letter `l`, it is a symbolic link to a directory somewhere else on the filesystem.

The next nine spaces are divided into three sets of three as shown in Figure 4.9. The first set of three is the read, write, and execute permissions for the owner of the file. The second set of three is the read, write, and execute permissions for anyone who belongs to the user group for the file. (For more information on the relationship between users and groups, refer to Chapter 9, "Managing Users and Groups.") The last set of permissions is for anyone who has a login to the system.

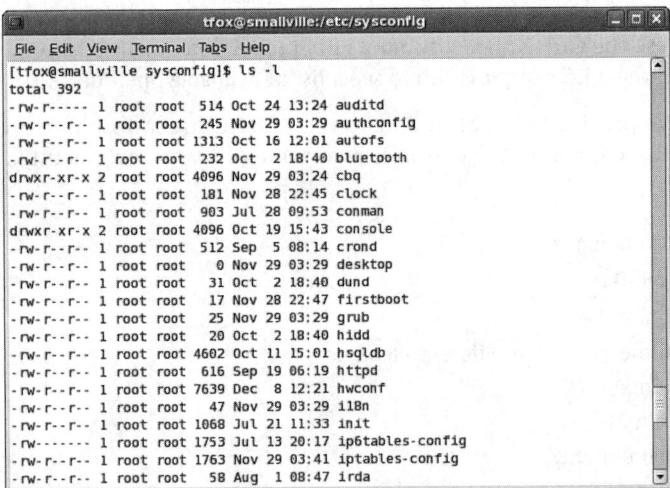

FIGURE 4.9 File Permissions

As you can probably guess, within each set of permissions, the r stands for read, the w stands for write, and the x stands for execute. If the file is a script or command, you must have execute permission to run it. You must also have execute permission to change into a directory.

To change file permissions, you must be the owner of the file or directory or be the root user. The chmod utility is used to modify file permissions. The basic syntax is as follows:

```
chmod [ugoa][+-=]<permissions> filename
```

For the first argument, choose one or more of the letters ugoa, where u stands for the user who owns the file (the first set of permissions), g stands for everyone in the file's group (the second set of permissions), o stands for other users not in the file's group (the third set of permissions), and a stands for all users (all three sets of permissions). The difference between specifying o and a is that o changes the third set of permissions for everyone and a changes the permissions for all three sets.

The second argument must be one of +, -, or =. If the plus sign (+) is used, the permissions that follow it are added for the users and groups provided by the first argument. If the minus sign (-) is used, the permissions that follow are removed for the users and groups in the first argument. Normally, when the chmod command is used, the permissions are added to the existing ones. However, if the equals sign (=) is used, the file will only have the permissions being specified (the existing permissions are overwritten and not retained).

The last argument is a filename or group of filenames on which to set the permissions. Multiple filenames can be listed using the * wildcard character such as *.txt for all files ending in .txt.

The third argument <permissions> is the list of permissions for the users and groups from the first argument. The list can consist of one or more of the permissions in Table 4.4.

TABLE 4.4 chmod File Permissions

Permission	Description
r	Read
w	Write
x	Execute (also gives permission to change into a directory)
X	Execute only if it is a directory or has execute permission for some user
s	Set user or group ID on execution
t	Sticky bit
u	Permissions granted to user who owns the file
g	Permissions granted to users in the file's group
o	Permissions granted to the owner of the group and the users in the file's group

The first three (r, w, x) are self-explanatory. Use them to set read, write, and execute permissions.

The s permission is used on directories to retain the user or group ID for a file created in the directory. To set the user ID for any new files created in the directory to the owner of the directory, use the `chmod u+s <directory>` command. To set the group ID for any new files created in the directory to the directory's group, use the `chmod g+s <directory>` command.

The sticky bit permission for files is no longer used. It was used on older systems to store executables in memory so they run faster, but with the current virtual memory system, the sticky bit is no longer needed. If the sticky bit (the t permission) is set for a directory, the directory can only be unlinked or renamed by the root user or the owner of the directory. If the sticky bit is not set for a directory, anyone with write permission can delete or rename the directory. If the sticky bit is set for a directory, the permissions listing looks similar to the following (notice the t in the last set of permissions) :

```
drwxrwxrwt 22 root root 4096 Mar 30 10:57 /tmp
```

The last three permissions (u, g, o) are only used with the = operator to set permissions for the owner, group, others, or everyone equal to the existing permissions for the owner, group, others, or everyone. For example, `chmod g=u <filename>` sets the group permissions to the current permissions for the owner of the file.

TIP

To change permissions recursively (on all the files in a directory, all the files in its subdirectories, all the files in the subdirectories of the subdirectories, and so on) use the `-R` option to `chmod` such as `chmod -R g+w output.txt`.

Examples include the following:

- `chmod ug+rw <filename>`

  Gives the user and group read and write permissions

- `chmod -R g+r *`

  Gives the group read permissions for all files in the current directory and any files and directories in the current directory, recursively

- `chmod o-x <directory>`

  Does not let users who aren't the owner or in the group change into the directory

File permissions can also be set graphically using the Nautilus file browser. From the desktop, click on the **Places** menu on the top panel and select **Home Folder**. Navigate to the file you want to view or change permissions for, right-click on it, and select **Properties**. Click on the **Permissions** tab as shown in Figure 4.10 to view the existing permissions or change them.

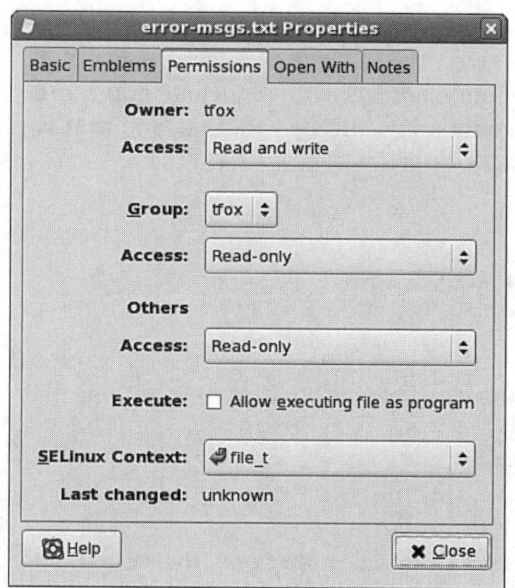

FIGURE 4.10 Changing File Permissions

Depending on how your system is configured, files might also have access control lists or Security-Enhanced Linux rules associated with them. Refer to the next section on "Access Control Lists" and Chapter 23, "Protecting Against Intruders with Security-Enhanced Linux," for details.

Initialization Scripts

Network services such as the Apache HTTP Server and DHCP along with other programs such as cron and syslog require a *daemon* to be running at all times. The daemon performs actions such as listening for connections to a service on specific ports, making sure commands are executed at specific times, and capturing data such as log messages when they are sent out by other programs.Programs that require a daemon to be started have an *initialization script* in the `/etc/rc.d/init.d/` directory. An initialization script can also be used to run a command at boot time such as the `readahead_early` and `readahead_later` scripts, which run the `readahead` utility so that programs used at startup are loaded into memory before they are needed. Doing so decreases the amount of time it takes to start the system. When you boot a Red Hat Enterprise Linux system, the `init` program is run last in the kernel boot process. This program first executes the `/etc/rc.d/rc.sysinit` script to perform actions such as loading kernel modules for hardware support, loading the default keymap, and setting the hostname. The `/etc/inittab` script is run next, which then tells `init` which runlevel to start. The runlevel defines which services to start at boot time, or which initialization scripts to execute. Refer to the later section "Runlevels" for details on how runlevels are configured.

Lastly, the `/etc/rc.d/rc.local` script is executed. Commands can be added to this file for custom initialization.

The initialization scripts can also be used to start, stop, and restart services after the system has booted. These actions are performed with the `service` command as the root user. Each script has its own list of actions. Common actions defined include `start`, `stop`, `conrestart` (which stops and starts the service only if it is already running), and `status`. To perform an action, use the following syntax:

```
service <service> <action>
```

For example, the following starts the OpenSSH service:

```
service sshd start
```

As each service with an initialization script is discussed in this book, a list of actions that can be performed with the script is given.

Runlevels

How does the system know which initialization scripts to run so that only the desired services are started at boot time? Linux uses the concept of *runlevels* to define which services to start at boot time. There are 7 runlevels, with each having its own general purpose:

- 0: Halt the system
- 1: Single-user mode (see Chapter 10, "Techniques for Backup and Recovery" for details)
- 2: Not used
- 3: Multi-user mode with text login
- 4: Not used
- 5: Multi-user mode with graphical login
- 6: Reboot

Each runlevel has its own directory named `rcX.d` in `/etc/rc.d/`, where `X` is the runlevel number. Each of these directories contains symbolic links to the actual initialization scripts in `/etc/rc.d/init.d/`. Each symbolic link start with the letter `S` or `K` followed by a number. The `S` stands for *start*, and the `K` stands for *kill*, which means to stop a process. When a runlevel is initialized, all the services starting with `K` are stopped first, and then all the services starting with `S` are started. The number following the letter determines the order in which the stop and start actions are performed. The lower the number, the sooner it is executed.

Changing the Default Runlevel

By default, Red Hat Enterprise Linux boots into runlevel 5 with a graphical login screen and a graphical desktop once the user successfully authenticates. Runlevel 3 is essentially the same except the text login is used. Runlevels 2 and 4 are not reserved for a specific mode, but they can be defined for specific purposes if needed.

The default runlevel is configured on the following line from the /etc/inittab file:

```
id:5:initdefault:
```

To change the default runlevel, modify this line. The next time the system is booted, it is booted into the new default runlevel. To change to a different runlevel without rebooting the system, execute the following command as root, where <runlevel> is a number from 0 to 6:

```
init <runlevel>
```

Configuring the Runlevels

To configuring which services are started for a runlevel, use one of three programs: chkconfig (command line only), ntsysv (simple text-based application that doesn't require a graphical desktop), or the Service Configuration Tool (graphical application).

The chkconfig command can be used to configure runlevels and list the current runlevel configuration. It must be run as root if modifying a runlevel. Otherwise commands such as listing whether a service is started at boot time can be run as a non-root user.

To list the status of all services, execute the chkconfig --list command. A line is output for each service such as the following for the Apache HTTP Server:

```
httpd          0:off   1:off   2:off   3:off   4:off   5:off   6:off
```

To list the status for just one service, provide the name of the service:

```
chkconfig --list <service>
```

To modify whether the service is turned on or off for the runlevel, specify the service name and then on, off, or reset. Set it to on to have the service started at boot time. Set it to off to have the service stopped at boot time. Setting it to reset resets the values of all runlevels to the defaults from the initialization script. The syntax is as follows:

```
chkconfig <service> [on¦off¦reset]
```

If no runlevels are given, runlevels 2, 3, 4, and 5 are modified. To only modify one or more runlevels, use the following syntax where levels is a list of runlevel numbers not separated by spaces or commas such as 35 for runlevels 3 and 5:

```
chkconfig —level <levels> <service> [on¦off¦reset]
```

To run the Service Configuration Tool, select **Administration**, **Server Settings**, **Services** from the **System** menu on the top panel of the desktop. Or, execute the system-config-services command. If running as a non-root user, you must enter the root password before continuing. The application allows you to configure which services are started for runlevels 3, 4, and 5. **On the Background Services** tab, it also allows you to start and stop services. The **On Demand Services** tab provides an interface for enabling or disabling any xinetd services on the system.

Runlevel 5 is configured by default. To edit a different runlevel, select it from the **Edit Runlevel** menu. As shown in Figure 4.11, the check box is selected next to each service configured to start at boot time for the runlevel. Click on a service to display a brief description of it and its status. After making any changes, click the **Save** button to enable the changes.

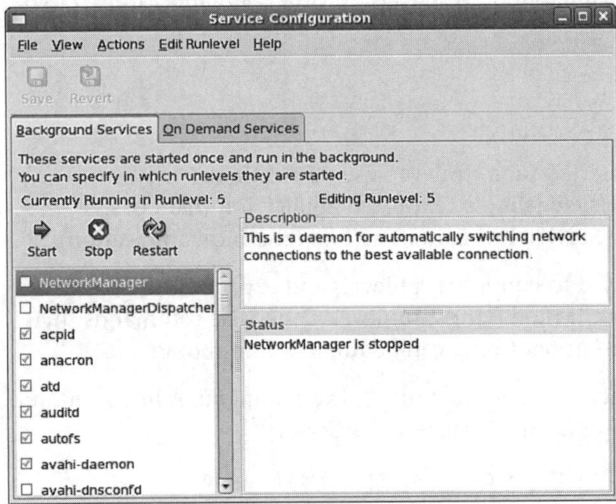

FIGURE 4.11 Changing File Permissions

Service Configuration Tool

To immediately start, stop, or restart a service, select it from the list and click the **Start**, **Stop**, or **Restart** button. This does not affect whether it is started or stopped at boot time.

If you do not have the graphical desktop installed or just prefer a more simplistic interface, `ntsysv` can be used to configure runlevels. The program must be run as the root user. If the `ntsysv` command is run without any command-line arguments, the current runlevel is configured. To configure a different runlevel or multiple runlevels, use the following syntax, where `<levels>` is a list of runlevel numbers without any spaces or commas such as `35` for runlevels 3 and 5:

```
ntsysv --level <levels>
```

A list of services is shown with an asterisk next to those configured to start at boot time (see Figure 4.12). If multiple runlevels are being configured, an asterisk indicates that the service is enabled for at least one of the runlevels, but not necessarily all of them.

Use the up and down arrow keys to move through the list. Use the spacebar to toggle the asterisk, enabling or disabling the service at boot time for the desired runlevel. Press the Tab key when finished to highlight the **Ok** button. Click Enter to save the changes and exit.

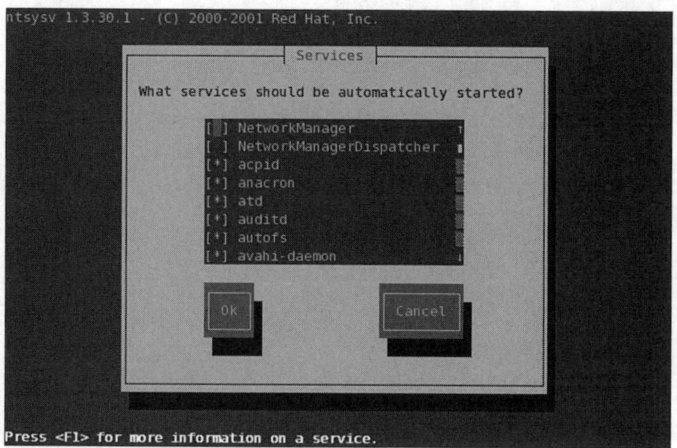

FIGURE 4.12 ntsysv

Summary

The rest of the book assumes you have an understanding of the basic concepts covered in this chapter such as how to navigate around the shell prompt, use man pages, modify file permissions, and execute initialization scripts. If you were not already familiar with them before reading this chapter, use this chapter to learn them before continuing. Refer back to this chapter when necessary.

CHAPTER 5

Working with RPM Software

IN THIS CHAPTER

- Understanding How RPM Works
- Finding the Software
- Installing Software
- Updating Software
- Removing Software
- Verifying Software Files
- Querying Package Files
- Building RPM Packages

A large part of a system administrator's job is to maintain the software on a company's servers as well as the software on the users' desktops. This can be a very daunting task, especially for a large corporation. The software must be updated for security fixes, compatibility with other software, and feature enhancements if they are needed. Before the software updates are applied to production systems, the updated software must be tested and verified to be compatible with the existing programs. To efficiently maintain the software on a Red Hat Enterprise Linux system, Red Hat Network (RHN) should be used as discussed in Chapter 3, "Operating System Updates." Red Hat Network is based on a software maintenance utility called *RPM* (Red Hat Package Manager). Entire books have been written on RPM, so this chapter will not attempt to cover every aspect of the software packaging tool. Instead, it gives an overview of the basic topics with which an administrator should be familiar.

Understanding How RPM Works

How does RPM work? Each software program consists of files and directories, most of which must be located in a particular place on the filesystem. If the software program is distributed in RPM format, these files are compressed together into one RPM file along with instructions on where the files should be located on the filesystem and any additional scripts or executables that must be run before or after the files are installed. These RPM files are often referred to as packages.

A software program, such as the Firefox web browser, might consist of one RPM file. However, some programs are divided into multiple RPM files to allow the administrator to customize which parts are necessary for the system's usage. For example, the GNOME graphical desktop is divided into many packages that contain parts of the overall desktop. For example, the `gnome-menus` package contains the files necessary for the desktop menus, while `gnome-panel` provides the files necessary for the panels. Some GNOME packages supply additional functionality not absolutely necessary for the desktop to function properly. Dividing the desktop until these specialized packages allows the administrator to only install the software essential for each computer.

A proper RPM file should follow a specific naming convention:

```
<packagename>-<version>-<release>.<arch>.rpm
```

For example, `pciutils-2.2.1-1.2.i386.rpm` is the RPM filename for the 1.2 release of version 2.2.1 of the PCI utilities software package built for the i386 architecture.

In our example, 2.2.1 is the version of `pciutils`, and 1.2 is the build version. The version number is similar to what you might have encountered with other software. The major version number is incremented when major features are added or it becomes incompatible with previous versions. It usually maps to specific package and distribution independent upstream version numbers. The minor version number is usually distribution dependent and changes for bug fixes, minor feature additions, and general maintenance. The release version starts at 1 for each version number change and is incremented every time that version is built for Red Hat Enterprise Linux. This small change allows the developer and users to know the package has been rebuilt while still keeping the version number the same.

The next part of the RPM filename is the architecture for which the package is built. Because different processors must use different software libraries, have different system calls, and utilize different optimizations, software must be built with the proper version of the compiler compatible with the architecture. There are some exceptions such as software written in an interpreted language such as Python, which is not compiled. For software written in this type of language, the correct version of the software that interprets the code must be installed while the RPM package that installs the code can be platform-independent. The most popular architectures abbreviations used by RPM are explained in Table 5.1.

TABLE 5.1 System Architectures Used by RPM

Architecture	Description
noarch	Architecture-independent, can run on any architecture
i386	Generic build for a 32-bit x86 system
i586	Sometimes used when building kernels for older x86 processors
i686	Intel® Pentium® II, Intel Pentium III, Intel Pentium 4, AMD® Athlon, and AMD Duron systems (Most RPMs for these architectures are built using the i386 architecture, with the kernel for these architectures being built with the i686 for optimal performance.)
x86_64	64-bit processors such as AMD Athlon64, AMD Opteron, and Intel EM64T
ia64	Intel® Itanium™
ppc	32-bit IBM® POWER, IBM eServer™ pSeries®, and IBM eServer iSeries
s390x	64-bit IBM eServer System z

Finding the Software

Before learning how to install and maintain RPM packages, you need to know where to find the packages. With an enterprise system, it is crucial to only install software from a reliable source. In the case of Red Hat Enterprise Linux, the trusted source is straight from Red Hat or a certified software partner or from a Red Hat certified ISV. If you are installing custom software built inside your company, be sure it goes through testing before installing it on production systems. Installing software from other sources is most likely not supported by your Red Hat Enterprise Linux support contract.

NOTE

For more information on downloading software directly from Red Hat, refer to Chapter 3. For information on software from other vendors, contact the vendor directly for Linux versions of their software.

Installing Software

Installing an RPM package can be done via the command line or a graphical program. Because some systems such as servers do not always have a graphical desktop installed, it is important to learn at least the basics of how to use the command-line version of RPM.

The command is simple to remember: It is the `rpm` command.

NOTE

Root access is required when installing, upgrading, or removing a package with the `rpm` command.

Before installing any software, confirm that it was packaged by a trusted source and has not been altered since the trusted source built it. This process is done by checking the GPG *signature* of the package.

First, as the root user, import the GPG signature of the trusted party with the `rpm --import <keyfile>` command, where `<keyfile>` is the file containing the key. If you do not know where to securely obtain the key file, ask your trusted RPM source.

NOTE

Key files for software distributed by Red Hat can be found in the root directory of the first installation CD:

```
RPM-GPG-KEY-fedora
RPM-GPG-KEY-fedora-test
RPM-GPG-KEY-redhat-auxiliary
RPM-GPG-KEY-redhat-beta
RPM-GPG-KEY-redhat-former
RPM-GPG-KEY-redhat-release
```

5

To verify that the key was imported properly, execute the rpm -qa gpg-pubkey* command. If you imported the RPM-GPG-KEY-redhat-release key, the output will be similar to the following:

```
gpg-pubkey-37017186-45761324
```

To view the details of the key, execute the rpm -qi gpg-pubkey-37017186-45761324 command (output is in Listing 5.1).

LISTING 5.1 Details of RPM GPG Key

```
Name        : gpg-pubkey                   Relocations: (not relocatable)
Version     : 37017186                          Vendor: (none)
Release     : 45761324               Build Date: Wed 28 Feb 2007 12:36:35 AM EST
Install Date: Wed 28 Feb 2007 12:36:35 AM EST      Build Host: localhost
Group       : Public Keys                   Source RPM: (none)
Size        : 0                                License: pubkey
Signature   : (none)
Summary     : gpg(Red Hat, Inc. (release key) <security@redhat.com>)
Description :
-----BEGIN PGP PUBLIC KEY BLOCK-----
Version: rpm-4.4.2 (beecrypt-4.1.2)

mQGiBEV2EyQRBAD4/SR69qoLzK4HIa6g9iS+baiX0o3NjkLftFHg/xy+IMOMg//i4c5bUpLK
DTMH3+yT0G8qpul/RALUFOESKFkZm3/SlkJKuroXcB8U6s2dh5XX9DDBISqRwL7M5qB8rfDP
KHN+k/XwJ9CNpHMdNxnnc2WhnnmHNp6NrD/bUEH4vwCglMa0rFRXPaN7407DARGHvW/jugsE
ANFaeZsFwos/sajL1XQRfHZUTnvDjJgz31IFY+OLDlOVAOtV/NaECMwIJsMIhoisW4Luwp4m
75Qh3ogq3bwqSWNLsfJ9WFnNqXOgamyDh/F4q492z6FpyIb1JZLABBSH7LEQjHlR/s/Ct5JE
Wc5MyfzdjBi6J9qCh3y/IYL0EbfRA/4yoJ/fH9uthDLZsZRWmnGJvb+VpRvcVs8IQ4aIAcOM
bWu2Sp3U9pm6cxZFN7tShmAwiiGj9UXVtlhpj3lnqulLMD9VqXGF0YgDOaQ7CP/99OEEhUjB
j/8o8udFgxc1i2WJjc7/sr8IMbDv/SNToi0bnZUxXa/BUjj92uaQ6/LupbQxUmVkIEhhdCwg
SW5jLiAocmVsZWFzZSBrZXkpIDxzZWN1cml0eUByZWRoYXQuY29tPohfBBMRAgAfBQJFdhMk
AhsDBgsJCAcDAgQVAggDAxYCAQIeAQIXgAAKCRBTJoEBNwFxhogXAKCDTuYeyQrkYXjg9JmO
dTZvsIVfZgCcCWKJXtfbC5dbv0piTHI/cdwVzJo=
=mhzo
-----END PGP PUBLIC KEY BLOCK-----
```

After importing the key, the signature on the package can be verified with the rpm -K <rpmfile> command. If the package has not been corrupted since it was signed, the output will include the phrase md5 gpg OK.

If the package is not signed, the output will include output such as:

```
NOT OK
```

If you haven't imported the corresponding public key, the following message is given:

```
MISSING KEYS
```

After verifying that the package is trustworthy, install it with this command:

```
rpm -Uvh <rpmfile>
```

The -Uvh arguments tell the rpm command to install the package, display verbose information about the installation, and display the progress of the installation with hash marks.

The output will look similar to Listing 5.2.

LISTING 5.2 Installing an RPM Package

```
Preparing...                ########################################### [100%]
   1:example                ########################################### [100%]
```

Sometimes a package requires additional RPM packages to be installed or updated as shown in Listing 5.3.

LISTING 5.3 Dependencies Needed

```
error: Failed dependencies:
        example-core = 1:2.0.0-3.2.1 is needed by example-filters-2.0.0-3.2.1.i386
```

Download the additional package as well and install all the packages at the same time:

```
rpm -Uvh <rpmfile1> <rpmfile2>
```

TIP

The -U argument installs the software if it is not already installed. If it is already installed and you only want to upgrade the package , use the -F argument instead:

```
rpm -Fvh <packagename>-<version_number>.<arch>.rpm
```

Additional options to the rpm command can be specified when installing packages. Some of these options are described in Table 5.2.

TABLE 5.2 Optional rpm Arguments When Installing or Updating

Argument	Description
--nodeps	Install or upgrade the package without checking for dependencies. The software will most likely not function properly without the software dependencies installed. If you contact Red Hat support with problems, they will most likely ask you to reproduce the problem on a system where all package dependencies have been satisified.
--noscripts	Do not execute any of the scripts before or after installation, upgrade, or removal.
--excludedocs	Do not install packages marked as documentation files such as man pages.

TABLE 5.2 Continued

Argument	Description
`--oldpackage`	Allow a package to be replaced with an older version.
`--test`	Check for potential conflicts such as package dependencies but do not install the package.

Installing an RPM package without Red Hat Network to resolve dependencies can be quite frustrating because sometimes the package name is listed as a dependency and sometimes just a filename is listed as a dependency; the administrator has to determine which package provides the file. If the package you are trying to install is provided with Red Hat Enterprise Linux, refer to Chapter 3 for details on installing it and automatically resolving its package dependencies with RHN or the `yum` command-line utility.

If the package is not part of Red Hat Enterprise Linux, you still might be able to use RHN to resolve the software dependencies. Open the Nautilus file browser by selecting **Home Folder** or **Desktop** from the **Places** menu on the top panel of the desktop. Browse to the directory containing the RPM to be installed. Double-click on it to open the Software Installer as shown in Figure 5.1.

FIGURE 5.1 Installing an RPM Package with Software Installer

Click **Apply** to install the package. If additional packages are required as dependencies, the program will try to use `yum` to find the additional software. For this feature to work, the system must be registered to use RHN (refer to Chapter 3). If the dependencies are found, they are listed so that you can confirm their installation as well. When the installation is finished, a completion message will appear.

Installing a New Kernel

There is a `-i` argument to RPM to install packages, but it is more convenient to use `-U` when installing and upgrading software because `-U` installs or upgrades the package depending on whether or not it is already installed. However, there is an exception: installing a new kernel. When installing a new kernel, you should keep the current kernel installed in case the new kernel does not work with the system's hardware, does not perform as well as the current kernel, or causes other problems. When you use the `-U` argument to RPM, the older version of the software package is no longer available.

For most packages, you will receive an error message when trying to use the `-i` argument to upgrade a package if you already have an older version installed. With the kernel package, you will not receive this error because it is possible to have multiple versions of the kernel installed. Thus, it is recommended that you always use the `rpm -ivh kernel-<version>-<release>.<arch>.rpm` command when upgrading the kernel so the older kernel remains on the system. The system must be rebooted to enable the new kernel. After rebooting, you will notice the new kernel in the list of possible boot choices. By default, the system boot loader is configured to boot the new kernel. To modify which kernel is booted by default, edit the boot loader configuration file for your architecture. Chapter 2, "Post-Installation Configuration," contains example boot loader files for all architectures.

For x86 and x86_64 systems, modify the value of the `default` option in `/etc/grub.conf` file. Each kernel installed has a section in `/etc/grub.conf` starting with a title line such as the one shown in Listing 5.4. The value of the `default` option is the number of the title section, with the count starting at 0 and going from the first title section listed to the bottom of the file.

5

LISTING 5.4 Kernel Section in Bootloader Configuration File

```
title Red Hat Enterprise Linux (2.6.16-1.2096)
        root (hd0,0)
        kernel /boot/vmlinuz-2.6.16-1.2096 ro root=LABEL=/ rhgb quiet
        initrd /boot/initrd-2.6.16-1.2096.img
```

If you are unable to boot the new kernel to modify the bootloader configuration file, you can choose a different kernel using the up and down arrow keys at the bootloader screen shown as the system is booting and before the kernel is loaded.

Updating Software

If an RPM package is already installed, it can be updated to a newer version. With RPM, there isn't the concept of using a different file or set of files to perform a software upgrade. The same RPM file or files used to install a program can be used to update the program as well.

To update to a newer version of a package already installed:

```
rpm -Uvh <packagename>-<version>-<release>.<arch>.rpm
```

The same additional arguments available when installing packages can be used when upgrading. They are listed in Table 5.1.

Some of the files in an RPM package are marked according to what type of files they are. For example, configuration files can be marked as configuration files by the person who created the RPM package. If a configuration file is part of the package being upgraded, RPM checks the file to determine if it has been modified. So, what happens to the configuration files when a package is upgraded? Here are the possible scenarios:

- Current file has not been modified

  Regardless of whether the file from the updated package has changed from the file installed by the original package, the configuration file is replaced with the file from the updated package.

- Current file has been modified but the file from the updated package hasn't changed from the file installed by the original package

  Because the configuration file hasn't changed from version to version, the modified file on the system is left alone.

- Current file has been modified and the file from the updated package has changed from the file installed by the original package

  Because the configuration file has changed from version to version, it is not known whether the current configuration file will work with the new version of the software. The modified file on the system is renamed with the `.rpmsave` file extension, and the configuration file from the new package version is installed over the modified file on disk. If you are using the command-line version of RPM, a message is displayed with the old and new filenames.

Removing Software

To remove a package, issue the following command:

```
rpm -e <packagename>
```

Notice that this time, only `<packagename>` is used, not the full name of the file used to install the software. When this command is issued, the RPM database is searched for the files associated with this package, and they are removed.

If multiple versions of a package are installed, such as the kernel, the package version can also be specified to make sure the correct version is removed:

```
rpm -e <packagename>-<version>-<release>
```

As previously discussed, sometimes packages must have additional packages installed for them to function properly. If you try to remove a package that is needed by a package installed, a message similar to the following is shown:

```
error: Failed dependencies:
        example-filters is needed by example-core = 1:2.0.0-3.2.1
```

If the package that depends on the package you are trying to remove is still needed on the system, you should not try to remove the package. If the package that depends on the package you are trying to remove is also not needed, both must be removed at the same time to resolve the dependency:

```
rpm -e <packagename1> <packagename1>
```

Even if the packages are not dependent on each other, multiple packages can be removed at the same time by specifying them in the same command separated by a space.

If a configuration file is part of the package being removed but it has been modified, the file will be renamed instead of removed with the `.rpmsave` extension, and a message similar to the following is displayed:

```
warning: /etc/sysconfig/samba saved as /etc/sysconfig/samba.rpmsave
```

Verifying Software Files

What if you want to verify that the files associated with a package haven't been corrupted or compromised? For example, if you suspect your system has been accessed by a nonauthorized user, you can verify that the files from a package have not been changed with the RPM verify feature. Of course, if the unauthorized user altered the RPM database, the results may not be accurate. It is always best to back up to a known secure state of the filesystem if you suspect foul play.

If the verify function is used, file properties such as file size, MD5 sum, file permissions, file type, and file ownership are compared to the original values stored in the RPM database. To verify that the files are associated with a package, use the following command:

```
rpm -V <packagename>
```

If no output is returned, the files from the package have not been modified since installation. If a file, such as a configuration file, has been modified, the output is similar to Listing 5.5.

LISTING 5.5 Output from `rpm -V httpd`

```
.M.....T  c /etc/httpd/conf/httpd.conf
```

To verify the files from all the packages installed, use the `rpm -Va` command. The output is similar to Listing 5.6.

LISTING 5.6 Sample Output from `rpm -Va`

```
....L...  c /etc/pam.d/system-auth
..5....T  c /etc/inittab
missing     /usr/lib/mozilla-1.7.12/chrome/overlayinfo/browser
missing     /usr/lib/mozilla-1.7.12/chrome/overlayinfo/browser/content
missing     /usr/lib/mozilla-1.7.12/chrome/overlayinfo/browser/skin
missing     /usr/lib/mozilla-1.7.12/chrome/overlayinfo/cookie
```

LISTING 5.6 Continued

```
missing     /usr/lib/mozilla-1.7.12/chrome/overlayinfo/cookie/content
missing     /usr/lib/mozilla-1.7.12/chrome/overlayinfo/editor
missing     /usr/lib/mozilla-1.7.12/chrome/overlayinfo/editor/content
missing     /usr/lib/mozilla-1.7.12/chrome/overlayinfo/global
missing     /usr/lib/mozilla-1.7.12/chrome/overlayinfo/global/content
missing     /usr/lib/mozilla-1.7.12/chrome/overlayinfo/global/skin
S.5....T  c /etc/ntp/ntpservers
S.5....T  c /etc/audit.rules
```

In Listing 5.5, the `c` to the left of the filename indicates that the file is a configuration file. Other possible attribute markers include `d` for documentation files, `g` for ghost files (file contents are not included in the package payload), `l` for license files, and `r` for readme files.

The letters, numbers, and dots at the beginning of each line detail how the file differs from the original state of the file. As shown in Listing 5.6, if a file is no longer installed, the word `missing` appears instead of the sequence of codes. Otherwise the eight letters, numbers, and dots represent eight different tests performed to verify the file. Table 5.3 explains the codes that appear in the sequence in the order in which they appear if any of the tests fail. If a dot is shown instead of a code letter or number, the test passed.

TABLE 5.3 RPM Verification Codes

Code	Explanation
S	File size has changed
M	Mode has changed, including file permissions and file type
5	MD5 sum has changed
D	Device major or minor number has changed
L	The path of the symbolic link has changed
U	The owner of the file has changed
G	The group of the file has changed
T	The last modified time has changed

Querying Package Files

You now know that an RPM database on the system keeps track of which files are associated with each RPM installed, but how do you know which files are associated with which RPM packages? You can query the RPM database and find out with the following command:

```
rpm -qf <filename>
```

The `<filename>` must be the full path to the file. If the file is associated with an RPM package installed, the name of the package and the version installed is displayed. For example, if the `rpm -qf /etc/crontab` command is issued, the output is `crontabs-<version>-<release>`, where `<version>-<release>` is the version and release of the `crontabs` package installed.

TIP

If the file is a command already in your PATH environment variable, use the following syntax instead of typing the entire path to the file,:

```
rpm -qf `which <filename>`
```

Notice the command contains back ticks, not apostrophes. The back ticks tell the shell to execute the command inside them and use that as part of the overall command.

You also know that configuration files are marked as configuration files in the RPM database when they are installed. To retrieve a list of configuration files from a package installed, use the following command:

```
rpm -qc <packagename>
```

If any files from the package were marked as configuration files when the package was created, a list of them will be displayed.

A similar query can be performed to list any documentation files installed with a package:

```
rpm -qd <packagename>
```

Documentation files include man pages and text or HTML formatted files in `/usr/share/doc/` installed by the package.

Each time a package is changed, the developer is responsible for adding a changelog entry to describe the change. This becomes part of the information provided by the RPM package. The query option has the ability to show the changelog for the package with the following command:

```
rpm -q --changelog <packagename>
```

These query commands can also be performed on an RPM package file instead of on the package name of the package already installed. To do so, add the `-p` argument followed by the full or relative path to the package file. For example, to view the changelog of a package before installing it, use the following command:

```
rpm -q --changelog -p <packagename>-<version>-<release>.<arch>.rpm
```

Building RPM Packages

Finally, although building packages is usually left to the software distributor or software developer, it is useful for an administrator to know how to build a basic RPM package.

Think beyond traditional software programs. RPM packages can be used to install user files required for a corporate workstation, custom VPN software or configuration files, corporate templates for internal and external communications, and so on.

Advantages of distributing custom scripts, corporate templates, configuration files, and the like in RPM format instead of just copying them to each system include

- Version control. The RPM version number can help you keep track of the version number for debugging or determining which systems need to be updated.
- Easier distribution. Installing an RPM can be done remotely from an SSH session or via Red Hat Network Satellite.
- Consistency. By defining where the files are installed when building the RPM package, administrators can find them in the same location on any system. This can be especially useful if multiple administrators are responsible for installing and using the software.
- Verification. Using the verify option previously discussed, administrators can quickly determine if the files have been altered (assuming the RPM database was not modified to hide the file modifications).

The program necessary for building RPM packages is not installed by default. Before building your RPM packages or following the example in this section, install the `rpm-build` package and its dependencies. If your system is registered with RHN, install the package with the `yum install rpm-build` command or refer to Chapter 3 for instructions on how to schedule its installation with the RHN website.

NOTE

The example files used in this section can be downloaded from the book's website.

This section discusses the following steps for building an RPM:

1. Setting up the build environment.
2. Creating a spec file that defines the package name, version, release number, description, and more.
3. Creating a Makefile that contains target actions such as building the source and binary RPM files.
4. Creating a tarball of all the source files.
5. Running the appropriate Makefile target to build the source RPM, binary RPM, or both.

Setting Up the Build Environment

Before building the package, set up your build environment. By default, the `/usr/src/redhat/` directory is used and contains the following subdirectories: `BUILD`, `RPMS`, `SOURCES`, `SPECS`, and `SRPMS`. However, these directories are owned by the root user and are only writable by the root user. When building RPMs, it is best to build as a non-root user such as your user account or perhaps a special user account set up for building RPM. This is to make sure the build process does not accidentally corrupt the filesystem or overwrite critical files owned by root. A small error in a script can do unintentional damage that might be irreversible.

To set up build directories for your own personal use, create a .rpmmacros file in your home directory with the contents from Listing 5.7, replacing <username> with your username. This file must be created by each user building packages.

LISTING 5.7 ~/.rpmmacros File

```
%_topdir /home/<username>/RPMBUILD
```

The line in Listing 5.7 defines the directory to use when building the RPM files. You need to create this directory and some additional subdirectories. Change into your home directory and then execute the following commands:

```
mkdir RPMBUILD
mkdir -p RPMBUILD/{BUILD,RPMS/x86_64,SOURCES,SRPMS,SPECS}
```

The command assumes you are using a x86_64 system. RPMs build for the x86_64 architecture are saved to the /home/<username>/RPMBUILD/RPMS/x86_64/ directory. If you need to build RPMs for different architectures compatible with your system such as the noarch or i386 architectures on an x86_64 system, create directories for them as well. The directory names should be the same as the RPM architecture abbreviations in Table 5.1. In our example, the RPMBUILD/RPMS/noarch/ directory must be created since the example package is a noarch RPM.

TIP

Additional macros can be defined in the .rpmmacros file. Refer to /usr/lib/rpm/macros file for a full list. For example, if you want to save the SRPMs in a different directory, you can add the following line to your .rpmmacros file:

```
%_srcrpmdir /home/<username>/SRPMS
```

The .rpmmacros file and the build directories only need to be created once. After that, your build environment is set up for any RPMs and SRPMs you need to create.

Creating the Spec File

Building a package requires a package specification file (often called a *spec file* for short) and the files to be included in the package. For example, you might want to package a custom VPN script used by laptop users to connect to the company's private network while traveling or working from home. The name of the script is called startvpn. Every VPN solution is a bit different, so for the purpose of this example, use Listing 5.8 for the contents of this script. It does not actually start a VPN, but it does display a message so that we can test our RPM file.

LISTING 5.8 Example startvpn Script

```
#!/bin/bash

echo "startvpn script executed"
```

This example package depends on the vpnc package to work properly. An example spec file, startvpn.spec, can be found in Listing 5.9.

NOTE

This is a very simplistic example that does not require the code to be compiled or any post commands to be executed. It is intended to illustrate how building an RPM can be useful for a system administrator. For more advanced building options, refer to the RPM Guide available at http://fedora.redhat.com/docs/drafts/rpm-guide-en/ from the Fedora Project.

LISTING 5.9 Example spec File

```
Name: startvpn
Summary: Custom script to start VPN
Version: 1.1
Release: 1
License: GPL
Group: Applications/Internet
URL: http://www.example.org/
Source0: %{name}-%{version}.tar.gz
BuildRoot: %{_tmppath}/%{name}-%{version}-%{release}
BuildArch: noarch
Requires: bash
Requires: vpnc

%description
Custom script to start VPN and connect to company's private network.
For company use only.

%prep
%setup -q

%install
#rm -fr $RPM_BUILD_ROOT
make INSTROOT=$RPM_BUILD_ROOT install

%clean
rm -fr $RPM_BUILD_ROOT
```

LISTING 5.9 Continued

```
%files
%defattr(-,root,root,-)
/usr/local/bin/%{name}

%changelog
* Thu Apr 27 2006 Tammy Fox <tfox@example.org>
- updated routes
* Wed Feb 22 2006 Tammy Fox <tfox@example.org>
- first build of VPN script
```

The following describes the fields and sections from the spec file in Listing 5.9:

`Name`

Package name. The name can not contain spaces.

`Summary`

Short phrase describing the purpose of the package.

`Version`

Software version of the package.

`Release`

Build number. Every time the package is rebuilt with the same version number, this number should be incremented so that it is clear a rebuild has occurred even if the code has not changed. If a new version is built, this number goes back to 1 because the version number indicates a code change and a rebuild.

`License`

License for the software such as GPL, LGPL, or FDL for documentation.

`Group`

The software group for the package. It must be a valid group from the `/usr/share/doc/rpm-<version>/GROUPS` file.

`URL`

Website location for the software, if one exists.

`Source0`

Name of the file that contains the source and other files to be installed. The file is usually a tar file compressed with either gzip or bzip2. Always use macros in the filename such as `%{name}` and `%{version}` when possible. Doing so will result in minimal changes to the spec file when other parameters change. If multiple source tarballs exist, list them on separate lines and increment the number for each file such as `Source0`, `Source1`, `Source2`, and so on.

`BuildRoot`

Directory location of where to build the package. As code is compiled, it is set up in this directory so the RPM package can be built. Be sure to use the macro `%{_tmppath}` for the temporary directory to make sure the correct directory is used on the build server. As shown in Listing 5.9, be sure to include the name and version of the package in the build root directory to ensure the package is built in a unique directory that another package build is not using.

`BuildArch`

Architecture from Table 5.1 for which the package should be built. In our example, the `BuildArch` is `noarch` because the bash script can be run on any architecture.

`Requires`

If additional software needs to be installed for the software to run, list the packages that provide the additional software with this field. List each package on separate lines with this keyword. If additional software is necessary to build the source code while building the package, use the `BuildRequires` field instead.

`%description`

Description of the package. It shouldn't be more than 10 to 15 lines. This description is displayed when the `rpm -qi <packagename>` command is executed.

`%prep`

How to unpack the source code from the source files listed with `Source0`, `Source1`, and so on. Usually done with the `%setup` macro in quiet mode:

```
%setup -q
```

`%install`

Instructions for installing the files in the package. It is a good idea to clean out the build root just in case a previous build left files in it:

```
rm -rf $RPM_BUILD_ROOT
```

If using `make` to install the files, be sure to specify the RPM build root as the INSTROOT for it:

```
make INSTROOT=$RPM_BUILD_ROOT install
```

The `install` target of the `Makefile` creates the `/usr/local/bin/` directory in the `INSTROOT` and then installs the script in the directory. Because the name of the script file is the same as the package name, the `${PKGNAME}` macro is used.

`%clean`

Command to clean up the build root. Usually the following will work:

```
rm -rf $RPM_BUILD_ROOT
```

`%files`

The list of files installed by the RPM package. These are the files associated with the package in the RPM database and listed when the `rpm -ql <packagename>` command is run. When listing files, be sure to use macros such as `%{name}` and `%{version}` when possible.

Use the `%defattr` macro to set the default file permissions for the files installed. For most packages it should be

```
%defattr(-,root,root,-)
```

The fields inside the parentheses stand for the file permissions, owner, group, and directory permissions. A dash for the file and directory permissions causes the permissions of the files and directories inside the BuildRoot to be retained. This macro is usually listed first under the `%files` section for easy readability.

To mark files as special file types, include the following macros before the filename: `%doc` for documentation files, `%config` for configuration files, `%config(noreplace)` for configuration files that should not be replaced when upgrading the package.

If a directory is listed, place the `%dir` macro in front of it.

If a specific file needs different attributes, they can be listed with the `%attr` macro in front of the filename in the list such as:

```
%attr(0644,root,root)%config(noreplace) /etc/sysconfig/%{name}
```

Macros for special directories should be used in case their locations change or differ on different versions of the operating system. This prevents files from being installed in the wrong location should a special directory such as the man page directory change locations. It also helps the files stay FHS-compliant. These macros include `%{_bindir}` for the system `bin` directory, `%{_mandir}` for the man page directory, `%{_datadir}` for the `share` directory, and `%{_defaultdocdir}` for the documentation directory.

`%changelog`

Every time the package is built, a changelog entry should be added to the spec file in the format shown in Listing 5.9. Even if the rebuild is for the same version with a different release number, a changelog entry should be added to describe why the rebuild occurred. The entries should be as specific as possible. For example, instead of `random bug fixes`, the entry should include information such as `fixed traceback error when log file doesn't exist` so the administrator can determine whether the update is necessary or whether the update will fix a program he is having with the software. If a bug tracking system is used for the software, include the bug number with the changelog entry.

Additional parameters that can be set in the spec file include

`%build`

Instructions for building the package. Usually the `make` command is used to run the default target of the `Makefile`, or the `%configure` macro is used if automake and autoconf are used. For our example, this parameter is not used since the program being installed is a script and does not need to be compiled.

`BuildRequires`

If a package such as one that provides a compiler or a library necessary to build the package is needed, use this field to list them. Each package should be listed on its own line with the `BuildRequires` keyword. If a package is required to run the software after it is installed, use the `Requires` field instead.

`Patch0`

If a patch should be applied to the source code during the build process, list it with this field. If more than one patch is necessary, list them separate and increment the patch number in the field name such as `Patch0`, `Patch1`, `Patch2`, and so on.

`Obsoletes`

If the package name has changed, this field can be used to list the old package name. When performing a package update, if the old package is installed, it will be removed and replaced with the updated package with the new package name.

`%pre`

Command that needs to be run before the package is installed.

`%post`

Command run immediately after the package is installed. For example, an initialization script to start a daemon.

`%preun`

Commands run right before the package is removed.

`%postun`

Commands run right after a package is removed.

In the sections `%pre`, `%post`, `%preun`, and `%postun`, always use the full path to commands, never output messages to standard out, and never make the scripts interactive. If the RPM installation, upgrade, or removal is part of a bigger script run or is performed from a graphical interface, messages to standard out are not seen, including prompts for the user to interact with the script.

Creating the Makefile

The `Makefile` is similar to a script. It contains variables that define values such as the name of the package. It also contains stanzas called *targets*. Each target has a unique name that represents an action such as `install` for installing the software or `rpm` for building the RPM file. Each target contains a list of commands to run to perform the action.

Listing 5.10 contains a simple `Makefile` for our example `startvpn` program.

CAUTION

When creating the `Makefile`, be sure to use tabs instead of spaces to indent the lines for each target. Also, the commands for each target must be started on the next line as shown in Listing 5.10.

LISTING 5.10 Example Makefile

```
PKGNAME=startvpn
VERSION=$(shell awk '/Version:/ { print $$2 }' ${PKGNAME}.spec)

default: install

install:
	echo "hello"
	echo $(INSTROOT)
	mkdir -p $(INSTROOT)/usr/local/bin
	install ${PKGNAME} $(INSTROOT)/usr/local/bin/${PKGNAME}
srpm:
	@rpmbuild -ts ${PKGNAME}-${VERSION}.tar.gz
rpm:
	@rpmbuild -tb ${PKGNAME}-${VERSION}.tar.gz
```

The example `Makefile` starts off by defining the name of the package as the `PKGNAME` variable and the version of the package as the `VERSION` variable. Notice that the version number is retrieved from the package spec file using an `awk` command. Using this command prevents you from getting the package versions listed in the spec file and `Makefile` out of sync. Because the `Makefile` retrieves the version number from the spec file, you just need to change the version number in the spec file each time it needs to be incremented.

Because our example program is only one file, the `install` target creates the directory for the file and then installs the file into the directory. The `srpm` and `rpm` targets execute the corresponding `rpmbuild` commands.

Creating the Source Tarball

Creating the source tarball is as easy as creating a directory with the package name and version in it such as `startvpn-1.1`, copying all the source files including the `Makefile` and the spec file in it, and using the following command to create the compressed archive file whose filename also includes the package name and version number:

```
tar czvf <packagename>-<version>.tar.gz <packagename>-<version>
```

In our example, the command would be

```
tar czvf startvpn-1.1.tar.gz startvpn-1.1
```

Notice that the `startvpn-1.1/` directory is retained for the files in the tarball. When the tarball is uncompressed and unarchived, this directory must be created. To test the tarball, execute the `tar tzvf startvpn-1.1.tar.gz` command. You should see the following:

```
startvpn-1.1/
startvpn-1.1/startvpn
startvpn-1.1/startvpn.spec
startvpn-1.1/Makefile
```

Building the Package

Now that the spec file has been created, the Makefile has been written, and the source files have been archived and compressed into a source tarball, it is time to build the source RPM (also referred to as the SRPM) and the RPM used to install the software.

The `rpmbuild` command is used to actually build the SRPM and RPM files. It is provided by the `rpm-build` package, so make sure the `rpm-build` package is installed. Notice that the `Makefile` in our example from Listing 5.10 includes `srpm` and `rpm` targets that execute the `rpmbuild` command for building the SRPM and RPM for our package. So, to build the SRPM file, make sure you are in the directory that contains the Makefile, the spec file, and the source tarball you just created, and execute the `make srpm` command. Listing 5.11 shows the output when building the SRPM, assuming the user building the package is tfox. If you are using the `.rpmmacros` file from Listing 5.7, the SRPM file will be saved to the `/home/<username>/SRPMS/` directory.

LISTING 5.11 Building the SRPM

```
Wrote: /home/tfox/RPMBUILD/SRPMS/startvpn-1.1-1.src.rpm
```

To build the RPM used to install the software, execute the `make rpm` command. The RPM will be saved in the /home/`<username>/RPMS/<arch>` directory, where `<arch>` is the architecture specified by the `BuildArch` parameter in the spec file. In our example, the `<arch>` is `noarch`. Listing 5.12 shows the output while building the RPM, assuming the user building the package is tfox.

LISTING 5.12 Building the RPM

```
Executing(%prep): /bin/sh -e /var/tmp/rpm-tmp.38985
+ umask 022
```

LISTING 5.12 Continued

```
+ cd /home/tfox/RPMBUILD/BUILD
+ cd /home/tfox/RPMBUILD/BUILD
+ rm -rf startvpn-1.1
+ /bin/gzip -dc /home/tfox/startvpn/startvpn-1.1.tar.gz
+ tar -xf -
+ STATUS=0
+ '[' 0 -ne 0 ']'
+ cd startvpn-1.1
+ exit 0
Executing(%install): /bin/sh -e /var/tmp/rpm-tmp.38985
+ umask 022
+ cd /home/tfox/RPMBUILD/BUILD
+ cd startvpn-1.1
+ make INSTROOT=/var/tmp/startvpn-1.1-1 install
make[1]: Entering directory `/home/tfox/RPMBUILD/BUILD/startvpn-1.1'
echo /var/tmp/startvpn-1.1-1
/var/tmp/startvpn-1.1-1
mkdir -p /var/tmp/startvpn-1.1-1/usr/local/bin
install startvpn /var/tmp/startvpn-1.1-1/usr/local/bin/startvpn
make[1]: Leaving directory `/home/tfox/RPMBUILD/BUILD/startvpn-1.1'
+ exit 0
Processing files: startvpn-1.1-1
Requires(rpmlib): rpmlib(CompressedFileNames) <= 3.0.4-1 rpmlib(PayloadFile-
sHavePrefix) <= 4.0-1
Requires: /bin/bash bash vpnc
Checking for unpackaged file(s): /usr/lib/rpm/check-files /var/tmp/startvpn-1.1-1
Wrote: /home/tfox/RPMBUILD/RPMS/noarch/startvpn-1.1-1.noarch.rpm
Executing(%clean): /bin/sh -e /var/tmp/rpm-tmp.38985
+ umask 022
+ cd /home/tfox/RPMBUILD/BUILD
+ cd startvpn-1.1
+ rm -fr /var/tmp/startvpn-1.1-1
+ exit 0
```

Signing the Package

After building the package, while not required, it is recommended that you sign the package. Signing the package allows anyone installing it to verify that the package has not been modified in any way after being signed by you. Each time you build the package, you need to sign it.

If you do not already have a GPG key or want to use a different one for signing packages, use the following command to generate a GPG key:

```
gpg --gen-key
```

Be sure to run this command as root so that the memory used to generate the key can be locked. Non-root users can not lock access to memory, giving someone the opportunity to read the memory used to generate the key. Unlocked memory might also be written to disk. Listing 5.13 shows what is displayed after executing the command.

LISTING 5.13 Generating a GPG Key

```
gpg (GnuPG) 1.4.5; Copyright (C) 2006 Free Software Foundation, Inc.
This program comes with ABSOLUTELY NO WARRANTY.
This is free software, and you are welcome to redistribute it
under certain conditions. See the file COPYING for details.
gpg: directory `/root/.gnupg' created
gpg: new configuration file `/root/.gnupg/gpg.conf' created
gpg: WARNING: options in `/root/.gnupg/gpg.conf' are not yet active during this run
gpg: keyring `/root/.gnupg/secring.gpg' created
gpg: keyring `/root/.gnupg/pubring.gpg' created
Please select what kind of key you want:
   (1) DSA and Elgamal (default)
   (2) DSA (sign only)
   (5) RSA (sign only)
Your selection?
```

Select the default key type by typing `1` when prompted. Next, you are prompted for a key size. The longer the key size, the more secure. A size of at least 1024 bits is recommended.

A key can have an expiration date. If an expiration date is entered, everyone with the public key is notified of its expiration when they try to use the public key after the expiration date. Unless you have a specific reason to make the key expire, enter `0` for the expiration date, meaning that there is not expiration date for the key. Type `y` to confirm that the key will not expire.

The following message appears next:

```
You need a user ID to identify your key; the software constructs the user ID
from the Real Name, Comment and Email Address in this form:
    "Heinrich Heine (Der Dichter) <heinrichh@duesseldorf.de>"
```

This user ID can be read by everyone with the public key, so choose it carefully. If you are generating this for your company, instead of using your name, use the company name. Use an email address that will still be active after several years such as security@example.com. The individual email address that receives the email can change over the years, while the generic email address stays the same.

You are prompted for each of these three items individually. After entering all three, you can change any of them, confirm them by typing `O` for OK, or quit.

If you type `O`, next enter a passphrase. Just like a password, a passphrase should contain a combination of upper- and lowercase letters, numbers, and special characters. A passphrase is used instead of a password because a passphrase can be and should be longer than a user password. Instead of just using one word, try to use a passphrase based on a long phrase. Just be sure it is one you can remember because it must be typed each time you sign an RPM package. After entering the passphrase and entering it again to confirm it, the following message is displayed:

```
We need to generate a lot of random bytes. It is a good idea to perform
some other action (type on the keyboard, move the mouse, utilize the
disks) during the prime generation; this gives the random number
generator a better chance to gain enough entropy.
++++++++++++++++++++++++++++++++++++++++++++++++++++++++++++.+++++..++++++++++
++++++++++++++++++++++++++++++.+++++++++++++++++++++++++>+++++.+++++
```

As the message says, try to perform disk and I/O operations while the key is being generated. After the key is generate, a message similar to the following is displayed:

```
gpg: /root/.gnupg/trustdb.gpg: trustdb created
gpg: key AADA3407 marked as ultimately trusted
public and secret key created and signed.

gpg: checking the trustdb
gpg: 3 marginal(s) needed, 1 complete(s) needed, PGP trust model
gpg: depth: 0  valid:   1  signed:   0  trust: 0-, 0q, 0n, 0m, 0f, 1u
pub   1024D/AADA3407 2007-02-28
      Key fingerprint = AA96 00FF 5934 440D DE40  C4EA 13FB 19C1 AADA 3407
uid                  TCBF Computers (TCBF) <security@example.com>
sub   2048g/1A85EDF8 2007-02-28
```

The public and private keys are written to the `/root/.gnupg/` directory. To write the public key to a file named `public_key.txt`, execute the following (replace `Name` with the real name you used when generating the key):

```
gpg --export -a 'Name' > public_key.txt
```

CAUTION

Be sure to back up the private and public keys in a secure location. The private key is required when signing RPM packages.

Anyone wanting to verify the signature of your RPM files, including yourself, must have this key imported into the RPM keyring with the following command run as root:

```
rpm --import public_key.txt
```

Refer to the "Installing Software" section in this chapter for instructions on verifying that the key is imported.

Now the rpm utility must be set up to use this new key when signing packages. First, determine the unique GPG name given to the key by executing the following command as root:

```
gpg --list-keys
```

The output looks similar to the following, and the unique GPG name you need to look for is after the slash on the line starting with sub:

```
/root/.gnupg/pubring.gpg
------------------------
pub   1024D/AADA3407 2007-02-28
uid                  TCBF Computers (TCBF) <security@example.com>
sub   2048g/1A85EDF8 2007-02-28
```

In our example, 1A85EDF8 is the name you need to reference. In the /root/.rpmmacros file, include the following lines (replace the name with your GPG name):

```
%_signature gpg
%_gpg_name 1A85EDF8
```

To sign a package, execute the following as root:

```
rpm --resign <rpmfile>
```

Enter the passphrase used to generate the key when prompted. If you enter the correct passphrase for the GPG key named in the /root/.rpmmacros file, the message Pass phrase is good is displayed.

Testing the Package

After building and signing the RPM, install it on a test system to be sure all the files are installed and it performs as expected. First, check the signature on the package with the rpm -K <rpmfile> command. Remember to import your own key as described in the previous section before checking the signature. If the package has not been modified or corrupted since it was signed, the output will include the phrase md5 gpg OK:

```
startvpn-1.1-1.noarch.rpm: (sha1) dsa sha1 md5 gpg OK
```

If the package is not signed, the output will include output such as:

```
NOT OK
```

If you haven't imported the corresponding public key, the following is displayed:

```
MISSING KEYS
```

When installing the example package, if you do not have the vpnc package installed, the following error is displayed:

```
error: Failed dependencies:
        vpnc is needed by startvpn-1.1-1.noarch
```

You can force the installation of the package so that you can test the package you built from this example:

```
rpm -Uvh --nodeps startvpn-1.1-1.noarch.rpm
```

Now that the package is installed, execute the `rpm -qi startvpn` command. The correct output is shown in Listing 5.14. The build host will be the hostname of the system used to build the package.

LISTING 5.14 Information About startvpn RPM

```
Name        : startvpn                      Relocations: (not relocatable)
Version     : 1.1                                Vendor: (none)
Release     : 1                              Build Date: Wed 28 Feb 2007 12:16:12 AM
EST
Install Date: Wed 28 Feb 2007 12:16:38 AM EST     Build Host: build.example.org
Group       : Applications/Internet          Source RPM: startvpn-1.1-1.src.rpm
Size        : 45                                License: GPL
Signature   : (none)
URL         : http://www.example.org/
Summary     : Custom script to start VPN
Description :
Custom script to start VPN and connect to company's private network.
For company use only.
```

The command `rpm -ql startvpn` shows that only one file was installed:

```
/usr/local/bin/startvpn
```

Summary

If you use Red Hat Network, you may never have to use the command-line version of RPM, but hopefully, this chapter has given you a basic understanding of it so that you can better understand Red Hat Network. If you have custom software to distribute within your company, consider distributing it in an RPM package to ensure consistent installation across all systems and easily keep track of what versions are installed.

Summary

CHAPTER 6

Analyzing Hardware

IN THIS CHAPTER

- Listing Devices
- Detecting Hardware
- Gathering Information from the BIOS
- Listing and Configuring Kernel Modules
- HAL

Similar to other operating systems, Red Hat Enterprise Linux must be configured to use drivers, also known as *kernel modules*, for each supported device. If the device is connected to the system during the installation process, the installation program will attempt to configure the system to automatically load the device driver on startup. One convenience of Linux is that most drivers are included with the operating system. There is no need to remember where you put a driver disk or search for a driver on the manufacturer's website. Red Hat Enterprise Linux includes drivers that are compatible with the kernel version.

What happens when you add new hardware after installation? Is there a program that can tell you what devices are connected to the PCI and USB buses? What does the operating system know about the BIOS? How do you know what drivers are being used? This chapter answers these questions and more.

This chapter discusses how to determine what hardware Red Hat Enterprise Linux recognizes and supports, how that hardware is configured, and what to do when new hardware is added.

TIP

This chapter only gives instruction on how to gather information about hardware, add new hardware, determine what hardware is recognized by the operating system, and configure it. To learn more about monitoring the usage of hardware such as memory and CPU, refer to Chapter 20, "Monitoring System Resources."

Listing Devices

PCI and USB devices can be probed for information such as an identification number, chipset revision number, and amount of on-board memory. This information can then be used to properly configure the driver and settings used for the device.

This section discusses the `lspci` utility for listing PCI devices and the `lsusb` command for probing USB devices for information.

Listing PCI Devices

Many devices such as network and video cards are attached to the PCI bus. It is important that the operating system load the correct driver for each device so that the proper device settings are configured. For example, if your server contains a Gigabit network card connected to a Gigabit network switch, you can use a few simple Linux utilities to verify and, if necessary, change the transfer rate of the NIC.

To list all the PCI buses on the system and all the devices attached to them, use the `lspci` utility from the `pciutils` package. Install this package via Red Hat Network if necessary as described in Chapter 3, "Operating System Updates."

If run with no command-line options, the output includes one line per PCI device with basic information such as the vendor and product name as shown in Listing 6.1.

LISTING 6.1 Sample `lspci` Output

```
00:00.0 Host bridge: Intel Corporation 82975X Memory Controller Hub
00:01.0 PCI bridge: Intel Corporation 82975X PCI Express Root Port
00:1b.0 Audio device: Intel Corporation 82801G (ICH7 Family) High Definition
Audio Controller (rev 01)
00:1c.0 PCI bridge: Intel Corporation 82801G (ICH7 Family) PCI Express
Port 1 (rev 01)
00:1c.4 PCI bridge: Intel Corporation 82801GR/GH/GHM (ICH7 Family) PCI Express
Port 5 (rev 01)
00:1c.5 PCI bridge: Intel Corporation 82801GR/GH/GHM (ICH7 Family) PCI Express
Port 6 (rev 01)
00:1d.0 USB Controller: Intel Corporation 82801G (ICH7 Family) USB UHCI #1 (rev 01)
00:1d.1 USB Controller: Intel Corporation 82801G (ICH7 Family) USB UHCI #2 (rev 01)
00:1d.2 USB Controller: Intel Corporation 82801G (ICH7 Family) USB UHCI #3 (rev 01)
00:1d.3 USB Controller: Intel Corporation 82801G (ICH7 Family) USB UHCI #4 (rev 01)
00:1d.7 USB Controller: Intel Corporation 82801G (ICH7 Family) USB2 EHCI
Controller (rev 01)
00:1e.0 PCI bridge: Intel Corporation 82801 PCI Bridge (rev e1)
00:1f.0 ISA bridge: Intel Corporation 82801GH (ICH7DH) LPC Interface Bridge (rev
➥01)
00:1f.1 IDE interface: Intel Corporation 82801G (ICH7 Family) IDE Controller (rev
➥01)
00:1f.2 IDE interface: Intel Corporation 82801GB/GR/GH (ICH7 Family) Serial ATA
```

LISTING 6.1 Continued

```
Storage Controller IDE (rev 01)
00:1f.3 SMBus: Intel Corporation 82801G (ICH7 Family) SMBus Controller (rev 01)
01:00.0 VGA compatible controller: nVidia Corporation G70 [GeForce 7600 GT] (rev
➥a1)
04:00.0 Ethernet controller: Intel Corporation 82573L Gigabit Ethernet Controller
05:04.0 FireWire (IEEE 1394): Texas Instruments TSB43AB23 IEEE-1394a-2000
➥Controller (PHY/Link)
05:05.0 RAID bus controller: Silicon Image, Inc. SiI 3114 [SATALink/SATARaid]
Serial ATA Controller (rev 02)
```

To display more verbose information about the devices such as the amount of internal memory, use the command `lspci -v`. Listing 6.2 shows the verbose output for the RAID controller from Listing 6.1.

LISTING 6.2 Verbose `lspci` Output

```
05:05.0 RAID bus controller: Silicon Image, Inc. SiI 3114
[SATALink/SATARaid] Serial ATA Controller (rev 02)
        Subsystem: Intel Corporation Unknown device 7114
        Flags: bus master, 66MHz, medium devsel, latency 32, IRQ 17
        I/O ports at 1018 [size=8]
        I/O ports at 1024 [size=4]
        I/O ports at 1010 [size=8]
        I/O ports at 1020 [size=4]
        I/O ports at 1000 [size=16]
        Memory at 92004800 (32-bit, non-prefetchable) [size=1K]
        Expansion ROM at fff80000 [disabled] [size=512K]
        Capabilities: [60] Power Management version 2
```

To display everything the system knows about the devices, use the command `lspci -vv`. Listing 6.3 shows the even more verbose output for the same RAID controller.

LISTING 6.3 Even More Verbose `lspci` Output

```
05:05.0 RAID bus controller: Silicon Image, Inc. SiI 3114 [SATALink/SATARaid]
Serial ATA Controller (rev 02)
        Subsystem: Intel Corporation Unknown device 7114
        Control: I/O+ Mem+ BusMaster+ SpecCycle- MemWINV- VGASnoop- ParErr-
Stepping- SERR- FastB2B-
        Status: Cap+ 66MHz+ UDF- FastB2B+ ParErr- DEVSEL=medium >TAbort-
<TAbort- <MAbort- >SERR- <PERR-
        Latency: 32, Cache Line Size: 64 bytes
        Interrupt: pin A routed to IRQ 17
        Region 0: I/O ports at 1018 [size=8]
        Region 1: I/O ports at 1024 [size=4]
```

LISTING 6.3 Continued

```
        Region 2: I/O ports at 1010 [size=8]
        Region 3: I/O ports at 1020 [size=4]
        Region 4: I/O ports at 1000 [size=16]
        Region 5: Memory at 92004800 (32-bit, non-prefetchable) [size=1K]
        Expansion ROM at fff80000 [disabled] [size=512K]
        Capabilities: [60] Power Management version 2
                Flags: PMEClk- DSI+ D1+ D2+ AuxCurrent=0mA
                PME(D0-,D1-,D2-,D3hot-,D3cold-)
                Status: D0 PME-Enable- DSel=0 DScale=2 PME-
```

The `lspci` utility works by probing the device for its PCI ID. Then, this ID number is cross-referenced with the `/usr/share/hwdata/pci.ids` file from the `hwdata` package. This file contains the vendor, device, subvendor, subdevice, and class identifiers for all known PCI IDs.

TIP

To change the output of `lspci` to a format easier to parse using a script, use the `-m` switch. This argument will place quotation marks around each device property.

Listing USB Devices

Because USB devices are connected to a separate controller, a different command, `lsusb`, must be used to list them. The `lsusb` utility is provided by the `usbutils` package. Install this package via Red Hat Network if necessary as described in Chapter 3.

If executed without arguments, the `lsusb` command displays each USB bus and any devices attached to them on a separate line as shown in Listing 6.4.

LISTING 6.4 USB Device List

```
Bus 002 Device 001: ID 0000:0000
Bus 003 Device 001: ID 0000:0000
Bus 004 Device 001: ID 0000:0000
Bus 005 Device 001: ID 0000:0000
Bus 001 Device 001: ID 0000:0000
Bus 001 Device 004: ID 046d:c501 Logitech, Inc. Cordless Mouse Receiver
```

Similar to PCI devices, each USB device has a unique ID. `lsusb` probes for this ID and references the `/usr/share/hwdata/usb.ids` file for the vendor, product name, and model number. If this information is found for the ID, this more user-friendly information is displayed in the `lsusb` output as shown in the last line of Listing 6.4 for the cordless mouse.

To view more information about each bus, use the command `lsusb -v`. For example, Listing 6.5 shows the verbose output for the cordless mouse from Listing 6.4.

LISTING 6.5 Verbose Output for a USB Device

```
Bus 001 Device 004: ID 046d:c501 Logitech, Inc. Cordless Mouse Receiver
Device Descriptor:
  bLength                18
  bDescriptorType         1
  bcdUSB               1.10
  bDeviceClass            0 (Defined at Interface level)
  bDeviceSubClass         0
  bDeviceProtocol         0
  bMaxPacketSize0         8
  idVendor           0x046d Logitech, Inc.
  idProduct          0xc501 Cordless Mouse Receiver
  bcdDevice            9.10
  iManufacturer           1 Logitech
  iProduct                2 USB Receiver
  iSerial                 0
  bNumConfigurations      1
  Configuration Descriptor:
    bLength                 9
    bDescriptorType         2
    wTotalLength           34
    bNumInterfaces          1
    bConfigurationValue     1
    iConfiguration          0
    bmAttributes         0xa0
      Remote Wakeup
    MaxPower               50mA
    Interface Descriptor:
      bLength                 9
      bDescriptorType         4
      bInterfaceNumber        0
      bAlternateSetting       0
      bNumEndpoints           1
      bInterfaceClass         3 Human Interface Devices
      bInterfaceSubClass      1 Boot Interface Subclass
      bInterfaceProtocol      2 Mouse
      iInterface              0
        HID Device Descriptor:
          bLength                 9
          bDescriptorType        33
          bcdHID               1.10
          bCountryCode            0 Not supported
          bNumDescriptors         1
          bDescriptorType        34 Report
          wDescriptorLength      82
      Report Descriptors:
```

LISTING 6.5 Continued

```
        ** UNAVAILABLE **
      Endpoint Descriptor:
        bLength                 7
        bDescriptorType         5
        bEndpointAddress     0x81  EP 1 IN
        bmAttributes            3
          Transfer Type            Interrupt
          Synch Type               None
          Usage Type               Data
        wMaxPacketSize     0x0008  1x 8 bytes
        bInterval              10
```

Listing Storage Devices

To list the drives connected to the system, use the `fdisk -l` command as root. Each disk is listed along with its capacity and partitions. In Listing 6.6, there is one disk, `/dev/sda`, with eight partitions. The top line shows the capacity of the disk: 120 GB.

LISTING 6.6 List of Connected Disks from `fdisk`

```
Disk /dev/sda: 120.0 GB, 120034123776 bytes
255 heads, 63 sectors/track, 14593 cylinders
Units = cylinders of 16065 * 512 = 8225280 bytes

   Device Boot      Start         End      Blocks   Id  System
/dev/sda1   *           1          13      104391   83  Linux
/dev/sda2              14        1925    15358140   83  Linux
/dev/sda3            1926        2179     2040255   82  Linux swap
/dev/sda4            2180       14593    99715455   83  Linux
/dev/sda5            2180        2192      104391   83  Linux
/dev/sda6            2193        2702     4096543+  83  Linux
/dev/sda7            2703        2715      104391   83  Linux
/dev/sda8            2716        3097     3068383+  83  Linux
```

A list of partitions for a device can also be listed using the `parted` utility. Executing the `parted <device-name>` command as the root user gives you a `parted` prompt on which to issue commands for the specified device. For example, to specify the first device on the SCSI bus, use the `parted /dev/sda` command. While in `parted`, use the `print` command to list the disk geometry and partitions on the device. Listing 6.7 shows output from parted for a 300 GB disk partitioned to use LVM.

LISTING 6.7 List of Partitions from `parted`

```
GNU Parted 1.7.1
Using /dev/sda
```

LISTING 6.7 Continued

```
Welcome to GNU Parted! Type 'help' to view a list of commands.
(parted) print

Disk /dev/sda: 300GB
Sector size (logical/physical): 512B/512B
Partition Table: msdos

Number  Start   End    Size    Type     File system  Flags
 1      32.3kB  107MB  107MB   primary  ext3
 3      107MB   100GB  99.9GB  primary               lvm
 2      100GB   300GB  200GB   primary  ntfs         boot
```

Detecting Hardware

After the installation program probes for hardware and maps the IDs to the appropriate kernel module (if available), the kernel module information is written to the `/etc/modprobe.conf` file so it can be used on subsequent boots.

TIP

For a list of all kernel modules loaded, issue the `lsmod` command as described in the "Listing and Configuring Kernel Modules" section later in this chapter.

But, what should you do if a device is not configured by the installation program? You can use tools to probe the hardware and discover information that can be used to manually configure the device. This section discusses two tools for this purpose: Kudzu and `ddcprobe`.

Detecting Hardware with Kudzu

What happens when you add a new device after installation? The Kudzu program runs each time the system boots and performs a hardware probe. If new hardware is found, Kudzu attempts to map it to a kernel module. If successful, the information is saved, and the device is configured.

The Kudzu program includes an initialization script, `/etc/rc.d/init.d/kudzu`, which is run at boot time (unless disabled). A list of configured hardware for the system is stored in `/etc/sysconfig/hwconf`, a file maintained by Kudzu. If Kudzu finds new hardware not in this file, it prompts the administrator to configure it. If Kudzu detects removed hardware, it prompts the administrator to remove the configuration. If the administrator confirms the removal, it is removed from the `hwconf` file as well.

Instead of reading `/etc/sysconfig/hwconf`, issue the `kudzu --probe` command to view the list of hardware detected by Kudzu. To narrow down the results, you can also specify the bus or class:

```
kudzu --probe --bus=<BUS>
```

or

```
kudzu --probe --class=<CLASS>
```

For example, `kudzu --probe --bus=PCI` only displays the device on the PCI bus. Or, the command `kudzu --probe --class=VIDEO` only displays the video devices as demonstrated in Listing 6.8.

LISTING 6.8 Kudzu Probe for a Video Device

```
class: VIDEO
bus: PCI
detached: 0
driver: nvidiafb
desc: "nVidia Corporation G70 [GeForce 7600 GT]"
video.xdriver: nv
vendorId: 10de
deviceId: 0391
subVendorId: 1682
subDeviceId: 2220
pciType: 1
pcidom:    0
pcibus:  1
pcidev:  0
pcifn:  0
```

If new hardware is detected, Kudzu references the hardware lookup tables in the `/usr/share/hwdata/` directory installed by the `hwdata` software package and tries to map the hardware ID to a kernel module. If a driver is found, a configuration line for the hardware is added to the `/etc/modprobe.conf` so the same driver can be used on subsequent boots.

Kudzu does have a small configuration file `/etc/sysconfig/kudzu` with one option: SAFE. By default, SAFE is set to `no`. Set it to `yes` to enable the safe probe mode. The safe probe mode disables serial port, DDC monitor, and PS/2 probing.

TIP

If a kernel module is not available for an added piece of hardware, try updating the kernel and the `hwdata` RPM package. Support may have been recently added for the hardware.

Detecting Hardware with `ddcprobe`

Kudzu runs at boot time to detect and configure new hardware, including video cards. But, what if you suspect that Kudzu was unable to properly detect the video card or monitor in your system?

To view the video card and monitor information found by Kudzu, use the `ddcprobe` command. You must be root to run this command. Provided by the `rhpxl` package, `ddcprobe` is a script written to call the Kudzu's probing function and display the results in a user-friendly output. If the `rhpxl` package is not installed, install it via Red Hat Network as described in Chapter 3.

NOTE

The `ddcprobe` utility doesn't work on some laptops and LCD monitors. It is only available on x86 and x86_64 hardware.

Along with the manufacturer and product name of the video card and monitor, `ddcprobe` displays information such as the amount of memory the video card has and the monitor refresh rates as shown in Listing 6.9.

LISTING 6.9 Video Card Probe Results

```
Videocard DDC probe results
Description:  Intel Corporation Intel(r)865G Graphics Controller
Memory (MB):  15

Monitor DDC probe results
ID: DEL3007
Name: Dell 1702FP (Analog)
Horizontal Sync (kHZ): 30-80
Vertical Sync (HZ)   : 56-76
Width (mm): 340
Height(mm): 270
```

If the `ddcprobe` output is not correct for the monitor or video card, run the `system-config-display` utility by selecting the **System** menu from the top panel of the desktop and then selecting **Administration**, **Display** or by executing the `system-config-display` command. You must enter the root password to proceed if you are not already root when you run the program. Manually select the correct monitor or video card so that the correct settings are written to the configuration file.

Gathering Information from the BIOS

When a computer first starts, the first program that runs, and the first one you see, is the *BIOS*, or the *Basic Input/Output System*. Most BIOSes also have an *SMBIOS* (*System Management BIOS*) or a *DMI* (*Desktop Management Interface*) that generates a table of data about the BIOS and computer system in a standard format.

For a system with a BIOS, it is possible to request information directly from it and the SMBIOS or DMI instead of the physical hardware in the system. The `dmidecode` RPM package contains utilities to perform these queries. The `dmidecode`, `biosdecode`, `ownership`, and `vpddecode` commands are provided by this package. Install it with RHN (refer to Chapter 3) if it is not already installed. This section discusses each of these programs.

CAUTION

The output of the biosdecode and dmidecode utilities may not be 100% accurate. For example, sometimes the BIOS returns the highest possible processor speed the motherboard allows, not the actual processor speed of the processor installed. Use its output with caution.

Querying the BIOS

As the root user, execute the `biosdecode` command to query the BIOS for system information. Listing 6.10 shows example output.

LISTING 6.10 Output from biosdecode

```
# biosdecode 2.7
ACPI 1.0 present.
        OEM Identifier: INTEL
        RSD Table 32-bit Address: 0x7FEFDE48
PNP BIOS 1.0 present.
        Event Notification: Not Supported
        Real Mode 16-bit Code Address: F000:A6DC
        Real Mode 16-bit Data Address: 0040:0000
        16-bit Protected Mode Code Address: 0x000FA6E7
        16-bit Protected Mode Data Address: 0x00000400
        OEM Device Identifier: SST2400
SMBIOS 2.3 present.
        Structure Table Length: 1616 bytes
        Structure Table Address: 0x000E34F0
        Number Of Structures: 34
        Maximum Structure Size: 150 bytes
```

The output for each system will vary, depending on what type of data the BIOS returns and what features the BIOS and system hardware have. In Listing 6.10, information about the ACPI, PNP BIOS, and SMBIOS are given. The following types of data can be displayed if returned by the BIOS:

- SMBIOS
- DMI
- SYSID
- PNP
- ACPI
- BIOS32
- PIR
- 32OS (Compaq-specific)
- SNY
- VPD (IBM-specific)

Querying the SMBIOS or DMI

If the output from `biosdecode` shows a SMBIOS or DMI, further information can be retrieved from the SMBIOS or DMI with the `dmidecode` command. The `dmidecode` command must be run as the root user as well. It displays information about each structure found such as the processor and BIOS structures shown in Listing 6.11.

LISTING 6.11 Output from dmidecode

```
Handle 0x0000, DMI type 4, 35 bytes.
Processor Information
        Socket Designation: J3E1
        Type: Central Processor
        Family: Unknown
        Manufacturer: Intel(R) Corporation
        ID: F6 06 00 00 FF FB EB BF
        Version: Intel(R) Core(TM)2 CPU          6600  @ 2.40GHz
        Voltage: 1.6 V
        External Clock: 266 MHz
        Max Speed: 4000 MHz
        Current Speed: 2400 MHz
        Status: Populated, Enabled
        Upgrade: Other
        L1 Cache Handle: 0x0002
        L2 Cache Handle: Not Provided
        L3 Cache Handle: Not Provided
        Serial Number: Not Specified
        Asset Tag: Unknown
        Part Number: Not Specified

Handle 0x0003, DMI type 0, 20 bytes.
BIOS Information
        Vendor: Intel Corp.
        Version: BX97510J.86A.0618.2006.0223.1728
        Release Date: 02/23/2006
        Address: 0xF0000
        Runtime Size: 64 kB
        ROM Size: 512 kB
        Characteristics:
                PCI is supported
                BIOS is upgradeable
                BIOS shadowing is allowed
                Boot from CD is supported
                Selectable boot is supported
                EDD is supported
                8042 keyboard services are supported (int 9h)
                Serial services are supported (int 14h)
                Printer services are supported (int 17h)
                CGA/mono video services are supported (int 10h)
                ACPI is supported
                USB legacy is supported
                ATAPI Zip drive boot is supported
                BIOS boot specification is supported
                Function key-initiated network boot is supported
```

6

For each structure listed, the following information is presented:

- *Handle*: Unique value for each structure so other structures can reference each other.
- *Type*: The SMBIOS or DMI type number as defined by the SMBIOS or DMI specifications.
- *Size*: Size of the structure. Each one has a 4-byte header that stores the handle, type, and size. The remainder of the size stores the actual data about the structure, which varies, so the size varies.
- *Decoded values*: Information about the structure. Varies according to the type as shown in Listing 6.11.

The `dmidecode` output can be narrowed down by a few command-line options such as `dmidecode -q` to not display unknown, inactive, and OEM-specific values. Table 6.1 shows all the command-line options for `dmidecode`.

TABLE 6.1 Command-Line Options for `dmidecode`

Command Line Option	Description
`-d <file>`	Read memory from a different device file. The default file read is `/dev/mem`.
`-q`	Quiet mode. Does not display unknown, inactive, and OEM-specific values.
`-s <keyword>`	Only show values with `<keyword>`. `<keyword>` can be one of the following: `bios-vendor`, `bios-version`, `bios-release-date`, `system-manufacturer`, `system-product-name`, `system-version`, `system-serial-number`, `baseboard-manufacturer`, `baseboard-product-name`, `baseboard-version`, `baseboard-serial-number`, `baseboard-asset-tag`, `chassis-manufacturer`, `chassis-version`, `chassis-serial-number`, `chassis-asset-tag`, `processor-manufacturer`, `processor-version`. Not all keywords return a value on all systems. To list valid keywords for a system, execute `dmidecode -s` (don't list a `<keyword>`). This option can only be used once per command execution.
`-t <type>`	Only show entries of type <type>. <type> can be one of the following: `bios`, `system`, `baseboard`, `chassis`, `processor`, `memory`, `cache`, `connector`, `slot`. Specify more than one type by separating them with commas. To list valid types for a system, execute `dmidecode -t` (don't give a `<type>`). Refer to the `dmidecode` man page for a list of types along with their associated type number value.
`-u`	Dump data as hexadecimal instead of decoding them. Mostly used for debugging purposes.
`-h`	Show brief usage information for `dmidecode`.
`-V`	Show version of `dmidecode`.

Querying Vendor-Specific Data

The dmidecode RPM package also includes the ownership and vpddecode utilities. The ownership utility is a specialized command for Compaq computers. If biosdecode displays information about 32OS data, the ownership command can retrieve the Compaq ownership tag. The vpddecode utility is also for a specific set of computers. It only works on IBM computers to display the vital product data from the system. If VPD data is found in the biosdecode query, use the vpddecode command to query for more information. The output includes the BIOS build ID, product name, box serial number, motherboard serial number, and machine type/model. Some systems output more information such as BIOS release date.

Listing and Configuring Kernel Modules

For a piece of hardware to work properly in Red Hat Enterprise Linux, the associated kernel module must be loaded. The kernel module allows the kernel and end-user programs to interact with the hardware.

To view a list of all currently loaded kernel modules, use the lsmod command. It can be run as a normal user or as root, but if run as a non-root user, you might need to specify the full path to the command, /sbin/lsmod, because /sbin/ is not in the default path of a non-root user.

9

TIP

To manually load a module, use the modprobe <modulename> command. The specified module will be loaded along with any module dependencies.

The module to use for some hardware such as network cards, sound cards, and USB controllers are saved in /etc/modprobe.conf so they don't have to be configured each time the system boots. Other modules are loaded as needed from the utilities that require them. For example, when the mount command is used to mount a Samba share, the smbfs module is loaded.

Kernel module options can also be added to /etc/modprobe.conf to tweak the module settings. To determine what parameters are available, use the modinfo <modulename> command. The beginning of the modinfo outputs displays the full path to the kernel module, software license for the module, description, and author as shown in Listing 6.12 for the 3c59x module.

LISTING 6.12 Beginning of Module Information for 3c59x Module

```
filename:      /lib/modules/2.6.18-1.2839.el5xen/kernel/drivers/net/3c59x.ko
license:       GPL
description:   3Com 3c59x/3c9xx ethernet driver
author:        Donald Becker <becker@scyld.com>
```

The output also includes lines that begin with the parm keyword. These lines describe possible kernel module options and the value type each accepts. For example, the modinfo output for 3c59x contains the lines in Listing 6.13.

LISTING 6.13 3c59x Module Options

```
parm:           debug:3c59x debug level (0-6) (int)
parm:           options:3c59x: Bits 0-3: media type, bit 4: bus mastering,
bit 9: full duplex (array of int)
parm:           global_options:3c59x: same as options, but applies to all
NICs if options is unset (int)
parm:           full_duplex:3c59x full duplex setting(s) (1) (array of int)
parm:           global_full_duplex:3c59x: same as full_duplex, but applies to all
NICs if full_duplex is unset (int)
parm:           hw_checksums:3c59x Hardware checksum checking by adapter(s) (0-1)
(array of int)
parm:           flow_ctrl:3c59x 802.3x flow control usage (PAUSE only) (0-1)
(array of int)
parm:           enable_wol:3c59x: Turn on Wake-on-LAN for adapter(s) (0-1)
(array of int)
parm:           global_enable_wol:3c59x: same as enable_wol, but applies to all
NICs if enable_wol is unset (int)
parm:           rx_copybreak:3c59x copy breakpoint for copy-only-tiny-frames (int)
parm:           max_interrupt_work:3c59x maximum events handled per interrupt (int)
parm:           compaq_ioaddr:3c59x PCI I/O base address (Compaq BIOS problem
workaround) (int)
parm:           compaq_irq:3c59x PCI IRQ number (Compaq BIOS problem workaround)
➥(int)
parm:           compaq_device_id:3c59x PCI device ID (Compaq BIOS problem
➥workaround) (int)
parm:           watchdog:3c59x transmit timeout in milliseconds (int)
parm:           global_use_mmio:3c59x: same as use_mmio, but applies to all
NICs if options is unset (int)
parm:           use_mmio:3c59x: use memory-mapped PCI I/O resource (0-1)
(array of int)
```

For example, the full_duplex module is for setting the network card to full duplex, and its value type must be an array of integers. The integer value in parentheses for full_duplex tells us that a value of 1 sets the network card to full duplex mode.

The parameters for each kernel module are different, so be sure to check the modinfo output for the module before trying to add options to a module. After determining the parameter name and possible values, they can be added to /etc/modprobe.conf if necessary. For example, the line for the 3c59x module might look similar to the following:

```
alias eth0 3c59x full_duplex=1
```

HAL

If the kernel knows about a piece of hardware, how does an application gain access to it? As a user or administrator, you want it to "just work." This is now possible with *HAL* (Hardware Abstraction Layer). HAL was introduced in Fedora Core 3 and Red Hat Enterprise Linux 4.

HAL works by broadcasting a signal to the system message bus when a new device is added. Then, an application can connect to the message bus instead of the kernel to learn about the hardware. Just like Kudzu runs at boot time to detect new hardware, the HAL daemon runs while the system is running to detect new hardware. The HAL daemon collects information about the device from the kernel as well as other resources. This allows the system bus to send as much information as possible to the application, and the application only needs to gather information from one place.

For developers who need to use HAL, the `hal-gnome` package includes an example program and development tool for HAL. It can be started by executing the `hal-device-manager` command. As shown in Figure 6.1, it provides a tree view of all the devices HAL knows about. Because it is a Python program, the `hal-gnome` package installs the source files for the program in `/usr/share/hal/device-manager/`. They can be used to understand how to interact with devices via HAL.

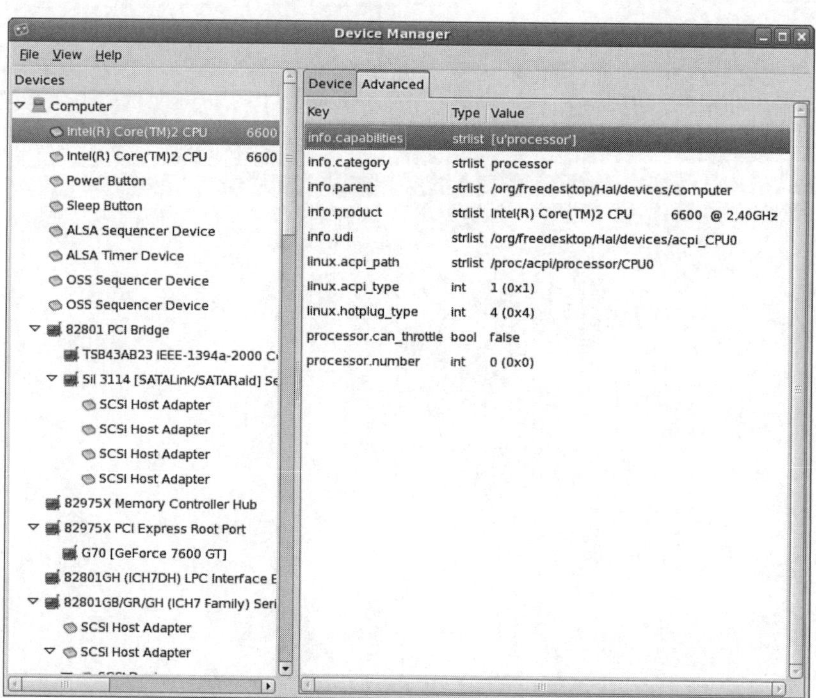

FIGURE 6.1 HAL Device Manager

Summary

This chapter was all about hardware. It described how to list the devices detected by Red Hat Enterprise Linux with `lspci` and `lsusb`, detect hardware with Kudzu and `ddcprobe`, retrieve information from the BIOS, and list the currently configured and loaded kernel modules. It also provided information about the recently developed Hardware Abstraction Layer (HAL).

Without hardware, a computer system could not exist. But, without an operating system such as Red Hat Enterprise Linux to interact with the hardware and allow the hardware to interact with each other, the hardware would be useless.

CHAPTER 7

Managing Storage

IN THIS CHAPTER

- Understanding Partitioning
- Understanding LVM
- Understanding RAID
- Understanding Clustering and GFS
- Using Access Control Lists
- Using Disk Quotas

Managing storage is an important responsibility. The right solution works seamlessly with little gratitude. The wrong solution can lead to many headaches and late nights of trying to recover from failed file systems or inadequate storage allocation.

During installation, you are asked which partitioning method to use. You must choose to remove Linux partitions on selected drives and create the default layout, remove all partitions on selected drives and create the default layout, use free space on selected drives and create the default layout, or create a custom layout. If you choose to create the default layout, the Logical Volume Manager (LVM) is used to divide the hard drive, and then the necessary Linux mount points are created. Alternatively, if you choose custom layout, you can instead use software RAID or create partitions directly on the hard drives. Global File Systems (GFS) and clustering are two more storage solutions available with Red Hat Enterprise Linux.

This chapter explains these partitioning options so you can determine which is best for you and you can learn how to manage them. It also discusses how to use access control lists to limit access to filesystems as well as how to enforce disk usage limits known as quotas. Analyze how your company uses storage and decide which options are best for you.

Understanding Partitioning

LVM and RAID offer benefits such as resizing, striping, and combining multiple hard drives into logical physical devices. Sometimes it is necessary to just create partitions on the hard drives. Even when using RAID, partitions are created before the LVM or RAID layer is implemented.

To view a list of partitions on the system, use the `fdisk -l` command as root. As you can see from Listing 7.1, the output shows each partition along with its device name, whether it is a bootable partition, the starting cylinder, the ending cylinder, the number of blocks, the filesystem identification number used by `fdisk`, and the filesystem type.

LISTING 7.1 Partitioning Scheme with Standard Partitions

```
Disk /dev/sda: 100.0 GB, 100030242816 bytes
255 heads, 63 sectors/track, 12161 cylinders
Units = cylinders of 16065 * 512 = 8225280 bytes

   Device Boot      Start         End      Blocks   Id  System
/dev/sda1   *           1        1147     9213246   83  Linux
/dev/sda2            1148        4334    25599577+  83  Linux
/dev/sda3            4335        4399      522112+  82  Linux swap / Solaris
/dev/sda4            4400       12161    62348265    5  Extended
/dev/sda5            4400       12161    62348233+  83  Linux
```

If the system uses LVM or RAID, the `fdisk -l` output will reflect it. For example, Listing 7.2 shows the output for a system partitioned with LVM. There are fewer partitions shown because the logical volumes are inside the logical volume group. The first partition shown is the `/boot` partition because it can't be inside a logical volume group.

LISTING 7.2 Partitioning Scheme with LVM

```
Disk /dev/sda: 300.0 GB, 300090728448 bytes
255 heads, 63 sectors/track, 36483 cylinders
Units = cylinders of 16065 * 512 = 8225280 bytes

   Device Boot      Start         End      Blocks   Id  System
/dev/sda1               1          13      104391   83  Linux
/dev/sda2              14       36482   292937242+  8e  Linux LVM
```

During installation, the hard drives can be partitioned, given a filesystem type for formatting, and assigned a mount point as described in Chapter 1, "Installing Red Hat Enterprise Linux." If hard drives are added to the system after installation or a hard drive has to be replaced, it is important to understand how to perform these functions post-installation.

CAUTION

Perform all these actions in rescue mode without the filesystem mounted or ensure the entire device is not mounted before manipulating the partition table for it. Refer to Chapter 10, "Techniques for Backup and Recovery," for instructions on booting into rescue mode. Most changes to the partition table require a reboot. When you exit rescue mode, the system will reboot.

Creating Partitions

A partition can be created from free space on a hard drive. You might need to create a partition if you add a new hard drive to the system, if you left unpartitioned space on the system during installation and want to partition it, or if you are using LVM and want to create the physical volumes on a partition instead of an entire raw device.

There are two partitioning utilities in Red Hat Enterprise Linux: `parted` and `fdisk`. The `parted` utility is used in this chapter because it includes a resize utility and is a bit more user-friendly. For more information on `fdisk`, refer to the man page with the `man fdisk` command.

As root, issue the `parted` command followed by the device name such as

```
parted /dev/sda
```

You are now in an interactive `parted` shell, in which the commands executed manipulate the device specified. To view existing partitions from this interactive shell, type the `print` command at the `(parted)` prompt. The output should look similar to Listing 7.3. If you compare this output to the output in Listing 7.1 and Listing 7.2 from the `fdisk -l` command, you will see that the `parted` output is a little easier to read because it includes the size in user-friendly units such as megabytes and gigabytes instead of the beginning and ending cylinders from the `fdisk -l` output.

LISTING 7.3 Partition Table from `parted` for Standard Partitions

```
Using /dev/hda
(parted) print
Disk geometry for /dev/hda: 0kB - 100GB
Disk label type: msdos
Number  Start   End     Size    Type      File system  Flags
1       32kB    9434MB  9434MB  primary   ext3         boot
2       9434MB  36GB    26GB    primary   ext3
3       36GB    36GB    535MB   primary   linux-swap
4       36GB    100GB   64GB    extended
5       36GB    100GB   64GB    logical   ext3
```

Once again, the output will differ depending on the partitioning scheme being used. Listing 7.4 shows output from a system using LVM and can be compared to Listing 7.2, which shows the same output from `fdisk -l`.

LISTING 7.4 Partition Table from `parted` for LVM

```
Disk /dev/sda: 300GB
Sector size (logical/physical): 512B/512B
Partition Table: msdos

Number  Start   End     Size     Type     File system  Flags
 1      32.3kB  107MB   107MB    primary  ext3
 3      107MB   300GB   299.9GB  primary               lvm
```

To create a partition in parted, issue the following command at the interactive parted prompt:

```
mkpart <part-type> <fs-type> <start> <end>
```

`<part-type>` must be one of `primary`, `logical`, or `extended`. `<fs-type>` must be one of `fat16`, `fat32`, `ext2`, `HFS`, `linux-swap`, `NTFS`, `reiserfs`, or `ufs`. The `<start>` and `<end>` values should be given in megabytes and must be given as integers.

The ext3 filesystem is the default filesystem for Red Hat Enterprise Linux. It is the ext2 filesystem plus journaling. To create an ext3 filesystem, use `ext2` as the `<fs-type>` and then use the `-j` option to `mke2fs` to make the filesystem ext3 as described in the next section.

After creating the partition, use the `print` command again to verify that the partition was created. Then type `quit` to exit parted.

Creating a Filesystem on a Partition

Next, create a filesystem on the partition. To create an ext3 filesystem (default used during installation), as root, execute the following, where `<device>` is the device name for the partition such as `/dev/sda1`:

```
mke2fs -j <device>
```

If the partition is to be a swap partition, format it with the following command as root:

```
mkswap <device>
```

Labeling the Partition

To label the partition, execute the following as root:

```
e2label <device> <label>
```

While labeling is not required, partition labels can be useful. For example, when adding the partition to `/etc/fstab`, the label can be listed instead of the partition device name. This proves useful if the partition number is changed from repartitioning the drive or if the partition is moved.

If the `e2label` command is used with just the partition device name as an argument, the current label for the partition is displayed.

Creating a Mount Point

Now that the partition is created and has a filesystem, as root, create a directory so it can be mounted:

```
mkdir <dir-name>
```

Then, mount the new partition:

```
mount <device> <dir-name>
```

such as:

```
mount /dev/sda5 /tmp
```

Access the directory and make sure you can read and write to it.

Finally, add the partition to the `/etc/fstab` file so it is mounted automatically at boot time. For example:

```
LABEL=/tmp              /tmp                    ext3    defaults        1 2
```

If a new swap partition is added, be sure to use `swap` as the filesystem type instead:

```
LABEL=swap2             swap                    swap    defaults        0 0
```

Resizing Partitions

The `parted` utility can also be used to resize a partition. After starting `parted` as root on the desired device, use the following command to resize a specific partition:

```
resize <minor-num> <start> <end>
```

To determine the `<minor-num>` for the partition, look at the partition table with the `print` command such as the output shown in Listing 7.3 and Listing 7.4. The `<start>` and `<end>` values should be the start and end points of the partition, in megabytes.

Removing Partitions

To use `parted` to remove a partition, start `parted` on the desired device as root, and issue the following command at the interactive prompt:

```
rm <minor-num>
```

The minor number for the partition is displayed when you execute the `print` command to list partitions. The data on the partition will no longer be accessible after the partition is removed, so be sure to back up any data you want to keep before removing the partition.

Understanding LVM

Logical Volume Manager, or LVM, is a storage management solution that allows administrators to divide hard drive space into *physical volumes* (*PV*), which can then be combined into *logical volume groups* (*VG*), which are then divided into *logical volumes* (*LV*) on which the filesystem and mount point are created.

As shown in Figure 7.1, because a logical volume group can include more than one physical volume, a mount point can include more than one physical hard drive, meaning the largest mount point can be larger than the biggest hard drive in the set. These logical volumes can be resized later if more disk space is needed for a particular mount point. After the mount points are created on logical volumes, a filesystem must be created on them.

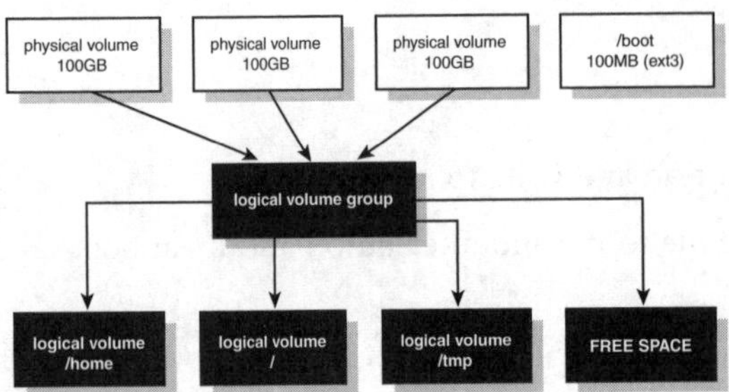

FIGURE 7.1 How Logical Volume Manager Works

LVM is used by default during installation for all mount points except the /boot partition, which cannot exist on a logical volume. This section discusses how to perform LVM operations after installation such as creating a physical volume for a newly added hard drive, expanding logical volumes, and generating LV snapshots.

Table 7.1 summaries the LVM tools available after installation.

TABLE 7.1 LVM Tools

LVM Tool	Description
`pvcreate`	Create physical volume from a hard drive
`vgcreate`	Create logical volume group from one or more physical volumes
`vgextend`	Add a physical volume to an existing volume group
`vgreduce`	Remove a physical volume from a volume group
`lvcreate`	Create a logical volume from available space in the volume group
`lvextend`	Extend the size of a logical volume from free physical extents in the logical volume group
`lvremove`	Remove a logical volume from a logical volume group, after unmounting it
`vgdisplay`	Show properties of existing volume group
`lvdisplay`	Show properties of existing logical volumes
`pvscan`	Show properties of existing physical volumes

Adding Additional Disk Space

One big advantage of using LVM is that the size of a logical volume can be increased and logical volumes can be added to create additional mount points. To modify the LVM configuration post-installation, the `lvm2` package needs to be installed. Refer to Chapter 3, "Operating System Updates," for details on installing packages.

TIP

If possible, leave free disk space when partitioning during installation so logical volume sizes can be increased without adding additional hard drives.

To increase the size of an existing logical volume or to add a logical volume, you first need free disk space. This free disk space can either be disk space that already exists in the system as unpartitioned space (not part of an existing logical volume), an unused partition, physical volume that is not already a member of a logical volume, or disk space as a result of installing one or more additional hard drives to the system. The disk space can come from removing a logical volume to create space in the logical volume group, however, this is not common because if the LV already exists, it is most likely already being used and cannot be easily deleted without losing data.

After deciding which free disk space to use, the basic steps for increasing the size of a logical volume are as follows:

1. Create new physical volume from free disk space.
2. Add physical volume to the logical volume group.
3. Expand the size of the logical volume to include the newly added disk space in the volume group.
4. Expand the filesystem on the logical volume to include the new space.

To add a logical volume, use the following steps:

1. Create new physical volume from free disk space.
2. Add physical volume to the logical volume group.
3. Create a logical volume with the new space in volume group.
4. Create a filesystem on the logical volume.
5. Create a mount point.
6. Mount the logical volume.
7. Test the filesystem.
8. Add the new mount point to `/etc/fstab`.

TIP

If you prefer a graphical interface, the `system-config-lvm` utility can be used to modify your LVM configuration.

Creating a Physical Volume

To create a new physical volume from free hard drive space or a hard drive partition, use the `pvcreate` command:

```
pvcreate <disk>
```

Replace `<disk>` with the device name of the hard drive:

```
pvcreate /dev/sda
```

7

or the partition name:

```
pvcreate /dev/sda1
```

The `<disk>` specified can also be a meta device or loopback device, but using an entire hard disk or partition is more common. After creating a physical volume, you can either add it to an existing volume group or create a new volume group with the physical volume.

Creating and Modifying Volume Groups

A volume group can be created from one or more physical volumes. To scan the system for all physical volumes, use the `pvscan` command as root. It displays all PVs on the system. If the PV is part of a VG, it will display the name of the VG next to it.

To create a VG, execute the `vgcreate` command as root, where `<vgname>` is a unique name for the volume group and `<pvlist>` is one or more physical volumes to use, each separated by a space:

```
vgcreate <vgname> <pvlist>
```

For example, to create a VG with the name `DatabaseVG` from the first and second SCSI hard drives:

```
vgcreate DatabaseVG /dev/sda /dev/sdb
```

NOTE

If the volume group was created during installation, the installation program names the first volume group `VolGroup00`, the second one `VolGroup01`, and so on.

If a volume group already exists but needs to be expanded, use the `vgextend` command to add additional physical volumes to it:

```
vgextend <vgname> <pvlist>
```

To remove a physical volume from a volume group:

```
vgreduce <vgname> <pvlist>
```

Use caution when reducing a volume group because any logical volume using the PVs are removed from the VG and can no longer be accessed.

Creating and Modifying Logical Volumes

Now that the physical volumes are formed into volume groups, the volume groups can be divided into logical volumes, and the logical volumes can be formatted with a filesystem and assigned mount points.

Use the `lvcreate` command to create a logical volume. Each LV must have a unique name. If one is not specified with the `-n <name>` option, a name will be assigned to it. To create a logical volume from the volume group `<vgname>` of a certain size, specify the size unit after the value of the size such as **300G** for 300 gigabytes:

```
lvcreate -n <lvname> --size <size> <vgname>
```

Each physical volume consists of *physical extents*, which are 4 megabytes in size by default. When the size is given in gigabytes, this size must be converted to physical extents, meaning that some amount of disk space may not be used. So, the number of physical extents to use when creating the logical volume can be given with the `-l <numpe>` option:

```
lvcreate -n <lvname> -l <numpe> <vgname>
```

To determine the number of physical extents in a logical volume group, issue the following command as root:

```
vgdisplay <vgname>
```

The `Total PE` line shows the number of physical extents for the volume group. The output should look similar to Listing 7.5, which shows a total of 1189 physical extents. Look for the `Free PE / Size` line to determine whether any free PEs are available to allocate to a new logical volume. Listing 7.5 shows 220 free physical extents.

LISTING 7.5 Example `vgdisplay` Output

```
--- Volume group ---
VG Name               VolGroup00
System ID
Format                lvm2
Metadata Areas        1
Metadata Sequence No  5
VG Access             read/write
VG Status             resizable
MAX LV                0
Cur LV                2
Open LV               2
Max PV                0
Cur PV                1
Act PV                1
VG Size               37.16 GB
PE Size               32.00 MB
Total PE              1189
Alloc PE / Size       969 / 30.28 GB
Free  PE / Size       220 / 6.88 GB
VG UUID               N60y5U-2sM2-uxHY-M1op-Q1v3-uVV2-Zkahza
```

7

TIP

Each LV has a device name in /dev/ with the format /dev/<vgname>/<lvname>.

By default, logical volumes are created linearly over the physical volumes. However, they can be striped over multiple PVs:

```
lvcreate -i<stripes> -I<stripesize> -l <numpe> -n <lvname> <vgname> <pvlist>
```

The -i<stripes> option sets the number of stripes, or physical volumes to use. The -I<stripesize> is the stripe size, which must be 2^n, where n is an integer from 2 to 9. Provide the number of PEs to use with the -l <numpe> option or give the size of the LV with the --size <size> option. The -n <lvname> option specifies the LV name, and <vgname> represents the name of the VG to use. Optionally, list the PVs to use, <pvlist>, at the end of the command separated by spaces. The number of PVs listed should be equal to the number of stripes.

After creating the logical volume, you must create a filesystem on it. To create an ext3 filesystem, execute the following as root:

```
mke2fs -j /dev/<vgname>/<lvname>
```

If the LV is to be used as swap, execute the following as root instead:

```
mkswap /dev/<vgname>/<lvname>
```

Next, still as the root user, create an empty directory as its mount point with the mkdir command, and use the mount command to mount the filesystem:

```
mount /dev/<vgname>/<lvname> /mount/point
```

If it mounts properly, the last step is to add it to /etc/fstab so it is mounted automatically at boot time. As root, add a line similar to the following, replacing with the appropriate values:

```
/dev/<vgname>/<lvname> /mount/point                    ext3    defaults        1 2
```

To extend a logical volume, expand the volume group if necessary, and then use the lvextend command. Either specify the final size of the logical volume:

```
lvextend --size <size> /dev/<vgname>/<lvname>
```

or specify how much to expand the logical volume:

```
lvextend --size +<addsize> /dev/<vgname>/<lvname>
```

Just like physical volumes are composed of 4KB physical extents, logical volumes consist of *logical extents*, which also have a default size of 4KB. Instead of specifying the size or amount of space to add in gigabytes, it is also possible to use the -l <numle> to provide the final number of logical extents or -l +<numle> to expand the logical volume by a certain number of logical extents.

After extending the logical volume, the filesystem on it must be expanded as well. If it is an ext3 filesystem (default filesystem for Red Hat Enterprise Linux), it can be expanded while it is still mounted (also known as *online*). To do so, execute the following as root:

```
resize2fs /dev/<vgname>/<lvname>
```

The filesystem is expanded to fill the entire logical volume unless a size is listed after the logical volume device name (be sure to list the size unit such as G for gigabyte after the size):

```
resize2fs /dev/<vgname>/<lvname> <size>
```

To remove a logical volume from a volume group, first unmount it with the umount command:

```
umount /dev/<vgname>/<lvname>
```

and then use the lvremove command:

```
lvremove /dev/<vgname>/<lvname>
```

To view the existing logical volumes along with information about them such as what VG they are a member of, the number of logical extents, and their size in gigabytes, execute the lvdisplay command as root as shown in Listing 7.6.

LISTING 7.6 Example lvdisplay Output

```
  --- Logical volume ---
  LV Name                /dev/VolGroup00/LogVol00
  VG Name                VolGroup00
  LV UUID                tugMFo-PESp-3INs-nrGF-K0Wh-s3U0-l9FsTc
  LV Write Access        read/write
  LV Status              available
  # open                 1
  LV Size                12.94 GB
  Current LE             414
  Segments               1
  Allocation             inherit
  Read ahead sectors     0
  Block device           253:0

  --- Logical volume ---
  LV Name                /dev/VolGroup00/LogVol01
  VG Name                VolGroup00
  LV UUID                fdKfYP-wIP9-M4Da-eoV3-pP99-w8Vb-0yhgZb
  LV Write Access        read/write
```

LISTING 7.6 Continued

```
  LV Status              available
  # open                 1
  LV Size                78.12 GB
  Current LE             2500
  Segments               1
  Allocation             inherit
  Read ahead sectors     0
  Block device           253:1

  --- Logical volume ---
  LV Name                /dev/VolGroup00/LogVol02
  VG Name                VolGroup00
  LV UUID                bzr4Ag-rDKT-y8zY-F3e8-SaBI-QY51-r6lJ3T
  LV Write Access        read/write
  LV Status              available
  # open                 1
  LV Size                1.94 GB
  Current LE             62
  Segments               1
  Allocation             inherit
  Read ahead sectors     0
  Block device           253:2
```

Creating Snapshots

With LVM, it is possible to take a snapshot of a logical volume while the LV is still in read-write mode and being accessed by the system. As the root user, issue the following command:

```
lvcreate --size <size> -s -n <snapshotname> <lvname>
```

The `lvcreate` command is used to create a new logical volume, meaning there must be free physical extents in the logical volume group to create a snapshot. The `-s` option means that the LV is a snapshot, `<snapshotname>` is the name of the new LV created, and `<lvname>` is the name of the LV from which to create the snapshot.

A snapshot is not a copy of the entire LV. Instead, it keeps track of the changes from the time the snapshot is taken and the present time. Thus, the size of the snapshot LV does not need to be as large as the LV from which it is created. It just needs to be as big as all the changes from the time the snapshot is taken until the snapshot is used. Snapshots are not intended to be left around for long periods of time. Reasons to create snapshots include performing backups (most common), creating virtual machines using the Virtualization feature (refer to Appendix B, “Creating Virtual Machines”), creating a duplicate testing system, and transferring data from one logical volume group (and possibly a different hard drive) to another.

If a snapshot LV reaches disk capacity, it will become unusable. When the backup or data transfer has been completed, the snapshot logical volume should be unmounted and removed with the `lvremove /dev/<vgname>/<lvname>` command. Because the snapshot LV is storing a copy of all changes made to the original LV, performance for the original LV can be reduced because of this copy process.

Understanding RAID

RAID (Redundant Array of Independent Disks) allows an administrator to form an array of several hard drives into one logical drive recognized as one drive by the operating system. It also spreads the data stored over the array of drives to decrease disk access time and accomplish data redundancy. The data redundancy can be used to recover data should one of the hard drives in the array crash.

There are two types of RAID: *hardware RAID* and *software RAID*. Hardware RAID is implemented through the disk controller for the system. Instructions for configuring hardware RAID differ from controller to controller, so refer to the manual for your disk controller for instructions. Software RAID is implemented through the operating system and does use some processor and memory resources, although some software RAID implementations can produce faster disk access times than hardware RAID.

During installation, it is possible to configure software RAID as discussed in Chapter 1. This section explains the different RAID levels available with software RAID so you can decide which level is best for you. Software RAID allows for RAID levels 0, 1, 5, and 6.

RAID *level 0*, or *striping*, means that data is written across all hard drives in the array to accomplish the fast disk performance. No redundancy is used, so the size of the logical RAID drive is equal to the size of all the hard drives in the array. Because there is no redundancy, recovering data from a hard drive crash is not possible through RAID.

RAID *level 1*, or *mirroring*, means that all data is written to each disk in the array, accomplishing redundancy. The data is "mirrored" on a second drive. This allows for easy recovery should a disk fail. However, it does mean that, for example, if there are two disks in the array, the size for the logical disk is size of the smaller of the two disks because data must be mirrored to the second disk.

RAID *level 5* combines striping and *parity*. Data is written across all disks as in RAID 0, but parity data is also written to one of the disks. Should a hard drive failure occur, this parity data can be used to recover the data from the failed drive, including while the data is being accessed and the drive is still missing from the array.

RAID *level 6* is RAID level 5 with *dual parity*. Data is written across all disks as in RAID 5, but two sets of parity data is calculated. Performance is slightly worse than RAID 5 because the extra parity data must be calculated and written to disk. RAID 5 allows for recovery using the parity data if only one drive in the array fails. Because of the dual parity, RAID 6 allows for recovery from the failure of up to two drives in the array.

Setting Up RAID Devices

For best results, software RAID should be configured during installation, but it can be configured after installation if necessary. To set up software RAID devices after installation, install the mdadm software package. Refer to Chapter 3 for instructions on installing packages. This section provides an overview of post-installation software RAID configuration. It shows you how to create a RAID array and then move the data from the existing filesystem onto it. Be sure to test the process on a test system before attempting it on a production system.

CAUTION

Remember to back up all data before converting partitions to software RAID devices. As with any process that modifies disk partitions and partition tables, data loss is possible.

Before starting the conversion, add the appropriate number of hard drives with the proper sizes for the RAID level. For example, two partitions are needed for RAID 1 (mirroring) and at least three partitions are needed for RAID 5. To use all the benefits of RAID, each partition in a RAID device should be on separate hard drives so each member of the RAID device can be written to at the same time and there is redundancy across separate hard drives should one fail.

It is possible to configure a RAID array with a missing partition so that the data on the existing partition can be copied to the degraded array. The existing partition is reconfigured as a RAID partition and then added to the RAID array to complete it. However, the process for doing so is more complicated and not recommended because it is easier to lose the existing data. It is recommended that new drives be used to set up the RAID device and for the existing data to then be copied to the new RAID device.

When creating partitions to use for the RAID device, make sure they are of type `Linux raid auto`. In `fdisk`, this is partition id `fd`. After creating the partitions for the RAID device, use the following syntax as the root user to create the RAID device:

```
mdadm --create /dev/mdX --level=<num> --raid-devices=<num> <device list>
```

The progress of the device creation can be monitored with the following command as root:

```
tail -f /proc/mdstat
```

For example, to create a RAID level 1 device `/dev/md0` from three partitions, use the following command:

```
mdadm --create /dev/md0 --level=1 --raid-devices=3 /dev/sda5 /dev/sda6 /dev/sda7
```

The command `cat /proc/mdstat` should show output similar to Listing 7.7.

LISTING 7.7 Creating a RAID Array

```
Personalities : [raid0] [raid1]
md0 : active raid1 sda7[2] sda6[1] sda5[0]
      10241280 blocks [3/3] [UUU]
      [>....................]  resync =  0.0% (8192/10241280) finish=62.3min
speed=2730K/sec

unused devices: <none>
```

The RAID device `/dev/md0` is created. Next, create a filesystem on it. To create an ext3 filesystem, execute the following as root:

```
mke2fs -j /dev/md0
```

If the new RAID device is to be used as the swap partition, use the following command as root instead:

```
mkswap /dev/md0
```

Copy any data over to the new device and be sure to change all references to the old partition to the new RAID device, including `/etc/fstab` and `/etc/grub.conf`. It is recommended that the `/boot` and the `/` filesystems remain on their original filesystems to ensure the system can still boot after added the RAID devices. Partitions such as `/home` will benefit from RAID more because data on it changes frequently.

Adding and Failing RAID Partitions

To add a partition to a RAID device, execute the following as root after creating the partition of type `Linux raid auto` (`fd` in `fdisk`):

```
mdadm /dev/mdX -a <device list>
```

To add `/dev/sda8` to the `/dev/md0` RAID device created in the previous section:

```
mdadm /dev/md0 -a /dev/sda8
```

Listing 7.8 shows the output from `cat /proc/mdstat`. The `/dev/sda8` partition is now a spare partition in the RAID array.

LISTING 7.8 Adding a Spare Partition

```
Personalities : [raid0] [raid1]
md0 : active raid1 sda8[3](S) sda7[2] sda6[1] sda5[0]
      10241280 blocks [3/3] [UUU]
      [>....................]  resync =  0.6% (66560/10241280) finish=84.0min
speed=2016K/sec

unused devices: <none>
```

7

If a partition in the array fails, use the following to remove it from the array and rebuild the array using the spare partition already added:

```
mdadm /dev/mdX -f <failed device>
```

For example, to fail /dev/sda5 from /dev/md0 and replace it with the spare (assuming the spare has already been added):

```
mdadm /dev/md0 -f /dev/sda5
```

To verify that the device has been failed and that the rebuild has been complete and was successful, monitor the /proc/mdstat file (output shown in Listing 7.9):

```
tail -f /proc/mdstat
```

Notice that /dev/sda5 is now failed and that /dev/sda8 has changed from a spare to an active partition in the RAID array.

LISTING 7.9 Failing a Partition and Replacing with a Spare

```
Personalities : [raid0] [raid1]
md0 : active raid1 sda8[3] sda7[2] sda6[1] sda5[4](F)
      10241280 blocks [3/2] [_UU]
      [>....................]  recovery =  0.2% (30528/10241280) finish=11.1min
speed=15264K/sec

unused devices: <none>
```

Monitoring RAID Devices

The following commands are useful for monitoring RAID devices:

- cat /proc/mdstat: Shows the status of the RAID devices and the status of any actions being performed on them such as adding a new member or rebuilding the array.
- mdadm --query /dev/mdX: Displays basic data about the device such as size and number of spares such as:

  ```
  /dev/md0: 9.77GiB raid1 3 devices, 1 spare.
  ```

  Add the --detail option to display more data (mdadm --query --detail /dev/mdX):

  ```
  /dev/md0:
          Version : 00.90.03
    Creation Time : Mon Dec 18 07:39:05 2006
       Raid Level : raid1
       Array Size : 10241280 (9.77 GiB 10.49 GB)
  ```

```
    Device Size : 10241280 (9.77 GiB 10.49 GB)
   Raid Devices : 3
  Total Devices : 4
Preferred Minor : 0
    Persistence : Superblock is persistent

    Update Time : Mon Dec 18 07:40:01 2006
          State : clean, degraded, recovering
 Active Devices : 2
Working Devices : 3
 Failed Devices : 1
  Spare Devices : 1

 Rebuild Status : 49% complete

           UUID : be623775:3e4ed7d6:c133873d:fbd771aa
         Events : 0.5

    Number   Major   Minor   RaidDevice State
       3       8       8        0      spare rebuilding   /dev/sda8
       1       8       6        1      active sync   /dev/sda6
       2       8       7        2      active sync   /dev/sda7

       4       8       5        -      faulty spare   /dev/sda5
```

- `mdadm --examine <partition>`: Displays detailed data about a component of a RAID array such as RAID level, total number of devices, number of working devices, and number of failed devices. For example, the output of `mdadm --examine /dev/sda6` shows the following:

```
/dev/sda6:
          Magic : a92b4efc
        Version : 00.90.00
           UUID : be623775:3e4ed7d6:c133873d:fbd771aa
  Creation Time : Mon Dec 18 07:39:05 2006
     Raid Level : raid1
    Device Size : 10241280 (9.77 GiB 10.49 GB)
     Array Size : 10241280 (9.77 GiB 10.49 GB)
   Raid Devices : 3
  Total Devices : 4
Preferred Minor : 0

    Update Time : Mon Dec 18 07:40:01 2006
          State : active
 Active Devices : 2
Working Devices : 3
```

```
   Failed Devices : 0
    Spare Devices : 1
         Checksum : ee90b526 - correct
           Events : 0.5


        Number   Major   Minor   RaidDevice State
this     1        8       6        1        active sync   /dev/sda6

   0     0        0       0        0        removed
   1     1        8       6        1        active sync   /dev/sda6
   2     2        8       7        2        active sync   /dev/sda7
   3     3        8       8        3        spare   /dev/sda8
```

Using MD Multipath

The hard drives in a system are connected to the rest of the system hardware via a disk controller. If the controller fails, the system can no longer communicate with the drives connected to it. However, some systems offer multipath disk access in which more than one controller is connected to the disks. If the active controller fails, a spare one replaces it, allowing continued access to the storage attached.

An example usage of MD Multipath is when a system is connected to a storage area network (SAN) via Fiber Channel Protocol or Cards. The multipath device can represent one interface that connects to the SAN using multiple physical cables. If one or more of the physical connections stops working or gets disconnected, the other physical cables are still active, and the storage is still accessible.

The Linux kernel offers Multiple Device (MD) Multipathing via its software RAID feature. MD Multipathing allows a device to be set up with multiple spares so that if the active device fails, I/O requests do not fail. If the active partition fails, the kernel activates one of the spare partitions as the active one.

To set up an MD Multipath device:

```
mdadm --create /dev/mdX --level=multipath --raid-devices=<num> <device list>
```

For example, use the following to set up `/dev/md0` with three drives, two of which become spares:

```
mdadm --create /dev/md0 --level=multipath --raid-devices=3 /dev/sda1 /dev/sdc1
➥/dev/sdd1
```

The kernel monitors the failure of the partition and activates a spare when it fails. However, the `mdmpd` daemon from the `mdadm` RPM package must be running to automatically add a failed partition back to the array when it becomes available again.

Understanding Clustering and GFS

In some enterprise infrastructures, high-performance, reliable, scalable servers and shared storage are necessary, with minimal downtime. Although RAID offers redundancy and NFS offers shared storage, they have limitations. For example, NFS transfer and access rates are slower than I/O to local disks and can have even slower rates depending on the number of simultaneous connections.

The Red Hat Cluster Suite offers application failover across multiple servers. Common servers that use clustering include web servers, database servers, and file servers such as GFS, or Global File Systems.

GFS is a scalable shared storage solution with I/O performance comparable to local disk access. It is usually combined with clustering to provide even more reliable storage with failover, redundancy, and simultaneous shared access to a GFS filesystem. When combined with clustering, the GFS filesystem is used on one or more file servers acting as the storage pool accessed by all the cluster nodes via a Storage Area Network (SAN). In addition to its ability to scale to meet the storage needs of hundreds or more servers simultaneously, the size of each GFS filesystem can be expanded while still in use.

The easiest way to start using the Red Hat Cluster Suite and Red Hat GFS is to install the packages from RHN using the Cluster Suite and GFS software channels. Refer to Chapter 3 for details on installing all the packages from a child software channel.

After installing the appropriate RPM packages, set up the cluster using the Cluster Configuration Tool (`system-config-cluster`) before configuring GFS. The exact configuration of Cluster Suite and GFS depends on a great deal of factors including the needs of your infrastructure, budget allocated to the system group, amount of shared storage needed plus extra for future expansion, and what type of application servers are to be run on the cluster servers. Refer to the *Documentation* and *Knowledgebase* sections of redhat.com for detailed instructions.

Using Access Control Lists

On an ext3 filesystem, read, write, and execute permissions can be set for the owner of the file, the group associated with the file, and for everyone else who has access to the filesystem. These files are visible with the `ls -l` command. Refer to Chapter 4, "Understanding Linux Concepts," for information on reading standard file permissions.

In most cases, these standard file permissions along with restricted access to mounting filesystems are all that an administrator needs to grant file privileges to users and to prevent unauthorized users from accessing important files. However, when these basic file permissions are not enough, *access control lists*, or *ACLs*, can be used on an ext3 filesystem.

ACLs expand the basic read, write, and execute permissions to more categories of users and groups. In addition to permissions for the owner and group for the file, ACLs allow for permissions to be set for any user, any user group, and the group of all users not in the group for the user. An effective rights mask, which is explained later, can also be set to restrict permissions.

To use ACLs on the filesystem, the `acl` package must be installed. If it is not already installed, install it via Red Hat Network as discussed in Chapter 3.

Enabling ACLs

To use ACLs, they must be enabled when an ext3 filesystem is mounted. This is most commonly enabled as an option in `/etc/fstab`. For example:

```
LABEL=/share   /share          ext3          acl            1 2
```

If the filesystem can be unmounted and remounted while the system is still running, modify `/etc/fstab` for the filesystem, unmount it, and remount it so the changes to `/etc/fstab` take effect. Otherwise, the system must be rebooted to enable ACLs on the desired filesystems.

If you are mounting the filesystem via the `mount` command instead, use the `-o acl` option when mounting:

```
mount -t ext3 -o acl <device> <partition>
```

Setting and Modifying ACLs

There are four categories of ACLs per file: for an individual user, for a user group, via the effective rights mask, and for users not in the user group associated with the file. To view the existing ACLs for a file, execute the following:

```
getfacl <file>
```

If ACLs are enabled, the output should look similar to Listing 7.10.

LISTING 7.10 Viewing ACLs

```
# file: testfile
# owner: tfox
# group: tfox
user::rwx
group::r-x
mask::rwx
other::r-x
```

To set or modify existing ACLs, use the following syntax:

```
setfacl -m <rules> <file>
```

Other useful options include `--test` to show the results of the command but not change the ACL and `-R` to apply the rules recursively.

Replace `<file>` with one or more space-separated file or directory names. Rules can be set for four different rule types. Replace `<rules>` with one or more of the following, and replace `<perms>` in these rules with one or more of `r`, `w`, and `x` (which stand for read, write, and execute):

- For an individual user:

  `u:<uid>:<perms>`

- For a specific user group:

  `g:<gid>:<perms>`

- For users not in the user group associated with the file:

  `o:<perms>`

- Via the effective rights mask:

  `m:<perms>`

The first three rule types (individual user, user group, or users not in the user group for the file) are pretty self-explanatory. They allow you to give read, write, or execute permissions to users in these three categories. A user or group ID may be used, or the actual username or group name.

CAUTION

If the actual username or group name is used to set an ACL, the UID or GID for it are still used to store the ACL. If the UID or GID for a user or group name changes, the ACLs are *not* changed to reflect the new UID or GID.

But, what is the *effective rights mask*? The effective rights mask restricts the ACL permission set allowed for users or groups other than the owner of the file. The standard file permissions are not affected by the mask, just the permissions granted by using ACLs. In other words, if the permission (read, write, or execute) is not in the effective rights mask, it appears in the ACLs retrieved with the `getfacl` command, but the permission is ignored. Listing 7.11 shows an example of this where the effective rights mask is set to read-only, meaning the read-write permissions for user brent and the group associated with the file are effectively read-only. Notice the comment to the right of the ACLs affected by the effective rights mask.

LISTING 7.11 Effective Rights Mask

```
# file: testfile
# owner: tammy
# group: tammy
user::rw-
user:brent:rw-                    #effective:r--
group::rw-                        #effective:r--
mask::r--
other::rw-
```

The effective rights mask must be set *after* the ACL rule types. When an ACL for an individual user (other than the owner of the file) or a user group is added, the effective rights mask is automatically recalculated as the union of all the permissions for all users other than the owner and all groups including the group associated with the file. So, to make sure the effective rights mask is not modified after setting it, set it after all other ACL permissions.

If the ACL for one of these rule types already exists for the file or directory, the existing ACL for the rule type is replaced, not added to. For example, if user 605 already has read and execute permissions to the file, after the `u:605:w` rule is implemented, user 605 only has write permissions.

Setting Default ACLs

Two types of ACLs can be used: *access ACLs,* and *default ACLs.* So far, this chapter has only discussed access ACLs. Access ACLs are set for individual files and directories. Directories, and directories only, can also have default ACLs, which are optional. If a directory has a default ACL set for it, any file or directory created in the directory with default ACLs will inherit the default ACLs. If a file is created, the access ACLs are set to what the default ACLs are for the parent directory. If a directory is created, the access ACLs are set to what the default ACLs are for the parent directory *and* the default ACLs for the new directory are set to the same default ACLs as the parent directory.

To set the ACL as a default ACL, prepend `d:` to the rule such as `d:g:500:rwx` to set a default ACL of read, write, and execute for user group 500. If any default ACL exists for the directory, the default ACLs must include a user, group, and other ACL at a minimum as shown in Listing 7.12.

LISTING 7.12 Default ACLs

```
# file: testdir
# owner: tfox
# group: tfox
user::rwx
group::r-x
mask::rwx
other::r-x
default:user::rwx
default:group::r-x
default:other::r--
```

If a default ACL is set for an individual user other than the file owner or for a user group other than the group associated with the file, a default effective rights mask must also exist. If one is not implicitly set, it is automatically calculated as with access ACLs. The same rules apply for the default ACL effective rights mask: It is recalculated after an ACL for any user other than the owner is set or if an ACL for any group including the group associated with the file is set, meaning it should be set last to ensure it is not changed after being set.

Removing ACLs

The setfacl -x <rules> <file> command can be used to remove ACL permissions by ACL rule type. The <rules> for this command use the same syntax as the setfacl -m <rules> <file> command except that the <perms> field is omitted because all rules for the rule type are removed.

It is also possible to remove all ACLs for a file or directory with:

```
setfacl --remove-all <file>
```

To remove all default ACLs for a directory:

```
setfacl --remove-default <dir>
```

Preserving ACLs

The NFS and Samba file sharing clients in Red Hat Enterprise Linux recognize and use any ACLs associated with the files shared on the server. If your NFS or Samba clients are not running Red Hat Enterprise Linux, be sure to ask the operating system vendor about ACL support or test your client configuration for support.

The mv command to move files preserves the ACLs associated with the file. If it can't for some reason, a warning is displayed. However, the cp command to copy files does *not* preserve ACLs.

The tar and dump commands also do *not* preserve the ACLs associated with files or directories and should not be used to back up or archive files with ACLs. To back up or archive files while preserving ACLs use the star utility. For example, if you are moving a large number of files with ACLs, create an archive of all the files using star, copy the star archive file to the new system or directory, and unarchive the files. Be sure to use getfacl to verify that the ACLs are still associated with the files. The star RPM package must be installed to use the utility. Refer to Chapter 3 for details on package installation via Red Hat Network. The star command is similar to tar. Refer to its man page with the man star command for details.

Using Disk Quotas

Part of managing storage is determining how the available storage can be used. Although setting the size of filesystems such as /tmp and /home can limit storage for certain types of data, it is sometimes necessary to enable disk usage per user or per user group. This is possible with disk quotas. To use quotas, the quota RPM package must be installed. Refer to Chapter 3 for details on installing packages.

Enabling Quotas

To use quotas, they must be enabled in /etc/fstab, which is read at boot time to mount filesystems. This enables quotas in the kernel booted for the system. To add as an option in /etc/fstab, for example (as the root user):

```
/dev/VolGroup00/LogVol01 /home            ext3    usrquota,grpquota        1 2
```

The usrquota mount option enables user quotas, and the grpquota option enables group quotas. One or both can be used. Either reboot the system to enable the quotas or remount each filesystem as root with the following command:

```
mount -o remount,acl,usrquota,grpquota,rw <mountpoint>
```

Once again, one or both of usrquota or grpquota can be used. In our example, <mountpoint> would be /home. To verify that the remount enabled quotas, execute the following command:

```
mount ¦ grep <mountpoint>
```

or use such as mount ¦ grep home if you are following the example. The output shows which mount options were used to mount the filesystem:

```
/dev/VolGroup00/LogVol01 on /home type ext3 (rw,acl,acl,usrquota,grpquota)
```

Creating Quota Database Files

The first time the system is booted with quotas enabled in /etc/fstab, quotas are not turned on because the quota database files for the filesystem do not exist. The quotacheck command is used to create these files.

After rebooting with quotas enabled in /etc/fstab and before executing the quotaon command to turn on quotas, the filesystem must be initialized to use quotas. If they do not already exist, the aquota.user and aquota.group files are created in the root directory of the filesystem. These are database files used to enforce quotas.

Refer to the quotacheck man page for a list of all options and determine which options are best for your situation. By default, only user quotas are checked and initialized. If you need to initialize user group quotas as well, specify it with the -g option. A typical command to run with options, as the root user, would be:

```
quotacheck -uvg <devicename>
```

such as:

```
quotacheck -uvg /dev/VolGroup00/LogVol02
```

Because disk usage can change when the filesystem is mounted in read-write mode, it is recommended that quotacheck be run when the filesystem is mounted read-only. If the filesystem is mounted when quotacheck is run, quotacheck will try to mount it read-only before starting the scan. It then remounts it in read-write mode after the scan is complete.

If it is unable to mount it read-only, a message similar to the following appears:

```
quotacheck: Cannot remount filesystem mounted on /home read-only
so counted values might not be right.
Please stop all programs writing to filesystem or use -m flag to force checking.
```

If `quotacheck` can't remount the filesystem read-only before starting, you can force the quota check anyway by using the `-m` command-line option.

The `quotacheck` utility should be run on a regular basis to keep quotas accurate or after a system crash in which the filesystem was not unmounted cleanly. To make sure it is done on a schedule, setup a cron task that is run automatically at set times. Refer to Chapter 11, "Automating Tasks with Scripts," for details on setting up a cron task.

After creating the quota database files, be sure to turn quotas on as described in the next section. After the quota database files are created, subsequent boots with the `usrquota` and/or `grpquota` mount options in `/etc/fstab` will automatically have quotas turned on for those filesystems.

Turning Quotas On and Off

Quotas can be turned on and off without rebooting the system with the `quotaon` and `quotaoff` commands, but only for filesystems that meet two conditions: The filesystem must be mounted at boot time with the `usrquota` and/or `grpquota` mount options in `/etc/fstab`, and the filesystem must have the `aquota.user` and/or `aquota.group` files in the root of the filesystem.

To turn quotas on for an already mounted filesystem, the `quotaon` utility can be used. As root, use the following to enable user and group quotas:

```
quotaon -vug <devicename>
```


To temporarily turn off quotas, execute the following command as root:

```
quotaoff -vug <devicename>
```

The `-vug` options specify that messages should be displayed showing that the quotas are being turned off as well as error messages if they exist and that both the user and group quotas should be turned off.

`To verify that the quotas have been turned on or off, execute the mount command and read the mount options used such as the following:/dev/VolGroup00/LogVol01 on /home type ext3 (rw,acl,acl,usrquota,grpquota)`

Setting and Modifying Quotas

Quotas can be set per user, group, or filesystem with the `edquota` command. The user or group name can be used or the UID or GID for the user or group. To set or modify the quota for a user, execute the following as root:

```
edquota <username>
```

To set or modify the quota for a user group, execute the following as root:

```
edquota -g <groupname>
```

When the edquota command is executed, the default text editor is opened as determined by the $EDITOR environment variable. In Red Hat Enterprise Linux, the default editor is Vi. To set the default editor to a different editor, execute the following command, replacing emacs with the editor of your choice (this setting is per user):

```
export EDITOR="emacs"
```

When this command is executed, it only changes the default editor for that login session. When the system is rebooted, this setting is lost. To permanently change the default editor, add the command as a line to your .bashrc file in your home directory. The .bashrc file is only read when a user logs in, so to enable changes to the file after you have already logged in, execute the source ~/.bashrc command.

When setting quotas, there are two types of limits: *soft limits* and *hard limits*. When the soft limit is reached, the user is warned and allowed to exceed the soft limit for a *grace period*, which is set to 7 days by default in Red Hat Enterprise Linux. This grace period allows the user or group time to reduce disk usage and return to below the soft limit. A hard limit is the absolute maximum amount of disk usage the user or group is allowed. After it is reached, no more disk space is allocated to the user or group.

If a user or group still exceeds the soft limit after the grace period has expired, the soft limit is treated as a hard limit, and the user or group is not allowed additional disk usage until the disk usage falls below the soft limit.

When the edquota command is executed, the output looks similar to Listing 7.13, which shows content for modifying quotas for the user tfox.

LISTING 7.13 Setting Disk Quotas

```
Disk quotas for user tfox (uid 501):
  Filesystem                   blocks       soft     hard   inodes    soft    hard
  /dev/mapper/VolGroup00-LogVol02  59403        0        0        0       0       0
```

There are seven columns of information. The first column shows the filesystem in question. The next three columns are for setting quotas according to block size, with the first being the current block usage for the user or group. The next two are for setting the soft and hard limits for block usage. The last three columns are for inode usage, with the first being the current usage for the user or group, and the last two being the soft and hard limits. Setting any of these limits to 0, the default, means there is no limit. The block and inode usage columns are for reference only and should not be modified. Change the values of the limits, save the file, and exit.

To modify the grace period for a filesystem, execute the following as root:

```
edquota -t
```

This grace period is used for all users and groups. To set the grace period for a specific user, execute the following as root, where <username> is a username or UID:

```
edquota -T <username>
```

To set the grace period for a specific user group, execute the following as root, where <groupname> is a group name or GID:

```
edquota -T -g <groupname>
```

Displaying Quotas

To display all quotas along with user and group usage, execute the following as root:

```
repquota -a
```

The output should look similar to Listing 7.14.

LISTING 7.14 Reporting Disk Usage and Quotas

```
*** Report for user quotas on device /dev/mapper/VolGroup00-LogVol01
Block grace time: 7days; Inode grace time: 7days
                            Block limits                File limits
User            used        soft      hard  grace    used  soft  hard  grace
----------------------------------------------------------------------------
root        --   189192         0         0           336     0     0
bfox        -- 3216936    40000000 45000000         26383     0     0
tfox        -- 36329868   40000000 45000000         56253     0     0
```

Summary

After reading this chapter, you now have an understanding of the many storage configuration schemes in Red Hat Enterprise Linux, some of which can be combined. Standard partitions are straightforward and necessary for some mount points but lack the option to resize without destroying the existing partitions. LVM is the default partitioning scheme for Red Hat Enterprise Linux. Logical volumes can be resized easily. Software RAID offers redundancy and some speed advantages. Global File Systems and clustering offer scalable, reliable storage for enterprises.

CHAPTER 8

64-Bit, Multi-Core, and Hyper-Threading Technology Processors

IN THIS CHAPTER

- 64-Bit Processors
- Multi-Core Processors
- Processors with Hyper-Threading Technology

As systems, both servers and desktops, require more processing power, large file sizes, and access to more and more memory, CPU manufacturers have been developing processors to address these needs. Red Hat Enterprise Linux has also evolved to support these technologies.

64-Bit Processors

In 2004, the 64-bit processor was introduced into the computer market. In the beginning, these 64-bit processors were only used for servers, but ones such as the AMD Athlon™ 64 are now being used for desktop computers as well.

Red Hat Enterprise Linux supports both 32-bit and 64-bit processors. If you have a system with a 64-bit processor, install the 64-bit version of the operating system if you want the 64-bit kernel, libraries, and available applications to be installed.

Most of the modern 64-bit processors such as the AMD64 and EM64T can also run 32-bit applications if the operating system also supports it. 32-bit support is installed by default when installing the 64-bit version of Red Hat Enterprise Linux.

To run both 32-bit and 64-bit applications, both sets of libraries must be installed. Having both the 64-bit and 32-bit versions of a library installed at the same time is known as *multilib*. Red Hat Enterprise Linux allows for this by following the FHS guidelines. 32-bit libraries are installed in `/lib/` and `/usr/lib/`, and 64-bit libraries are installed in `/lib64/` and `/usr/lib64/`.

NOTE

For the complete FHS guidelines explanation of how 32-bit and 64-bit libraries coexist, refer to `http://www.pathname.com/fhs/pub/fhs-2.3.html#LIB64`.

Some packages have been compiled for the 64-bit architecture but are available in a 32-bit version as well. When using Red Hat Network to install a package on a 64-bit system with the 64-bit version of the OS installed, the 64-bit version of the package is installed if available. If the 32-bit version is the only one available, it is installed. If both versions are available, the architecture can be specified if installing from Red Hat Network:

```
yum install <package_name>.<arch>
```

Replace `<arch>` with the 32-bit architecture compatible with your 64-bit processor such as `i386` for Intel Itanium, AMD64, and EM64T systems. If you are selecting a package to install via the RHN website, the architecture is included in the package name such as `glibc-2.3.4-2.i686` and `glibc-2.3.4-2.ia64`. If you are installing software directly from the RPM package file, remember that the filename includes the architecture such as `glibc-2.3.4-2.i686.rpm`. Table 8.1 shows the architecture abbreviations used in the RPM filename and in the package name listed on the RHN website. It also shows the compatible 32-bit architectures.

TABLE 8.1 Compatible Architectures

Processor	RPM Architecture	Compatible 32-Bit Architectures
Intel Itanium	ia64	i386, i686
AMD64, EM64T	x86_64	i386, i686
IBM POWER	ppc64	ppc
IBM zSeries	s390x	s390

After installing both versions of a library, how can you verify they are both installed? The `rpm -q <package-name>` command doesn't display the architecture of the package by default. But, the command can be configured to show this information by using the `--queryformat` option:

```
rpm -q <package-name> --queryformat='%{NAME}-%{VERSION}.%{ARCH}\n'
```

This changes the format displayed to also include a period at the end of the package name followed by the architecture such as the following for two different builds of `glibc`:

```
glibc-2.3.4-2.19.i686
glibc-2.3.4-2.19.x86_64
```

This option is very useful, but it is not easy to remember. Luckily, this format can be saved as the default for each user. In your home directory, create a `.rpmmacros` file if you don't already have one. In this file, add the following line:

```
%_query_all_fmt %%{name}-%%{version}-%%{release}.%%{arch}
```

Duplicate this file for each user who wants to view the architecture of the packages queried.

TIP

Add this formatting line to the `.rpmmacros` file for the root user as well if you often perform RPM queries as root.

Multi-Core Processors

A multi-core processor is a processor that contains one or more processor cores on a single processor chip, with each core having its own dedicated cache. The advantages of using multi-core processors include the following:

- More processor cores on a single processor means a smaller physical footprint for a multi-processor machine. More processor cores can fit in a single unit.
- If combined with Virtualization or a similar technology, each processor core can be dedicated to a virtual machine. Just switching to dual-core processors doubles the number of virtual machines with a dedicated processor. Refer to Appendix B, "Creating Virtual Machines," for details on implementing the Virtualization layer.

The Linux kernel recognizes the number of physical processors, the number of processor cores on each physical processor, and the total number of processor cores. It uses each processor core as it would a separate physical processor. In addition to the processor vendor, speed, and cache size, the `/proc/cpuinfo` virtual file shows information about the processor cores. To view the contents of this virtual file, use the `cat /proc/cpuinfo` command.

Listing 8.1 shows the output on a system with two processors, with each processor having two processor cores. The `processor` field counts the total number of processor cores for the entire system. In Listing 8.1, this value starts with 0 and ends with 3, for a total of four processor cores. The total number of physical processors is two, as shown by the `physical id` field starting at 0 for the first processor core and ending at 1 for the last processor core. The value of the `cpu cores` field is the total number of processor cores on the physical processor. The `core id` field counts the number of processor cores for each physical processor.

8

LISTING 8.1 Contents of `/proc/cpuinfo` for a 2-Processor, Dual-Core System

```
processor       : 0
vendor_id       : AuthenticAMD
cpu family      : 15
model           : 33
model name      : AMD Opteron(tm) Processor 860
stepping        : 2
cpu MHz         : 1607.417
```

LISTING 8.1 Continued

```
cache size       : 1024 KB
physical id      : 0
siblings         : 2
core id          : 0
cpu cores        : 2
fpu              : yes
fpu_exception    : yes
cpuid level      : 1
wp               : yes
flags            : fpu vme de pse tsc msr pae mce cx8 apic sep mtrr pge \
   mca cmov pat pse36 clflush mmx fxsr sse sse2 ht syscall nx mmxext lm \
   3dnowext 3dnow pni
bogomips         : 3218.03
TLB size         : 1088 4K pages
clflush size     : 64
cache_alignment : 64
address sizes    : 40 bits physical, 48 bits virtual
power management: ts ttp

processor        : 1
vendor_id        : AuthenticAMD
cpu family       : 15
model            : 33
model name       : AMD Opteron(tm) Processor 860
stepping         : 2
cpu MHz          : 1607.417
cache size       : 1024 KB
physical id      : 0
siblings         : 2
core id          : 1
cpu cores        : 2
fpu              : yes
fpu_exception    : yes
cpuid level      : 1
wp               : yes
flags            : fpu vme de pse tsc msr pae mce cx8 apic sep mtrr pge mca \
   cmov pat pse36 clflush mmx fxsr sse sse2 ht syscall nx mmxext lm 3dnowext \
   3dnow pni
bogomips         : 3214.44
TLB size         : 1088 4K pages
clflush size     : 64
cache_alignment : 64
address sizes    : 40 bits physical, 48 bits virtual
```

LISTING 8.1 Continued

```
power management: ts ttp

processor       : 2
vendor_id       : AuthenticAMD
cpu family      : 15
model           : 33
model name      : AMD Opteron(tm) Processor 860
stepping        : 2
cpu MHz         : 1607.417
cache size      : 1024 KB
physical id     : 1
siblings        : 2
core id         : 0
cpu cores       : 2
fpu             : yes
fpu_exception   : yes
cpuid level     : 1
wp              : yes
flags           : fpu vme de pse tsc msr pae mce cx8 apic sep mtrr pge mca \
   cmov pat pse36 clflush mmx fxsr sse sse2 ht syscall nx mmxext lm 3dnowext \
   3dnow pni
bogomips        : 3214.42
TLB size        : 1088 4K pages
clflush size    : 64
cache_alignment : 64
address sizes   : 40 bits physical, 48 bits virtual
power management: ts ttp

processor       : 3
vendor_id       : AuthenticAMD
cpu family      : 15
model           : 33
model name      : AMD Opteron(tm) Processor 860
stepping        : 2
cpu MHz         : 1607.417
cache size      : 1024 KB
physical id     : 1
siblings        : 2
core id         : 1
cpu cores       : 2
fpu             : yes
fpu_exception   : yes
cpuid level     : 1
wp              : yes
```

LISTING 8.1 Continued

```
flags           : fpu vme de pse tsc msr pae mce cx8 apic sep mtrr pge mca \
   cmov pat pse36 clflush mmx fxsr sse sse2 ht syscall nx mmxext lm 3dnowext \
   3dnow pni
bogomips        : 3214.42
TLB size        : 1088 4K pages
clflush size    : 64
cache_alignment : 64
address sizes   : 40 bits physical, 48 bits virtual
power management: ts ttp
```

Processors with Hyper-Threading Technology

Processors with Hyper-Threading Technology (HT Technology) are seen by the operating system as two logical processors. These processors are different from multi-core processors because processors with HT Technology do not contain all the components of two separate processors. Only specific parts of a second processor are included so that two process threads can be executed at the same time.

When Red Hat Enterprise Linux detects a processor with HT Technology, it configures the system as a multi-processor system, and therefore uses the SMP kernel. This can be seen in the output of the `/proc/cpuinfo` virtual file as shown in Listing 8.2.

LISTING 8.2 Contents of `/proc/cpuinfo` for a Process with HT Technology

```
processor       : 0
vendor_id       : GenuineIntel
cpu family      : 15
model           : 3
model name      : Genuine Intel(R) CPU 3.20GHz
stepping        : 3
cpu Mhz         : 2793.829
cache size      : 1024 KB
physical id     : 0
siblings        : 2
core id         : 0
cpu cores       : 1
fdiv_bug        : no
hlt_bug         : no
f00f_bug        : no
coma_bug        : no
fpu             : yes
fpu_exception   : yes
cpuid level     : 5
wp              : yes
flags           : fpu vme de pse tsc msr pae mce cx8 apic mtrr pge mca
```

LISTING 8.2 Continued

```
cmov pat pse36 clflush dts acpi mmx fxsr sse sse2 ss ht tm pbe pni
monitor ds_cpl cid
bogomips        : 5592.02

processor       : 1
vendor_id       : GenuineIntel
cpu family      : 15
model           : 3
model name      : Genuine Intel(R) CPU 3.20GHz
stepping        : 3
cpu Mhz         : 2793.829
cache size      : 1024 KB
physical id     : 0
siblings        : 2
core id         : 0
cpu cores       : 1
fdiv_bug        : no
hlt_bug         : no
f00f_bug        : no
coma_bug        : no
fpu             : yes
fpu_exception   : yes
cpuid level     : 5
wp              : yes
flags           : fpu vme de pse tsc msr pae mce cx8 apic mtrr pge mca
cmov pat pse36 clflush dts acpi mmx fxsr sse sse2 ss ht tm pbe pni
monitor ds_cpl cid
bogomips        : 5585.63
```

Similar to the previous example for the multi-core processors, look at the `processor`, `physical id`, `core id`, and `cpu cores` fields to verify that the system is recognized as one with HT Technology. The `processor` count goes from 0 to 1, indicating that, as far as the operating system is considered, there are two processors to send data to for execution. The `physical id` is 0 for both, meaning that there is only one physical processor. The value of `cpu cores` is 1, and the value of `core id` is 0 for both, meaning that the processor is not a multi-core processor. Thus, the processor must have HT Technology because the virtual processor count is 2 with only one processor core.

Hyper-Threading can be disabled at boot-time with a kernel option passed to the kernel using the GRUB boot loader. This process only disables Hyper-Threading for one boot instance. It must be repeated on subsequent boots to continue disabling Hyper-Threading. The steps are as follows:

1. When the GRUB boot menu appears, use the up and down arrows to select the kernel to boot.

2. Press the E key to add a kernel option to the kernel selected.
3. At the end of the line, add a space and then the `noht` kernel option.
4. Press Enter to return to the GRUB boot menu.
5. Press the B key to boot the system.

Hyper-Threading can be disabled for all subsequent boots if the kernel option is added to the GRUB configuration file. As root, open the `/etc/grub.conf` file and find the kernel stanza for which you want to disable Hyper-Threading. Find the kernel line for the stanza, add a space to the end, and add the `noht` kernel option as shown in Listing 8.3.

LISTING 8.3 Disabling Hyper-Threading with GRUB

```
default=0
timeout=15
splashimage=(hd0,0)/boot/grub/splash.xpm.gz
hiddenmenu
title Red Hat Enterprise Linux (2.6.16-1.2133)
        root (hd0,0)
        kernel /boot/vmlinuz-2.6.16-1.2133 ro root=LABEL=/ rhgb quiet noht
        initrd /boot/initrd-2.6.16-1.2133.img
```

Summary

This chapter explained what to look for when using Red Hat Enterprise Linux on 64-bit and multi-core systems as well as systems with Hyper-Threading Technology. Install Red Hat Enterprise Linux on these systems as you would for any other system. For the 64-bit system, be sure to install the 64-bit version of the operating system. For a multi-core system, the number of processor cores is detected, and the appropriate kernel is installed.

PART III

System Administration

IN THIS PART

CHAPTER 9

Managing Users and Groups

IN THIS CHAPTER

With Red Hat Enterprise Linux, all users must enter a username and password combination to use the operating system and applications for security. Privileges and access to specific files and directories can be granted or denied based on a person's username. Thus, part of an administrators' duties is to manage their company's database of users and groups as employees change, request more storage, and transfer to different departments. Although adding users and groups seems like a simple task on the surface, it does require forward planning and preparation for a large user group such as one for a large company or corporation or for an organization that requires users to have access to multiple computers throughout the same building or even a set of worldwide offices.

This chapter explains how to manage *local* users and groups. Local users and groups are authenticated by the system on which they are logging in to. The files storing usernames, groups, and passwords are all on the local system. Users and groups can also be authenticated from a network server. For details on network services that allow identity management from a central server, refer to Chapter 12, "Identity Management."

Even if you are using remote identity management, it is recommended that you read the first section "What Are Users and Groups?" and the last section "Best Practices." The last section provides tips on managing usernames, managing passwords, deleting accounts, and structuring home directories. The methods in this section apply to user management regardless of whether the authentication takes place on the local system or from a remote server.

What Are Users and Groups?

In addition to a Red Hat Enterprise Linux system having a username for each user allowed access to a system, each system has *user groups*. A user group is a group of one or more users. A user can be a member of more than one group. As discussed in the section "File Permissions" of Chapter 4, "Understanding Linux Concepts," file and directory permissions can be granted for the owner of the file, the group associated with the file, and all users on the system.

User groups can be any grouping of users on which you decide: groups of users in a functional department, groups in the same physical location, or groups based on security access. It is important to plan the user groups for your company carefully before implementing them because changing them means changing the groups associated with files, which can sometimes lead to incorrect group permissions if they are not changed correctly.

Managing Users

Each user on a Red Hat Enterprise Linux system is assigned a unique user identification number, also known as a *UID*. UIDs below 500 are reserved for system users such as the root user. System users also include those added for a specific service such as the `nfsnobody`, `rpc`, and `rpcuser` users for the NFS service.

By default in Red Hat Enterprise Linux, when a user is added, a *private user group* is created—meaning that a user group of the same name is created and that the new user is the sole user in that group.

Red Hat Enterprise Linux includes a graphical program for managing users and groups. The `system-config-users` package is required to do so. Install it using the RHN website or YUM as described in Chapter 3, "Operating System Updates." Start the user and group tool from the **System** menu on the top panel of the desktop by selecting **Administration**, **Users and Groups** or execute the command `system-config-users`. If the program is run as a non-root user, enter the root password when prompted. As shown in Figure 9.1, all existing users are listed on the **Users** tab.

By default, system users are not shown in the list of users. To show system users in the list, select **Edit**, **Preferences** from the pull-down menu. In the **Preferences** dialog, unselect the **Hide system users and groups** option, and click **Close**.

Adding and Modifying Users

To add a new user, click **Add User** to display the dialog window in Figure 9.2.

Configure the username, full name, and password for the new user. The default login shell for new users is bash. By default, the directory `/home/<username>/` is created as the user's home directory, and a private group is created for the user. These options can be modified as shown in Figure 9.2. A UID above 500 is automatically selected for the user. To manually set the UID, select the **Specify user ID manually** option and then select a UID. Click **OK** to add the user to the system. The user immediately appears on the **Users** tab of the main window, and is also added to the system.

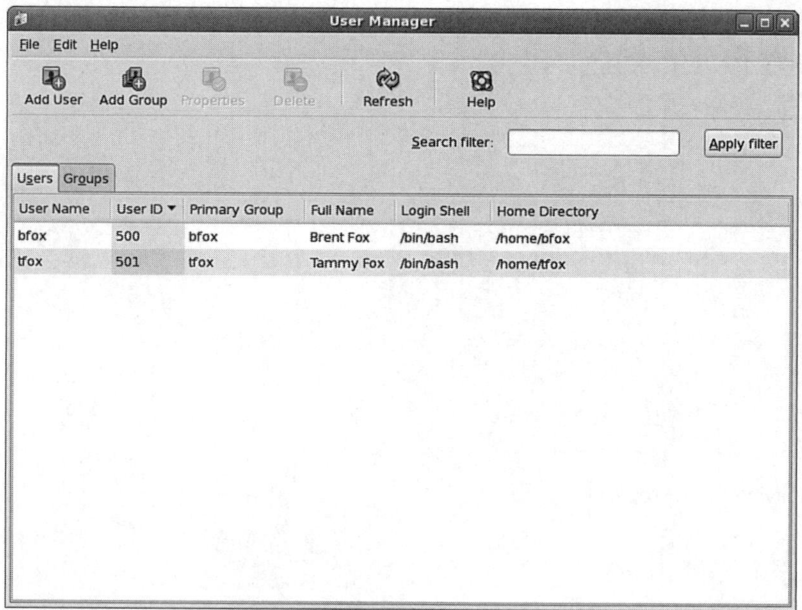

FIGURE 9.1 List of Existing Users

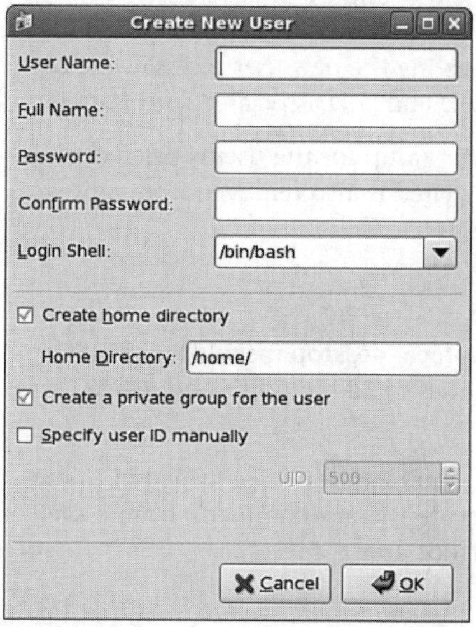

FIGURE 9.2 Adding a New User

To configure more advanced user options for the new user or any existing user, select him from the list on the Users tab and click **Properties**. The dialog box in Figure 9.3 appears and displays the options currently configured for the user. Features such as account expiration, password locking, password expiration, and groups to which the user is a member are configurable from the **User Properties** dialog box.

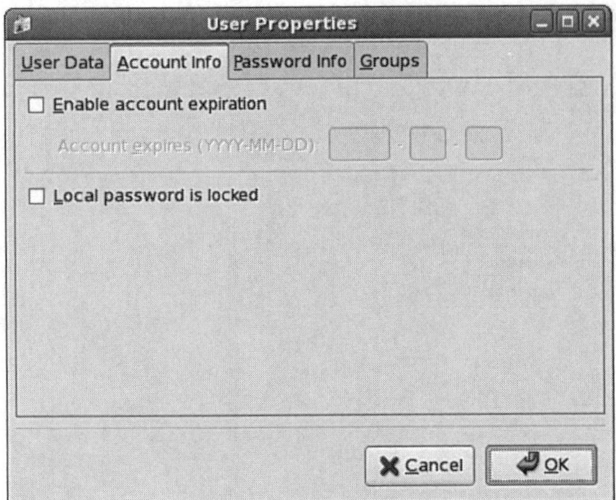

FIGURE 9.3 Modifying User Properties

Deleting Users

To delete a user, select her from the list and click **Delete**. When deleting a user, you have the option of deleting the user's home directory, mail spool, and temporary files. Changes take effect immediately, so clicking **Yes** will remove the user and the user's files. Any remaining files will still exist with the user's old UID, so be careful when creating new users. If the UID is reused for a different user, you might be giving the new user access to the old user's files because file permissions are based on the UID and GID associated with the file.

When using the graphical application, the private user group for the user is deleted when the user is deleted from the system. The user being deleted is also removed from any other groups of which it was a member.

Configuring via the Command Line

If you prefer the command line or do not have a graphical desktop installed on the system, the `shadow-utils` RPM package provides utilities to add, modify, and delete users from a shell prompt.

The commands discussed in this section require the administrator to be logged in as the root user. If you are logged in as a non-root user, execute the `su-` command from a shell prompt, and enter the root password to become the root user.

Adding Users

To add a new user, use the `useradd` command. The basic syntax is `useradd <username>`. The username is the only information required to add a new user; however, Table 9.1 shows additional command-line arguments for `useradd`. The `useradd` command creates the account, but the account is locked. To unlock the account and create a password for the user, use the command `passwd <username>`. By default, the user's home directory is created and the files from `/etc/skel/` are copied into it. The two exceptions are if the `-M` option is used and if the home directory already exists.

TABLE 9.1 Options for useradd

Command-Line Option	Description
-c <fullname>	Full name of the user (or a comment about the user). If more than one word is needed, place quotation marks around the value.
-d <directory>	Home directory for the user. The default value is /home/<username>/.
-e <date>	Date on which the user account will expire and be disabled. Use the format YYYY-MM-DD (default: never expire or disable).
-f <numdays>	Number of days after the password expires until the account will be disabled. 0 disables the account immediately after the password expires. -1 disables this feature (default: -1).
-g <group>	Default group for the user specified as a group name or group ID number. The group name or GID must already exist. The default is to create a private user group. If a private user group is not created, the default is the users group.
-G <group>	Comma-separated list of additional group names or GIDs to which the user will be a member. Groups must already exist.
-M	Do not create a home directory for the user. By default, a home directory is created unless this option is used or unless the directory already exists.
-m	Create a home directory for the user if it doesn't exist. Files from /etc/skel/ are copied into the home directory.
-n	Do not create a private user group for the user. By default, a private user group is created for the user.
-o	Allow the creation of a user with a UID that already exists for another user. By default, the UID must be unique.
-p <password>	Specify an encrypted password for the user as returned by the crypt utility. By default, the account is locked until the passwd command is used to set the user's password.
-r	Add the user as a system user with a UID below 500 and with a password that never expires. The user's home directory is not created unless the -m option is used. The default is UID 500 or higher for a non-system user.
-l	Do not add the user to the last login log file. The default is to add the user to the last login log file.
-s <shell>	Specify the user login shell for the user. The default shell if not specified is /bin/bash.
-u <uid>	Integer to use for the user ID. Must be unique unless -o is used. Values less than 500 are reserved for system users.

Modifying Users

The usermod command can also be used to modify options for an existing user with the usermod <options> <username> command. Most of the useradd options from Table 9.1 can be used with usermod. Table 9.2 lists additional usermod options.

TABLE 9.2 Additional Options for Modifying Users

Command-Line Option	Description
`-l <loginname>`	Change the user's username to `<loginname>`. You should consider changing the user's home directory and name of the user private group to reflect username change.
`-L`	Lock the user's password by placing the `!` character in front of it in `/etc/shadow` or `/etc/passwd`. User can no longer log in to the system with the old password.
`-U`	Unlock the user's password so the user can log in to the system again. Removes the `!` character in front of it in `/etc/shadow` or `/etc/passwd`.

Password Aging

Optionally, password aging can also be configured with the `chage` command. If the `chage` command is immediately followed by a username, the administrator will be interactively prompted for the password aging values as shown in Listing 9.1. The command-line options in Table 9.3 can also be used with `chage`.

TIP

To list current password aging values, use the `chage -l <username>` command.

LISTING 9.1 Interactive Password Aging Configuration

```
Changing the aging information for testuser
Enter the new value, or press ENTER for the default

        Minimum Password Age [0]:
        Maximum Password Age [99999]:
        Last Password Change (YYYY-MM-DD) [2006-02-12]:
        Password Expiration Warning [7]:
        Password Inactive [-1]:
        Account Expiration Date (YYYY-MM-DD) [1969-12-31]:
```

TABLE 9.3 Command-Line Options for Password Aging

Command-Line Option	Description
`-d <day>`	Number of days since January 1, 1970 when the password was changed or the date when the password was last changed in the format YYYY-MM-DD.
`-E <date>`	Number of days since January 1, 1970 on which the account will be locked or the date on which the account will be locked in the format YYYY-MM-DD.
`-I <days>`	Number of inactive days since the password has expired before the account is locked. `-1` disables this feature.

TABLE 9.3 Continued

Command-Line Option	Description
`-m <days>`	Minimum number of days between password changes. `0` allows user to change password as many times as he wants.
`-M <days>`	Maximum number of days between password changes, after which the user will be forced to change password before being allowed to log in again.
`-W <days>`	Number of days before password change is required to warn user of upcoming password expiration.

Deleting Users

The `userdel` command is available for deleting users using the `userdel <username>` syntax. If no command line options are used, the user is deleted and can no longer log into the system. The private user group for the user is also deleted, and the user is removed from any other groups of which he was a member. However, the user's home directory and any other files the user owned are not deleted from the system.

To remove the user's home directory and mail spool, use the `userdel -r <username>` command. All other files owned by the user must be deleted manually if the administrator needs them removed. However, use caution when removing files owned by a removed user, they might be shared files still needed by others in the group.

Managing Groups

As previously mentioned, a new group with the same name as the user is created by default when a new user is added. This new group is referred to as a private user group. Every user has a default group, which is usually the user's private user group, but every user can also be a member of more than one group. When a file or directory is created by a user, the user's default group becomes the group associated with the file unless the directory is configured to with the `s` option to `chmod` that sets the group ID of files in that directory upon creation. The additional groups a user is a member of allows the user to have access to files associated with the group and with the proper group file permissions.

A unique integer known as a GID is associated with each group. GIDs below 500 are reserved for system groups just like UIDs below 500 are reserved for system users.

To start the graphical application for managing users and groups, select **Administration, Users and Groups** from the **System** menu on the top panel of the desktop, or execute the command `system-config-users`. If the program is run as a non-root user, enter the root password when prompted. As shown in Figure 9.4, select the **Groups** tab to view all existing groups.

By default, system groups are not displayed in the list. To show system users in the list, select **Preferences, Filter system users and groups**.

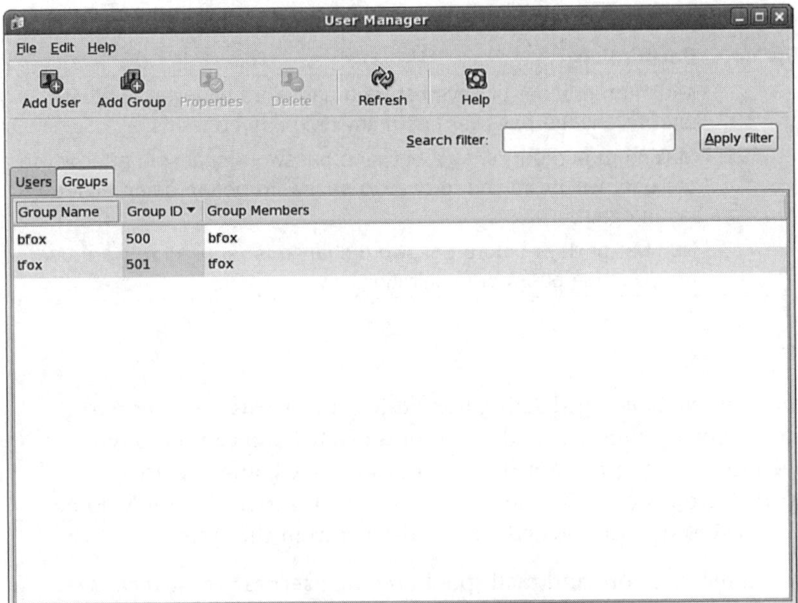

FIGURE 9.4 List of Existing Groups

Adding and Modifying Groups

To add a group, click Add Group to display the dialog box in Figure 9.5.

FIGURE 9.5 Adding a Group

In this dialog box, type the name of the new group. If the option to specify the GID is not selected, the next available GID above 500 is used. Click **OK** to add the group. The changes take place immediately, and the group is added to the list of existing groups in the main window.

To add a user to an existing group or change the name of the group, select him from the list on the **Groups** tab of the main application window, and click **Properties**. On the **Group Users** tab, select the users who should be members of the group, and click **OK** to enable the changes. The **Group Data** tab allows an administrator to change the name of the group. Once again, the changes take place immediately.

Deleting Groups

To delete a group, select it from the list on the **Groups** tab, and click the **Delete** button in the toolbar. Click **Yes** to confirm the deletion. The changes take place immediately, and the group is removed from the list of existing groups.

CAUTION

The application will not let you remove a group if it is the primary group for an existing user.

Configuring via the Command Line

If you prefer command-line configuration or just don't have the X Window System installed on the system, this section describes the command-line utilities that can be used to manage groups.

The commands discussed in this section must be executed by the root user.

Adding Groups

The `groupadd` command can be used to add user groups to the system. The basic syntax is `groupadd <groupname>`. If no command-line options are used, the group is created with the next available GID above 499. To specify a GID, use the `groupadd -g <gid> <groupname>` command. To add a system group, use the `groupadd -r <groupname>` command. The first available GID below 500 is used for the system group. To add a system group and specify the GID, use the `groupadd -r -g <gid> <groupname>` command. Even if you specify a GID for the system group, the GID still needs to be below 500 to follow the numbering convention.

To add users to a group, use the `usermod -G <groups> <username>` command as previously discussed in this chapter or the `gpasswd` command as discussed in the next section "Modifying Groups."

Modifying Groups

Other than adding users to the group, the name of the group and the GID of the group can be changed with the `groupmod` command. To change the GID of a group, use the `groupmod -g <gid> <groupname>` command. To change the name of the group, use the `groupmod -n <newname> <groupname>` command.

Red Hat Enterprise Linux also includes the `gpasswd` command for managing groups. It allows an administrator to configure group administrators, group members, and a group password. Group administrators can add and delete users as well as set, change, or remove the group password. A group can have more than one group administrator.

To add group administrators, use the `gpasswd -A <users> <groupname>` command, where `<users>` is a comma-separated list of existing users you want to be group administrators. Don't use any spaces between the commas.

The root user or a group administrator can add users to the group with the `gpasswd -a <user> <groupname>` command. Using this method, only one user can be added at a time. Similarly, to remove a user from a group, use the `gpasswd -d <user> <groupname>` command.

It is also possible for the root user (not a group administrator) to modify the members of a group with the `gpasswd -M <users> <groupname>` command, where `<users>` is a comma-separated list of *all* the users in the group. Notice the word *all*. When this command is executed, the group members list changes to the users listed in this command. Any existing members not listed will be removed.

To add or change the password for a group, the root user or a group administrator can use the `gpasswd <groupname>` command. When changing the password, the old password is not needed. To remove the group password, use the `gpasswd -r <groupname>` command.

If a user is a member of a group, she can use the `newgrp <groupname>` command to make that group her default group for that login session. If the group has a password, the user must enter the correct password before successfully switching groups. If the group has a password, users who aren't members of the group can also make the group their default group with the `newgrp` command. If the group doesn't have a password configured, only users who are members of the group can use the `newgrp` command to change groups for that login session. To disable the use of the `newgrp` command for a group, use the `gpasswd -R <groupname>` command.

Deleting Groups

To delete an existing group, use the `groupdel <groupname>` command. The group is removed, and the users in the group are no longer members of the group.

How It All Works

A list of all local users is stored in the `/etc/passwd` file. This file is in plain text format and is readable by anyone logged in to the system because it is referenced by user-accessible utilities such as `ls` and `who` to map user and group IDs to usernames and group names. Each user is listed on a separate line, with the following format:

```
username:password:uid:gid:real_name:/home/directory:shell
```

Table 9.4 describes these fields.

TABLE 9.4 `/etc/passwd` Fields

Field	Description
`username`	Login name for the user. Can't contain spaces or tabs.
`password`	The `x` character that denotes the encrypted password is stored in `/etc/shadow`. If shadow passwords are not used, this field contains the encrypted user password.
`uid`	Unique integer used as the user ID.
`gid`	Unique integer used as the group ID.
`real_name`	Full name of the user (not required).
`/home/directory`	Full path to the home directory of the user.
`shell`	Login shell for the user. `/bin/bash` is the default.

If shadow passwords are used (the default), the encrypted passwords are stored in the /etc/shadow file, readable only by root for security reasons. This file can also store optional password expiration data.

All user groups are stored in the /etc/group file, readable by everyone but only writable by root for the same reason /etc/passwd has these permissions—user utilities need to be able to map group IDs to group names. Each group is listed on a separate line in the following format:

```
groupname:password:gid:users
```

The group name is the actual name of the user group, the password field contains the x character if shadow passwords are used or the encrypted password if shadow passwords are not used. The gid is the unique group ID for the group, and the users field is a comma-delimited list of users in the group.

If shadow passwords are used for group passwords (the default), they are stored in /etc/gshadow, a file readable only by the root user.

When a new user is added, files from the /etc/skel/ directory are copied to the user's home directory unless the administrator chooses not to create one.

NOTE

By default, a home directory is created when a user is added. If the user's home directory already exists (for example, the /home/ directory was preserved during reinstallation), the files from /etc/skel/ are *not* copied to the existing home directory so that the existing files are not overwritten. This behavior has changed in recent versions of useradd, so use caution when performing this same operation on older versions of Red Hat Enterprise Linux.

The default values used when adding a user are stored in the /etc/default/useradd file. By default, it contains the values in Listing 9.2.

LISTING 9.2 Default Values When Adding a User

```
# useradd defaults file
GROUP=100
HOME=/home
INACTIVE=-1
EXPIRE=
SHELL=/bin/bash
SKEL=/etc/skel
CREATE_MAIL_SPOOL=no
```

These default values can be modified with the useradd -D <options> command. Available options for modifying default values are in Table 9.5.

TABLE 9.5 Options for Modifying Default Values When Adding a User

Command-Line Option	Directive	Default Value	Description
`-g <group>`	`GROUP`	`100`	Default group name or GID for the user if a user private group is not created for the user
`-d <directory>`	`HOME`	`/home`	Path prefix to use when creating the user's home directory unless the `-d` option is used to specify a different home directory
`-f <days>`	`INACTIVE`	`-1`	Number of days after the password expires before the account is disabled (`-1` disables the feature, `0` disables the account immediately after the password expires)
`-e <date>`	`EXPIRE`	Never expire	Date on which the user account is disabled
`-s <shell>`	`SHELL`	`/bin/bash`	Default shell to use when creating user accounts

Additional default values for creating users and groups are located in the `/etc/login.defs` file. This file is documented with comments above each directive, which should be easy to follow if modifications are needed. The following can be modified with options from this file:

- Mail spool directory
- Maximum number of days a password can be used
- Minimum number of days between password changes
- Minimum password length accepted
- Number of days to warn user before password expires
- Maximum UID for automatic selection by useradd
- Minimum UID for automatic selection by useradd
- Maximum GID for automatic selection by groupadd
- Minimum GID for automatic selection by groupadd
- Whether to remove cron and print jobs owned by user when user is removed
- Whether or not to create the home directory by default

Best Practices

Over time, every administrator develops her own method for managing users and groups from naming conventions to using subdirectories to divide users by departments to customized scripts for removing users who are no longer with the company. This section briefly describes a few practices to think about when developing your management style.

Managing Usernames

There are many username styles:

- First name of the user such as tammy
- First initial of the first name followed by the last name such as tfox
- Three-letter initials for the user such as tcf
- First name followed by a period followed by the last name such as tammy.fox
- First name followed by a period, followed by a middle initial, followed by the last name such as tammy.c.fox

When selecting a style to use, be sure to ask yourself if it is scalable. For a home computer, using the first name of each user might work because most members of a family don't have the same name. However, this method does not scale in a corporate environment that might have five to ten people named Joe. Using the first initial of the first name followed by the last name might work for a corporation as long as there is an alternative style if more than one person has the same username combination. For example, what do you do with a Joe Smith and a Jocelyn Smith? Unless they start at exactly the same time, the first one to join the company will have jsmith for a username. For the next person, consider using his middle initial as well or spelling out his first name if it is short. A similar concern exists for the three initial method—more than one employee might have the same three initials.

In the end, try to be consistent with the style you choose.

Managing Passwords

By default, a user account is enabled when the password is set with the `passwd` command, the password does not expire, and the account is never disabled due to lack of activity. Enterprise administrators are constantly considering the security implications of their procedures. Thus, consider forcing users to change their passwords on a regular basis such as every quarter to increase security. Also consider locking the account if the user does not change his password after it has expired.

Another good practice is educating users on why they should not give their passwords to anyone else and why they should not write it down anywhere others can find it. If users do not understand the security risks, they are less likely to keep their passwords secure.

When asking users to set or change their passwords, give them tips for selecting a good password such as the following:

- Use a combination of letters, numbers, and special characters to make it harder for someone to guess your password.
- Do not use obvious passwords such as any combination of your name or the name of a family member.
- Do not use your birthday or a family member's birthday.

- Do not use the date of a special occasion people know about such as your wedding date.
- Try using the first letter of each word in a catchy phrase you can easily remember so your password is not a dictionary word.
- Try replacing a few letters of a real word with numbers or special characters to help you remember it.

Consider posting these simple tips on the company's intranet so users can refer to them when changing their passwords.

Deleting Accounts

When an employee is terminated or quits the company, time is of the essence when it comes to disabling and deleting the user's account. As an administrator, you will develop a step-by-step process for systematically removing users if you haven't done so already. A few actions to consider include disabling the account as soon as you are told that the employee no longer works for the company. This can be done by simply adding the `!` character to the beginning of the password field for the user in `/etc/shadow`. The user can no longer log in, but all the user's data is still intact. This does not terminate any existing login sessions, so be sure to also determine whether the user is already logged in to any systems on the network and terminate those sessions.

After disabling the account, determine whether the files owned by the user such as files in the user's home directory and email need to be saved. If the answer is yes, be sure to back them up before removing the user account and the files associated with the user account such as the home directory, mail spool, and temporary files.

When removing files owned by the user, do not just search for them and delete them all from the system or a shared filesystem. If functional groups inside the organization have a shared directory setup, the former employee might have owned some of the files a group is using and still needs. If files of this type are found, be sure to assign the files to a new owner still in the functional group and verify that the permissions allow the group to continue working.

Also look for cron jobs set up by the user. Before deleting them, again, make sure they are not used by a group instead of the individual user. If any of them are for group use, the cron task will need to be set up with a different owner.

Structuring Home Directories

The `/home` directory, or whatever directory you have chosen to store users' home directories, can either be on the local filesystem or on a remote filesystem mounted by all necessary clients. In an enterprise environment, the remote filesystem is more likely because it is more scalable—one large storage system is easier to back up on a regular, automated basis, each client system has less to configure, users can log in to more than one system and have access to the same home directory, among other things.

If your company is quite large, you might also want to consider using subdirectories within `/home` to organize users by departments or groups. For example, `/home/eng/` can be used for all users within the engineering department and `/home/mktg/` can be used for users within the marketing department. This can also help the administrator keep track of disk quotas for each department if necessary or determine which department has the most storage needs.

Summary

This chapter explains the many tools included with Red Hat Enterprise Linux to successfully manage users and groups. As you have read, it is much more than just adding and removing them when employees within the company come and go. If the company is large, it might be necessary to document a process for managing users and groups such as a naming convention for usernames or structure of home directories.

CHAPTER 10

Techniques for Backup and Recovery

IN THIS CHAPTER

- Writing a Backup Plan
- Using Amanda for Backups
- Other Linux Backup Utilities
- Recovery and Repair

When hardware components or security measures fail, every administrator must be prepared to recover a system as quickly and efficiently as possible. Preparing for a disaster means having a solid backup procedure and a well-tested recovery process.

Because you can't always detect when a failure will occur, it is important to create backups on a regular basis depending on how often the data changes and how much time it takes to complete the backup. All the files on the system don't have to be included in every backup. Consider how often the files change. For example, operating system files such as files in `/bin/` and "virtual" files in `/proc/` and `/dev/` do not need to be backed up because they can easily be reinstalled; this also ensures they have not be compromised if you are restoring after a security breach.

For home directories that constantly change, daily or even hourly backups might be necessary. For the payroll database or LDAP server, weekly backups might be sufficient. Ultimately, it is up to the system administrator or the system administration team to decide. Each organization has a different set of systems, custom configurations, and a required length of time in which the system must be restored.

TIP

Remember to test your recovery plan *before* a system recovery is needed. Finding out that your backups do not include all the files necessary for a successful recovery while you are recovering can cause more downtime than anticipated, which can mean even more loss of data, poor customer service, or a significant loss of revenue.

This chapter provides you with concepts to consider when creating a custom backup and recovery process as well as Linux tools that can be used for backup and recovery.

Writing a Backup Plan

The backup plan you write and commit to will be specialized to your needs, your company's resources, the number of systems to back up, the operating systems running on those systems, and much more. You will probably go through many versions of your plan before finalizing it. This section provides a few concepts to think about when deciding what data to back up and whether to perform incremental or full backups.

> **TIP**
>
> If your systems are subscribed to the Provisioning module of Red Hat Network (not included with your Red Hat Enterprise Linux subscription), you can use Red Hat Network to assist with configuration management.

What Data to Back Up

Deciding what data to back up is nontrivial and might vary for each system. Here is a list of data to consider:

- Home directories
- Email spools and IMAP directories
- `/etc/` directory for various configuration files
- Shared directories
- Database files
- Cron scripts
- Content management directories such as CVS or Subversion

Other thoughts to consider when devising a backup plan:

- Does your backup plan include backups on an offsite server in case of natural disaster or physical damage to the office building or server room?
- Is redundant hardware part of your plan in case of unrecoverable hardware failure?
- Is the total recovery time from backup acceptable for the needs of the company?
- Are you alerted when a system failure occurs?
- Are you alerted when a failure occurs during the backup procedure?
- What is the initial cost of equipment and software?
- What is the total annual cost of the backup media? Does it fit in your allotted budget?
- Does the plan scale if additional systems need to be added?

- Do multiple administrators have the knowledge to recover each system in case of personnel changes or vacation times?
- Are the processes well-documented so they can be easily accessed and reviewed on a regular basis?

Incremental versus Full Backups

If your organization is large or modifies the same subset of data frequently, you might want to consider *incremental backups*. You start off with a full backup and then only back up the data that has changed since the last backup. This often saves disk space on the backup servers and shortens the time it takes to perform backups.

Even if you implement incremental backups, it is a good idea to perform a full backup less frequently (for example, every one or two months if the incremental backups are performed weekly). Each time you perform a full backup, the subsequent incremental backups are based on the last full backup. When you do have to recover the system, the restoration process begins with the last full backup and then all the incremental backups are applied. The time it takes to recover will depend on how many incremental backups you must apply.

Using Amanda for Backups

Red Hat Enterprise Linux includes AMANDA, or the Advanced Maryland Automatic Network Disk Archiver, for assisting in backups. AMANDA works by setting up a master backup server on the network and backing up systems running different versions of UNIX (using `tar` or `dump`) and Microsoft Windows (using SAMBA) to tape or hard disk. This section covers setting up the server and clients on Red Hat Enterprise Linux. Refer to www.amanda.org for setup instructions for other operating systems.

NOTE

Extensive documentation is available on www.amanda.org. This section provides enough information to get you started. Refer to the website for more details.

CAUTION

The `tar` and `dump` utilities do not preserve access control lists (ACLs) associated with files. Refer to Chapter 7, "Managing Storage" for details on ACLs.

10

Setting up the Amanda Server

Backups done by Amanda are done in parallel to holding discs on the hard drives, and the data is then written to the tape or backup media. Software or hardware compression can be used, with hardware compression using fewer CPU resources.

The Amanda backup server must have the tape drive or other backup media attached to it. It must also have the `amanda-server` RPM package installed. Refer to Chapter 3, "Operating System Updates," for details on package installation.

The server configuration files for Amanda are installed in the `/etc/amanda/` directory. The `/etc/amanda/DailySet1/` directory contains two files: `amanda.conf` and `disklist`. The `DailySet1` directory name is the default configuration name and can be changed as long as the file permissions and ownership remains the same for the directory and the configuration files in it. Create a new directory with a unique name for each configuration, and then copy the default configuration files from the `DailySet1/` directory into it. The default configuration files are just examples and must be modified to work properly.

The `disklist` file is used to define the clients to be backed up and is discussed in the section "Setting Up the Amanda Clients" later in this chapter.

The `amanda.conf` file is the main configuration file for the Amanda server and contains server configuration parameters. Read the brief descriptions of each parameter in the example file and refer to the `amanda.conf` man page for more details. Table 10.1 describes some of the most common parameters.

CAUTION

The default `amanda.conf` uses the directories in `/usr/adm/amanda/` for many default values. The `/etc/amanda/` directory is used instead of this directory in Red Hat Enterprise Linux. Any values with `/usr/adm/amanda/` should be modified.

TABLE 10.1 Common Amanda Configuration Parameters

Parameter	Description
`org`	Descriptive name of the configuration. Used in the subject of emails generated for this configuration. Each configuration should have a unique org name.
`mailto`	Email addresses of all the administrators who should receive reports from this configuration. Separate each email address by a space.
`dumpcycle`	Number of days between full backups.
`runspercycle`	Number of runs per cycle, with the cycle defined by `dumpcycle`.
`netusage`	Maximum amount of network bandwidth that can be used by Amanda.
`maxdumps`	Maximum number of backups Amanda will attempt to run at the same time.
`logdir`	Directory to write logs. Directory from default value in `amanda.conf` does not exist. Change to existing `/var/log/amanda` directory or another existing directory.

Saving to Tape

If using a tape drive, be sure to use a non-rewinding tape drive that does not automatically rewind when closed. Amanda uses a new tape for each run and can not be configured to append a second run to a tape.

Table 10.2 contains common parameters that can be used to customize the tape drive settings. Refer to the `amanda.conf` man page for a full list of parameters for configuring a tape drive.

TABLE 10.2 Tape Drive Parameters for Amanda

Parameter	Description
`tapedev`	Path to the tape device to use. Must be a non-rewinding tape device.
`tapetype`	Type of tapes to be used. Must be set to a `tapetype` definition from `amanda.conf`.
`tapelist`	Filename for the `tapelist` file. Maintained by Amanda and should not be modified.
`tapebufs`	Number of buffers used by the backup process to hold data before it is written to tape. Buffer is in the shared memory region.
`tapecycle`	Size of the tape rotation. Must be larger than the number of tapes it takes for a full backup.
`runtapes`	Maximum number of tapes to be used for a single backup run. If this number is larger than one, a tape changer must be configured with the `tpchanger` parameter.

Saving to Other Media

Amanda was originally written to be used with a tape device, but it can be configured to back up to other media such as a set of hard drives. To configure Amanda to back up to a media type other than a tape, the parameters in Listing 10.1 must be set.

LISTING 10.1 Using the Hard Drive as a Virtual Tape

```
tpchanger chg-disk
tapedev "file:/backups/DailySet1"
tapetype HD
define tapetype HD {
    comment "use hard drive as tape"
    length 2048 mbytes
}
```

The `tpchanger` specifies which script to use to change the virtual tape device. Several scripts are provided in `/usr/lib/amanda/` by the `amanda-server` RPM package. The `chg-disk` script is recommended when using the hard drive as a virtual tape.

Set the `tapedev` parameter in `amanda.conf` to use the `file` driver with the name of an *existing* directory to store backups. In Listing 10.1, the `/backups/DailySet1/` directory is used. This directory must be created and configured as a virtual tape before running `amdump` to generate backups, and the directory and all the files in it must be owned by the amanda user so `amdump` has permission to write to it. Use the following steps as the root user to create the virtual tape (assuming `/backups/DailySet1/` is being configured as the virtual tape):

10

1. Create the directory being used to emulate the tape device:

```
mkdir /backups
mkdir /backups/DailySet1
```

2. Create an empty file named `info` in the virtual tape device directory:

```
touch /backups/DailySet1/info
```

3. Create an empty file to represent the tape list:

```
touch /etc/amanda/DailySet1/tapelist
```

4. Create a directory for each virtual tape (where `X` starts with `1` and increases by 1 for each tape):

```
mkdir /backups/DailySet1/slotX
```

5. "Load" the first virtual tape so the backups will start with it:

```
ln -s /backups/DailySet1/slot1 /backups/DailySet1/data
```

6. Make sure the amanda user owns all the files:

```
chown -R amanda.disk /backups
```

7. Become the amanda user:

```
su amanda
```

8. Label each virtual tape with the naming convention set by the `labelstr` parameter in `amanda.conf` (where `X` starts with `1` and increases by 1 for each tape):

```
amlabel DailySet1 DailySet1-0X slot X
```

9. Test the virtual tape setup:

```
amcheck DailySet1
```

10. If errors occur, fix them and rerun `amcheck`. Repeat until no errors exist.
11. Exit back to root shell instead of being the amanda user:

```
exit
```

A `tapetype` definition for the hard drive must also be specified as shown in Listing 10.1. The length is the maximum amount of disk space to be used by Amanda to emulate the tape device. In Listing 10.1, 2,048 megabytes is listed to give Amanda 2 gigabytes of space for backups. Also set the `tapetype` parameter in `amanda.conf` to the name of this `tapetype` definition.

Setting Up Holding Disks

If holding disks are used, backups are written to the holding disks and then flushed to the tapes, reducing total dump time and the wear on the tape and drive. Dumps from more than one system can only be done in parallel if a holding disk is used.

Holding disks are defined in the `amanda.conf` file, and one or more holding disks can be defined. The holding disc on the tape server should be large enough to hold the two largest backups simultaneously, if possible. The holding disk should also be dedicated to backups. If a dump is too big for the holding disk, the backup is written directly to tape.

TIP

If the backup server crashes or a tape fails during backup, the `amflush` utility can be used to write data from the holding disk to tape.

For example, Listing 10.2 defines the `/dumps/DailySet1` as a holding disk directory. The directory must already exist and must be owned by the amanda user because `amdump` is run as the amanda user. After creating the directory as root, change the ownership with the following command:

```
chown amanda.disk /dumps/DailySet1
```

LISTING 10.2 Holding Disk Definition

```
holdingdisk hd1 {
    comment "first holding disk"
    directory "/dumps/DailySet1"
    use -200 Mb
    chunksize 1Gb
    }
```

The `use` parameter specifies the amount of size that can be used by Amanda. If the value is a negative number as in Listing 10.2, Amanda uses all available space except for the value specified. To split large dumps into multiple files, specify the maximum file size for each chunk with the `chunksize` parameter, whose value must end in `Kb`, `Mb`, `Gb`, or `Tb`. The maximum value of `chunksize` is the maximum file size the kernel can allow minus 1 megabyte.

Setting Up the Amanda Clients

This section discusses the configuration of a Red Hat Enterprise Linux Amanda client. To configure clients of a different operating system, refer to www.amanda.org. Each client must have the `amanda-client` RPM package installed. Refer to Chapter 3 for details on installing software.

Before configuring the clients, decide the following for each client:

- Which files and directories to back up
- Whether to use dump or GNU tar to create backups

- Whether to use compression (GNU zip) or no compression
- If compression is used, whether to compress the files on the client or server
- Priority level if all backups can't be performed

All of these options and more are configured in user-defined *dumptypes* in the `amanda.conf` file on the backup server. There are some predefined dumptypes in the example `amanda.conf` file to use as a reference. Each dumptype is given a unique name and can optionally be based on a different dumptype. To base a dumptype on one already defined, list the name of the existing dumptype as the first parameter of the definition. A parameter can be redefined in the new dumptype, overriding the value in the original dumptype for clients using the new dumptype. For example, Listing 10.3 shows an example dumptype named `tar-compress`. It includes the parameters from the `global` dumptype definition and adds archiving with `tar` and `fast` compression on the client.

LISTING 10.3 Example Dumptype

```
define dumptype tar-compress {
    global
    program "GNUTAR"
    comment "tar and compressed"
    compress client fast
}
```

The possible dumptype parameters are listed in Table 10.3.

TABLE 10.3 Dumptype Parameters

Dumptype Parameters	Description
`auth`	Authentication scheme between server and client. Either `bsd` or `krb4`, with `bsd` being the default.
`comment`	Short description.
`comprate`	Compression rate specified as two numbers separated by commas. The first number is the full compression rate, and the second number is the incremental rate.

`compress`	Whether or not to compress the files. If compression is used, decide whether to compress on the client or server and whether the best compression (and probably slowest) or fast compression should be used. Possible values:
	`none`
	`client best`
	`client fast`
	`server best`
	`server fast`

`dumpcycle`	Number of days between full backups.

TABLE 10.3 Continued

Dumptype Parameters	Description
estimate	How Amanda determines estimates: client: use defined dumping program on client (from program parameter), which is the most accurate, but might take the longest calcsize: faster than client, but might be less accurate server: use statistics from previous run, which is not very accurate if disk usage changes from day to day
exclude	If GNU tar is used, lists files and directories to exclude from backup run.
holdingdisk	Whether or not to use the holding disk. Possible values: yes or no
ignore	Don't back up this filesystem.
index	Create an index of files backed up.
kencrypt	Encrypt the data sent between the server and client.
maxdumps	Maximum number of dumps to run at the same time.
maxpromoteday	Maximum number of days for a promotion. Set to 0 for no promotion. Set to 1 or 2 if the disk is overpromoted.
priority	Priority level used if there is no tape to write to. Backups are performed until holding disks are full, using the priority to determine which filesystems to back up first. Possible values: low, medium, high.
program	Whether to use dump or tar.
record	Record backup in time-stamp-database (/etc/dumpdates for dump and /var/lib/amanda/gnutar-lists/ directory for GNU tar).
skip-full	Skip the disk when a level 0 is due.
skip-incr	Skip the disk when a level 0 is not due.
starttime	Amount of time to delay the start of the dump.
strategy	Dump strategy from one of the following: standard: Default strategy nofull: Level 1 dumps every time skip: Skip all dumps incronly: Incremental backups only

After defining dumptypes, define the clients to be backed up in the /etc/amanda/<configname>/disklist (/etc/amanda/DailySet1/disklist in our example) file on the Amanda server, one client on each line in the following format:

```
<hostname> <area> <dumptype>
```

Replace <hostname> with the hostname or IP address of the client. If a hostname is used, the server must be able to resolve it to an IP address. Replace <area> with a disk name such as sda, a device name such as /dev/sda, or a logical name such as /etc to back up. Replace <dumptype> with a dumptype name as defined in amanda.conf on the server.

To allow the Amanda server access to the client, use the .amandahosts file in the home directory of the amanda user on each client, even if the client is also the server. The home directory of the amanda user on the client is set to /var/lib/amanda/, and the file /var/lib/amanda/.amandahosts already exists with localhost and localhost.localdomain already configured as possible Amanda servers. List each Amanda server on separate lines in the following format:

```
<hostname> amanda
```

where <hostname> is the hostname or IP address of the Amanda server. If using a hostname, the client must be able to resolve it to an IP address. The username amanda follows the hostname to list the username under which the backups are done. This corresponds the dumpuser value in amanda.conf on the server.

Finally, the amanda xinetd service must be started on clients. Configure it to start automatically at boot time with the chkconfig amanda on command as root. Because it is an xinetd service instead of a standalone daemon, make sure it is also enabled at boot time with the chkconfig xinetd on command as root. Restart xinetd with the service xinetd restart command at root to enable Amanda immediately. If you are not already using xinetd, be sure the other xinetd services are disabled if you do not want them to be turned on, and then start xinetd with the service xinetd start command.

Executing the Backup

To start the backup process immediately, use the following command on the Amanda server, replacing DailySet1 with the name of your configuration:

```
su amanda -c "amdump DailySet1"
```

This command can be used to immediately start a dump for testing or to create the first set of backups. After that, cron can be configured to run the backups at the desired intervals.

The su amanda part of the command is used to run the process as the amanda user. If you are the root user when you execute this command, you will not be prompted for amanda user's password. If you are a non-root user, you will be prompted for the amanda user's password. However, a password was not created when the amanda user was added. If you want the amanda user to have a password, execute the passwd amanda command as root to set it.

The amanda-server package installs a sample cron task file at /etc/amanda/crontab.sample, which contains the following:

```
# This is an example for a crontab entry for automated backup with amanda
# With these cron lines, Amanda will check that the correct tape is in
# the drive every weekday afternoon at 4pm (if it isn't, all the
# operators will get mail).  At 12:45am that night the dumps will be run.
#
# This should be put in user operator's crontab
#
0 16 * * 1-5    /usr/sbin/amcheck -m DailySet1
45 0 * * 2-6    /usr/sbin/amdump DailySet1
```

As you can see from the example file, the `amcheck` utility runs a self-check, and the `-m` argument causes any errors to be emailed to all the administrators listed in `amanda.conf`. The `amdump` utility starts the actual backup process. Create a similar cron task on your Amanda server. The `amdump` command must be run by the amanda user, so be sure to add the cron task to the list of jobs for the amanda user. For details on configuring a cron task, refer to Chapter 11, "Automating Tasks with Scripts."

Table 10.4 contains brief descriptions of the Amanda utilities that can be used on the Amanda server.

TABLE 10.4 Amanda Server Utilities

Server Utility	Description
`amdump`	Usually used in scripts to start the backup process on all configured clients. Email is sent upon completion, reporting successes and failures.
`amcheck`	Run before `amdump` to verify the correct tape is mounted and client filesystems are ready.
`amcheckdb`	Check that each tape in the Amanda database is listed in the `tapelist` file.
`amcleanup`	If `amdump` fails before completion, use this command to clean up.
`amdd`	Amanda version of `dd`. Use for full restore if the standard `dd` program is not available.
`ammt`	Amanda version of `mt`. Use for full restore if the standard `mt` program is not available.
`amadmin`	Interactive command to perform admin tasks such as forcing a full backup, checking backup status of clients, and determining which tape will be used for the next backup run.
`amflush`	Write files from holding disk to tape or backup media. Use if a tape failure occurs and after fixing the problem with the tape device.
`amgetconf`	Look up the value of an Amanda parameter.
`amlabel`	Label tapes to use with Amanda. Tapes must be labeled before Amanda can use them. Must use label naming convention defined by `labelstr` in `amanda.conf`.
`amoverview`	Display list of hosts and filesystems backed up, along with their backup schedule.
`amplot`	Produce a graph, using `gnuplot`, to show Amanda performance. Can be used to determine if performance can be improved with different settings.
`amreport`	Email a statistics report for an Amanda run to the administrator.
`amrmtape`	Delete a tape from the backup rotation.
`amstatus`	Determine status of previous or running backup run.
`amtoc`	Produce a TOC for a backup run. Usually run after `amdump` in cron script.
`amverify`	Check all tapes for errors.
amverifyrun	Check the tapes used by the last run for errors.
`amtape`	Perform tape changer tasks such as resetting, ejecting, and cleaning.
`amtapetype`	Create a tapetype definition for use in `amanda.conf`.

Restoring from Backup

Now that you have learned how to perform backups with Amanda, the next step is to learn about restoring from backup. Remember to test the restore process before a system failure occurs.

There are two utilities for restoring with Amanda: `amrestore` and `amrecover`. The `amrestore` utility can be used to restore entire images from the backup server; `amrecover` is an interactive command run on the client and used to recover specific files.

Using `amrestore`

Before using `amrestore`, determine which tape has the image you want to restore using either `amadmin` or `amtoc`. Make sure the tape is mounted on the server before restoring an image. To retrieve all images for the host named wudan, use the following command:

```
amrestore <tape-device> wudan
```

Refer to the man page for `amrestore` with the `man amrestore` for additional options.

Using `amrecover`

To use `amrecover`, the `index` parameter must be set to `yes` for the dumptype defined in `amanda.conf` and set for the client in the `disklist` file. Because the root user on the client must run `amrecover`, be sure the root user is allowed as a remote user on the client in the `.amandahosts` file on the server.

To start `amrecover`, log in as root on the client, start a shell prompt, change to the directory that should contain the file or files you want to restore, and type the `amrecover <configname>` command such as `amrecover DailySet1`. If connection is successful, you will receive the `amrecover>` prompt.

The default restore date is set to the current day. Use the `setdate` command to change the date from which you want to restore files, use the `cd` command to change directories to find the files on the server, and use the `ls` command to list files in the current directory on the server. After finding the file to recover, use the `add <command>` command to add the file to the list of files to recover, and use the `extract` command to retrieve the file. Refer to the man page with the `man amrecover` command for a full list of possible commands.

Other Linux Backup Utilities

If you write your own custom scripts or software for performing backups, many Linux utilities can be used including `tar` and `rsync`. Use this section to learn more about them and determine if they can be useful for you.

The `tar` Utility

When backing up data that is no longer being used or data that is not frequently changed, consider creating a compressed archive file using the `tar` archive utility in combination with one of the compression tools such as `gzip` or `bzip2`. Creating a compressed archive file results in one file that must be decompressed and unarchived before files can be restored from it. The compression of the files saves room on the backup media. To use `tar`, the `tar` RPM package must be installed. It should be installed on your system unless you chose to only install a specific set of packages.

CAUTION

The `tar` utility does not preserve access control lists.

To archive a set of files and compress it with `bzip2`:

```
tar cjvf <filename>.tar.bz <files>
```

The `tar` arguments used are as follows:

- `c`: create the archive
- `j`: use bzip2 compression
- `v`: be verbose and show the progress
- `f`: files to archive will follow

A filename for the compressed archive must be given. Try to be as descriptive yet brief as possible. The commonly used extension for a tar file compressed with `bzip2` is `.tar.bz`.

For `<files>`, multiple files and directories can be specified. If a directory is specified, all the files and subdirectories are archives as well by default.

To uncompress and unarchive a tar file compressed with `bzip2`:

```
tar xjvf <filename>.tar.bz
```

When the files are unarchived, the original directory structure is retained. For example, if you specified the directory `templates/` as the files to be archived, when the tar file is unarchived, the directory `templates/` is created in the current working directory, and all the original files in the directory are written in the newly created directory.

File ownership is also retained by UID and GID. Keep in mind that if a tar file is created on one system and then unarchived on a different system, the file ownership might change if the UID or GID is mapped to a different user or group on the second system.

To list the contents of the file without uncompressing or unarchiving it:

```
tar tjvf <filename>.tar.bz
```

10

The `rsync` Utility

When developing backup scripts, consider using the `rsync` utility. The `rsync` utility allows you to copy from the local system to a remote system or copy between two local directories. If the files exist in the destination directory, `rsync` only transfers the differences in the files, which is ideal for backups. The `rsync` RPM package is required and should already be installed on your system.

After the `rsync` command-line arguments are listed, the first directory listed is the source, and the second directory listed is the destination. If either directory is preceded by a hostname and a colon (`:`), the directory is a remote directory. For example, to transfer all home directories to the `backup/` directory on the remote server `backup.example.com`:

```
rsync -avz /home backup.example.com:backups/
```

The `-a` argument stands for "archive" mode, meaning that `rsync` performs a recursive transfer (the source directory, its subdirectories, the subdirectories of the subdirectories, and so on are transferred), symbolic links are preserved, permissions and time stamps are preserved, groups are preserved, file ownership is preserved if it is root, and devices are preserved if they are owned by root. If the `-v` argument is used, progress messages are displayed including how much data is sent and received and the average transfer rate. Using the `-z` argument compresses the data to be transferred, speeding up the time it takes to transfer the files or the file differences.

When transferring files with `rsync`, whether or not a trailing slash is included on the source directory is important. In our example, a trailing slash is not used on the source directory so that the directory `backups/home/` is created on the remote server and all the files in the `/home/` directory on the local system are recursively copied into `backups/home/` on the remote server. If a trailing slash is specified on the source directory such as the following:

```
rsync -avz /etc/sysconfig/ backup.example.com:backups/configfiles/
```

The source directory specified is *not* created in the destination directory. In our example, all the files in `/etc/sysconfig/` on the local system are recursively copied into the `backups/configfiles/` directory on the remote server.

TIP

Consider using `rsync` in a custom shell script or as a cron task to schedule backups. Refer to Chapter 11 for details.

For more information on `rsync`, including how to use the `rsync` daemon for transfers, refer to the manual page by using the `man rsync` command at a shell prompt.

Recovery and Repair

To analyze or repair a system failure, you might need to boot into the system. But, what if the boot loader is corrupt or what if the filesystem can't be mounted anymore? Red Hat Enterprise Linux includes alternative boot methods for system repair: *rescue mode*, *single-user mode*, and *emergency mode*.

After booted into one of these modes, a set of commonly used editors such as Emacs and Vi are available along with commonly used utilities such as `e2fsck` for repairing a filesystem and `grub-install` for repairing the boot loader on an x86 or x86_64 system.

Rescue Mode

Rescue mode allows the administrator to bypass the boot loader by instead booting off an installation media. Possible reasons to use rescue mode include

- Corrupt boot loader that needs repair
- Corrupt filesystem that can not be mounted and needs repair

To start rescue mode, boot from the first Red Hat Enterprise Linux installation CD. After booting off the CD, the command used to enter rescue mode differs by architecture. Refer to Table 10.5 for the command for your architecture.

TABLE 10.5 Booting into Rescue Mode per Architecture

Architecture	Rescue Mode Command
x86, x86_64	Type `linux rescue` at GRUB prompt
Intel Itanium	Type elilo linux rescue at EILO prompt
IBM POWER (IBM eServer iSeries, IBM eServer pSeries)	Append `rescue` after kernel name at YABOOT prompt
IBM System z	Add `rescue` to the CMS conf parameter file

After booting into rescue mode, select the language and keyboard layout to use during rescue mode. Next, decide whether to start the network. If the system has been compromised, you probably don't want to start a network connection in case a program that sends data to another system over the network has been added to the system. If you need to copy data to another system to save it before reinstalling or copying files to the system to repair it, you will need to start the network.

The next question is whether or not to try and mount the Linux filesystem. You can select to skip this step, mount the filesystem, or mount the filesystem read-only. If you are not sure whether the filesystem can be mounted, you can select to mount it. If it can't be mounted, a message is displayed, and you are allowed to go back and select to skip mounting the filesystem. If the filesystem is successfully mounted, it is mounted under the `/mnt/sysimage/` directory. If you need to execute a command from the installed system, remember the path to the command should be prepended with `/mnt/sysimage/`.

A shell prompt is displayed next. Use this shell to repair your system. Type `exit` to exit rescue mode and reboot the system.

Alternatively, you can boot from a disk created from the `boot.iso` image found in the `images/` directory of the first installation CD and then use the command from Table 10.5. After selecting the language and keyboard, select the location of the rescue image. Choose from the CD-ROM drive, hard drive, NFS, FTP, or HTTP. The location specified must contain the installation source files for the same version of Red Hat Enterprise Linux as the `boot.iso` you used to create the boot media. Refer to Chapter 1, "Installing Red Hat Enterprise Linux," for details on setting up the installation source.

TIP

If using NFS, FTP, or HTTP, remember to allow the system being booted into rescue mode access to the directory containing the installation files.

If you select NFS, FTP, or HTTP, a network connection will be established, if possible, before continuing. If the location does not require a network connection, rescue mode optionally allows the administrator to start a network connection. After choosing whether to start the network, select whether to mount the filesystem. As with using rescue mode from the installation CD or DVD, use the shell to repair the system, and type `exit` to reboot the system when finished.

Single-User Mode

Single-user mode is equivalent to runlevel 1 on the system. If runlevel 1 is not configured properly, you will not be able to boot into single-user mode. Rescue mode requires a boot media, but single-user mode is specified as a kernel option using the installed boot loader and does not require additional boot media. However, it does require that the boot loader is working properly and that the filesystem be mounted. It does not provide the ability to start a network connection.

Possible reasons to use single-user mode include

- Forgot root password
- Repair runlevel other than runlevel 1

To boot into single-user mode, boot the system with the `single` kernel parameter. Specifying a boot parameter differs from architecture to architecture. Refer to Table 10.6 to determine the correct method for your architecture.

TABLE 10.6 Booting into Single-User Mode per Architecture

Architecture	Single-User Mode Command
x86, x86_64	Press any key at the `Booting Red Hat Enterprise Linux (<kernel-version>)` message to view the GRUB menu. Press the `E` key to edit the currently selected boot line. Append the line with the word `single`, and press `B` to boot the system.
Intel Itanium	At the EFI shell prompt, type `elilo linux single`.
IBM POWER (IBM eServer iSeries, IBM eServer pSeries)	Append a space and the number 1 after the kernel name at YABOOT prompt.
IBM System z	Create another boot stanza in `/etc/zipl.conf` identical to the default stanza except append a space and the number 1 at the end of the parameters. Refer to Chapter 2, "Post-Installation Configuration," for a sample `/etc/zipl.conf` file. Be sure to run the `/sbin/zipl` command as root to enable the change.

Once in single-user mode, your filesystems are mounted, so any installed applications should be available. Use the `exit` command to exit single-user mode and reboot the system.

Emergency Mode

Emergency mode is similar to single-user mode except the root filesystem is mounted read-only and runlevel 1 is not used. Boot into emergency mode using the same method as single-user mode except replace the word `single` with `emergency` in the boot method. Because the filesystem is mounted read-only, files can not be changed or repaired, but files can be retrieved off the system.

Filesystem Repair

If one or more filesystems are corrupt, boot into rescue mode and do not mount the filesystem. Even if you can boot into single-user mode, do not use it because the filesystem can not be repaired if it is mounted.

The `e2fsck` utility can be used to check and repair an ext2 or ext3 (default for Red Hat Enterprise Linux) filesystem. It must be run as root, and the filesystem being checked should *not* be mounted. The basic syntax is as follows:

```
e2fsck <device>
```

where `<device>` is the device filename for the filesystem such as `/dev/hda1` for the first partition on the first IDE drive or `/dev/sda2` for the second partition on the first SCSI drive. As the utility finds errors such as bad inodes, it prompts the administrator to confirm the fix. To automatically answer yes to all questions and cause the utility to be non-interactive (for example, you want to call it from a non-interactive script), use the `-y` command-line argument. To print verbose information while the filesystem check and repair is occurring, use the `-v` command-line argument. Additional arguments can be found in the `e2fsck` man page called from the `man e2fsck` command.

Boot Loader Repair

If your system does not display the GRUB interface when booting, if GRUB won't boot into Red Hat Enterprise Linux properly, or if you have another problem with the GRUB boot loader on an x86 or x86_64 system, try booting into rescue mode and reinstalling GRUB with the following command:

```
grub-install --root-directory=/boot '<device-name>'
```


The `--root-directory=/boot` option specifies that the GRUB images should be installed in the `/boot` directory. Replace `<device-name>` with the device name on which to install the GRUB images. The device name can be either the GRUB device name such as `hd0` or `sd0` or the system device name such as `/dev/hda` or `/dev/sda`. For example, for the GRUB device named `sd0`, the command would be

```
grub-install --root-directory=/boot '(sd0)'
```

Summary

This chapter has started you on the right path toward developing a backup and recovery plan for your Red Hat Enterprise Linux systems. Either use a program such as Amanda or a third-party backup program or write your own custom scripts. As your company and number of users expand, be sure to test your plan to ensure it can scale properly.

CHAPTER 11
Automating Tasks with Scripts

IN THIS CHAPTER

When an administrator has to perform the same task on hundreds, possibly thousands, of systems, automating everyday maintenance and deployment operations is a necessity. Red Hat Network allows Red Hat Enterprise Linux administrators to schedule package updates, package installations, operating system installations, and more, but what about other tasks such as monitoring disk space, performing backups, and removing users?

This chapter explains how to automate these tasks and others like it as scripts. It also gives step-by-step instructions for scheduling the execution of the scripts using the cron daemon.

Red Hat Enterprise Linux offers a multitude of options for the scripting language, each with its strengths and weaknesses. This chapter focuses on Bash because it is the most commonly used for system administration tasks, and it also gives an overview of other popular languages.

Writing Scripts with Bash

The GNU Bourne Again Shell (Bash) scripting language is useful when trying to automate a sequence of commands or when you want to execute the same command over and over again until a certain limit is reached.

Because the default shell in Red Hat Enterprise Linux is Bash, the `bash` RPM package is most likely already installed on your system. You might also want to check out the many commands from the `coreutils` and the `util-linux` packages such as `rename` to rename a group of files and `basename` to return the basename of a file without its extension.

CAUTION

When writing a Bash script, use a text editor such as Vi, Emacs, or gEdit (select **Accessories**, **Text Editor** from the **Applications** menu). Using a more complex word processing application such as OpenOffice.org Writer is not recommended because it automatically wraps lines or tries to correct capitalization and spelling of words. Because spacing and end-of-line characters are used in Bash to form structures such as loops, the built-in formatting of a word processor can cause syntax errors in Bash scripts.

All Bash scripts must start with a line that defines it as a Bash script:

```
#!/bin/bash
```

Any other lines that begin with the hash mark (#) are considered comments and are not processed as lines of code. For example, you can add a small description of what the program does, the author, when it was last modified, and a version number to the top of the script:

```
#!/bin/bash
# This program creates daily backups for Company Name
# For internal use only
# Author: Your Name Here
# Last modified: May 15, 2006
# Version: 1.5
```

TIP

For a complete Bash reference, refer to the "Bash Reference Manual" at http://www.gnu.org/software/bash/manual/.

Executing Commands in a Bash Script

To execute a series of commands in a Bash script, list each command on a separate line. For example, Listing 11.1 shows the very basic Bash script that gathers information about system resources.

LISTING 11.1 Generating a System Resources Report, Version 1

```
#!/bin/bash
#Script to generate a system resources report
#Author: Tammy Fox

uptime
mpstat
sar
free -m
df -h
vmstat -d
```

TIP

The system monitoring utilities used in Listing 11.1 are explained in Chapter 20, "Monitoring System Resources," along with many other monitoring tools.

As you can see, the commands are listed in the script, each on separate lines. Although the resulting file is useful to an administrator if generated on a regular basis, it would be more useful if the output were put into context. A useful Bash command when writing scripts is the `echo` command. Any text in quotation marks following the `echo` command is displayed to the terminal.

If used on the command line, the `echo` command can be used to display messages to the terminal. If used in a Bash script, the `echo` command can be used to write messages to a file if the output is redirected to a file. It can be used to add messages to the report as shown in Listing 11.2.

TIP

To exclude the end-of-line character, use the `-n` option such as `echo -n "message"`.

LISTING 11.2 Generating a System Resources Report, Version 2

```
#!/bin/bash

#Script to generate a system resources report
#Author: Tammy Fox

uptime

echo ""
echo "PROCESSOR REPORT:"
echo "----------------------------------------------"

echo "Output from mpstat:"
mpstat
echo ""

echo "Output from sar:"
sar
echo ""

echo ""
echo "MEMORY REPORT:"
echo "----------------------------------------------"

echo "Output from free -m:"
```

LISTING 11.2 Continued

```
free -m
echo ""

echo ""
echo "DISK USAGE REPORT:"
echo "---------------------------------------------"

echo "Output from df -h:"
df -h
echo ""

echo "Output from vmstat -d:"
vmstat -d
echo ""
```

The echo command has other benefits. For example, the echo command can be used to print a message at the beginning and end of the program so the user running it knows the status of the program. Additional usages of echo will also be discussed as this chapter explores other Bash programming features.

Variables

An administrator would most likely want to run this script on more than one system. But how can he keep track of which file was generated from each system? Because each system has a unique hostname, he can add the hostname to the report. At the top of the script, before the uptime command, the following line can be added:

```
echo "System Resources Report for $HOSTNAME"
```

$HOSTNAME in this line is a variable, denoted by the dollar sign in front of it. In this case, the variable is an environment variable given its default value by the system. Other variables can be declared and given values in a Bash script and then referenced later in the script as shown in Listing 11.3.

LISTING 11.3 Using Variables in Bash

```
#!/bin/bash
VARIABLE=value
echo "The value of $VARIABLE is $VARIABLE"
```

Table 11.1 lists additional environment variables that are useful when writing scripts.

TABLE 11.1 Command Environment Variables for Scripts

Environment Variable	Description
`$HOSTNAME`	Hostname of the system
`$USER`	Username of the user currently logged in
`$UID`	User ID of the user currently logged in
`$LANG`	Language set for the system such as `en_US.UTF-8`
`$HOME`	Home directory for the user currently logged in
`$0`	The command executed to run the script, without any command-line arguments
`$1, $2, etc.`	$1 is the value of the first command-line argument to the script, $2 is the value of the second argument, and so on.

Running the Script

Before going any further, it is a good idea to test the script. It is also beneficial to test the script as you add functionality to make it easier to find errors if they exist.

First, select a directory location for the script. As mentioned in Chapter 4, "Understanding Linux Concepts," the Filesystem Hierarchy System (FHS) guidelines designate `/usr/local/` for locally installed software independent of operating system updates. Because this script is a command, it should be in a `bin` directory as well. Also, pick a descriptive name for the script such as `get-resources`. So, saving it as `/usr/local/bin/get-resources` allows you to place it in a consistent location across systems and allows other administrators to find it easily.

The next step is to make it executable with the command `chmod +x get-resources`. If you aren't in the `/usr/local/bin/` directory when you execute this command, either change into that directory or give the full path to the script. This command allows anyone on the system to execute the script. To restrict file permissions further, refer to the "File Permissions" section in Chapter 4.

To run the script, either give its full path `/usr/local/bin/get-resources` or execute the command `./get-resources` if it is in the current working directory. If executing it from another script or specifying it in a crontab as discussed in this chapter, be sure to use the full path.

When you execute the script, you can redirect the output to a file such as:

```
./get-resources.sh > /var/log/resources
```

If the commands are run without syntax error, the `/var/log/resources` file should contain all the output. Also watch the command line from which you execute the script for any messages about syntax errors.

Optionally, you can also use the `$HOSTNAME` variable to create a unique filename for each file generated by replacing `/var/log/resources` with `/var/log/resources-$HOSTNAME` in the script. This proves useful if all the files are written to a remote shared directory from each system running the script.

Because this script writes the output file to the `/var/log/` directory, it must be run as root as non-root users do not have permission to write to this directory. If you want non-root users to be able to run the script, change the output file to a location writable by all such as the `/tmp/` directory, and make the output filename unique to each user such as `/tmp/resources-$HOSTNAME-$USER`, where `$USER` is an environment variable for the username of the user currently logged in.

Conditionals

Similar to other programming languages, Bash allows for conditionals, or if/then statements. If a condition is met, then the commands are executed. Optionally, you can use an `else` statement to provide commands if the condition is not met or use an `elif` statement to provide additional conditionals. Listing 11.4 shows the basic syntax and structure.

LISTING 11.4 Bash Syntax for Conditionals

```
if [ <condition> ];then
   ...
elif
   ...
else
   ...
fi
```

Table 11.2 lists commonly used conditions (`<condition>`). For a complete list, refer to the "Conditional Expressions" section of the Bash man page or the "Bash Conditional Expressions" section of the "Bash Reference Manual" at `http://www.gnu.org/software/bash/manual/`.

TABLE 11.2 Command Environment Variables for Scripts

Conditional	**Description**
`-d "filename"`	Returns true if file exists and is a directory
`-e "filename"`	Returns true if file exists
`-r "filename"`	Returns true if file exists and is readable
`-s "filename"`	Returns true if file exists and is bigger than zero bytes
`-w "filename"`	Returns true if file exists and is writable
`-x "filename"`	Returns true if file exists and is executable
`-N "filename"`	Returns true if file exists and has been modified since it was last read
`-n "$VARIABLE"`	Returns true if string is non-zero
`"$VAR1" == "$VAR2"`	Returns true if strings are equal
`"$VAR1" != "$VAR2"`	Returns true if strings are not equal
`"$VAR1" < "$VAR2"`	Returns true if the first string sorts before the second string lexicographically according to the system's locale such as alphabetically for the en_US.UTF-8 locale
`"$VAR1" > "$VAR2"`	Returns true if the first string sorts after the second string lexicographically according to the system's locale such as alphabetically for the en_US.UTF-8 locale

TABLE 11.2 Continued

`$NUM1 -eq $NUM2`	Returns true if the two integers are equal in value
`$NUM1 -ne $NUM2`	Returns true if the two integers are not equal in value
`$NUM1 -lt $NUM2`	Returns true if the first integer is less than the second integer
`$NUM1 -le $NUM2`	Returns true if the first integer is less than or equal to the second integer
`$NUM1 -gt $NUM2`	Returns true if the first integer is greater than the second integer
`$NUM1 -ge $NUM2`	Returns true if the first integer is greater than or equal to the second integer

TIP

Be sure to include the spaces around the operators and operand. Also, unless you are using the operands to compare integers, be sure to place quotation marks around the variables when comparing their values because the values compared are expected to be strings. For example,

```
if [ "$VAR1" == "$VAR2" ]then
   ...
fi
```

is the proper syntax to determine if two variables are equal.

To keep a copy of the last system resource report generated, you can add the following line to the beginning of the script:

```
mv /var/log/resources /var/log/resources.old
```

However, you will receive an error from the `mv` command if the file doesn't exist such as the very first time you run the script. To make the script more robust, you can use a conditional to check for the existence of the file before renaming it as shown in Listing 11.5.

LISTING 11.5 Check for Existence of File

```
#Keep previously generated report
if [ -e "/var/log/resources" ];then
   mv /var/log/resources /var/log/resources.old
fi
```

Loops

Another useful part of the Bash scripting language is the inclusion of loops. There are three types of loops: `while`, `for`, and `until`.

A `while` loop allows you to execute a sequence of commands while a test is true such as while an integer is larger than another integer or while a string does not equal another string. Listing 11.6 shows the basic syntax of a `while` loop.

LISTING 11.6 Syntax of a while Loop

```
while <test>
do
   ...
done
```

The <test> can be any of the string or integer comparisons from Table 11.2. For example, Listing 11.7 shows a while loop that iterates until the INT variable reaches the value of 4.

LISTING 11.7 Example while Loop

```
#!/bin/bash
INT=1
while [ $INT -lt 5 ]
do
   echo $INT
   INT=$((INT+1))
done
```

The until loop is similar to the while loop except that the code in the loop is executed until the test is true. For example, the loop is run until the INT variable reaches the value of 4 in Listing 11.8.

LISTING 11.8 Example until Loop

```
#!/bin/bash
INT=1
until [ $INT -gt 4 ]
do
   echo $INT
   INT=$((INT+1))
done
```

The for loop in Bash changes the value of a variable to a defined list of values, one at a time, until the end of the list. Listing 11.9 shows the basic syntax of a for loop.

LISTING 11.9 Syntax of a for Loop

```
for X in <list> ; do
   ...
done
```

For example:

```
#!/bin/bash
for X in dog cat mouse ; do
   echo "$X"
done
```

The asterisk can be used as a wildcard when defining the list. For example, `*.html` can be used to iterate through all the HTML files in the current directory.

Additional Scripting Languages

When automating system administration tasks, scripting languages such as Bash are most commonly used because they are efficient at executing a series of commands. However, other languages, both scripting and compiled, offer functions such as finding phrases in text files and replacing them with a different word or phrase, which can be helpful when you want to customize configuration files.

This section gives a brief overview of a few of the other scripting languages used in Red Hat Enterprise Linux along with some of their advantages and disadvantages for system administrators.

Writing Scripts with Python

Compared to Bash scripting, the syntax and features of Python look and feel more like a real programming language. Because the code is interpreted, not compiled into byte code, it can be used as a scripting language similar to Bash and can run on multiple platforms including Linux, Mac OS X, and the Microsoft Windows variants. Or, the programmer can choose to utilize the object-oriented nature of Python and write more complex user-end applications complete with graphical interfaces. In fact, all of the `system-config-*` configuration tools from Red Hat are written in Python.

One of Python's strengths is its easy-to-read syntax. Instead of having to use semicolons and remembering what keyword is used to end a loop, the programmer simply uses consistent indentation to tell the interpreter what lines are part of which functions or loops.

The `python` RPM package needs to be installed to use Python. If you don't have it installed, refer to Chapter 3, "Operating System Updates," for instructions. There are also packages that provide additional Python modules such as `rpm-python` for developing Python programs to interface with the RPM packages or database. Install these additional packages if you require their functionality.

Documentation for Python can be found at http://python.org/doc/, by installing the `python-docs` RPM package, and in books dedicated to teaching Python.

Writing Scripts with Perl

Similar to Python, Perl is available for many different operating systems, so its code can be easily ported to multiple operating systems. Perl's strengths include its process, file, and text-manipulation abilities. It is commonly used to write system management programs, scripts to access databases, and CGI scripts for the web. For example, the `logwatch` utility discussed in Chapter 20, "Monitoring System Resources," includes Perl scripts to generate log file reports.

The `perl` RPM package needs to be installed to use Perl. Optionally, packages that include additional Perl modules can be installed such as `perl-DBI` for accessing databases with Perl and `perl-HTML-Parser` for parsing HTML files in Perl.

Documentation for Perl can be found in the many man pages that come with the `perl` package. Start by executing the `man perl` command. The main Perl man page provides a list of other man pages and their purposes. More information and further documentation can be found at http://www.perl.org/.

Writing Scripts with Sed

A stream editor, Sed, reads the input of text sequentially line by line and processes it through a set of text transformation rules. All the rules are applied to the text with one pass of the text file from start to finish. Sed can be used on the command line from the `sed` command or it can be called from a script such as a Bash script, which was discussed earlier in this chapter. The `sed` RPM package must be installed to use Sed. Install it from Red Hat Network if it is not already installed. Software installation instructions can be found in Chapter 3.

To use a Sed rule from the command line, use the following format, which saves the new content in a separate file:

```
sed -e '<rules>' original.txt > newfile.txt
```

Alternatively, you can output the contents of a file and pipe it through Sed:

```
cat original.txt | sed -e '<rules>' > newfile.txt
```

To apply Sed rules to a file "in-place," use the following format (the changes are made to the same file):

```
sed -i -e '<rules>' file.txt
```

NOTE

If you do not redirect the results into a new file, it is displayed to *standard out*, or displayed on the command line before returning to the command prompt.

Sed commands can also be called from a script file by using a Bash script. The first line of the file must be

```
#!/bin/bash
```

After that, the syntax for calling the command is the same as from the command line. Refer to the "Executing Commands in a Bash Script" section earlier in this chapter for further explanation of the file format.

Listing 11.10 provides some sample Sed commands that can be invoked from the command line. They can also be executed from a script as previously described. Lines beginning with # in Listing 11.10 are comments to explain the commands.

LISTING 11.10 Example Sed Commands

```
#double space a text file that is single spaced
sed -e G singlespace.txt > doublespace.txt

#replace the word one with the number 1
sed -s 's/one/1/g' old.txt > new.txt

#replace the word old with the word new but only for the first instance on each
➥line
sed -s 's/old/new/' old.txt > new.txt
```

For a Sed reference including a list of regular expressions accepted by Sed, refer to the Sed manual at http://www.gnu.org/software/sed/manual/sed.html.

Writing Scripts with Awk

Compared to Sed, Awk is a more complete language with arrays, built-in functions, and the ability to print from an Awk program. It, too, can be called directly from the command line or from a Bash script. Install the gawk package to use Awk (Red Hat Enterprise Linux includes the GNU version of Awk called Gawk). To use Awk from the command line, invoke the `awk` command followed by the code inside curly brackets, inside single quotation marks:

```
awk '{<code>}'
```

To use Awk from a Bash script, use the same syntax as if from the command line. Refer to the "Executing Commands in a Bash Script" section earlier in this chapter for further explanation on including commands in a Bash script.

Listing 11.11 shows a simple `awk` command to parse through the output of the `uptime` command and only display the number of days since the last reboot.

LISTING 11.11 Awk Program to Parse Output of `uptime` Command

```
#only print how long the system has been running from the uptime command
uptime | awk '{print $3 " " $4}'
```

Because the output of uptime is always in the same format, you know that the third and fourth fields in the space-separated list contain the number of days that the system has been running and the word "days." This data is displayed using the Awk `print` command.

For a complete Gawk reference including a list of built-in functions, refer to the Gawk manual at http://www.gnu.org/software/gawk/manual/.

Scheduling Tasks with Cron

Now that you understand the basics of automating tasks with a script or program, the next step is to know how to schedule the tasks so they are executed at a specific time or on a set schedule. Some scripts such as removing users may not need to be scheduled, but others such as performing backups might work better on a schedule so users can anticipate them or so they can be run during a time when they won't interfere with the daily workload of the system.

Your Red Hat Enterprise Linux system should have the packages called `vixie-cron` and `crontabs` installed by default because basic system maintenance such as rotating log files is automated through the cron daemon.

The `vixie-cron` package installs a daemon called `crond`. This daemon references a set of files that contains lists of tasks to run every hour, every day, every week, every month, or at a specific time. If a specific time is listed, the minute, hour, day of the month, month, and day of the week can be scheduled. It also provides the initialization script used to start the daemon at boot time and the `crontab` executable used by non-root users to schedule cron tasks.

The `crontabs` package sets up the basic directory structure for the cron files. The following directories are created:

```
/etc/cron.daily
/etc/cron.hourly
/etc/cron.monthly
/etc/cron.weekly
```

Along with these directories, the `/etc/crontab` and the `/usr/bin/run-parts` files are installed. The `/etc/crontab` file defines the `SHELL`, `PATH`, `MAILTO`, and `HOME` variables and then defines when to run the hourly, daily, weekly, and monthly cron tasks. The `/usr/bin/run-parts` file is a bash script called by the `/etc/crontab` file to run the tasks in the hourly, daily, weekly, and monthly cron directories.

Because you have root privileges to the system as the administrator, you can add your custom script to one of the directories set up by the `crontabs` package or add a specially formatted file in the `/etc/cron.d/` directory.

After adding your custom script to the appropriate directory, it is executed when the tasks for each directory are scheduled to run as defined in `/etc/crontab`. The following log entry in `/var/log/cron` confirms that the daemon executed the daily scripts (this example was added to `/etc/cron.daily/`):

```
May 15 04:02:01 goofy crond[447]: (root) CMD (run-parts /etc/cron.daily)
```

To use a specially formatted file in the `/etc/cron.d/` directory instead, create a file in the directory with a unique, descriptive name such as backup for a cron task that creates backup. For example, to echo a message to a file 47 minutes after every hour, create a file called `testing` containing the following:

```
47 * * * * root echo "testing from cron.d" >> /tmp/testing
```

The contents of each file in the `/etc/cron.d/` directory must use the following format:

```
* * * * * username command
```

The five asterisks should be replaced by the minute, hour, day of the month, month, and day of the week on which to execute the command.

The following entry in /var/log/cron confirms the addition and the execution of the task:

```
May 13 15:37:01 goofy crond[1824]: (*system*) RELOAD (/etc/cron.d/testing)
May 13 15:47:01 goofy crond[6977]: (root) CMD (echo "testing from cron.d" >>
/tmp/testing)
```

NOTE

The cron daemon (crond) looks for new cron tasks every minute, so a log entry confirming the addition of a cron task will not appear until the daemon re-reads the task lists.

Finally, if you want to add a cron task as a user, execute the crontab -e command as a non-root user. This utility allows each user to have his or her own list of cron tasks. For example, suppose the user tfox executes crontab -e and enters the content from Listing 11.12. Note that the default editor used is Vi.

LISTING 11.12 Example crontab -e Entry

```
SHELL=/bin/bash
MAILTO=tfox
22 15 13 5 *    echo "testing" >> /tmp/testing
```

The format for each entry is similar to the format used for the files in /etc/cron.d/ except the username is not specified since each crontab file created with the crontab -e command is specific to a user. Because the file is specific to the user, variables such as what shell to use and who to email if the tasks generate output can be given values at the top of the file as shown in Listing 11.12.

After the user saves the entry, it is written to the /var/spool/cron/<username> file, /var/spool/cron/tfox in the example. For security reasons, the/var/spool/cron/ directory is only readable by the root user, but non-root users can execute the crontab -e command at any time to review their cron tasks.

This simple example creates the file /tmp/testing with a line that reads testing in the file. It is set to execute on May 13 at 3:22 p.m. After adding and saving the entry and after it is executed, the content from Listing 11.13 appears in the /var/log/cron log file.

LISTING 11.13 Log Entries after Adding a User Cron Task

```
May 13 15:20:09 goofy crontab[6588]: (tfox) BEGIN EDIT (tfox)
May 13 15:20:42 goofy crontab[6588]: (tfox) REPLACE (tfox)
May 13 15:20:42 goofy crontab[6588]: (tfox) END EDIT (tfox)
May 13 15:21:01 goofy crond[1824]: (tfox) RELOAD (cron/tfox)
May 13 15:22:01 goofy crond[6631]: (tfox) CMD (echo "testing" >> /tmp/testing)
```

The last two examples in this section show how to add a simple command as the cron task. Let's go back to the example bash script you have been working on to gather system resources. You can configure cron to execute the script using one of the previously mentioned methods and then as part of that same cron task have the file emailed to the administrator.

For example, if you are adding the file `resources` to the `/etc/cron.d/` directory to control precisely when the script runs, modify the following entry and save it in a file named `/etc/cron.d/resources`:

```
47 02 * * * root /usr/local/bin/get-resources > /var/log/resources; \
cat /var/log/resources | mail -s "Resources report for `echo $HOSTNAME`" \
admin@example.com
```

The `mail` command is provided by the `mailx` package. For this command to work, the system must be properly configured to send email. Refer to Chapter 18, "Setting Up an Email Server with Sendmail" for details.

Summary

This chapter provided you with an overview of some common scripting languages available for Red Hat Enterprise Linux to help you start writing your own scripts. Think about tasks you perform on a regular basis and whether they can be automated with a script. If they can be scripted, also consider automating their execution at set intervals using the cron utility.

PART IV

Network Services

IN THIS PART

CHAPTER 12

Identity Management

IN THIS CHAPTER

- Understanding PAM
- Enabling NIS
- Enabling LDAP
- Enabling Kerberos
- Enabling SMB or Winbind Authentication
- Enabling with Authentication Tool

Managing user accounts, including passwords, on individual systems does not scale well when an administrator must maintain hundreds or thousands of users on hundreds or thousands of systems, often around the world. Many services are available for Red Hat Enterprise Linux to allow users to authenticate from a central, remote server, which can also store user information that can be retrieved from client systems.

Some of the advantages of using a network service for user information and authentication include only having to back up this data from one system, updating the information on the server updates the information for all clients, and implementing higher security on the server containing user information.

If local authentication is what you require, refer to Chapter 9, "Managing Users and Groups," for details. Even if you are not using local users and groups, it is recommended that you read the "What Are Users and Groups" section for a description of Linux users and groups and the "Best Practices" section of Chapter 9 for suggested methods for establishing username conventions, setting password expiration, selecting secure password, deleting accounts, and structuring home directories.

Red Hat Enterprise Linux includes many network services for remote identity management. This chapter discusses the NIS, LDAP, Kerberos, Hesiod, SMB, and Winbind authentication services.

Understanding PAM

PAM, or *Pluggable Authentication Modules*, is an authentication layer that allows programs to be written independent of a specific authentication scheme. Applications request authentication via the PAM library, and the PAM library determines whether the user is allowed to proceed. If an administrator wants to implement a different authentication scheme, he just changes the PAM configuration files and the existing programs work seamlessly.

All applications and services that depend on PAM for authentication have a file in the `/etc/pam.d/` directory, with the filename being exactly the same as the application or service. Filenames must be in all lowercase. The RPM for the application or service is responsible for installing its own configuration file in this directory. For example, the `reboot` command is PAM-aware and thus the `usermode` package that included `reboot` installs the `/etc/pam.d/reboot` file.

Contents of the `/etc/pam.d/` configuration files are case-sensitive, and each line uses the following format:

```
<type> <control> <module> <module_options>
```

Each line calls a module located in the `/lib/security/` or `/lib64/security/` directory, depending on whether the system is 32-bit or 64-bit and whether the module is 32-bit or 64-bit (32-bit modules can exist on a 64-bit system). Module calls can be stacked so that multiple criteria must be verified before allowing authentication. The modules calls are processed from top to bottom, so the order matters. Options for the module can also be specified.

The `<type>` must be one of the following management groups:

- `account`: Non-authentication account management such as verifying the location of the request or whether system resources are available for the request.
- `auth`: Authenticate the requested user based on a password or other form of authentication. Also can grant privileges to authorized users.
- `password`: Required for managing passwords or other authentication tokens.
- `session`: Manage actions before and after a user is granted or denied access to a service such as logging and mounting directories.

Each module returns a success or failure status. The `<control>` determines whether or not the next module should be called to continue the authentication process. The `<control>` is usually one of the following:

- `required`: If the module returns success, the next module in the stack is called if it exists or the authentication is successful if it is the last module called. Return authentication failure if the module returns failure but only after calling the remaining modules in the stack.
- `requisite`: Similar to required except that control is immediately sent back to the application or service requesting authentication instead of calling the remaining modules.
- `sufficient`: If the module returns a failure, the authentication can still be successful if all the required modules in the stack return success.

- `optional`: Results of the module is ignored.
- `include`: Include lines from the given configuration file in the same `/etc/pam.d/` directory such as `include system-auth`.

The `<control>` can also be in the following form:

```
[value1=action1 value2=action2 ... ]
```

The value should be the return code from the function called in the module. Refer to the pam.conf man page by executing the `man pam.conf` command for details.

Enabling NIS

NIS, or *Network Information Systems*, is a network service that allows authentication and login information to be stored on a centrally located server. This includes the username and password database for login authentication, database of user groups, and the locations of home directories.

To allow users to log in to any system on the network seamlessly, NIS and NFS can be used together. The NIS server provides the network service for logging in to the system, and NFS can be used to export user home directories from a central server. If used together, users can access any system with the same username and password, system groups remain the same across the network, and users' home directories are exactly the same regardless of which system they log in to. If using SELinux, the `use_nfs_home_dirs boolean` SELinux boolean must be set to 1 on each NFS client mounting the home directories. Refer to Chapter 13, "Network File Sharing" for details.

NIS and SELinux

In Red Hat Enterprise Linux 5, NIS is protected by the default Security-Enhanced Linux (SELinux) policy, known as the targeted policy. Refer to Chapter 23 for more information on SELinux.

By default, this targeted policy does not allow NIS connections. To use NIS, you must set the `allow_ypbind` SELinux boolean to `1` with the following command:

```
setsebool -P allow_ypbind 1
```

To verify that the setting has been changed, execute the following:

```
getsebool allow_ypbind
```

If enabled, the output should be the following:

```
allow_ypbind --> on
```

Other SELinux booleans for NIS include the following (they are set to `0` by default) :

- `yppasswdd_disable_trans`: Disable SELinux protection for `yppasswd` if set to `1`.

- ypxfr_disable_trans: Disable SELinux protection for ypxfr if set to 1.
- ypbind_disable_trans: Disable SELinux protection for ypbind if set to 1.

You can also change the values of these booleans by running the SELinux Management Tool. Start it by selecting **Administration, SELinux Management** from the **System** menu on the top panel of the desktop or by executing the system-config-selinux command. Enter the root password when prompted if running as a non-root user. Select **Boolean** from the list on the left. On the right, click the triangle icon next to **NIS**. The SELinux booleans affecting NIS appear.

TIP

The SELinux booleans that affect NIS are described in the ypbind_selinux man page viewable with the man ypbind_selinux command.

Allowing NIS Connections

By default, the ports used by NIS are selected at random by portmap. If you are using firewall rules that only allow connections on specific ports, static ports can be set for the ypserv and ypxfrd services but not for yppasswdd. Refer to the /etc/services file for a list of ports already reserved for other services on the system and then select available ports. To assign ports to ypserv and ypxfrd, add the following lines to /etc/sysconfig/network:

```
YPSERV_ARGS="-p <port>"
YPXFRD_ARGS="p <port>"
```

If the services are already running, they must be restarted for the changes to take effect. After restarting them, use the rpcinfo -p <hostname> command to verify that the selected ports are being used.

If custom IPTables rules are being used, refer to Chapter 24, "Configuring a Firewall," for details on how to allow these ports.

If the default security level is enabled instead of custom IPTables rules, use the Security Level Configuration tool to allow NIS connections. Start it by selecting **Administration, Security Level and Firewall** from the **System** menu on the top panel of the desktop or by executing the system-config-securitylevel command. Enter the root password when prompted if running as a non-root user. In the **Other ports** area, click **Add** to specify these two ports.

Configuring the NIS Server

To configure a system as an NIS server, first install the ypserv RPM package via RHN, which installs the portmap package as a dependency. Also install the ypbind via RHN, which installs the yp-tools package as a dependency. The ypserv service provides the NIS server, and ypbind provides the necessary client utilities.

TIP

Log messages for ypserv and its related services are written to the /var/log/messages file.

The NIS server must have a domain name (which is different from the domain name of a FQDN as discussed in Chapter 16, "Hostname Resolution with BIND"). The domain name is used along with its IP address or hostname by clients to connect to it. Set the NIS domain name in /etc/sysconfig/network by adding the following line as root (replace <domain> with a unique name):

```
NISDOMAIN="<domain>"
```

The server must be set up as a client of itself, so add the following line to /etc/yp.conf:

```
ypserver 172.0.0.1
```

The local files from which NIS gets its information to share with clients must be configured, including /etc/passwd, /etc/shadow, /etc/group, and /etc/hosts. In other words, users must be added to the NIS server with the desired passwords, groups must be added, and any IP address and hostname combinations to be shared must be added to /etc/hosts.

Next, start the portmap, yppasswdd, and ypserv services by executing the following as root for each of them:

```
service <service> start
```

Be sure these services are started at boot time with the following command as root for each service:

```
chkconfig <service> on
```

Lastly, create the NIS database (on a 64-bit system, the lib directory will be lib64 instead):

```
/usr/lib/yp/ypinit -m
```

Enter the requested information and answer the questions appropriately when prompted. The output should look similar to Listing 12.1.

LISTING 12.1 Creating the NIS Database

```
At this point, we have to construct a list of the hosts which will run NIS
servers.  smallville.example.net is in the list of NIS server hosts.
Please continue to add the names for the other hosts, one per line.
When you are done with the list, type a <control D>.
        next host to add:  smallville.example.net
        next host to add:
The current list of NIS servers looks like this:
```

LISTING 12.1 Continued

```
smallville.example.net

Is this correct?  [y/n: y]  y
We need a few minutes to build the databases...
Building /var/yp/example/ypservers...
Running /var/yp/Makefile...
gmake[1]: Entering directory `/var/yp/example'
Updating passwd.byname...
Updating passwd.byuid...
Updating group.byname...
Updating group.bygid...
Updating hosts.byname...
Updating hosts.byaddr...
Updating rpc.byname...
Updating rpc.bynumber...
Updating services.byname...
Updating services.byservicename...
Updating netid.byname...
Updating protocols.bynumber...
Updating protocols.byname...
Updating mail.aliases...
gmake[1]: Leaving directory `/var/yp/example'

smallville.example.net has been set up as a NIS master server.

Now you can run ypinit -s smallville.example.net on all slave server.
```

The NIS map files are created in the `/var/yp/<domain>/` directory. After the NIS database has been created, the server must be told about changes to the data being shared. To update the NIS maps after modifying files on the server, change to the `/var/yp/` directory and type the `make` command as the root user. To keep the NIS information updated on a regular basis, consider creating a cron task to execute this command periodically. The update frequency depends on how often the information is updated. You can also run `make` in the `/var/yp/` directory after each change if you need them to take place immediately or if you don't update the data very often. Refer to Chapter 11, "Automating Tasks with Scripts," for details on setting up a cron task.

From the client side, the `ypcat` command can be used to view the contents of the NIS maps. For example, execute `ypcat passwd.byname` to view the user entries from `/etc/passwd` on the server. A full list of maps to query can be retrieved from the `ypwhich -m` command on the client. Entry names such as `passwd.byname` are not always easy to remember, so the `/var/yp/nicknames` file on the NIS server can be used to set up aliases or nicknames so they can be used to query the server for information lists. For example, the nickname `passwd` is set up by default for `passwd.byname`. View the contents of the

/var/yp/nicknames file for a complete list of aliases set up by default. From the client, the ypwhich -x command lists the available nicknames. Remember to run the make command in the /var/yp/ directory on the server after modifying the /var/yp/nicknames file to update the NIS map file for it.

The ypserv service also has a configuration file, /etc/ypserv.conf. The default file contains comments that detail the available options. The ypserv.conf man page provides descriptions of them as well. Access control lists can also be added to this file. Refer to the "Restricting Access to NIS Server" section for details.

The yppasswdd daemon allows users on the NIS clients to change their passwords and other user information stored on the server. Refer to the "Connecting to the NIS Server" section for instructions on using the client-side utility. When passwords and user information are changed with yppasswd, the daemon assumes the /etc/passwd and /etc/shadow files by default. If the server uses different file locations, set them in /etc/sysconfig/yppasswdd. This configuration file also contains an option to pass arguments to the daemon when it is started. A list of these arguments can be found in the yppasswdd man page.

Adding Optional NIS Slave Servers

The NIS server where the master copy of the user information is stored and can be modified is called the *master server*, and each NIS domain can only have one master server. However, slave NIS servers can be added to the network.

These slave servers retrieve their data from the master server and are useful if the master server fails or needs to be taken down for maintenance; the slave server can act in its place. NIS clients will try to find a different server for its NIS domain if the server it is connected to is responding slowly or not at all. If slave servers for the domain exist, they can help handle the heavy request load.

Configuring NIS Slave Servers

To configure a slave server, first configure the master server for the domain. If slave servers are to be set up for the domain, the ypxfrd service can be run on the NIS server to allow for NIS database transfers. Start it on the master server as root with the service ypxfrd start command. Also, make sure it is started at boot time with the chkconfig ypxfrd on command, also as root.

Also on the master server, add the hostname of the slave server to the list of NIS servers in the /var/yp/ypservers file. Enable this change by switching to the /var/yp/ directory with the cd /var/yp command and running the make command as root. Make sure the hostname of the slave server is in /etc/hosts or can be resolved via DNS.

The same set of RPM packages required on the master server must also be installed on each slave server. Make sure the hostname of the master server can be resolved to its IP address on the slave server via DNS or the /etc/hosts file. Then, copy the NIS databases from the master server by executing the following as root on each slave server, where <master> is the hostname of the master NIS server (on a 64-bit system, the lib directory will be lib64 instead) :

```
/usr/lib/yp/ypinit -s <master>
```

Change the NIS server for the slave server to itself in the /etc/yp.conf file. If a different NIS server is already configured, comment it out by added a # character in front of the line, or delete the line. The following line in /etc/yp.conf configures the slave server as its own NIS server:

```
ypserver 127.0.0.1
```

On the slave server, the ypserv service must be started before the ypbind service. As root, execute the following sequence of commands:

```
service ypbind stop; service ypserv start; service ypbind start
```

Verify that the slave server is now using itself as the NIS server by executing the ypwhich command. It should return the hostname of the slave server.

Updating NIS Maps from Master

To update the NIS maps on a slave server from the master server, the ypxfrd service must be running on the master server as previously mentioned. This daemon listens for client requests. On each slave server, the ypxfr command must be run as root for each map file to be updated (on a 64-bit system, the lib directory will be lib64 instead):

```
/usr/lib/yp/ypxfr <mapname>
```

To verify that the map was updated, execute the ypcat <mapname> command and look for the newly added data. As previously mentioned, a list of maps can be retrieved with the ypwhich -m command.

Instead of executing the ypxfr command manually every time a map file is changed, you can configure a cron task to execute it periodically for each map file. The interval at which it is executed depends on how often you update the map files on the master server. Because the xpxfr command must be executed for each map file, all the map files do not have to be updated at the same time. Refer to Chapter 11 for details on setting up a cron task.

CAUTION

Remember, if shared data is modified on the server, the make command must be run in the /var/yp/ directory on the server to update the master NIS maps before the updated map files can be transferred to the clients.

Restricting Access to NIS Server

By default, anyone with access to the network on which the NIS server is running can query the server and query for data in the NIS maps. To restrict connections to specific clients, create a /var/yp/securenets file. Lines beginning with # are comments. The file should contain the following line to allow the local host to connect:

```
host 127.0.0.1
```

To accept requests from additional hosts, add a line with a netmask, followed by a space, followed by a network pair for each set of hosts such as

```
255.255.255.0 192.168.10.0
```

If clients not in the `/var/yp/securenets` file try to connect, the request is ignored, and a warning message is logged on the server.

Access control lists for NIS can also be set in `/etc/ypserv.conf`. Each access control line is in the following format:

```
host:domain:map:security
```

The `host` field can be an individual IP address such as 192.168.10.2, an IP address range and netmask such as 192.168.10.0/255.255.255.0, or the beginning of the IP address range such as 192.168, which translates to 192.168.0.0/255.255.0.0. The `domain` field is the NIS domain for which this rule applies. An asterisk (`*`) can be used as the domain name to match any domain. The map field must be an NIS map name or an asterisk for all NIS maps. Security must be `none`, `port`, or `deny`. If set to `none`, clients matching the rule are allowed access. If set to `port`, clients matching the rule are allowed from ports less than 1024 only. If set to `deny`, clients matching the rule are denied access to the NIS server.

Connecting to the NIS Server

The `ypbind` RPM package must be installed on each NIS client so that the `ypbind` service can be run to connect to the NIS server. The client connects to the NIS server based on the hostname of the NIS server and optionally the domain name if more than one domain is on the network.

To configure the NIS server for the client, edit the `/etc/yp.conf` file as root to include the following line, replace `<nis-server>` with the IP address or hostname of the server:

```
ypserver <nis-server>
```

or to specify the domain as well:

```
domain <domain> server <nis-server>
```

Next, start the service with the `service ypbind start` command as root. Also execute `chkconfig ypbind on` as root to make sure it is started at boot time.

To verify that you are connected to the NIS server, execute the `ypwhich` command. It displays the name of the NIS server to which you are connected. The `ypcat <mapname>` command as previously mentioned can be used on the client to display various maps and configuration files from the server. To view a list of available maps, execute the `ypwhich -m` command on the client.

To change user data from an NIS client, use the following command:

```
yppasswd <option> <username>
```

The command doesn't have to be executed as root on the client, but the root password of the NIS server must be entered before data can be changed. If `<username>` is not given, the username of the user executing the `yppasswd` command is used.

Replace `<option>` with one of the following:

- `-p`: Change user's password, implied if no option is given.
- `-l`: Change user's login shell.
- `-f`: Change user's full name and related information displayed by the `finger` utility. The current value for each field is shown. To accept it, press Enter. To change it, type a new value and then press Enter. To clear the field, type `none` and then press Enter.

Using NIS with autofs

NIS can also be configured to serve configuration files for other services such as autofs, allowing NIS clients to receive the master configuration file `auto.master` and any additional automount files such as `auto.home` from the NIS server. If mount points, server names, or directory locations change, one update to the NIS server changes the data for the entire network, and the client can retrieve the updated data by executing the `service autofs reload` command, or they will receive it automatically the next time the system is rebooted. Not having to change this data on each client system saves valuable time and effort.

First, configure autofs on the NIS server as described in Chapter 13, "Network File Sharing," and verify that the autofs service works on the client. Then, configure the NIS server to create the autofs NIS map files by modifying the `/var/yp/Makefile` file:

Near the top of the file is a list of variables for the autofs configuration files referenced in the `Makefile`. By default, the following autofs files are declared:

```
AUTO_MASTER = $(YPSRCDIR)/auto.master
AUTO_HOME   = $(YPSRCDIR)/auto.home
AUTO_LOCAL  = $(YPSRCDIR)/auto.local
```

If you are using additional `auto.*` files, add them to the list of file variables using the same format. For example, add the following for `auto.shares`:

```
AUTO_SHARES   = $(YPSRCDIR)/auto.shares
```

Modify the `all` target to include all the `auto.*` files being used on the server. By default, the `all` target looks like the following:

```
all:  passwd group hosts rpc services netid protocols mail \
        # netgrp shadow publickey networks ethers bootparams printcap \
        # amd.home auto.master auto.home auto.local passwd.adjunct \
        # timezone locale netmasks
```

Because the lines that begin with # are comments, the `auto.*` files listed by default are not built into NIS maps. They are just shown as examples of files that can be shared by NIS. Add `auto.master` and any other `auto.*` files being used by autofs at the end of the first line before the \ character.

If you added any `auto.*` file variables in the first step and then added those files to the `all` target, you also need to add a target for each additional file. These individual targets are near the end of the file such as the following:

```
auto.home: $(AUTO_HOME) $(YPDIR)/Makefile
        @echo "Updating $@..."
        -@sed -e "/^#/d" -e s/#.*$$// $(AUTO_HOME) ¦ $(DBLOAD) \
                -i $(AUTO_HOME) -o $(YPMAPDIR)/$@ - $@
        -@$(NOPUSH) ¦¦ $(YPPUSH) -d $(DOMAIN) $@
```

Create a new stanza for each additional autofs file by copying this one and replacing `auto.home` with the name of the autofs file and `AUTO_HOME` with the name of the variable you created in the first step. Be sure to use tabs instead of spaces to indent the lines or you will receive a syntax error when reloading the autofs files.

Reload the autofs files with the `service autofs reload` command as root. Or, if it is not already started, execute `service autofs start` as root on the NIS server.

To ensure autofs is started by boot time, execute `chkconfig autofs on` as root.

In the `/var/yp/` directory on the NIS server, type the `make` command as root to create NIS map files from the autofs files. Listing 12.2 shows the output of the `make` command after adding `auto.master` and `auto.home` to the `all` target.

LISTING 12.2 Creating the autofs NIS map

```
gmake[1]: Entering directory `/var/yp/example'
Updating passwd.byname...
Updating passwd.byuid...
Updating group.byname...
Updating group.bygid...
Updating hosts.byname...
Updating hosts.byaddr...
Updating rpc.byname...
Updating rpc.bynumber...
Updating services.byname...
Updating services.byservicename...
Updating netid.byname...
Updating protocols.bynumber...
Updating protocols.byname...
Updating mail.aliases...
Updating auto.master...
Updating auto.home...
gmake[1]: Leaving directory `/var/yp/example'
```

Each time the `auto.*` files are modified on the server, the `service autofs reload` command must be run to reload the files and the `make` command must be run in the `/var/yp/` directory to update the NIS map files. If an `auto.*` file is removed from the autofs configuration, the NIS map file for the deleted file in `/var/yp/<domain>/` must be deleted before running `make` in the `/var/yp/` directory to update the NIS maps. If slave NIS servers exist, use `ypxfr` as described in the earlier "Configuring NIS Slave Servers" section to update the NIS maps on the slave servers as well.

From the NIS client, the `ypcat` command can be used to view the contents of these files such as the following:

```
ypcat auto.master
```

Now that the NIS client has the autofs configuration files, stop the autofs service if it is already running with local files:

```
service autofs stop
```

Remove the local autofs configuration files so the autofs service knows to get them via NIS. It is a good idea to back them up in case you need to reference them later:

```
rm /etc/auto.*
```

Start the autofs service on the client with the `service autofs start` command as root. To ensure autofs is started by boot time, execute `chkconfig autofs on` as root as well.

Enabling LDAP

LDAP, or *Lightweight Directory Access Protocol*, is a server-client service that provides a directory of information such as user data and user authentication. If the LDAP server being contacted does not have the requested information, it can forward the request to a different LDAP server on the same network or on the Internet. Even though requests can be forwarded to other LDAP servers, the most common application of LDAP is an internal directory for large organizations such as a business office (from one office to multiple offices around the world) or a university. Instead of having to find a traditional phone directory or phone book, information about other employees or students can be quickly referenced online using LDAP. Instead of updating the file for the directory and reprinting it for everyone, the central directory is updated, and all users have access to the newly updated information instantly.

Allowing LDAP Connections

By default, OpenLDAP uses TCP and UDP port 389 for unencrypted connections and TCP and UDP port 636 for secure, encrypted connections.

If custom IPTables rules are being used, refer to Chapter 24 for details on how to allow these ports.

If the default security level is enabled instead of custom IPTables rules, use the Security Level Configuration tool to allow LDAP connections. Start it by selecting **Administration**, **Security**

Level and Firewall from the **System** menu on the top panel of the desktop or by executing the `system-config-securitylevel` command. Enter the root password when prompted if running as a non-root user. Click **Add** next to the **Other ports** table to add a port.

Configuring the LDAP Server

On Red Hat Enterprise Linux, OpenLDAP is used to implement an LDAP server. OpenLDAP is an open source implementation of LDAP. The `openldap` and `openldap-servers` RPM packages must be installed on the system to configure it as an LDAP server.

Setting Up the LDAP Configuration Files

The LDAP daemon, `slapd`, uses `/etc/openldap/slapd.conf` as its main configuration file. There are many configuration options available for `slapd.conf`. Refer to the `slapd.conf` man page for a complete list. At a minimum, the following need to be set:

- At least one suffix must be defined with the domain for which the LDAP directory is providing entries. Replace the sample `suffix` line with the information for your domain, such as the following for example.com:

  ```
  suffix          "dc=example,dc=com"
  ```

- Define a user who has complete control over the directory. This user is not subject to access control or other restrictions. Replace the sample `rootdn` line with the superuser for LDAP and the domain name for the directory such as the following:

  ```
  rootdn          "cn=root,dc=example,dc=com"
  ```

- If you plan to perform maintenance on the directory remotely, an encrypted password can be set so the user defined with the `rootdn` option has to provide a password before modifying the database. If you don't need remote maintenance, this option is not necessary. To generate the encrypted version of the password, execute the `slappasswd` command. Be sure to copy and paste the entire output as the value of the `rootpw` option, including the encryption method such as the following:

  ```
  rootpw        {SSHA}vhSdnGD3mNZpvxF63OmuaAUlNF16yVVT
  ```

Even though the password is encrypted in the configuration file, it is still sent unencrypted from the client to the server unless encryption is enabled. Refer to the "Enabling TLS Encryption for LDAP" section for details.

Also create a `DB_CONFIG` file in the `/var/lib/ldap/` directory (or the directory defined with the `directory` option in `slapd.conf`). This file contains tuning options for the directory. The example file, `/etc/openldap/DB_CONFIG.example` is included with the `openldap-servers` package. Use it as a starting point and modify the settings for your LDAP directory environment. If this file doesn't exist, an error message such as the following is shown each time `slapcat`, `slapadd`, and other administrative utilities are run:

```
bdb_db_open: Warning - No DB_CONFIG file found in directory /var/lib/ldap: (2)
Expect poor performance for suffix dc=example,dc=com.
```

Adding LDAP Entries

Each item in the directory is called an *entry*, and each entry is composed of *attributes* such as a name and location. Attributes can be required or optional. An LDAP entry is identified by its *Distinguished Name* (*DN*), which must be unique for each entry.

Entries added to the directory must follow a *schema*, which defines available attribute types. Some schema files are included with OpenLDAP in the `/etc/openldap/schema/` directory. To use the attribute types in one of the schemas, the `slapd.conf` file must reference them such as the following:

```
include         /etc/openldap/schema/core.schema
```

The `core`, `cosine`, `inetorgperson`, and `nis` schemas are referenced in the default `slapd.conf` file so that the entry types, called *object classes*, in these files can be used. Add `include` lines to reference additional schema files if necessary for your directory configuration. Additional packages can add includes to `slapd.conf` as well. For example, the `bind-sdb` package adds an include for the `dnszone.schema` file.

TIP

The software packages for some services such as Samba include LDAP schema files so that the OpenLDAP can be set up to share its configuration files. Execute `rpm -ql <packagename>` on the name of the RPM package for the services you use to determine if they provide a schema file.

The included schemas can be extended or new schemas can be created, depending on what type of data you are storing in your LDAP directory. To extend or create a new schema, create a new schema file in the `/etc/openldap/schema/` directory with the same file permissions as the existing schema files. Refer to http://www.openldap.org/doc/admin23/schema.html for details on writing a custom schema file. The existing files provided with OpenLDAP should not be modified. Be sure to reference the new file in `/etc/openldap/slapd.conf` file with an `include` line as previously mentioned.

To read the schema files, consider this basic example. Listing 12.3 includes excerpts from `core.schema` and `inetorgperson.schema`. In `core.schema`, the object class (this is the entry type) of `person` is defined as a subclass of the `top` object class as shown by the line starting with the keyword `SUP`. Then, in `inetorgperson.schema`, the object class `inetOrgPerson` is defined as a subclass of `person`, inheriting the attributes list from its parent object class `person`.

LISTING 12.3 Object Class Definitions

```
objectclass ( 2.5.6.6 NAME 'person'
        DESC 'RFC2256: a person'
        SUP top STRUCTURAL
        MUST ( sn $ cn )
        MAY ( userPassword $ telephoneNumber $ seeAlso $ description ) )
```

LISTING 12.3 Continued

```
objectclass ( 2.5.6.7 NAME 'inetOrgPerson'
        DESC 'RFC2256: an organizational person'
        SUP person STRUCTURAL
        MAY ( title $ x121Address $ registeredAddress $ destinationIndicator $
                preferredDeliveryMethod $ telexNumber $ teletexTerminalIdentifier $
                telephoneNumber $ internationaliSDNNumber $
                facsimileTelephoneNumber $ street $ postOfficeBox $ postalCode $
                postalAddress $ physicalDeliveryOfficeName $ ou $ st $ l ) )
```

Attributes for an object class can be required or optional. The attributes listed within the parentheses after the `MUST` keyword are required. The attributes listed within the parentheses after the `MAY` keyword are optional. In Listing 12.3, the `sn` (surname) and `cn` (common name) attributes are required for both the person and `inetOrgPerson` object classes. To find a brief description for each attribute listed, look for its `attributetype` definition such as the one for `sn` in Listing 12.4, which is found in `core.schema`.

LISTING 12.4 Attribute Type Definition for the sn Attribute

```
attributetype ( 2.5.4.4 NAME ( 'sn' 'surname' )
        DESC 'RFC2256: last (family) name(s) for which the entity is known by'
        SUP name )
```

Entries are added to a directory using a file formatted in the *LDIF* (*LDAP Data Interchange Format*) style, which is demonstrated in Listing 12.5. Lines beginning with a # character are comments.

LISTING 12.5 LDIF Style

```
dn: <dn>
<attribute>: <value>
<attribute>: <value>
<attribute>: <value>
```

Each entry in the LDIF file starts with a DN, which is a unique value for the entry used to identify it such as a person's name. Each entry in the file is separated by one or more blank lines. The value of an attribute can be specified as UTF-8 text, base64 encoded data, a URL of the location of the value, or the file location of the value with `file:///` at the beginning of the full path to the file.

For example, Listing 12.6 shows an example LDIF file to create an employee directory. It uses the `organizationalUnit` object class to define the purpose of the directory, an employee directory. It uses the `organizationalRole` object class to define the departments within the company and the `inetOrgPerson` object class to add entries for each employee within each department.

CAUTION

Whitespace is not trimmed when saving values. Any unnecessary whitespace at the beginning or end of the attribute value will be included in the value.

LISTING 12.6 LDIF File for Creating an Employee Directory

```
# organization: example, com
dn: dc=example, dc=com
objectClass: top
objectClass: dcObject
objectClass: organization
dc: example
o: TCBF, Inc.

# organizationalUnit: employeedir
dn: ou=employeedir, dc=example, dc=com
objectClass: top
objectClass: organizationalUnit
ou: employeedir

# organizationalUnit: finance
dn: ou=finance, ou=employeedir, dc=example, dc=com
objectClass: top
objectClass: organizationalUnit
ou: finance

# organizationalUnit: engineering
dn: ou=engineering, ou=employeedir, dc=example, dc=com
objectClass: top
objectClass: organizationalUnit
ou: engineering

# start adding employees here

dn: cn=Jane Doe, ou=engineering, ou=employeedir, dc=example, dc=com
objectClass: top
objectClass: inetOrgPerson
cn: Jane Doe
sn: Doe
telephoneNumber: 919-555-1234
mail: jane.doe@example.com
title: Level II systems engineer
physicalDeliveryOfficeName: Raleigh 3rd floor

dn: cn=Evan Wolf, ou=engineering, ou=employeedir, dc=example, dc=com
```

LISTING 12.6 Continued

```
objectClass: top
objectClass: inetOrgPerson
cn: Evan Wolf
sn: Wolf
telephoneNumber: 919-555-4567
mail: evan.wolf@example.com
title: Level II systems engineer
physicalDeliveryOfficeName: Raleigh 3rd floor

dn: cn=Ed Money, ou=finance, ou=employeedir, dc=example, dc=com
objectClass: top
objectClass: inetOrgPerson
cn: Ed Money
sn: Money
telephoneNumber: 919-555-9876
mail: ed.money@example.com
title: Accounts Payable
physicalDeliveryOfficeName: Raleigh 2nd floor

dn: cn=Seymour Air, ou=finance, ou=employeedir, dc=example, dc=com
objectClass: top
objectClass: inetOrgPerson
cn: Seymour Air
sn: Air
telephoneNumber: 919-555-1470
mail: seymour.air@example.com
title: Accounts Receivable
physicalDeliveryOfficeName: Raleigh 2nd floor
```

Before adding entries, stop the LDAP service with the `service ldap stop` command run as root. Then, use the `slapadd` utility to add the entries from the file you created in LDIF format:

```
slapadd -v -l example.ldif
```

If the syntax of the file is correct, the following type of message is shown for each entry successfully added:

```
added: "cn=Seymour Air,ou=finance,ou=employeedir,dc=example,dc=com" (0000000a)
```

If you see any error message instead, go back and fix the error. But, remember that the entries are added as they are successfully read from the file. So, be sure to comment out or delete any entries from the LDIF file that have already been added. If the LDIF file contains entries that already exist in the directory, all entries after the already added entry are not added to the directory, and the following error is shown:

```
=> bdb_tool_entry_put: id2entry_add failed: DB_KEYEXIST: Key/data pair
already exists (-30996)
=> bdb_tool_entry_put: txn_aborted! DB_KEYEXIST: Key/data pair already
exists (-30996)
slapadd: could not add entry dn="dc=example,dc=com" (line=6): txn_aborted!
DB_KEYEXIST: Key/data pair already exists (-30996)
```

As you are adding entries, use the `slapcat` command to view all the entries in the directory. Because the output is in LDIF format, this utility can also be used to create a backup file of the entries in the directory.

The database files for the entries added are created in the `/var/lib/ldap/` directory with read permissions only for the file owner. The OpenLDAP daemon runs as the ldap user for security reasons, and the entry files must be readable by the ldap user. Because entries are added as the root user, use the following command to change the owner of the database files to ldap:

```
chown ldap.ldap /var/lib/ldap/*
```

After adding all the entries to create the directory, start the daemon again with the `service ldap start` command run as root. If you fail to change the owner of the database files, a message similar to the following appears when `slapd` is started again:

```
/var/lib/ldap/__db.005 is not owned by "ldap"              [WARNING]
```

After the daemon is back up and running, the `ldapsearch` utility can be used to query the database by specific parameters. Refer to the `ldapsearch` man page for a list of all command-line options. The `openldap-clients` package must be installed to use this command. An example query:

```
ldapsearch -b 'dc=example,dc=com' '(objectclass=*)'
```

If encryption has not been enabled, the `-x` option must also be specified to use simple authentication instead:

```
ldapsearch -x -b 'dc=example,dc=com' '(objectclass=*)'
```

Modifying and Deleting LDAP Entries

To modify or delete an entry, use the `changetype` attribute after the DN in the LDIF file. It should be set to one of `add`, `modify`, `delete`, or `modrdn`. The `add` type is only used when adding a new entry. Note that it can't be used to add new attributes to entries. Use the `modify` type for adding new attributes and their values, changing the value of an attribute, and deleting existing attributes for a specific entry. The `delete` type is used to delete an entire entry. The `modrdn` type is used to change the DN of an entry. Listing 12.7 shows some examples. Notice that a blank line separates the entries for each change.

LISTING 12.7 Modifying an Entry

```
#change the title of an employee after a promotion
dn: cn=Evan Wolf,ou=engineering,ou=employeedir,dc=example ,dc=com
changetype: modify
replace: title
title: Level III systems engineer

#change the dn of an employee after he has changed departments
dn: cn=Seymour Air, ou=finance, ou=employeedir, dc=example, dc=com
changetype: modrdn
newrdn: cn=Seymour Air
deleteoldrdn: 0
newsuperior: ou=engineering, ou=employeedir, dc=example, dc=com

#now change the title and location of the same employee
dn: cn=Seymour Air, ou=engineering, ou=employeedir, dc=example, dc=com
changetype: modify
title: Level I systems engineer
physicalDeliveryOfficeName: Raleigh 3rd floor

#delete an employee after he no longer works for the company
dn: cn=Ed Money, ou=finance, ou=employeedir, dc=example, dc=com
changetype: delete

#add a new employee
dn: cn=Nick Burns, ou=engineering, ou=employeedir, dc=example, dc=com
changetype: add
objectClass: top
objectClass: inetOrgPerson
cn: Nick Burns
sn: Burns
telephoneNumber: 919-555-9010
mail: nick.burns@example.com
title: Engineering Administrator
physicalDeliveryOfficeName: Raleigh 3rd floor

#add the manager attribute to an employee
dn: cn=Seymour Air, ou=engineering, ou=employeedir, dc=example, dc=com
changetype: modify
add: manager
manager: cn=Evan Wolf,ou=engineering,ou=employeedir,dc=example,dc=com
```

To make the changes in Listing 12.7, execute the following:

```
ldapmodify -D 'cn=root,dc=example,dc=com' -W -f modify.ldif
```

Unlike `slapadd`, `ldapmodify` must be run while the daemon is running. It connects to the daemon for modification of the database. If encryption is not being used, also specify the `-x` option to use simple authentication. The value following `-D` must be the value of `rootdn` from `slapd.conf`. The `-W` option specifies that the user should be prompted for the password from the `rootpw` option in `slapd.conf`, which is more secure than listing it on the command line with the `-w` option. If the password is listed on the command line, it is stored in the user's command history, which can be read by unauthorized users easier than `slapd.conf`. Also remember that, even if you are prompted for the password, the password is sent unencrypted over the network unless encryption is enabled as described in the "Enabling TLS Encryption for LDAP" section.

As with `slapadd`, the `slapcat` or `ldapsearch` utilities can be used to verify if the entries have been modified or deleted. The `slapcat` command works regardless of whether the service is started. The `ldapsearch` command only works if `slapd` is running.

Customizing LDAP Indexing

The directory can be indexed based on particular attributes so that searches with `ldapsearch` are faster. Keep in mind that too much indexing can slow down performance. Indexing should only be enabled for frequent searches.

Indexing is defined in `slapd.conf` in the following format:

```
index <attributes> <indices>
```

Replace `<attributes>` with an attribute name or a list of attributes separated by commas. Replace `<indices>` with one of the following or a comma-separated list of two or more:

- `pres`: Use if searches have the form `objectclass=person` or `attribute-mail`
- `approx`: Must be used for searches with the form `sn~=person`
- `eq`: Use for equality searches without wildcards
- `sub`: Use for searches with wildcard substitutions
- `nolang`: Can be used for searches with lang subtype
- `nosubtypes`: Can be used for searches with subtypes

Optionally, the keyword `default` can be placed between the attributes and indices lists to define a set of default indices to use if an attribute is given on subsequent lines without indices:

```
index <attributes> default <indices>
```

Listing 12.8 shows examples, which are also the defaults in the `slapd.conf` file.

LISTING 12.8 Default Indexing Settings

```
# Indices to maintain for this database
index objectClass                      eq,pres
index ou,cn,mail,surname,givenname     eq,pres,sub
index uidNumber,gidNumber,loginShell   eq,pres
index uid,memberUid                    eq,pres,sub
index nisMapName,nisMapEntry           eq,pres,sub
```

Each time indexing options are modified, the indexes have to be regenerated as the root user on the server with the `slapindex` utility, and the daemon has to be stopped with the `service slapd stop` command before running `slapindex`.

Enabling TLS Encryption for LDAP

By default, all data sent between the OpenLDAP server and its clients are sent unencrypted in plain text that can be read by anyone who intercepts the packets on the network. If the server is internal only, this might not be a concern for you. A *TLS*, or *Transport Layer Security*, certificate can be used to enable authentication using *SASL* (*Simple Authentication and Security Layer*) EXTERNAL.

First, create an SSL certificate for the server. It can be one from a certificate authority (CA) such as VeriSign or it can be a self-signing certificate created with a program such as OpenSSL. Refer to openssl.org for details on the latter.

The `cn` attribute of the server must be the FQDN of the server, and the DN of the server certificate must be exactly the same as the `cn` attribute of the OpenLDAP server. Alias names and wildcards can be specified using the `subjectAltName` certificate extension. The clients can also have a certificate to authenticate with SASL EXTERNAL.

TIP

A dummy certificate, `/etc/pki/tls/certs/slapd.pem`, is included with the `openldap-servers` package and can be used for testing purposes.

To enable TLS encryption so data, including the password used to administer the directory from a remote system, is encrypted between the server and the client, uncomment the following lines in `/etc/openldap/slapd.conf`:

```
TLSCACertificateFile /etc/pki/tls/certs/ca-bundle.crt
TLSCertificateFile /etc/pki/tls/certs/slapd.pem
TLSCertificateKeyFile /etc/pki/tls/certs/slapd.pem
```

If unchanged, after restarting the service with `service ldap restart`, the dummy certificate installed for testing is used. Otherwise, copy your certificates to the `/etc/pki/tls/certs/` directory and change the values of the options to appropriate filenames.

The client must be configured to trust the server certificate. Refer to "Connecting to the LDAP Server" for details.

Starting and Stopping the LDAP Server

As previously mentioned, to start the LDAP server daemon, `slapd`, execute `service ldap start` as root.

The following commands can also be run from the initialization script in the format `service ldap <command>`:

- `configtest`: Test for common configuration errors.
- `start`: Start `slapd`.
- `stop`: Stop `slapd`.
- `status`: Show whether the service is running.
- `restart`: Stop and then start `slapd`.
- `condrestart`: If `slapd` is already running, restart it. Otherwise, do nothing.

Be sure to execute `chkconfig ldap on` as root to make sure the daemon is started automatically at boot time.

Connecting to the LDAP Server

Clients wishing to connect to an OpenLDAP server must have the `openldap-clients` and `nss_ldap` packages installed. These clients can run the available remote OpenLDAP utilities such as `ldapadd` and `ldapsearch`. They can also connect to the directory from a user-end application such as the Evolution email application.

To configure a Red Hat Enterprise Linux system as an LDAP client, configure the following options in `/etc/openldap/ldap.conf` and `/etc/ldap.conf` (replace `<server-ip>` with the IP address of the LDAP server):

```
URI ldap://<server-ip>/
BASE dc=example,dc=com
```

If TLS encryption is to be used, also add the following line to `/etc/openldap/ldap.conf` and copy the certificate files in the defined directory:

```
TLS_CACERTDIR /etc/openldap/cacerts
```

TIP

Additional options for `ldap.conf` can be found in the `ldap.conf` man page.

To use LDAP for login user authentication, edit `/etc/nsswitch.conf` as root and add `ldap` to the `passwd`, `shadow`, and `group` lines:

```
passwd: files ldap
shadow: files ldap
group: files ldap
```

Many applications can connect to an LDAP server to query the database such as Evolution. Some applications can retrieve and modify entries in the directory. Others, like Evolution, can just request entries. Refer to the documentation for each application for details on configuring it to connect to your LDAP server.

Customizing LDAP Logging

Log messages for the OpenLDAP service are sent to `/var/log/messages` by default using the syslog mechanism. The log level can be set in `slapd.conf` using the following syntax:

```
loglevel <level>
```

where `<level>` determines what type of messages to log and is one or more of the following (two or more should be space separated):

- `1`: trace function calls
- `4`: heavy trace debugging
- `8`: connection management
- `16`: packets sent and received
- `32`: search filter processing
- `64`: configuration file processing
- `128`: access control list processing
- `256`: statistics for log connections, operations, and results
- `512`: statistics for log entries sent
- `1024`: communication with shell backends
- `2048`: entry parsing
- `4096`: caching (unused)
- `8192`: data indexing (unused)
- `16384`: LDAPSync replication
- `32768`: log messages logged regardless of log level

The log levels or combinations of log levels can be represented by values other than integers. See the `slapd.conf` man page for details.

To write log messages to a separate file, add the following line to `/etc/syslog.conf`:

```
local4.*                /var/log/slapd.log
```

Enabling Kerberos

Unlike other authentication systems, Kerberos is designed to allow authorized users access to systems and services based on an encrypted ticketing system. The *key distribution center* (*KDC*) stores the Kerberos database, and the *ticket-granting server* (*TGS*) issues tickets to clients.

Each client requests a ticket from the KDC. The client must enter a valid password after the request, and the password is used as the key to encrypt the ticket. A *ticket-granting ticket* (*TGT*) is granted by the KDC, encrypted with the user's password, and sent back to the client. The client decrypts it with the password. The TGT and the corresponding *ticket session key* (TSK) on the client are called *credentials*. The credentials automatically time out after a configured amount of time, which is set to 10 hours by default. Each Kerberos server is responsible for granting access for a particular *realm*, or network that utilizes Kerberos.

Usually, the realm name is the same as the domain name. To distinguish between realm names and domain names, realms are written in all uppercase letters, and domain names are written in all lowercase letters. Be sure to use this convention when modifying configuration files.

NOTE

If SELinux, a mandatory access control security mechanism, is set to enforcing mode, Kerberos is protected by it. For the default targeted policy, the system is allowed to work with Kerberos by setting the SELinux boolean `allow_kerberos` to `1`. Refer to Chapter 23 for details on SELinux. Execute the `man kerberos_selinux` command for more information on how SELinux affects Kerberos.

Allowing Kerberos Connections

Kerberos uses TCP and UDP port 88 by default. The `kpasswd` user application for changing the user's password uses TCP and UDP port 464. The `kadmin` program uses TCP port 749. If `klogin` is used, it used TCP port 543 or TCP port 2105 for the encrypted version. If additional Kerberized applications are enabled, refer to `/etc/services` for their port numbers.

If custom IPTables rules are being used, refer to Chapter 24 for details on how to allow connections from a specific port.

If the default security level is enabled instead of custom IPTables rules, use the Security Level Configuration tool to allow Kerberos connections. Start it by selecting **Administration, Security Level and Firewall** from the **System** menu on the top panel of the desktop or by executing the `system-config-securitylevel` command. Enter the root password when prompted if running as a non-root user. Click **Add** next to the **Other ports** table to add a port.

Configuring the Kerberos Server

Before setting up a Kerberos server or client, the clock on the server and all the clients must be in sync. If the clock between the server and client are too far apart (5 minutes by default), the credentials are ignored and the client is not authenticated. It is recommended that administrators use the *Network Time Protocol* (*NTP*) on the server and clients to keep the clocks in sync. Refer to Chapter 19, "Explaining Other Common Network Services," for details on configuring NTP.

Customizing the Kerberos Configuration Files

On the system you are setting up as a Kerberos server, install the `krb5-server` and `krb5-workstation` RPM packages. The `/etc/krb5.conf` file is the main configuration file for the server. This file is formatted using the following style:

```
[section]
   tag=value
   tag=value
   tag=value
```

The following sections exist:

- `[libdefaults]`: Default values for Kerberos.
- `[login]`: Default values for the Kerberos login program.
- `[appdefaults]`: Default values for applications that use Kerberos.
- `[realms]`: Define the server location of each Kerberos realm.
- `[domain_realm]`: Associates subdomains and domain names to Kerberos realm names. Required if domain names are not used as realm names.
- `[logging]`: Logging preferences. Refer to "Logging Kerberos Connections" for details.
- `[cpaths]`: Paths to authentication certificates, if used.

At a bare minimum, replace all the example.com domain references and EXAMPLE.COM realm references in the existing `/etc/krb5.conf` file with your domain. The file is case-sensitive so be sure to preserve the upper- or lowercase.

Also configure the realm and other settings for the KDC in `/var/kerberos/krb5kdc/kdc.conf`. The following sections can be defined:

- `[kdcdefaults]`: Default values for the KDC.
- `[realms]`: Define the server locations for each Kerberos realm.

At a bare minimum, replace EXAMPLE.COM with your realm name in the existing `kdc.conf`, which is usually a domain name, in all uppercase letters.

Creating the Kerberos Database

To create the Kerberos database, use the kdb5_util command. Optionally, also create a *stash file*, or an encrypted file containing a copy of the master keys. The stash file also serves as an automatic authentication system for the KDC to itself when the Kerberos daemons are started. Because the stash file contains the master key, be sure it is only readable by the root user and is on the local file system for the KDC. Do not include the stash file in your backup plan unless access to the file system containing the backup files are heavily restricted to trusted administrators because it can be used to gain access to the entire Kerberos database. To create the database and stash file, use the following command as root (replace <realm_name> with the name of the realm such as EXAMPLE.COM):

```
/usr/kerberos/sbin/kdb5_util create -r <realm_name> -s
```

The -s option creates the stash file. If you don't want to create one, do not include the -s option. The utility prompts you for the master key as shown in Listing 12.9.

LISTING 12.9 Creating the Kerberos Database and Stash File

```
Loading random data
Initializing database '/var/kerberos/krb5kdc/principal' for realm 'EXAMPLE.COM',
master key name 'K/M@EXAMPLE.COM'
You will be prompted for the database Master Password.
It is important that you NOT FORGET this password.
Enter KDC database master key:
Re-enter KDC database master key to verify:
```

The utility creates the following files in the /var/kerberos/krb5kdc/ directory:

- principal: Kerberos database file.
- principal.ok: Kerberos database file.
- principal.kadm5: Kerberos administrative database file.
- principal.kadm5.lock: Kerberos administrative database lock file.
- .k5.<realm_name>: Stash file (if -s is used). Replace <realm_name>.

Managing Kerberos Principals

Kerberos users allowed access to the database are called principals, which are divided into three components in the form <primary>/<instance>@<REALM>. Principals can have multiple instances: a null instance represented by a username and realm such as tfox@EXAMPLE.COM, an admin instance represented by a username followed by /admin and a realm such as tfox/admin@EXAMPLE.COM, and a root instance represented by a username followed by /root and a realm such as tfox/root@EXAMPLE.COM. Having an admin and root instance for users allows them to authenticate as a different principal when performing administrative tasks but use a non-privileged principal when performing user operations. This is similar to the non-root user and root user concept: Only perform actions as a privileged user when necessary to prevent unintended operations.

Principals must be explicitly added using the `add_principal` command to `kadmin` or `kadmin.local`. The `kadmin` and `kadmin.local` utilities offer the same functionality except that the `kadmin.local` utility can only be run on the master KDC and does not authenticate through Kerberos. Because the KDC service hasn't been started yet, add at least one administrative principal using the `kadmin.local` utility. Additional principals, both administrators and non-administrators, can be added during this setup phase, or they can be added later.

NOTE

If the `kadmin` command is used, the principal adding, modifying, or deleting principals must have permission to do so using the Kerberos ACLs as described in the "Setting Access Control Lists for Kerberos" section.

Start the `kadmin` shell by executing `kadmin.local` as the root user on the KDC server. To add a principal, use the following command:

```
add_principal <options> <principal>
```

TIP

To view a list of valid commands while in the `kadmin` or `kadmin.local shell`, press the Tab key twice.

Replace `<principal>` with the username such as `tfox/admin`. Table 12.1 shows available `<options>`.

TABLE 12.1 Principal Options

Restriction Flags	Description
`-expire <time>`	Set expiration date for the principal.
`-pwexpire <time>`	Set the password expiration date.
`-maxlife <time>`	Set maximum ticket life for the principal.
`-maxrenewlife <time>`	Set maximum renewable ticket life for the principal.
`-kvno <kvno>`	Set the key version number.
`-policy <policy>`	Set policy for the principal. If no policy is set, the policy name default is used if it exists. A warning message is printed if a principal doesn't have a policy.
`-clearpolicy`	Do not assign the principal the "default" policy if one is not specified with `-policy <policy>`.
`-allow_postdated`	Do not allow the principal to retrieve post-dated tickets. `+allow_postdated` clears this preference.
`-allow_forwardable`	Do not allow the principal to retrieve forwardable tickets. `+allow_forwardable` clears this preference.
`-allow_renewable`	Do not allow the principal to retrieve renewable tickets. `+allow_renewable` clears this preference.

TABLE 12.1 Continued

Restriction Flags	Description
-allow_proxiable	Do not allow the principal to retrieve proxiable tickets. +allow_proxiable clears this preference.
-allow_dup_skey	Do not allow user-to-user authentication for the principal by not allowing the principal to retrieve a session key from another user. +allow_dup_skey clears this preference.
+requires_preauth	Principal must preauthenticate before calling kinit. -requires_preauth clears this preference.
+requires_hwauth	Principal must preauthenticate using a hardware device before calling kinit. -requires_hwauth clears this preference.
-allow_svr	Do not allow the principal to issue service tickets. +allow_svr clears this preference.
-allow_tgs_req	Do not allow the principal to request a service ticket from a TGS. +allow_tgs_req clears this preference.
-allow-tix	Do not allow the principal to issue any tickets. +allow-tix clears this preference.
+needchange	Force a password for the principal. -needchange clears the preference.
+password_changing_service	Marks the principal as a password change service principal. -password_changing_service clears the preference.
-randkey	Set the key of the principal to a random value.
-pw <password>	Set the key of the principal to <password> and do not prompt for a password.
-e <list>	Use the <list> as <enctype>:<salttype> pairs to set the key of the principal.

To modify a principal, use the following command inside the `kadmin` or `kadmin.local` shell (the same options from Table 12.1 can be used):

```
modify_principal <options> <principal>
```

To delete a principal, use the following command inside the `kadmin` or `kadmin.local` shell:

```
delete_principal <principal>
```

You must confirm the deletion unless the `-force` option is specified before the name of the principal.

Setting Access Control Lists for Kerberos

The Kerberos ACL file `kadm5.acl` is located in the `/var/kerberos/krb5kdc/` directory. At least one Kerberos administrator must be added to this access control file, and all principals listed must exist in the database. The order of the access control lines matters. The first match takes precedence. Each line in the file uses the following format:

```
<principal>     <permissions>     <target_principal>     <restrictions>
```

In the ACL file, the * wildcard can be used when specifying the principal such as `*/admin@EXAMPLE.COM` for all admin instances of valid users.

Table 12.2 shows the available permissions. Uppercase letters are used for negative permissions. To specify more than one permission, do not separate them by any spaces or punctuation such as `ad`.

TABLE 12.2 Kerberos ACL Permissions

Permission	Description
a	Allow the user to add principals or policies.
A	Do not allow the user to add principals or policies.
d	Allow the user to delete principals or policies.
D	Do not allow the user to delete principals or policies.
m	Allow the user to modify principals or policies.
M	Do not allow the user to modify principals or policies.
c	Allow the user to change the passwords for principals.
C	Do not allow the user to change the passwords for principals.
i	Allow the user to query the database.
I	Do not allow the user to query the database.
l	Allow the user to list principals or policies.
L	Do not allow the user to list principals or policies.
s	Allow the user to explicitly set the key for a principal.
S	Do not allow the user to explicitly set the key for a principal.
*	All permissions.
x	All permissions. The same as *.

The `<target_principal>` is only applicable if the permission has a target and is therefore optional. For example, a principal can be granted the ability to change passwords but only for specific users provided as the `<target_principal>`. Each component of the `<principal>` can be referenced in the `<target_principal>` with the `*<num>` wildcard such as `*1` for the first component of the principal.

The `<restrictions>` restrict, add, or modify actions granted and are also optional. They are in the format `+<flag>` or `-<flag>`. The same options used when adding or modifying a principal can be used as restrictions when adding ACLs. They are listed in Table 12.1.

Starting and Stopping the Kerberos Server

To start the Kerberos server, execute the following as root to start the appropriate daemons:

```
service krb5kdc start
service kadmin start
```

Be sure to configure the system to start these services at boot time:

```
chkconfig krb5kdc on
```

```
chkconfig kadmin on
```

For these services to start at boot time, a stash file must exist as described earlier.

Connecting to the Kerberos Server

Each Kerberos client must have the `krb5-workstation` RPM package installed to provide the Kerberos user commands for requesting and managing tickets. It also provides Kerberized versions of authentication utilities such as `rlogin` and `ftp`.

On each client, edit the `/etc/krb5.conf` file to set the realm and the location of the server for the realm. Replacing the example.com and EXAMPLE.COM instances in the default `krb5.conf` file is usually sufficient.

The Kerberized applications must be enabled on each client. For example, to enable the Kerberized telnet, make sure the `krb5-telnet` service is enabled and make sure users execute `/usr/kerberos/bin/telnet` instead of `/usr/bin/telnet`. To ensure the Kerberized programs are executed, verify that each user's path includes `/usr/kerberos/bin/` before any of the other directories containing the non-Kerberized versions of the commands such as `/usr/bin/` or `/usr/local/bin/`. Other Kerberized applications include `ftp`, `rsh`, and `rcp`.

If Kerberos is used, users must use the `kpasswd` command to change their password instead of `passwd`. They must also use `ksu` instead of `su` to change to the root user.

If the clients are configured to use `klogin` instead of `login`, each user is granted a ticket, and using the ticket is transparent to the user. Otherwise, the user must explicitly request a ticket with the `kinit` utility. The user executes the `kinit` command, is prompted for his password, and is granted a ticket if the correct password is entered. The user is then authenticated for all Kerberized programs until the ticket expires, which is ten hours by default.

A user can view his tickets and expiration dates with the `klist` command. A user can also cancel his tickets immediately at any time by executing the `kdestroy` command. Because the user does not have to enter a password or any other form of identification for Kerberized programs, users need to be careful about who has access to their computers or login sessions. If a user is going to be away from his computer, executing `kdestroy` to expire his Kerberos tickets is recommended so that someone else can't use his authentication while he is away.

Logging Kerberos Connections

In the `/etc/krb5.conf` configuration file, the following logging section exists:

```
[logging]
 default = FILE:/var/log/krb5libs.log
 kdc = FILE:/var/log/krb5kdc.log
 admin_server = FILE:/var/log/kadmind.log
```

As you can see, the following entities can be set:

- `default`: Default logging if additional settings are configured.
- `kdc`: How to handle logging for the KDC.
- `admin_server`: How to handle logging for the administrative server.

By default, these three entities are set to write logs to three different files. The following values are allowed for each of the entities:

- Write to a file:

  `FILE:<filename>`

- Write to a standard error:

  `STDERR`

- Write to the console:

  `CONSOLE`

- Write to specified device:

  `DEVICE=<devicename>`

- Write to the system log using syslog with the specified severity and facility (valid severities and facilities are in the syslog man page):

  `SYSLOG:<severity>:<facility>`

Enabling SMB or Winbind Authentication

Chapter 13 discusses the basics of configuring a Samba (SMB) server for file sharing, including allowing connections and logging customization. It also discusses connecting to existing shared directories on an SMB server on the network. This section discusses how to authenticate users via an SMB server or the Winbind service on a Samba server.

The `pam_smb` RPM package is required for SMB authentication. The `samba-common` package is required for Winbind authentication. Install the package containing the authentication method of your choice via RHN if it is not already installed.

Enabling SMB

Other than the documentation files, the `pam_smb` package contains two files: the `/etc/pam_smb.conf` configuration file and `/lib/security/pam_smb_auth.so` (`/lib64/security/pam_smb_auth.so` on 64-bit systems).

The /etc/pam_smb.conf file should contain three lines. The first should be the workgroup name for the SMB server, and the next two lines should be the IP addresses or hostnames of the primary and secondary domain controllers:

```
<workgroup>
<primary-server>
<secondary-server>
```

The /etc/pam.d/system-auth file is the main PAM authentication configuration file. If you view the contents of the other files in /etc/pam.d/, you will notice that most have a line to include this file. If you have used the authconfig tool as discussed in the "Enabling with the Authentication Tool" section, this file is removed and symbolically linked to /etc/pam.d/system-auth-ac, which is modified by authconfig.

Because using authconfig removes the /etc/pam.d/system-auth file and because you might need to revert back to the original file, be sure to make a backup copy of the file before modifying it. Also, leave a terminal open with root already logged in while modifying the file until you have tested the new configuration to make sure you can still log in to the system. If you create a syntax error in the file, you might not be able to log in again and will need the already opened root terminal to fix the file.

In /etc/pam.d/system-auth (or /etc/pam.d/system-auth-ac), add the following line to enable SMB authentication:

```
auth        sufficient    pam_smb_auth.so use_first_pass nolocal
```

The users still need to be in /etc/passwd. Users with a starred password are authenticated with the SMB server. Otherwise, local authentication is used.

Enabling Winbind

Enabling Winbind is similar to enabling SMB authentication. Add the following line to /etc/pam.d/system-auth (or /etc/pam.d/system-auth-ac):

```
auth        sufficient    pam_winbind.so use_first_pass nolocal
```

The Winbind users should not be added as local users, but their home directories as configured on the Samba server must be created on the Linux client. If the winbind use default domain option in smb.conf is set to false (the default), Winbind users must log in with a username in the format <domain>+<username> such as EXAMPLE+tfox for the tfox user.

TIP

For more details about Winbind, refer to http://samba.org/samba/docs/man/Samba3-HOWTO/winbind.html.

Enabling with the Authentication Tool

All of these user information databases and authentication methods can be easily set up with the Authentication Configuration (`system-config-authentication`) tool, which has a text-based, graphical, and a command-line version. The text-based or command-line versions are useful when running them remotely over SSH without X forwarding enabled or when running them from a console instead of the graphical desktop. The command-line version, which is executed with the `authconfig` command, can be non-interactive for use in scripts or kickstart.

To use this utility, install the `authconfig` RPM package as described in Chapter 3, "Operating System Updates." Also install the `authconfig-gtk` package if you want to use the graphical version.

When the application is started, you are prompted for the root password before continuing if you are not already logged in as root. This section assumes you are using the graphical version of the tool. The same general steps apply for the text-based version, but the interface might differ slightly.

Figure 12.1 shows the graphical application. As you can see, three tabs divide the application into functional groups: **User Information**, **Authentication**, and **Options**. It is assumed that the administrator has installed all necessary RPM packages for any service required before enabling them with this tool. All services and options are shown in the interface regardless of which packages are currently installed. Refer to the sections earlier in the chapter for a list of packages necessary for each type of identity management service.

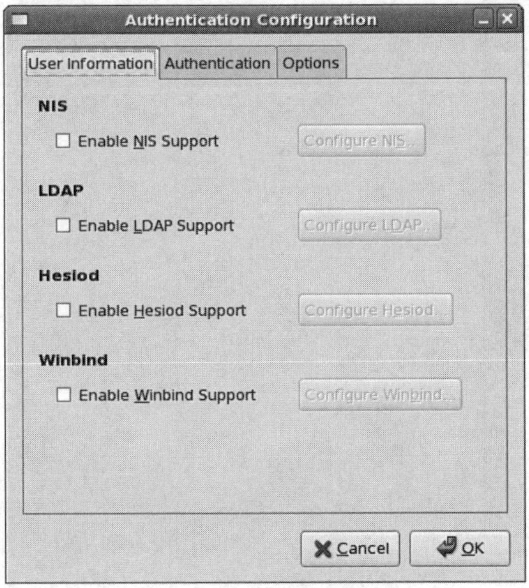

FIGURE 12.1 User Information

CAUTION

Most changes take effect immediately after you click **OK**. The network services enabled are started and configured to start at boot time. If a service is already enabled, but its settings are modified, the service is restarted with the new settings. If a service is disabled in the interface, the service is not always stopped immediately after you click **OK** or configured not to start at boot time. Be sure to stop the service explicitly and use chkconfig <service> off to disable it at boot time.

As shown in Figure 12.1, the NIS, LDAP, Hesiod, and Winbind network services are available for user information. Refer to their corresponding sections earlier in this chapter for more information about each of them. To retrieve user information from a remote server (such as the information displayed with the finger <username> command), click the **Enable** check box next to the desired method or methods. Then, click the **Configure** button for the method. The required settings differ per support option. Enter the requested information for each one enabled. For example, after enabling NIS, enter the NIS domain and server to connect to.

To configure a remote authentication method, go to the **Authentication** tab as shown in Figure 12.2. The Kerberos, LDAP, SmartCard, SMB (Samba), and Winbind network services are available for user authentication. Click the **Enable** check box next to the desired support option. Then, click the **Configure** button for the method and enter the requested information.

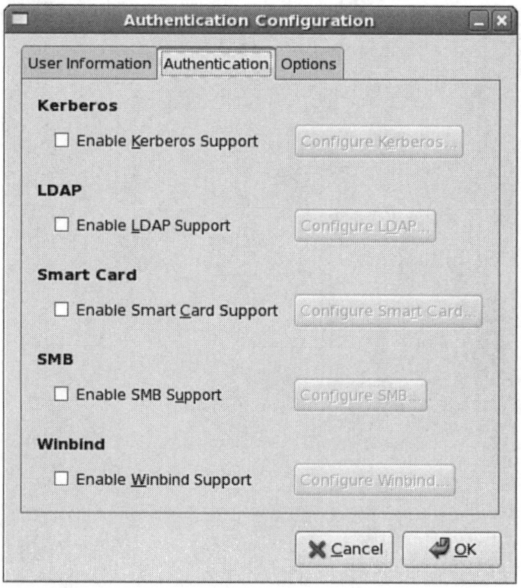

FIGURE 12.2 Authentication Configuration

Lastly, the **Options** tab allows an administrator to customize identity management for the system. The following options are available:

- **Cache User Information**: Enable the name caching daemon (`nscd`) and configure it to start at boot time. When enabled, this daemon can be configured to cache information about `/etc/passwd`, `/etc/group`, and hostname resolution. If this option is selected, all three are cached. The `/etc/nscd.conf` file can be modified by root to customize the caching such as the time-to-live values and which of the three to cache.

CAUTION

The Winbind authentication method and `nscd` will not work together properly. If they are both running at the same time, the system will not be able to resolve domain users and groups.

- **Use Shadow Passwords**: Enabled by default during installation using the `shadow-utils` package. If enabled, instead of encrypted passwords being stored in the `/etc/passwd` file, which is readable by everyone, they are located in the `/etc/shadow` file, which is readable by the root user only.
- **Use MD5 Passwords**: Enabled by default. If enabled, passwords can be 256 characters instead of just 8 characters. This enhances security on the system because it is harder to guess longer passwords.
- **Local authorization is sufficient for local users**: Allow local users to be authenticated with local files instead of with the network authentication service.
- **Authenticate system accounts by network services**: Authenticate system accounts (user accounts under UID 500) with the enabled network authentication service instead of local files.

Using the Command-Line Version

As previously mentioned, the command-line version of the Authentication Configuration tool allows you to configure the same settings as the graphical interface. Command-line options are used so that the commands are non-interactive, making it possible to use in an automated script or a kickstart file.

Table 12.3 contains the available command-line options. These options can also be found in the `authconfig` man page or by executing the `authconfig --help` command. They are invoked by executing the `authconfig` command as root followed by one or more options:

```
authconfig <options> --update
```

If the `--update` option is not listed, the settings are not updated. If `--test` is used instead, the settings are not updated, but the listed changes are displayed in a summary report. The `--test` option can also be used without any other options to display the current authentication settings. If `--probe` is used instead, the network is probed via DNS and other services for configuration information about the system. If any information is found, it is displayed. If none are found, no information is displayed.

If enabling a service, be sure to also specify its required settings such as `--ldapserver=<server>` and `ldapbasedn=<dn>` with `--enableldapauth`. Because the command-line version is intended to be non-interactive, no error messages or warnings appear if you don't provide the necessary information for a service. The service is just not enabled or started. Be sure to test all commands being used in scripts or kickstart before relying on them to work.

TABLE 12.3 authconfig Command-Line Options

Command-Line Option	Description
`--help`	Display all command-line options and brief descriptions.
`--enableshadow`	Enable shadow passwords (the default).
`--disableshadow`	Disable shadow passwords.
`--enablemd5`	Enable MD5 passwords (the default).
`--disablemd5`	Disable MD5 passwords.
`--enablenis`	Enable NIS for user information.
`--disablenis`	Disable NIS for user information.
`--nisdomain=<domain>`	Specify NIS domain if enabling NIS.
`--nisserver=<server>`	Specify NIS server if enabling NIS.
`--enableldap`	Enable LDAP for user information.
`--disableldap`	Disable LDAP for user information.
`--enableldapauth`	Enable LDAP for authentication.
`--disableldapauth`	Disable LDAP for authentication.
`--ldapserver=<server>`	Provide LDAP server if enabling LDAP.
`--ldapbasedn=<dn>`	Provide LDAP base DN if enabling LDAP.
`--enableldaptls`	Enable use of TLS with LDAP.
`--disableldaptls`	Disable use of TLS with LDAP.
`--ldaploadcacert=<url>`	Load CA certificate from URL provided if enabling LDAP.
`--enablesmartcard`	Enable smart card authentication.
`--disablesmartcard`	Disable smart card authentication.
`--enablerequiresmartcard`	Require smart card authentication.
`--disablerequiresmartcard`	Do not require smart card authentication.
`--smartcardmodule=<module>`	Specify smart card module to use if enabling it.
`--smartcardaction=<action>`	Set action to take when smart card is removed. Set `<action>` to `0` to lock or `1` to ignore.
`--enablekrb5`	Enable Kerberos authentication.
`--disablekrb5`	Disable Kerberos authentication.
`--krb5kdc=<server>`	Set Kerberos KDC when enabling Kerberos authentication.

TABLE 12.3 Continued

Command-Line Option	**Description**
`--krb5adminserver=<server>`	Set Kerberos admin server when enabling Kerberos authentication.
`--krb5realm=<realm>`	Set Kerberos realm when enabling Kerberos authentication.
`--enablekrb5kdcdns`	Enable use of DNS to determine Kerberos KDCs.
`--disablekrb5kdcdns`	Disable use of DNS to determine Kerberos KDCs.
`--enablekrb5realmdns`	Enable use of DNS to determine Kerberos realms.
`--disablekrb5realmdns`	Disable use of DNS to determine Kerberos realms.
`--enablesmbauth`	Enable Samba authentication.
`--disablesmbauth`	Disable Samba authentication.
`--smbservers=<servers>`	Set Samba server when enabling Samba authentication.
`--smbworkgroup=<workgroup>`	Set which workgroup the Samba authentication server is in when enabling Samba authentication.
`--enablewinbind`	Enable Winbind for user information.
`--disablewinbind`	Disable Winbind for user information.
`--enablewinbindauth`	Enable Winbind for authentication.
`--disablewinbindauth`	Disable Winbind for authentication.
`--smbsecurity=<mode>`	Set security mode for Samba or Winbind. Must be one of `user`, `server`, `domain`, or `ads`.
`--smbrealm=<realm>`	Set realm for Samba and Winbind when security mode is set to ads.
`--smbidmapuid=<range>`	Provide UID range from lowest to highest to assign to Winbind users when security is set to `domain` or `ads`.
`--smbidmapgid=<range>`	Provide GID range from lowest to highest to assign to Winbind users when security is set to `domain` or `ads`.
`--winbindseparator=<char>`	Set character used to separate domain and user part of usernames created by Winbind if `winbinduserdefaultdomain` is not enabled.
`--winbindtemplatehomedir=<dir>`	Set home directory for users created by Winbind. For example, `/home/%D/%U`.
`--winbindtemplateprimarygroup=<group>`	Set primary group for users created by Winbind such as the nobody group.
`--winbindtemplateshell=<shell>`	Set login shell of users created by Winbind such as `/bin/false`.
`--enablewinbindusedefaultdomain`	If Winbind is enabled, users with no domain in their usernames are domain users.

TABLE 12.3 Continued

Command-Line Option	Description
`--disablewinbindusedefaultdomain`	If Winbind is enabled, users with no domain in their usernames are not domain users.
`--winbindjoin=<admin>`	When joining the Winbind domain or ads realm, join as specified administrator.
`--enablewins`	Enable WINS hostname resolution.
`--disablewins`	Disable WINS hostname resolution.
`--enablehesiod`	Enable Hesiod for user information.
`--disablehesiod`	Disable Hesiod for user information.
`--hesiodlhs=<lhs>`	Set Hesiod LHS when enabling Hesiod.
`--hesiodrhs=<rhs>`	Set Hesiod RHS when enabling Hesiod.
`--enablecache`	Enabling caching of user information with `nscd`.
`--disablecache`	Disabling caching of user information with `nscd`.
`--enablelocauthorize`	Enable local authorization for local users.
`--disablelocauthorize`	Disable local authorization for local users.
`--enablesysnetauth`	Enable network authentication for system users.
`--disablesysnetauth`	Disable network authentication for system users. System users are authorized by local files only.
`--nostart`	Do not start or stop `portmap`, `ypbind`, or `nscd`.

Summary

The NIS, LDAP, Kerberos, Hesiod, SMB, and Winbind network authentication services discussed in this chapter can centralize user information, including passwords. This allows for easier maintenance and backup procedures. They also allow for identical authentication from any system on the network.

Review each of these authentication services and decide which one works best for your network.

CHAPTER 13

Network File Sharing

IN THIS CHAPTER

- Network File System
- Samba File Sharing

In an enterprise computing environment, it is common to share files between computers or allow several users to access the same set of files on a central server and have all changes be visible to all users immediately. In a pure UNIX environment, including those consisting solely of Red Hat Enterprise Linux systems, this can be achieved via Network File System (NFS). If sharing files between Red Hat Enterprise Linux and Microsoft Windows systems is desired, Samba can be used to achieve connectivity.

Network File System

NFS, or *Network File System*, is a server-client protocol for sharing files between computers on a common network. It is available on a variety of UNIX-based operating systems, not just Linux. The server and client do not have to use the same operating system. The client system just needs to be running an NFS client compatible with the NFS server.

The NFS server *exports* one or more directories to the client systems, and the client systems *mount* one or more of the shared directories to local directories called *mount points*. After the share is mounted, all I/O operations are written back to the server, and all clients notice the change as if it occurred on the local filesystem. A manual refresh is not needed because the client accesses the remote filesystem as if it were local. Access is granted or restricted by client IP addresses.

One advantage of NFS is that the client mounts the remote filesystem to a directory thus allowing users to access it in the same method used to access local files. Furthermore, because access is granted by IP address, a username and password are not required. However, there are security risks to consider because the NFS server knows nothing about the users on the client system. The files from the NFS server retain their file permissions, user ID, and group ID when mounted. If the client uses a different set of user and group IDs, file ownership will change.

For example, if a file is owned by user ID 500 on the NFS server, the file is exported to the clients with that same user ID. If user ID 500 maps to the user bsf on the NFS server but maps to the user akf on the remote client, user akf will have access to the file on the remote client. Thus, it is crucial that the NFS server and all its clients use the same user database so the user and group IDs are identical no matter which machine is used to access the files. The administrator can assign identical user and group IDs on systems on the network, but this can be a tedious and time-consuming task if the network has more than a few users. A more error-proof and manageable method is to use NIS as discussed in Chapter 12, "Identity Management."

NOTE

NFS does not have its own log file. Instead, the commands used by NFS such as `rpc.mountd` to mount client requests are logged in the system log file `/var/log/messages`. Kernel messages from `nfsd` are also logged to this file.

NFS and SELinux

In Red Hat Enterprise Linux 5, NFS is protected by the default Security-Enhanced Linux (SELinux) policy, known as the targeted policy. Refer to Chapter 23, "Protecting Against Intruders with Security-Enhanced Linux" for more information on SELinux.

By default, this targeted policy allows NFS connections to the server by setting the `nfs_export_all_ro` and `nfs_export_all_rw` SELinux booleans to `1`.

If you are sharing home directories over NFS while using SELinux, you must set `use_nfs_home_dirs boolean` to `1` on each client connecting to the NFS server sharing the home directories. Execute the following command as root:

```
setsebool -P use_nfs_home_dirs boolean 1
```

To verify that the setting has been changed, execute the following:

```
getsebool use_nfs_home_dirs boolean
```

If enabled, the output should be the following:

```
use_nfs_home_dirs --> on
```

You can also change this setting by running the SELinux Management Tool. Start it by selecting **Administration**, **SELinux Management** from the **System** menu on the top panel of the desktop or by executing the `system-config-selinux` command. Enter the root password when prompted if running as a non-root user. Select **Boolean** from the list on the left. On the right, click the triangle icon next to **NFS**. The SELinux booleans affecting NFS appear. Click the check box next to **Support NFS home directories**. The change takes place immediately.

TIP

The SELinux booleans that affect NFS are described in the nfs_selinux man page viewable with the `man nfs_selinux` command.

The SELinux implementation in Red Hat Enterprise Linux does not require the files shared with NFS to be labeled with a specific security context. However, if more than one file-sharing protocol is configured to share the same set of files such as FTP and Samba, the security context of the files must be set to `public_content_t` or `public_content_rw_t` instead. Additional SELinux booleans must be enabled as well. Refer to the "Security Context for Multiple File-Sharing Protocols" section in Chapter 23 for complete instructions.

Allowing NFS Connections

Before configuring the NFS server, configure your firewall settings to allow the incoming connections. While `portmapper` and the `nfs` daemon use static ports, NFS also employs four additional services: `statd`, `mountd`, `rquotad`, and `lockd`. They are assigned a random port by `portmapper`, which makes it difficult for firewall configuration. However, it is possible to configure these four daemons to use static ports. Refer to the "Assigning Static NFS Ports" section later in this chapter for details.

The `portmapper` service uses UDP and TCP port 111, and the `nfs` daemon uses UDP and TCP port 2049 by default. If custom IPTables rules are being used, refer to Chapter 24, "Configuring a Firewall," for details on how to allow these ports.

If the default security level is enabled instead of custom IPTables rules, use the Security Level Configuration tool to allow NFS connections. Start it by selecting **Administration**, **Security Level and Firewall** from the System menu on the top panel of the desktop or by executing the `system-config-securitylevel` command. Enter the root password when prompted if running as a user. In the **Other ports** area, click **Add** to specify each NFS port. Remember, the ports will differ depending on which ones you choose.

TIP

To retrieve a list of clients connected to the NFS server, use the `showmount` command from a shell prompt. To also show the directories the clients are connected to, use the `showmount -a` command.

Using a Graphical Tool to Configure the NFS Server

To use a system as an NFS server, the `nfs-utils` RPM package must be installed. If it is not installed, install it with Red Hat Network as described in Chapter 3, "Operating System Updates." To configure it via the NFS Server Configuration graphical tool, the `system-config-nfs` RPM package must also be installed. If you prefer to edit the configuration file directly, skip to the later section "Configuring the NFS Server on the Command Line."

To start the tool, select **Administration**, **Server Settings**, **NFS** from the **System** menu on the top panel of the desktop. Alternatively, execute the command `system-config-nfs` from a shell prompt.

Root privileges are required to modify the NFS server settings, so you must have root access to use this tool. If you are not root when you start the program, you will be prompted for the root password.

All currently configured shares are shown each time the program is started as shown in Figure 13.1.

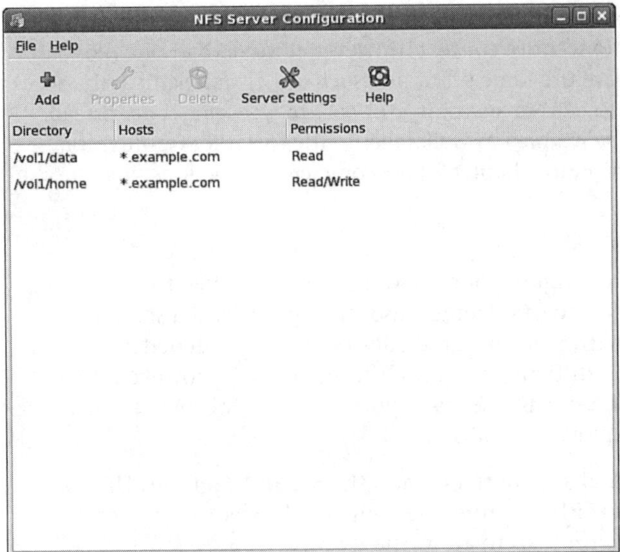

FIGURE 13.1 NFS Server Configuration Tool

NOTE

This graphical interface interacts with the `/etc/exports` file directly. Any changes made directly to the configuration file after the graphical tool is used will appear in the graphical tool the next time it is used.

Adding a New NFS Share

To add a new share, click the **Add** button in the toolbar. The Add dialog window appears as shown in Figure 13.2.

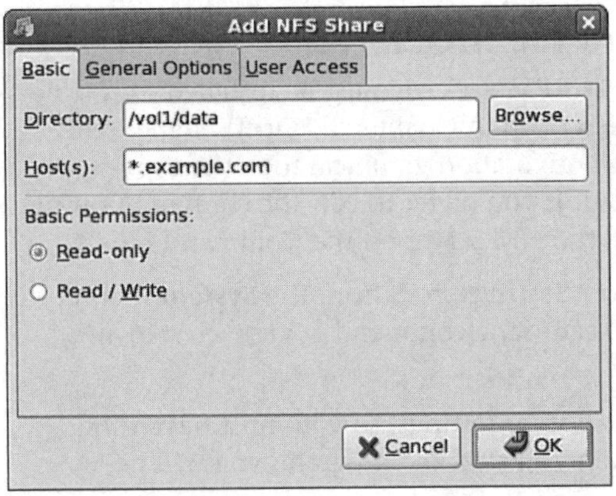

FIGURE 13.2 Adding an NFS Share

On the **Basic** tab, specify a directory to share, configure the allowed clients, and select whether the clients should be allowed read-only or read-write access.

The IP address range for the allowed clients must be in one of the following formats:

- Specific IP address or hostname: Provide the IP address, the fully qualified domain name (FQDN), or hostname of the allowed client. If the FQDN or hostname is used, the server must be able to resolve it to an IP address.
- FQDNs specified by wildcards: Use the * or ? special character to list a set of FQDNs such as `*.example.com`. Dots are not included in the wildcard. (Note: Wildcards can not be used with IP addresses.)
- IP networks: Specify an IP network with its network netmask or the number of bits in the netmask such as 192.168.1.0/255.255.255.0 or 192.168.1.0/24.
- Netgroups: Specify an NIS netgroup such as @example_group_name.

NOTE

As the NFS server options are discussed, the corresponding option in the `/etc/exports` configuration file is provided in brackets such as `[option]`.

As shown in Figure 13.3, the **General Options** tab allows the administrator to configure the following options:

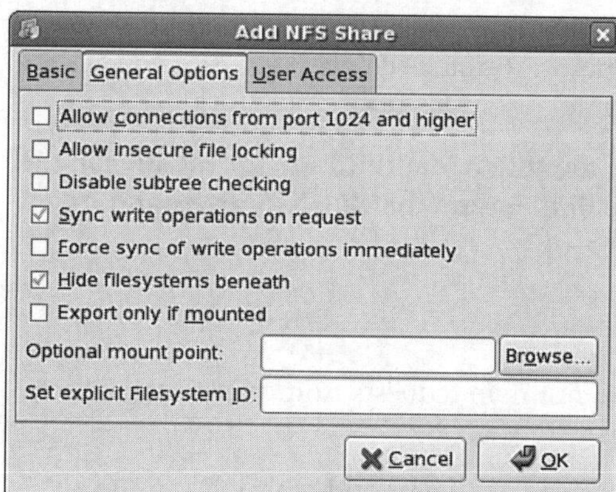

FIGURE 13.3 NFS General Options

- **Allow connections from port 1024 and higher**: By default, the NFS server requires root privileges to start, stop, or modify. If this option is selected, a user other than root can start the server. `[insecure]`
- **Allow insecure file locking**: Lock requests are not required. `[insecure_locks]`
- **Disable subtree checking**: By default, NFS performs a subtree check, meaning that if a subdirectory is shared, but the entire filesystem isn't, the server verifies that the

requested file is in the exported tree. When subtree checking is enabled, it also makes sure files inside directories with root-only access can only be accessed when exported with the `no_root_squash` option, which is not a default option. This option disables subtree checking. [`no_subtree_check`]

- **Sync write operations on request**: Wait until operation is written to disk before responding to client. Enabled by default because it is part of the NFS protocol and a required option. [`sync`]
- **Force sync of write operations immediately**: By default, write operations are delayed slightly if the server might receive another related write request or if one is already in progress. The writes are performed in one operation, which might improve performance. When this option is enabled, the server does not delay when writing to disk. This option can not be used if the `async` option is enabled. [`no_wdelay`]
- **Hide filesystems beneath**: If a subdirectory of a directory already exported is also configured as a mount point, by default, the subdirectory is accessible without having to specifically mount it. If this option is enabled, the subdirectory must be mounted separately from the parent directory. If it is not, the subdirectory will appear empty to NFS clients. [`hide` if checked, `no_hide` if unchecked]
- **Export only if mounted**: Export a directory only if it has been successfully mounted on the NFS server. This option prevents an empty directory from being exported should the filesystem being exported fail to mount on the NFS server. [`mp`]
- **Optional mount point**: If Export Only If Mounted is selected, a mount point can be specified if it differs from the export point. If not specified, it is assumed that the mount point and export point are the same. [`mountpoint`]
- **Set explicit Filesystem ID**: Override the filesystem identification for the file handle and file attributes with this number. Useful to ensure that the NFS server and its failover use identical NFS file handles. [`fsid`]

The **User Access** tab contains the following options:

- **Treat remote root user as local root**: Do not map requests from root to the anonymous user and group ID. [`no_root_squash`]
- **Treat all client users as anonymous users**: Map all user and group IDs to the anonymous user and group ID. [`all_squash`]
- **Local user ID for anonymous users**: If Treat All Client Users As Anonymous Users is enabled, use this user ID for the anonymous user. [`anonuid`]
- **Local group ID for anonymous users**: If Treat All Client Users As Anonymous Users is enabled, use this group ID for the anonymous user. [`anongid`]

Click **OK** to add the share to the list. After clicking **OK**, the settings are automatically saved to the `/etc/exports` file and the daemon is automatically reloaded so the new share is available. The old configuration file is written to `/etc/exports.bak`.

Editing and Deleting NFS Shares

To modify an existing share, select it from the list and click the **Properties** button in the toolbar. The existing settings for the share are shown and can be modified. After you click **OK**, the changes take place immediately.

To delete a share, select it from the list and click **Delete**. The shared directory is removed from the list. Once again, the change takes place immediately.

Configuring the NFS Server on the Command Line

To configure a Red Hat Enterprise Linux system as an NFS server via the command line, make sure the `nfs-utils` RPM package is installed.

The server configuration file, `/etc/exports`, uses the following format:

```
shared_directory allowed_hosts(options)
```

where `shared_directory` is the name of the directory to be shared, `allowed_hosts` is the IP address range of the allowed clients, and `options` is a list of NFS options for the exported directory. Obviously, the exported directory must exist. Refer to the previous section on graphical configuration for valid IP address range configuration. You must be root to modify this file.

For example, the following `/etc/exports` line allows all systems with 192.168.1.* IP addresses read-write access to the `/shared/` directory:

```
/shared 192.168.1.0/255.255.255.0(sync,rw)
```

CAUTION

Notice that `allowed_hosts` and `(options)` do not have a space between them. If a space is included, the options are applied to any and all IP addresses, which can be quite dangerous if write permission is granted.

The `sync` or `async` option must be specified as an NFS option. If `sync` is specified, the server waits until the request is written to disk before responding to the client. The `sync` option is recommended because it follows the NFS protocol.

To grant read-write access for the exported directory, use the `rw` option. For additional options, refer to the previous section on graphical configuration. For a full list of NFS server options, refer to the exports man page with the command `man exports`. Options should be separated by commas.

Starting and Stopping the NFS Server

The root user must execute the commands to start, stop, and reload the NFS server. To start the NFS server, execute the command `service nfs start`. To stop the server, execute the command `service nfs stop`. If the server is already started and the `/etc/exports` configuration file is altered, the NFS server must be informed. Use the command `service nfs reload` to force the server to reread the configuration file.

To have the service start automatically at boot time, use `chkconfig` as the root user:

```
chkconfig nfs on
```

To verify that the NFS server is running, issue the command `service nfs status`.

Assigning Static NFS Ports

Refer to `/etc/services` for a list of ports already reserved for other services on the system and then select ports over 1024 to assign to the `statd`, `mountd`, `rquotad`, and `lockd` services. In this example, the following ports will be used:

- TCP and UDP port 38001 for `statd`
- TCP and UDP port 38002 for `statd` (outgoing)
- TCP and UDP port 38003 for `mountd`
- TCP and UDP port 38004 for `rquotad`
- TCP port 38005 for `lockd`
- UDP port 38006 for `lockd`

The NFS initialization scripts check for the configuration file `/etc/sysconfig/nfs` for static port assignments. If the file is not found, random ports are used for `statd`, `mountd`, `rquotad`, and `lockd`. To assign static ports, create the file `/etc/sysconfig/nfs` with the lines from Listing 13.1. Replace the port numbers with the ones you decided to use after examining `/etc/services`.

LISTING 13.1 Assigning Static Ports for NFS

```
STATD_PORT=38001
LOCKD_TCPPORT=38005
LOCKD_UDPPORT=38006
MOUNTD_PORT=38003
```

If you are using disk quota as discussed in Chapter 7, "Managing Storage," you also need to assign a static port to `rquotad`, the daemon used to determine quotas for a remotely mounted NFS filesystem. In addition to the lines in Listing 13.1, also add the following line to `/etc/sysconfig/nfs`:

```
RQUOTAD_PORT=38004
```

Use the command `rpcinfo -p localhost` to verify that the port numbers for the `portmapper`, `status`, `rquotad`, `nlockmgr`, and `mountd` services are correct. Because `lockd` is a kernel module, a reboot might be needed for the changes to take effect.

Static ports can also be assigned with the graphical NFS configuration tool. After starting the tool, click the **Server Settings** button on the toolbar. The dialog shown in Figure 13.4 appears.

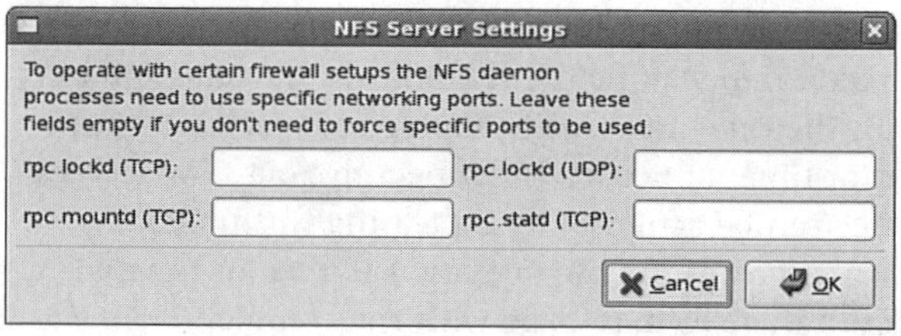

FIGURE 13.4 Assigning Static NFS Ports

Provide the ports you want to use, and click **OK**.

Connecting to the NFS Shares

There are three ways to mount an NFS export on a client system, assuming the server has given the client permission to do so:

- Use the `mount` command along with the server name, exported directory, and local mount point.
- Add the export to `/etc/fstab` so it is automatically mounted at boot time or is available to be mounted.
- Use the autofs service to mount the share when a user attempts to access it from a client.

Using `mount` to Connect to the NFS Share

If you only need to mount the share occasionally (or if you are testing the export), use the `mount` command. Create a directory to mount the share, then, as root, execute the following command:

```
mount -o <options> server.example.com:/exporteddir /mountpoint
```

replacing the server name, exported directory, and the local mount point. By default, the share is mounted in read-write mode, meaning that all file permissions are retained from the server. It is important to know that the file permissions are based on the user ID and group ID numbers, not the user and group *names* used on the NFS server. If the client is allowed access by the server, the shared directory will then be available from the specified mount point on the client.

Any NFS mount options can also be used in place of <options> including the following:

- `rsize=8192`
- `wsize=8192`
- `timeo=14`
- `intr`

The `rsize` value is the number of bytes used when reading from the server. The `wsize` value is the number of bytes used when writing to the server. The default for both is

1024, but using 8192 greatly improves throughput and is recommended. The `timeo` value is the amount of time, in tenths of a second, to wait before resending a transmission after an RPC timeout. After the first timeout, the timeout value is doubled for each retry for a maximum of 60 seconds or until a major timeout occurs. If connecting to a slow server or over a busy network, better performance can be achieved by increasing this timeout value. The `intr` option allows signals to interrupt the file operation if a major timeout occurs for a hard-mounted share. Refer to the NFS man page with the command `man nfs` for a full list of available options.

Using `/etc/fstab` to Connect to the NFS Share

After you have verified that the client can mount the share, you can configure the system to mount it at boot time by modifying the `/etc/fstab` file as follows:

```
server:/exported/dir    /mountpoint   nfs    rsize=8192,wsize=8192,timeo=14,intr
```

Replace the server name, exported directory, and mount point with the appropriate values. The third column indicates that the mount point is of the type `nfs`.

The last column contains a comma-separated list of NFS options. The options in our example were explained in the previous section, "Using `mount` to Connect to the NFS Share."

After the entry is added to `/etc/fstab`, use the command `mount /mountpoint` as root to mount the share immediately. Unless the `noauto` option is specified, it is automatically mounted at boot time.

TIP

The `user` option can also be used to allow a non-root user to mount the share with the `mount /mountpoint` command. This is useful if the `noauto` option is used to not mount the share at boot time.

Using autofs to Connect to the NFS Share

The last option is to use autofs. The autofs service works by using the `automount` daemon to monitor preconfigured NFS mount points. They are only mounted when a user attempts to access the local mount point directory.

There are several advantages to using autofs instead of configuring shares in `/etc/fstab`. Because shares are only mounted when they are accessed, system boot time is faster. The system doesn't have to wait for each NFS server to respond and the mount to succeed. Secondly, it is more secure. Users on the client systems must know what directory is configured to mount the share before changing into that directory to force the mount. On the other hand, if all shares are mounted on bootup, users can browse the contents of the shared directory if they have permission. If the system is compromised by an unauthorized user, having the shares pre-mounted makes it that much easier for the intruder to find the shared files. Finally, if the clients are configured to use NIS for user authentication, NIS can also be configured to provide the `/etc/auto.*` files necessary for autofs. So, when a share needs to be added, modified, or removed, the administrator just needs to update the configuration files on the NIS server, and they are populated to all clients after the NIS service is restarted on the clients. The update is almost seamless to the end user.

The master configuration file is `/etc/auto.master`, Listing 13.2 shows the default `auto.master` file .

LISTING 13.2 Default `auto.master` File

```
#
# $Id: auto.master,v 1.4 2005/01/04 14:36:54 raven Exp $
#
# Sample auto.master file
# This is an automounter map and it has the following format
# key [ -mount-options-separated-by-comma ] location
# For details of the format look at autofs(5).
#
/misc   /etc/auto.misc
/net    -hosts
#
# Include central master map if it can be found using
# nsswitch sources.
#
# Note that if there are entries for /net or /misc (as
# above) in the included master map any keys that are the
# same will not be seen as the first read key seen takes
# precedence.
#
+auto.master
```

As you can see, the mounts for the `/misc/` directory are defined in a different file. One additional configuration file per directory is controlled by autofs. The `/misc/` directory in Red Hat Enterprise Linux is reserved for autofs mounts. Because `/etc/auto.misc` is already created, add NFS mounts to it in the following format:

```
mountdir   <options>   server.example.com:/exporteddir
```

Replace `mountdir` with the name of the `/misc/` subdirectory you want the share to be mounted. For example, to use the directory `/misc/data/`, replace `mountdir` with `data`. This subdirectory is dynamically created when the share is mounted. Do not create it on the local filesystem.

Replace `<options>` with a list of comma-separated NFS options discussed previously in this chapter and found in the NFS man page (accessed with the `man nfs` command). Replace the server name and exported directory as well.

If a directory is used by autofs as a mount point, the directory should not be written to unless the remote filesystem is mounted in that directory. Consider it a reserved directory for autofs.

To start the `automount` daemon, use the command `service autofs start`. To stop it, use the command `service autofs stop`. If the service is already running when the `auto.master` file or any of the files it includes such as `auto.misc` is modified, use the command `service autofs reload` to force a reread of the configuration files. To configure the system to start it at boot time, execute `chkconfig autofs on` as the root user.

Samba File Sharing

Samba is the file-sharing protocol used by the Microsoft Windows operating system. Because some network environments include more than one operating system, Red Hat Enterprise Linux provides a way to use alternative file-sharing methods. If only sharing between Linux and other UNIX variants, it is recommended that NFS be used instead.

TIP

For additional information on Samba, refer to the `/usr/share/doc/samba-<version>/` directory. Among other resources, it contains a PDF of the *Samba-3 by Example* book.

Samba and SELinux

Samba file sharing is protected by SELinux, a mandatory access control security mechanism. Refer to Chapter 23 for details on how SELinux works.

If SELinux is set to the enforcing mode, the files shared via Samba must be labeled with the correct SELinux security context. After configuring Samba to share a directory, execute the following command to change the security context of the files in the shared directory:

```
chcon -R -t samba_share_t <directory>
```

If the directory is inside a home directory, you might need to set the security context of the entire home directory:

```
chcon -R -t samba_share_t <home_directory>
```

CAUTION

If the filesystem is relabeled for SELinux, the security context changes you make will be overwritten. To make your changes permanent even through a relabel, refer to the "Making Security Context Changes Permanent" section in Chapter 23.

Execute the following command to allow home directories or directories inside home directories to be shared:

```
setsebool -P samba_enable_home_dirs=1
```

To verify that the setting has been changed, execute the following:

```
getsebool  samba_enable_home_dirs
```

If enabled, the output should be the following:

```
samba_enable_home_dirs --> on
```

If more than one file sharing protocol is configured to share the same set of files such as FTP and Samba, the security context of the files must be set to `public_content_t` or `public_content_rw_t` instead. Additional SELinux booleans must be enabled as well. Refer to the "Security Context for Multiple File-Sharing Protocols" section in Chapter 23 for complete instructions.

To use Samba to mount home directories from a Samba server, the `use_samba_home_dirs` boolean must be set to 1 on each system mounting the home directories.

Any of these SELinux booleans can also be modified by running the SELinux Management Tool. Start it by selecting **Administration**, **SELinux Management** from the **System** menu on the top panel of the desktop or by executing the `system-config-selinux` command. Enter the root password when prompted if running as a non-root user. Select **Boolean** from the list on the left. On the right, click the triangle icon next to **Samba**. The SELinux booleans affecting Samba appear. A check box appears next to each boolean enabled. Changes take place immediately after modifying the check box.

TIP

The SELinux booleans that affect Samba are described in the samba_selinux man page viewable with the `man samba_selinux` command.

Allowing Samba Connections

Before configuring the Samba server, configure your firewall settings to allow the incoming connections. The following ports must be opened:

- UDP port 137 for `netbios-ns`, the NETBIOS Name Service
- UDP port 138 for `netbios-dgm`, the NETBIOS Datagram Service
- TCP port 139 for `netbios-ssn`, the NETBIOS session service
- TCP port 445 for `microsoft-ds`, the Microsoft Domain Service

If custom IPTables rules are being used, refer to Chapter 24 for details on how to allow these ports.

If the default security level is enabled instead of custom IPTables rules, use the Security Level Configuration tool to allow Samba connections. Start it by selecting **Administration**, **Security Level and Firewall** from the **System** menu on the top panel of the desktop or by executing the `system-config-securitylevel` command. Enter the root password when prompted if running as a non-root user. In the **Other ports** area, click **Add** to specify each Samba port.

Using a Graphical Tool to Configure the Samba Server

To use a system as a Samba server, the `samba` RPM package must be installed. If it is not installed, install it with Red Hat Network as described in Chapter 3. To configure it via the Samba Server Configuration graphical interface, the `system-config-samba` RPM package must also be installed.

To start the tool, select **Administration**, **Server Settings**, **Samba** from the **System** menu on the top panel of the desktop. Alternatively, execute the command `system-config-samba` from a shell prompt. All configured shares are listed when the tool starts as shown Figure 13.5.

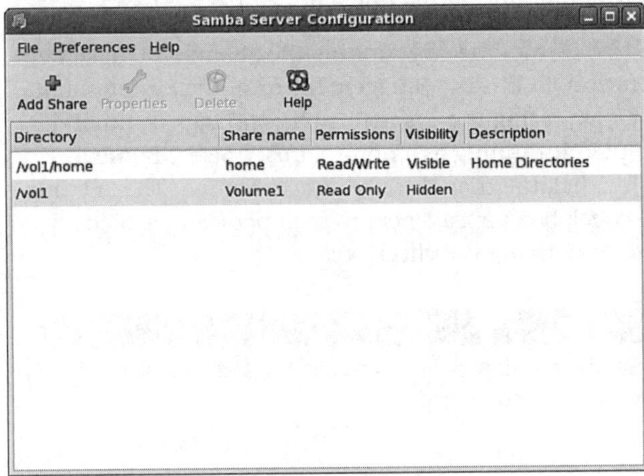

FIGURE 13.5 Samba Server Configuration Tool

Root privileges are required to modify the Samba server settings, so you must have root access to use this tool. If you are not root when you start the program, you will be prompted for the root password.

Configuring the Samba Server Settings

The first step when setting up Samba is to configure the server settings. Select **Preferences, Server Settings** from the pull-down menu to display the **Server Settings** dialog window as shown in Figure 13.6.

On the **Basic** tab, configure the workgroup name for the server and give a brief description.

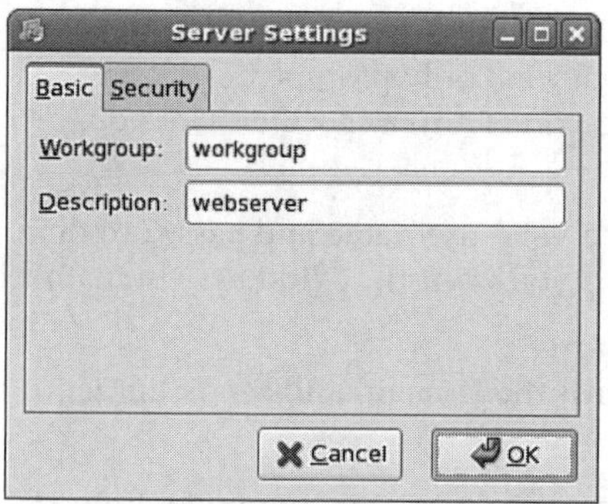

FIGURE 13.6 Samba Server Settings

On the **Security** tab, configure the following:

- **Authentication Mode**: Select one of the following:
  - **ADS:** The Samba server acts as a domain member in an Active Directory Domain (ADS) realm. Kerberos must be installed and properly configured on the server for this authentication mode to work. In addition, use the net utility to make Samba a member of the ADS realm. The net utility can be installed with the `samba-common` package. Refer to the man page for net (use the command `man net`) for details. Be sure to also set the Kerberos Realm, which must be in all uppercase letters, such as EXAMPLE.COM.

NOTE

This option does not configure Samba to be an ADS Controller.

  - **Domain:** Authentication is achieved by passing the username and password combination to a Windows NT Primary or Backup Domain Controller just like a Windows NT Server. A valid Linux system account must exist on the Samba server so the Windows Domain Controller account can be mapped to it. Set the Authentication Server field to the NetBIOS name of the Primary or Backup Domain Controller that will perform the authentication.

    If this option is selected, the Samba server must be added to the Windows NT Domain with the `net` utility provided by the `samba-common` package. Also, Encrypted Passwords must be set to **Yes**.
  - **Server:** Account verification is passed to another Samba server. If that fails, the server tries to authenticate locally using the User mode. Set the Authentication Server field to the NetBIOS name of the remote Samba server that will perform the authentication. Encrypted Passwords must be set to **Yes** if the remote server used for authentication supports it.

- **Share:** Samba users can browse the shared directories without having to enter a username and password combination. They are only prompted for a username and password when they attempt to connect to a specific shared directory from a Samba server.
- **User:** (Default) Samba users must provide a valid username and password on a per-Samba-server basis. Select this option if you want the Windows Username option to work.

- **Authentication Server**: Used in conjunction with the Domain and Server authentication modes.
- **Kerberos Realm:** Used in combination with the ADS authentication mode. It must be in all uppercase letters, such as EXAMPLE.COM.
- **Encrypt Passwords**: Set to `yes` by default. If set to `no`, passwords are sent over the network in plain text and can be intercepted by a simple packet sniffer. It is highly recommended not to change this setting.
- **Guest Account**: To configure the server to allow a guest account to connect, select a system user from the pull-down menu. When a guest connects to the server, the guest user will be mapped to this system user with all the permissions the system user has.

Click **OK** to save the settings. The settings take place immediately: If the service is not started, clicking OK starts it. If the service is already started, clicking **OK** forces a reload of the configuration file.

Adding Samba Users

After configuring the server settings, the next step is to configure the Samba users. If the authentication type is set to `user`, access to Samba shares are allowed by a username and password combination. These users must be configured as Samba users. Each Samba user maps to an existing user on the Samba server, so a user account must exist for each Samba user added before adding the Samba user in this graphical program. Refer to Chapter 9, "Managing Users and Groups," for more information on adding system users.

To add Samba users, select **Preferences**, **Samba Users** from the pull-down menu. Click **Add User** and provide the following:

- **Unix Username**: The existing user to map the Samba user to.
- **Windows Username**: The username to be used for Samba authentication. This option is useful if the user already has an account on the Windows system connecting to the server, but the username on the Windows system is different from the username on the Linux Samba server. For this to work, the Authentication Mode on the Security tab of the Server Settings preferences must be set to **User**.
- **Samba Password**: A password for the Samba user to be used for Samba authentication. For higher security, this should be different from the user's system password.
- **Confirm Samba Password**: Enter the password again to make sure it is recorded without typos.

Clicking **OK** saves the new user to /etc/samba/smbusers, making the changes take place immediately. Repeat this process for each Samba user you want to configure.

Adding a Samba Share

All currently configured shares are shown each time the program is started as shown in Figure 13.5. To add a new share, click the **Add Share** button in the toolbar. The **Create Samba Share** dialog window appears as shown in Figure 13.7.

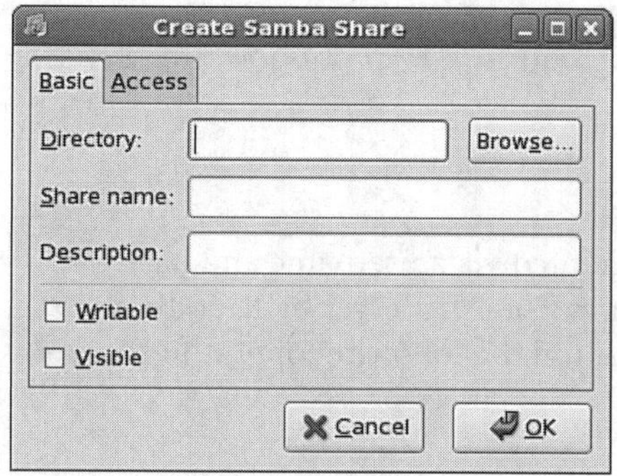

FIGURE 13.7 Adding a Samba Share

The **Create Samba Share** dialog window includes two tabs for configuring the options for each share. The **Basic** tab contains the following options:

- **Directory**: The directory to share via Samba. The directory must already exist.
- **Share name**: The share name visible to the Samba clients.
- **Description**: Brief description for the share.
- **Writable**: If selected, client systems can write back to the directory. If not selected, the shared directory is read-only.
- **Visible**: If selected, the share will appear when a system on the network browses for Samba shares. If not selected, the user must know the share name to access it.

On the **Access** tab, indicate whether everyone or only specific users should be allowed access to the share. If **Only allow access to specific users** is selected, select them for the list of existing Samba users on this tab as well.

TIP

To find out who is connected to the Samba server, use the smbstatus command from a shell prompt. It will list all active connections, including usernames and IP addresses.

Configuring the Samba Server with the Command Line

To configure a Red Hat Enterprise Linux system as a Samba server, the `samba` RPM package must be installed.

The configuration files for Samba are located in the `/etc/samba/` directory with the main configuration file being `/etc/samba/smb.conf`.

The options in the `[global]` section of the file apply to all shares unless an individual share section overrides the global option.

In the `[global]` section of `smb.conf`, specify a workgroup and description for the server:

```
workgroup=WORKGROUP
server string=DESCRIPTION
```

Even though access to a specific share directory is granted via a username and password combination, access can also be restricted to all shares from the server by IP address. To grant only certain systems from accessing the server, use the following option in the `[global]` section of `smb.conf`:

```
hosts allow = <IP addresses>
```

where `<IP addresses>` can be the hostnames, IP addresses, or IP address ranges. If hostnames are used, the system must be able to resolve them to IP addresses. All acceptable formats can be listed with the command `man 5 hosts_access`. The `hosts allow` option can also be used in the individual share sections.

TIP

Use the command `man smb.conf` to view a complete list of the many configuration options for Samba.

Adding Samba Users

Samba uses its own user database, including passwords. However, a system user with the same username must exist before a corresponding Samba user can be added to the server.

To add a Samba user, create a system user with the same username if it doesn't already exist, and then use the following command as root:

```
smbpasswd -a <username>
```

This writes an encrypted password for the user to the `/etc/samba/smbpasswd` file. By default, Samba encrypts passwords. The use of encrypted passwords does not need to be explicitly included in the configuration file, but it can be set with the following line in the `[global]` section:

```
encrypted passwords = yes
```

If users will be connecting to the Samba shares from a Microsoft Windows system, it is possible to map Windows usernames to Samba usernames. This is useful if the Windows system is configured with different usernames. To map Windows usernames to Samba usernames, add them to `/etc/samba/smbusers` with the following format:

```
username = Windows_name1
```

To map more than one Windows username to the same Linux system username, separate them by spaces:

```
username = Windows_name1 Windows_name2
```


Adding a Samba Share

To add a shared directory, include a section in `smb.conf`:

```
[sharename]
path = <path>
```

The `sharename` should be descriptive and easy to remember. Table 13.1 includes other common options.

TABLE 13.1 Common Samba Share Options

Command	Description
`comment`	Brief description of the share displayed when browsing for the share.
`valid users`	List of Samba users allowed access to the share.
`invalid users`	List of Samba users denied access the share. If a user is listed in the `valid users` and the `invalid users` list, the user is denied access.
`public`	If set to `yes`, password authentication is not required. Access is granted through the guest user with guest privileges. (default=no)
`read only`	If set to `yes`, client users can not create, modify, or delete files in the share. (default=yes)
`printable`	If set to `yes`, client users can open, write to, and submit spool files on the shared directory. (default=no)
`hosts allow`	List of clients allowed access to share. Use the command `man 5 hosts_access` for details on valid IP address formats.
`browseable`	If set to no, the share will not be visible by a net view or a browse list. (default=yes)

For example, Listing 13.3 contains a section to share a data directory between the users bsf and akf. This directory is not visible in a net view or browse list.

LISTING 13.3 Private Samba Share

```
[data]
   comment=Private share for bsf and akf
   path=/shares/data
```

LISTING 13.3 Continued

```
   read only = no
   valid users = bsf akf
   browseable = no
```

Listing 13.4 shows a more open share of the Samba servers `/tmp` directory. All valid Samba users are allowed read-write access, and it is visible in a net view or browse list.

LISTING 13.4 Samba Share for /tmp/

```
[tmp]
   comment=Shared temporary disk space
   path=/tmp
   read only = no
   browseable = yes
```

Testing the Samba Configuration File

After modifying the `smb.conf` file, test for syntax errors with the `testparm` command. By default, it looks for the configuration file in `/etc/samba/smb.conf`. To force it to look at a different file, specify it as a command-line argument such as `testparm /etc/samba/smb.conf.new`. This allows an administrator to test multiple files or create a new Samba configuration file elsewhere before committing it to the actual configuration file. Listing 13.5 shows the output of `testparm`.

LISTING 13.5 Testing a Samba Configuration File

```
Load smb config files from /etc/samba/smb.conf
Processing section "[homes]"
Processing section "[printers]"
Processing section "[tmp]"
Loaded services file OK.
Server role: ROLE_STANDALONE
Press enter to see a dump of your service definitions
```

After the testing is done, it prompts the administrator to press Enter to display the service definitions. If Enter is pressed, the global options are shown followed by a list of configured Samba shares for the server as shown in Listing 13.6.

LISTING 13.6 List of Samba Shares

```
# Global parameters
[global]
        workgroup = WUDAN
        server string = Jadefox Samba Server
        log file = /var/log/samba/%m.log
```

LISTING 13.6 Continued

```
        max log size = 50
        socket options = TCP_NODELAY SO_RCVBUF=8192 SO_SNDBUF=8192
        printcap name = /etc/printcap
        dns proxy = No
        cups options = raw

[homes]
        comment = Home Directories
        read only = No
        browseable = No

[printers]
        comment = All Printers
        path = /var/spool/samba
        printable = Yes
        browseable = No

[tmp]
        comment = Temporary file space
        path = /tmp
        read only = No
```


Starting and Stopping the Samba Server

To start the Samba server, execute the command `service smb start`. To stop the server, execute the command `service smb stop`.

To have the service start automatically at boot time, use `chkconfig`:

```
chkconfig smb on
```

To determine whether or not the Samba server is running, use the command `service smb status`. If the `smb.conf` configuration file is modified after the service is started, use the command `service smb reload` to force a reread of the configuration file so the changes take effect.

Logging Samba Connections

The system log file, `/var/log/messages`, contains messages from the Samba services `smbd`, `nmbd`, and `mount.cifs` as well as kernel messages about the smb service.

By default, a log file is created for each system that connects to the server. The log files are located in the `/var/log/samba/` directory, with the naming convention of `<client_name>.log` for the individual log files. This default is configured in `smb.conf` with the following line:

```
log file = /var/log/samba/%m.log
```

To use one log file for all clients instead, change this line to the following:

```
log file = /var/log/samba/log.smbd
```

The log files are rotated once a week and kept on disk for four weeks by the `logrotate` utility.

Connecting to the Samba Shares

Connecting to a Samba share in Windows varies with the different versions. Refer to the documentation for your version of Windows for detailed information on connecting to a Samba share. The method for connecting to a Windows Samba server and Linux Samba server are the same. This section goes into detail about how to connect to a Samba server, Linux or Windows, from a Red Hat Enterprise Linux system.

NOTE

Connecting to a Samba share with the Desktop File Browser and `smbclient` do not require root privileges. However, the `mount.cifs` and `mount -t cifs <share>` commands must be run as the root user.

Connecting Using the Desktop File Browser

To view all available shares on the network (except those that have visibility disabled), select **Places, Network Servers** from the desktop menu. As shown in Figure 13.8, each server icon represents a share server. Double-click on it to view the shared directories on the server. Depending on what authentication type the server is configured for, you might be prompted for a username and password.

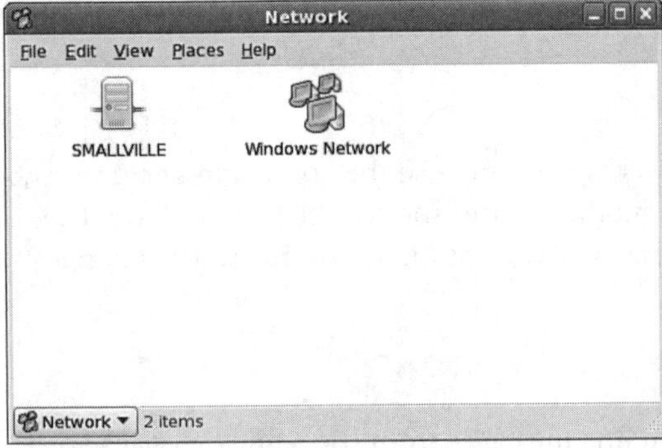

FIGURE 13.8 Browsing Samba Servers

To narrow down the list of servers by workgroup, double-click on the **Windows Network** icon. A list of workgroups will appear. Double-click on the workgroup to view the Samba servers in that workgroup.

If you know the name of the server you want to connect to, you can connect to it directly and create a shortcut on the desktop. This is also useful for servers that are configured to not be visible and thus don't appear when you browse the network. Select **Places, Connect to Server** from the desktop menu. Then select **Windows share** as the **Service type**, and enter the name of the server as shown in Figure 13.9.

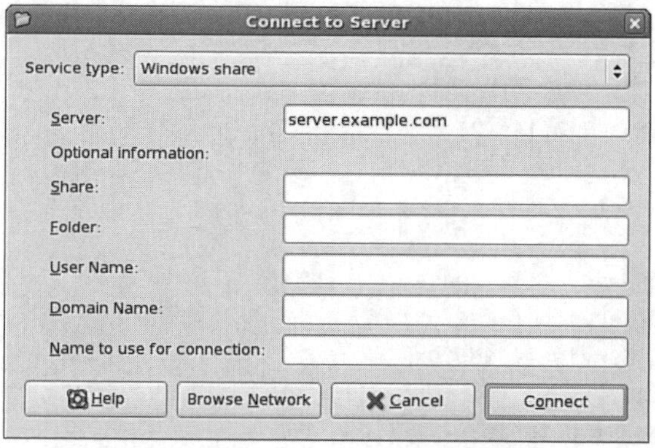

FIGURE 13.9 Connecting Directly to a Samba Share

Under the Optional information section, the following can be configured:

- **Share**: The name of the Samba share.
- **Folder**: The folder to open inside the Samba share.
- **User Name**: The username to use for authentication when connecting. If a username is not provided, the connection is made with the guest account if it is enabled, which usually has limited permissions.
- **Name to use for the connection**: Connection name to use when labeling the temporary mount point in the Places menu and on the desktop.

An icon will appear on the desktop using the name of the server or, if provided, the name in the **Name To Use For The Connection** field. A shortcut is also listed under the **Places** menu item in the desktop menu.

NOTE

To unmount the share, right-click on its desktop icon and select **Unmount Volume**. If the share is not unmounted, it will remain in the **Places** menu on reboot, but you must reauthenticate to access the share after rebooting.

Connecting with `smbclient`

The `smbclient` command provides an FTP-like interface to the server. It is provided by the `samba-client` package. Install it via RHN if not already installed.

Before you can connect to a Samba share, you must know its name. If you only know the name of the Samba server, use `smbclient` to display a list of available shares and the workgroup for the Samba server, and replace the `<servername>` and `<username>`:

```
smbclient -L <servername> -U <username>
```

The output will look similar to Listing 13.7.

LISTING 13.7 Output from `smbclient -L`

```
Domain=[JADEFOX] OS=[Unix] Server=[Samba 3.0.14a-2]

        Sharename       Type      Comment
        ---------       ----      -------
        tmp             Disk      Temporary file space
        IPC$            IPC       IPC Service (Jadefox)
        ADMIN$          IPC       IPC Service (Jadefox)
        printer         Printer   printer
        tfox            Disk      Home Directories
Domain=[JADEFOX] OS=[Unix] Server=[Samba 3.0.23c-2]

        Server               Comment
        ---------            -------

        Workgroup            Master
        ---------            -------
        WUDAN              JADEFOX
```

If the `-U <username>` option is not used, the connection is attempted as a guest user. If a username is specified, enter the correct password when prompted.

To connect to a specific share using `smbclient`, use the following:

```
smbclient //<servername>/<sharename> -U <username>
```

A successful connection is indicated by the `smb: \>` prompt. Once connected, the commands are similar to a command-line FTP client. Table 13.2 lists common commands .

TABLE 13.2 Common `smbclient` Commands

Command	Description
`pwd`	Display current remote directory
`cd <directory_name>`	Change directories if it is accessible
`lcd <directory_name>`	Change current local directory
`get <file>`	Retrieve `<file>` from current remote directory to current local directory
`mget <files>`	Retrieve multiple files, will be prompted for each matching file unless prompt is disabled

TABLE 13.2 Continued

`put <file>`	Upload local file to the current remote directory
`mput <files>`	Upload multiple local files to the current remote directory; you will be prompted for each matching file unless prompt is disabled
`prompt`	Toggle prompting confirmation for each file with `mget` and `mput` commands
`ls`	List files in current remote directory
`exit`	Close connection to Samba server and exit

Mounting the Samba Share

To mount a Samba share to a local directory similar to mounting an NFS share, use the following command (you must be root):

```
mount -t cifs //servername/sharename /mountpoint -o username=<username>
```

Replace the `servername`, `sharename`, `mountpoint`, and `username`. You will be prompted for the password. Remember that the user must exist as a Samba user on the Samba server. After it is mounted, the files on the mount can be accessed just like local files in the directory given as the mount point. All updates to the share automatically appear on the clients.

To unmount the share, use the command `umount /mointpoint` (replace `/mountpoint`). This mount is not persistent—it will not be remounted on reboot.

Alternatively, the `mount.cifs` command from the `samba-client` package can perform the same mount. It is just a shortcut to `mount -t cifs`. It must be run as the root user as well:

```
mount.cifs //servername/sharename /mountpoint -o username=<username>
```

To create a persistent mount that is automatically mounted at boot time, add an entry to `/etc/fstab`:

```
//servername/sharename     /mountpoint   cifs   defaults   0 0
```

Replace `servername`, `sharename`, and `mountpoint`. To make the mount read-write, replace `defaults` with `rw`. Because including the password is a security risk, and just giving the username will prompt for a password, this configuration mounts the share as a guest user.

Because mounting as a guest only gives the user the permissions of user `nobody` on the Samba server, it is possible to configure a credentials file that includes the username and password (and any other options necessary for the mount):

```
//servername/sharename     /mountpoint    cifs    credentials=/etc/smbcreds   0 0
```

This configuration will refer to the file `/etc/smbcreds` for Samba options. The file should include the following lines (replace `<username>` and `<password>`):

```
username=<username>
password=<password>
```

This file can have a different filename and be located anywhere on the filesystem. However, to prevent other users from getting the password be sure to change the permissions of the credential file with the command `chmod 600 <filename>` so only the owner can read it. For extra security, be sure the password used is not used for access to other systems in case it is compromised or read by someone else.

NOTE

Adding an entry for a Samba mount point to `/etc/fstab` does not automatically mount the share. It will be mounted the next time the system is booted. To mount the share immediately, use the following command as root (replace `/mountpoint`):

```
mount /mountpoint
```

Yet another option for configuring a Samba mount is to use autofs. The share can be mounted in any directory reserved for autofs. For example, to mount it in `/misc/<mount_dir>/`, make sure the following line exists and is not commented out in `/etc/auto.master`:

```
/misc   /etc/auto.misc
```

Then, in `/etc/auto.misc`, add the following line:

```
mount_dir   -fstype=cifs,credentials=/etc/smbcreds   ://<servername>/<sharename>
```

As shown, a credentials file can also be used with autofs. If the autofs service is already started, be sure to reload the configuration files with the command `service autofs reload`. Refer to the "Using autofs to Connect to the NFS Share" section in this chapter for more details on how autofs works.

Summary

In this chapter, both the NFS and Samba protocols for sharing files across a network were discussed. NFS should be used for file sharing among UNIX-based operating systems. However, if the clients include Microsoft Windows clients, a Red Hat Enterprise Linux system can be configured as a Samba server, and Red Hat Enterprise Linux can also serve as a Samba client to connect to a Linux or Windows Samba server.

CHAPTER 14

Granting Network Connectivity with DHCP

IN THIS CHAPTER

- Allowing Connections
- Configuring the Server
- Logging Connections

DHCP, or *Dynamic Host Configuration Protocol*, allows an administrator to configure network settings for all clients on a central server. The DHCP clients request an IP address and other network settings from the DHCP server on the network. The DHCP server in turn leases the client an IP address within a given range or leases the client an IP address based on the MAC address of the client's network interface card (NIC). If an IP address is assigned according to the MAC address of the client's NIC, the same IP address can be leased to the client every time the client requests one.

DHCP makes network administration easier and less prone to error. For example, when network settings or the IP address range of a network changes, instead of changing the configuration files on each client, the administrator simply changes the configuration on the DHCP server and applies the changes. If your network consists of hundreds of clients, it is easy to see the benefits.

From the user's point of view, DHCP can be useful for mobile computing. If a laptop is configured to use DHCP for its network settings, it can easily move from one network to another without reconfiguration or user intervention as long as the network includes a DHCP server with an available IP address for the laptop.

NOTE

If SELinux, a mandatory access control security system, is enabled, the default targeted policy protects the DHCP daemon. Refer to Chapter 23, "Protecting Against Intruders with Security-Enhanced Linux," for details.

Allowing Connections

By default, the DHCP server listens for requests on UDP port 67. Verify that your firewall settings allow incoming requests from this port.

NOTE

If the `local-port` parameter (discussed in the next section) is used in the configuration file to change the port number, adjust your firewall settings for the defined port instead.

If custom IPTables rules are being used, refer to Chapter 24, "Configuring a Firewall," for details on how to allow these ports.

If using a default security level in Red Hat Enterprise Linux, use the Security Level Configuration tool. Start it by selecting **Administration**, **Security Level and Firewall** from the **System** menu on the top panel of the desktop or by executing the `system-config-securitylevel` command. Enter the root password when prompted if running as a non-root user. In the **Other ports** area, click **Add** to specify the DHCP port. After adding the port, it appears in the **Other ports** list as shown in Figure 14.1.

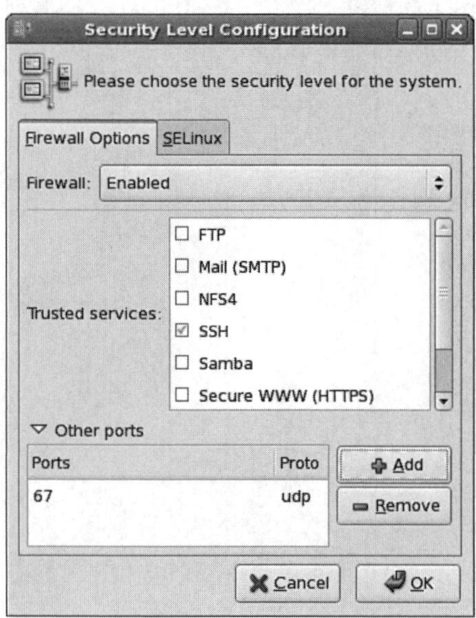

FIGURE 14.1 Allowing DHCP Requests

Configuring the Server

To configure a Red Hat Enterprise Linux system as a DHCP server, the `dhcp` RPM package must be installed. If it is not installed, use Red Hat Network to install it as discussed in

Chapter 3, "Operating System Updates." The DHCP server can allow any system on the network to retrieve an IP address, assign systems the same IP address each time one is requested, or a combination of the two.

The DHCP service uses the `/etc/dhcpd.conf` configuration file. A file without any configuration options is installed at this location with the `dhcp` package, and a sample file is provided in `/usr/share/doc/dhcp-<version>/dhcpd.conf.sample`.

NOTE

Because brackets and curly brackets are used to define statement groupings and relationships, blank lines and extra spacing including tabs can be used to format the file so it is easier to read. Lines that begin with # are considered comments.

In older versions of DHCP, the `ad-hoc` DNS update scheme was available. In the current version, it is depreciated and does not work. Thus, the `interim` scheme is highly recommended. For more details, refer to the `dhcpd.conf` man page with the command `man dhcpd.conf`. As you can see from the sample configuration file `/usr/share/doc/dhcp-<version>/dhcpd.conf.sample`, the first line of `/etc/dhcpd.conf` should define the DNS update scheme:

```
ddns-update-style interim;
```

Listing 14.1 contains an example DHCP configuration file. In this example, three subnets are defined, two of which are on the same physical network. In the 192.168.0.0 subnet declaration, several options including the gateway, subnet mask, and DNS server are configured for all clients in the subnet. Clients in the subnet who request an IP address are leased an IP address in the 192.168.0.128 to 192.168.0.254 range with the exception of the system defined in the `host` statement. If the system with the MAC address listed in the `host` statement connects, it is leased the 192.168.0.4 IP address each and every time.

TIP

To obtain the MAC address of a network interface card in a Red Hat Enterprise Linux client, use the command `ifconfig <interface-name>`, where `<interface-name>` is the device name for the NIC such as `eth0`.

LISTING 14.1 Example DHCP Configuration File

```
ddns-update-style interim;
authoritative;


subnet 192.168.0.0 netmask 255.255.255.0 {
   #global parameters for the subnet
   option routers                   192.168.0.1;
   option subnet-mask               255.255.255.0;
```

LISTING 14.1 Continued

```
   option domain-name              "example.com";
   option domain-name-servers      192.168.1.1;
   range dynamic-bootp 192.168.0.128 192.168.0.254;
   default-lease-time 21600;
   max-lease-time 43200;

   # fixed address example
   host jadefox {
      next-server ns.example.com;
      hardware ethernet 12:34:56:78:AB:CD;
      fixed-address 192.168.0.4;
   }
}
shared-network third-floor {
   #global parameters for the shared network
   option routers                  192.168.0.1;
   option subnet-mask              255.255.255.0;
   option nis-domain               "example.com";
   option domain-name              "example.com";
   option domain-name-servers      192.168.1.1;
   default-lease-time 21600;
   max-lease-time 43200;

   subnet 192.168.10.0 netmask 255.255.255.0 {
      range dynamic-bootp 192.168.10.1 192.168.10.254;
   }

   subnet 192.168.20.0 netmask 255.255.255.0 {
      range dynamic-bootp 192.168.20.1 192.168.20.254;
   }
}
```

In Listing 14.1, the two subnets in the `shared-network` grouping are on the same physical network and share all the parameters defined before the first subnet declaration within the `shared-network` declaration. Each subnet then has an IP address range defined for its clients.

To configure global settings for multiple declaration groups, use the `group` statement as shown in Listing 14.2. In this example, all the options outside the two `host` declarations apply to both `host` declarations. The `group` statement is not limited to `host` statements. It can be used to declare the same options for multiple subnets, for example.

LISTING 14.2 Example group Declaration

```
group {
  #common parameters for both host declarations
  option routers                192.168.10.254;
  option subnet-mask            255.255.255.0;
  option domain-name            "example.com";
  option domain-name-servers     192.168.10.24;
  default-lease-time 21600;
  max-lease-time 43200;

  host printer {
    option host-name "printer.example.com";
    hardware ethernet 01:BE:BB:5E:1A:CC;
    fixed-address 192.168.10.7;
  }

  host payroll {
    option host-name "payroll.example.com";
    hardware ethernet 02:B4:7C:43:DD:FF;
    fixed-address 192.168.10.10;
  }
}
```

Common DHCP parameters are described in Table 14.1. For a complete list, refer to the `dhcpd.conf` man page with the command `man dhcpd.conf`.

TABLE 14.1 Common DHCP Parameters

Command	Description
`routers`	Router or gateway for the client's network configuration.
`domain-name`	Domain name for the client's network configuration.
`domain-name-servers`	DNS servers for the client's network configuration.
`default-lease-time <time>`	Length of client lease, in seconds, if client does not request a different lease length.
`max-lease-time <time>`	Maximum amount of time, in seconds, the server will lease an IP address.
`min-lease-time <time>`	Minimum amount of time, in seconds, the server will lease an IP address.
`local-port`	By default, DHCP listens for request on UDP port 67. Use this option to listen on a different UDP port.
`range <start-ip> <end-ip>`	Range of IP addresses to lease to clients.
`log-facility <facility>`	Instead of logging to `/var/log/messages`, log to the specified facility. Refer to the "Logging Connections" section of this chapter for details.
`host-name`	Specify a hostname for the client within a `host` declaration.

14

TABLE 14.1 Continued

Command	Description
`hardware <type> <address>`	Specify the hardware address of a client such as the MAC address of an Ethernet card. `<type>` can be either `ethernet` or `token-ring`.
`fixed-address <IP-address>`	IP address that should be assigned to a specific host. Only valid within a `host` declaration.

After a client has successfully leased an IP address from the server, that IP address is reserved for the MAC address of the client for a specific amount of time as determined by a combination of the `default-lease-time`, `maximum-lease-time`, and `minimum-lease-time` parameters. This information is recorded in the `/var/lib/dhcp/dhcpd.leases` file on the DHCP server to make sure an IP address isn't assigned to more than one system at the same time.

NOTE

For DHCP client configuration, refer to Chapter 2, which provides instructions for network configuration.

Starting and Stopping the Server

Like the other services in Red Hat Enterprise Linux, DHCP can be started, stopped, and restarted with the `service` command as root. To start the server, use the `service dhcpd start` command. Each time the server is started, it looks for the `/var/lib/dhcp/dhcpd.leases` file. If it is not found, the service is not started. Before the service is started for the first time, the file must be created with the command `touch /var/lib/dhcp/dhcpd.leases`.

The command `service dhcpd status` displays whether the service is running. The command `service dhcpd restart` restarts the service, including re-reading the configuration file. Remember that the `dhcpd` service must be restarted after the configuration file is modified.

To configure the DHCP service to start automatically at boot time, use the command:

```
chkconfig dhcpd on
```

The DHCP server also looks for the `/etc/sysconfig/dhcpd` configuration file on startup. It is not required, but it can be used to define command-line options to `dhcpd`. The default file contains the following lines:

```
# Command line options here
DHCPDARGS=
```

For example, to only listen for connections on a specific network interface:

```
DHCPDARGS=eth0
```

This argument is useful for a DHCP server with separate network cards for traffic inside and outside a private network. For security reasons, the DHCP server should only listen for client connections on the NIC configured for internal traffic.

Additional command-line options are explained in the man page for `dhcpd`. Use the command `man dhcpd` to read it.

Logging Connections

By default, log messages from the DHCP server are written to `/var/log/messages`. However, DHCP supports logging to a separate file by adding the following statement to the top of `dhcpd.conf`:

```
log-facility <facility>;
```


For example, to use the local7 facility of syslog, use the following line:

```
log-facility local7;
```

The `/etc/syslog.conf` file must also be modified to include the following:

```
#Log DHCP daemon messages to separate file
local7.*          /var/log/dhcpd.log
```

You can use a different name for the log file, but the `syslog.conf` line must include its full path and it must be created with the same permissions as the `/var/log/messages` file. Also restart syslog to enable the change (as the root user):

```
service syslog restart
```

Because the `log-facility` statement is not read until `dhcpd.conf` is read, all logs before reading the configuration file are still written to `/var/log/messages`.

For more details on log facilities, refer to the `syslog` and `syslog.conf` man pages.

Summary

When configuring a large network of systems, DHCP can be used to quickly and easily configure client network settings. Clients can be assigned a specific IP address based on the MAC addresses of their network cards or can be assigned a random IP address from a defined range. Administrators benefit from this configuration because changes can be made on a central server instead of on each individual client.

For more information, refer to the `dhcpd` and `dhcpd.conf` man pages with the commands `man dhcpd` and `man dhcpd.conf`. For a complete list of DHCP options, use the command `man dhcp-options`.

CHAPTER 15

Creating a Web Server with the Apache HTTP Server

IN THIS CHAPTER

- Apache HTTP Server and SELinux
- Allowing Connections
- Configuring the Server
- Logging Connections
- Starting and Stopping the Server

When you view a web page over the Internet, the code to create that page must be retrieved from a server somewhere on the Internet. The server that sends your web browser the code to display a web page is called a *web server*. There are countless web servers all over the Internet serving countless websites to people all over the world.

A web server can also be set up on an internal network so that it is only accessible by the computers inside the private network. If this internal network is inside a company or corporation, it is often called an *intranet*.

Whether you need a web server to host a website on the Internet or to host a company portal inside its internal network, a Red Hat Enterprise Linux server can function as a web server using the Apache HTTP server. The Apache HTTP server is a popular, open source server application that runs on many UNIX-based systems as well as Microsoft Windows. This chapter explains how to get a web server up and running on Red Hat Enterprise Linux.

Apache HTTP Server and SELinux

If SELinux, a mandatory access control security system, is enabled, the default targeted policy protects the Apache HTTP daemon. Refer to Chapter 23, "Protecting Against Intruders with Security-Enhanced Linux," for details about SELinux.

All files accessed via the web server must be labeled with the proper security context. For example, if SELinux is enabled and the `DocumentRoot` location is modified, the SELinux security context of the new location must be changed. A list of valid security contexts and their usages are given in the httpd_selinux man page read with the `man httpd_selinux` command. Refer to the "Modifying Security Contexts" section of Chapter 23, for step-by-step instructions on changing the `DocumentRoot`.

The targeted SELinux policy allows for CGI scripts and allows the Apache HTTP Server to read home directories. Other features such as allowing Apache to run as an FTP server are not allowed by default to increase security. SELinux booleans must be explicitly set to `1` to allow these additional features. All of the SELinux booleans that affect the Apache HTTP server are described in the httpd_selinux man page viewable with the `man httpd_selinux` command.

These SELinux booleans can be set with the `setsebool` command or with the SELinux Management Tool, both of which are discussed in Chapter 23. To use the SELinux Management Tool, start it by selecting **Administration**, **SELinux Management** from the System menu on the top panel of the desktop or by executing the `system-config-selinux` command. Enter the root password when prompted if running as a non-root user. Select **Boolean** from the list on the left. On the right, click the triangle icon next to HTTPD Service to view a list of booleans.

Allowing Connections

By default, the Apache HTTP server uses TCP and UDP port 80 for HTTP transfers and TCP and UDP port 443 for HTTPS secure transfers. Verify that your firewall settings allow incoming requests from port 80 if serving non-encrypted web pages and port 443 if serving encrypted pages.

If custom IPTables rules are being used, refer to Chapter 24, "Configuring a Firewall," for details on how to allow these ports.

If using a default security level in Red Hat Enterprise Linux, use the Security Level Configuration tool to allow the system to serve web pages. Start the application by clicking on the **System** menu on the top panel of the desktop and then selecting **Administration**, **Security Level and Firewall** or by executing the `system-config-securitylevel` command. Enter the root password when prompted if running as a non-root user.

As shown in Figure 15.1, select the **WWW (HTTP)** option in the **Trusted services** section to allow requests on port 80, and select the **Secure WWW (HTTPS)** option to allow secure requests on port 443. Click **OK** to enable the changes immediately.

FIGURE 15.1 Allowing HTTP Requests

Configuring the Server

To configure a Red Hat Enterprise Linux system as a web server, the `httpd` RPM package must be installed. If it is not installed, use Red Hat Network to install it (refer to Chapter 3, "Operating System Updates").

The main configuration file used by the web server is `/etc/httpd/conf/httpd.conf`. It is a plain text file that can be edited with a simple text editor such as Emacs or Vi. Refer to Chapter 4, "Understanding Linux Concepts," for more information on using these text editors.

NOTE

Red Hat Enterprise Linux includes version 2.2 of the Apache HTTP server. When consulting any documentation, make sure it is for version 2.2 because directives can change from version to version. To determine what version you have installed, execute the command `rpm -q httpd` on the command line.

The configuration options in the `/etc/httpd/conf/httpd.conf` configuration file are called *directives*. The file is divided into three main parts, or sets of directives:

- Global configuration options for the server process
- Main server options, which are also defaults for the virtual hosts
- Virtual host definitions

The default configuration file is divided into these three categories, in the order listed previously. The Apache HTTP server in Red Hat Enterprise Linux has been customized for Red Hat Enterprise Linux. Thus, the default values in the default configuration file might differ from the default values in other documentation such as the ones found at apache.org.

NOTE

For a complete list of directives, go to http://httpd.apache.org/docs/2.2/mod/directives.html. When this chapter references the apache.org directive page, go to this page and click on the name of the directive for more detailed information. This chapter describes some of the more common directives to help get you started. It is by no means a substitution for reading the apache.org directive documentation.

Listing 15.1 shows common global configuration and main server directives that are explained in this chapter. Any line that begins with the # character is considered a comment.

Listing 15.1 Sample Apache HTTP Server Configuration File

```
#Section 1. Global configuration options
ServerRoot /etc/httpd
Listen 80
Timeout 120
KeepAlive Off
MaxKeepAliveRequests 100
KeepAliveTimeout 15
User apache
Group apache

#Section 2. Main server configuration options
ServerAdmin webmaster@example.com
ServerName example.com
DocumentRoot /var/www/html
DirectoryIndex index.html index.php index.txt
ErrorDocument 404 /errors/404.html
Options Indexes MultiViews
```

Global Configuration Section

Common directives for the global configuration section include the following. The default values reflect the values found in the default configuration file included with Red Hat Enterprise Linux.

`ServerRoot`

Directory that contains the configuration files, error messages, and log files. Do not add a forward slash at the end of the directory path. Default value: `/etc/httpd`

`Listen`

Port number on which to listen for nonsecure (http) transfers. To specify multiple ports, list them on separate lines with the `Listen` directive. To only listen on a specific network interface, specify it before the port number such as `Listen 192.168.1.1:80`. Default value: `80`

`SecureListen`

Optional directive to configure a secure, encrypted SSL connection on a specific port, usually port 443.

`Timeout`

Amount of time, in seconds, the server will wait for the following events before failing:

- Receive a GET request
- Receive TCP packets on a POST or PUT request
- Receive ACKs on transmissions of TCP packets in responses

Default value: `120`

`KeepAlive`

If set to `On`, more than one request is allowed per connection, also known as a persistent connection. Default value: `Off`

`MaxKeepAliveRequests`

If `KeepAlive` is set to `On`, number of requests allowed per connection. To allow unlimited requests, set this directive to `0`. Default value: `100`

`KeepAliveTimeout`

If `KeepAlive` is set to `On`, the amount of time, in seconds, the server will wait for additional requests from the same connection. The higher the number, the more `httpd` processes will wait for subsequent connections instead of accepting connections from new clients. Use caution when setting this value because waiting too long for subsequent connections might result in a slow response to new connections. Default value: `15`

`LoadModule`

Module to be loaded. Specify multiple modules on separate lines. Be sure the module can be used for the version of Apache you are running. To specify multiple modules, list them on separate lines preceded by the `LoadModule` directive. Refer to the "Loading Modules" section later in this chapter for details.

`User`

Username or UID of the Apache process (`httpd`) owner. After the service is started as root, the process changes ownership to this user with fewer privileges. Default value: `apache`

`Group`

Group name or GID of the Apache process (`httpd`) group. To be used in conjunction with the `User` directive. Default value: `apache`

Main Server Section

Common directives for the main server section include

`ServerAdmin`

Email address or URL to be used as the contact link for the server administrator in error messages sent to clients. This directive can also be used in a virtual host declaration so each site can have different contact links.

`ServerName`

Hostname and port the server uses to identify itself to clients. This directive can also be specified in a virtual host section.

`DocumentRoot`

Location of files accessible by clients. By default, the Apache HTTP server in Red Hat Enterprise Linux is configured to serve files from the `/var/www/html/` directory. The default web page of the server such as http://www.example.com/ must be located in this directory with a filename defined with the `DirectoryIndex` directive such as `index.html`. If subdirectories are created within `/var/www/html/`, they are also available on the website as subdirectories. For example, the `/var/www/html/about/` directory translates to the http://www.example.com/about/ URL.

CAUTION

If SELinux is enabled and the `DocumentRoot` location is modified, the SELinux security context of the new location must be changed. Refer to the "Modifying Security Contexts" section of Chapter 23 for instructions.

`DirectoryIndex`

List of index files to use when a directory such as http://www.example.com/ or http://www.example.com/about/ is requested. Multiple index pages can be listed, separated by a space. Possible values include `index.html`, `index.php`, and `index.txt`. This directive can be set inside a virtual host or directory section as well. It requires the `mod_dir` module to be loaded.

`ErrorDocument`

Provide a custom message, web page, or remote URL to display for HTTP error codes. If this directive is not defined, a default error message is displayed. This directive can be defined in a virtual host or directory section to further customize error messages. Specify different error codes and how to handle them on separate lines. The format is as follows:

```
ErrorDocument <code> <page>
```

where <code> is the HTTP error code such as 404 for page not found and 500 for a server error. The <page> can be one of the following:

- Location of a web page from the same server, starting with a forward slash. The page is relative to the `DocumentRoot`. It can be a server-side script. Example: /errors/404.html
- Remote URL. Specify the entire URL, including the http://. Example: http://errors.example.com/404.html
- Custom error message contained in quotation marks. Example: `"Page not found on this server"`
- The keyword `default` to display the default error message from the Apache HTTP server.

`Options`

Allow a particular server feature for the main server, in a virtual host declaration, or in a directory section. List multiple options on the same line separated by spaces. The following `Options` are available:

`All`

All options except `MultiViews`.

`ExecCGI`

Allow for the execution of CGI scripts using the `mod_cgi` module.

`FollowSymLinks`

Follow symbolic links in the directory.

`Includes`

Allow server-side includes with the `mod_includes` module.

`IncludesNOEXEC`

Allow server-side includes except for `#exec cmd` and `#exec cgi`. Using `#include virtual`, CGI scripts from directories listed with the `ScriptAlias` directive are still allowed.

`Indexes`

If the `DirectoryIndex` directive is not used to define valid index pages, allow the `mod_autoindex` module to generate the index pages list.

`MultiViews`

As provided by the `mod_negotiation` module, allow for the selection of the content according to what works best for the client based on the client's browser, language, preferred encoding, and more.

`SymLinksIfOwnerMatch`

Only follow symbolic links if the target file or directory is owned by the same user as the file or directory requested.

Directory Sections

In the main server section, each directory that contains files accessible to remote systems from the Apache HTTP server can be configured separately as shown in the `<Directory>` sections in Listing 15.2. `<Directory>` sections can also be configured within a virtual host section.

CAUTION

Do not end the directory name with a trailing forward slash.

LISTING 15.2 Example `<Directory>` Section

```
# Defaults for all directories
<Directory />
    Options FollowSymLinks
</Directory>

# Settings for DocumentRoot
<Directory "/var/www/html">
    Options Indexes MultiViews
</Directory>

# Settings for /legal/
<Directory "/var/www/html/legal">
    DirectoryIndex index.html
    ErrorDocument 404 /errors/legal/404.html
</Directory>
```

As you can see from Listing 15.2, it is wise to set defaults for the root directory of the files accessible by Apache and then modify them per directory and subdirectory. Directives configured for a directory apply to that directory and any subdirectories unless a separate set of directives is provided for the subdirectory. If a directive is defined in the main server section as well as within a directory declaration, the value in the directory declaration is used for that particular directory.

Virtual Host Sections

To serve more than one website from the same Apache HTTP server, you need to configure *virtual hosts*. There are two types of virtual hosts: *name-based* and *IP-based*. Name-based virtual host means that multiple names are running on each IP address. IP-based virtual host means that a different IP address exists for each website served. Most configurations are named-based because it only requires one IP address, which is the type discussed in this section.

Virtual hosts are configured one at a time usually at the end of the `httpd.conf` file. An example is shown in Listing 15.3.

LISTING 15.3 Example Virtual Host

```
#Enable name-based virtual hosting
NameVirtualHost *.80

<VirtualHost *:80>
    ServerName www.example.org
    DocumentRoot /var/www/example.org
    #add other directives here
</VirtualHost>
```

Notice the `NameVirtualHost` directive must be set to enable name-based virtual hosting. The `*` in the value (and in the `<VirtualHost>` values) means requests are answered from all server IP addresses that the Apache HTTP server is configured to listen on with the `Listen` and `SecureListen` directives.

Most of the directives that can be configured in the main server section can be configured in a virtual host section. The `ServerName` and `DocumentRoot` directives are required in a virtual host section so the server knows which website the virtual host is for and where the files being served for the site are located.

Loading Modules

The Apache HTTP server supports the loading of modules to implement additional features. Examples include `mod_log_config` for customizing log files, `mod_alias` for URL redirection, and `mod_cgi` for executing CGI scripts.

NOTE

For a list of modules available for version 2.2 of the Apache HTTP server, go to http://httpd.apache.org/docs/2.2/mod/.

For each module you want to load, add a line similar to the following in the global configuration section of `httpd.conf` (replace `module_name` and `module_filename.so`):

```
LoadModule module_name modules/module_filename.so
```

After listing the module with the `LoadModule` directive, include any of the directives from the module in the appropriate `httpd.conf` sections.

Logging Connections

By default, log messages from the Apache HTTP server are written to the `/var/log/httpd/` directory. When a file is transferred to a client, information such as the IP address of the client, the file transferred, a time stamp, and the client's browser are written to the transfer log. By default, the transfer log is set to `access_log` in the `/var/log/httpd/` directory. Error messages and messages from starting and stopping the server are written to the `error_log` file. If you have enabled SSL connections on the web server, any secure transfers are recorded in `ssl_access_log`, and any server messages are written to `ssl_error_log`.

These log files are rotated using the `logrotate` utility. By default, new log files are started every week, and four weeks of log files are kept.

The following directives control logging:

`TransferLog`

Filename for the transfer log. If the filename does not begin with a forward slash (/), it is relative to the server root. Default value: `logs/access_log`

NOTE

Because the default value of `logs/access_log` does not start with a forward slash, it is relative to the server root, which is `/etc/httpd` by default. However, the `/etc/httpd/logs/` directory is a symbolic link to the `/var/log/httpd/` directory to allow Apache to follow the FHS guidelines of log files being located in `/var/log/`. Thus, the full path to the default transfer log is `/var/log/httpd/access_log`.

`ErrorLog`

Filename for the error log. If the filename does not begin with a forward slash (/), it is relative to the server root. Default value: `logs/error_log`

`LogFormat`

Format used when writing log messages. Refer to the apache.org directive page for details on the available formats. The `mod_log_config` module must be loaded for this directive.

`LogLevel`

Level of log messages written to the error log file. Possible values include `debug`, `info`, `notice`, `warn`, `error`, `crit`, `alert`, and `emerg`. The `debug` log level produces the most messages, and `emerg` only logs messages about the system being unusable. Default value: `warn`

`CustomLog`

Sets the filename of the transfer log and format of the log file. Can be used instead of using both `TransferLog` and `LogFormat`. Refer to the apache.org directive page for details. The `mod_log_config` module must be loaded for this directive.

Starting and Stopping the Server

Even though a non-root user such as apache owns the `httpd` processes, you still must be root to start and stop the service. Now that you have the basic settings configured, use the `service httpd start` command as root to start the server. If all goes well, the server will start. If you have a syntax error in the configuration file, a message is displayed to let you know the server hasn't been started and a gives a hint on where the syntax error is located. Also check the error log file as defined with the `ErrorLog` directive for messages.

If the web server is already running, the `service httpd reload` command must be run before the changes take effect. To stop the server, use the `service httpd stop` command.

To configure the web service to start automatically at boot time, execute the `chkconfig httpd on` command as root.

Summary

This chapter provided a basic understanding of the Apache HTTP server and how it is configured in Red Hat Enterprise Linux. The list of required configuration options is short. However, as you have read, the Apache HTTP server can be customized in numerous ways. It can be configured to serve multiple websites, and modules can be added to the Apache HTTP server to enhance its functionality. What and how log messages are written can even be customized.

CHAPTER 16

Hostname Resolution with BIND

IN THIS CHAPTER

- ▶ Understanding DNS Concepts
- ▶ Allowing Connections
- ▶ Configuring BIND
- ▶ Configuring BIND Graphically
- ▶ Logging Connections

Every computer on a network, whether it be a public-facing system on the Internet or one only accessible from an internal network, has a series of numbers called an *IP address* that identifies it to all other systems on the network. Each computer on the network must have a unique IP address.

To make it easier to remember and identify systems, each IP address can be resolved to a *hostname* such as server.example.com, which must also be unique per network. IP addresses can be translated, or *resolved*, to hostnames, and vice versa, via the Internet Domain Name System, or *DNS*. DNS is a set of distributed databases with a hierarchy that dictates which server is more authoritative for a particular set of systems.

To set up a DNS server, also referred to as a *name server*, on Red Hat Enterprise Linux, use *BIND* (Berkeley Internet Name Domain). This chapter first explains the basics of how DNS works. Then, it guides you through configuration of Red Hat Enterprise Linux as a DNS server using BIND.

Understanding DNS Concepts

A *DNS server*, or *name server*, is used to resolve an IP address to a hostname or vice versa. Before configuring BIND to create a DNS server, you must understand some basic DNS concepts.

When talking to another person, you usually refer to him by his first name even though he has a surname and sometimes a middle name as well. Similarly, administrators often refer to systems by the first part of their hostnames such as talon for talon.example.com. The entire hostname with its domain such as talon.example.com is called a *fully qualified domain name (FQDN)*. The right-most part of the

FQDN such as .com or .net is called the *top level domain*, with the remaining parts of the FQDN, which are separated by periods, being *sub-domains*.

These sub-domains are used to divide FQDNs into *zones*, with the DNS information for each zone being maintained by at least one *authoritative name server*. Multiple authoritative name servers for a zone can be implemented and are useful when server or network failures occur. The authoritative server that contains the master *zone file*, which can be modified to update DNS information about the zone, is called the *primary master server*, or just *master server*. The additional name servers for the zone are called *secondary servers* or *slave servers*. Secondary servers retrieve information about the zone through a *zone transfer* from the master server or from another secondary server. DNS information about a zone is never modified directly on the secondary server because it would then be out of sync with the master server, which is considered to be the most authoritative.

Some name servers cache lookup data because they depend on other name servers for information and can't talk to authoritative servers directly. The amount of time a record is stored in cache is set with the *Time To Live* (*TTL*) field for each resource record. There are also name servers that forward requests to one or more name servers in a list until the lookup is achieved or until all the name servers in the list have been contacted.

A name server can act in multiple roles. For example, a server can be an authoritative server for some zones but a slave server for others. Or, a slave server can also be a caching server.

Allowing Connections

DNS servers use port 53 by default. Incoming and outgoing packets should be allowed on port 53. Also allow connections on port 921 if you configure a lightweight resolver server. The DNS control utility, `rndc`, connects to the DNS server with TCP port 953 by default. If you are running `rndc` on the name server, connections on this TCP port from localhost should be allowed. If you are running `rndc` on additional systems, allow connections to port 953 (or whatever port you have chosen to configure) from these additional systems.

If custom IPTables rules are being used, refer to Chapter 24, "Configuring a Firewall," for details on how to allow connections from a specific port.

If using a default security level in Red Hat Enterprise Linux, use the Security Level Configuration tool. Start it by selecting **Administration, Security Level and Firewall** from the **System** menu on the top panel of the desktop or by executing the `system-config-securitylevel` command. Enter the root password when prompted if running as a user. Click the **Add** button next to the **Other ports** table to add a port.

Configuring BIND

BIND uses `/etc/named.conf` as its main configuration file, the `/etc/rndc.conf` file as the configuration file for name server control utility `rndc`, and the `/var/named/` directory for zone files and the like. All these files can be configured with a simple text editor, or they can be configured with the graphical Red Hat tool, `system-config-bind`. Refer to the section "Configuring BIND Graphically" at the end of this chapter for details on using `system-config-bind`.

Install the `bind` package, the `bind-utils` package, and their software dependencies using RHN (refer to Chapter 3, "Operating System Updates") to set up BIND.

This chapter focuses on basic DNS configuration via the configuration files to help you get started. However, you should also read the "BIND 9 Administrator Reference Manual" that comes with the `bind` package in the `/usr/share/doc/bind-<version>/arm/Bv9ARM.pdf` file. It includes everything from DNS fundamentals and BIND resource requirements to configuring and securing the name server.

Configuring named.conf

The `/etc/named.conf` file is the main configuration file for BIND. It should be owned by the named user because the `named` service is run by this user. The file permissions for `named.conf` should only allow the owner to read and write to the file (which also allows the root user to modify the file).

To add comments to `named.conf`, the following methods can be used:

- `/* This is a comment. */`
- `// This is a comment.`
- `# This is a comment.`

The following statements are allowed in `named.conf`:

- `acl`: IP address list used for access control. For example:

  ```
  acl <name> {
     <acl_list>
  };
  ```

  Replace `<name>` with a unique name for the list, and replace `<acl_list>` with a semicolon-separated list of elements, which can include IP addresses, IP address prefixes in the form X.X.X.X/X, one of the predefined list names (`any`, `none`, `localhost`, and `localnets`), the name of a key defined in the top-level of `named.conf`, or a nested address list in braces. Any of these elements can be negated by prefixing it with an exclamation point and a space such as `! 192.168.0.2` to exclude 192.168.0.2 from the list. When the match is being made, the matching stops at the first element in the list it matches: Be careful with the order of the elements.

  These defined ACLs can later be used to allow or deny access with the `allow-transfer`, `allow-recursion`, `allow-query`, and other statements.

- `controls`: Define control channels for the `rndc` utility. Refer to the next section "Configuring Control Channels" for details.
- `include`: Include the contents of a separate file, which can have more restrictive permissions to protect sensitive data. The `<filename>` must include the full path to the file.

  ```
  include "<filename>"
  ```

- `key`: Define a shared secret key to use with TSIG or the control channel. The secret must be a base-64 encoding of the encryption key, enclosed in double quotation marks. It can be generated with the `rndc-confgen` command as described in the "Configuring `rndc.conf`" section.

  Replace `<key-id>` with a unique name for the key:

  ```
  key <key-id> {
     algorithm hmac-md5
     secret "<secret>"
  };
  ```

  The `key` statement must be inside a `view` statement, inside a `server` statement, or at the top-level of `named.conf`. Keys inside `view` statements can only be used by requesters matching the view definition. Keys inside `server` statements are used to sign requests sent to that server. Top-level statements can be referenced inside other statements by the `<key-id>`. For example, to use a top-level key inside the `server` statement:

  ```
  server <ip> {
     keys { <key-id> };
  };
  ```

- `logging`: Customize logging. Refer to the "Logging Connections" section for details.
- `lwres`: Configure the name server to act as a lightweight resolver server. Multiple `lwres` statements can be declared.

  ```
  lwres {
       listen-on { <ip> port <port_num> ; <ip> port <port_num> };
       view <view-name>;
       search { <domain_name> ; <domain_name2> };
       ndots <num>;
  };
  ```

  The `listen-on` statement declares a semicolon-separated list of IP addresses and port numbers for the IPs from which the lightweight resolver accepts requests. If a port number is not given, the default port (port 921) is used. If the `listen-on` statement is missing, only requests from the local loopback (127.0.0.1) on port 921 are accepted.

  To bind this lightweight resolver to a view so the response is formatted according to the view, use the `view` statement to list the name of the view declared in the top-level of `named.conf`. If no view is listed, the default view is used.

  Use the `search` statement to list domain names used to convert hostnames to FQDNs when they are sent in requests. This is the same as the `search` statement in `/etc/resolv.conf`. Multiple domain names can be listed, separated by semicolons.

  The `ndots` statement sets the minimum number of periods in a domain name that should match exactly before the domain names declared with the search statements are added to the end of it. This is the same as the `ndots` statement in `/etc/resolv.conf`:

- masters: List a set of master name servers to use for stub and slave zones.

```
masters <name> port <port_num> {
<ip> port <port_num> key <key>
};
```

When declaring a master server for a stub or slave server, the port numbers and keys are optional. The IP address of the master server is the only required component.

- options: The options statement can be used to set global options for the server and defaults for other statements. Options include additional servers to query if the server doesn't have the data, zone transfer settings, settings to limit system resources for the name server, and time-to-live values. Refer to the "BIND 9 Administrator Reference Manual" included with the bind package in the /usr/share/doc/bind-<version>/arm/Bv9ARM.pdf file for a complete list of global options.

```
options {
   <options>
};
```

- server: Set properties of a remote name server. These statements can be top-level statements or inside view statements. The bogus statement should be set to yes or no, with yes meaning that queries should not be sent to it. If the local server is a master name server, set provide-ixfr to yes to allow incremental transfers to this server. If the local server is a slave and the remote server is a master, set request-ixfr to yes to request incremental transfers from the remote master server.

Set ends to yes to allow the local server to use EDNS (an extension of DNS) when communicating with the remote server. Set transfer-format to one-answer or many-answers to control how many DNS messages per resource record are transferred at one time. The many-answers option is only supported by some versions of BIND. Set transfers to the maximum number of simultaneous inbound zone transfers allowed. Set the keys statement to the key to use when signing requests to the server.

Use the transfer-source statement to set the IPv4 source address used for zone transfers or transfer-source-v6 to set the IPv6 source address used for zone transfers:

```
server <ip> {
   bogus <value>;
   provide-ixfr <value>;
   request-ixfr <value>;
   edns <value>;
   transfers <num>;
   transfer-format <format>;
   keys { <key-id-list> } ;
   transfer-source <ip> port <port_num>;
   transfer-source-v6 <ip> port <port_num>;
};
```

- `trusted-keys`: Set DNSSEC (DNS Security) security roots. A security root is a public key for a non-authoritative zone, which is known but can not be securely retrieved via DNS. If it is listed as a trusted key, it is thought to be valid and secure. The `<key-list>` is a semicolon-separated list of keys with each entry in the format `<domainname> <flags> <protocol> <algorithm> <key-id>`.

```
trusted-keys {
    <key_list>
};
```

- `view`: A view defines what data is sent in a response to a DNS request. Multiple views can be set. Refer to the "Configuring Views" section for details.
- `zone`: Declare the zone type for the server, which can have multiple zones. Refer to the "Configuring Zones" section for details.

Configuring Control Channels

Use the `controls` statement in `named.conf` to define control channels for the server. Control channels accept commands from the `rndc` utility. Only the `inet` control channel is currently available. Multiple control channels can be defined in the `controls` statement by declaring multiple `inet` clauses in it. Refer to the "Configuring `rndc.conf`" section for an explanation of the `rndc` utility. The `controls` statement uses the following syntax:

```
controls {
   inet <ip-addr> port <port-num> allow { <address-list>} keys { <key-list> };
};
```

Replace `<ip-addr>` with the IP address of the name server. Using the loopback address 127.0.0.1 is recommended for high security. A port number does not have to list with `<port-num>` unless you are not using the default port of 953.

Replace `<address-list>` with a semicolon-separated list of IP address elements: either individual addresses or address ranges in the form X.X.X.X/X. Only `rndc` connection requests from these addresses are allowed, and then only if they authenticate with a key from `<key-list>`.

Replace `<key-list>` with a semicolon-separated list of key names for keys declared elsewhere in the `named.conf` file. These are the authentication keys used by the `rndc` utility when requesting connection to the name server. Only `rndc` utilities authenticating with these keys are allowed to send commands to the name server.

TIP

If the `named.conf` file contains secret keys, be sure to set its file permissions as restrictive as possible so that non-authorized users can not read the key.

If no `controls` statement is present, only `rndc` connections from the localhost using the authentication key in `/etc/rndc.key` are accepted.

Configuring Views

On a BIND server, *views* can be created to customize the data sent to different requesters based on the source and destination IP addresses. Most of the global option statements can also be used inside a view to override the default value or the value set as a global option. They have the following syntax:

```
view <name> <class> {
      match-clients { <ip_list> } ;
      match-destinations { <ip_list> } ;
      match-recursive-only <value> ;
      <options>
      <zone-statements>
};
```

The `<name>` must be unique per view and should be a short, descriptive word describing the view specifications. The `<class>` is optional and defaults to `IN`.

Use the `match-clients` clause to define the source address to match. Use the `match-destinations` clause to define the destination address of the request. If the source address is not specified, requests from any source match. If the destination address is not specified, requests to be sent to any address match.

The order in which views are listed in `named.conf` matters. The first view that matches the source and/or destination addresses of the server requesting the data is used to format the response. So, `view` statements should go from the most restrictive to the least restrictive. If you want to declare a `view` statement without a `match-clients` or `match-destinations` statement as a "catch-all" for requesters that don't match any of the other statements, it should be the last `view` statement in `named.conf`, or the other `view` statements will be ignored because all requests will match the "catch-all" statement.

The `keys` statement allows clients a way to select the view. If the `match-recursive-only` statement is set to `yes`, only recursive requests match. If any views are defined, all `zone` statements must be inside `view` statements. Zones defined inside views can only be accessed by clients that match the view specifications.

16

Configuring Zones

A `zone` statement is used to define a zone and its properties. Some global options apply to zones unless they are overridden inside the `zone` statement. Zone files are written to the `/var/named/` directory.

The statements have the following syntax:

```
zone <name> <class> {
   type <type>
   <options>
};
```

The `<name>` must be unique and must be the domain name for the zone such as example.com or host.example.com. It is used to complete hostnames that are not FQDNs.

The <class> is optional. It can be one of the following:

- IN: Internet zone. The default class if one is not given.
- HS: Hesiod zone. Hesiod is a service used to distribute system information such as user and group definition and password files and print configuration files.
- CHAOS: CHAOSnet zone. CHAOSnet is a LAN protocol.

The <type> must be one of the following:

- master: Authoritative name server for the zone.
- slave: Secondary name server for the zone. Retrieve zone data from the master server.
- hint: Provide a list of root name servers, which are used to find a root name server and retrieve a list of the most recent root name servers.
- stub: Like a slave zone except it only retrieves the NS records from the master zone. Not a standard DNS zone: specific to BIND.
- forward: Set forwarding for the domain given as the zone name.
- delegation-only: Use to enforce delegation-only status of infrastructure zones such as COM and NET. Does not affect answers from forwarders.

A full list of options for <options> is available in the "BIND 9 Administrator Reference Manual" included with the bind package in the /usr/share/doc/bind-<version>/arm/Bv9ARM.pdf file.

Configuring rndc.conf

The name server control utility, rndc, sends named digitally signed commands over a TCP connection. Its configuration file /etc/rndc.conf stores configuration information such as the name server to connect to and which key to use for the digital signature. The utility is started when named is started using the initialization script.

The rndc.conf file uses syntax similar to named.conf. The same comment styles are available, statements are within braces, and the semicolon is used as the terminating character. Only three types of statements can be declared:

NOTE

The preferences in rndc.conf can be overridden by specifying values on the command line when rndc is started. Refer to Table 16.1 for a list of command-line options.

- options: The options statement can have three clauses. The default-server clause defines the IP address of the name server to which the rndc should connect to and sends commands. The default-key clause lists the key-id of the key to use if a key statement is not listed in the server statement for the name server. If default-key is used, a key statement with the same key-id must be declared in the same rndc.conf file.

The default-port clause specifies the port number to use when connecting to the name server. If a port clause is not listed in the server statement for the name server, this default port is used when connecting. If no port is given, the default is 953.

```
options {
    default-server <ip>;
    default-key <key-id>;
    default-port <port-num>;
};
```

- server: A server statement can be defined for the name server, with <ip> being the IP address of the name server to which rndc is configured to connect. The key clause should be used to provide the key-id of the key to use for authentication with the name server. The port clause lists the port to use when connecting to the name server.

TIP

Instead of declaring a server statement, you can just declare the key and port in the options statement.

```
server <ip> {
    key <key-id>;
    port <port-num>;
};
```

- key: Each key statement must have a unique key name, or key-id. The algorithm clause provides the encryption algorithm to use for the key. Currently, only hmac-md5 is supported by BIND. The secret clause must be a base-64 encoding of the encryption key, enclosed in double quotation marks.

```
key <key-id> {
    algorithm hmac-md5;
    secret "<secret>";
};
```

An rndc.conf file can be generated with a random key with the rndc-confgen command. It outputs the rndc.conf file and the corresponding key and controls statements for the named.conf file. Either cut and paste the output to the appropriate files or redirect the output into a file named rndc.conf, and remove the extra statements for named.conf:

```
rndc-confgen > rndc.conf
```

Table 16.1 shows the available rndc command-line options such as rndc status to show the server's status.

TABLE 16.1 Command Line-Options for rndc

Option	Description
-c <config-file>	Specify the full path of the configuration file to use. Default: /etc/rndc.conf.
-k <key-file>	If /etc/rndc.conf doesn't exist to list the default key to use, /etc/rndc.key is used as the authentication key. Use this option to use a different key file if the configuration file is missing.
-s <server>	IP address of a server statement in rndc.conf to connect to as the name server.
-p <port>	Provide a different port to use instead of the default TCP port of 953.
-y <key-id>	Which key to use. A key with the given <key-id> must be declared in rndc.conf.
-V	Turn on verbose logging.
reload	Reload the configuration file and zones.
reload <zone> <class> <view>	Reload a specific zone. The <class> and <view> are optional.
refresh <zone> <class> <view>	Schedule immediate maintenance for a specific zone. The <class> and <view> are optional.
retransfer <zone> <class> <view>	Retransfer a specific zone without checking the serial number. The <class> and <view> are optional.
freeze <zone> <class> <view>	Temporarily stop updates to a zone. The <class> and <view> are optional.
thaw <zone> <class> <view>	Re-enable transfers to a zone that is frozen, and reload its configuration files and zones. The <class> and <view> are optional.
reconfig	Reload configuration files but only reload new zones.
stats	Save server statistics to the statistics file.
querylog	Enable query logging.
dumpdb <-all¦-cache¦ -zones> <view>	Dump cache to the named_dump.db file. The <view> is optional.
stop	Save pending updates to master files, and stop the server.
stop -p	Save pending updates to master files, stop the server, and report process ID (PID).
halt	Stop the server without saving pending updates to the master files.
halt -p	Stop the server without saving pending updates to the master files, and report process ID (PID).
trace	Increase debugging level by one.
trace <level>	Set debugging level to <level>.
notrace	Set debugging level to 0.
flush	Flush server's cache.
flush <view>	Flush server's cache for a specific view.
flushname <name>	Flush <name> from the server's cache.
status	Show server status.
recursing	Dump queries currently being recursed.

Starting and Stopping the Server

The BIND daemon is called named, which can be controlled by its initialization script with the following command:

```
service named <command>
```

Replace <command> with one of the following:

- start: Start the name server.
- stop: Stop the name server.
- status: Show the status of the name server.
- restart: Stop the server if it is running, then start named. If the server is not already running, the stop action will fail, but the start action will still be called.
- condrestart: If the server is already running, and only if the server is already running, restart it.
- reload: Reload the server configuration to enable changes to the configuration files.

To have BIND start at boot time, execute the following as root:

```
chkconfig named on
```


Configuring BIND Graphically

Even if you use the graphical tool to configure BIND, it is recommended that you read the previous section "Configuring BIND" to understand the configuration options the tool is manipulating.

In addition to installing the bind package, bind-utils package, and their software dependencies, install the system-config-bind RPM package if you want to use the graphical configuration tool.

To start the tool, go to the **System** menu on the top panel of the desktop and select **Administration, Server Settings, Domain Name System**. Alternatively, execute the system-config-bind command. If you are not already logged in as the root user, the correct root password must be entered before you are allowed to use the tool.

The application comes with a detailed manual in PDF format in the /usr/share/doc/system-config-bind-<version>/scb_manual.pdf file. This section highlights some of its features, but the manual should be consulted for complete instructions.

When the tool starts, it reads the existing /etc/named.conf file and loads the current configuration. However, if the file contains a syntax error, the error is displayed instead. After fixing the error, start the tool again to proceed. Because the configuration file is read each time the tool starts, it can be modified manually with a text editor before or after using system-config-bind without losing the changes the next time the tool is started.

The first time you start the application, the default settings are shown as in Figure 16.1. Before the default settings are shown, a message appears stating that no default configuration was found if the `/etc/named.conf` file doesn't exist,. If you click **OK** to the message, a `/etc/named.conf` file is created with default values.

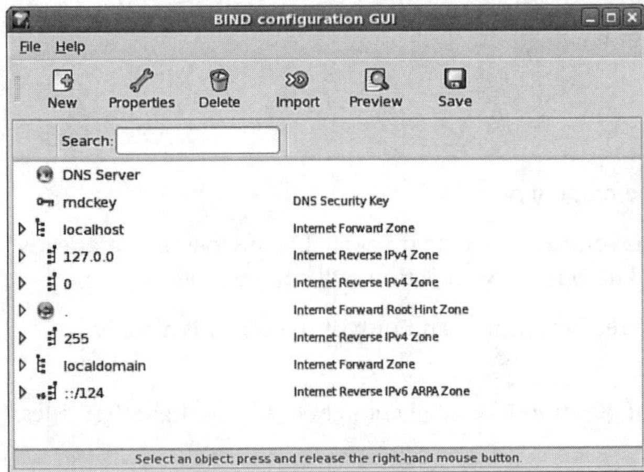

FIGURE 16.1 Default Settings

To add, edit, or delete properties, select an entry from the list in the main window and right-click on it to view an action menu. The actions in the menu vary depending on what is selected.

Importing Defined Hosts

The **Import** button on the toolbar can be used to import a list of IP addresses and their hostnames in the format of the `/etc/hosts` file. After clicking the button, use the **Open** button to select the file containing hosts to import.

To import all the hosts listed in the selected file, click **OK** and notice that the hosts appear in the zone list of the main window. The list of imported hosts from the given file can be filtered so that only specific hosts matching a pattern, or not matching a given pattern, are imported. To set up a filter, first select one of the filter types from the **New List Element** list. The input fields in the **Edit List Element** area changes depending on which filter type is selected. For example, selecting **IPV4 Address Filter** changes the **Edit List Element** frame to look like Figure 16.2.

For any of the filter types, enter the pattern to match and click **OK** in the **Edit List Element** frame to add it to the **Filter List**. When the filter is added, if the unlabeled button is clicked to the left of the input fields in the **Edit List Element** frame, an exclamation point appears as the label of the button. If a filter is added with the exclamation point instead of adding the hosts that match the filter, hosts that match the pattern are not added. If **Match ALL Filters** is selected, hosts are added only if they match all the patterns in the list. If **Match ANY Filters** is selected, hosts are added if they match at least one of the filters. After configuring the filters, click **OK** on the bottom right of the dialog window to add the desired hosts to the zone list in the main window.

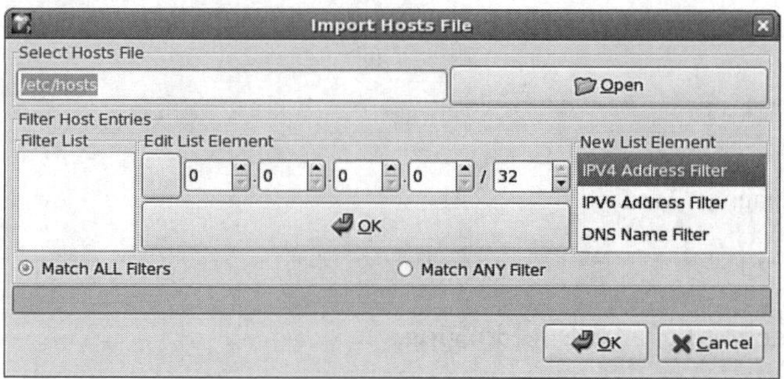

FIGURE 16.2 Importing Defined Hosts

Saving Changes

After configuring the DNS server or making changes to its settings, click the **Save** button in the toolbar of the main window. Configuration files whose settings were modified are saved and the previous version is saved as `<filename>.<timestamp>` such as `named.conf.2006-11-17_11.0.0`. If the `named` service is already running, it is restarted to enable the changes.

Starting and Stopping the Server

To start the server, select **DNS Server** from the zone list, and right-click on it to display a menu. Select **Start Server** from the menu. If the server is already running, options to restart, reload, or stop the server are available instead.

If changes are saved and the named service is already running, the daemon is restarted after the changes are saved.

Logging Connections

By default, the `named` service writes log messages to `/var/log/messages`. Logging may be customized with the `logging` statement in `named.conf`. If `named.conf` has syntax errors, messages about the errors will go to `/var/log/messages` or standard error regardless of the `logging` statement.

The location of log messages can be modified by defining one or more `channel` statements inside the `logging` statement. Listing 16.1 shows the basic syntax with required and optional statements.

LISTING 16.1 Basic Syntax of a Logging Statement

```
logging {
   channel <channel-name> {
      <destination>;
   };
   severity <sev>;
```

LISTING 16.1 Continued

```
   print-category <value>;
   print-severity <value>;
   print-time <value>;
   category <category-name> <channel-list>;
};
```

Listing 16.2 defines the four predefined channels for logging.

LISTING 16.2 Predefined Logging Channels

```
channel default_syslog {
    syslog daemon;          // send to syslog's daemon
                            // facility
    severity info;          // only send priority info
                            // and higher
};

channel default_debug {
    file "named.run";       // write to named.run in
                            // the working directory
                            // Note: stderr is used instead
                            // of "named.run"
                            // if the server is started
                            // with the '-f' option.
    severity dynamic;       // log at the server's
                            // current debug level
};

channel default_stderr {
    stderr;                 // writes to stderr
    severity info;          // only send priority info
                            // and higher
};

channel null {
   null;                    // toss anything sent to
                            // this channel
};
```

You can also define your own custom channel. When creating user-defined channels, use a unique channel name, and replace `<destination>` from Listing 16.1 with one of the following:

- Send messages to a file:

```
file <filename> versions <num> size <num>
```

Only the filename is required. Optionally, set how many old log files are kept on disk with `versions <num>`. Set `<num>` to `unlimited` to keep all old log files. If `versions` is not configured, no backup log files are saved. The `size` option must be set for this to work.

If `size` is set and `versions` is set to more than 0, a new log file is created when it reaches the given size and the old file is renamed `<filename>.0`. If the log file reaches the given size and `versions` is not set to start a new file, the log file remains on disk, but it is not written to after it reaches the given size. The log file must be renamed manually or somehow reduced in size for logging to resume. If `size` is not set, the log file size is not limited. When setting, the number should be followed by `k` for kilobytes, `m` for megabytes, and so on such as `10m` for 10 megabytes.

- Send messages to a specific syslog facility:

  ```
  syslog <facility>
  ```

  Replace `<facility>` with the syslog facility to use: `auth`, `authpriv`, `cron`, `daemon`, `kern`, `lpr`, `mail`, `news`, `syslog`, `user`, `uucp`, and `local0` through `local7`. The list is also in the `syslog.conf` man page. The `/etc/syslog.conf` file must then be modified to determine how syslog handles the messages through the set facility. Refer to the `syslog.conf` man page for details.

- Send messages to standard error:

  ```
  stderr
  ```

  This method is usually only used when `named` is running in the foreground while you are actively monitoring `stderr`, such as during debugging.

- Throw out messages and do not write them anywhere:

  ```
  null
  ```

Optionally, if writing messages to a file, a log severity level can be set with the `severity <sev>` statement inside the `logging` statement to determine what type of messages are processed by each channel. If syslog is being used, the priority set for it is also factored into the decision.

When customizing logging, the `print-category`, `print-severity`, and `print-time` statements can each be optionally set to `yes` or `no`. If `print-category` is set to `yes`, the category of the message is logged. If `print-severity` is set to `yes`, the severity level of each messages is logged. If `print-time` is set to `yes`, a time stamp is written with each message.

The `category` statement inside the `logging` statement is used to associate channels with log message categories. As shown in Listing 16.1, the statement takes the form:

```
category <category-name> <channel-list>
```

If a channel is not listed for a category, the predefined channels of `default_syslog` and `default_debug` are used unless the `default` category is redefined. Otherwise, replace `<channel-list>` with a semicolon-separated list of predefined and/or user-defined channels.

Replace <category-name> with one of the following:

- `default`: Set which channels to use if none are set for a category. If this category is not defined, the `default_syslog` and `default_debug` predefined channels are used for other nondefined categories.
- `general`: Messages that don't fall into any of the other categories are in this category.
- `database`: Messages about the internal database used by named to keep track of zones and cache data.
- `security`: Messages about whether requests are approved or denied.
- `config`: Messages about the configuration file such as syntax errors.
- `resolver`: Messages about DNS resolution.
- `xfer-in`: Messages about zone transfers received by the server.
- `xfer-out`: Messages about zone transfers sent by the server.
- `notify`: Messages about the NOTIFY protocol.
- `client`: Messages about client requests.
- `unmatched`: Messages for which there is no matching view or for which the daemon can't figure out the class. If a message is in this category, a one line message is also set to the client category. By default, these messages are sent to the `null` channel.
- `network`: Messages about network operations.
- `update`: Messages about dynamic updates.
- `update-security`: Messages about whether update requests were approved or denied.
- `queries`: Messages about queries, including the IP address and port of the client, query name, class, and type.
- `dispatch`: Messages about the dispatching of incoming packets to the server modules.
- `dnssec`: Messages about the DNSSEC and TSIG protocols.
- `lame-servers`: Messages about the lame servers.
- `delegation-only`: Messages about log queries forced to NXDOMAIN from the delegation-only zone and a delegation-only in a hint or stub zone.

Summary

This chapter explains DNS and the BIND implementation of the name server. Information such as access control lists and logging preferences can be set in the BIND configuration file, `named.conf`. The `/etc/rndc.conf` file customizes the name server control utility `rndc`, while zone files are located in the `/var/named/` directory. If you prefer a graphical tool, the `system-config-bind` utility provides a graphical interface to the same configuration options.

CHAPTER 17

Securing Remote Logins with OpenSSH

IN THIS CHAPTER

- Allowing Connections
- Configuring the Server
- Connecting from the Client
- Logging Connections

OpenSSH is the open source version of SSH, or *Secure Shell*. Connectivity tools such as Telnet and FTP are well-known, but they send data in plain text format, which can be intercepted by someone using another system on the same network, including the Internet. On the other hand, all data transferred using OpenSSH tools is encrypted, making it inherently more secure. The OpenSSH suite of tools includes `ssh` for securely logging in to a remote system and executing remote commands, `scp` for encrypting files while transferring them to a remote system, and `sftp` for secure FTP transfers.

OpenSSH uses a server-client relationship. The system being connected *to* is referred to as the *server*. The system *requesting* the connection is referred to as the *client*. A system can be both an SSH server and a client.

OpenSSH also has the added benefits of *X11 forwarding* and *port forwarding*. X11 forwarding, if enabled on both the server and client, allows users to display a graphical application from the system they are logged in to on the system they are logged in from. Port forwarding allows a connection request to be sent to one server but be forwarded to another server that actually accepts the request.

This chapter discusses how to use OpenSSH, both from the server-side and the client-side.

Allowing Connections

By default, the OpenSSH server listens for requests on port 22 and port 6010 for X11 forwarding.

If custom IPTables rules are being used, refer to Chapter 24, "Configuring a Firewall," for details on how to allow these ports.

If using a default security level in Red Hat Enterprise Linux, use the Security Level Configuration tool to allow SSH connections. Start it by selecting **Administration**, **System Settings**, **Security Level** from the System menu on the top panel of the desktop or by executing the `system-config-securitylevel` command. Enter the root password when prompted if running as a non-root user. SSH is allowed by default if the default security level is enabled as shown in Figure 17.1. On the Firewall Options tab, make sure the SSH service in the Trusted services section has a check mark beside it. If not, click the check box beside **SSH**, and click **OK** to enable the changes.

FIGURE 17.1 Allowing SSH Requests

Configuring the Server

The `openssh-server` RPM package is required to configure a Red Hat Enterprise Linux system as an OpenSSH server. If it is not already installed, install it with Red Hat Network as described in Chapter 3, "Operating System Updates."

After it is installed, start the service as root with the command `service sshd start`. The system is now an SSH server and can accept connections if the server allows connections on port 22 as described in the "Allowing Connections" section of this chapter.

To configure the server to automatically start the service at boot time, execute the command `chkconfig sshd on` as root. To stop the server, execute the command `service sshd stop`. To verify that the server is running, use the command `service sshd status`.

Retaining Keys After Reinstalling

When the OpenSSH server package is installed, server authentication keys are generated. The keys are generated when the OpenSSH server package is installed and are unique to the server. They are used to verify that the server being connected to is the intended server. The first time a client connects to an OpenSSH server, it must accept the public key. If accepted, the client stores the public key and uses it to verify the identity of the server with each connection.

When a system acting as an OpenSSH server is reinstalled, the files storing the OpenSSH identification keys are re-created as well. Because the SSH clients use these keys to identify the server before connecting to it, they will see the warning message in Listing 17.1 after the operating system reinstallation, which generates new keys.

LISTING 17.1 Warning About Keys Not Matching

```
@@@@@@@@@@@@@@@@@@@@@@@@@@@@@@@@@@@@@@@@@@@@@@@@@@@@@@@@@@@
@    WARNING: REMOTE HOST IDENTIFICATION HAS CHANGED!     @
@@@@@@@@@@@@@@@@@@@@@@@@@@@@@@@@@@@@@@@@@@@@@@@@@@@@@@@@@@@
IT IS POSSIBLE THAT SOMEONE IS DOING SOMETHING NASTY!
Someone could be eavesdropping on you right now (man-in-the-middle attack)!
It is also possible that the RSA host key has just been changed.
The fingerprint for the RSA key sent by the remote host is
66:50:c5:dc:ba:36:d4:3f:ea:93:1d:d8:56:e3:38:56.
Please contact your system administrator.
Add correct host key in /home/tfox/.ssh/known_hosts to get rid of this message.
Offending key in /home/tfox/.ssh/known_hosts:73
RSA host key for 172.31.0.1 has changed and you have requested strict checking.
Host key verification failed.
```

After the message is displayed, the program exits. If you are sure that the key on the server changed, edit the `known_hosts` file in the `.ssh` directory of your home directory such as `/home/tfox/.ssh/known_hosts`. The warning message gives the line number that contains the stored key for the server, or you can search for the hostname or IP address of the server, whichever one you use to connect to it. Delete the line, save the file, and exit the text editor. The next time you try to connect to the server via SSH, you will need to accept the new RSA server key.

17

CAUTION

Before removing a stored RSA key for a server and accepting a new one, verify with the administrator of the server that the key has changed and that the new key you are accepting is correct. Otherwise, the system could have been compromised, and you might be compromising your system by accepting the different key and connecting to a different server.

Instead of communicating a new key to users every time a server is reinstalled, an administrator can retain the host keys generated for the system before reinstalling. To save the keys before reinstalling, save the `/etc/ssh/ssh_host*key*` files on another system or backup media. After reinstalling, restore these files to their original locations on the server to retain the system's identification keys. If this process is used, clients will not receive the warning message when trying to connect to the system after it is reinstalled.

Connecting from the Client

This section discusses how to connect to an SSH server from a Red Hat Enterprise Linux system. The SSH server can be any server running an SSH daemon, including a Red Hat Enterprise Linux system running OpenSSH.

To connect to an SSH server, the `openssh-clients` RPM package must be installed. Install it via Red Hat Network if it is not already installed. This package provides the SSH utilities discussed in this section and summarized in Table 17.1.

TABLE 17.1 OpenSSH Client Utilities

OpenSSH Utility	Description
`ssh`	Securely log in to a remote system or execute a command on a remote system
`slogin`	Alias to the `ssh` command
`scp`	Copy files from one computer to another while encrypting the data
`sftp`	Securely transfer files from one system to another
`ssh-add`	Add RSA or DSA identities to the authentication agent
`ssh-agent`	Remember private keys for public key authentication
`ssh-keyscan`	Gather public SSH keys

Logging In to a Remote System

The most common OpenSSH utility is `ssh`, a secure replacement for `rlogin`, `rsh`, and `telnet`. The `ssh` command allows users to remotely log in to a system from another system using an encrypted transfer protocol. Every transfer starting with the username and password sent for authentication is encrypted so it can't be easily read if intercepted. The system being connected to is considered the *server*. The system being connected from is called the *client*.

To log in to a system with `ssh`, use the following command, where `<hostname>` is the hostname, fully qualified domain name, or IP address of the remote system:

```
ssh <hostname>
```

If the hostname or fully qualified domain name is used, the client must be able to resolve it to a valid IP address. The first time a user tries to connect via `ssh` to another system, the message in Listing 17.2 is displayed.

LISTING 17.2 Connecting to an SSH Server for the First Time

```
The authenticity of host '172.31.0.1 (172.31.0.1)' can't be established.
RSA key fingerprint is 66:50:c5:dc:ba:36:d4:3f:ea:93:1d:d8:56:e3:38:56.
Are you sure you want to continue connecting (yes/no)?
```

If the user types `yes`, the client saves the server's public RSA key, and the server responds by requesting the user's password. If the correct password is entered, the server accepts the request, and the user receives a shell prompt to the remote system. The server's public key is added to the `.ssh/known_hosts` file in the user's home directory. After this public key is written to this file, the message in Listing 17.2 is no longer displayed when a connection is requested.

When the `ssh` command is executed, the username of the user currently logged in to the client is sent to the remote server as the username requesting connection. To use a different username on the remote server, use the command `ssh username@<hostname>`.

Executing a Command Remotely

The `ssh` utility also allows users to execute commands remotely using the following syntax:

```
ssh <hostname> <command>
```

If the command contains any wildcards, redirects, or pipes, it must be in quotation marks such as the following:

```
ssh myserver.example.com "cat /proc/cpuinfo | grep flags"
```

After authenticating with a password or passphrase, the results of `<command>` are displayed to the client.

Transferring Files Securely

The `scp` utility provides the ability to transfer files from one system to another system running an SSH server such as OpenSSH. The command has many variations, but the basic syntax is as follows:

```
scp <local-file> <username>@remote.example.com:<remote-file>
```

Like `ssh`, if a username is not specified for the remote server, the current username is assumed. If only a directory path is given for `<remote-file>`, the same filename is used to transfer the file to the specified directory on the remote server.

The wildcard character `*` can be used to specify multiple files for `<local-file>` and `<remote-file>`.

The `scp` command can also be used to transfer remote files to the local system. Just reverse the syntax:

```
scp <username>@remote.example.com:<remote-file> <local-file>
```

A few command-line options to `scp`, such as `-l`, limit the amount of bandwidth it is allowed to use. Refer to its man page with the `man scp` command for a full list with descriptions.

TIP

If the path for the <remote-file> does not begin with a /, it is assumed that the path is relative to the user's home directory. For example, to transfer the file `ProjectSchedule.odt` to your home directory on a remote system, use the `scp ProjectSchedule.odt remote.example.com:` command.

The `sftp` utility can also be used to transfer files via an encrypted connection. It differs from `scp` and is similar to `ftp` in that it uses an interactive shell. To connect via `sftp` to a remote system, use the command `sftp username@<remote-system>`. Again, if no username is specified, the username of the current user on the client is assumed for the remote system. After authenticating correctly, the `sftp>` prompt is displayed, giving the user an interactive session to the remote system (see Listing 17.3). The interactive commands are similar to `ftp`. Table 17.2 lists common `sftp` commands.

LISTING 17.3 `sftp` Session

```
Connecting to fileserver.example.com...
tfox@fileserver's password:
sftp>
```

TABLE 17.2 Common `sftp` Commands

`sftp` **command**	**Description**
`pwd`	Display current remote directory
`lpwd`	Display current local directory
`cd <directory_name>`	Change to remote directory
`lcd <directory_name>`	Change current local directory
`get <file>`	Retrieve `<file>` from current remote directory to current local directory
`mget <files>`	Retrieve multiple files
`put <file>`	Upload local file to the current remote directory
`mput <files>`	Upload multiple local files to the current remote directory
`ls`	List files in current remote directory
`exit`	Close connection to SSH server and exit

As you can tell, the commands are similar to `ftp` with a few exceptions, such as the user is not prompted to confirm actions by default—there is no need to disable prompting with the `prompt` command before using `mget` and `mput`. Hash marks can't be displayed to show progress, but progress in terms of percentage of total transfer, total kilobytes already transferred, transfer rate, and time remaining is automatically displayed, as in the following:

```
/tmp/samplefile                          100% 1888KB    1.8MB/s    00:01
```

It is also possible to connect to an FTP server using `sftp` from the Nautilus file browser. Select **Places, Connect to Server** from the desktop menu, and select **SSH** as the service type.

Type the IP address or full hostname of the FTP server in the Server field as shown in Figure 17.2.

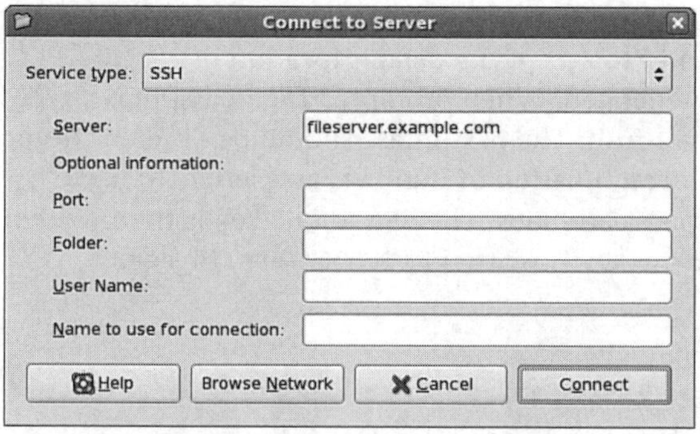

FIGURE 17.2 Connecting to an sftp Server

Under the Optional information section, the following can be configured:

- **Port**: Specify the server port to connect to if different than the default FTP port 21.
- **Folder**: The folder to open after logging in to the FTP server.
- **User Name**: The username to use for authentication when connecting. You will be prompted for the password later.
- **Name to use for the connection**: Connection name to use when labeling the mount point in the Places menu and on the desktop.

An icon will appear on the desktop using the name of the server or, if provided, the name in the Name To Use For The Connection field. A shortcut is also listed under the Places menu item in the desktop menu. Double-clicking on the desktop icon or selecting the shortcut item in the Places menu will open a file browser window with the files from the FTP server. Depending on your file permissions from the server, you can open, copy, delete, rename files and directories, and more.

To unmount the share, right-click on its desktop icon and select **Unmount Volume**. If the share is not unmounted, it will remain in the Places menu on reboot, but you must reauthenticate to access the share after rebooting.

Creating a Passphrase

Instead of using a password to authenticate, OpenSSH allows the use of a passphrase. Why use a passphrase? Unlike a password, a passphrase can contain spaces and tabs and is usually much longer than a password, hence the word *phrase* in the name. The added length along with the spaces and tabs makes a passphrase more secure and harder to guess.

Passphrases are unique per user and must be created by each user while logged in with the corresponding username. Red Hat Enterprise Linux 5 uses SSH Protocol 2 and RSA keys by default. To generate an RSA key pair for SSH version 2, use the following command:

```
ssh-keygen -t rsa
```

As demonstrated in Listing 17.4, press Enter to accept the default location of `$HOME/.ssh/id_rsa` after the key pair is generated. When prompted for a passphrase, type a passphrase to use and type it again to confirm. The passphrase should be different from the user's password and should contain a combination of numbers and letters to make it more secure. Remember it can contain spaces and tabs. The RSA public key is then written to `$HOME/.ssh/id_rsa.pub` while the private key is written to `$HOME/.ssh/id_rsa`.

LISTING 17.4 Generating a Passphrase

```
Generating public/private rsa key pair.
Enter file in which to save the key (/home/tfox/.ssh/id_rsa):
Enter passphrase (empty for no passphrase):
Enter same passphrase again:
Your identification has been saved in /home/tfox/.ssh/id_rsa.
Your public key has been saved in /home/tfox/.ssh/id_rsa.pub.
The key fingerprint is:
ed:09:c2:a8:31:1f:11:85:0a:5e:c0:ab:16:b6:f1:98 tfox@rhel5
```

CAUTION

The private key file should never be accessible by anyone other than the user who created it. It is created with read-write file permissions for the user only. These permissions should not be altered.

After successfully generating the key pair, copy the contents of the public key file `$HOME/.ssh/id_rsa.pub` to `$HOME/.ssh/authorized_keys` on all the systems you want to connect to with the SSH tools. If the `authorized_keys` file already exists, append it with the contents of `$HOME/.ssh/id_rsa.pub`. If the `.ssh/` directory does not exist in your home directory on the remote systems, it must be created so that only you, the owner, can access it. To change the permissions for it, execute the command `chmod 0700 $HOME/.ssh` on the remote system. The `$HOME/.ssh/authorized_keys` file on each remote system must have the same permissions as the `$HOME/.ssh/id_rsa.pub` file created by `ssh-keygen`. Change its permissions with the `chmod 644 $HOME/.ssh/authorized_keys` command on each remote system to which you will be connecting.

After creating an RSA key pair and distributing the public key to the remote systems, when the `ssh <hostname>` command is executed, the user will be prompted for the passphrase used to create the key pair instead of being prompted for a password for authentication.

Remembering the Passphrase

Instead of entering the passphrase each time you connect to a remote system, the `ssh-agent` utility from the `openssh-clients` package can be used to remember the passphrase.

Additionally, if a graphical desktop is used and the `openssh-askpass` package is installed, the desktop can be configured to prompt the user for the passphrase after the user logs in to the graphical interface. While that graphical login session is active, the passphrase will be remembered for all terminals opened within that graphical session. To configure `ssh-agent` as a startup program, use the following steps:

1. Verify that the `openssh-askpass` package is installed. If it isn't, install it via Red Hat Network.
2. From the System menu on the top panel of the desktop, select **Preferences**, **More Preferences**, **Sessions**.
3. When the Sessions window appears, select the **Startup Programs** tab.
4. Click **Add** and enter **`/usr/bin/ssh-add`** as the startup command. Click **OK**. The window will look similar to Figure 17.3.
5. Click **Close** to save the settings and exit.

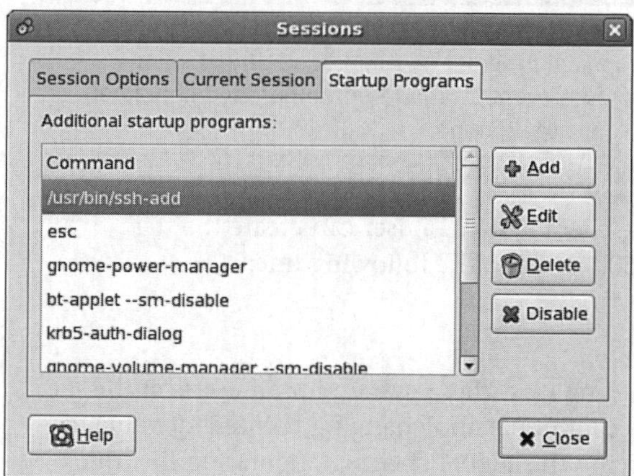

FIGURE 17.3 Adding `ssh-add` to the Startup Programs

The next time the user logs in to the graphical desktop, a dialog window will appear prompting the user for the passphrase. If the correct passphrase is entered, the user will not have to type the passphrase again when connecting to systems that contain the corresponding `$HOME/.ssh/authorized_keys` file.

If a graphical interface is not being used, the passphrase can be remembered by executing the following commands:

```
exec /usr/bin/ssh-agent $SHELL
ssh-add
```

17

After you enter the correct passphrase, it will be remembered for that session or terminal window.

X11 Forwarding

X11 forwarding means that graphical programs can be executed on a remote system and displayed on the local client system. Even though the interface appears on the client, it is running on the remote server. For example, if you want to enable Kdump on a remote system, you can log in to it remotely using `ssh`, execute the `system-config-kdump` command on the remote system, and the graphical program appears on your local computer. Configure the Kdump settings for the remote system, save the settings, and you are done without having to physically move to the remote system to get a graphical desktop. X11 forwarding must be enabled on both the client and server system for it to work.

By default, X11 forwarding is not enabled on the client. If the server supports X11 forwarding, the user can enable it with the `-Y` command-line option:

```
ssh -Y <hostname>
```

TIP

When you execute a graphical program from a remote login session, the program is displayed on the client, but while the graphical program is being used, the session cannot be used to run other commands. To prevent this, add an ampersand character (&) after the command such as `system-config-kdump&`.

To always enable X11 forwarding on the client system, a user can create the file `$HOME/.ssh/config` with permissions 0600 and add the following line:

```
ForwardX11 yes
```

An administrator can enable X11 forwarding on a client system for all users on the system by modifying the `/etc/ssh/ssh_config` file and changing the default value of `ForwardX11` from `no` to `yes`. After modifying this global client configuration file, the service must be restarted for the changes to take effect with the `service sshd restart` command. Settings in this global file apply to all users unless the values are overridden in the `$HOME/.ssh/config` user file.

NOTE

The OpenSSH client tools check the file permission for the `$HOME/.ssh/config` file if it exists. If the file has write permissions for the group or other category, the program will exit instead of connecting to the server. It is recommended that the file have the permissions 0600, which can be modified with the `chmod` command.

After enabling X11 forwarding, if a user is logged in to a remote system via ssh and executes a graphical program, the program is run on the remote system, but the graphical interface is displayed on the client system the user is logged in to. This has many benefits including being able to run graphical system administration tools remotely.

To allow X11 forwarding on server, the X11Forwarding option must be set to yes in the /etc/ssh/sshd_config file on the OpenSSH server. According to the sshd_config man page, the default value for X11Forwarding is no. However, the default value in Red Hat Enterprise Linux is set to yes. After modifying the configuration file, execute the command service sshd restart to enable the change.

TIP

To learn about the other options in /etc/ssh/ssh_config on the client and /etc/ssh/sshd_config on the server, read their man pages with the man ssh_config and man sshd_config commands.

Port Forwarding

In addition to X11 forwarding, ssh can also be used to forward connections from one port to another, otherwise known as *port forwarding* or *tunneling*. Port forwarding can be used to make an otherwise unencrypted connection secure by encrypting it via ssh. It can also be used to connect to a server behind a firewall.

The basic syntax is as follows:

```
ssh -L <localport>:<remotehost>:<remoteport> <username>@<otherhost>
```

When a connection is made to port <localport> on the local system, the connection goes over an encrypted tunnel to the <otherhost> and then is forwarded to port <remoteport> on the <remotehost> after successful authentication for username@otherhost.

For an example, refer to Figure 17.4. In this figure, an SSH tunnel is established between the source host and the SSH server. The destination host can be any type of server configured to accept connections on a static port such as a POP3 email server, a web server, or even another SSH server.

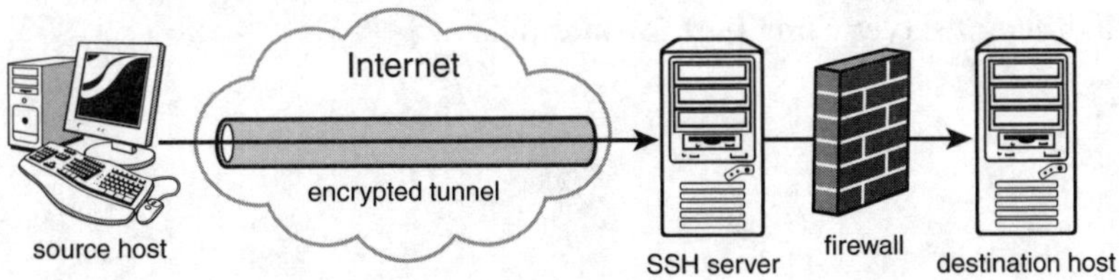

FIGURE 17.4 Establishing an SSH Tunnel

17

The destination host allows connections from the SSH server through the firewall, but the firewall does not allow connections from the source host. So, an encrypted SSH tunnel is established between the source host and the SSH server. Then, packets intended for the destination host are sent over the encrypted tunnel to the SSH server and then forwarded to the destination host on the other side of the firewall. The connection between the SSH server and the destination host is not necessarily encrypted because 'an SSH tunnel has not been established between them. However, the connection can be secured with additional software such as a VPN solution. If the destination host is another SSH server, the connection between the connecting SSH server and the destination host is encrypted because of the SSH connection.

TIP

To disable port forwarding on an OpenSSH server, add the following line to `/etc/ssh/sshd_config`:

```
AllowTcpForwarding no
```

Logging Connections

By default, the OpenSSH daemon (`sshd`) uses syslog to write messages to `/var/log/messages` when sessions are opened and closed for users as well as when an authentication attempt has failed.

To modify the type of messages logged, set the `LogLevel` directive in the `/etc/ssh/sshd_config` file. By default, it is set to `INFO`. The possible values in order of verbosity are `QUIET`, `FATAL`, `ERROR`, `INFO`, `VERBOSE`, `DEBUG`, `DEBUG1`, `DEBUG2`, and `DEBUG3`. `DEBUG` and `DEBUG1` are the same. Logging with any of the `DEBUG` levels violates user privacy and is not recommended.

Summary

When administering UNIX-based systems such as those running Red Hat Enterprise Linux, SSH tools such as the OpenSSH suite are essential. It can help you perform a variety of tasks such as logging in to a system to monitor system performance, remotely running graphical configuration tools, applying system updates, or even checking email. It can also allow you to display a graphical application remotely with X11 forwarding and redirect requests to a different server using port forwarding.

CHAPTER 18

Setting Up an Email Server with Sendmail

IN THIS CHAPTER

- Understanding Email Concepts
- Configuring Sendmail
- Using POP and IMAP
- Logging Sendmail Connections
- Allowing Email Connections

In a corporate environment, email is an essential component to the work day. Email is used to schedule and remind employees of meetings, communicate with both internal employees and external customers, and enable remote employees to participate in company discussions; it has even taken the place of water cooler talk for some employees.

The first part of this chapter outlines how an email message reaches its destination email server. The second part of the chapter explains how to set up Red Hat Enterprise Linux to send and receive email with Sendmail. Finally, users must retrieve email off an email server from an email client using a protocol such as POP or IMAP. Configuring the email server to allow POP and IMAP connections is discussed in the last part of this chapter.

Understanding Email Concepts

When a person wants to send an email to someone else on the Internet, she opens an email client, which is also called a *Mail User Agent* (*MUA*), such as Evolution or Thunderbird. Instead of using a standalone email client, you can also use a web browser to access a web-based email client or even an application on a portable Internet device such as a cell phone or PDA.

After you send an email, the email is formatted into a standard format so that all the other email servers on the Internet can read it.

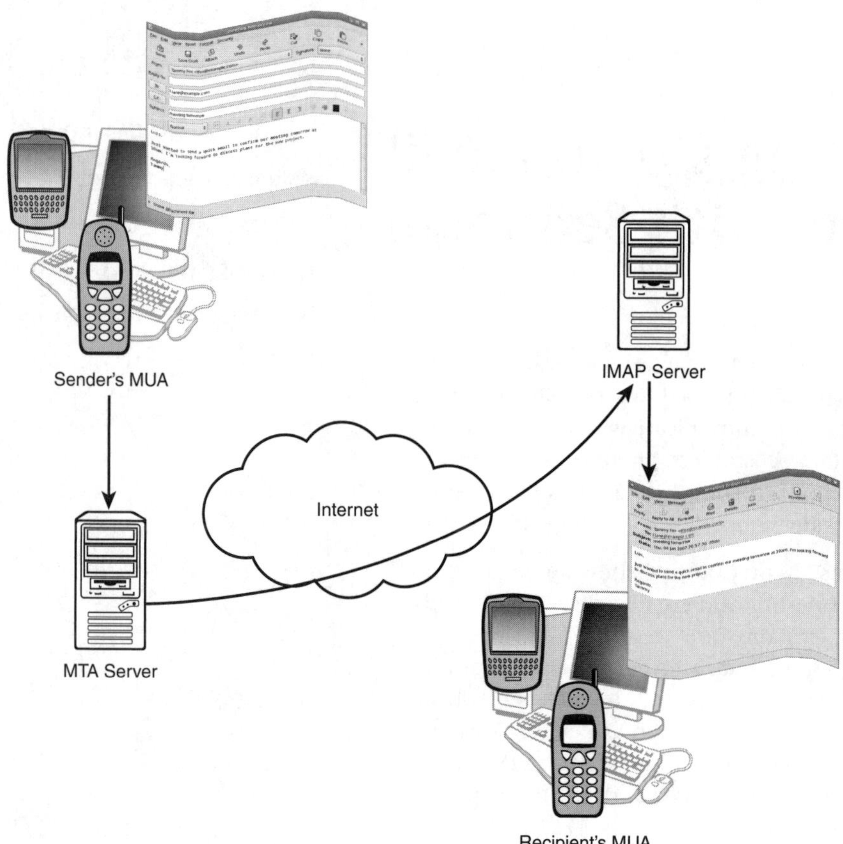

FIGURE 18.1 Sending an Email

As shown in Figure 18.1, after the message is formatted and optionally encrypted, it is sent to a *Mail Transport Agent* (*MTA*) using the Simple Mail Transfer Protocol (SMTP). The email application used is configured to send all outgoing emails to a specific MTA server. After that, the email may be transferred to several MTA servers before reaching the MTA for the domain of the email recipient. After the email reaches its destination MTA, it is stored on the server and waits for the recipient to retrieve it.

The email transfer in Figure 18.1 shows the initial MTA inside the same private network as the device used to send the email. However, the MTA doesn't have to be inside the private network. It only needs to be accessible by the system sending the email. For example, home users are given an MTA server (sometimes called an SMTP server) to use, which is accessible over the Internet.

If you are administering systems for a company that transfers a large amount of email as well as company confidential email, you will need to set up an MTA inside the company's private network. As shown in Figure 18.2, if an employee sends an email to another employee inside the private network with an MTA server, the email goes through the private MTA server and is never transmitted across the Internet, thus making it harder for someone outside the company to intercept and read the email containing confidential information.

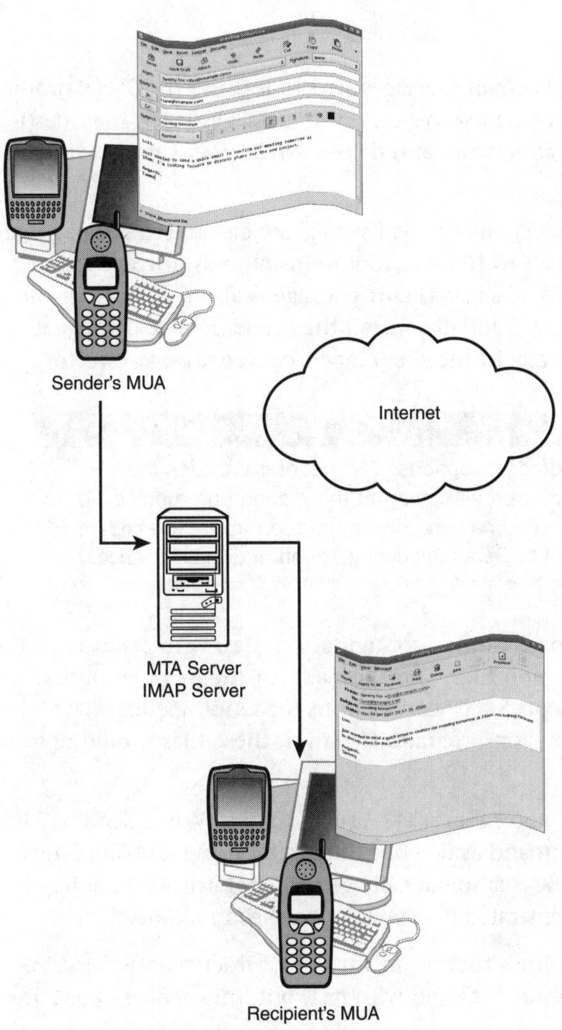

FIGURE 18.2 Sending an Internal Email

To read the email, the recipient uses an MUA, commonly known as an email client. It must be configured to download the email using a protocol accepted by the MTA storing the email. Most MTAs accept the POP3 protocol, the IMAP protocol, or both. The differences between these two protocols are discussed later in the "Using POP and IMAP" section.

After the recipient reads the email, he has many options. For example, he can choose to make a copy of it on his local filesystem, keep the message on the server, delete the message from the server, forward the email to a different person, or reply to the person who sent the email.

Configuring Sendmail

Sendmail™ is an MTA, meaning it accepts email messages sent to it using the SMTP protocol and transports them to another MTA email server until the messages reach their destinations. It also accepts email for the local network and delivers them to local mail spools, one for each user.

To configure a Red Hat Enterprise Linux system as a mail server, the `sendmail` RPM package must be installed. If it is not installed, use Red Hat Network to install it as discussed in Chapter 3, "Operating System Updates." The `sendmail-cf` package is also necessary if you plan to change the default configuration. Optionally, install the `sendmail-doc` package if you want the Sendmail docs installed locally in the `/usr/share/doc/sendmail/` directory.

NOTE

Sendmail is quite configurable with hundreds of options. This chapter provides the essential information necessary to get your email server off the ground and running. To explore more of its functionality, consult sendmail.org, documentation from the `sendmail-docs` package, or a book dedicated to Sendmail configuration and maintenance.

The `/etc/mail/` directory contains all the Sendmail configuration files, with `sendmail.cf` and `submit.cf` being the main configuration files. The `sendmail.cf` file includes options for the mail transmission agent and accepts SMTP connections for sending email. The `submit.cf` file configures the mail submission program. However, these files should not be edited directly.

Instead, edit the `/etc/mail/sendmail.mc` and `/etc/mail/submit.mc` files. When Sendmail is started or restarted with the `service` command as described in the "Starting and Stopping the Server" section, a new `sendmail.cf` file is automatically generated if `sendmail.mc` has been modified, and a new `submit.cf` is generated if `submit.mc` has been modified.

In the `sendmail.mc` and `submit.mc` files, lines that begin with `dnl`, which stands for *delete to new line*, are considered comments. Some lines end with `dnl`, but lines *ending* in `dnl` are not comments.

Only the root user can modify files in the `/etc/mail/` directory. The `/etc/mail/` directory also includes the following configuration files:

- `access`

  List of hosts that are allowed to send email from this server. Refer to `/usr/share/doc/sendmail/README.cf` from the `sendmail-docs` package for details.

- `domaintable`

  Table of old domain names and their new domain names in case they have changed.

- `helpfile`

  Text file containing the content displayed for the `SMTP HELP` command.

- `local-host-names`

  If the email server should be known by different hostnames, list the hostnames in this file, one line per hostname. Any email sent to addresses at these hostnames is treated as local mail. The `FEATURE(`use_cw_file')` option must be enabled in the `sendmail.mc` file for this file to be referenced.

- `mailertable`

  Table of domains and what mailer and domain they should be routed to. `FEATURE(`mailertable')` must be enabled in `sendmail.mc`.

- `trusted-users`

  List of users that can send email as other users without a warning including system users such as apache for the Apache HTTP Server.

- `virtusertable`

  List of email address or domain names (meaning all email addresses at that domain) along with an email address to forward them to or an error code to return for the email address.

TIP

Further details about all these files can be found in `/usr/share/doc/sendmail/README.cf` from the `sendmail-docs` package.

Some of these configuration files are similar to `sendmail.mc` and `submit.mc` in that they are not the actual files referenced by Sendmail. If the `access`, `domaintable`, `mailertable`, or `virtusertable` file is modified, the corresponding database file referenced by Sendmail must be regenerated. When the `service sendmail {start,reload,restart}` command is executed, the initialization script calls the `makemap` utility to regenerate these database files.

18

An additional configuration file, `/etc/aliases`, can be used to redirect email from one user to another. By default, it includes redirects for system accounts to the root user. It can then be used to redirect all email for the root user to the user account for the system administrator. If this file is modified, the Sendmail service must be restarted so that the initialization script runs the `newaliases` utility to rebuild the aliases database referenced by Sendmail.

By default, Sendmail in Red Hat Enterprise Linux is configured to only accept connections from the local system through the loopback device (127.0.0.1). To modify this behavior, locate the following line in `/etc/mail/sendmail.mc`:

```
DAEMON_OPTIONS(`Port=smtp,Addr=127.0.0.1, Name=MTA')dnl
```

Either comment out the line completely by prepending it with `dnl` and a space or by changing the loopback address (127.0.0.1) to the IP address of the network device listening for Sendmail connections.

Sendmail can only deliver email to a user's mail spool in `/var/spool/mail/` if the user exists on the system. For each email account, create a user account or configure network authentication such as NIS for the system. The directories that contain email such as `/var/spool/mail/` and, by default, the `Mail/` directory in each user's home directory if you are using IMAP should not be located on an NFS share because the user or group ID of the files can be duplicated on a system mounting the share, granting anyone access to the email files. Also, it is good practice to only allow the root user to log in to the email server for better security. Users should retrieve their email from an email client running on another system and should have no need to log in to the email server directly.

Using SSL Encryption

Sendmail can be configured to encrypt email sent and received using SSL (secure sockets layer). First, generate an SSL certificate. You can either create a self-signed certificate or purchase one from verisign.com or other similar third-party companies.

To generate a self-signed certificate, open a terminal and use the `su -` command to change to the root user if you are logged in as a non-root user. Change into the `/etc/pki/tls/certs/` directory, and execute the `make sendmail.pem` command. You will be prompted for information such as the location of the company, company name, and email address. Listing 18.1 shows this process with the example data provided in bold.

LISTING 18.1 Generating a Self-Signed SSL Certificate

```
umask 77 ; \
PEM1=`/bin/mktemp /tmp/openssl.XXXXXX` ; \
PEM2=`/bin/mktemp /tmp/openssl.XXXXXX` ; \
/usr/bin/openssl req -utf8 -newkey rsa:1024 -keyout $PEM1 -nodes \
-x509 -days 365 -out $PEM2 -set_serial 0 ; \
cat $PEM1 >  sendmail.pem ; \
echo ""    >> sendmail.pem ; \
cat $PEM2 >> sendmail.pem ; \
rm -f $PEM1 $PEM2
Generating a 1024 bit RSA private key
.......++++++
........................++++++
writing new private key to '/tmp/openssl.y25478'
-----
You are about to be asked to enter information that will be incorporated
into your certificate request.
What you are about to enter is what is called a Distinguished Name or a DN.
There are quite a few fields but you can leave some blank
For some fields there will be a default value,
If you enter '.', the field will be left blank.
-----
Country Name (2 letter code) [GB]:US
State or Province Name (full name) [Berkshire]:North Carolina
```

LISTING 18.1 Continued

```
Locality Name (eg, city) [Newbury]:Raleigh
Organization Name (eg, company) [My Company Ltd]:TCBF Computers, Inc.
Organizational Unit Name (eg, section) []:
Common Name (eg, your name or your server's hostname) []:My Hostname
Email Address []:admin@example.com
```

Next, configuration changes in `/etc/mail/sendmail.mc` must be made. Uncomment the following line by removing the `dnl` prefix:

```
dnl DAEMON_OPTIONS(`Port=smtps, Name=TLSMTA, M=s')dnl
```

After removing the `dnl` prefix, it should look like the following:

```
DAEMON_OPTIONS(`Port=smtps, Name=TLSMTA, M=s')dnl
```

Also uncomment the following lines so Sendmail knows how to locate the SSL certificate just generated:

```
define(`confCACERT_PATH',`/etc/pki/tls/certs')dnl
define(`confCACERT',`/etc/pki/tls/certs/ca-bundle.crt')dnl
define(`confSERVER_CERT',`/etc/pki/tls/certs/sendmail.pem')dnl
define(`confSERVER_KEY',`/etc/pki/tls/certs/sendmail.pem')dnl
```

CAUTION

The formatting of the `sendmail.mc` file is sensitive. Be sure not to use extra white-space or blank lines. Doing so will cause errors when the file is converted to the `sendmail.cf` file.

Sendmail must be restarted for the changes to take effect. Restart it by executing the `service sendmail restart` command as the root user.

Starting and Stopping the Server

Sendmail can be started, stopped, and restarted with the `service` command as root. After configuring Sendmail, start the server with the `service sendmail start` command. When the Sendmail service is started with this command or restarted with `service sendmail restart`, changes to the configuration files in `/etc/mail/` are automatically enabled as previously discussed.

The command `service sendmail status` displays whether the service is running. The command `service sendmail reload` enables any changes made to the `/etc/mail/` configuration files.

To configure the Sendmail service to start automatically at boot time, use the following command as root:

```
chkconfig sendmail on
```

Using POP and IMAP

After the emails arrive on the server, users can retrieve them with an email client such as Evolution or Thunderbird. While some email clients can be configured to read email directly from the user's spool file in `/var/spool/mail/`, this can be inconvenient because the mail client must be run on the email server and the emails have not been run through any filters to sort them into easier-to-manage email folders. All emails are aggregated into one file, and when the number of emails becomes large (greater than 1,000), reading email directly from the mail spool can be inefficient. Two popular protocols for retrieving email are *POP* and *IMAP*.

The latest version of POP, or Post Office Protocol, is pop3. It works by "popping" the email messages off the user's spool on the email server and saving them in folders on the user's local system running the email client. By default, the email is deleted from the email server after it is saved locally. Optionally, the email client can be configured to filter the mail into different mail folders before saving them on the local system. By default, emails retrieved using POP are not encrypted, but an encrypted version of pop3 can be set up on the server and used if the email client supports it.

Because the email is stored in local mail folders, one disadvantage is that the user must always check email from the same computer (locally or remotely). Because the email is removed from the email server by default (clients can be configured to leave the email on the server even after it is copied locally), a disk failure on the user's computer can result in loss of email unless the email folders are part of a routine backup plan.

IMAP, or Internet Message Access Protocol, can also be used to retrieve email from a server. However, unlike POP, the messages are kept on the server, including the email folders used to organize the messages. The main advantage of IMAP is that users can open any email client with IMAP support on any computer that has access to the email server and see all their email, complete with email folders and sent mail. Because all the email is stored on the server, the client is simply used to allow the user to read email off the server. Messages can optionally be copied to the user's local system so they can be read while not connected to the network, but the email is still kept on the server unless specifically deleted by the user.

By default, the IMAP connection is not encrypted, but an encrypted version of IMAP can be configured on the server. IMAP also simplifies an administrator's backup procedure because he only needs to back up the directories that store email on the email server instead of on each user's computer. If a user has a disk failure on her computer, she can log in to another computer and continue reading her email while the disk failure is fixed.

Enabling POP and IMAP

After setting up Sendmail on the email server, install the `dovecot` RPM package to set up the IMAP and/or POP protocols. Refer to Chapter 3, "Operating System Updates," for details on how to install an RPM package.

In `/etc/dovecot.conf` find the following line and uncomment it (lines that begin with # are comments):

```
protocols = imap imaps pop3 pop3s
```

By default, the line lists the protocols for IMAP, IMAP over SSL, POP, and POP over SSL. If you don't want to enable all of these, remove the unwanted ones from the list. Next, start Dovecot with the service dovecot start command as root.

The /etc/dovecot.conf file contains many more options for customizing Dovecot. The comments in the configuration file offer brief descriptions of the variables. Refer to the /usr/share/doc/dovecot-<version>/configuration.txt, the other files in the /usr/share/doc/dovecot-<version>/ directory, and dovecot.org for details.

Enabling POP and IMAP with SSL

To use the secure versions of POP and IMAP (pop3s and imaps), you need to generate an SSL certificate. Dummy certificates are generated when the dovecot RPM package is installed, but they should only be used for testing purposes because they do not show the correct hostname for the email server or location. A self-signed certificate can be generated with the /usr/share/doc/dovecot-<version>/examples/mkcert.sh script. An SSL certificate issued by a trusted third party can be purchased from sites such as verisign.com.

Before running the mkcert.sh script, modify /etc/pki/dovecot/dovecot-openssl.cnf with the correct values for your server. For example, the CN option for Common Name needs to be set to the domain name of the email server. Also, in mkcert.sh, you need to modify the location of the SSLDIR variable to the default directory Dovecot expects the SSL keys to be located in. It should read as follows:

```
SSLDIR=${SSLDIR-/etc/pki/dovecot}
```

The mkcert.sh script will not override existing keys, so move the default keys created, /etc/pki/dovecot/certs/dovecot.pem and /etc/pki/dovecot/private/dovecot.pem, into a backup directory or rename them. The script also assumes the dovecot-openssl.cnf file is in the current working directory, so change into the /etc/pki/dovecot/ directory as root, and execute the script using the full path to its location: /usr/share/doc/dovecot-<version>/examples/mkcert.sh, where <version> is the version of Dovecot installed. If the script successfully creates the keys, the output will look similar to the following:


```
Generating a 1024 bit RSA private key
....++++++
.......................................................++++++
writing new private key to '/etc/pki/dovecot/private/dovecot.pem'
-----

subject= /C=US/ST=North Carolina/L=Raleigh/OU=IMAP
server/CN=host.example.com/emailAddress=postmaster@example.com
SHA1 Fingerprint=B3:93:A8:A8:51:1F:28:08:41:12:14:B5:72:5E:5B:4B:83:B0:88:4B
```

To test the connection, use the command telnet localhost <port>, where <port> is 110 for POP, 143 for IMAP, 995 for POP over SSL, and 993 for IMAP over SSL. If Dovecot is configured properly and listening for connections, you should see the following:

```
Trying 127.0.0.1...
Connected to localhost.localdomain (127.0.0.1).
Escape character is '^]'.
+OK Dovecot ready.
```

Also, test the protocols from an email client. If imaps or pop3s is enabled, the client will ask you to accept the SSL certificate before prompting for a password.

CAUTION

If the /etc/dovecot.conf file is modified while the service is running, be sure to enable the changes with the `service dovecot reload` command as root.

Logging Sendmail Connections

Sendmail uses the syslog facility to write log entries to the `/var/log/maillog` file. Each entry includes information such as the recipient of the email, when it was sent, and the delivery status. For example:

```
maillog:May 23 22:46:27 examplehostname sendmail[29858]: k402kMUr029858:
to=tfox@linuxheadquarters.com, ctladdr=tfox (501/501), delay=00:00:05,
xdelay=00:00:05, mailer=relay, pri=42830, relay=[127.0.0.1] [127.0.0.1],
dsn=2.0.0, stat=Sent (k402kMrC029859 Message accepted for delivery)
```

Because the syslog facility is used, the log file is rotated periodically, and the previous five log files are kept. The old log files are named `maillog.X`, where `X` is a number. The larger the number, the older the log file.

The log level can be set in `sendmail.mc` and defaults to level 9. Levels under 10 are considered useful, levels 11–64 are verbose, and levels above 64 are for debugging. Further explanation on the commonly used log levels can be found in `/usr/share/doc/sendmail/doc/op/op.ps`. Remember to enable the changes with the `service sendmail reload` command if you modify the log level.

Basic statistics are also recorded for Sendmail in the `/var/log/mail/statistics` file. The file is not stored in plain text, so the `mailstats` utility must be used to read it. As root, execute the `mailstats` command to display the Sendmail stats. By default, it reads the statistics from the `/var/log/mail/statistics` file (or whatever file is specified for `StatusFile` in `sendmail.mc`). To specify a different file, use the `mailstats -f <filename>` command, where `<filename>` is the alternate file name and location. Listing 18.2 shows sample output.

LISTING 18.2 Example Sendmail Statistics

```
Statistics from Sat Mar 25 16:04:28 2006
 M   msgsfr  bytes_from   msgsto    bytes_to  msgsrej msgsdis msgsqur  Mailer
 4     1054       5467K     1004       6030K        0       0       0  esmtp
```

LISTING 18.2 Continued

```
 9     2079       7248K     2075        8230K         0         0         0  local
=====================================================================
 T      3133      12716K     3079      14260K         0         0         0
 C      3133                 3079                     0
```

As you can see from Listing 18.2, the `mailstats` output starts with the date on which the statistics shown began. The next lines before the line of equals (=) characters contain statistics for each mailer with the columns described in Table 18.1.

TABLE 18.1 `mailstats` Columns

Column	Description
`M`	Mailer number
`msgsfr`	Number of messages received from the mailer
`bytes_from`	Kilobytes received from the mailer
`msgsto`	Number of messages to the mailer
`bytes_to`	Kilobytes sent to the mailer
`msgsrej`	Number of rejected messages
`msgsdis`	Number of discarded messages
`msgsqur`	Number of quarantined messages (specific messages marked as quarantined so they are not delivered or displayed)
`Mailer`	Name of the mailer

The line that begins with `T` lists the totals for all the mailers, and the last row that begins with `C` shows the number of TCP connections.

By default, Dovecot also logs to the `/var/log/maillog` file such as the following entry for a login attempt:

```
Jun 12 13:52:26 hostname dovecot: imap-login: Login: user=<tfox>, method=PLAIN,
rip=::ffff:127.0.0.1, lip=::ffff:127.0.0.1, TLS
```

To write Dovecot log files to a separate log file, use the `log_path` variable in `/etc/dovecot.conf` such as

```
log_path = /var/log/dovecot
```

Allowing Email Connections

By default, Sendmail uses TCP and UDP port 25 for non-encrypted transfers. If the Sendmail server is configured to use SSL for encrypting email sent and received, it uses port 465. If you also enable the POP protocol for users to retrieve email, allow port 110 for insecure POP connections or port 995 for secure POP over SSL. If you enable IMAP, allow port 143 for insecure IMAP connections or port 993 for secure IMAP over SSL. Verify that your firewall settings on the mail server allow incoming and outgoing requests on the appropriate port.

If custom IPTables rules are being used, refer to Chapter 24, "Configuring a Firewall," for details on how to allow these ports.

If using a default security level in Red Hat Enterprise Linux, use the Security Level Configuration tool. Start it by selecting **Administration**, **Security Level and Firewall** from the System menu on the top panel of the desktop or by executing the `system-config-securitylevel` command. Enter the root password when prompted if running as a user. Click **Add** next to the Other ports table to add the appropriate ports.

TIP

If setting up an internal email server, be sure to configure it to accept connections from IP addresses within your private network. If the email server is accessible over the Internet and accepts email to be sent from any computer, it could be used by unauthorized users to send spam, or junk email, to people.

Summary

In most companies today, email is vital to internal communications. In many companies, it has replaced paper memos and bulletin board notices. This chapter described the path an email takes after being sent. It then provides steps for setting up an email server on Red Hat Enterprise Linux using Sendmail. If used in conjunction with Dovecot, the same server used to send email can also support the IMAP and POP protocols for retrieving email. Sendmail, POP, and IMAP can all be configured with an SSL certificate so email sent and received is encrypted, making it harder to read if intercepted over the network.

CHAPTER 19

Explaining Other Common Network Services

IN THIS CHAPTER

- The xinetd Super Server
- Transferring Files with FTP
- Keeping Accurate Time with NTP
- Creating a Network Printer with CUPS

This chapter describes the xinetd, FTP, NTP, and CUPS network services including how to configure them, how to connect to them, and what ports they use so administrators can configure firewalls settings for them.

These four services have one thing in common—when configured, they generally do not require much maintenance other than checking for security updates via Red Hat Network.

The xinetd Super Server

Not all services have their own initialization script for starting, stopping, and checking the status of the daemon. Some network services are controlled by *xinetd*, also known as the *super server*. Running services through xinetd allows the administrator to utilize xinetd features such as access control, custom logging, and the incoming connection rate.

The xinetd service listens on all ports used by the daemons it controls. When a connection is requested, xinetd determines if the client is allowed access. If the client is allowed access, xinetd starts up the desired service and passes the client connection to it.

The `xinetd` RPM package must be installed to use this super server. If it is not, install it via Red Hat Network as discussed in Chapter 3, "Operating System Updates."

Configuring the xinetd Server

The xinetd super daemon uses the `/etc/xinetd.conf` file as the master configuration file and the `/etc/xinetd.d/` directory for configuration files per service controlled by xinetd. This section discusses how to use these files to configure xinetd and its services.

NOTE

For both /etc/xinetd.conf and the files in the /etc/xinetd.d/ directory, lines that begin with a hash mark (#) are considered comments and ignored. Blank lines are also ignored.

Master xinetd Configuration File

Listing 19.1 shows the default xinetd global configuration file, /etc/xinetd.conf. This file contains settings that apply to all services controlled by xinetd unless the file in /etc/xinetd.d/ for a specific service overrides these default values. If changes are made to this file, execute the `service xinetd reload` command to enable the changes.

LISTING 19.1 xinetd Global Configuration File

```
#
# This is the master xinetd configuration file. Settings in the
# default section will be inherited by all service configurations
# unless explicitly overridden in the service configuration. See
# xinetd.conf in the man pages for a more detailed explanation of
# these attributes.

defaults
{
# The next two items are intended to be a quick access place to
# temporarily enable or disable services.
#
#       enabled         =
#       disabled        =

# Define general logging characteristics.
        log_type        = SYSLOG daemon info
        log_on_failure  = HOST
        log_on_success  = PID HOST DURATION EXIT
# Define access restriction defaults
#
#       no_access       =
#       only_from       =
#       max_load        = 0
        cps             = 50 10
        instances       = 50
        per_source      = 10

# Address and networking defaults
#
#       bind            =
#       mdns            = yes
```

LISTING 19.1 Continued

```
        v6only          = no

# setup environmental attributes
#
#       passenv         =
        groups          = yes
        umask           = 002

# Generally, banners are not used. This sets up their global defaults
#
#       banner          =
#       banner_fail     =
#       banner_success  =
}

includedir /etc/xinetd.d
```

NOTE

Each of the attributes in Listing 19.1 is explained in the following text. However, notice that some are commented out by default because setting them to a blank value has meaning.

The first two options inside the default section of `xinetd.conf` are `enabled` and `disabled`. Enabling and disabling xinetd services should be done in the individual services files in the `/etc/xinetd.d/` directory with the `disable` attribute set to `yes` or `no` as described in the next section "Individual xinetd Service Files." Using the `enabled` and `disabled` options in `xinetd.conf` is only recommended for temporary situations such as testing or if you think your system has been compromised and need to turn off all the unnecessary services. To use one or both of these attributes, uncomment one or both of them first.

The `enabled` option can be used to list services that are allowed to accept connections. The services listed with this option still need to be enabled in their individual services files in `/etc/xinetd.d/` by setting the `disable` attribute to `no` and making sure the `DISABLE` flag is not listed in the `flags` attribute. If the `disabled` option is not set, only the xinetd services in the `enabled` list are allowed to accept connections.

If the `disabled` option is set, only the xinetd services in the `enabled` list accept connections *unless* they are also in the `disabled` list. All services listed with the `disabled` option are not allowed to accept connection requests.

Both attributes accept a space-separated list of service IDs. For both these options, the service ID must be used, not the service name. In the individual service files in `/etc/xinetd.d/`, the `id` attribute sets the service ID to a unique identifier. If an ID is not given, the ID defaults to the service name. Most service IDs are the same as the service names, but be sure to double-check when using them with the `enabled` and `disabled` attributes.

The next set of attributes in the default settings control logging. They are as follows:

- `log_type`: Set the log service. If set to `SYSLOG <facility>`, the syslog facility specified is used. If set to `FILE <file>`, logs are written to the specified file.
- `log_on_failure`: Set the log service. If set to `SYSLOG <facility>`, the syslog facility specified is used. If set to `FILE <file>`, logs are written to the specified file.
- `log_on_success`: Set what type of messages are logged when an xinetd service is started or when one of them exists. Refer to the man page for `xinetd.conf` for a complete list of values. With the default `xinetd.conf` settings, the remote host address and the service process ID are logged.

The next group of attributes sets the defaults for access control. Refer to the "Allowing xinetd Connections" section later in this chapter for details.

The next three attributes are address and network default values. The `bind` and `mdns` attributes are listed but commented out by default. The usage of these attributes is as follows:

- `bind`: To only listen for connections on a specific interface, set this value to the IP address of the interface.
- `mdns`: Set to `yes` to enable mdns registration, which is currently only available on Mac OS X. Set to `no` to disable mdns registration.
- `v6only`: Set to `yes` to use IPv6 only. Set to `no` by default to use both IPv4 and IPv6.

Three environmental attributes are listed as well:

- `passenv`: Commented out by default. If set to a list of environment variables, the values are passed to the service started by xinetd when a connection is requested and allowed to be passed on. If set to a blank value, no variables are passed on except those listed with the `env` attribute.
- `groups`: If set to `yes`, the server is executed with access to the groups accessible by the effective UID of the server. If set to `no`, the server does not have access to any additional groups. If set to a list of group names, the server is given access to the groups listed.
- `umask`: Set the default umask for the xinetd services. (The umask can be set for individual services in the individual service file in the `/etc/xinetd.d/` directory.)

The very last line in `xinetd.conf` utilizes the `includedir` attribute. It tells the super daemon to use the individual service files in the `/etc/xinetd.d/` directory.

Individual xinetd Service Files

Each xinetd service has a configuration file in the `/etc/xinetd.d/` directory. For example, the xinetd configuration file for `rsync` is `/etc/xinetd.d/rsync` as shown in Listing 19.2.

LISTING 19.2 xinetd Configuration File for rsync

```
# default: off
# description: The rsync server is a good addition to an ftp server, as it \
#       allows crc checksumming etc.
service rsync
{
        disable = yes
        socket_type     = stream
        wait            = no
        user            = root
        server          = /usr/bin/rsync
        server_args     = —daemon
        log_on_failure  += USERID
}
```

Any of the default attributes from /etc/xinetd.conf can be overwritten in these individual service files. Refer to the xinetd.conf man page with the man xinetd.conf command for a complete list of attributes.

Important attributes listed in the configuration file for each xinetd service include disable, user, and server. The disable attribute determines whether or not the service is accepting incoming connections via xinetd. If set to no, xinetd will hand off connections to it if the client first passes through the xinetd access control. Setting it to yes disables the service. The user specified with the user attribute can be set to a username or a UID. If set to a username, it must be resolvable to a UID from /etc/passwd. This UID owns the server process for the individual xinetd service. The server attributes specifies the program executed if the service is enabled. To enable changes made to the configuration files in /etc/xinetd.d/, use the service xinetd reload command.

Starting and Stopping xinetd

To start, stop, and restart xinetd, use the following command as root:

```
service xinetd <command>
```

Replace <command> with one of the following:

- start: Start the xinetd service.
- stop: Stop the xinetd service.
- status: Show the status of xinetd.
- restart: Stop the service if it is running, then start xinetd. If the service is not already running, the stop action will fail, but the start action will still be called.
- condrestart: If the service is already running, and only if the service is already running, restart it.
- reload: Reload the server configuration to enable changes to the configuration files.

To have xinetd start at boot time, execute the following as root:

```
chkconfig xinetd on
```

Allowing xinetd Connections

Access control can be configured in the individual files in the `/etc/xinetd.d/` directory. When a request is made, the TCP wrappers access control configuration is checked first. If the client is denied access from the TCP wrappers rules, the connection is denied. If the client is allowed access from the TCP wrappers rules, the attributes in the individual `/etc/xinetd.d/` files and the `/etc/xinetd.conf` file are checked. Both forms of access control can be used in conjunction with each other.

TCP Wrappers and xinetd

The xinetd services are protected by *TCP wrappers*, which provide a mechanism for allowing and denying access to the services. Two files are used to control access: `/etc/hosts.allow` and `/etc/hosts.deny`.

> **NOTE**
>
> xinetd is not the only network service protected by TCP wrappers. For example, in Red Hat Enterprise Linux, both `vsftpd` and `sshd` are compiled against the TCP wrappers library.

As the names imply, the `hosts.allow` file contains a list of clients allowed access to specific daemons, and the `hosts.deny` file contains rules denying client access. The files are read from top to bottom, so as soon as a rule to allow or deny access is found, that rule is applied, and the rest of the file is not read.

The `hosts.allow` file is read first. If both files contain rules that contradict each other, the first rule in `hosts.allow` takes precedence. If no rules are found for a client, access is granted. The access files are referenced each time a request is made, so changes to them take effect immediately without restarting any daemons.

Both `hosts.allow` and `hosts.deny` use the same file format. Blank lines and lines that begin with the hash mark (#) are ignored. If a line ends with the backslash character (\), the next line is considered a continuation of the previous line without the new line character. All other lines have the following format:

```
daemon_list : client_list [: options]
```

Only the `daemon_list` and `client_list` are required. The `daemon_list` is a list of one or more daemons separated by commas. Wildcards can be used for this list. The `client_list` is a list of hostnames, IP addresses, patterns, or wildcards allowed or denied access (depending on the file in which is it listed) to the daemons in the `daemon_list`.

In the `client_list`, the following patterns can be used:

- A pattern that begins with a period specifies all hostnames that end with the pattern. For example, the pattern .example.com matches the hostname host.example.com.
- A pattern that ends with a period specifies all IP address that begin with the pattern. For example, the pattern 192.168. includes 192.168.0.2.
- A pattern that begins with the @ character is used to specify an NIS netgroup name.
- A pattern in the form of a netmask pair such as 192.168.1.0/255.255.255.0 can be used to specify a subnet.
- A pattern in the form of a [net]/prefixlen pair or [n:n:n:n:n:n:n:n]/m can be used to specify a network.
- A pattern is considered a filename if it begins with a forward slash (/). The file should contain zero or more lines with zero or more hostname or address patterns separated by whitespace.
- Some patterns can use the * or ? character as a wildcard. It can't be used in conjunction with the following patterns: netmask matching, hostname pattern that begins with a period, or IP address pattern that ends with a period.

In the `daemon_list` and `client_list`, the following wildcards can be used:

- `ALL`: The universal wildcard, always matches.
- `LOCAL`: Any hostname that doesn't contain a dot character.
- `UNKNOWN`: Any user whose name is unknown and any host whose name or address is unknown.
- `KNOWN`: Any user whose name is known and any host whose name and address are known. Use this pattern with caution: Hostnames may be temporarily unavailable due to DNS issues.
- `PARANOID`: Any hostname that doesn't match its address.

In both `daemon_list` and `client_list`, the `EXCEPT` operator can be used to exclude names from the list. However, use caution with this operator because it makes it more difficult for administrators to read the access rules.

19

TIP

Use the command `man 5 hosts_access` to learn more about the `hosts.allow` and `hosts.deny` files.

Individual Access Control for xinetd

The default `/etc/xinetd.conf` file lists most of the access control attributes. They can be given default values in `/etc/xinetd.conf` and can also be given values per individual service in the individual service files in the `/etc/xinetd.d/` directory.

The `no_access` and `only_from` attributes can be used together to accept or deny connections from specific hosts. Hosts in the `no_access` list are not granted connectivity to xinetd services by default. Hosts in the `only_from` list are granted access to xinetd services by default.

Remember these attributes can be redefined in the individual service files to grant or deny hosts access to specific xinetd services. The `no_access` and the `only_from` attributes are commented out by default because setting `only_from` to a blank value denies all hosts. Both accept a list of hosts in the following formats:

- IPv4 or IPv6 individual IP address, such as 192.168.10.4.
- IPv4 address range denoted by using 0 as a wildcard in the right-most numbers of the IP address, such as 192.168.10.0 to match 192.168.10.1 through 192.168.10.254. 0.0.0.0 matches all IP addresses.
- Factorized IPv4 address, such as the form X.X.X.{X,X,X,...}, where the last number in the IP address is factorized. If all four integers in the IP are not specified, the remaining integers are assumed to be 0, which is interpreted as a wildcard. For example, 192.168.10.{1,5,6} represents the 192.168.10.1, 192.168.10.5, and 192.168.10.6 addresses.
- Network name from `/etc/networks`. Only works for IPv4 addresses.
- Specific hostname such as server.example.com.
- Domain such as example.com. All hosts with this domain such as server.example.com match.
- IP address/netmask range such as 192.168.10.0/32 for IPv4 and 1234::/46 for IPv6.

If an IP address or hostname matches both lists, the more specific match takes precedence. For example, assume that the `no_access` attribute includes 192.168.10.0 and the `only_from` attribute includes 192.168.10.4. If the host 192.168.10.4 tries to connect to an xinetd service, it is granted access because it matches both lists but the specific IP address is in the `only_from` list.

The other attributes for access control are as follows:

- `max_load`: Commented out by default. If set to a floating point value that represents the one minute load average, the service stops accepting connections when this load is reached.
- `cps`: Set the rate of the incoming connections. Two integer values must be specified. The first integer is the number of connections per second to allow. If the rate of incoming connections exceeds this number, the service is temporarily disabled. The second number is the number of seconds to wait before re-enabling the service.
- `instances`: Maximum number of xinetd connections allowed to be active. If set to `UNLIMITED`, there is no limit.

- per_source: Set the maximum number of service instances per IP address.
- access_times: Set the time intervals when the service is available in the form hour:min-hour:min. Connections are accepted at the bounds of the interval.

Transferring Files with FTP

FTP stands for *File Transfer Protocol*. An FTP server allows clients to connect to it either anonymously or with a username and password combination. After successful authentication, files can be transferred back and forth between the server and client. The files are neither encrypted nor compressed.

CAUTION

Because the files are not encrypted, use caution when transferring files if they contain sensitive information. Anyone on the same network, including the Internet if the transfer goes over the public Internet, can intercept the files as well as the username and password used to connect to the FTP server.

FTP and SELinux

If SELinux, a mandatory access control security mechanism, is set to enforcing mode, the FTP daemon is protected by it. Refer to Chapter 23 for details on SELinux.

If the FTP daemon is configured to share files anonymously, the shared files must be labeled with the public_content_t security context such as the following for the /var/ftp/ directory:

```
chcon -R -t public_content_t /var/ftp/
```

After setting up an uploads directory, you must set the security context of it to public_content_rw_t such as the following for the /var/ftp/incoming/ directory:

```
chcon -R -t public_content_rw_t /var/ftp/incoming/
```

CAUTION

If the filesystem is relabeled for SELinux, the security context changes you make will be overwritten. To make your changes permanent even through a relabel, refer to the "Making Security Context Changes Permanent" section in Chapter 23.

To allow users to write to the uploads directory, you must also enable the allow_ftpd_anon_write boolean with the following command:

```
setsebool -P allow_ftpd_anon_write=1
```

To verify that the setting has been changed, execute the following:

```
getsebool allow_ftpd_anon_write=1
```

If enabled, the output should be the following:

```
allow_ftpd_anon_write —> on
```

To share home directories on the FTP server, execute the following:

```
setsebool -P ftp_home_dir=1
```

You can also change these boolean values by running the SELinux Management Tool. Start it by selecting **Administration**, **SELinux Management** from the **System** menu on the top panel of the desktop or by executing the `system-config-selinux` command. Enter the root password when prompted if running as a non-root user. Select **Boolean** from the list on the left. On the right, click the triangle icon next to **FTP**. The SELinux booleans affecting FTP appear. Changes take effect immediately after changing the value of the check box next to the boolean.

TIP

The SELinux booleans that affect the FTP server are described in the ftpd_selinux man page viewable with the `man ftpd_selinux` command.

Configuring the FTP Server

Red Hat Enterprise Linux 5 includes the `vsftpd` FTP service. If the `vsftpd` package is not already installed, install it with Red Hat Network as discussed in Chapter 3.

The FTP server uses the `/etc/vsftpd/vsftpd.conf` configuration file. Using this file, you can set options for displaying a custom banner message after users log in, setting the default file permissions for uploaded files, and setting the port on which to listen for incoming connections.

For a full list of available directives, read the man page with the `man vsftpd.conf` command. The `vsftpd` package installs a basic configuration file on the system with a few commonly used directives set and explained with comments. Table 19.1 also includes some commonly used directives.

TABLE 19.1 Common `vsftpd` Directives

`vsftpd` **Directive**	**Default Value**	**Description**
`listen_port`	21	Port on which to listen for incoming FTP connection requests.
`ftpd_banner`	(none)	Use this string as the greeting message after users log in to the server.

TABLE 19.1 Continued

local_enable	NO	If set to YES, local users on the FTP server are allowed to log in to the server via FTP. Even though the default is NO, the sample configuration file enables this feature. Use caution when enabling this feature because all communications including the username and password authentication are not encrypted.
hide_ids	NO	If set to YES, all user and group file ownership is shown as ftp to hide the real owners and groups.
max_clients	0	Maximum number of clients that can connect at one time. If set to 0, the number of clients is unlimited.

To start the FTP server, use the `service vsftpd start` command as root. To stop the server, use the `service vsftpd stop` command. To have it automatically started at boot time, use the `chkconfig vsftpd on` command.

If the configuration file is modified after the server is started, use the `service vsftpd restart` command to enable the configuration changes.

Allowing Anonymous FTP

Some FTP servers are configured to allow users to access a set of files even though they do not have a username and password for the server. Instead, the user enters the username `anonymous`. Then, the FTP server usually asks for the person's email address as the password. Unless the server is configured to deny access to that particular email address password, the user is allowed to browse all the files in a directory set up for anonymous users. Depending on its purpose, the FTP server can be configured to allow anonymous users read-only access or can be configured to allow users to upload files.

Anonymous FTP is enabled by default by setting the `anonymous_enable` directive in `/etc/vsftpd/vsftpd.conf` to `YES`. To disable it, set the directive to `NO`.

If anonymous users are allowed, you can set the default directory into which the users are placed after logging in. This is set with the `anon_root` directive in `vsftpd.conf`. If this directive is not set to a directory, anonymous users are placed into the `/var/ftp/` directory, created when the `vsftpd` package is installed. By default, this directory is owned and can only be written to by root, but is readable by everyone.

If anonymous users are allowed to upload files, consider creating a separate directory such as `/var/ftp/pub/uploads/` for anonymous uploads. It should be writable by everyone, but it does not have to be readable by everyone. Making it not readable by the anonymous users will discourage people from finding the FTP server and using it for unauthorized users such as pirating illegal software.

Table 19.2 provides a list of directives for configuring anonymous FTP.

19

TABLE 19.2 Anonymous FTP Directives

vsftpd **Directive**	**Default Value**	**Description**
anonymous_enable	YES	Set to YES to enable anonymous FTP access.
allow_anon_ssl	NO	If ssl_enable and allow_anon_ssl are set to YES, anonymous users are allowed to use secure SSL connections. For these options to work, vsftpd must be compiled against OpenSSL, and the client connecting must have SSL support.
anon_mkdir_write_enable	NO	If set to YES along with write_enable, anonymous users can create directories if the anonymous FTP user has write permissions on the parent directory.
anon_other_write_enable	NO	If set to YES, anonymous users can write more than just directories and files. They can delete, rename, and more. Use caution when enabling this option.
anon_upload_enable	NO	If set to YES along with write_enable, anonymous users can upload files under certain conditions. Anonymous FTP users must have proper permissions in the directory being uploaded to.
anon_world_readable_only	YES	If set to YES, anonymous users can only download files that are world readable.
chown_uploads	NO	If set to YES, all files uploaded by anonymous users will be owned by the user set with chown_username.
deny_email_enable	NO	If set to YES, email addresses listed in the file set with banned_email_file and used as the anonymous user password are denied login. The default banned email file is /etc/vsftpd/banned_emails.
force_anon_data_ssl	NO	If set to YES along with ssl_enable, all anonymous users are forced to use SSL for data transfers.
force_anon_logins_ssl	NO	If set to YES along with ssl_enable, all anonymous users are forced to use SSL when sending the password.
no_anon_password	NO	If set to YES, anonymous users do not have to provide a password. They are logged in after specifying anonymous as the username.
secure_email_list_enable	NO	If set to YES, only anonymous users with email passwords listed in the file set by email_password_file are allowed to log in. By default, the email password file is set to /etc/vsftpd/email_passwords.

TABLE 19.2 Continued

vsftpd **Directive**	**Default Value**	**Description**
anon_max_rate	0	Maximum transfer rate allowed for anonymous users, in bytes per second. If set to 0, the maximum rate is unlimited.
anon_umask	077	Umask value for files created by anonymous users.
anon_root	(no default)	Default directory for anonymous users.
banned_email_file	/etc/vsftpd/banned_emails	If deny_email_enable is set to YES, this file contains the list of email passwords denied FTP login.
email_password_file	/etc/vsftpd/email_passwords	If secure_email_list_enable is set to YES, this file contains all the email passwords allowed FTP login.
chown_username	root	If chown_uploads is set to YES, all files uploaded by an anonymous user are owned by this user.

Allowing FTP Connections

To deny specific users access to the FTP server, add their usernames to the /etc/vsftpd/ftpusers file. By default, system users such as root and nobody are included in this list.

The /etc/vsftpd/user_list file is also used to allow or deny access to specific users. If the userlist_enable directive in /etc/vsftpd/vsftpd.conf is set to YES, the /etc/vsftpd/user_list file is read to determine if a user is allowed FTP access. If the userlist_deny is set to YES (the default), users listed in /etc/vsftpd/user_list are denied access before they are asked for a password. If userlist_deny is set to NO, only users explicitly listed in the /etc/vsftpd/user_list file are allowed access.

FTP uses two ports, 20 and 21. By default, the FTP server listens for requests on port 21. After a connection is established, the client sends commands to the server on port 21. However, port 20 is used when the server sends data back to the client. If a firewall exists on the client, be sure to allow connections on port 20 so data can be sent to it.

If custom IPTables rules are being used, refer to Chapter 24, "Configuring a Firewall," for details on how to allow these ports. If FTP clients connect in passive mode and the server has IPTables active, the ip_conntrack_ftp kernel module must be loaded on the FTP server. It can be added to the IPTABLES_MODULES directive in /etc/sysconfig/iptables-config.

If using a default security level in Red Hat Enterprise Linux, use the Security Level Configuration tool. Start it by selecting **Administration**, **Security Level and Firewall** from the **System** menu on the top panel of the desktop or by executing the system-config-securitylevel command. Enter the root password when prompted if running as a user. On the **Firewall Options** tab, check the **FTP** service in the **Trusted services** section as shown in Figure 19.1. Click **OK** to enable the changes.

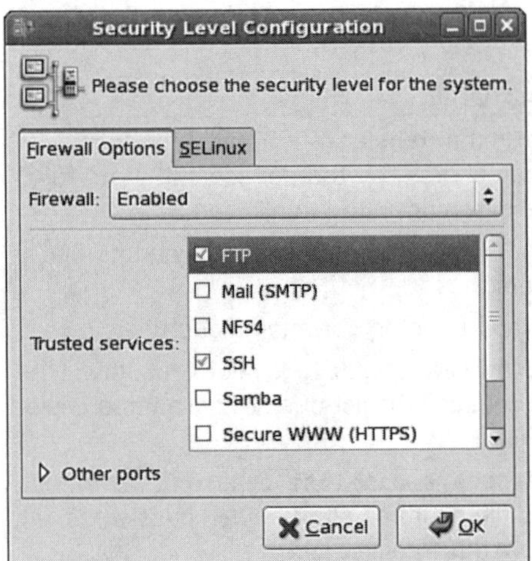

FIGURE 19.1 Allowing FTP Connections

Connecting from an FTP Client

To connect to an FTP server, an FTP client program is required. There are numerous FTP clients available for Linux and other operating systems. By default, Red Hat Enterprise Linux includes the command-line clients `ftp` and `lftp` as well as a method for connectng to FTP servers from the desktop file browser.

Connecting via FTP from the Command Line

The `ftp` and `lftp` command-line utilities for connecting to an FTP server use the same basic commands. However, `lftp` is more user-friendly so it will be discussed in this section. For example, `lftp` has tab completion similar to the Bash shell, shows the download progress by default, automatically assumes anonymous login unless a username is specified, and restarts downloads at the break point if the download is not completed on the first attempt.

To connect to an FTP server, use the `lftp <ftpserver>` command, where `<ftpserver>` is the IP address or hostname of the FTP server. If using a hostname, the client must be able to resolve it to an IP address. If the `lftp` prompt appears, the server has accepted the connection, and you are logged in as an anonymous user.

To log in to the server using a specific username, either use the `lftp -u <username> <ftpserver>` command to connect or wait until you are connected as an anonymous user and then type the `user <username>` command at the `lftp` prompt. Both methods will prompt you for a password to authenticate.

After you are logged in to the server, basic shell commands such as `ls` to list the files and `cd` to change directories can be used to find the files to download or to change to the location into which you want to upload files. Pressing the up arrow will toggle through a list of commands previously executed during the current FTP session.

To download a file from the server (assuming you have permission to), use the `get <file>` command. To retrieve several files on the server, use the command `mget <files>`, where `<files>` is a list of files separated by spaces. One or all of the multiple files can be specified with wildcards such as `mget *.pdf`.

When downloading files, the files are saved to the current directory on the local system. By default, this is the directory you were in before you executed the `lftp` command. After logged in to the FTP server, it is possible to change the local working directory with the `lcd <directory>` command. To determine what the local working directory is set to, use the `lpwd` command.

Uploading files to the server has a similar syntax: `put <file>` or `mput <files>`. The files can either be specified relative to the current local working directory or the full path to the files can be specified with the `put` and `mput` commands. Files are uploaded to the current working directory on the server. To determine what directory this is, use the `pwd` command.

TIP

For a complete list of `lftp` commands, refer to the man page with the `man lftp` command.

Listing 19.3 shows an example FTP session. In this example, anonymous user access is granted, and the `get` command is used to download the `debuginfo RPM` for xinetd.

LISTING 19.3 Example FTP Session

```
$ lftp ftp.redhat.com
lftp ftp.redhat.com:~> ls
drwxr-xr-x    4 ftp      ftp          4096 Nov 04  2005 pub
lftp ftp.redhat.com:/>
cd pub/redhat/linux/enterprise/5Server/en/os/x86_64/Debuginfo/
cd ok, cwd=/pub/redhat/linux/enterprise/5Server/en/os/x86_64/Debuginfo
lftp ftp.redhat.com:/pub/redhat/linux/enterprise/5Server/en/os/x86_64/
Debuginfo> get xinetd-debuginfo-2.3.14-10.el5.x86_64.rpm
314618 bytes transferred in 2 seconds (199.3K/s)
lftp ftp.redhat.com:/pub/redhat/linux/enterprise/5Server/en/os/x86_64/
Debuginfo>
```

Connecting via FTP Using the Desktop File Browser

To connect to an FTP server using the desktop file browser, select **Places, Connect to Server** from the top panel of the desktop. Select **Public FTP** for anonymous user login or **FTP (with login)** for access via username and password authentication. Type the IP address or full hostname of the FTP server in the **Server** field as shown in Figure 19.2.

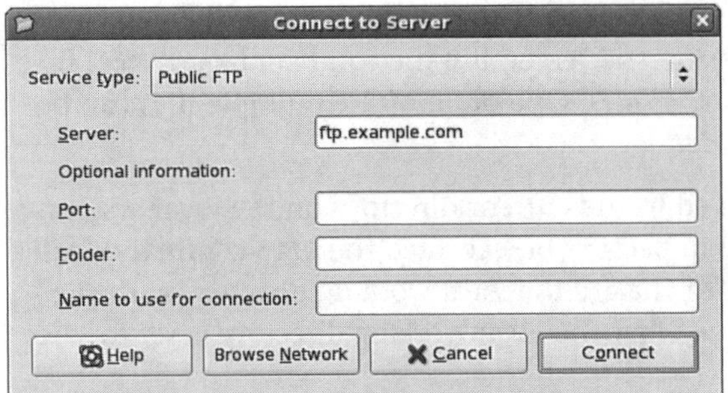

FIGURE 19.2 Connecting to an FTP Server

Under the **Optional information** section, the following can be configured:

- **Port**: Specify the server port to connect to if different than the default FTP port 21.
- **Folder**: The folder to open after logged in to the FTP server.
- **User Name**: The username to use for authentication when connecting. You will be prompted for the password later. Only shown when **FTP (with login)** is selected.
- **Name to use for connection**: Connection name to use when labeling the mount point in the **Places** menu and on the desktop.

Click **Connect** to establish an FTP connection. An icon will appear on the desktop using the name of the server or, if provided, the name in the **Name to use for connection** field. A shortcut is also listed under the **Places** menu item in the desktop menu. Double-clicking on the desktop icon or selecting the shortcut item in the **Places** menu will open a file browser window with the files from the FTP server. Depending on your file permissions from the server, you can open, copy, delete, and rename files and directories, and more.

To unmount the share, right-click on its desktop icon and select **Unmount Volume**. If the share is not unmounted, it will remain in the **Places** menu on reboot, but you must reauthenticate to access the share after rebooting.

Logging FTP Connections

If the `xferlog_enable` directive in `vsftpd.conf` is set to `YES`, file transfers using the FTP protocol are logged to `/var/log/xferlog`. The default value for this directive is `NO`, but the sample configuration file installed on Red Hat Enterprise Linux enables it. Information such as a time stamp, IP address of the client, the file being transferred, and the username of the person who authenticated the connection is included in the log entry.

To modify the name of the log file, set the `xferlog_file` directive in `vsftpd.conf` to the full path and filename of the alternate log file.

The log file is rotated every week, and four weeks of backlogs are kept as configured by the `/etc/logrotate.d/vsftpd.log` file.

Keeping Accurate Time with NTP

The system clock has a variety of uses. It can be used for simple tasks such as including the time stamp in a log entry or in an email sent to another user. It is also used for more system-critical tasks. If the system time on the nodes of a cluster are too far apart, the cluster might think one of the nodes is not responding and attempt to reboot it. When committing changes to a CVS server, if the time difference between the client and server is too skewed, the CVS server might refuse to commit the changes. Having an inaccurate system time can cause unpredictable behavior that can be difficult to diagnosis.

NTP, or *Network Time Protocol*, allows a system to sync its time with a time server. In Red Hat Enterprise Linux, this operation is performed by the `ntpd` service. This daemon polls the server at certain intervals. If the system time differs from the NTP server, the time is slowly synchronized in small steps. If the time difference is greater than 1,000 seconds, the daemon will exit and write a message to the system log. More than one NTP server can be specified to retrieve the most accurate time.

Where do the time servers retrieve its time? Part of the U.S. Commerce Department's Technology Administration, the National Institute of Standards and Technology (NIST) provides the Internet Time Service (ITS), which can be used to synchronize the system clock of a computer from an Internet server. The time signal maintained by NIST is considered a Stratum 0 source. Any time sources that retrieve their signals from this Stratum 0 source are considered Stratum 1. Time sources that retrieve their signals from a Stratum 1 source are considered Stratum 2, and so on. NIST provides Stratum 1 servers as part of their ITS. The lower the stratum number, the more accurate the time is.

Even though public time servers are available to allow administrators to synchronize the time on their servers with a known reference, sometimes it is necessary to configure an internal time server. For example, if all clients synchronize from the same server, they will all receive the same time so that their system times are as close as possible. Also, an administrator might need to set up his own time server if the clients are inside a firewall and do not have Internet access.

This section first discusses how to configure a system to connect to an NTP server to keep accurate time. Then, it describes how to configure the NTP service on a Red Hat Enterprise Linux server.

Connecting to NTP from a Client

To configure the system to use one or more NTP servers via a graphical interface, go to the **System** menu on the top panel of the desktop and select **Administration**, **Date & Time**. The command `system-config-date` can also be executed from a shell prompt to start the program. Go to the **Network Time Protocol** tab as shown in Figure 19.3. The `system-config-date` RPM package is needed to use this program, but it is installed by default along with the graphical desktop.

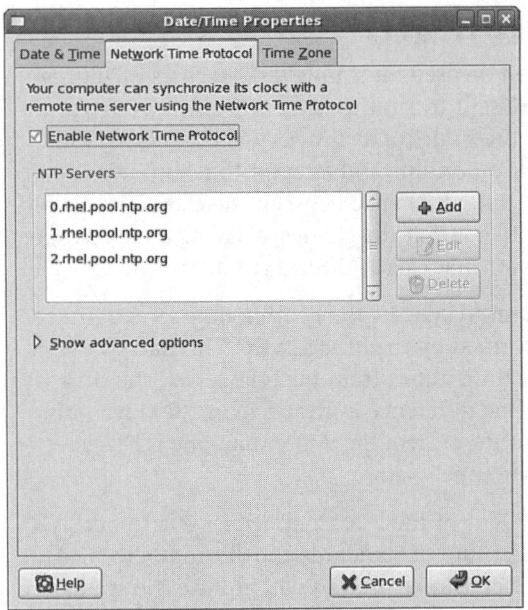

FIGURE 19.3 Enabling NTP

Check the **Enable Network Time Protocol** box. A list of NTP servers accessible over the Internet is already provided as shown in the **NTP Servers** frame.

If the client is a desktop system or another type of computer for which the time is not crucial, the default time server will work fine. However, if the client is a server that requires an accurate time source, go to http://www.ntp.org/ and http://tf.nist.gov/service/time-servers.html for a list of time servers. Be sure you have permission to connect to the time server before using it, and remember that the smaller the stratum number, the more accurate the time.

To add additional servers, click **Add**. To remove an NTP server from the list, select it from the list, and click **Delete**. Clicking **OK** saves and enables the changes immediately.

If you prefer command-line configuration, only the `ntp` RPM package is needed. NTP comes with a default configuration file. Either modify it or create your own. To configure an NTP client, the following lines must exist in `/etc/ntp.conf` for each NTP server:

```
restrict <servername> mask 255.255.255.255 nomodify notrap noquery
server <servername>
```

Refer to the documentation in /usr/share/doc/ntp-<version>/ for more configuration options in `/etc/ntp.conf`.

Before starting the service, roughly sync the time with a server with the following command:

```
ntpd -q <ntpserver>
```

After the time is roughly synchronized, the daemon will exit.

If the current system time and the time retrieved from the NTP server are more than 1,000 seconds apart, `ntpd` will exit and not modify the system time. To force the time to sync regardless of the time difference, use the `-g` option in addition to the `-q` option:

```
nptd -g -q <ntpserver>
```

Then, start the service with the `service ntpd start` command. To stop the service, use the `service ntpd stop` command. To enable the service to start automatically at boot time, execute the `chkconfig ntpd on` command.

Configuring the NTP Server

Because an NTP server must retrieve its time from somewhere, it is also an NTP client. Configure the system as an NTP client first, and then follow the instructions from this section. As with the NTP client, the `ntp` package must be installed on the system to configure an NTP server.

An NTP server can be configured so that each client must specify its IP address or hostname for access, or an NTP server can be configured in multicast mode to allow clients to find it.

The default `/etc/ntp.conf` file contains the following line near the top of the file:

```
restrict default nomodify notrap noquery
```

This line configures default restrictions for all connections with the `default` keyword. The default restrictions can be overridden with restrict statements about specific network ranges. The `nomodify`, `notrap`, and `noquery` access control options mean that the server can not be modified, control message trap service is denied, and all time sync queries are denied.

If a subnet is specified and the `noquery` keyword is omitted, the server is allowed to accept connections from the specified subnet (replace subnet):

```
restrict 192.168.0.0 mask 255.255.255.0 nomodify notrap
```

Multiple `restrict` lines can be added to allow multiple subnets to connect to the NTP server. 19

To configure the NTP daemon to work in multicast mode where clients can find it without knowing its hostname or IP address, use the following line in `/etc/ntpd.conf`:

```
broadcast 224.0.1.1 ttl 4
```

Notice the 244.0.1.1 address. The Internet Assigned Numbers Authority (IANA) has assigned the multicast group address 224.0.1.1 for IPv4 and ff05::101 (site local) for IPv6 exclusively to NTP.

After modifying the `ntp.conf` file, use the `service ntpd restart` command to enable the changes.

To start the server, execute the `service ntpd start` command. To stop it, use the `service ntpd stop` command. To configure the system to start the NTP server at boot time, run the `chkconfig ntpd on` command.

TIP

Check `/var/log/messages` for messages from `ntpd` to verify its status or to read error messages.

Allowing NTP Connections

Both the NTP server and clients connecting to an NTP server need to allow incoming and outgoing UDP connections on port 123.

If custom IPTables rules are being used, refer to Chapter 24 for details on how to allow these ports.

If using the Security Level Configuration tool, start it by selecting **Administration, Security Level and Firewall** from the **System** menu on the top panel of the desktop or by executing the `system-config-securitylevel` command. Enter the root password when prompted if running as a user. In the **Other ports** area, click **Add** to specify the NTP port.

Creating a Network Printer with CUPS

In Chapter 2, "Post-Installation Configuration," you learned how to configure a local printer or connect to a shared printer. The same graphical interface can also be used to share a printer with other systems on the network using the Common UNIX Printing System, also known as *CUPS*. The `cups` RPM package must be installed.

From the **System** menu on the top panel of the desktop, select **Administration, Printing** to start the tool, or execute the command `system-config-printer`. The root password is required to continue. The interface shows all configured printers, both locally attached and shared printers accessible by the system.

To share a printer over the network, first configure it as a local printer as described in the "Printer Configuration" section of Chapter 2. After the local printer is added, select the printer and make sure the **Shared** state is checked at the bottom of the **Settings** tab.

Then click on **Server Settings** in the left menu as shown in Figure 19.4 and select **Share published printers connected to this system**. Click **Apply** to enable the changes. All printers with shared state enabled are broadcast over the network for others to connect to for printing.

By default, if sharing is enabled, anyone can print to the shared printers on the server. To restrict printer access based on the user sending the print request, select the printer from the list on the left, and go to the **Access control** tab. There are two options:

- Allowing printing for everyone except these users
- Deny printing for everyone except these users

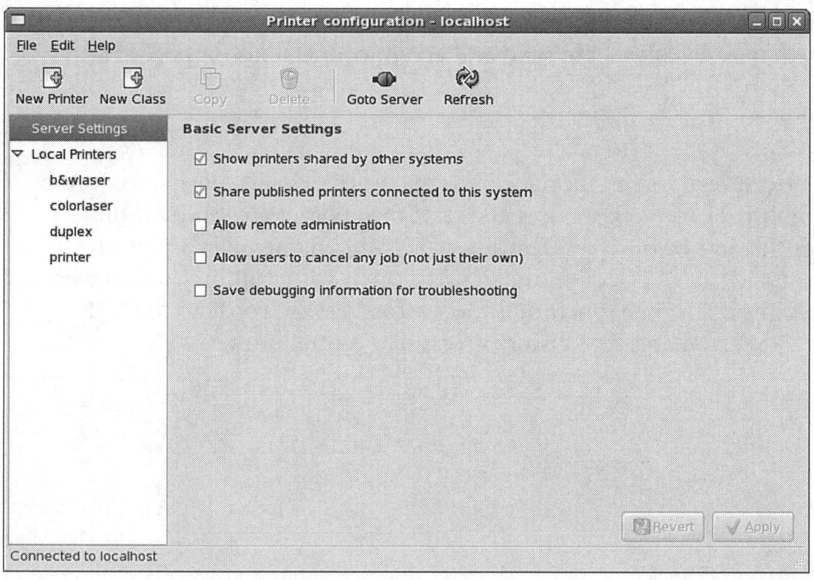

FIGURE 19.4 Server Settings

Select one of these options and add users to the desired list as shown in Figure 19.5. Clicking **Apply** enables the changes immediately. Notice that this access control list is per shared printer, so this step must be repeated for each printer if more than one is being shared.

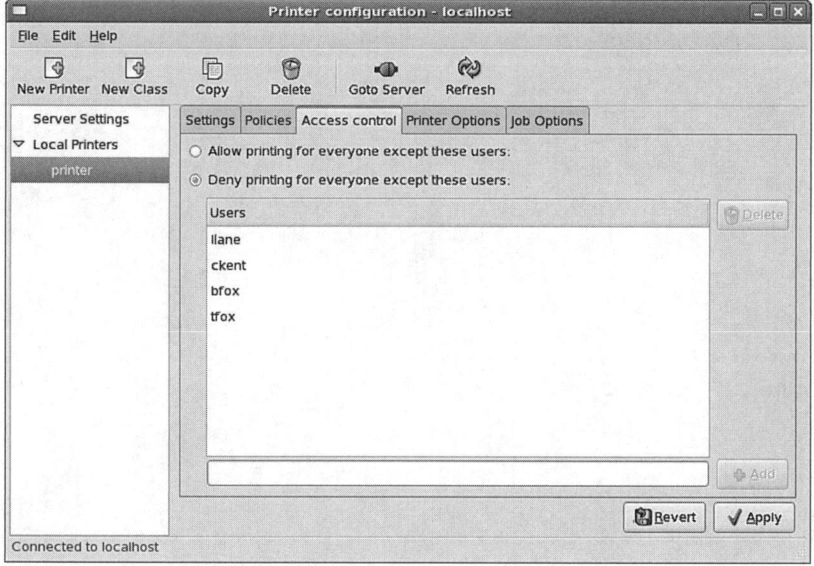

FIGURE 19.5 Access Control for Shared Printer

19

The printer server must be configured to send and receive connections on incoming UDP port 631. All clients must be allowed to send and accept connections on port 631.

Summary

This chapter detailed several important network services. The xinetd super server can be used to monitor traffic for network services and start the appropriate service if the connection passes the host-based access control rules. To share files over a private network or the Internet, the FTP service can be used. Use it with caution because files are transferred unencrypted. For time synchronization across servers, consider the NTP service. Finally, CUPS is available for network access to a central printer.

PART V

Monitoring and Tuning

IN THIS PART

CHAPTER 20

Monitoring System Resources

IN THIS CHAPTER

- Reporting Filesystem Usage
- Reporting Disk Performance
- Reporting System Processes
- Reporting on the System Processors
- Reporting Memory Usage
- Reporting on the Network Subsystem
- Generating a System Report
- Locating Log Files
- Viewing Log Files with Logwatch

Although most users only think about their administrators when a problem occurs or when they suspect their system has been compromised, administrators spend a considerable portion of their time monitoring system resources to prevent failures. It is often a thankless job, but it can be very rewarding for everyone, especially the administrator who doesn't have to get out of bed at 3 a.m. to fix a critical problem that could have been prevented by intelligent monitoring.

This chapter discusses how to monitor filesystems, system processes, CPU utilization, physical and virtual memory, and the network subsystem in Red Hat Enterprise Linux. It also details how to generate a system report for troubleshooting and where to find log files.

Consider using all or some of the commands provided in this chapter in custom scripts to alert you of problems that may arise. Refer to Chapter 11, "Automating Tasks with Scripts," for more information about writing custom scripts and scheduling their execution at set intervals.

Reporting Filesystem Usage

One of the most critical system components to monitor is the filesystem. If the filesystem becomes unavailable, the system is most likely incapacitated. Discovering problems before the system goes down is key to being a successful administrator. For example, adding additional storage or cleaning off unneeded files when a disk has almost reached capacity is much better than waiting for the all disk space to be used and then hearing from everyone that they can't write files to the disk. The first requires a scheduled action during a scheduled maintenance time, and the later requires an immediate emergency operation, which can occur at any time, including when access to the system is most required.

Determining Filesystem Usage

To determine how much disk space is being used for a given partition, logical volume, or NFS mount, use the `df` command. If no arguments are given to the command, disk usage for all mounted partitions is displayed in 1 kilobyte blocks. Listing 20.1 shows output from two logical volumes: the `/boot` partition and an NFS mounted directory from the production.example.com server.

LISTING 20.1 Disk Space Usage

```
Filesystem           1K-blocks      Used Available Use% Mounted on
/dev/mapper/VolGroup00-LogVol00
                      13140720   3097624   9364800  25% /
/dev/sda1               101086     18536     77331  20% /boot
tmpfs                   962696         0    962696   0% /dev/shm
/dev/mapper/VolGroup00-LogVol01
                      79354688  60896492  14362196  81% /home
production.example.com:/vol
                     38587596 26164688 1242290784  68% /data
```

To display the output in "human readable" format, use the `-h` argument to `df`. The output is then displayed in kilobytes, megabytes, gigabytes, or terabytes depending on the size of the filesystem. The same mount points from Listing 20.1 are shown in Listing 20.2 in human readable format.

LISTING 20.2 Disk Space Usage in Human Readable Format

```
Filesystem            Size  Used Avail Use% Mounted on
/dev/mapper/VolGroup00-LogVol00
                       13G  3.0G  9.0G  25% /
/dev/sda1              99M   19M   76M  20% /boot
tmpfs                 941M     0  941M   0% /dev/shm
/dev/mapper/VolGroup00-LogVol01
                       76G   59G   14G  81% /home
production.example.com:/vol
                      3.6T  2.5T  1.2T  68% /data
```

The default output includes the size of the partition, how much space is used, how much space is available, the percentage of space used, and on what directory the filesystem is mounted. To display the filesystem type as well, such as `ext3` or `nfs`, use the `-T` argument. To limit the output to specific filesystem types, use the `-t=<type>` option. To exclude certain filesystem types from the output, use the `-x-<type>` argument.

Some of the mounted filesystems might not be local such as NFS mounts. To limit the output to local filesystems, use the `-l` option. To calculate disk usage for a specific partition, include it as an argument to the command such as `df /dev/sda1`.

To view the same information from a graphical application, select **Administration, System Monitor** from the **System** menu on the top panel of the desktop. Click on the **File Systems** tab as shown in Figure 20.1.

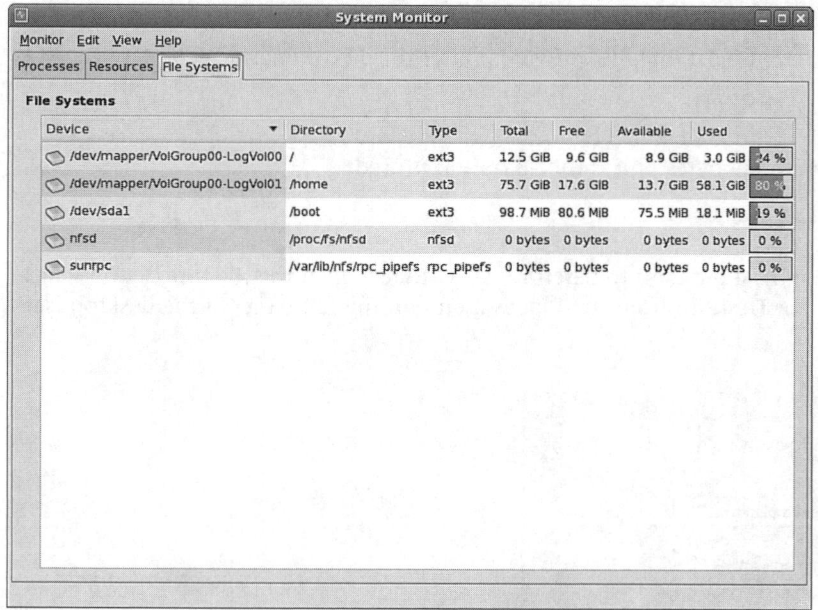

FIGURE 20.1 Graphical Display of Disk Usage

Although the `df` command is useful in determining how much space is being used for each partition, sometimes it is necessary to know what the size of a file, group of files, or directory is. By default, if no command-line options are used, the `du` command displays the disk usage totals for each subdirectory and finally the total usage for the current directory. Values are in kilobytes. Listing 20.3 shows the disk usage of the `/etc/sysconfig/` directory.

LISTING 20.3 Disk Usage of a Directory

```
388     ./network-scripts
24      ./cbq
8       ./console
16      ./modules
8       ./rhn/clientCaps.d
52      ./rhn
8       ./networking/devices
24      ./networking/profiles/default
32      ./networking/profiles
48      ./networking
880     .
```

20

To display the information in an easier-to-read format (megabytes, gigabytes, and terabytes), use the `-h` argument. To display only the grand total for the current directory without the usage for each subdirectory, use the `-s` argument. Combine these two arguments with the `du -hs` command, and only the grand total for the current directory is displayed in megabytes or gigabytes.

To determine the size of just one file, provide it after the `du` command such as

```
du /vol1/group1/examplefile
```

The value is given in kilobytes unless the `-h` option is used:

```
du -h /vol1/group1/examplefile
```

If you prefer a graphical program to determine disk usage, open the file browser by selecting **Home Folder** or **Desktop** from the **Places** menu on the top panel of the desktop (see Figure 20.2).

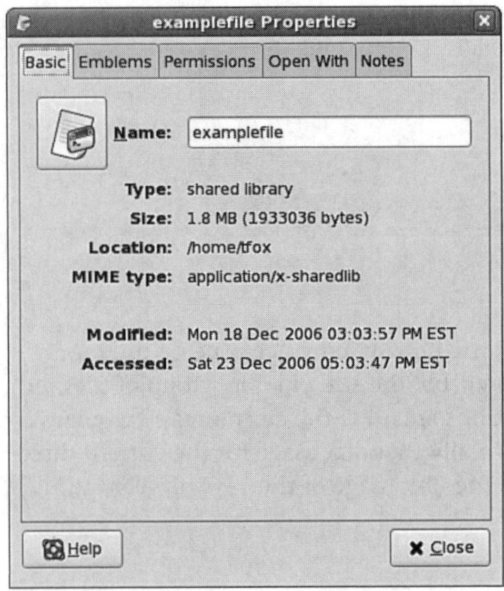

FIGURE 20.2 Graphical Display of File Size

The name, file type, size, location, MIME type, last modified date, and last accessed date are shown for the file. If a directory is selected instead, folder is shown as the file type. Also, the number of items in the folder, size of all the files and directories in the directory, location, volume, free size, and last modified date are displayed.

Reporting Open Files

The `lsof` command can be used to list open files, including library and network files. If an error occurs because a device is already in use, `lsof` can be used to determine which process is using it and who owns that process. By default, all open files for all active processes are listed. Use the `grep` command to search for a specific file.

TIP

Narrow down the output even more using one of the command-line arguments listed in the `lsof` man page.

For example, if you need to unmount an NFS volume but receive an error message that it is already in use, use the following to determine which users are still accessing it (replace `<nfs_mounted_dir>` with the directory in which the NFS share is mounted):

```
lsof | grep <nfs_mounted_dir>
```

All processes using the NFS mounted directory are shown such as the following for a bash session open by user tfox:

```
bash      12165     tfox     cwd      DIR     0,18  10240  1856 /data/group1
 (fileserver.example.com:/vol1/data)
```

Reporting Disk Performance

Disk performance should be constantly monitored over time to determine disk or controller problems. For example, if the access time for a drive suddenly drops, an administrator must quickly start troubleshooting the problem to determine if it is a software or hardware issue or simply due to lack of free space on the disk.

Using `iostat`

Part of the `sysstat` RPM package, the `iostat` utility can be used to gather performance statistics for devices or partitions. Use it in conjunction with `netstat` and `vmstat` to narrow down the problem to a possible I/O, network, or memory error. Install the `sysstat` RPM package with RHN as described in Chapter 3, "Operating System Updates," if it is not already installed. For each invocation of the `iostat` command, the first report given is always the average values from the system boot, while each additional report is the instantaneous change from the previous report. If the command is given without any command-line options, only the report of average values is displayed as shown in Listing 20.4.

LISTING 20.4 Example `iostat` Output

```
avg-cpu:  %user   %nice    %sys %iowait   %idle
           2.47    0.00    0.33    0.43   96.77

Device:          tps   Blk_read/s   Blk_wrtn/s   Blk_read   Blk_wrtn
sda             1.41        79.37        38.15   41006531   19710528
sdc             0.07        16.96         0.00    8762116          0
```

The first part of the report shows CPU usage. If the system has more than one processor, the performance percentages shown are averages from all the processors. The rest of the report shows information about each device on the system. Table 20.1 explains its output.

To create continuous reports, specify a time interval in seconds after the command. For example, to generate `iostat` reports every minute, use the command `iostat 60`. Press Ctrl+C to stop the output. Alternatively, specify the number of intervals as well with the format `iostat <interval> <iterations>` such as `iostat 60 5` to generate a report every 60 seconds for 5 iterations. As mentioned previously, after the first report of averages, each report is the instantaneous change from the previous report.

To include a line of values for the entire device along with the statistics for each partition, use the `iostat -p <device>` command such as the following for `/dev/sda`:

```
iostat -p /dev/sda
```

To display the statistics for more than one device, replace `<device>` with a space-separated list of device names.

TABLE 20.1 Explanation of `iostat` Headers

`iostat` Header	Explanation
`%user`	Percentage of CPU usage at the user level
`%nice`	Percentage of CPU usage at the user level with nice priority
`%sys`	Percentage of CPU usage at the system level
`%iowait`	Percentage of time the CPU(s) were idle while the system had an outstanding I/O request
`%idle`	Percentage of time the CPU(s) were idle while the system did not have an outstanding I/O request
`tps`	Transfers per second
`Blk read/s`	Amount of data read from the device in number of blocks per second
`Blk wrtn/s`	Amount of data written to the device in number of blocks per second
`Blk read`	Number of blocks read
`Blk wrtn`	Number of blocks written

TIP

In addition, the command `vmstat -d` reports additional disk usage, and `vmstat -p <device>` such as `vmstat -p sda1` reports disk usage for a specific partition.

Using `sar`

Also part of the `sysstat` commands, the `sar` utility produces system reports about the I/O, CPU, and memory. The data can be collected at specific intervals, thus making it easy to determine performance at specific load times. For example, if a system's usage peaks at a specific time everyday, the `sar` output can be analyzed to determine if more resources are necessary to handle the highest load.

Before using `sar`, it must be initialized with the following commands (replace `lib` with `lib64` for 64-bit system):

```
/usr/lib/sa/sa1 1 1
/usr/lib/sa/sa2 -A
```

These are automatically run by the cron script located at /etc/cron.d/sysstat. However, if you just installed the sysstat package and don't want to wait on the cron job to initialize sar, run the commands as root.

Because of the cron job, sar reports are generated every day at 23:53 and stored in the directory /var/log/sa/ using the filename convention sa<date>, where <date> is the two-digit representation of the day's date. For example, sar31 is used for December 31. The year is not used in the filename because only the last nine reports are kept. However, sar can easily be used in a script to produce custom reports. A custom script can also be written to copy the reports to a different location or server before they are removed by sar.

If the sar command is run on the command line, the output shows system information in ten-minute intervals as shown in Listing 20.5.

LISTING 20.5 Example sar Output

```
12:00:02 AM     CPU     %user     %nice   %system   %iowait     %steal     %idle
12:10:01 AM     all      2.95      0.00      0.32      0.05       0.01     96.69
12:20:01 AM     all      2.78      0.00      0.29      0.05       0.01     96.88
12:30:01 AM     all      2.80      0.00      0.31      0.00       0.01     96.89
12:40:01 AM     all      2.98      0.00      0.32      0.48       0.01     96.22
12:50:01 AM     all      2.83      0.00      0.31      0.10       0.01     96.76
```

To specify the time interval and number of iterations displayed:

```
sar <interval> <iterations>
```

For example, sar 60 5 displays 5 iterations at 60 second intervals.

To only take a snapshot for a specific processor, specify it with the -P <num> argument. For example, sar -P 0 60 5 displays 5 iterations at 60 second intervals for the first processor only. The processor numbering starts at 0.

By default, sar shows CPU information. Refer to Table 20.2 for other common display options.

TABLE 20.2 Command-Line Options for sar

Command-Line Option	Description
-u	Show CPU statistics (default)
-b	Show I/O and transfer rate statistics
-r	Show memory and swap space statistics
-R	Show memory statistics

20

NOTE

Other arguments are available; refer to the sar man page for details. It can be accessed by executing the man sar command at a shell prompt.

Reporting System Processes

The ps command outputs data about active processes. By default, it only displays processes associated with the current terminal and owned by the user executing the command. To view all processes on the system from all users, use the command ps -aux. The output for all users and processes can be long. Piping it through less will help you scroll through the output: ps -aux ¦ less. Piping it through grep can help you search for a specific process or user: ps -aux ¦ grep bash. You can also redirect the output to a file for further analysis: ps -aux > psoutput.txt.

NOTE

Numerous arguments to ps can be used to customize the output. A complete list is available in the ps man page.

Alternatively, the top command shows similar information but on a continuous basis, and the data can be sorted by memory usage, CPU usage, process ID, and more. While ps can be used to generate snapshots of usage, top can be used to actively monitor the system. To stop top, press the q key. Example output is shown in Listing 20.6.

LISTING 20.6 Example top Output

```
top - 15:41:45 up 16 days,  3:20,  6 users,  load average: 0.12, 0.18, 0.09
Tasks: 183 total,   1 running, 182 sleeping,   0 stopped,   0 zombie
Cpu(s):  8.5%us,  1.8%sy,  0.0%ni, 89.6%id,  0.0%wa,  0.0%hi,  0.0%si,  0.0%st
Mem:   1541120k total,  1521532k used,    19588k free,    67880k buffers
Swap:  2031608k total,      140k used,  2031468k free,   335872k cached

  PID USER      PR  NI  VIRT  RES  SHR S %CPU %MEM    TIME+  COMMAND
 3183 root      15   0  425m  80m  12m S   14  5.3  54:58.87 Xorg
 6584 tfox      15   0  269m  14m 9748 S    7  0.9   0:10.49 gnome-system-mo
 3543 tfox      16   0  290m  24m 9508 S    0  1.7   0:11.80 gnome-terminal
 5326 root      20   0  267m 7020 1172 S    0  0.5   5:35.15 python
 6566 root      15   0 12708 1124  796 R    0  0.1   0:00.39 top
    1 root      15   0 10300  656  544 S    0  0.0   0:00.16 init
    2 root      RT   0     0    0    0 S    0  0.0   0:00.03 migration/0
    3 root      34  19     0    0    0 S    0  0.0   0:00.00 ksoftirqd/0
    4 root      RT   0     0    0    0 S    0  0.0   0:00.00 watchdog/0
```

An explanation of the headers displayed by top is in Table 20.3.

TABLE 20.3 Explanation of `top` Headers

`top` **Header**	**Explanation**
PID	Process ID
USER	Owner of process
PR	Process priority
NI	Nice value
VIRT	Virtual memory used by process
RES	Non-swapped physical memory used by the process
SHR	Shared memory used by the process
S	Status of process
%CPU	Percentage of CPU usage
%MEM	Percentage of physical memory usage
TIME+	Total CPU time used by process
COMMAND	Command used to start the process

`top` is also interactive. For example, pressing Shift+M sorts the output by memory usage. Other sorting options are listed in Table 20.4.

TABLE 20.4 Interactive `top` Commands

`top` **Command**	**Explanation**
Shift+M	Sort by memory usage
Shift+P	Sort by CPU usage
Shift+N	Sort by PID
Shift+T	Sort by TIME+
k	Kill a specific process by PID
u	Sort by specific user
spacebar	Immediately refresh the output
h	Show help
q	Quit top

To view the same information graphically, select **Administration**, **System Monitor** from the **Systems** menu on the top panel of the desktop. As shown in Figure 20.3, the **Processes** tab shows the information from the `top` command in an easier to read format. Click on a column name to sort the information by the data in the column.

All of these tools can be used to determine if one or a small group of processes is consuming the majority of the system resources. This is especially useful on a server shared by many.

20

TIP

Want to quickly find out who owns the process taking up the most resources? Try the `w` command. It lists all users currently logged on and all their processes.

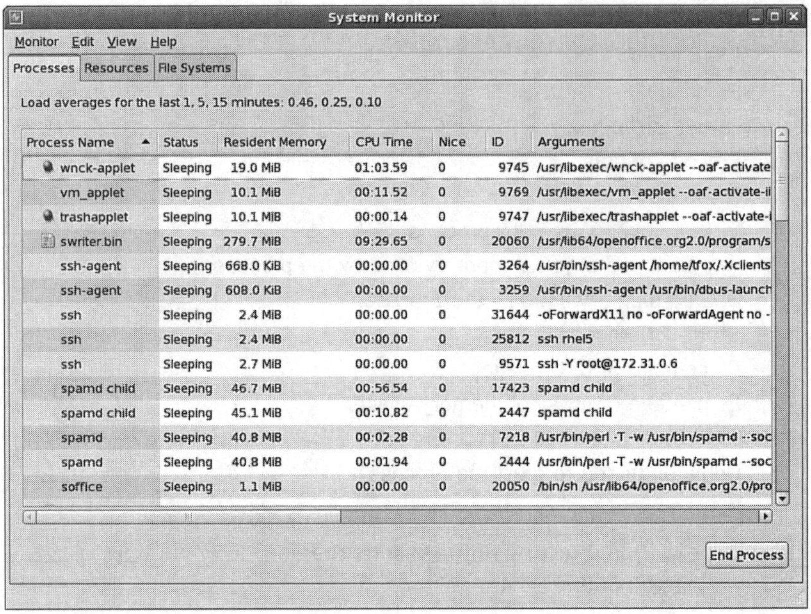

System Monitor

Monitor Edit View Help

Processes | Resources | File Systems

Load averages for the last 1, 5, 15 minutes: 0.46, 0.25, 0.10

Process Name	Status	Resident Memory	CPU Time	Nice	ID	Arguments
wnck-applet	Sleeping	19.0 MiB	01:03.59	0	9745	/usr/libexec/wnck-applet --oaf-activate
vm_applet	Sleeping	10.1 MiB	00:11.52	0	9769	/usr/libexec/vm_applet --oaf-activate-ii
trashapplet	Sleeping	10.1 MiB	00:00.14	0	9747	/usr/libexec/trashapplet --oaf-activate-i
swriter.bin	Sleeping	279.7 MiB	09:29.65	0	20060	/usr/lib64/openoffice.org2.0/program/s
ssh-agent	Sleeping	668.0 KiB	00:00.00	0	3264	/usr/bin/ssh-agent /home/tfox/.Xclients
ssh-agent	Sleeping	608.0 KiB	00:00.00	0	3259	/usr/bin/ssh-agent /usr/bin/dbus-launch
ssh	Sleeping	2.4 MiB	00:00.00	0	31644	-oForwardX11 no -oForwardAgent no -
ssh	Sleeping	2.4 MiB	00:00.00	0	25812	ssh rhel5
ssh	Sleeping	2.7 MiB	00:00.00	0	9571	ssh -Y root@172.31.0.6
spamd child	Sleeping	46.7 MiB	00:56.54	0	17423	spamd child
spamd child	Sleeping	45.1 MiB	00:10.82	0	2447	spamd child
spamd	Sleeping	40.8 MiB	00:02.28	0	7218	/usr/bin/perl -T -w /usr/bin/spamd --soc
spamd	Sleeping	40.8 MiB	00:01.94	0	2444	/usr/bin/perl -T -w /usr/bin/spamd --soc
soffice	Sleeping	1.1 MiB	00:00.00	0	20050	/bin/sh /usr/lib64/openoffice.org2.0/pro

End Process

FIGURE 20.3 Graphical Display of System Processes

Reporting on the System Processors

As explained the previous sections, the interactive `top` command and `iostat` provide information about the processor or processors in the system. The `uptime` and `mpstat` commands can also be useful when analyzing the CPU.

`uptime` is a simple program that displays the current time, system uptime, number of users logged on, and average CPU load for the past 1, 5, and 15 minutes:

```
22:52:42 up 8 days,  1:04,  5 users,  load average: 0.18, 0.36, 0.34
```

Another member of the `sysstat` family, `mpstat` provides statistics about each processor in the system as shown in Listing 20.7.

LISTING 20.7 Example `mpstat` Output

```
12:24:49 AM  CPU  %user  %nice %system %iowait  %irq  %soft  %steal  %idle   intr/s
12:24:49 AM  all   3.20   0.00    0.59    0.73  0.03   0.00    0.01  95.45  1020.55
```

Similar to `iostat` and `sar`, you can tell `mpstat` to run for a specific number of iterations at specific time intervals with the format `mpstat <interval> <interations>`.

Reporting Memory Usage

Two types of system memory exist: physical and virtual. To display the amount of free and used memory, both physical and virtual (swap), use the `free` command. Example output is shown in Listing 20.8.

LISTING 20.8 Example `free` Output

```
                total       used       free     shared    buffers     cached
Mem:          1541120    1521476      19644          0      68280     335948
-/+ buffers/cache:       1117248     423872
Swap:         2031608        140    2031468
```

By default, the output is shown in kilobytes. To show megabytes instead, use the command `free -m`. The total amount of memory, amount of memory used, and amount of memory free is shown first for the physical memory and then for the swap space. The statistics for the physical memory also include the amount of shared memory, the buffers used by the kernel, and amount of memory caches.

The content displayed by `free` is a snapshot. To output memory usage in specific intervals, use the command `free -s <interval>`, where `<interval>` is the amount of delay, in seconds, between output. To stop the continuous output, press Ctrl+C.

To report more detailed statistics about the physical and virtual memory, use `vmstat`, which is part of the `procps` package. Listing 20.9 shows example output in the default mode (without arguments).

LISTING 20.9 Example `vmstat` Output

```
procs -----------memory---------- ---swap-- -----io---- --system-- ----cpu----
 r  b   swpd   free   buff  cache   si   so    bi    bo   in    cs us sy id wa st
 0  0 496956   5828   2748  68632    2    2    50    21   24    41  3  1 96  1 1
```

By default, the values are in kilobytes. To use megabytes instead, use the command `vmstat -S M`.

Two columns are under the `procs` header: `r` and `b`. The value under the `r` column indicates the number of processes waiting for runtime. The value under the `b` column tells you the number of processes in uninterruptible sleep.

The following values are under the `memory` header:

`swpd`	Amount of virtual memory used
`free`	Amount of free memory
`buff`	Amount of memory used in buffers
`cache`	Amount of memory used as cache

Under the swap header:

- `si` Amount of memory swapped in from the disk
- `so` Amount of memory swapped to the disk

Under the io header:

- `bi` Number of blocks received from a block device
- `bo` Number of blocks sent to a block device

Under the system header:

- `in` Number of interrupts per second
- `cs` Number of context switches per second

Under the cpu header:

- `us` Percentage of time the processor(s) spent running non-kernel code
- `sy` Percentage of time the processor(s) spent running kernel code
- `id` Percentage of time spent not running any code
- `wa` Percentage of time spent waiting for I/O
- `st` Percentage of time the processor(s) spent running kernel code

Just like `free`, the content displayed by `vmstat` is a snapshot. To generate output at specific intervals, use the command `vmstat <interval>`, where `<interval>` is the amount of delay, in seconds, between output. To stop the continuous output, press Ctrl+C.

To specify the number of intervals, use the format `vmstat <interval> <iterations>`. For example, `vmstat 60 5` produces statistics every 60 seconds for 5 iterations and then stops.

TIP

Another great argument to `vmstat` is `-s`. `vmstat -s` outputs a quick summary of the system's memory as shown in Listing 20.10.

LISTING 20.10 Example output from `vmstat -s`

```
514188  total memory
491292  used memory
327068  active memory
105080  inactive memory
 22896  free memory
 14444  buffer memory
192768  swap cache
522104  total swap
224240  used swap
```

LISTING 20.10 Continued

```
      297864 free swap
     2638363 non-nice user cpu ticks
        3764 nice user cpu ticks
      503661 system cpu ticks
    78527688 idle cpu ticks
      647000 IO-wait cpu ticks
       26495 IRQ cpu ticks
           0 softirq cpu ticks
    40496151 pages paged in
    16937888 pages paged out
      678133 pages swapped in
      399395 pages swapped out
   840250343 interrupts
   326447770 CPU context switches
  1135738065 boot time
  109526 forks
```

Reporting on the Network Subsystem

In an enterprise company with offices all around the world, the network subsystem is one of the most carefully monitored system resources. Without network connectivity, some companies could not perform their day-to-day tasks from something as simple as email to something more critical such as accessing patient records.

While `ifconfig` can be used to configure network devices as discussed in Chapter 2, "Post-Installation Configuration," it can also be used to quickly determine if the device has an IP address or to retrieve the MAC address of an interface as shown in Listing 20.11.

LISTING 20.11 Example Output from `ifconfig`

```
eth0      Link encap:Ethernet  HWaddr 00:A0:CC:28:3D:44
          inet addr:192.168.0.4  Bcast:192.168.0.255  Mask:255.255.255.0
          inet6 addr: fe80::2a0:ccff:fe28:3d44/64 Scope:Link
          UP BROADCAST RUNNING MULTICAST  MTU:1500  Metric:1
          RX packets:1699162 errors:1 dropped:0 overruns:0 frame:0
          TX packets:2743880 errors:3 dropped:0 overruns:3 carrier:0
          collisions:3153 txqueuelen:1000
          RX bytes:335440321 (319.9 MiB)  TX bytes:3356790591 (3.1 GiB)
          Interrupt:9 Base address:0x6c00

lo        Link encap:Local Loopback
          inet addr:127.0.0.1  Mask:255.0.0.0
          inet6 addr: ::1/128 Scope:Host
          UP LOOPBACK RUNNING  MTU:16436  Metric:1
```

LISTING 20.11 Continued

```
          RX packets:89409 errors:0 dropped:0 overruns:0 frame:0
          TX packets:89409 errors:0 dropped:0 overruns:0 carrier:0
          collisions:0 txqueuelen:0
          RX bytes:34682468 (33.0 MiB)  TX bytes:34682468 (33.0 MiB)
```

The eth0 device is the first Ethernet device in the system. If additional Ethernet devices are available, they are referred to as eth1, eth2, and so on. The lo device is the local loopback device.

If the device has an IP address, it is listed after `inet addr:` as shown for eth0 in Listing 20.11. The MAC address is listed after `Hwaddr` for each device.

By default, `ifconfig` only displays devices with IP addresses. To list the information for a specific device such as one without an IP, specify it after the command such as `ifconfig eth1`.

To monitor traffic on a network, use the `tcpdump` utility. It enables the promiscuous mode of the network card to capture all the packets sent across the network. You must run `tcpdump` as the root user. This can be useful when trying to determine if packets are reaching their destinations and to check response times.

When run with no arguments, `tcpdump` runs continuously until you press Ctrl+C. To limit the number of packets captured, use the `-c <count>` argument. After `<count>` number of packets are captured, `tcpdump` stops. To save the output to a file instead of displaying it on the command line, use the `-w <file>` option, and then use the `-r <file>` argument to read it back from the file.

To only capture packets on a specific interface, use the command `tcpdump -D` to list the interfaces `tcpdump` can listen to. In this output, each interface is preceded by a number. Specify this number as `<interface>` with the command `tcpdump -i <interface>` to only capture packets on the specified interface.

If you prefer a graphical, interactive application to view packet transfers, try Wireshark. Use Red Hat Network as discussed in Chapter 3 to install the `wireshark-gnome` package if it is not already installed. It will also install the `wireshark` package (non-GUI version).

After installing the RPM packages, select **Internet**, **Wireshark Network Analyzer** from the **Applications** menu on the top panel of the desktop. You can also execute the `wireshark` command to start the program. If you run the program as a non-root user, you are prompted for the root password to continue.

As shown in Figure 20.4, Wireshark uses the same format as `tcpdump`, so if you use `tcpdump -w <file>` to save the output, you can then open it in Wireshark to take advantage of its easy-to-read color coding and interactive features such as filtering.

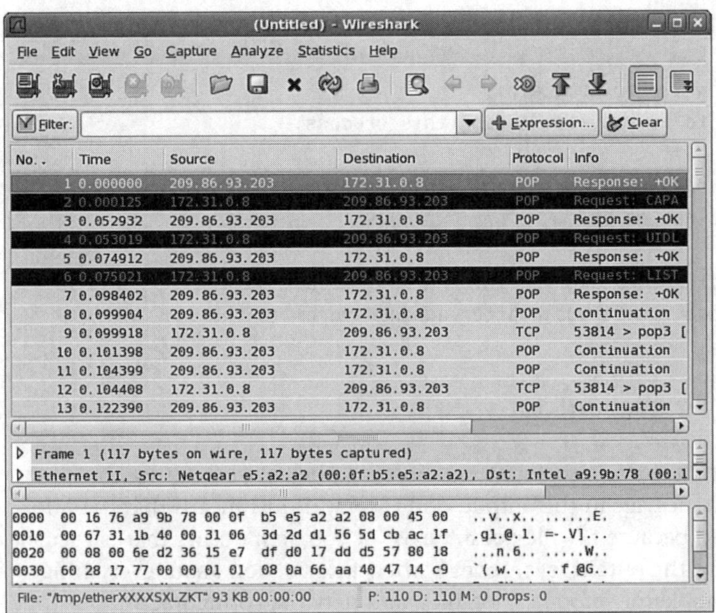

FIGURE 20.4 Wireshark After Capturing Packets

Generating a System Report

When troubleshooting a system, it is often useful to generate a system report so that data can be analyzed as a whole or to send to other administrators on the team or a customer support representative. The `sysreport` program is often used by the Red Hat support team and can be invaluable when searching for the root of a problem.

The program is provided by the `sysreport` RPM package. If it is not installed, install it using Red Hat Network (refer to Chapter 3).

The `sysreport` command must be run as the root user because it must be able to gather configuration information only accessible by the root user. The program itself is actually a shell script written by Red Hat as a tool that allows customers to easily send their support representative detailed information about the hardware and software on a given system. This allows customers to execute one command for common troubleshooting data instead of a series of commands they may not be familiar with.

After you execute the command `sysreport` as root, you will see the following message:

```
This utility will go through and collect some detailed information
about the hardware and setup of your Red Hat Linux system.
This information will be used to diagnose problems with your system
and will be considered confidential information.  Red Hat will use
this information for diagnostic purposes ONLY.
```

```
Please wait while we collect information about your system.

This process may take a while to complete....
No changes will be made to your system during this process.

NOTE: You can safely ignore a failed message. This only means a file
we were checking for did not exist.

If your system hangs while gathering rpm information, please abort
the script with CTRL-C and run it again after adding -norpm to the
sysreport command line

Press ENTER to continue, or CTRL-C to quit.
```

Press Enter to start generating the report. As information is gathered, you can see the progress. If you see a failed message in the output, don't worry. It just means that the information can not be gathered because the file doesn't exist or you aren't using that particular service. As you can see from the output, `sysreport` gathers information about everything including the kernel version, kernel modules, log files, and network configuration.

After `sysreport` finishes, you will be prompted to enter a case number if you have one from Red Hat Customer Service. After entering one and pressing Enter, a message will appear telling you the filename of the report in the format `/root/<hostname>-<casenum>.<date>.tar.bz2`. To view the contents of the report, execute the command `tar xjvf <filename>`, where `<filename>` is the name of the file generated. This command creates the subdirectory with the same filename as the archive file but without the `.tar.bz2` extension. This subdirectory contains all the information gathered by `sysreport`.

Locating Log Files

It is extremely important to keep a watch on the system's log files. If you are familiar with them, it is much easier to spot a change should a problem arise or should you think your system has been compromised. Log files are also useful when configuring a new device or kernel module. Error messages are written to log files and can be used to troubleshoot. You must be root to read most log files.

As the system boots, it writes to the log file `/var/log/dmesg`. This file contains information about the machine as it boots such as the kernel version, options passed to the boot loader, the type of processor detected, hard drive partitions found, and which partitions are mounted.

The default system log file is `/var/log/messages`. It contains information such as when a user logs in, when a USB device is inserted, and when a removable device is mounted.

Additional log files are located in the `/var/log/` directory, with some services having their own subdirectory such as `/var/log/cups/` for the printing subsystem. Some log files are rotating log files—meaning that only a certain number are kept on the disk to conserve disk space. If all logs were kept forever, they would eventually consume the entire disk.

For a list of logs that are rotated, refer to `/etc/logrotate.conf` and the `/etc/logrotate.d/` directory.

Viewing Log Files with Logwatch

To keep watch on all the log files on each system for which you are responsible, you can write customized scripts as cron tasks that execute on a regular basis as discussed in Chapter 11, or you can use the Logwatch program to analyze log files and generate reports about them. The Logwatch program is provided by the `logwatch` RPM package. Install if it is not already installed.

This section describes how to customize how log files are analyzed and reported, how to customize the scripts used, and how to add additional log files for Logwatch to monitor.

Understanding the Logwatch Configuration

The Logwatch program includes a script to execute the program once a day and email reports to the administrator. Installing the `logwatch` package is all it takes to have the program up and running. This subsection outlines the files used by Logwatch.

Most of the Logwatch files are installed into the `/usr/share/logwatch/` directory with the following subdirectories:

- `default.conf/`: Default configuration files.
- `dist.conf/`: Distribution-specific configuration files. (Red Hat Enterprise Linux does not include any.)
- `lib/`: Perl library files used by the scripts.
- `scripts/`: Executable scripts used by Logwatch. Most are written in Perl.

The `default.conf/` directory contains the following files and directories:

- `logfiles/`: Directory that contains configuration files for log file groups. Each log file group configuration file lists one or more log files that use the same format. Some log file group configuration files may be used by more than one service.
- `services/`: Directory that contains configuration files for each service whose log files are monitored by Logwatch such as one for the Apache HTTP server and one for the Samba file-sharing service.
- `logwatch.conf`: Configuration file that contains the default settings for Logwatch.

Customizing Logwatch Configuration

Logwatch is configured for the default log file locations in Red Hat Enterprise Linux, so no customization is required. The main reasons to customize it are if you have modified any service to use a non-default log file, if you want to change the type of data Logwatch looks for in the log files, and if you need to add a new set of log files to watch.

Even though the /usr/share/logwatch/ directory contains the configuration files, the ones in this directory are the defaults and should not be modified. To customize the Logwatch configuration, instead edit the files in /etc/logwatch/, which contains two directories: conf/ and scripts/. The /etc/logwatch/conf/ directory contains the files to customize the configuration files. The /etc/logwatch/scripts/ directory does not contain any files by default, but custom scripts can be added to it as explained in the "Customizing the Logwatch Scripts" section later in this chapter.

The configuration files use the following conventions:

- If a line begins with #, the entire line is a comment.
- If a line begins with $, the rest of the word is a variable.
- If a line begins with *, what follows is an executable.

All the variables set in the files in the /etc/logwatch/conf/ directory and subdirectories override the values from the /usr/share/logwatch/default.conf/ directory and subdirectories. To modify a value in logwatch.conf, copy it in the /etc/logwatch/conf/logwatch.conf file while preserving any subdirectories and modify its value. The next time Logwatch is executed by the daily cron job, the new values will be used instead of the defaults.

To change a value in any of the files in the logfiles/ or services/ directory, create the same file, including subdirectories in the /etc/logwatch/conf/ directory, and, in the file, declare the variables you want to change. For example, the /usr/share/logwatch/default.conf/services/iptables.conf file contains the lines from Listing 20.12 to define a variable that blocks hosts with less than a certain number of hits between all ports.

LISTING 20.12 IPTables Variable from Logwatch

```
# Set this to enable a filter on iptables/ipchains displays
# This will block out hosts who have less than the specified
# number of hits between all ports.  Defaults to 0.
$iptables_host_min_count = 0
```

To change this value, create the /etc/logwatch/conf/services/iptables.conf file. Copy these lines into the newly created file, and change the value of 0 to a different integer. The next time Logwatch is executed by the daily cron job, the new value will be used instead of the default.

TIP

Alternatively, copy the entire file from the /usr/share/logwatch/default.conf/ file and modify the values of the variables. This method is useful if many variables within a file need to be modified.

In addition to the `logfiles/` directory, `services/` directory, and `logwatch.conf` file found in `/usr/share/logwatch/default.conf/`, the `/etc/logwatch/conf/` directory contains two additional configuration files: `ignore.conf` and `override.conf`. In `ignore.conf`, if any Logwatch output from any service matches the regular expressions in this file, they are ignored and not included in the report generated.

To modify the value of a variable: Instead of declaring it again in the `/etc/logwatch/conf/logwatch.conf` directory or re-creating in the `logfiles/` or `services/` directory, all changed values can be declared in the one file, the `/etc/logwatch/conf/override.conf` file, using one of the following prefixes for each line (the colon must be included in the prefix followed by a space and then the entire line as it appears in the default configuration file):

- `logwatch`: This variable overwrites the one found in the default `logwatch.conf` file.
- `services/<filename>`: This variable overwrites the one found in the default `services/<filename>` (replace `<filename>` with the specific name of the file) file.
- `logfiles/<filename>`: This variable overwrites the one found in the default `logfiles/<filename>` (replace `<filename>` with the specific name of the file) file.

Customizing the Logwatch Scripts

The `/usr/share/logwatch/scripts/` directory contains the following directories:

- `services/`: Directory that contains the executable scripts for each service monitored by Logwatch.
- `shared/`: Directory that contains the executable scripts that might be used by more than one service.
- `logfiles/`: Directory that contains subdirectories named for log file groups. The executables in the subdirectories are executed when running a service that uses the log file group.

The same method for overwriting variable values is used for the scripts. To modify a default script, copy it from the `/usr/share/logwatch/scripts/` directory into the `/etc/logwatch/scripts/` directory while preserving any subdirectories and then modify the script. If a script with the exact same filename and relative path is found in `/etc/logwatch/scripts/`, it is used instead of the default script.

Creating Service Filters

As mentioned earlier, the `/usr/share/logwatch/default.conf/services/` directory contains a file for each service whose log files are analyzed by Logwatch. The `/usr/share/logwatch/scripts/services/` directory contains the executable scripts run for each service. To configure Logwatch to monitor log files for additional services, create a configuration file in `/etc/logwatch/conf/services/` and a corresponding executable in `/etc/logwatch/scripts/services/`. You can base the added files on existing files for a different service.

Summary

Red Hat Enterprise Linux includes several utilities necessary for adequately monitoring and tuning system resources.

The `df` and `du` commands calculate used and free space on partitions and in directories. The `lsof` utility lists open files for active processes. The `sysstat` programs `iostat` and `sar` help monitor disk load and performance.

Use `ps` and `top` to monitor processes. The `uptime` and `mpstat` utilities can help keep tabs on the processor or processors in the system while `free` and `vmstat` provide information about physical and virtual memory. To analyze network configuration and traffic, use a combination of `ifconfig` and `tcpdump`.

The `sysreport` program gathers all system information in one archive file for further analysis by an administrator or customer support representative. In addition, becoming familiar with log files can help you learn how your system works and allow you to recognize changes quickly.

The `logwatch` utility can be used to generate log file reports.

CHAPTER 21

Monitoring and Tuning the Kernel

IN THIS CHAPTER

- Using the /proc Directory
- Optimizing Virtual Memory
- Managing Memory with NUMA
- Using AltSysRq to Execute System Requests
- Saving Kernel Dumps for Analysis
- Setting SMP IRQ Affinity
- Enabling NMI Watchdog for Locked Systems

The previous chapter, "Monitoring System Resources," details how to monitor filesystems, system processes, CPU utilization, physical and virtual memory, and the network subsystem. This chapter dives even deeper into the system by discussing the monitoring and tuning of the kernel including how it manages memory, how it assigns processes to each processor in a multi-processor system, and how to gather information from the kernel when the system appears to be unresponsive.

Using the `/proc` Directory

Instead of executing utilities such as `free` and `top` to determine the status of system resources or `fdisk` to view disk partitions, an administrator can gather system information directly from the kernel through the `/proc` filesystem.

The `/proc` directory can be thought of as a window into what the kernel sees on the system. Even though the directory appears to contain files and directories, they are not ordinary files. You will notice that most of them are 0 bytes. You will also notice that it is mounted as a pseudo-filesystem in `/etc/fstab`:

```
proc          /proc          proc    defaults        0 0
```

When you view the contents of files in `/proc`, you are really asking the kernel what the current state is for that particular device or subsystem. To view the contents of a special file in `/proc`, use the `cat`, `less`, or `more` file viewing utilities.

For example, the `cat /proc/meminfo` command displays the current state of the system memory as shown in Listing 21.1.

LISTING 21.1 Current State of Memory from /proc/meminfo

```
MemTotal:        2057004 kB
MemFree:           42468 kB
Buffers:          177332 kB
Cached:           973368 kB
SwapCached:            0 kB
Active:          1060956 kB
Inactive:         796132 kB
HighTotal:             0 kB
HighFree:              0 kB
LowTotal:        2057004 kB
LowFree:           42468 kB
SwapTotal:       2031608 kB
SwapFree:        2031480 kB
Dirty:                44 kB
Writeback:             0 kB
AnonPages:        698652 kB
Mapped:           122272 kB
Slab:             105120 kB
PageTables:        29852 kB
NFS_Unstable:          0 kB
Bounce:                0 kB
CommitLimit:     3060108 kB
Committed_AS:    1436088 kB
VmallocTotal: 34359738367 kB
VmallocUsed:        1376 kB
VmallocChunk: 34359736971 kB
HugePages_Total:       0
HugePages_Free:        0
HugePages_Rsvd:        0
Hugepagesize:       2048 kB
```

Other virtual /proc files of interest include the following:

- /proc/cpuinfo: Information about the system's processors such as how many physical processors exist and how many processor cores exist.
- /proc/cmdline: Boot parameters passed to the kernel at boot time.
- /proc/sys/: Directory containing parameters that can be modified by sysctl. Refer to the "Using sysctl to Change Values" section for details.
- /proc/vm/: Directory containing virtual memory management configuration. The "Optimizing Virtual Memory" section later in this chapter discusses how to modify the virtual files in /proc/sys/vm/ to configure how the kernel manages virtual memory.

- /proc/net/: Directory containing network settings.
- /proc/irq/: Directories contain a subdirectory for each used IRQ, with the subdirectory containing information about the specific IRQ.

Using sysctl to Change Values

It is also possible to use the virtual /proc filesystem to change how the kernel behaves. The value of some files can be changed by redirecting data into it such as `echo 1 > /proc/sys/net/ipv4/ip_forward` to enable IP forwarding. However, these values are not persistent after a reboot.

To modify the values of the virtual files in /proc/sys/, the `sysctl` command can also be used by the root user to modify and test the values. Again, these changes are only used until the system is rebooted. To make the values persist between reboots, modify the /etc/sysctl.conf file as root. Changes to this file do not take place immediately. Either use the `sysctl -p` command to enable all changes in the file or echo the new values into the appropriate /proc file for the changes to take place immediately.

To retrieve a list of all values that can be modified in this manner, execute the `sysctl -a` command. Notice that the type of value each parameter is set to differs. Be extremely careful to set these parameters to proper values and test them before setting them on production systems. It is possible to lock up the system or cause severe system performance issues if incorrect values are given to them.

To map the parameters listed with the `sysctl -a` command to the virtual file locations, replace each dot (.) with a forward slash (/) and pre-pend the results with /proc/sys/. For example, the kernel.exec-shield parameter maps to the /proc/sys/kernel/exec-shield file.

TIP

To list the /proc/sys/ tunables for a specific function such as virtual memory, use grep to only show those options and redirect it into a file:

```
systctl -a ¦ grep vm > vm-tunables.txt
```

To use the `sysctl` command-line utility to assign values to these kernel parameters, use the following syntax as the root user:

```
sysctl -w <parameter>="<value>"
```

Changes can be saved for subsequent reboots by adding them to the /etc/sysctl.conf file with the following syntax:

```
<parameter> = <value>
```

For example, the following command increases how much the system should use its swap space from the default value of 60% to 70%:

```
sysctl -w vm.swappiness="70"
```

This command enables the change immediately. To save the setting so that it is remembered even if the system is rebooted, add the following line to /etc/sysctl.conf:

```
vm.swappiness = 70
```

If you add the change to /etc/sysctl.conf without executing the sysctl -w vm.swappiness="70" command, the change will not go into effect unless the sysctl -p command is also executed as root.

Optimizing Virtual Memory

As discussed in the "Using the /proc Directory" section earlier in this chapter, the settings in /proc/sys/ can be modified with the sysctl -w <parameter>="<value>" command or in the /etc/sysctl.conf file so that the change persists between reboots. One of the subdirectories, /proc/sys/vm/, can be used to optimize how the virtual memory is managed by the kernel.

Table 21.1 shows all the kernel virtual memory settings that can be configured in /etc/sysctl.conf and their default values. The virtual memory setting names are the ones used with the sysctl utility.

TIP

To retrieve a list of all the kernel virtual memory settings for your system, use the command sysctl -a | grep vm > sysctl_vm.txt. The resulting sysctl_vm.txt file will contain the list along with their current values.

TABLE 21.1 Virtual Memory Settings

Virtual Memory Setting	Default Value
vm.swap_token_timeout	300
vm.legacy_va_layout	0
vm.vfs_cache_pressure	100
vm.block_dump	0
vm.laptop_mode	0
vm.max_map_count	65536
vm.percpu_pagelist_fraction	0
vm.min_free_kbytes	2894
vm.drop_caches	0
vm.lowmem_reserve_ratio	256 256 32
vm.hugetlb_shm_group	0

TABLE 21.1 Continued

vm.nr_hugepages	0
vm.swappiness	60
vm.nr_pdflush_threads	2
vm.dirty_expire_centisecs	3000
vm.dirty_writeback_centisecs	500
vm.dirty_ratio	40
vm.dirty_background_ratio	10
vm.page-cluster	3
vm.overcommit_ratio	50
vm.overcommit_memory	0
vm.min_slab_ratio	5*
vm.min_unmapped_ratio	1*
vm.panic_on_oom	0

These tunables are only available for kernels with NUMA support.

The following explains each of these settings:

- `vm.swap_token_timeout`

  Length of the swap out protection token, in seconds. Used to prevent needless page faults in a thrashing state.

- `vm.legacy_va_layout`

  If the system's architecture allows it, this parameter allows the 2.4 kernel layout algorithm for allocating virtual memory for processes.

- `vm.vfs_cache_pressure`

  Controls how aggressive the kernel is in reclaiming memory used as cache for directory and inode objects. The higher the value, the more aggressive the kernel is in reclaiming this type of memory.

- `vm.block_dump`

  If set to a non-zero value and syslog is set to record debug messages from the kernel, messages about I/O requests and page writes are logged in `/var/log/messages`.

- `vm.laptop_mode`

  Minimizes power consumption used for writes to the disk such as performing write operations when the disk is already being used. Automatically enabled when the laptop is using the battery if the system uses ACPI. For more details, install the kernel-doc package and read the `/usr/share/doc/kernel-doc-<version>/Documentation/laptop-mode.txt` file.

- `vm.max_map_count`

  Maximum number of memory map areas the kernel will allocate each process.

- `vm.percpu_pagelist_fraction`

  Maximum pages allocated in each zone for any `per_cpu_pagelist`, as a fraction. For example, if this value is 50, a maximum of 1/50 of the pages in each zone can be allocated for each `per_cpu_pagelist`. Minimum value it can be set to is 8.

- `vm.min_free_kbytes`

  Minimum number of kilobytes to keep free so the kernel can reserve pages for each lowmem zone.

- `vm.drop_caches`

  Used to manually free page cache, dentries, and inodes. Does not free dirty objects, so the sync command should be run first to force dirty objects to be written to disk. Use the `echo` command as root to set it to one of the following values (such as, `echo 1 > /proc/sys/vm/drop_caches`):

  1: Free page cache

  2: Free dentries and inodes

  3: Free page cache, dentries, and inodes

- `vm.lowmem_reserve_ratio`

  Sets ratio of total pages to free pages for each memory zone.

- `vm.hugetlb_shm_group`

  Group ID of the non-root group allowed to allocate huge pages for SHM_HUGETLB shm segments. Useful when using the Oracle® Database.

- `vm.nr_hugepages`

  Current number of reserved hugetlb pages. Change this value to allocate or deallocate hugepages.

- `vm.swappiness`

  How much the kernel should swap memory into swap space. The value is a percentage of physical memory.

- `vm.nr_pdflush_threads`

  Number of pdflush threads running. Cannot be changed because it is a count of running threads. Will be between the minimum and maximum pdflush threads allowed. Useful in monitoring disk activity.

- `vm.dirty_expire_centisecs`

  When dirty data can be written to disk by pdflush, in 100th of a second. After dirty data has been in memory for this amount of time, it is written to disk the next time the pdflush daemon writes dirty data to disk.

- `vm.dirty_writeback_centisecs`

  How long a disk buffer can stay in RAM in a dirty state, specified in 100th of a second. If this time is exceeded, the buffer is written back to disk when the pdflush daemon runs next.

- `vm.dirty_ratio`

  Limit at which processes with dirty buffers start writing to disk (all at the same time) instead of waiting on pdflush. The value is a percentage of total memory.

- `vm.dirty_background_ratio`

  Percentage of memory. When this percentage is reached, dirty data is written out in the background using the pdflush daemon.

- `vm.page-cluster`

  Set to an integer value that controls the number of pages read at the same time, minimizing the number of disk reads. The number of pages read at once is equal to `2^<page-cluster>`. For example, if this parameter is set to 3, 8 pages are read at once.

- `vm.overcommit_memory`

  This parameter sets how the kernel handles memory allocation. If set to 0, the kernel will only assign memory to a program if there is enough free memory. If set to 1, the kernel will allocate memory even if all the memory has already been allocated to other programs. If set to 2 and all the physical memory and swap space have already been allocated, the kernel will allow a certain amount of additional memory to be allocated based on the value of `vm.overcommit_ratio`. If set to 2, the swap space should be the amount of physical memory plus the amount of memory the kernel is allowed to overcommit.

CAUTION

Use caution when allowing the kernel to overallocate memory. If programs actually use all the memory they request, overallocating will slow down the performance of the system as memory has to be constantly swapped in and out as programs try to compensate for the lack of available memory.

- `vm.overcommit_ratio`

  If `vm.overcommit_memory` is set to 2, for which the kernel allows memory allocations larger than the total amount of available memory, this percentage value determines how much additional memory can be allocated. It is expressed as a percentage of physical RAM. For example, if a system has 8GB of RAM and 10 GB of swap space, a value of 25 would allow the kernel to allocate an additional 2GB of memory (25% of 8GB).

- `vm.min_slab_ratio`

  Only for NUMA kernels. The percentage of total pages in each memory zone. If more than this percentage of zone pages are reclaimable slab pages, slabs are reclaimed when a zone reclaim occurs.

- `vm.min_unmapped_ratio`

  Only for NUMA kernels. The percentage of total pages in each memory zone. If, and only if, more than this percentage of zone pages are file backed and mapped, zone reclaim occurs. This setting ensures local pages are still available for file input and output even if a node is overallocated.

- `vm.panic_on_oom`

  If set to 0, the Out of Memory (OOM) killer is enabled. The OOM killer is enabled by default in the Red Hat Enterprise Linux kernel. When there is no memory left on the system and more memory is requested by an application, the kernel uses a complex algorithm to determine which process to kill based on the usage of the process and how much memory it has been allocated. This usually allows the system to stay up and running. If set to 1, the kernel panics when out-of-memory occurs.

- `vm.zone_reclaim_mode`

  Sets how memory is reclaimed when a zone runs out of memory. If set to `0`, no reclaim occurs, and memory is allocated from other zones or nodes on the system.

  The value of this setting should be the `ORed` value from the following:

  - `1`: Zone reclaim enabled. Easily reusable pages are reclaimed before allocating pages in a different node.

  - `2`: Zone reclaim writes dirty pages out. Dirty pages are written out if a zone fills up and slows down the system.

  - `4`: Zone reclaim swaps pages. Swapping pages limits allocations on local nodes.

  The default value is sometimes 1 instead of 0 if the kernel determines at bootup that pages from remote zones will cause a significant decrease in performance.

Managing Memory with NUMA

Non-Uniform Memory Access (NUMA) is a memory management technology available for some multi-processor systems. NUMA works by having dedicated memory for each processor to decrease access time and limit delays by preventing more than one processor from trying to access the same memory at the same time. When the same data in memory is needed by more than one processor, the data must be moved between memory banks, which slows down the process. The time saved by using NUMA depends on many factors including how many processors would otherwise be sharing the same memory bus, how often memory is accessed, whether the applications running were written for a NUMA system, and how much data in memory must be shared between processors.

NUMA is enabled by default in Red Hat Enterprise Linux 5. In some older versions of Red Hat Enterprise Linux, NUMA is disabled by default. Be sure to read the Release Notes to determine whether NUMA is enabled or disabled by default.

If it is enabled, in some cases, you might need to disable it. To disable NUMA, boot with the `numa=off` kernel boot parameter. Refer to "Adding Boot Parameters" in Chapter 2, "Post-Installation Configuration" for step-by-step instructions on adding this boot parameter to the boot loader configuration file. Alternatively, use the `numa=on` kernel boot parameter to explicitly enable NUMA.

To verify that NUMA is enabled on your system, use the `numactl --show` command from the `numactl` package. If it is not installed on your system, refer to Chapter 3, "Operating System Updates," for details on installing additional software. If NUMA is available and is enabled on the system, the output should look similar to Listing 21.2. If NUMA is not available on the system or it is disabled, the following message is displayed:

```
No NUMA support available on this system.
```

LISTING 21.2 NUMA Enabled on System

```
policy: default
preferred node: current
physcpubind: 0 1
cpubind: 0
nodebind: 0
membind: 0
```

To show the size of each memory node and how much memory is free in each node, use the `numactl --hardware` command. For example, Listing 21.3 shows four memory nodes on a system with four processors.

LISTING 21.3 NUMA Nodes and Free Memory on Each Node

```
available: 4 nodes (0-3)
node 0 size: 2047 MB
node 0 free: 1772 MB
node 1 size: 2047 MB
node 1 free: 1712 MB
node 2 size: 2047 MB
node 2 free: 1756 MB
node 3 size: 2047 MB
node 3 free: 1973 MB
```

The `numactl` utility also allows the administrator to tweak the NUMA policies such as setting up interleave memory nodes and configuring a preferred node on which to allocate memory if possible. For descriptions of these additional options, refer to the `numactl` man page with the `man numactl` command.

To display statistics for each NUMA node, execute the `numastat` command. It reads the `/sys/devices/system/node/` subdirectories and displays their data in a more user-friendly format as shown in Listing 21.4 for a system with four memory nodes.

LISTING 21.4 NUMA Statistics

```
                        node3       node2       node1       node0
numa_hit              2246949     2628316     2088387     2741816
numa_miss                   0           0           0           0
numa_foreign                0           0           0           0
interleave_hit          38494       39397       39650       39722
local_node            2217592     2597994     2056904     2713781
other_node              29357       30322       31483       28035
```

Using AltSysRq to Execute System Requests

When your system seems unresponsive or is unresponsive to other monitoring tools, using system requests can be useful to diagnose the problem. System requests are activated by special key combinations. When activated, anyone at the console can execute these system requests without being logged into the system and without entering additional authentication information. Thus, it should only be enabled to diagnose problems with the system and when the physical system is in a secure location or being monitored by an administrator.

To enable, execute the following command:

```
echo 1 > /proc/sys/kernel/sysrq
```

As previously discussed, modifying the value of a `/proc` virtual file with the echo command takes effect immediately but does not save the change after the system is rebooted. To make the change persist after a reboot, add the following line to `/etc/sysctl.conf`:

```
kernel.sysrq=1
```

If this file is modified, either execute the `sysctl -p` command to enable immediately or use the `echo` command to modify the value of the virtual file.

To execute these system requests on an x86 or x86_64 system, use the key combination Alt-SysRq-<commandkey>. Most modern keyboards have the SysRq key labeled. If yours does not, it is the same as the PrintScreen key. Key combinations for other architectures vary. However, on any architecture, you can always use the `echo` command to change the value of `/proc/sysrq-trigger` to the "command key" part of the key combination. For example, to execute the Alt-SysRq-m system request, use the following command:

```
echo m > /proc/sysrq-trigger
```

Table 21.2 lists the available command keys for executing system requests.

TABLE 21.2 List of AltSysRq Keys

Key	Description
r	Turn off raw mode for the keyboard and turn on XLATE.
k	Secure Access Key (SAK). Kill all programs on the current virtual console.
b	Immediately reboot the system without syncing memory to disk or unmounting disks. The command keys s and u to sync and remount all filesystems as read-only should be attempted first.
c	Perform a Kexec reboot so a crash dump can be taken.
o	Shut down the system.
s	Sync all mounted filesystems, if possible. Should be used before rebooting to try and minimize data loss. When the sync is finished the `OK` and `Done` messages will appear.
u	Remount all mounted filesystems as read-only, if possible.
p	Display value of all current registers and flags to the console.
t	Display current task list to the console.
m	Display current memory information to the console.
v	Display Voyager SMP processor information to the console.
0-9	Set what type of kernel messages are displayed to the console, or the console log level. If set to `0`, only emergency messages such as PANICs or OOPSes are printed. The higher the number, the more messages are printed.
f	Execute the OOM killer.
e	Terminate all processes except init with a SIGTERM signal.
i	Kill all processes except init with a SIGKILL signal.
l	Kill all processes including init with a SIGKILL signal, causing the system to be nonfunctional.
h	Display help.

Saving Kernel Dumps for Analysis

When the kernel crashes, sometimes a snapshot, or "dump" of the system memory, can be used to determine why the kernel crashes without having to reproduce the problem. Red Hat Enterprise Linux includes the Kdump utility to save the kernel dump. It replaces the Netdump and Diskdump utilities from previous versions of Red Hat Enterprise Linux. The kernel dump file can be analyzed by the `crash` program after it is saved.

Kdump has two major advantages over netdump and diskdump. First, the same program can be used to save the kernel dump to a local file or over the network. Previously, diskdump had to be used to save to a local file and netdump had to be used to save over the network. Second, Kdump uses Kexec to boot in to a second kernel without rebooting the crashed kernel, thus giving you a better chance of capturing the dump file.

Kdump and Kexec are features compiled into the kernel. However, the `kexec-tools` RPM package must also be installed because it includes the utilities to configure Kexec and Kdump. On the ppc64 architecture only, the `kernel-kdump` RPM package is also required for Kdump to function properly. The `kexec-tools` package (and the `kernel-kdump` package for ppc64) should already be installed. If it is not, refer to Chapter 3 for instructions on installing RPM packages from Red Hat Network.

This section describes how to capture a kernel dump when the system crashes and then how to analyze its contents.

NOTE

Kdump is only available for the i686, x86_64, ia64, and ppc64 kernels in Red Hat Enterprise Linux.

The Kdump program cannot be used with the Virtualization kernels. If the output of the `uname -r` command ends in `xen`, you are running a Virtualization kernel. Refer to the "Installing a New Kernel" section of Chapter 5 for details on booting a different kernel.

Booting with Kexec

Kexec is usually used in conjunction with Kdump to boot into a secondary kernel so that the memory from the initial kernel is preserved. However, it can be used alone to perform a *warm reboot*. A warm reboot uses the context of the running kernel to reboot the system without going through the BIOS, resulting in a faster boot time.

To perform a warm reboot with Kexec, use the following steps:

1. Load the kernel to boot in to the currently running kernel (must be executed as the root user):

   ```
   kexec -l /boot/vmlinuz-`uname -r` --initrd=/boot/initrd-`uname -r`.img \
           --command-line="`cat /proc/cmdline`"
   ```

   Notice that the command includes three commands in back quotes (`uname -r` twice and `cat /proc/cmdline`). Because these commands are in back quotes, the results of the commands replace the back quotes and the commands when the entire command is executed. Because `uname -r` returns the currently running kernel, this `kexec` command will reboot into the same kernel version. To boot in to a different kernel, use the different kernel version instead.

   The `cat /proc/cmdline` command embedded in the `kexec` command sets the kernel parameters to be used for the warm reboot to the parameters used to boot the currently running kernel. To use different parameters, list them instead.

2. Reboot the system and watch the warm reboot. This can be performed by executing the reboot command as root from the command line or selecting **System, Shut Down** from the desktop menus.

As the system reboots, you will notice that after going through the normal shutdown process, you see the Linux startup messages immediately. You do not see the system BIOS or the GRUB boot loader.

The Kexec program has command-line options in addition to the `-l` option to load a new kernel. Command-line options for all architectures can be found in Table 21.3. Additional command-line options exist per architecture. Execute the `kexec -h` command to view a list of these arch-specific options.

TABLE 21.3 Command-Line Options for `kexec`

Command-Line Option	Description
`-h`	Display list of command-line options with brief descriptions.
`-v`	Display the Kexec version.
`-f`	Force an immediate warm boot without calling shutdown.
`-x`	Do not bring down the network interfaces. Must be the last option specified.
`-l <vmlinuz-file>`	Load the specified kernel into the current loaded kernel.
`-p`	Load the new kernel for use on panic.
`-u`	Unload the currently loaded Kexec kernel.
`-e`	Execute the currently loaded Kexec kernel. The `kexec -e` command will reboot the system with the kernel loaded with the `-l` command.
`-t=<type>`	Provide the type of the kernel loaded with the `-l` option.
`--mem-min=<addr>`	Provide the lowest memory address to load code into.
`--mem-max=<addr>`	Provide the highest memory address to load code into.

Reserving Memory for the Secondary Kernel

Even though Kdump is compiled into the kernel, you must enable it and configure a few settings such as how much memory to reserve for the second kernel booted with Kexec and where to save the kernel dump file.

If Kdump is activated, when a crash occurs, Kexec is used to boot in to a second kernel. This second kernel captures the kernel dump file. This is possible because the first kernel reserves memory for the second kernel to boot. The second kernel can boot with very little memory. Because the reserved memory is used to boot the second kernel, the memory contents of the first kernel are still available for the second kernel to create the dump file.

The amount of reserved memory is set as a kernel parameter in the boot loader configuration file. For x86 and x86_64, edit the `/etc/grub.conf` file as root and append the following to the end of the `kernel` line in the active boot stanza:

```
crashkernel=128M@16M
```

For ia64 systems, edit `/etc/elilo.conf` as root and add the following to the end of the line starting with `append` in the active boot stanza:

```
crashkernel=256M@256M
```

For ppc64 systems, edit the `/etc/yaboot.conf` file as root and add the following to the end of the line starting with `append` in the active boot stanza (remember to enable the changes by executing `/sbin/ybin` after saving the changes to the file):

```
crashkernel=128M@16M
```

The two values in this parameter represent the amount of memory to reserve for the secondary kernel and the memory offset at which to start the reserved memory, respectively. Notice that at least 128 MB should be reserved for x86, x86_64, and ppc64 systems. At least 256 MB must be reserved for the ia64 architecture.

The system must be rebooted with this new boot parameter so that the set amount of memory is reserved. After rebooting, notice that the amount of free memory is the total amount of memory for the system minus the amount of reserved memory.

Selecting Location for Dump File

Next, decide whether to save the dump file to a local or remote filesystem. Both local and remote filesystems have their advantages. Writing to the local filesystem doesn't require the network connection to be functioning properly after a kernel crash. It can be much faster and more reliable depending on your network transfer speeds and the state of the network card driver. Imagine the impact of saving a 36 GB file over the network. It could cause the rest of the network to slow to a halt. If the system is in production, this could mean failure for all other packet transfers. If network transfer is critical to the system, such as a system accepting orders or stock trades, slowing down the network isn't acceptable. Also, if the network is not working properly on the system, the crash file might not ever get written to the remote filesystem.

TIP

If you need to send the crash file to someone such as Red Hat Support, you can compress the file to make it smaller with the `gzip` or `bzip` utilities.

However, writing to a local filesystem also means having enough dedicated disk space on the system for the kernel dump file. If you have a network file server set up on your network, it might be more convenient to write to a dedicated directory on it instead. Writing to a network location also has the advantage of being able to write all kernel dumps from all systems on the network to one central location.

NOTE

The dump file can be quite large—the size of the physical memory plus a header field, so saving the file might take a considerable amount of time and require a significant amount of available disk space. Be sure you have plenty of free disk space in the configured location. It should be at least as big as the total memory for the system.

If no location is specified, the dump file is written to the /var/crash/ directory, which must exist on a mounted filesystem. The following alternate location types can be set in /etc/kdump.conf:

CAUTION

If you modify the contents of /etc/kdump.conf after Kdump is already running, be sure to enable the changes by executing the service kdump restart command.

- *Dedicated partition*: The partition should be formatted but not mounted. The /var/crash/<date>/ directory is created on the partition, and the core dump file is written to the directory. Multiple dump files can be written to the partition assuming it has enough disk space. Specify the filesystem type for the partition (acceptable types are ext2, ext3, vfat, msdos, and cramfs) as well as the partition device name, disk label, or UUID:

  ```
  <fstype> <partition>
  ```

  Some examples include the following:

  ```
  ext3 /dev/sda5
  ext3 LABEL=kdump
  vfat UUID=b97e45eb-6610-4a3b-ad27-6cab8e7f2faf
  ```

- *Raw disk partition*: The partition should exist on the local system, but it should not be formatted. When a crash occurs, the dump file is written to the raw partition using the dd utility. One more dump file can be written to the raw partition at a time. In kdump.conf, replace <partition> with the partition device name such as /dev/sda5:

  ```
  raw <partition>
  ```

- *NFS mounted filesystem*: The NFS server must accept connections from the system and allow the root user of the crashed system to write to it. The NFS share does not have to be mounted. It will be mounted before attempting to write the dump file to it. If a hostname is used as the server name, the system must be able to resolve it to an IP address, or an IP address can be used.

  Each dump file is written to /var/crash/<host>-<date>/ in the specified NFS shared directory. The hostname of the crash system and the date are used in the directory path so that the server can store multiple dump files, assuming enough disk space is available. Replace the NFS server and directory name such as fileserver.example.com:/kdump:

  ```
  net <nfsserver>:<nfsdir>
  ```

- *Remote SSH filesystem*: The SSH server must accept connections from the system, and SSH keys must be set up for the SSH user provided. After configuring SSH keys for the user as discussed in Chapter 17, "Securing Remote Logins with OpenSSH," execute the `service kdump propagate` command as the root user to enter the SSH passphrase and allow the specified user to transfer files to the SSH server without being prompted for a password or passphrase.

  Because this user now has SSH access to the SSH server without having to enter a password, it is recommended that you use a dedicated SSH user for Kdump. The user should only have access to write to the designated directory for saving dump files. The `scp` utility is used for the transfer.

  Each dump file is written to `/var/crash/<host>-<date>/` in the specified shared directory on the SSH server. The hostname of the crash system and the date are used in the directory path so that the server can store multiple dump files, assuming enough disk space is available. Replace the username and the server name such as `kdump@fileserver.example.com`:

  ```
  net <user@server>
  ```

For all of these location options except the raw partition, the `path` option in `kdump.conf` determines the directory path appended to the end of the desired location. If a path is not set, the core file is saved in the `/var/crash/` directory inside the set location. To change this directory, add the following line to `/etc/kdump.conf`:

```
path <directory>
```

Additional Kdump Options

Two more options exist in the `/etc/kdump.conf` file:

- *Compression and filtering*: Use the `makedumpfile` program included with the `kexec-tools` package to compress or filter the core dump file. Compression can greatly decrease the size of the dump file, which is useful for systems with limited disk space or network transfers. Cannot be used if the save location is a raw partition or a remote SSH filesystem. After specifying a location in `/etc/kdump.conf`, add the following line (execute the `makedumpfile -h` command to view a list of options) :

  ```
  core_collector makedumpfile <options>
  ```

- *Default action*: If Kdump is configured to save to the local filesystem, the system reboots after saving the file, regardless of whether the save was successful or not. For any of the other save locations fails, Kdump tries to save to the local filesystem and then reboots. If you want to Kdump to skip trying to save to the local filesystem after it fails to write to a different location, add the following line to the end of `/etc/kdump.conf`:

  ```
  default <action>
  ```

  Replace `<action>` with `reboot` to reboot the system after failing or `shell` so that you can try to save the dump file manually.

Starting and Stopping the Kdump Service

After dedicating memory for the secondary kernel started with Kexec and setting the location in which to save the dump file, start the Kdump service as root:

```
service kdump start
```

NOTE

Each time Kdump is started, the options from `/etc/sysconfig/kdump` are used such as any additional command-line options to pass to the kernel. For most cases, this file does not need to be modified. The file contains comments describing each option should you need to modify them.

Other commands include (use with `service kdump <command>`):

- `stop`: Stop the Kdump service.
- `status`: Determine whether or not the Kdump service is running.
- `restart`: Stop and start the Kdump service. Must be used to enable changes to the `/etc/kdump.conf` file.
- `condrestart`: If and only if the Kdump service is already running, restart it.
- `propagate`: If an SSH server is configured in `/etc/kdump.conf` as the remote location on which to save the dump file, this command must be run to enter the passphrase so the given user can transfer the dump file without being prompted for a passphrase or password.

To have Kdump start at boot time, execute the following as root:

```
chkconfig kdump on
```

Activating Kdump with a Graphical Application

Red Hat Enterprise Linux also includes a graphical program for configuring Kdump. Start it by selecting **Administration**, **Kdump** from the **System** menu on the top panel of the desktop or by executing the `system-config-kdump` command. If you are a non-root user, you are prompted for the root password to continue.

As you can see from Figure 21.1, all the previously discussed options can be set, starting with the amount of reserved memory. Click the **Edit Location** button to select a location other than the default `/var/crash/` directory. The **Default Action** pulldown menu is equivalent to the `default` option in `kdump.conf` previously described in the "Additional Kdump Options" section. The **Core Collector** field is equivalent to the `core_collector` option while the **Path** field is equivalent to the `path` option that lets you set a different directory to append to the selected location. Both of these options were also discussed in the previous section "Additional Kdump Options." The **Core Collector** and **Path** options will only accept input if they can be used with the selected location.

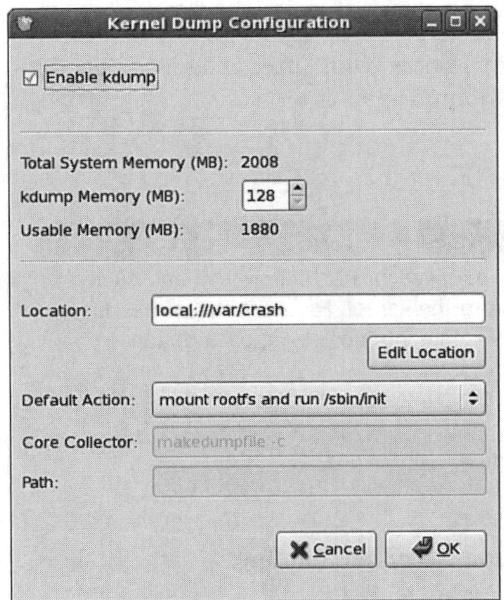

FIGURE 21.1 Kdump Graphical Configuration

Click **OK** to save the changes to the Kdump configuration file and the GRUB boot loader configuration file. If you just enabled Kdump or changed the amount of reserved memory, a message appears reminding you that you must reboot the system for the changes to take effect. This allows the set amount of memory to be reserved for the secondary kernel should a crash occur.

Testing Kdump

Because it is difficult to know whether Kdump is working before you have a kernel crash, there is a way to force a kernel crash.

```
echo c > /proc/sysrq-trigger
```

As soon as the command is execute, there should be a panic, and the system should be unresponsive. Then, the system should restart into the second kernel using Kexec. Because Kexec is used, you will not see the BIOS or GRUB boot screen. After the dump file is created and saved, the system is rebooted into the normal kernel. This time you will see the BIOS and GRUB screens. Depending on how big your system memory is, this entire process might take a while.

Refer to the next section "Analyzing the Crash" to learn how to gather information from this dump file.

Analyzing the Crash

The location of the dump file depends on the location you selected in `/etc/kdump.conf`. If no location is set in `kdump.conf`, the `vmcore` file is written to the `/var/crash/<date>/`

directory. If the location is set to a partition, the `vmcore` file can be found in the `/var/crash/<date>/` directory inside the directory in which the partition is mounted. If a network location (NFS or SSH) is configured, the `vmcore` file is transferred to the `/var/crash/<host>-<date>/` directory inside the directory specified along with the network server name. If a raw partition is used, the contents of the core dump are located on the raw partition. Remember that if an alternate directory is set with the `path` variable, the `/var/crash/` directory in these locations should be replaced with this different directory.

After a `vmcore` file is created, it can be interactively analyzed with the `crash` program. Make sure you have the `crash` RPM installed to use it. The `vmlinux` file for the kernel is also required to use `crash`. It is provided by the `kernel-debuginfo` package. A `kernel-debuginfo` package exists for each kernel version, so be sure to install the correct version. It is available via FTP from the ftp.redhat.com FTP server. After logging in as an anonymous user, change into the `pub/redhat/linux/enterprise/<version>/en/os/<arch>/Debuginfo/` directory, replacing `<version>` and `<arch>` with the appropriate values for your system such as 5Server for the `<version>` and `x86_64` for the `<arch>`. You can also view the list of packages by visiting http://ftp.redhat.com/ in a web browser.

To start analyzing the file, execute the command `crash <vmlinux> <vmcore>` as the root `user`. Be sure to use the full path to the `<vmcore>` if it is not in the current directory. (replace `<kernel-version>` with the kernel version that was running when the crash occurred):

```
crash /usr/lib/debug/lib/modules/<kernel-version>/vmlinux vmcore
```

Starting the utility displays the output from Listing 21.5.

LISTING 21.5 Starting the `crash` Utility

```
crash 4.0-3.11
Copyright  2002, 2003, 2004, 2005, 2006  Red Hat, Inc.
Copyright  2004, 2005, 2006  IBM Corporation
Copyright  1999-2006  Hewlett-Packard Co
Copyright  2005  Fujitsu Limited
Copyright  2005  NEC Corporation
Copyright  1999, 2002  Silicon Graphics, Inc.
Copyright  1999, 2000, 2001, 2002  Mission Critical Linux, Inc.
This program is free software, covered by the GNU General Public License,
and you are welcome to change it and/or distribute copies of it under
certain conditions.  Enter "help copying" to see the conditions.
This program has absolutely no warranty.  Enter "help warranty" for details.

GNU gdb 6.1
Copyright 2004 Free Software Foundation, Inc.
GDB is free software, covered by the GNU General Public License, and you are
welcome to change it and/or distribute copies of it under certain conditions.
```

LISTING 21.5 Continued

```
Type "show copying" to see the conditions.
There is absolutely no warranty for GDB.  Type "show warranty" for details.
This GDB was configured as "x86_64-unknown-linux-gnu"...

      KERNEL: /usr/lib/debug/lib/modules/2.6.18-1.2747.el5/vmlinux
    DUMPFILE: vmcore
        CPUS: 2
        DATE: Fri Jan 12 15:31:26 2007
      UPTIME: 00:04:20
LOAD AVERAGE: 0.31, 0.31, 0.14
       TASKS: 168
    NODENAME: myhostname
     RELEASE: 2.6.18-1.2747.el5
     VERSION: #1 SMP Thu Nov 9 18:52:11 EST 2006
     MACHINE: x86_64  (2400 Mhz)
      MEMORY: 2 GB
       PANIC: "SysRq : Trigger a crashdump"
         PID: 4254
     COMMAND: "bash"
        TASK: ffff81007fb02040  [THREAD_INFO: ffff810060036000]
         CPU: 0
       STATE: TASK_RUNNING (SYSRQ)
crash>
```

After you receive the `crash>` prompt, you can execute any of the `crash` commands listed in the man page (execute `man crash` to view) to analyze the `vmcore` file. For example, the `vm` command shows basic virtual memory information, and the `bt` command shows the backtrace. The information shown for each of these commands is what was stored in memory at the time of the system crash.

TIP

At the `crash>` prompt, type `help` at any time to display a list of commands. You can also type `help <command>` to display help for a specific command.

The default editor used when in a crash session is Vi. To change to the Emacs editor, create a `.crashrc` file in your home directory with the following line:

```
set emacs
```

This setting must be configured per user. To specifically set Vi as the editor during the `crash` session, include the following line in a `.crashrc` file in your home directory:

```
set vi
```

Setting SMP IRQ Affinity

If you have ever explored your system's BIOS or reviewed your system's configuration, you have probably noticed that hardware such as the Ethernet card or the sound card is assigned an *IRQ*. This IRQ allows the hardware to send event requests to the processor or processors in the system. When the hardware sends a request, it is called an *interrupt*.

For multi-processor systems, the Linux kernel balances interrupts across processors according to the type of requests. It is possible to configure the kernel to send interrupts from a specific IRQ to a designated processor or group of processors. This concept is known by the Linux kernel as *SMP IRQ affinity*. First, determine which IRQs are being used and by what hardware from the `/proc/interrupts` file.

CAUTION

Be extremely careful when using SMP IRQ affinity. Assigning too many interrupts to a single processor can cause a performance degradation. In most cases, the IRQ balancing done by the kernel is the most optimal solution.

In our example `/proc/interrupts` file as shown in Listing 21.6, the first column is a list of used IRQs, and the next two columns request the number of interrupts sent to each processor. SMP IRQ affinity is only possible with interrupts on the IO-APIC controller, which is displayed in the second to last column. The last column is the kernel module or device associated with the IRQ.

LISTING 21.6 Example `/proc/interrupts`

```
           CPU0       CPU1
  0:   10293911   10289264    IO-APIC-edge  timer
  1:       3958       4135    IO-APIC-edge  i8042
  8:          3          0    IO-APIC-edge  rtc
  9:          0          0   IO-APIC-level  acpi
 14:     148702     149207    IO-APIC-edge  ide0
 50:       6967       6924   IO-APIC-level  uhci_hcd:usb1, ehci_hcd:usb5
 58:        171          0   IO-APIC-level  HDA Intel
 66:    6222841          0         PCI-MSI  eth0
169:          0          0   IO-APIC-level  uhci_hcd:usb4
177:          0          0   IO-APIC-level  libata
225:          3          0   IO-APIC-level  uhci_hcd:usb3, ohci1394
233:      95803      90174   IO-APIC-level  libata, uhci_hcd:usb2
NMI:          0          0
LOC:   20654428   20654427
ERR:          0
MIS:          0
```

Each IRQ being used has its own directory in `/proc/irq/`, where the directory name is the IRQ number, and each of these directories has a file named `smp_affinity` in it. Each of these `smp_affinity` files contains a number in bitmask in hexadecimal format, representing which processor or processors to send interrupts to.

This bitmask number contains eight numbers, each representing four processors. The first four processors are represented by the right-most number, the second four processors are represented by the number to the left of that, and so on, for a total of 32 processors.

In hex notation, the numbers 0 through 9 represent the decimal numbers 0 through 9, and the numbers a through f represent the decimal numbers 10 through 15. To determine the hexadecimal number for each processor, its binary number must be converted to hex. Table 21.4 shows the binary to hex conversion.

TABLE 21.4 Binary to Hex Conversion

Processor Number	Binary	Hex
1	0001	1
2	0010	2
3	0100	4
4	1000	8

When setting SMP IRQ affinity, add the hexadecimal values of two or more processors if you want to assign more than one processor to an IRQ. For example, to represent the first and fourth processors, adding the hex numbers 1 and 8 results in the hex number 9. Adding hex numbers 4 and 8 for the third and fourth processors results in hex number c. All four processors are represented by the hex number f.

To set the SMP IRQ affinity for a specific interrupt, use the `echo` command to change the value of `/proc/irq/<irqnum>/smp_affinity`. In Listing 21.6, the Ethernet controller uses IRQ 66. Using the `cat /proc/irq/66/smp_affinity` command shows all Ethernet controller interrupts are sent to the first processor. To send interrupts to both processors, use the following command:

```
echo 2 > /proc/irq/66/smp_affinity
```

The `taskset` utility allows administrators to configure SMP IRQ affinity for a specific process by process ID (pid). Use the `ps` or `top` command to determine the pid of a process. To determine the SMP IRQ affinity for a running process, use the following command:

```
taskset -p <pid>
```

To set the SMP IRQ affinity for a running process:

```
taskset -p <bitmask> <pid>
```

To start a process with a specific SMP IRQ affinity:

```
taskset <bitmask> <command>
```

For the last two commands, instead of using the bitmask, the `-c <cpulist>` option can be used to specify the processors, where `<cpulist>` is a comma-separated list of processor numbers. The numbering starts at 0. So, `0` represents the first processor, `1` represents the second processor, and so on. A hyphen can be used to list sequential processor numbers such as `2-4`.

Enabling NMI Watchdog for Locked Systems

If you are experiencing hard system locks where the computer, even the keyboard, stops responding, it can be quite frustrating and difficult to diagnose. However, if you have an x86 and x86_64 system with APIC (Advanced Programmable Interrupt Controller), you most likely have a system capable of producing NMI (Non Maskable Interrupts) even if the system seems locked and unresponsive. The kernel can execute these interrupts and generate debugging information about the locked system.

NOTE

NMI watchdog and OProfile (discussed in Chapter 22, "Monitoring and Tuning Applications") cannot be run simultaneously. OProfile will automatically disable NMI watchdog if it is enabled when the OProfile daemon is started.

NMI watchdog has two modes:

- *Local APIC*: capable of generating inter-processor interrupts and external processor interrupts
- *I/O APIC*: capable of producing interrupts from I/O buses and redirecting them to the local APIC

To enable profiling and NMI watchdog, add the `profile=2` and `watchdog=1` boot options to the `kernel` line of the `/etc/grub.conf` boot loader configuration file for the default boot stanza being used as shown in Listing 21.7. The kernel line has been divided into two lines with a backward slash (\) for printing purposes. The content should be all on one line in your configuration file.

LISTING 21.7 Enabling Profiling and NMI Watchdog

```
default=0
timeout=5
splashimage=(hd0,0)/grub/splash.xpm.gz
hiddenmenu
title Red Hat Enterprise Linux (2.6.17-1.2174smp)
   root (hd0,0)
   kernel /vmlinuz-2.6.17-1.2174smp ro root=/dev/sda1 rhgb \
      quiet profile=2 nmi_watchdog=1
   initrd /initrd-2.6.17-1.2174smp.img
```

Setting nmi_watchdog to 1 enables I/O APIC. To enable local APIC instead, set its value to 2. To verify that NMI watchdog and profiling are enabled, make sure the /proc/profile file exists.

How does NMI watchdog work? A lockup is defined as the processor not executing the local timer interrupt more than 5 seconds from the last timer interrupt. If a lockup occurs, the NMI handler generates a kernel oops, writes debug messages, and kills the process causing the lockup. If the lockup is so bad an NMI interrupt can't be issued or the kernel can't write debug messages, NMI watchdog cannot work.

Local APIC works with the *cycles unhalted* processor event, meaning that it can only be triggered to write debug messages if the processor is not idle. If a system lockup occurs while the processor is idle, watchdog will not be triggered. On the other hand, the I/O APIC works with events outside the processor, but its frequency is higher, which can cause more impact on the overall performance of the system.

The /proc/profile file is not written in a human-readable format. The readprofile utility must be used to read the data. The System.map file for the currently running kernel must be specified with the -m <map> option such as the following:

```
readprofile -m /boot/System-map-`uname -r`
```

TIP

The output can be quite lengthy. To redirect the output to a file, append > filename.txt to the end of the command as follows:

```
readprofile -m /boot/System-map-`uname -r` > filename.txt
```

If no other options are passed to the command, the output is in three columns: the number of clock ticks, the name of C function in the kernel where those click ticks occurred, and the normalized load of the procedure as a ratio of the number of ticks to the procedure length. Table 21.5 describes the available command-line options.

TABLE 21.5 Command-Line Options for readprofile

Command-Line Option	Description
-m <map>	Provide the location of the System.map file for the running kernel.
-i	Output the profiling step used by the kernel. Use with -t to only print the number.
-a	List symbols in map file.
-b	List the individual histogram-bin counts.
-r	Reset the profiling buffer /proc/profile. Because only root can write to the file, this option can only be executed as root.
-M <multiplier>	Set the frequency at which the kernel sends profiling interrupts to the processor. Frequency should be set as a multiplier of the system clock frequency, which is in Hertz. Resets the buffer file as well. Only executable by root. Not available on all processors.

TABLE 21.5 Continued

-v	Display verbose output in four columns instead of three. The four columns, in the order in which they appear, are the RAM address of the kernel function, the name of the C function in the kernel where the clock ticks occurred, the number of clock ticks, and the normalized load of the procedure as a ratio of the number of ticks to the procedure length.
-p <file>	Use `<file>` instead of the default `/proc/profile` buffer file. For example, the kernel profile at a specific point in time can be saved by copying `/proc/profile` to a different file. Then, the data can be analyzed later.
-V	Output the version of `readprofile`.

The output can be further customized by piping the results through shell utilities such as `sort`, `head`, `tail`, `grep`, and `less`. For example, to sort the output by the number of clock ticks, list the highest numbers first:

```
readprofile -m /boot/System-map-`uname -r` | sort -nr
```

Or, to search for a specific function name:

```
readprofile -m /boot/System-map-`uname -r` | grep <function-name>
```

Profiling with SystemTap

Recently, kprobes, or kernel dynamic probes, have been added to the kernel. These probes allow you to add probes into the kernel for system diagnostics as a kernel module instead of having to modify the kernel source code before recompiling the kernel.

Since then, a project called SystemTap has been started to create a command-line interface and scripting language for kprobes, making it easier to use.

CAUTION

SystemTap is still in development and rapidly changing. It may not be available on all architectures. This section discusses how to get started and how to find the latest information on it. SystemTap is not ready for production systems and is subject to change during its development.

To use SystemTap, you need to install the following packages: `systemtap`, `kernel-debuginfo`, and `kernel-devel`. Refer to Chapter 3 for details on installing additional software. The `debuginfo` packages are not available from RHN. They can be downloaded via FTP from the ftp.redhat.com FTP server. After logging in as an anonymous user, change into the `pub/redhat/linux/enterprise/<version>/en/os/<arch>/Debuginfo/` directory, replacing `<version>` and `<arch>` with the appropriate values for your system. You can also view the list of packages by visiting http://ftp.redhat.com/ in a web browser, but it is recommended that you use an FTP client to download the files.

To configure kernel probes with SystemTap, you need to write a script using the SystemTap scripting language, which is similar to the Awk scripting language. When saving the script, save it as a text file with the `.stp` file extension. The functions available are defined in the stapfuncs man page accessible with the `man stapfuncs` command. The probe points available for monitoring can be viewed with the `man stapprobes` command. Example scripts can be studied with the `man stapex` command and at http://www.sourceware.org/systemtap/documentation.html.

After writing the script, as root, execute the following command:

```
stap <custom_script>
```

The `stap` program reads the script, converts it to a program written in the C language, compiles the C code into a kernel module, and loads the kernel module. This module is used to gather information about the probes. For more details about the `stap` program, refer to its man page with the `man stap` command. The script will run until the user stops it or if the `exit()` function is called in the script. By default, output from the script is displayed to the command line on which the `stap` command was executed.

Summary

The kernel controls many aspects of the operating system. It can be probed to determine the state of the various subsystems such as the amount of available memory and what processors are assigned to answer IRQ requests from specific hardware devices. While the kernel tries to manage the operating system as efficiently and fast as possible, its algorithms are designed to work for all types of systems. Some of the kernel management decisions can be tuned so they work better for your system's usage and load. Use this chapter to find out more about how your kernel works and if it can be tuned better for any of your systems. Remember to always test your kernel tweaks before modifying the kernel on a production system. Setting some kernel parameters to incorrect values can cause a slow down in performance or, in some cases, can cause the system to become unresponsive or lock up.

CHAPTER 22

Monitoring and Tuning Applications

IN THIS CHAPTER

- OProfile
- Valgrind
- Additional Programs to Consider

Chapter 20, "Monitoring System Resources," covered monitoring and tuning system resources, and Chapter 21, "Monitoring and Tuning the Kernel," discussed monitoring and tuning the kernel, but Part V, "Monitoring and Tuning," would not be complete without discussing application tuning. Because this is a book for administrators, this chapter explains in detail two programs for tuning applications, OProfile and Valgrind, which can also be beneficial for administrators. It also provides brief overviews of additional application tuning programs for those interested.

OProfile

OProfile accesses the performance monitoring hardware on the system's processor if available to gather performance-related data, which can then be used to identify areas for improvement.

To use OProfile, the `oprofile` RPM package must be installed. It can be installed via RHN as described in Chapter 3, "Operating System Updates." The `kernel-debuginfo` package must also be installed to adequately collect data from the kernel. It is available via FTP from the ftp.redhat.com FTP server. After logging in as an anonymous user, change into the /pub/redhat/linux/enterprise/<version>/en/os/<arch>/Debuginfo/ directory, replacing <version> and <arch> with the appropriate values for your system. You can also view the list of packages by visiting http://ftp.redhat.com/ in a web browser, but it is recommended that you download any files using an FTP client instead.

Setting Up OProfile

All OProfile commands must be run as the root user except the `opcontrol --dump`, `opcontrol --list-events`, and `ophelp` commands. Before each profile creation, make sure OProfile is not already running by executing the following command as root:

```
opcontrol --shutdown
```

Also clear any previous data:

```
opcontrol --reset
```

Provide the kernel to profile and set up the OProfile environment (`vmlinux` comes from `kernel-debuginfo`):

```
opcontrol --setup --vmlinux=/usr/lib/debug/lib/modules/`uname -r`/vmlinux
```

In addition to specifying the `vmlinux` file to use, this command loads the `oprofile` kernel module and sets up the `/dev/oprofile/` directory. To verify that the kernel module is loaded, run the command `lsmod | grep oprofile`. At this point, the `/root/.oprofile/daemonrc` file is created (or modified if it already exists) to save the settings as shown in Listing 22.1. As settings are changed as discussed later in this chapter, the values in this file are changed as well so they can be used for subsequent uses of OProfile.

LISTING 22.1 Default OProfile Settings

```
NR_CHOSEN=0
SEPARATE_LIB=0
SEPARATE_KERNEL=0
SEPARATE_THREAD=0
SEPARATE_CPU=0
VMLINUX=/usr/lib/debug/lib/modules/2.6.18-1.2747.el5/vmlinux
IMAGE_FILTER=
CPU_BUF_SIZE=0
CALLGRAPH=0
KERNEL_RANGE=c0400000,c0612de1
XENIMAGE=none
```

Setting Up Events to Monitor

Use the following command to determine the CPU type being used by OProfile:

```
cat /dev/oprofile/cpu_type
```

It displays the processor type such as `i386/p4` or `i386/core_2`. If `timer` is displayed, the processor does not have performance monitoring hardware, so the timer interrupt is being used.

The performance monitoring hardware on the processor contains counters, and the number of counters available depends on the processor type. The number of events that can be monitored by OProfile depends on the number of counters, and in some cases, certain events can only be monitored by a specific counter. If the timer interrupt is used by OProfile, the number of counters is 1.

Execute the ophelp command (equivalent to opcontrol --list-events) to display a list of available events for the system's processor type. The ophelp output is processor-specific and varies from system to system. If specific counters must be used for the event, they are listed with the event. For example, Listing 22.2 shows the MEMORY_COMPLETE event for an i386/p4 processor, which must be profiled with counters 2 and 6.

LISTING 22.2 Counter-Specific Event

```
MEMORY_COMPLETE: (counter: 2, 6)
        completed split (min count: 3000)
        Unit masks (default 0x3)
        ----------
        0x01: load split completed, excluding UC/WC loads
        0x02: any split stores completed
        0x04: uncacheable load split completed
         0x08: uncacheable store split complete
```

If any counter can be used, the keyword all is used for the counter numbers as shown in Listing 22.3 for the MEMORY_DISAMBIGUATION event on an i386/core2 processor.

LISTING 22.3 Event That Can Profiled with All Counters

```
MEMORY_DISAMBIGUATION: (counter: all)
        Memory disambiguation reset cycles. (min count: 1000)
        Unit masks (default 0x1)
        ----------
        0x01: RESET     Memory disambiguation reset cycles.
         0x02: SUCCESS   Number of loads that were successfully disambiguated.
```

For each counter available, the following command can be used to associate an event with it:

```
opcontrol -event=<name>:<sample-rate>:<unit-mask>:<kernel>:<user> \
--separate=<option>
```

The arguments for the command are as follows:

- --event=<name> sets which event to profile. Use the ophelp command to list available events for the system along with brief descriptions for each.
- <sample-rate> is the number of events between sampling. The lower the number, the more samples taken. Use caution when setting the sample rate. If it is set too low, sampling might occur too frequently and slow down the system or make the system appear unresponsive.

- `<unit-mask>` might be necessary for the event profiled. The unit masks for each event are listed with the events from the `ophelp` list. If the `timer` counter is used, a unit mask is not required.
- `<kernel>` set to `1` means that samples will be taken from kernel-space. If set to `0`, kernel-space samples are not gathered.
- `<user>` set to `1` means that samples will be taken from user-space. If set to `0`, user-space samples are not gathered.
- `--separate=<option>` argument can be used to separate kernel and library samples. The following options are available:
    - `none`: Kernel and library profiles are not separated (default).
    - `library`: Separate library samples with the applications they are associated with (recommended).
    - `kernel`: Separate kernel and kernel module samples with the applications they are associated with.
    - `all`: Equivalent to specifying both `library` and `kernel`.

For example, to monitor the `CPU_CLK_UNHALTED` event with a sample rate of `950000` and unit mask of `0` in both the kernel- and user-space, showing library samples with the applications using them, execute the following command:

```
opcontrol --event=CPU_CLK_UNHALTED:950000:0:1:1 --separate=library
```

The settings in `/root/.oprofile/daemonrc` are modified accordingly after specifying an event and options related to the event. If an event is not specified with the `opcontrol` command, the default event for the processor type is used. Table 22.1 shows the default event for some of the processor types. These defaults are all time-based events. The default event can also be retrieved with the following command:

```
ophelp -d -c <cpu_type>
```

Replace `<cpu_type>` with the processor type from the `cat /dev/oprofile/cpu_type` command. You can also combine these commands to get the default event:

```
ophelp -d -c `cat /dev/oprofile/cpu_type`
```

TABLE 22.1 Default Processor Events

Processor	**Default Event**
Intel Pentium Pro, Pentium II, Pentium III, AMD Athlon, AMD64, Core2 Duo	CPU_CLK_UNHALTED
Pentium 4 (HT and non-HT)	GLOBAL_POWER_EVENTS
Intel Itanium and Itanium 2	CPU_CYCLES
ppc64/power4	CYCLES

TABLE 22.1 Continued

ppc64/power5	CYCLES
ppc64/970	CYCLES
ppc64/power5+	CYCLES

Starting OProfile

Finally, to start the sampling process, execute the following as root:

```
opcontrol --start
```

The settings from `/root/.oprofile/daemonrc` are used, and the daemon `oprofiled` is started. The output should look similar to Listing 22.4.

LISTING 22.4 Starting OProfile

```
Using default event: CPU_CLK_UNHALTED:100000:0:1:1
Using 2.6+ OProfile kernel interface.
Reading module info.
Using log file /var/lib/oprofile/oprofiled.log
Daemon started.
Profiler running.
```

Gathering the Samples

The samples collected are written to the `/var/lib/oprofile/samples/` directory, and `/var/lib/oprofile/oprofiled.log` is used as the log file for the daemon.

To force the sample data to be written, use the following command as root:

```
opcontrol --save=<name>
```

The `/var/lib/oprofile/samples/<name>/` directory is created, and the sample data is written to the directory.

Analyzing the Samples

Before analyzing the samples in the `/var/lib/oprofile/samples/` directory, make sure all data has been written out by executing the following command as root (data is flushed to the `/var/lib/oprofile/samples/current/` directory):

```
opcontrol --dump
```

After running the OProfile daemon to collect your data and writing the data to disk, OProfile can be stopped by executing the following command as root:

```
opcontrol --stop
```

When OProfile is stopped, the daemon is stopped, meaning that it stops collecting samples. Reports can also be generated while the daemon is running if you need to collect samples at set intervals.

Two tools, `opreport` and `opannotate`, can be used to analyze the OProfile samples. The exact executables used to generate the samples must be used with these tools to analyze the data. If they need to be changed after collecting the data, back up the executables with the sample data before updating the executables on the system.

Using `opreport` to Analyze Samples

If `opreport` is run without any arguments, the number of samples per executable along with their percentages relative to the total number of samples are displayed as shown in Listing 22.5.

LISTING 22.5 Example Output from opreport

```
CPU: Core 2, speed 1596 MHz (estimated)
Counted CPU_CLK_UNHALTED events (Clock cycles when not halted)
with a unit mask of 0x00 (Unhalted core cycles) count 100000
CPU_CLK_UNHALT...¦
  samples¦      %¦
------------------
  1233664 50.0256 vmlinux
   286210 11.6059 libfb.so
   150459  6.1012 libc-2.5.so
   139635  5.6623 libpthread-2.5.so
   103056  4.1790 libglib-2.0.so.0.1200.3
    41031  1.6638 libperl.so
    34991  1.4189 libsw680lx.so
    34311  1.3913 libvcl680lx.so
    29216  1.1847 dbus-daemon
    28631  1.1610 Xorg
    25432  1.0313 libuno_sal.so.3
    25125  1.0188 libdbus-1.so.3.0.0
    19195  0.7784 libgobject-2.0.so.0.1200.3
    18094  0.7337 e1000
    17945  0.7277 libpython2.4.so.1.0
    13699  0.5555 libcairo.so.2.9.2
    13477  0.5465 libgklayout.so
    12966  0.5258 libata
    12545  0.5087 oprofiled
    11922  0.4834 libmozjs.so
     9604  0.3894 libX11.so.6.2.0
     8631  0.3500 libsfx680lx.so
     8023  0.3253 libgdk-x11-2.0.so.0.1000.4
     7880  0.3195 oprofile
[truncated due to length]
```

To further customize the report, provide the full path to an executable:

```
opcontrol <option> <executable>
```

The <executable> must include the full path and must be the exact executable used when collecting the samples.

The output can be customized in a variety of ways using command-line options such as opreport -a --symbols to list the symbols in addition to the default information shown. Refer to Table 22.2 for a list of command-line options for opreport.

TABLE 22.2 Command-Line Options for opreport

Command-Line Option	Description
-a	Display accumulated sample and percentage counts in the symbol list.
-g	Display source file and line number for each symbol in the symbol list.
-D <demangler>	Set <demangler> to none, smart, or normal. If set to none, there is no demangling. If set to normal, the default demangler is used. If set to smart, pattern-matching is used to make symbol demangling more readable.
-c	Display call graph data if available.
-d	Display per-instruction details for selected symbols.
-x	If --separate is used, using this option excludes application-specific images for libraries, kernel modules, and the kernel.
-e <symbols>	Exclude the comma-separated list of symbols from the symbols list.
-%	Calculate percentages as percentages relative to the entire profile.
--help	Display brief usage and command-line options list.
-p <paths>	Search for binaries in the comma-separated list of directory paths.
-i <symbols>	Only include these symbols in the symbols list. List should be comma separated.
-f	Display full paths instead of just filenames.
-m <profiles>	Merge comma-separated list of profiles that were separated with --separate. List of profiles can include lib, cpu, tid, tgid, unitmask, and all.
--no-header	Don't display header.
-o <file>	Write output to <file>.
-r	Sort in the reverse order.
-w	Display the VMA address of each symbol.
-s <sort>	Sort the symbols list by method given by <sort>. <sort> can be one of the following: vma: Sort by symbol address. sample: Sort by the number of samples. symbol: Sort by symbol name. debug: Sort by debug filename and line number. image: Sort by binary image filename.
-l	Display per-symbol information in list instead of binary image summary.

TABLE 22.2 Continued

`-t <percentage>`	Only display data for symbols with more than the provided percentage of total samples.
`-V`	Display verbose output. Useful for debugging.
`-v`	Display `opreport` version.

Using `opannotate` to Analyze Samples

The `opannotate` utility generates an annotated listing of the assembly or source code along with the samples. To compile an annotated list of the assembly, use the following command:

```
opannotate --assembly <executable>
```

Producing an annotated listing of the source code is possible with a similar command:

```
opannotate --source <executable>
```

However, the executable has to contain debug information. If the program is in C or C++, debug information can be created by using the `-g` option to `gcc`. By default, the software distributed with Red Hat Enterprise Linux is not compiled with debug information. However, the debug information necessary to produce meaningful output with `opannotate` can be installed using the associated `debuginfo` RPM packages. Just as the `kernel-debuginfo` package was installed so kernel data could be sampled, other packages have equivalent packages such as `bash-debuginfo` and `httpd-debuginfo`. The debug files from these packages are installed in the `/usr/lib/debug/` directory. Again, these `debuginfo` packages can be downloaded from the ftp.redhat.com FTP server using anonymous login.

> **TIP**
>
> Refer to the `opannotate` man page with the `man opannotate` command for more command-line options such as `-e <symbols>` to exclude certain symbols from the list.

OProfile Review

The following is a summary of all the commands necessary to use OProfile:

1. Before starting OProfile each time, make sure it is shut down and clear all previous data sampled:

   ```
   opcontrol --shutdown
   opcontrol --reset
   ```

2. Set up which kernel to profile:

   ```
   opcontrol --setup \
   --vmlinux=/usr/lib/debug/lib/modules/`uname -r`/vmlinux
   ```

3. Set up which processor event to sample and whether to separate kernel and library samples:

```
opcontrol -event=<name>:<sample-rate>:<unit-mask>:<kernel>:<user> \
--separate=<option>
```

4. Start the OProfile daemon, which starts the sampling process:

```
opcontrol --start
```

5. Write the samples to disk:

```
opcontrol --dump
```

6. Generate a report about the samples using `opreport`, `opcontrol`, and `opannotate`.

7. After collecting all your samples, stop the daemon and the sampling process:

```
opcontrol --stop
```

Using OProfile Graphically

If the `oprofile-gui` RPM package is installed, you can also use a graphical program to set up OProfile, start OProfile, flush the data to disk, and stop OProfile. You will still need to use `opreport`, `opcontrol`, and `opannotate` to generate reports after the data is flushed to disk.

To start the graphical interface, execute the `oprof_start` command as the root user. On the **Setup** tab shown in Figure 22.1, click on one or more processor events to monitor.

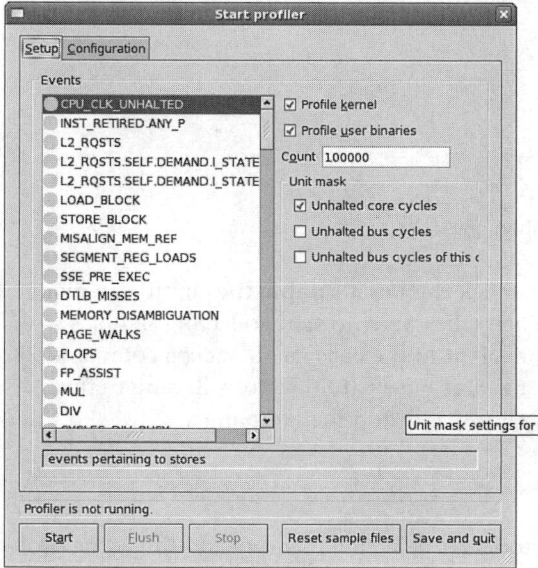

FIGURE 22.1 OProfile Graphical Setup

The interface will only let you select event combinations that work for the number of counters for your processor. If an event is already selected, click it again to unselect it. As you select events, the colored circle icon next to the all the events change colors. If the icon is green, the event may be selected in addition to the already selected ones. If the icon is red, the event cannot be selected in conjunction with the already selected ones.

Placing the mouse cursor over an event displays a brief description of the event at the bottom of the application window. Also notice that as you select events to monitor, you can also select the unit masks specific to the events on the right side of the window. On the right side, also select whether to profile the kernel and/or the user binaries.

On the **Configuration** tab as shown in Figure 22.2, provide the full path to the `vmlinux` file of the kernel to profile. Other configuration options available in the graphical interface include the buffer size and whether to separate the profiles per processor.

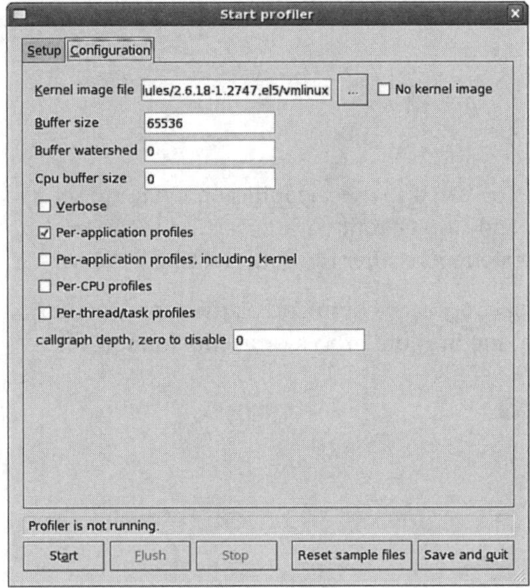

FIGURE 22.2 OProfile Graphical Configuration

After finishing the setup and configuration, click the **Reset sample files** button to make sure all previous sample files are cleared. Then, click **Start** to start collecting samples with the OProfile daemon. Clicking **Flush** is equivalent to the `opcontrol --dump` command. Data is flushed to the `/var/lib/oprofile/samples/current/` directory. Be sure to flush the data before clicking **Stop** to stop the daemon and stop the sampling.

Valgrind

Valgrind is set of debugging and profiling tools for detecting memory and threading problems and profiling programs to determine if their memory management can be improved. For system administrators, Valgrind is useful for analyzing frequently used programs to determine what processes are using the most memory on a system. This information can then be passed on to a development team or, if possible, the program can be replaced by one that requires less memory if necessary. Valgrind currently only works on the following architectures: x86, x86_64, ppc32, and ppc64.

To use Valgrind, start by installing the `valgrind` RPM package. Instructions for installing software can be found in Chapter 3, "Operating System Updates."

Valgrind includes the following tools:

- *Memcheck*: Memory debugging tool. Detects errors in memory management as they occur, giving the source code file and line number of the erroneous code along with a stack trace of functions leading up to that line of code. When using Memcheck, programs run 10 to 30 times slower than usual.
- *Massif*: Heap profiler. Takes snapshots of the heap and generates a graph to show heap usage over time. Also shows the program parts that allocate the most memory. When using Massif, programs run 20 times slower than usual.
- *Cachegrind*: Cache profiler. Identifies cache misses by simulating the processor's cache. When using Cachegrind, programs run 20 to 100 times slower than usual.
- *Callgrind*: Extension of Cachegrind. Provides all the information of Cachegrind plus data about callgraphs.
- *Helgrind*: Thread debugger. Detects memory locations that are used by more than one thread.

For each program to be debugged or profiled by Valgrind, you will need to install the associated `debuginfo` package. Again, these `debuginfo` packages can be downloaded from the ftp.redhat.com FTP server using anonymous login. If you are debugging or profiling a C or C++ program not distributed as a Red Hat Enterprise Linux RPM package, debug information can be compiled with the `-g` argument to `gcc`.

The `valgrind` executable is used to invoke each of these tools with the following syntax:

```
valgrind [options] <program> <program-args>
```

The Memcheck tool is used by default if no tool is specified. To use a different tool, use the `--tool=<name>` option:

```
valgrind --tool=<name> <program> <program-args>
```

The Valgrind program has options available for it, and each tool has specialized options as well. Refer to the Valgrind man page with the `man valgrind` command for the most updated list of options.

NOTE

Because Valgrind is still under development, refer to www.valgrind.org for instructions on how to read the output, detailed documentation on how each of the tools work, and for updates to the tools.

Additional Programs to Consider

Additional debugging and profiling tools exist in Red Hat Enterprise Linux. Some are still considered under development such as Frysk and some are tried-and-true tools such as gdb. Some of the most popular include the following:

- *Frysk:* Monitoring and debugging tool. Still in the early development stages and is not ready for production. It is included in Red Hat Enterprise Linux as a technology preview. For the latest version, additional information, and the status of the project, refer to http://sourceware.org/frysk/.
- *GNU Debugger*: Command-line debugging tool, which can be used as the program runs. Documentation, examples, and more are available at http://www.gnu.org/software/gdb/.
- *DejaGnu*: Testing framework used to create test suites. Part of the GNU family of programs. Go to http://www.gnu.org/software/dejagnu/ for details.
- *Dogtail*: Testing tool used to automate tests for programs with graphical interfaces. For more information, go to http://people.redhat.com/zcerza/dogtail/.
- *lcov*: Determines which parts of a program are executed during a test case. The program page is at http://ltp.sourceforge.net/coverage/lcov.php.

Summary

Even though it is not the primary goal of an administrator to debug programs, some might find these debugging and profiling tools useful when trying to track down a decrease in performance, especially after the addition of a software to the system. OProfile utilizes the performance monitoring hardware of supported processors to analyze program performance. Valgrind is useful for determining memory and threading problems or just comparing the memory usage of two or more programs.

PART VI

Security

IN THIS PART

CHAPTER 23

Protecting Against Intruders with Security-Enhanced Linux

IN THIS CHAPTER

- Selecting an SELinux Mode
- Selecting and Customizing the SELinux Policy
- Utilizing the SELinux Troubleshooting Tool
- Working with Security Contexts

On a system without *Security-Enhanced Linux* (SELinux) enabled, discretionary access control (DAC) is used for file security. Basic file permissions as discussed in Chapter 4, "Understanding Linux Concepts," and optionally access control lists as described in Chapter 7, "Managing Storage," are used to grant file access to users. Users and programs alike are allowed to grant insecure file permissions to others. For users, there is no way for an administrator to prevent a user from granting world-readable and world-writable permissions to his files. For programs, the file operations are performed as the owner of the process, which can be the root user, giving the program access to any file on the system.

SELinux is a mandatory access control (MAC) mechanism, implemented in the kernel. Programs protected by SELinux are only allowed access to parts of the filesystem they require to function properly, meaning that if a program intentionally or unintentionally tries to access or modify a file not necessary for it to function or a file not in a directory controlled by the program, file access is denied and the action is logged.

The ability to protect files with SELinux is implemented in the kernel. Exactly what files and directories are protected and to what extent they are protected is defined by the *SELinux policy*. This chapter gives instructions on how to enable the SELinux protection mechanism, describes the SELinux policies available in Red Hat Enterprise Linux, tells you how to read the SELinux permissions of a file, shows how the SELinux Troubleshooting Tool alerts you of SELinux errors, and steps you through how to change the security context of files.

Selecting an SELinux Mode

When your Red Hat Enterprise Linux system is booted for the first time, the Setup Agent is started as described in Chapter 2. When you reach the SELinux step, the SELinux mode is set to **Enforcing** by default. The following modes are available:

- **Enforcing**: Enable and enforce the SELinux security mechanism on the system, logging any actions denied because of it.
- **Permissive**: Enable SELinux but don't enforce the policy. Only warn about files protected by SELinux.
- **Disabled**: Turn off SELinux.

The SELinux mode can be changed at a later time by using the SELinux Management Tool, a graphical application for customizing SELinux. The `policycoreutils-gui` RPM package must be installed to use this program. Refer to Chapter 3 for details on package installation. Start the tool by executing the `system-config-selinux` command or selecting **Administration, SELinux Management** from the **System** menu of the top panel of the desktop. If you are not the root user, you are prompted to enter the root password before continuing. As shown in Figure 23.1, choose the SELinux mode for the following two options:

- **System Default Enforcing Mode**: The mode to use when the system is booted. Choose between **Enforcing**, **Permissive**, and **Disabled** (described earlier in this section). The mode change does not take place immediately. This preference is written to the `/etc//selinux/config` file. The next time the system is rebooted, this mode is used.

  If the mode is changed from **Disabled** to **Permissive** or **Enforcing**, the filesystem must be relabeled for SELinux during the reboot, which can be quite time-consuming depending on the size of the filesystem. It is highly recommended that the filesystem be backed up before changing modes in case of disk failure or other errors during the conversion process.
- **Current Enforcing Mode**: The SELinux mode current being implemented. If the system was booted into the enforcing or permissive mode, the current mode can be immediately changed between the two without a reboot.

TIP

The mode changes can be confirmed by executing the `sestatus` command.

If you do not have a graphical desktop, are logged in remotely without X forwarding, or just prefer the command line, these mode preferences can be made using the command line.

To change the currently running SELinux mode, use the `setenforce` command as the root user, replacing `<mode>` with either `Enforcing` or `Permissive`:

```
setenforce <mode>
```

To confirm the change, execute the `getenforce` command, which displays the current SELinux mode.

CAUTION

If using `setenforce`, be sure to change the mode in `/etc/selinux/config` as well so the change will persist after a reboot.

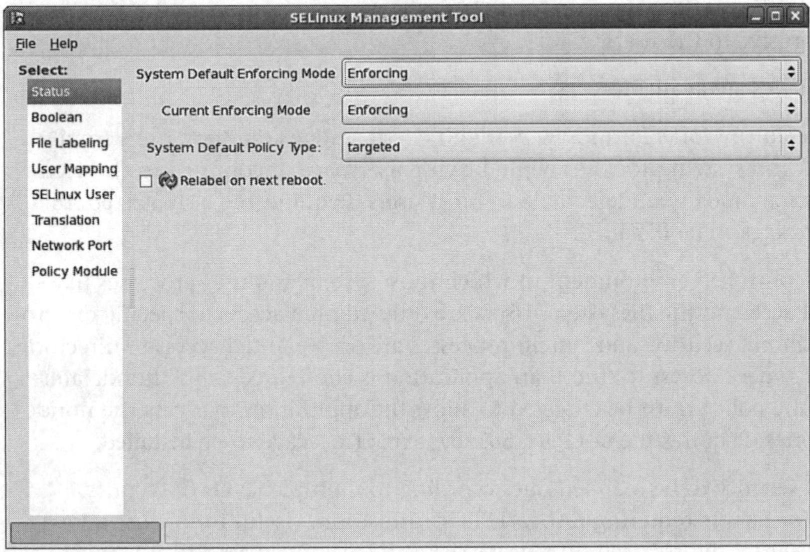

FIGURE 23.1 Selecting the SELinux Mode

The SELinux mode used at boot time can be set in the `/etc/selinux/config` file. As the root user, set the `SELINUX` option to `enforcing`, `permissive`, or `disabled` such as the following:

```
SELINUX=enforcing
```

After the reboot, verify the mode was changed with the `sestatus` command. The output should look similar to Listing 23.1.

LISTING 23.1 SELinux Status with `sestatus`

```
SELinux status:                 enabled
SELinuxfs mount:                /selinux
Current mode:                   enforcing
Mode from config file:          enforcing
Policy version:                 21
Policy from config file:        targeted
```

Selecting and Customizing the SELinux Policy

If permissive or enforcing mode is enabled, an SELinux policy must be selected to determine which programs are governed by SELinux and which are run in unconfined space. The SELinux policy sets what programs are protected under SELinux. The default policy, called the *targeted policy*, in Red Hat Enterprise Linux is designed to protect the system without being intrusive to the users.

The following policies are available:

- **targeted** (default): Works for most server and client systems. Protects users from applications and system processes while leaving userspace unconfined so the security measures are mostly undetectable to most users. Requires the `selinux-policy-targeted` package to be installed.
- **strict**: Very controlled environment in which most system and user processes have very limited access to the filesystem. Users are only granted access to specific directories for maximum security, and system processes are only granted access to directories to which they need access to run. If an application is configured to use nondefault directories, the policy must be changed to allow the application to access the nondefault directories. Requires the `selinux-policy-strict` package to be installed.
- **mls**: Allows security to be mapped out according to multiple levels of security. Developed for servers requiring EAL4+/LSPP certification. Useful for organizations that grant security rights based on a user's security level. Requires the `selinux-policy-mls` package to be installed.

To change the SELinux policy, first install the corresponding package. To change the policy from the SELinux Management Tool, go to the Status view and select the desired policy from the **System Default Policy Type** pull-down menu. Only installed policies are available for selection.

To change from the command line, set the `SELINUXTYPE` option in the `/etc/selinux/config` file to `targeted`, `strict`, or `mls` such as the following:

```
SELINUXTYPE=targeted
```

A reboot is required after selecting a different policy so that the filesystem can be relabeled. Remember to back up the filesystem before changing the SELinux policy. After the reboot, verify the policy was changed by executing the `sestatus` command. The output should look similar to Listing 23.1.

When changing the policy, setting the mode to permissive allows the administrator to test the policy without enabling it at first. After reviewing the SELinux alerts and system log files for any errors or warnings for a testing period, the mode can be changed from permissive to enforcing as described in the "Selecting an SELinux Mode" section.

Major modifications to the policy require the policy source to be modified and the source to be recompiled. However, policies do allow minor changes to it without recompiling by setting the boolean value (0 or 1) for optional features. For example, by default, the SELinux targeted policy does not allow the Apache HTTP Server to serve files from home directories. The value of the `httpd_enable_homedirs` boolean can be set to `1` to explicitly allow it. Changes to boolean values can be made with the SELinux Management Tool or the `setsebool` command.

Start the graphical tool with the `system-config-selinux` command or the **Administration, SELinux Management** menu item in the **System** menu of the top panel of the desktop. Select the **Boolean** view from the list on the left. A tree view of possible boolean modifications can now be seen. Click the triangle icon next to each category to view a list of boolean options. Boolean options with a checkmark beside them are enabled. Check an option to enable it, and uncheck an option to disable it. The changes take place immediately. For example, Figure 23.2 shows the values for the booleans that affect the NFS daemon.

NOTE

The values of the booleans are stored on the virtual filesystem `/selinux/boolean/` and can be viewed with the command `cat /selinux/boolean/<boolean_name>`.

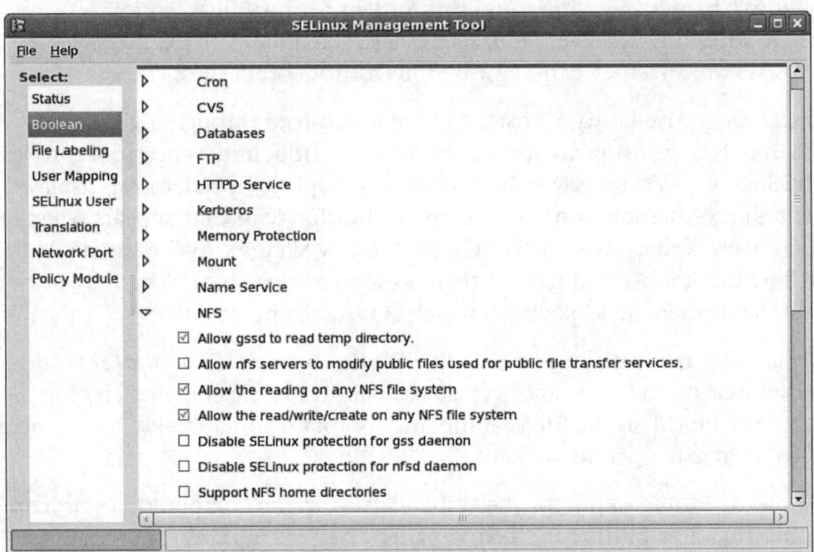

FIGURE 23.2 Modifying the SELinux Mode

Descriptions of each available boolean values can be found in the `BOOLEANS` section of the man page for the specific policy. For example, the `nfs_selinux` man page describes the `use_nfs_home_dirs` boolean, which translates to the **Support NFS home directories** option under the **NFS** category in the graphical application.

Alternatively, use the `setsebool` command to set the boolean to the desired value:

```
setsebool -P <boolean> <value>
```

To view the status of a boolean via the command line, execute the `getsebool` command:

```
getsebool use_nfs_home_dirs
```

To completely disable SELinux for a specific service, place a checkmark next to the corresponding boolean under the **SELinux Service Protection** category or the category for the specific service such as **Kerberos**. While this will allow the service to work with SELinux enabled, the service will no longer be protected by SELinux and is not recommended. If a service can not be started because of SELinux, look at the boolean values that can be changed for it. The SELinux Troubleshooting Tool summarizes why the action was blocked by the SELinux policy. It also offers possible solutions for the problem. Refer to the "Utilizing the SELinux Troubleshooting Tool" for details.

Utilizing the SELinux Troubleshooting Tool

Log messages for SELinux are written to `/var/log/messages` unless the Linux Auditing System is used (refer to Chapter 25, "Linux Auditing System," for details). If audit is enabled, messages are written to the `/var/log/audit/audit.log` file. The log messages are labeled with the `AVC` keyword so they can be easily filtered from other messages.

Starting with Red Hat Enterprise Linux 5, instead of having to read through log files to determine why SELinux is preventing an action, the SELinux Troubleshooting Tool can be used to analyze the SELinux AVC messages. It consists of a graphical interface for displaying these messages and possible solutions, a desktop notification icon that appears when there are messages to view, and a daemon that checks for new SELinux AVC messages so that you are alerted by the notification icon of them as soon as they occur. The tool is provided by the `setroubleshoot` RPM package, which is installed by default.

The daemon, `setroubleshootd`, is started by default with the `/etc/rc.d/init.d/setroubleshoot` initialization script. The `/var/log/setroubleshootd.log` file contains any log messages concerning the tool. This log file is automatically rotated on a weekly basis, and old log files for the previous two weeks are kept.

If you are working on the local desktop for the system(sitting at the computer), a star icon appears in the notification area of the top desktop panel when SELinux AVC messages are available for viewing. Click on it to view the SELinux Troubleshooting Tool as shown in Figure 23.3.

TIP

If working on the local desktop, you can also open the SELinux Troubleshooting Tool by selecting **Administration**, **SELinux Troubleshooting** from the **System** menu on the top panel.

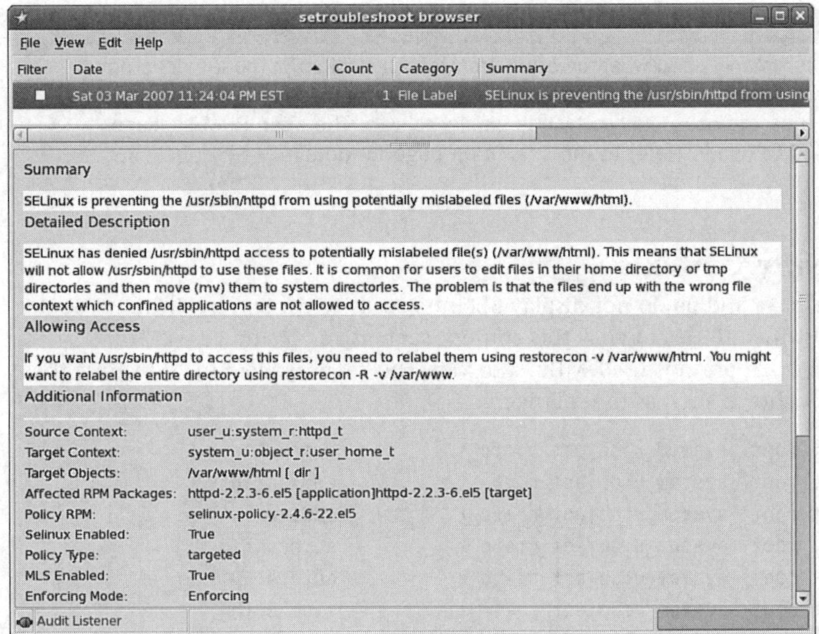

FIGURE 23.3 SELinux Troubleshooting Tool

If you are not working on the local desktop but have SSH access to the system with X forwarding, you can execute the `sealert -b` command to remotely view the graphical troubleshooting browser.

An example of using the SELinux Troubleshooting Tool is given in the "Modifying Security Contexts" section later in this chapter.

Working with Security Contexts

When SELinux is enabled, all files and objects have a security context. Security contexts for processes are called domains such as `httpd_t` for the Apache web server daemon processes. Security contexts for files are called file contexts and are stored in the extended attributes of the files. The security context has four parts to it separated by colons:

```
user:role:type:mls
```

Unless the MLS policy is being used, the last `mls` field is not used. The `user` field is the SELinux user who created the file. The `role` field is the role of the object or file, and the `type` field is the type of rule associated with the object or file. An example of a security context for the targeted policy would be the following:

```
system_u:object_r:etc_t
```

In this example, the file is a system file as indicated by the `system_u` user field, is a file object labeled with `object_r`, and is governed by the `etc_r` rule type because it is a file in the `/etc/` directory.

CAUTION

The `tar` utility commonly used when creating archives for backup purposes does not preserve extended attributes of the filesystem. To back up a filesystem and its SELinux labels, use the `star` utility, which is similar to `tar`. The `star` RPM package must be installed to use it. Refer to the `star` man page for details.

Viewing Security Contexts

File utilities such as `ls` and `ps` do not display SELinux security context by default. Use the `-Z` option for most file utilities to view this content such as `ls -Z` and `ps -Z`. For example, when the `-Z` option is used with `ls` to view the `/etc/sysconfig/` directory, the security context is shown such as the following:

```
-rw-r—r—    root root   system_u:object_r:etc_t          apmd
drwxr-xr-x  root root   system_u:object_r:etc_t          apm-scripts
-rw-r——-    root root   system_u:object_r:etc_t          auditd
-rw-r—r—    root root   system_u:object_r:etc_t          authconfig
-rw-r—r—    root root   system_u:object_r:etc_t          autofs
-rw-r—r—    root root   system_u:object_r:etc_t          bluetooth
```

The `cp` and `mv` commands for copying and moving files handle file contexts differently. By default, the `cp` command creates a new file in the desired location with a type based on the creating process and the parent directory of the desired location. For example, if the file is copied from the `/etc/` directory to a backup directory, the `type` field of the file changes from `etc_t` to whatever the default type is for the target directory. The `-Z` option to `cp` can be used to specify a type to use when copying the file:

```
cp -Z <context> file /new/location
```

The `mv` command to move files preserves the file context of the files by default. If the file needs a different type in the new location, be sure to relabel the file with the `chcon` command:

```
chcon -t <context> <file>
```

Modifying Security Contexts

To better understand the impact and usage of security contexts, consider an example concerning the Apache HTTP Server. If you are not familiar with the web server, refer to Chapter 15, "Creating a Web Server with Apache HTTP Server."

It is common to change the default DocumentRoot to something other than `/var/www/html/`. Perhaps you need files to come from network storage mounted in a different directory. SELinux protects the `httpd` process and only allows the web server to serve files and directories with a specific security context.

The security context of the default files in the `/var/www/` directory is shown in Listing 23.2. The output is from the `ls -d -Z /var/www;ls -Z /var/www` command.

LISTING 23.2 Security Context of Default DocumentRoot

```
drwxr-xr-x  root root system_u:object_r:httpd_sys_content_t /var/www
drwxr-xr-x  root root system_u:object_r:httpd_sys_script_exec_t cgi-bin
drwxr-xr-x  root root system_u:object_r:httpd_sys_content_t error
drwxr-xr-x  root root system_u:object_r:httpd_sys_content_t html
drwxr-xr-x  root root system_u:object_r:httpd_sys_content_t icons
```

TIP

The `secon -f <file>` command can also be used to view the security context of a file.

If you change the DocumentRoot to `/home/html/`, after restarting `httpd` and trying to view the pages from the new DocumentRoot from a web browser, the service will start, but the website will default to the test page instead of the index page of your website. The message from Listing 23.3 appear in `/var/log/messages`.

LISTING 23.3 System Error Messages After Changing DocumentRoot

```
Mar  6 14:54:07 localhost setroubleshoot:      SELinux is preventing
the /usr/sbin/httpd from using potentially mislabeled files
(/home/html/index.html).
For complete SELinux messages. run sealert -l e2d75f44-7c89-4fc1-a06b-23603ab00af8
```

If you have the Linux Auditing System enabled (the default), the `/var/log/audit/audit.log` file shows the SELinux AVC messages from Listing 23.4.

LISTING 23.4 Audit Error Messages After Changing DocumentRoot

```
type=AVC msg=audit(1173211195.225:286487): avc:  denied  { getattr } for
pid=19315 comm="httpd" name="index.html" dev=dm-1 ino=12845059
scontext=user_u:system_r:httpd_t:s0 tcontext=user_u:object_r:user_home_t:s0
tclass=file
type=SYSCALL msg=audit(1173211195.225:286487): arch=c000003e syscall=4
success=no exit=-13 a0=5555cc034d50 a1=7fff0cb47140 a2=7fff0cb47140
a3=5555cc034db8 items=0 ppid=19307 pid=19315 auid=501 uid=48 gid=48 euid=48
suid=48 fsuid=48 egid=48 sgid=48 fsgid=48 tty=(none) comm="httpd"
exe="/usr/sbin/httpd" subj=user_u:system_r:httpd_t:s0 key=(null)
type=AVC_PATH msg=audit(1173211195.225:286487):  path="/home/html/index.html"
type=AVC msg=audit(1173211195.225:286488): avc:  denied  { getattr } for
pid=19315 comm="httpd" name="index.html" dev=dm-1 ino=12845059 scontext=user_u:sys-
tem_r:httpd_t:s0 tcontext=user_u:object_r:user_home_t:s0
tclass=file
type=SYSCALL msg=audit(1173211195.225:286488): arch=c000003e syscall=6
success=no exit=-13 a0=5555cc034e18 a1=7fff0cb47140 a2=7fff0cb47140
```

LISTING 23.4 Continued

```
a3=5555cc034e22 items=0 ppid=19307 pid=19315 auid=501 uid=48 gid=48 euid=48
suid=48 fsuid=48 egid=48 sgid=48 fsgid=48 tty=(none) comm="httpd"
exe="/usr/sbin/httpd" subj=user_u:system_r:httpd_t:s0 key=(null)
type=AVC_PATH msg=audit(1173211195.225:286488):  path="/home/html/index.html
```

Notice that the end of the message from `/var/log/messages` in Listing 23.3 gives the `sealert -l e2d75f44-7c89-4fc1-a06b-23603ab00af8` command to execute for complete SELinux messages. The `sealert` command is part of the SELinux Troubleshooting Tool. If the `sealert -l <lookup-id>` command is used, the same information shown in the graphical program for the SELinux Troubleshooting Tool is displayed to the command line. The output from our example is shown in Listing 23.5.

LISTING 23.5 Analysis of AVC Messages

```
Summary
    SELinux is preventing the /usr/sbin/httpd from using potentially mislabeled
    files (/home/html/index.html).

Detailed Description
    SELinux has denied /usr/sbin/httpd access to potentially mislabeled file(s)
    (/home/html/index.html).  This means that SELinux will not allow
    /usr/sbin/httpd to use these files.  It is common for users to edit files in
    their home directory or tmp directories and then move (mv) them to system
    directories.  The problem is that the files end up with the wrong file
    context which confined applications are not allowed to access.

Allowing Access
    If you want /usr/sbin/httpd to access this files, you need to relabel them
    using restorecon -v /home/html/index.html.  You might want to relabel the
    entire directory using restorecon -R -v /home/html.

Additional Information

Source Context              user_u:system_r:httpd_t
Target Context              user_u:object_r:user_home_t
Target Objects              /home/html/index.html [ file ]
Affected RPM Packages       httpd-2.2.3-6.el5 [application]
Policy RPM                  selinux-policy-2.4.6-22.el5
Selinux Enabled             True
Policy Type                 targeted
MLS Enabled                 True
Enforcing Mode              Enforcing
Plugin Name                 plugins.home_tmp_bad_labels
Host Name                   smallville
```

LISTING 23.5 Continued

```
Platform                    Linux smallville 2.6.18-1.2961.el5 #1 SMP Wed Jan
                            3 14:35:32 EST 2007 x86_64 x86_64
Alert Count                 12
Line Numbers

Raw Audit Messages

avc: denied { getattr } for comm="httpd" dev=dm-1 egid=48 euid=48
exe="/usr/sbin/httpd" exit=-13 fsgid=48 fsuid=48 gid=48 items=0
name="index.html" path="/home/html/index.html" pid=19312
scontext=user_u:system_r:httpd_t:s0 sgid=48 subj=user_u:system_r:httpd_t:s0
suid=48 tclass=file tcontext=user_u:object_r:user_home_t:s0 tty=(none) uid=48
```

TIP

To save the output of the sealert -l <lookup-id> command, redirect it into a file such as:

```
sealert -l e2d75f44-7c89-4fc1-a06b-23603ab00af8 > httpd_selinux_errors.txt
```

You can also generate the output in HTML format by adding the -H command line option:

```
sealert -H -l e2d75f44-7c89-4fc1-a06b-23603ab00af8 >
➥httpd_selinux_errors.txt
```

Figure 23.4 shows the same analysis viewed from the graphical browser of the SELinux Troubleshooting Tool.

The description of the problem from the SELinux Troubleshooting Tool is correct. The files in the DocumentRoot for the web server are mislabeled. The instructions in the Allowing Access section are suggestions that may or may not fix the problem. In this case, using the restorecon command to relabel does not properly label the files for the DocumentRoot.

The security context of the new DocumentRoot must be changed so that SELinux recognizes the files in it as valid web pages to use with the Apache HTTP Server. The security context of the /home/html/ directory is the following (output from ls -d -Z /home/html command):

```
drwxr-xr-x  root root root:object_r:user_home_dir_t /home/html
```

Use the chcon command with the -R option to recursively change the security context of the directory. Since the -R option is used, the security context for all files and subdirectories is changed too. The command is as follows:

```
chcon -v -R —user=system_u —role=object_r —type=httpd_sys_content_t /home/html
```

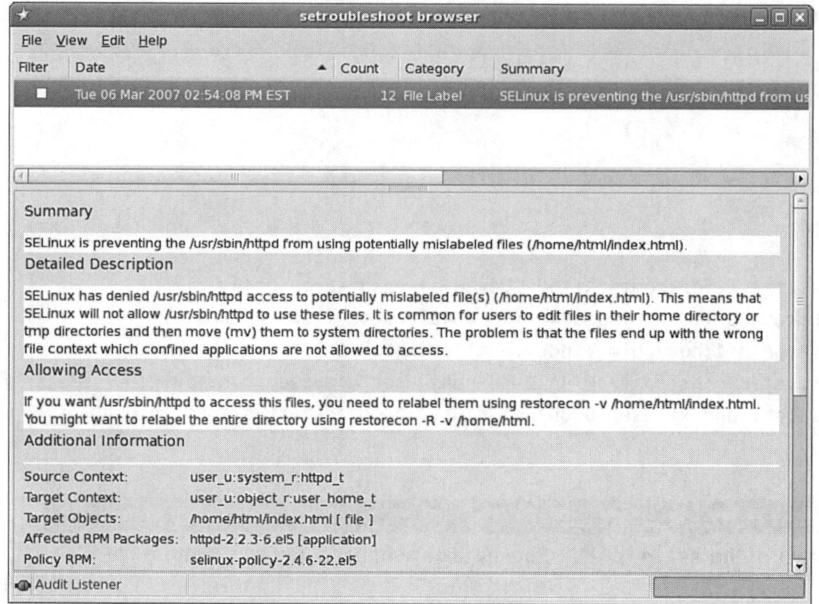

FIGURE 23.4 Error Analysis

Since the -v option was used, if the command is successful, the following types of messages are displayed:

```
context of /home/html changed to system_u:object_r:httpd_sys_content_t
context of /home/html/index.html changed to system_u:object_r:httpd_sys_content_t
```

As you might have noticed from Listing 23.2, the `cgi-bin` directory needs to have a different security context type since files in it can be executed. If you have a `cgi-bin` directory, use the following to change its security context:

```
chcon -R —type=httpd_sys_script_exec_t /home/html/cgi-bin
```

Because the user and role of the security context was already changed when you recursively changed the security context for the entire new DocumentRoot, this command only modifies the type.

TIP

A complete list of security contexts for the Apache HTTP server can be found in the httpd_selinux man page. View it with the `man httpd_selinux` command.

After fixing the security context of the web page files, test your changes by opening a web browser and trying to view the pages. Restarting `httpd` is not necessary after changing the security context of the files because SELinux checks the security context each time a request is made.

If you need to share the files in the DocumentRoot using another file sharing protocol such as FTP or NFS, the security context of the files need to be `public_content_t` or `public_content_rw_t`, depending on whether you need to give write access to users. Refer to the "Security Context for Multiple File Sharing Protocols" for details on using them.

Security Context for Multiple File Sharing Protocols

If more than one file sharing protocol (FTP, HTTP, NFS, rsync, and Samba) is used to share the same set of files, the security context must be set to `public_content_t` or `public_content_rw_t` instead of the security context specific to the protocol such as `samba_share_t` for Samba.

The `public_content_t` context only allows read access to the files. The `public_content_rw_t` context allows read and write access. To allow read and write access, you must also enable the `allow_<protocol>_anon_write` boolean, where `<protocol>` is one of `ftpd`, `httpd`, `nfsd`, `rsync`, or `smbd`. For example, to allow FTP and the Apache HTTP Server to share the same files, execute the following commands as root:

```
setsebool -P allow_ftpd_anon_write=1
setsebool -P allow_httpd_anon_write=1
```

CAUTION

If the filesystem is relabeled for SELinux, the security context changes you make will be overwritten. To make your changes permanent even through a relabel, refer to the "Making Security Context Changes Permanent" section.

Making Security Context Changes Permanent

Modifying the security context of files such as discussed in the previous section persists between reboots unless the filesystem is relabeled. A filesystem is relabeled for a variety of reasons including changing the SELinux policy. To make sure the security context of your files are not changed, you must set the default security context of the files by adding the file specification, file type, and SELinux security context to the `/etc/selinux/<policy>/contexts/files/file_contexts.local` file. Do not create or modify this file manually. Use the SELinux Management Tool or the `semanage` command.

After starting the SELinux Management Tool as previously described, click on **File Labeling** in the list on the left. Click the **Add** button and enter the following information as shown in Figure 23.5:

- **File Specification**: Enter `/home/html(/.*)?` to represent the `/home/html/` directory and all the files and directories in it.
- **File Type**: Leave as the default, **all files.**
- **SELinux Type**: Enter `httpd_sys_content_t` as the security context.
- **MLS**: Leave as default if you are not using the MLS policy.

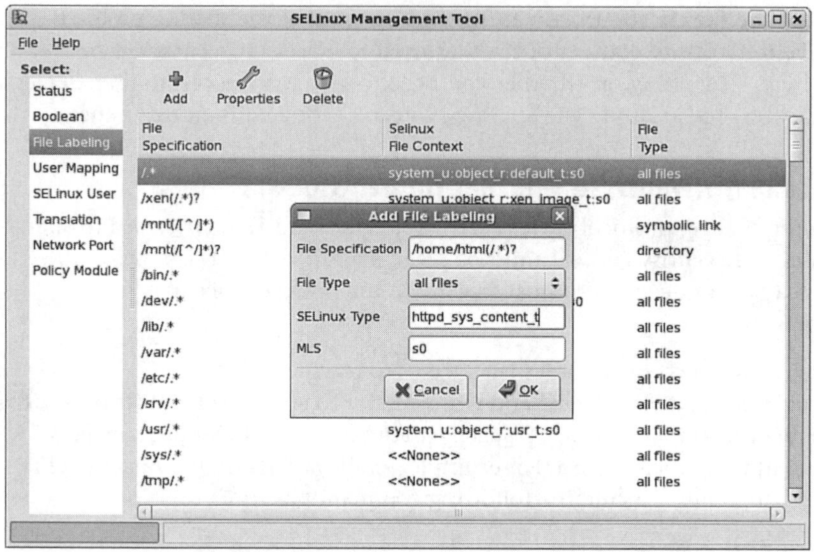

FIGURE 23.5 Adding Default Security Context

> **NOTE**
>
> The `restorecon` command can be used to manually relabel a filesystem using the default security contexts.

To perform the same action on the command line, execute the following command as the root user:

```
semanage fcontext -a -t httpd_sys_content_t '/home/html(/.*)?'
```

Either method creates the `/etc/selinux/<policy>/contexts/files/file_contexts.local` file if it doesn't already exist and adds the following line to it:

```
/home/html(/.*)?    system_u:object_r:httpd_sys_content_t:s0
```

If you require additional security contexts such as `httpd_sys_script_exec_t` for a `cgi_bin` directory, add those as well.

Summary

Implemented at the kernel level, SELinux provides the ability to define a policy from which the SELinux mechanism allows or denies file access to specific users and processes. The default policy in Red Hat Enterprise Linux, the targeted policy, restricts access to particular processes so that the security layer does not interfere with the day-to-day activities of most users. Basic options such as turning off protection for specific daemons and allowing certain service features that may be insecure can be enabled and disabled without writing a new policy.

CHAPTER 24

Configuring a Firewall

IN THIS CHAPTER

- Selecting a Table and Command for IPTables
- Selecting IPTables Options
- Using IPTables Match Extensions
- Using IPTables Target Extensions
- Starting and Stopping the IPTables Service
- Saving the IPTables Rules
- IPTables Examples
- Enabling the Default Firewall

As an administrator in today's world of networked computing and easy access to the Internet, security both internally and externally must be the first and last issue considered. Denying unauthorized access is the first step to keeping your system secure. The mechanism to prevent access to all or some network services on a system is called a *firewall*.

Every operating system allows for the implementation of a firewall differently. Red Hat Enterprise Linux uses *IPTables*, a network packet-filtering mechanism in the Linux kernel. IPTables can be used to allow or deny packets based on numerous factors including their destination, their source, which port they are trying to access, the user ID of the process that created the packet, and more.

Install the `iptables` RPM package to use IPTables. It includes utilities to configure which packets to filter. Refer to Chapter 3, "Operating System Updates," for instructions on installing packages.

The IPTables configuration consists of a series of *rules*. Each rule must be for a specific *table*, with each table having its own set of chains. A *chain* is a list of rules, which are compared to the packets passed through the chain. If a set of packets matches a chain, the *target* of the rule tells the system what to do with the packets, including passing it along to a different chain.

This chapter discusses how to write and enable IPTables rules. It also discusses the Red Hat Enterprise Linux security levels, which are predefined sets of IPTables rules. They can be used to quickly implement a basic firewall.

TIP

Log messages for IPTables are controlled by syslog and go to `/var/log/messages` by default.

Selecting a Table and Command for IPTables

The first part of an IPTables rule is defining the table with the `-t <table>` option:

```
iptables -t <table> ...
```

Choose from the following tables:

- `filter`: Default table used if `-t <table>` is not specified. Its predefined chains are `INPUT`, `FORWARD`, and `OUTPUT`.
- `nat`: Use when a packet tries to create a new connection. Its predefined chains are `PREROUTING`, `OUTPUT`, and `POSTROUTING`.
- `mangle`: Use for specialized packet altering such as changing the destination of the packet. Its predefined chains are `PREROUTING`, `OUTPUT`, `INPUT`, `FORWARD`, and `POSTROUTING`.
- `raw`: Use for exempting packets from connection tracking when the `NOTRACK` target is used. Its predefined chains are `PREROUTING` and `OUTPUT`.

Each rule must contain only one of the commands listed in Table 24.1 unless otherwise specified. The command should follow the table definition:

```
iptables -t <table> -A <chain> <rulespec> ...
```

TABLE 24.1 IPTables Commands

IPTables Command	Description
`-A <chain> <rulespec>`	Append rule to the end of the chain.
`-D <chain> <rulespec>`	Delete rule. The `<rule>` can be the rule number, with the count starting at 1.
`-I <chain> <rulnum> <rulespec>`	Insert a rule at a specific point in the chain.
`-R <chain> <rulenum> <rulespec>`	Replace a rule at a specific point in the chain.
`-L <chain>`	List all rules in the chain. The `-t <table>` option can be used to display rules for a given table.
`-F <chain>`	Delete, or flush, all the rules in the chain.
`-Z <chain>`	Set the packet and byte counters to zero in a specific chain or in all chains if no chain is given.
`-N <chain>`	Add a new chain. Name must be unique.
`-X <chain>`	Delete a given chain. Before a chain can be deleted, it cannot be referenced by any rules, and the chain must not contain any rules.

TABLE 24.1 Continued

IPTables Command	Description
`-P <chain> <target>`	Set the target policy for a given chain, or what to do with the packets if they match the rule.
`-E <old> <new>`	Rename a user-defined chain. New name must be unique.
`-h`	Show very brief description of command-line options.

The parameters in Table 24.2 should be used to form the rule specifications for the commands in Table 24.1 that are followed by `<rulespec>`.

CAUTION

Do not use hostnames when writing IPTables rules. IPTables is started before DNS, and the system will not be able to resolve the hostnames.

TABLE 24.2 IPTables Rule Parameters

Parameter	Description
`-p <protocol>`	Protocol for the packets. The most common ones are `tcp`, `udp`, and `icmp`. Protocols from `/etc/protocols` can also be used. If `all` is used, all protocols are valid for the rule. If an exclamation point and a space are before the protocol name, the rule matches all protocols except the one listed after the exclamation point.
`-s <address>`	Source of the packets. The `<address>` can be a network name, an IP address, or an IP address with a mask. If an exclamation point and a space are before the address, the rule matches all addresses except the one listed after the exclamation point.
`-d <address>`	Destination of the packets. The `<address>` can be in the same formats as for the `-s <address>` parameter.
`-j <target>`	Target of the rule, or what to do with the packets if they match the rule. Target can be a user-defined chain other than the one this rule is in, a predefined target, or an extension. Refer to the "Using IPTables Target Extensions" section for details on extensions. The following predefined targets are available: `ACCEPT`: Allow the packet through. `DROP`: Drop the packet and do nothing further with it. `QUEUE`: Pass the packet to userspace. `RETURN`: Stop processing the current chain and return the previous chain.
`-g <chain>`	Continue processing in the given chain.

TABLE 24.2 Continued

Parameter	Description
-i <name>	Interface on which the packet was received. If an exclamation point and a space are before it, the rule only matches if the packet was not received on the given interface. If a plus mark is appended to the interface name, the rule is true for any interface that begins with the name. If the interface name is not specified, packets received from any interface matches the rule. Only for packets entering the INPUT, FORWARD, and PREROUTING chains.
-o <name>	Interface on which the packet will be sent. If an exclamation point and a space is before it, the rule only matches if the packet was not received on the given interface. If a plus mark is appended to the interface name, the rule is true for any interface that begins with the name. If the interface name is not specified, packets to be sent from any interface matches the rule. Only for packets entering the INPUT, FORWARD, and PREROUTING chains.
-f	Rule only matches second and further fragmented packets. If an exclamation point is before the -f parameter, the rule only matches unfragmented packets.
-c PKTS BYTES	Used to initialize the packet and byte counters of the rule. Only for INSERT, APPEND, and REPLACE actions.

Selecting IPTables Options

Each rule may contain the options in Table 24.3, but they are not required. They should be listed in the rule after the command and any rule specifications for the command such as the following:

```
iptables -t <table> -A <chain> <rulespec> --line-numbers ...
```

TABLE 24.3 IPTables Options

IPTables Option	Description
-v	Show more details if available such as the interface name and counters when listing rules.
-n	Do not resolve IP addresses to hostnames, port numbers to service names, or network address to network names. Can be used to speed up output of commands such as listing the rules.
-x	Provide the exact values of the packet and byte counters. Only applicable to the -L command.
--line-numbers	When listing rules, display line numbers in front of each rule to show the position of the rule in the chain.
--modprobe=<command>	When adding or inserting rules, use the specified command to load additional kernel modules.

Using IPTables Match Extensions

Optionally, packet matching modules, or match extensions can be loaded. Depending on the module loaded, even more options are available. To find out what additional options are available, load the module, and then use the `iptables -h` command to learn more about the options.

The meaning of most of the match extensions can be inverted by adding an exclamation point before it. Extensions with this functionality are noted with a [!] where the optional exclamation point should go. Modules are loaded with the `-m` or `-p` options. Unless noted, the modules are loaded with the `-m <modulename>` option. The following match extensions are available:

account

Gather traffic statistics for all systems within a network defined by its network/netmask combination.

`--aaddr <network/netmask>`

Network for which to gather statistics.

`--aname <name>`

Name of the statistics table. If a name is not provided, `DEFAULT` will be used.

`--ashort`

Record short statistics.

addrtype

Match packets based on their source and/or destination address type. Address type can be one of the following: `UNSPEC`, `UNICAST`, `LOCAL`, `BROADCAST`, `ANYCAST`, `MULTICAST`, `BLACKHOLE`, `UNREACHABLE`, `PROHIBIT`, `THROW`, `NAT`, and `XRESOLVE`.

`--src-type <type>`

Type of source address used to match the rule.

`--dst-type <type>`

Type of destination address used to match the rule.

ah

Match based on SPIs in Authentication header of IPsec packets.

`--ahspi [!] <spi>:<spi>`

Define range of SPIs to match.

childlevel

Set connection level of packets to match. Most packets are level 0, with their children being level 1, and so on.

`--childlevel [!] <level>`

Define connection level on which to match.

24

comment

Add a comment to a rule.

`--comment <comment>`

Provide a comment of up to 256 characters.

condition

Match if the value of the specified `/proc` file is 0 or 1.

`--condition [!] <filename>`

Replace `<filename>` with the full path and filename of a file in the `/proc` directory.

connbytes

Match according to the number of bytes or packets transferred or by the average number of bytes per transfer.

`[!] --connbytes <from>:<to>`

Packets match if the number of packets, number of bytes, or average packet size is more than `<from>` but less than `<to>`. The `<to>` value for providing an upper limit is optional.

`--conbytes-dir <type>`

Replace `<type>` with `original`, `reply`, or `both` to match these types of packets.

`--connbytes-mode <mode>`

Replace `<mode>` with `packets`, `bytes`, or `avgpkt` to set what the lower and upper limits from the `--connbytes <from>:<to>` command should be compared to.

connlimit

Block a client by IP address or set a maximum number of TCP connections from a client.

`[!] --connlimit=above <num>`

Maximum number of TCP connections. If the connection number exceeds the limit, the packets do not match the rule.

`--connlimit-mask <bits>`

Network mask of the network to restrict.

connmark

Match netfilter mark for the connection.

`--mark <mark>`

Match packets with specific mark value.

connrate

Match current transfer rate for the connection.

`--connrate [!] <from>:<to>`

Match transfer rate greater than `<from>` but less than `<to>`.

conntrack

Match packet according to its connection state.

`--ctstate <state>`

Replace `<state>` with a comma-separated list of states. Possible states:

- `INVALID`: Packet is not associated with a known connection.
- `ESTABLISHED`: Packet is associated with an established connection, meaning it has sent packets in both directions.
- `NEW`: Packet is associated with a new connection that has not sent packets in any direction or has started a new connection.
- `RELATED`: Packet has started a new connection associated with an existing connection.
- `SNAT`: Original source address for the packet is different from the reply destination.
- `DNAT`: Original destination address for the packet is different from the reply source.

`--ctproto <proto>`

Match a given protocol by its name or number.

`--ctorigsrc [!] <address>/<mask>`

Match packets with a specified original source address. Address mask is optional.

`--ctorigdst [!] <address>/</mask>`

Match packets with a specific original destination address. Address mask is optional.

`--ctreplsrc [!] <address>/<mask>`

Match packets with a provided reply source address. Address mask is optional.

`--ctrepldst [!] <address>/<mask>`

Match packets according to reply destination address. Address mask is optional.

`--ctstatus <state>`

Match packets according to internal conntrack state.

`--ctexpire <time>:<time>`

Packets match if its remaining lifetime is within a range, provided in seconds. The maximum time is optional.

dccp

Match based on DCCP.

`--source-port,--sport [!] <port>:<port>`

Match according to minimum source port number or a range.

`--destination-port,--dport [!] <port>:<port>`

Match according to minimum destination port number or a range.

`--dccp-types [!] <mask>`

Match if DCCP packet type is `<mask>`, where `<mask>` is a comma-separated list of types. Valid types are `REQUEST`, `RESPONSE`, `DATA`, `ACK`, `DATAACK`, `CLOSEREQ`, `CLOSE`, `RESET`, `SYNC`, `SYNCACK`, and `INVALID`.

`--dccp-option [!] <num>`

Match if DCP option is set to `<num>`.

dscp

Match according to 6-bit DSCP field within the TOS field in the IP header.

`--dscp <value>`

Match if DSCP value matches.

`--dscp-class <class>`

Match if DSCP class matches the BE, EF, AFxx, or CSx class provided.

ecn

Match ECN bits of the IPv4 and TCP header.

`--ecn-tcp-cwr`

Match if the TCP ECN CWR bit is set.

`--ecn-tcp-ece`

Match if the TCP ECN ECE (ECN Echo) bit is set.

`--ecn-ip-ect <num>`

Match a specific IPv4 ECT (ECN-Capable Transport). The number must be between 0 and 3.

esp

Match the SPIs in the ESP header of IPsec packets.

`--espspi [!] <spi>:<spi>`

Set specific SPI or a range of SPIs to match.

fuzzy

Match the rate limit from the fuzzy logic controller.

`--lower-limit <num>`

Minimum rate limit in packets per second.

`--upper-limit <num>`

Maximum rate limit in packets per second.

hashlimit

Match based on upper limit of average packet transfer rate. Limit is for single destination system or a destination with its port. Similar to `limit`.

`--hashlimit <rate>`

Specify the rate as a number followed by `/<time>`, where `<time>` is `second`, `minute`, `hour`, or `day`.

`--hashlimit-burst <num>`

Maximum burst value, where the burst value is increased by 1 each time the defined rate limit is reached. Default value is 5.

`--hashlimit-mode <destination>`

Replace `<destination>` with destination IP address or IP address and port combination in the format `<ip>-<port>`.

`--hashlimit-name <name>`

Name for the `/proc/net/ipt_hashlimit/<name>` file.

`--hashlimit-htable-size <num>`

Number of buckets of the hash table.

`--hashlimit-htable-max <num>`

Maximum number of entries in the hash.

`--hashlimit-htable-expire <num>`

Hash entries expire after a defined number of milliseconds.

`--hashlimit-htable-gcinterval <num>`

Time interval between garbage collection in milliseconds.

helper

Match based on conntrack-helper.

`--helper <string>`

Replace `<string>` with name of service if it is using the default port or the name of the service followed by a hyphen and port number such as http-4343.

icmp

Match based on ICMP type. Must be used in conjunction with `--protocol icmp`.

`--icmp-type [!] <type>`

`<type>` can be a number or the ICMP type name.

iprange

Match according to IP (version 4) range.

`[!]--src-range <ip>-<ip>`

Match according to source IP within given range.

`[!]--dst-range <ip>-<ip>`

Match according to destination IP within given range.

ipv4options

Match based on IP (version 4) header options.

`--ssrr`

Match packets with the flag strict source routing.

`--lsrr`

Match packets with the flag loose source routing.

`--no-srr`

Match packets with no flag for source routing.

`[!] --rr`

Match packets with the RR flag.

`[!] --ts`

Match packets with the TS flag.

`[!] --ra`

Match packets with the router-alert option.

`[!] --any-opt`

Match packets with at least one IP option.

length

Match exact packet length or match packets based on a range of lengths.

`--length [!] <length>:<length>`

Define a length or range of lengths to match.

limit

Use with other parameters and targets to limit the value being matched.

`--limit <rate>`

Upper rate limit. Rate number can optionally be followed by `/<time>`, where `<time>` is `second`, `minute`, `hour`, or `day` to qualify rate.

`--limit-burst <num>`

Maximum burst value, where the burst value is increased by 1 each time the defined rate limit is reached. Default value is 5.

mac

Match the source MAC address of the packet. Only valid when using Ethernet devices and entering the PREROUTING, `FORWARD`, or `INPUT` chain.

`--mac-source [!] <address>`

`<address>` must be in the format XX:XX:XX:XX:XX:XX.

mark

Match the netfilter mark field of the packet.

`--mark <value>/<mask>`

Define the mark value. The `/<mask>` is the option.

mport

Match packets with specific source or destination ports. Must be used with the `-p tcp` or `-p udp` options. `<ports>` is a comma-separated list of port numbers.

`--source-ports <ports>`

Define source ports on which to match.

`--destination-ports <ports>`

Define destination ports on which to match.

`--ports <ports>`

Only match if source and destination ports match each other and are in the given list of ports.

nth

Match the nth packet.

`--every <n>`

Match every nth packet.

`--counter <num>`

Use specified counter. Must be from `0` to `15`. Defaults to `0`.

`--start <num>`

Start counter at `<num>`. Counter starts at `0` if not specified.

`--packet <num>`

Match if packet number is `<num>`.

osf

Match data from SYN packet to OS fingerprints.

`--log <num>`

If set to `0`, log all determined entries. If set to `1`, log only first determined entry. Logs are sent to syslog.

`--smart`

Use some smartness to determine remote OS. Use initial TTL only if connection source is in local network.

`--netlink`

Log all events through netlink.

`--genre [!] string`

Match an OS genre by passive fingerprinting.

owner

For packets created on this system, match characteristics of the packet creator. Only works in the OUTPUT chain. Some packets don't match because they don't have a creator.

--uid-owner <uid>

Matches if the process that created the packet is owned by the given user.

--gid-owner <gid>

Matches if the process that created the packet has the given effective group ID.

--pid-owner <pid>

Matches if the process that created the packet has the given process ID.

--sid-owner <sid>

Matches if the process that created the packet is in the given session group.

--cmd-owner <name>

Matches if the process that created the packet has the provided command name.

physdev

Match based on the bridge port input and output devices.

--physdev-in [!] <name>

Name of a bridge port from which the packet was received. Only works if the packet entered in the INPUT, FORWARD, or PREROUTING chain. If the name ends in a +, then any interface beginning with the given name matches.

--physdev-out [!] <name>

Name of the bridge port from which the packet is sent. Only works if the packet entered in the FORWARD, OUTPUT, or POSTROUTING chain. If the interface name ends in a +, then any interface beginning with this name will match.

[!] --physdev-is-in

Matches if the packet has entered through a bridge interface.

[!] --physdev-is-out

Matches if the packet will leave through a bridge interface.

[!] --physdev-is-bridged

Matches if the packet is being bridged and not routed. Only works in the FORWARD or POSTROUTING chain.

pkttype

Matches based on the link-layer packet type.

--pkt-type <type>

<type> must be one of unicast, broadcast, or multicast.

policy

Matches policy used by IPsec for packet handling.

--dir <direction>

<direction> must be in or out. Match if the policy is used for decapsulation or encapsulation. The value of in only works in the PREROUTING, INPUT, and FORWARD chains. The value of out only works in the POSTROUTING, OUTPUT, and FORWARD chains.

--pol <value>

Set <value> to ipsec to match packets subject to IPsec processing. Set <value> to none to match packets not subject to IPsec processing.

--strict

If used, the rule only matches the packet if the policy matches exactly. If not used, the rule matches if any rule of the policy matches the defined policy.

--reqid <id>

Match the reqid of the policy rule.

--spi <spi>

Match the SPI of the SA.

--proto <proto>

Match the encapsulation protocol, where <proto> is either ah, esp, or iocomp.

--mode <mode>

Match the encapsulation mode, where <mode> is tunnel or transport.

--tunnel-src <addr>/<mask>

Match the source end-point address of a tunnel mode SA. Can only be used if mode is set to tunnel. The mask is optional.

--tunnel-dst <addr>/<mask>

Match the destination end-point address of a tunnel mode SA. Can only be used if mode is set to tunnel.

--next

Start the next element in the policy specification. Only valid when --strict is also used.

psd

Try to detect TCP and UDP port scans.

--psd-weight-threshold <threshold>

When detecting a port scan sequence, the total weight of the latest TCP or UDP packets with different destination ports from the same host.

--psd-delay-threshold <delay>

When detecting a port scan sequence, the delay in hundredths of a second for the TCP or UDP packets with different destination ports from the same host.

`--psd-lo-ports-weight <weight>`

Weight of a packet with a privileged destination port, which are port numbers 1024 and under.

`--psd-hi-ports-weight <weight>`

Weight of a packet with a nonprivileged destination port, which are port numbers 1024 and above.

quota

Network quota calculated with a byte counter for each packet.

`--quota <bytes>`

Total bytes allowed for each packet.

random

Randomly match a defined percentage of packets.

`--average <percent>`

Defined percentage of packets to match. If not defined, 50% is used.

realm

Match the routing realm.

`--realm [!] <value>/<mask>`

Define the realm value to match. The mask is optional.

recent

Grant or deny access to a specific list of IP addresses, which can be modified at any time.

`--name <name>`

Name the list. `DEFAULT` is used if a name is not defined. The list is stored in the `/proc/net/ipt_recent/<name>` file. Use `--set` or `--remove` to add or remove the source address of the packet to the list.

Alternatively, to add IP addresses to the list (as root):

```
echo xx.xx.xx.xx > /proc/net/ipt_recent/<name>
```

To remove IP address from the list:

```
echo -xx.xx.xx.xx > /proc/net/ipt_recent/<name>
```

`[!] --set`

Add the source address of the packet to the list.

`[!] --rcheck`

Check if the source address of the packet is in the list.

`[!] --update`

If source address of the packet is in the list, update the "last seen" timestamp.

`[!] --remove`

If the source address of the packet is in the list, remove it from the list.

`[!] --seconds <seconds>`

Optional parameter that only allows a match if the address is in the list and was last seen within the defined number of seconds. Must be used with `--rcheck` or `--update`.

`[!] --hitcount <hits>`

Optional parameter that causes a match only if the address is in the list and the number of packets received is greater than or equal to the defined value. Must be used with `--rcheck` or `--update`.

`--rttl`

Optional parameter that allows a match only if the address is in the list and the TTL of the current packet matches that of the packet that hit the `--set` rule. Must be used with `--rcheck` or `--update`.

sctp

Use to match SCTP packets with the `-p` option: `-p sctp`

`--source-port [!] <port>:<port>`

Specify SCTP source port as an individual port or a range of ports.

`--destination-port [!] <port>:<port>`

Specify SCTP destination port as an individual port or a range of ports.

`--chunk-types [!] <all¦any¦only> <chunktype>:<flags>`

Specify `all`, `any`, or `only` to specify how to match the chunk type list. Replace `<chunktype>` with a comma-separated list of chunk types. Chunk types: DATA, INIT, INIT_ACK, SACK, HEARTBEAT, HEARTBEAT_ACK, ABORT, SHUTDOWN, SHUTDOWN_ACK, ERROR, COOKIE_ECHO, COOKIE_ACK, ECN_ECNE, ECN_CWR, SHUTDOWN_COMPLETE, ASCONF, ASCONF_ACK. The `<flags>` are optional and are specific to certain chunk types. If the flag is in uppercase, the flag is set to on. If the flag is in lowercase, the flag is set to off. The DATA chunk type has the flags U, B, E, u, b, and e. The ABORT and SHUTDOWN_COMPLETE chunk types both have the flags T and t.

set

Matches IP sets defined by `ipset`.

`--set <name> <flags>`

`<flags>` is an `src`, `dst`, or both separated by commas. If `src` is listed, packets match if the source address or port number is found in the IP set. If `dst` is listed, the packets match if the destination address or port number is found in the IP set.

state

Allows access to connection tracking state for packets when used with connection tracking.

`--state <state>`

Replace `<state>` with comma-separated list of connection states to match. Valid states are `INVALID`, `ESTABLISHED`, `NEW`, and `RELATED`. Refer to the `conntrack` entry for a description of the states.

string

Matches a user-defined string by using one of two pattern matching strategies.

`--algo <strategy>`

Replace `<strategy>` with `bm` to use the Boyer-Moore pattern matching strategy. Replace `<strategy>` with `kmp` to use the Knuth-Pratt-Morris pattern matching strategy.

`--from <offset>`

If set, start looking for a match after the defined offset. If not set, it starts at 0.

`--to <offset>`

If set, the offset is the length it looks for a match. If not set, the entire packet size is used to match the string.

`--string <pattern>`

Pattern to match.

`--hex-string <pattern>`

Pattern to match in hex notation.

tcp

If `-p tcp` is used, the following options can be used:

`--source-port [!] <port>:<port>`

TCP source port or port range to match. The port can be the service name or a port number.

`--destination-port [!] <port>:<port>`

TCP destination port or port range to match. The port can be the service name or a port number.

`--tcp-flags [!] <flags> <comp>`

Match TCP flags listed. `<flags>` should be a comma-separated list of flags to look at, and `<comp>` should be a comma-separated list of flags that must be set. To match, the flags in the `<flags>` list but not in `<comp>` must be unset and the flags in both lists must be set. Valid flags are `SYN`, `ACK`, `FIN`, `RST`, `URG`, `PSH`, `ALL`, and `NONE`.

`[!] --syn`

Match only if the SYN bit is set and the `ACK`, `RST`, and `FIN` bits are cleared. These packets are trying to initiate a TCP connection.

`--tcp-option [!] <num>`

Match if the TCP option listed is set.

`--mss <value>:<value>`

Match TCP SYN or TCP SYN/ACK packets with the given MSS value or value range.

tcpmss

Match the TCP MSS field of the TCP header. This field controls the maximum packet size for the connection.

`[!] --mss <value>:<value>`

Match based on a value or a value range.

time

Define a range of arrival times and dates for packets to match.

`--timestart <value>`

Match if start time is after defined time, which is in the format HH:MM.

`--timestop <value>`

Match if stop time is before defined time, which is in the format HH:MM.

`--days <days>`

Match if today is in the list of days, which is a comma-separated list of days. Correct day formats: `Mon`, `Tue`, `Wed`, `Thu`, `Fri`, `Sat`, `Sun`.

`--datestop <date>`

Match if stop date is before defined date in the format YYYY[:MM[:DD[:hh[:mm[:ss]]]]]. The h, m, and s values start counting at 0.

tos

Match the TOS (Type of Service) field in the IP header.

`--tos <tos>`

Name or number to match. Execute `iptables -m tos -h` for a list of valid values.

ttl

Match the TTL (Time To Live) field in the IP header.

`--ttl-eq <ttl>`

Match defined TTL value.

`--ttl-gt <ttl>`

Match if TTL is greater than defined value.

`--ttl-lt <ttl>`

Match if TTP is less than defined value.

u32

Extract quantities of up to 4 bytes from a packet, AND them with specific masks, shift them by defined amounts, and test whether the results are in a defined range.

udp

If -p udp is used, the following can be used:

--source-port [!] <port>:<port>

UDP source port or port range to match. The port can be the service name or a port number.

--destination-port [!] <port>:<port>

UDP destination port or port range to match. The port can be the service name or a port number.

unclean

Tries to match packets that are malformed or unusual. Experimental.

Using IPTables Target Extensions

In addition to the four predefined targets (ACCEPT, DROP, QUEUE, and RETURN), the following target extensions are available:

BALANCE

Balance DNAT connections in a round-robin over a given range of destination addresses.

--to-destination <ip>-<ip>

Address range to round-robin.

CLASSIFY

Set the skb->priority value, which classifies the packet into a specific CBQ class.

--set-class <major>:<minor>

Set the major and minor classes.

CLUSTERIP

Set up a cluster of nodes that share an IP and MAC address without an explicit load balancer in front of them. Connections are statically distributed between defined nodes.

--new

Create new cluster.

`--hashmode <hash>`

Hashing mode to use. Must be one of `sourceip`, `sourceip-sourceport`, or sourceip-`sourceport-destport`.

`--clustermac <mac>`

MAC address of cluster. Has to be a link-layer multi-cast address.

`--total-nodes <num>`

Number of nodes in the cluster.

`--local-node <num>`

Local node number in the cluster.

`--hash-init <rnd>`

Random seed to use when initializing hash.

CONNMARK

Set netfilter mark value for the connection.

`--set-mark <mark>/<mask>`

Set connection mark. The `<mask>` is optional. If the mask is defined, only bits in the mask are modified.

`--save-mark --mask <mask>`

Copy netfilter packet mark value to the connection mark. The mask value is optional. If the mask is defined, only bits in the mask are copied.

`--restore-mark --mask <mask>`

Copy the connection mark value to the packet. The mask value is optional. If the mask is defined, only bits in the mask are copied. Can only be used with the `mangle` table.

DNAT

Can only be used with the `nat` table and in the `PREROUTING` and `OUTPUT` chains or in user-defined chains called from these two chains. Modifies the destination address of the packet and all future packets in the connection. Rules will not be examined for these mangled packets.

`--to-destination <ipaddr>-<ipaddr>:<port>-<port>`

Define the new destination IP or an IP range. Optionally define a port range if `-p tcp` or `-p udp` is used.

DSCP

Alter the value of the DSCP field within the TOS header of the IP version 4 packet. Only valid with the `mangle` table.

`--set-dscp <dscp>`

Set DSCP to a decimal or hex number.

`--set-dscp-class <class>`

Set DSCP to the defined class.

ECN

Work around for known ECN blackholes. Only valid with the `mangle` table.

`--ecn-tcp-remove`

Remove all ENC bits from the TCP header. Only valid with `-p tcp`.

IPMARK

Mark a received packet based on its IP. Should be used in the `mangle` table with the `PREROUTING`, `POSTROUTING`, or `FORWARD` chains.

`--addr <address>`

Source or destination IP address.

`--and-mask <mask>`

`AND` the IP and defined mask.

`--or-mask <mask>`

`OR` the IP and defined mask.

IPV4OPTSSTRIP

Strip IP options from packet.

LOG

Enable kernel logging for matching packets. Logs go to dmesg or syslog.

`--log-level <level>`

Log level specified as a number or the syslog log level name.

`--log-prefix <prefix>`

Define a prefix for the log messages up to 29 letters.

`--log-tcp-sequence`

Log TCP sequence numbers.

`--log-tcp-options`

Log options from the TCP packet header.

`--log-ip-options`

Log options from the IP packet header.

`--log-uid`

Log UID of the process that generated the packet.

MARK

Set netfilter mark value for packet. Only valid with `mangle` table.

`--set-mark <mark>`

Define mark to use.

MASQUERADE

Masquerade the IP address of the network interface from which the packet is leaving. Connections are forgotten when the interface goes down. Only for dialup connections without a static IP address. For static IPs, use the `SNAT` target. Can only be used with the `nat` table in the `POSTROUTING` chain.

`--to-ports <port>-<port>`

Range of source ports to use. Only works if `-p tcp` or `-p udp` is used.

MIRROR

Invert the source and destination fields in the IP header and send the packet again. Can only be used in the `INPUT`, `FORWARD`, and `PREROUTING` chains or user-defined chains called from these chains. Experimental.

NETMAP

Statically map a network of address onto another one. Only works with the nat table.

`--to <address>/<mask>`

Which network address on which to map. The mask is optional.

NFQUEUE

Extension of the `QUEUE` target. Allows the packet to be placed in a specific queue.

`--queue-num <num>`

16-bit queue number in which to place the packet, from 0 to 65535. Defaults to 0.

NOTRACK

Disable connection tracking for packets matching the rule. Only works with the `raw` table.

REDIRECT

Redirect packet to the local host by modifying the destination IP to the primary address of the incoming network interface. Only works with the `nat` table in the `PREROUTING` and `OUTPUT` chains or a user-defined chain called from these chains.

`--to-ports <port>-<port>`

Individual destination port or port range. Must only be used with `-p tcp` or `-p udp`.

REJECT

If packet matches, an error packet is sent back as a response. Only works with the `INPUT`, `FORWARD`, and `OUTPUT` chains or a user-defined chain called from these chains.

`--reject-with <type>`

The error message sent back depends on the type chosen. The `icmp-port-unreachable` type is the default. Valid types: `icmp-net-unreachable`, `icmp-host-unreachable`, `icmp-port-unreachable`, `icmp-proto-unreachable`, `icmp-net-prohibited`, `icmp-host-prohibited`, `icmp-admin-prohibited`

ROUTE

Change the default routing. Must be used with the `mangle` table.

`--oif <nic>`

Route through the defined NIC.

`--iif <nic>`

Modify incoming interface of packet to defined NIC.

`--gw <ip>`

Route the packet through the defined gateway.

`--continue`

Act like a nonterminating target and keep processing the rules. Can't be used with `--iif` or `--tee`.

`--tee`

Route a copy of the packet to the given destination. The original packet acts like a nonterminating target and keeps processing the rules. Can't be used with `--iif` or `--continue`.

SAME

Gives each client the same source and destination address for each connection based on a range.

`--to <ip>-<ip>`

Range of IP address to use.

`--nodst`

When calculating the source address, don't take the destination address into consideration.

SET

Add or delete from IP sets defined by `ipset`.

`--add-set <setname> <flags>`

Add addresses or ports to the named set. `<Flags>` is a comma-separated list, which can be `src` and/or `dst`.

`--del-set <setname> <flags>`

Delete addresses or ports to the named set. `<Flags>` is a comma-separated list, which can be `src` and/or `dst`.

SNAT

Modify the source address of the packet and all new packets from the same connection. Do not process any more rules. Must be used in combination with the `nat` table in the `POSTROUTING` chain.

`--to-source <ipaddr>-<ipaddr>:<port>-<port>`

Define a new source IP or a range for the new source IP. Optionally, provide a port range, which can only be used with `-p tcp` or `-p udp`. If a port range is not defined, ports below 512 are changed to ports below 512, ports from 512 to 1023 are mapped to ports below 1024, and all other ports are mapped to port 1024 and above.

TARPIT

Without using local per-connection resources, capture and hold incoming TCP connections. After connections are accepted, they are instantly changed to the persist state so the remote side stops sending data but continues requests every 60 to 240 seconds. Requests to close the connection are not accepted, which causes the connection to time out in 12 to 24 minutes.

TCPMSS

Used to control the maximum connection size. Alter the MSS value of TCP SYN packets. Only valid with `-p tcp` in the `mangle` table.

`--set-mss <mss>`

Set MSS to defined value.

`--clamp-mss-to-pmtu`

Clamp MSS value to 40 less than path_MTU.

TOS

Set the 8-bit TOS field in IP header. Only works with the `mangle` table.

`--set-tos <tos>`

Numerical value of TOS to use or the TOS name. Use the `iptables -j TOS -h` command to retrieve a list of TOS names.

TRACE

Enable packet tracing for packets that match the rule.

TTL

Change the IP version 4 TTL (Time To Live) header field, which defines how many times a packet can be re-routed before its time to live expires. Must be used in conjunction with the `mangle` table. Dangerous. Use with extreme caution.

`--ttl-set <ttl>`

24

Set TTL value.

`--ttl-dec <amount>`

Decrease TTL value by defined amount.

`--ttl-inc <amount>`

Increase TTL by default amount.

ULOG

User-space logging for packets that match the rule. Packet is multicast through a netlink socket so userspace processes can subscribe to it and receive the packets.

`--ulog-nlgroup <nlgroup>`

Packet is sent to the chosen netlink group, defined by a number from 1 to 32. Defaults to 1.

`--ulog-prefix <prefix>`

Define a prefix up to 32 characters for the log messages to set them apart from other messages.

`--ulog-cprange <num>`

Number of bytes to copy to user-space. If set to 0, the whole packet is copied. Defaults to 0.

`--ulog-qthreshold <num>`

How many packets to queue inside the kernel before transmitting them as one multi-part netlink message. Defaults to 1.

XOR

Encrypt TCP and UDP traffic using XOR encryption.

`--key <string>`

Set a key.

`--block-size <size>`

Set block size.

Starting and Stopping the IPTables Service

The IPTables service can be started and stopped using the `iptables` service. The script to manage the service has many other options. As root, the following `<options>` can be used with the `service iptables <options>` command:

- `start`: Start service with the rules defined in `/etc/sysconfig/iptables`.
- `stop`: Flush firewall rules, delete chains, unload kernel modules, and set policy to accept all packets again.
- `restart`: Stop the service, then start it again.

- condrestart: Stop the service, then start it again but only if it is already running.
- save: Save current rules in /etc/sysconfig/iptables.
- status: If firewall is active, display output of rules.
- panic: Same as stop, but after the firewall is disabled, the policy is set to drop all packets.

To activate the firewall at boot time, execute the following as root:

```
chkconfig iptables on
```

Saving the IPTables Rules

IPTables rules can be set on the command line by issuing the iptables commands one by one as root. However, they are only in effect until the system is rebooted or the table of rules is cleared. They are not saved. Executing individual iptables commands is useful for testing the syntax of new rules or watching how they affect packets in real-time. However, at some point, the rules need to be saved so that they can be used on subsequent reboots. After setting up your rules, use the following command as root to save them to /etc/sysconfig/iptables:

```
service iptables save
```

The next time the system is rebooted and the iptables service is started, the rules are read from the file and re-enabled.

Alternately, you can add your IPTables rules directly to the /etc/sysconfig/iptables file.

IPTables Examples

With so many tables, chains, and targets, the possible IPTables rules seem endless. This section gives some common examples to help you understand how it all fits together.

- Flush rules for the INPUT, FORWARD, and OUTPUT chains:

```
iptables -F INPUT
iptables -F FORWARD
iptables -F OUTPUT
```

- Drop all incoming and forwarding packets but allow outgoing packets to be sent:

```
iptables -P INPUT DROP
iptables -P FORWARD DROP
iptables -P OUTPUT ACCEPT
```

- To allow incoming and outgoing connections to the port used for a network service:

```
iptables -A INPUT -p tcp --sport <port> -j ACCEPT
iptables -A OUTPUT -p tcp --dport <port> -j ACCEPT
```

For example, to allow SSH connections:

```
iptables -A INPUT -p tcp --sport 22 -j ACCEPT
iptables -A OUTPUT -p tcp --dport 22 -j ACCEPT
```

- On an internal webserver with eth1 connected to the internal network and eth0 connected to the Internet, only accept web connections from internal clients on port 80, assuming all internal packets are routed to eth1. Drop all packets coming from the Internet, regardless of the port.

```
iptables -A INPUT -i eth0 -j DROP
iptables -A INPUT -p tcp --sport 80 -i eth1 -j ACCEPT
iptables -A OUTPUT -p tcp --dport 80 -i eth1 -j ACCEPT
```

- Allow the server to masquerade packets from other systems using it as a gateway:

```
iptables -t nat -A POSTROUTING -o eth0 -j MASQUERADE
```

For this to work, IP forwarding must also be enabled in the kernel by changing the value of `net.ipv4.ip_forward` to 1 in `/etc/sysctl.conf` by the root user:

```
net.ipv4.ip_forward=1
```

Changes to this file do not take effect until the `sysctl -p` command is executed by root.

- Using the `connlimit` match extension, limit the number of simultaneous SSH connections to the server per client IP address to 3:

```
iptables -p tcp --syn --dport 22 -m connlimit --connlimit-above 3 -j REJECT
```

Enabling the Default Firewall

If you just need to set which ports should accept connections and which ports should deny requests for connections, you can enable the default Red Hat Enterprise Linux firewall and then specify specific ports on which to allow connections. This default firewall is a predefined set of IPTables rules. Using this default set of rules and then adding ports on which to accept connections instead of writing your own custom IPTables rules works best for desktop systems that aren't offering any server or network services and single-purpose systems that only need to accept connections on specific ports such as the FTP port for an FTP server.

To enable the default firewall, use the Security Level Configuration program in Red Hat Enterprise Linux. To start the program, select **Administration**, **Security Level and Firewall** from the **System** menu on the top panel on the desktop or execute the `system-config-securitylevel` command. This is the same application used in the Setup Agent the first time the system is booted as mentioned in Chapter 2, "Post-Installation Configuration." If you configured a security level with the Setup Agent, it can be modified with this tool at any time. To use this program, you must have the `system-config-securitylevel` RPM package installed. Refer to Chapter 3 for details on installing software.

As shown in Figure 24.1, there are two tabs in the application: **Firewall Options** and **SELinux**. The **Firewall Options** tab is for enabling or disabling the default firewall.

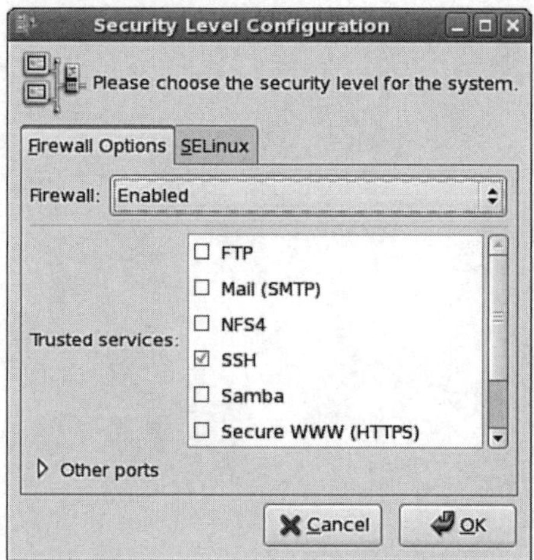

FIGURE 24.1 Enabling the Security Level

Start by selecting **Enabled** or **Disabled** from the **Firewall** pull-down menu. If you choose **Disabled**, a security level is not implemented and your system will accept connections to all ports with services running on them unless SELinux, custom IPTables rules, or other security measures have been enabled instead.

Selecting **Enabled** rejects all connections to all port except the ones selected from the **Trusted services** list or added to the **Other ports** list. Notice that SSH is selected by default. The following trusted services can be selected so their default ports accept connections:

- FTP
- Mail (SMTP)
- NFS4
- SSH
- Samba
- Secure WWW (HTTPS)
- Telnet
- WWW (HTTP)

To accept connections to additional ports, click the arrow beside **Other ports** to display the input box. For each port to add, click **Add**. A dialog window as shown in Figure 24.2 appears prompting for a port number and the protocol (tcp or udp). Click **OK** to add it to the port list.

24

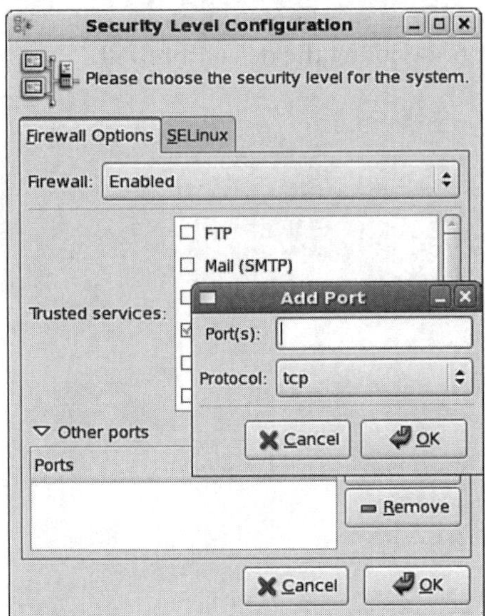

FIGURE 24.2 Adding Additional Ports

If you are logged in remotely via SSH, be sure to select SSH as a trusted device so you remain connected to the system. Finally, click **OK** in the main window to enable the firewall.

The security level tool uses IPTables rules to configure the firewall for commonly used services. After setting which services to allow, the rules are written to `/etc/sysconfig/iptables`. The `iptables` service must be running as discussed earlier in the chapter for the firewall to work. When the firewall is enabled in the `system-config-securitylevel` tool, the system is automatically configured to start the `iptables` service at boot-time, and it is immediately started if it is not already on.

CAUTION

Do not use the `system-config-securitylevel` program after writing and saving custom rules because the custom rules will be overwritten when a new `/etc/sysconfig/iptables` file is written by the program.

Summary

As you have read, IPTables offers very simple to extremely complex packet filtering. It can be used to block all connection requests, only allow requests for a specific port through, limit the number of simultaneous connections per client while logging the state of the connections, forward requests to a different server, modify the destination of a packet, and more.

If you just need a simple firewall to block all connections except ones on specific ports, you can enable the basic Red Hat Enterprise Linux firewall using the Security Level graphical application.

CHAPTER 25

Linux Auditing System

IN THIS CHAPTER

- Configuring the Audit Daemon
- Writing Audit Rules and Watches
- Starting and Stopping the Daemon
- Analyzing the Records
- Tracing a Process with Audit

The 2.6 Linux kernel has the ability to log events such as system calls and file access. These logs can then be reviewed by the administrator to determine possible security breaches such as failed login attempts or a user failing to access system files. This functionality, called the *Linux Auditing System*, is available in Red Hat Enterprise Linux 5.

To use the Linux Auditing System, use the following steps:

1. Configure the audit daemon.
2. Add audit rules and watches to collect desired data.
3. Start the daemon, which enables the Linux Auditing System in the kernel and starts the logging.
4. Periodically analyze data by generating audit reports and searching the logs.

This chapter discusses each of these steps in detail.

Configuring the Audit Daemon

The Linux Auditing System in the kernel is turned off by default in Red Hat Enterprise Linux 5. When the audit daemon is started, this kernel feature is enabled. To enable the Linux Auditing System at startup without using the daemon `auditd`, boot with the `audit=1` parameter. If this parameter is set to `1` and `auditd` is not running, the audit logs are written to `/var/log/messages`.

To use `auditd` and the utilities for generating log file reports, the `audit` RPM package must be installed. If it is not installed, refer to Chapter 3, "Operating System Updates," for instructions on package installation.

Using `auditd` allows the administrator to customize the audit logs produced. The following are just some of the customizations available:

- Setting a dedicated log file for audit messages
- Determining whether or not the log file is rotated
- Enabling warnings if the log files start to take up too much disk space
- Configuring audit rules to log more detailed information
- Activating file and directory watches

These settings and more are configured in the `/etc/audit/auditd.conf` file, which contains options to modify the behavior of the audit daemon. Each option should be on a separate line followed by an equals sign (=) and the value for the option. Listing 25.1 shows the default configuration file.

LISTING 25.1 Default Audit Daemon Parameters

```
#
# This file controls the configuration of the audit daemon
#

log_file = /var/log/audit/audit.log
log_format = RAW
priority_boost = 3
flush = INCREMENTAL
freq = 20
num_logs = 4
dispatcher = /sbin/audispd
disp_qos = lossy
max_log_file = 5
max_log_file_action = ROTATE
space_left = 75
space_left_action = SYSLOG
action_mail_acct = root
admin_space_left = 50
admin_space_left_action = SUSPEND
disk_full_action = SUSPEND
disk_error_action = SUSPEND
```

The following options can be configured (refer to Listing 25.1 for the default values):

`log_file`

Full path to the audit log file. If you configure the daemon to write logs to a directory other than the default `/var/log/audit/`, be sure to change the file permissions on it so that only root has read, write, and execute permissions. All other users should not be able to access the directory or the log files in the directory.

`log_format`

Format to use when writing logs. When set to `RAW`, the data is written to the log file in the exact format retrieved from the kernel. When set to `NOLOG`, data is not written to the log file, but data is still sent to the audit event dispatcher if one is specified with the `dispatcher` option.

`priority_boost`

How much of a priority boost the audit daemon should take. Must be a non-negative number with `0` indicating no change.

`flush`

How often to write data to log file. Value can be one of `NONE`, `INCREMENTAL`, `DATA`, and `SYNC`. If set to `NONE`, no special effort is made to flush data to the log file. If set to `INCREMENTAL`, the value of the `freq` option is used to determine how often a flush to disk occurs. If set to `DATA`, the audit data and log file are in constant synchronization. If set to `SYNC`, the data and meta-data are synchronized with every write to the log file.

`freq`

If `flush` is set to `INCREMENTAL`, the number of records the audit daemon receives from the kernel before writing them to the log file.

`num_logs`

Number of log files to keep if `max_log_file_action` is set to `ROTATE`. Must be a number from 0 to 99. If set to less than 2, logs are not rotated. If the number of log files is increased, it might be necessary to increase the kernel backlog setting in `/etc/audit/audit.rules` to allow time for the log rotation. If a `num_logs` value is not set, it defaults to `0`, which means the log file is never rotated.

`dispatcher`

Program started by the audit daemon when the daemon is started. All audit events are passed to the program. It can be used to further customize reports or produce them in a different format compatible with your custom analysis programs. Sample code for a customized program can be found in `/usr/share/doc/audit-<version>/skeleton.c`. The dispatcher program is run with root privileges, so practice extreme caution when using this option. This option is not required.

`disp_qos`

Controls the type of communication between the dispatcher and the audit daemon. Valid values are `lossy` and `lossless`. If set to `lossy`, incoming events sent to the dispatcher are discarded if the buffer between the audit daemon and dispatcher is full (the buffer is 128 kilobytes). However, events are still written to disk as long as `log_format` is not set to `nolog`. If set to `lossless`, the daemon waits for the buffer to have sufficient space before sending the event to the dispatcher and before writing the log to disk.

`max_log_file`

Maximum log file size, in megabytes. When this size is reached, the action specified with `max_log_file_action` is taken.

`max_log_file_action`

Action to take when the log file size from `max_log_file` is reached. Value must be one of `IGNORE`, `SYSLOG`, `SUSPEND`, `ROTATE`, and `KEEP_LOGS`. If set to `IGNORE`, no action is taken after the log file size reaches `max_log_file`. If set to `SYSLOG`, a warning is written to the system log `/var/log/messages` after the file size is reached. If set to `SUSPEND`, audit messages aren't written to the log file after the file size is reached. If set to `ROTATE`, the log file is rotated after reaching the specified file size, but only a certain number of old log files are saved as set by the `num_logs` parameter. The old log files will have the filename `audit.log.N`, where N is a number. The larger the number, the older the log file. If set to `KEEP_LOGS`, the log file is rotated, but the `num_logs` parameter is ignored so that no log files are deleted.

`space_left`

Amount of free disk space in megabytes. When this level is reached, the action from the `space_left_action` parameter is taken.

`space_left_action`

When the amount of free disk space reaches the value from `space_left`, this action is taken. Valid values are `IGNORE`, `SYSLOG`, `EMAIL`, `SUSPEND`, `SINGLE`, and `HALT`. If set to `IGNORE`, no action is taken. If set to `SYSLOG`, a warning message is written to the system log `/var/log/messages`. If set to `EMAIL`, an email is sent to the address from `action_mail_acct`, and a warning message is written to `/var/log/messages`. If set to `SUSPEND`, no more log messages are written to the audit log file. If set to `SINGLE`, the system is put in single user mode. If set to `HALT`, the system is shut down.

`action_mail_acct`

Email address of the administrator responsible for maintaining the audit daemon and logs. If the address does not have a hostname, it is assumed the address is local such as `root`. `sendmail` must be installed and configured to send email to the specified email address.

`admin_space_left`

Amount of free disk space in megabytes. Use this option to set a more aggressive action than `space_left_action` in case the `space_left_action` does not cause the administrator to free any disk space. This value should be lower than `space_left_action`. If this level is reached, the action from `admin_space_left_action` is taken.

admin_space_left_action

> Action to take when the amount of free disk space reaches admin_space_left. Valid values are IGNORE, SYSLOG, EMAIL, SUSPEND, SINGLE, and HALT. The actions associated with these values are the same as the ones from space_left_action.

disk_full_action

> Take this action if the partition containing the audit log file becomes full. Possible values are IGNORE, SYSLOG, SUSPEND, SINGLE, and HALT. The actions associated with these values are the same as the ones from space_left_action.

TIP

If the audit log files are not rotated, the partition containing the /var/log/audit/ can become full and cause system errors. Thus, it is recommended that /var/log/audit/ be a separate dedicated partition.

disk_error_action

> Action to take if an error is detected while writing audit logs or rotating the audit log files. The value must be one of IGNORE, SYSLOG, SUSPEND, SINGLE, and HALT. The actions associated with these values are the same as the ones from space_left_action.

The /etc/sysconfig/auditd file can be used to set command-line options for auditd with the EXTRAOPTIONS parameter. The only command line option, -f, puts the daemon in debugging mode. If debugging mode is enabled, messages go to standard error instead of the log file. The AUDITD_LANG setting can be used to change the locale for the daemon. If set to none, all locale information is removed from the audit environment. If the AUDITD_CLEAN_STOP option is set to yes, audit rules and watches are deleted when the audit daemon is stopped with the service auditd stop command. For more information on audit rules, refer to the next section.

Writing Audit Rules and Watches

The Linux Auditing System can be used to write rules for events such as system calls and to watch operations on files or directories using the auditctl command-line utility. If the initialization script is used to start auditd (using the service auditd start command), the rules and watches can be added to /etc/audit/audit.rules so they are executed when the daemon is started. Only the root user can read or modify this file.

Each rule and watch in /etc/audit/audit.rules must be on its own line, with lines beginning with # being ignored. The rules and watches are the auditctl command-line options without the auditctl command preceding them. They are read from the top of the file to the bottom. If one or more rules or watches conflict with each other, the first one found is used.

Writing Audit Rules

To add an audit rule, use the following syntax in the /etc/audit/audit.rules file:

```
-a <list>,<action> <options>
```

CAUTION

If you add rules /etc/audit/audit.rules while the daemon is running, be sure to enable the changes with the service auditd restart command as root. The service auditd reload command can also be used, but you will not be notified of configuration file errors.

The list name must be one of the following:

`task`

Per task list. It is only used when a task is created. Only fields known at creation time such as UID can be used with this list.

`entry`

System call entry list. Used when entering a system call to determine if an audit even should be created.

`exit`

System call exit list. Used when exiting a system call to determine if an audit even should be created.

`user`

User message filter list. The kernel uses this list to filter user space events before passing them on to the audit daemon. The only valid fields are `uid`, `auid`, `gid`, and `pid`.

`exclude`

Event type exclusion filter list. Used to filter events the administrator doesn't want to see. Use the `msgtype` field to specify message types you don't want to log.

The action must be one of the following:

`never`

Do not generate audit records.

`always`

Allocate audit context, always fill it in at system call entry, and always write an audit record at system call exit.

The `<options>` can include one or more of the following:

-S <syscall>

Specify a system call by name or number. To specify all system calls, use `all` as the system call name. Start an audit record if a program uses this system call. Multiple system calls can be specified for the same rule, and each one must start with `-S`. Specifying multiple system calls in the same rule instead of listing separate rules will result in better performance because only one rule has to be evaluated.

-F <name[=,!=,<,>,<=,>=]value>

Specify a rule field. If multiple fields are specified for a rule, all fields must be true to start an audit record. Each rule must start with `-F`, and up to 64 rules may be specified. If usernames and group names are used as fields instead of UIDs and GIDs, they are resolved to UIDs and GIDs for the matching. The following are valid field names:

`pid`

Process ID.

`ppid`

Process ID of the parent process.

`uid`

User ID.

`euid`

Effective user ID.

`suid`

Set user ID.

`fsuid`

Filesystem user ID.

`gid`

Group ID.

`egid`

Effective group ID.

`sgid`

Set group ID.

`fsgid`

Filesystem group ID.

`auid`

Audit ID, or the original ID the user logged in with.

`msgtype`

Message type number. Should only be used on the exclude filter list.

`pers`

OS Personality Number.

`arch`

Processor architecture of the system call. Specify the exact architecture such as `i686` (can be retrieved from the `uname -m` command) or `b32` to use the 32-bit system call table or `b64` to use the 64-bit system call table.

`devmajor`

Device Major Number.

`devminor`

Device Minor Number.

`inode`

Inode Number.

`exit`

Exit value from system call.

`success`

Success value of system call. Use `1` for true/yes and `0` for false/no.

`a0`, `a1`, `a2`, `a3`

First four arguments to the system call, respectively. Only numerical values can be used.

`key`

Set a filter key with which to tag audit log message for the event. See Listing 25.2 and Listing 25.3 for examples. Similar to the `-k` option used when adding watches. Refer to "Writing Audit Rules and Watches" for details about the `-k` option.

`obj_user`

SELinux user for the resource.

`obj_role`

SELinux role for the resource.

`obj_type`

SELinux type for the resource.

`obj_lev_low`

SELinux low level for the resource.

`obj_lev_high`

SELinux high level for the resource.

`subj_user`

SELinux user for the program.

`subj_role`

SELinux role for the program.

`subj_type`

SELinux type for the program.

`subj_sen`

SELinux sensitivity for the program.

`subj_clr`

SELinux clearance for the program.

The `-a` option appends the rule to the list. To add the rule to the beginning of the list, replace `-a` with `-A`. Deleting a rule has the same syntax except `-a` is replaced by `-d`. To delete all rules, specify the `-D` option. Listing 25.2 contains some example audit rules for `/etc/audit/audit.rules`.

LISTING 25.2 Example Audit Rules

```
#Record all file opens from user 501
#Use with caution since this can quickly
#produce a large quantity of records
-a exit,always -S open -F uid=501 -F key=501open
#Record file permission changes
-a entry,always -S chmod
```

TIP

If the `audit` package is installed, additional examples are in the `*.rules` files `/usr/share/doc/audit-<version>/` directory.

When an action from the defined rules occurs, it is sent through the dispatcher if one is defined in `/etc/audit/auditd.conf`, and then a log message is written to `/var/log/audit/audit.log`. For example, Listing 25.3 contains the log entries for the first rule in Listing 25.2, which logs file opens from user 501. The rule includes a filter key, which appears at the end of the log entry in Listing 25.3.

LISTING 25.3 Example Audit Rule Log Message

```
type=SYSCALL msg=audit(1168206647.422:5227): arch=c000003e syscall=2 success=no
exit=-2 a0=7fff37fc5a40 a1=0 a2=2aaaaaaab000 a3=0 items=1 ppid=26640 pid=2716
auid=501 uid=501 gid=501 euid=501 suid=501 fsuid=501 egid=501 sgid=501 fsgid=501
tty=pts5 comm="vim" exe="/usr/bin/vim" key="501open"
```

Writing Audit Watches

The Linux Auditing System also allows administrators to watch files and directories. If a watch is placed on a file or directory, successful and failed actions such as opening and executing the file or directory are logged. To add watches, use the `-w` option followed by a file or directory to watch.

CAUTION

If you add watches `/etc/audit/audit.rules` while the daemon is running, be sure to enable the changes with the `service auditd restart` command as root. The `service auditd reload` command can also be used, but you will not be notified of configuration file errors.

Listing 25.4 contains example watches for inclusion in the `/etc/audit/audit.rules` file. If the `-k` <key> option is used in conjunction with `-w`, all records produced by the watch will contain an alert word (limited to 31 bytes) so that the records for the watch can be easily filtered out of the audit log files. To limit file or directory watches to certain actions, use the `-p` option followed by one or more of the following: `r` to watch read actions, `w` to watch write actions, `x` to watch execute actions, and `a` to watch append actions. To delete a watch, use the `-W` option followed by the file or directory.

LISTING 25.4 Example Audit Watches

```
#Watch for changes to sysconfig files
-w /etc/sysconfig -k SYSCONFIG
#Watch for changes to audit config files
-w /etc/audit/audit.rules -k AUDIT_RULES
-w /etc/audit/auditd.conf -k AUDIT_CONF
-w /var/log/audit/ -k LOG_AUDIT
#Watch to see who tries to start the VPN client
-w /usr/bin/vpnc -k VPNC -p x
#Watch password files
-w /etc/group -k PASSWD
-w /etc/passwd -k PASSWD
-w /etc/shadow -k PASSWD
```

For example, Listing 25.4 includes a watch on the password files with the key filter `PASSWD`. Listing 25.5 contains the log entries from `/var/log/audit/audit.log` after deleting a user, which modifies these password files being watched. Just like the example in Listing 25.3 for a rule with a filter key, the key is added to the end of the log entry so it can be easily filtered from the rest of the log entries.

LISTING 25.5 Example Log Entries for Audit Watches

```
type=SYSCALL msg=audit(1168227741.656:17915): arch=c000003e syscall=82
success=yes exit=0 a0=7fff00975dd0 a1=60a700 a2=0 a3=22 items=5 ppid=26575
pid=4147 auid=501 uid=0 gid=0 euid=0 suid=0 fsuid=0 egid=0 sgid=0 fsgid=0
tty=pts4 comm="userdel" exe="/usr/sbin/userdel" key="PASSWD"
```

Customizing `auditctl`

Command-line options for configuring the audit system parameters can also be included in `/etc/audit/audit.rules`. Table 25.1 lists these options.

TABLE 25.1 `auditctl` Options for Configuring Audit System Parameters

Option	Description
`-b <backlog>`	Maximum number of outstanding audit buffers allowed. The default from the kernel is 64. If all buffers are full, the kernel refers to the failure flag set with the `-f` option to determine which action to take.
`-e [0,1]`	Set to 0 to disable auditing, or set to 1 to enable auditing. Useful for temporarily disabling audit for troubleshooting or other purposes.
`-f [0,1,2]`	Set the failure flag used to tell the kernel how to handle critical errors such as the audit buffers being full or being out of kernel memory. Valid values are `0` (no action), 1 (use printk to log messages to `/var/log/messages`), and 2 (panic). The default is 1, but 2 is more secure.
`-r <rate>`	Rate limit in messages/second. If set to 0, there is no limit. If the rate limit is exceeded, the kernel consults the failure flag from the `-f` option to determine which action to take.
`-i`	Ignore errors when reading rules from a file.

To verify they have been set, use the `auditctl -s` command to view the status. The output looks like the following:

```
AUDIT_STATUS: enabled=1 flag=1 pid=1954 rate_limit=0 backlog_limit=256
lost=0 backlog=0
```

Starting and Stopping the Daemon

After configuring the daemon and adding rules and watches, start the daemon with the `service auditd start` command as root. To stop it, use the `service auditd stop` command. To enable it to automatically start at boot time, execute the `chkconfig auditd on` command as root.

If the daemon is already running when you modify its configuration, use the `service auditd restart` command as root to enable the changes. To verify that the rules and watches have been modified, use the `auditctl -l` command as root to list all active rules and watches. For example, Listing 25.6 shows the `auditctl -l` output for the rules and watches in Listing 25.2 and 25.4.

LISTING 25.6 Listing Audit Rules and Watches

```
LIST_RULES: entry,always syscall=chmod
LIST_RULES: exit,always uid=501 (0x1f5) key=tfox syscall=open
LIST_RULES: exit,always watch=/var/log/audit perm=rwxa key=LOG_AUDIT
LIST_RULES: exit,always watch=/etc/sysconfig perm=rwxa key=SYSCONFIG
LIST_RULES: exit,always watch=/etc/passwd perm=rwxa key=PASSWD
LIST_RULES: exit,always watch=/etc/shadow perm=rwxa key=PASSWD
LIST_RULES: exit,always watch=/etc/group perm=rwxa key=PASSWD
LIST_RULES: exit,always watch=/etc/audit/audit.rules perm=rwxa key=AUDIT_RULES
LIST_RULES: exit,always watch=/etc/audit/auditd.conf perm=rwxa key=AUDIT_CONF
LIST_RULES: exit,always watch=/usr/bin/vpnc perm=x key=VPNC
```

Analyzing the Records

If `auditd` is used, audit messages are written to `/var/log/audit/audit.log` unless the filename is changed with the `log_file` parameter in `/etc/audit/auditd.conf`. The log file is a text file and can be read with the `less` utility or a text editor such as Emacs or Vi. The messages are written in the format received from the kernel in the order they are received. The `aureport` utility can be used to generate summary reports from the log file. The `ausearch` utility can be used to search for reports based on criteria such as the audit event ID, a filename, UID or GID, message type, and system call name.

Unless the daemon is configured to rotate the log files and remove old ones as previously described in the "Configuring the Audit Daemon" section, the log files in `/var/log/audit/` are never removed. Administrators should check the logs frequently and remove old ones or move them to backup storage. If the logs are not removed periodically, they can fill up the entire disk. Because of this, it is recommended that `/var/log/audit/` be a separate dedicated partition so it does not affect the writing of other log files or cause other system errors.

TIP

To force the log file to be rotated immediately, issue the `service auditd rotate` command as root. The old log files will have the filename `audit.log.N`, where `N` is a number. The larger the number, the older the log file.

Generating Reports

To generate reports of the audit messages, use the `aureport`. The `/var/log/audit/` directory and all the audit log files in it are only readable by the root user for security. Thus, you must be the root user to execute the `aureport` command. If `aureport` is executed without any options, a summary report as shown in Listing 25.7 is displayed.

LISTING 25.7 `aureport` Summary

```
Summary Report
======================
Range of time: 11/29/2006 03:40:18.155 - 01/07/2007 23:29:02.898
Number of changes in configuration: 71
Number of changes to accounts, groups, or roles: 14
Number of logins: 38
Number of failed logins: 0
Number of users: 3
Number of terminals: 35
Number of host names: 7
Number of executables: 55
Number of files: 1186
Number of AVC denials: 0
Number of MAC events: 70
Number of failed syscalls: 2594
Number of anomaly events: 46
Number of responses to anomaly events: 0
Number of crypto events: 0
Number of process IDs: 3734
Number of events: 33743
```


To generate a more specific report, execute the `aureport` command as root followed by one or more options from Table 25.2. These options narrow down the report to specific data such as system calls or configuration changes.

TABLE 25.2 `aureport` Options for Generating Specific Reports

Option	Description
`-a`	Report messages about access vector cache (AVC)
`-c`	Report messages about configuration changes
`-cr`	Report messages about crypto events
`-e`	Report messages about events
`-f`	Report messages about files
`-h`	Report messages about hosts
`-l`	Report messages about logins
`-m`	Report messages about account modifications
`-ma`	Report messages about Mandatory Access Control (MAC) events
`-p`	Report messages about processes
`-s`	Report messages about system calls
`-tm`	Report messages about terminals

To produce results in more human-readable format such as replacing UIDs with the usernames they map to, also use the -i option:

```
aureport -<flag> -i
```

To display the start and stop times for each log, add the -t option:

```
aureport -<flag> -i -t
```

To display events equal to or before a specific time, add the -te option followed by end date and end time. Use the numerical format for the date and time for your locale, and specify the time in the 24-hour format. For example, for the en_us.UTF-8 locale, use the date format MM/DD/YY:

```
aureport -<flag> -i -te <end date> <end time>
```

To display events equal to or after a specific time, add the -ts option followed by start date and time. The same date and time formatting rules apply as the ones for the -te option:

```
aureport -<flag> -i -ts <start date> <start time>
```

To display only failed events use --failed; notice this option is prefixed with two dashes instead of one:

```
aureport -<flag> -i --failed
```

To display only successful events use --success; notice this option is prefixed with two dashes instead of one:

```
aureport -<flag> -i --success
```

Some reports can also be generated in a summary format with the --summary option; notice this option is prefixed with two dashes instead of one:

```
aureport -<flag> -i --summary
```

To produce a main summary report instead of one about one area, use the -r option:

```
aureport -r -i
```

To produce reports from a log file other than the default, specify it with the -if option:

```
aureport -<flag> -i -if /var/log/audit/audit.log.1
```

Searching the Records

In addition to generating event reports and summaries with aureport, administrators can also search the audit records with ausearch. As root, execute the ausearch command followed by one or more options from Table 25.3. If more than one option is specified, the results shown match both requests. To retrieve results that match the search criteria of one option *or* another option, perform two different searches and combine the results yourself.

TABLE 25.3 ausearch Options

Option	Description
`-a <event id>`	Show messages with a specific event ID. Each message contains an identification string such as `msg=audit (1145758414.468:8758)`. The number after the colon, such as 8758 in this example, is the audit event ID. All events from an application's system call have the same audit event ID so they can be grouped together.
`-c <comm name>`	Show messages with a specific comm name, which is the executable's name from the task structure. The comm name such as `firefox-bin` or `vim` is shown when searching for a specific audit event ID.
`-f <filename>`	Show messages concerning a specific filename. Useful if watching a file with `auditctl`.
`-ga <group id>`	Show messages with either an effective group ID or group ID that matches the given GID.
`-ge <group id>`	Show messages with an effective group ID that matches the given GID.
`-gi <group id>`	Show messages with a group ID that matches the given GID.
`-h`	Display brief help.
`-hn <hostname>`	Show messages containing a specific hostname.
`-i`	Show results in human-readable format.
`-if <logfile>`	Read logs from `<logfile>` instead of `/var/log/audit/audit.log` or file set with the `log_file` parameter in `/etc/audit/auditd.conf.log`.
`-k <key>`	Show messages with `<key>`.
`-m <mess type>`	Show messages containing a specific message type such as `CONFIG_CHANGE` or `USER_ACCT`.
`-o <SELinux context>`	Show messages containing `SELinux tcontext (object)` that match the provided string.
`-p <pid>`	Show messages with a specific process ID.
`-sc <syscall>`	Show messages about a particular system call, specified by the system call name or its numeric value.
`-se <SELinux context>`	Show messages containing `SELinux scontext/subject` or `tcontext/object` that match the provided string.
`-su <SELinux context>`	Show messages containing `SELinux scontext (subject)` that match the provided string.
`-sv <success value>`	Show successful or failed events by specifying the value `yes` or `no` to this option. As shown in Listing 25.8, the `success` value is followed by the `res` keyword at the end of the message and can be either `success` or `failed`.

25

TABLE 25.3 Continued

Option	Description
-te <date> <time>	Show messages with timestamps equal to or before a given date and time. The date and time formats depend on the system's locale. Specify the time using a 24-hour clock such as 23:00:00. For the en_US.UTF-8 locale, the date format is the numerical equivalent of MM/DD/YY.
-ts <date> <time>	Show messages with timestamps equal to or after a given time. Time and date format rules from the -te option apply.
-tm <terminal>	Show messages with the specified terminal such as pts/6. Some executables such as cron and atd use the daemon name for the terminal.
-ua <uid>	Show messages whose user ID, effective user ID, or login UID (auid) matches the one specified.
-ue <uid>	Show messages whose effective user ID matches the one specified.
-ui <uid>	Show messages whose user ID matches the one specified.
-ul <login id>	Show messages whose login UID matches the one specified.
-v	Display ausearch version.
-w	If a string to be matched is specified, only display results that match the entire word.
-x	Show messages about an executable such as crond or sudo. The full path to the executable is provided after the exe keyword in the message such as "/bin/sudo" in Listing 25.8.

Similar to aureport, the -i option can be used to make the output more human-readable, and the -if <filename> option can be used to provide an alternate log file in which to search.

When the results are displayed, each record is separated by a line of four dashes, and a timestamp precedes each record as shown in Listing 25.8.

LISTING 25.8 Results from ausearch -x sudo

```
time->Fri Dec  1 00:01:01 2006
type=CRED_ACQ msg=audit(1145210930.022:2023): user pid=30718 uid=0
auid=4294967295 msg='PAM: setcred acct=root : exe="/usr/bin/sudo"
(hostname=?, addr=?, terminal=pts/3 res=success)'
----
time->Fri Dec  1 04:01:01 2006
type=USER_START msg=audit(1145210930.022:2024): user pid=30718 uid=0
auid=4294967295 msg='PAM: session open acct=root : exe="/usr/bin/sudo"
(hostname=?, addr=?, terminal=pts/3 res=success)'
----
time->Fri Dec  1 04:42:01 2006
```

LISTING 25.8 Continued

```
type=USER_END msg=audit(1145210930.022:2025): user pid=30718 uid=0
auid=4294967295 msg='PAM: session close acct=root : exe="/usr/bin/sudo"
(hostname=?, addr=?, terminal=pts/3 res=success)'
----
time->Fri Dec  1 05:01:01 2006
type=CRED_ACQ msg=audit(1145249595.972:2482): user pid=2062 uid=0
auid=4294967295 msg='PAM: setcred acct=root : exe="/usr/bin/sudo"
(hostname=?, addr=?, terminal=pts/6 res=success)'
----
time->Fri Dec  1 06:01:01 2006
type=USER_START msg=audit(1145249595.972:2483): user pid=2062 uid=0
auid=4294967295 msg='PAM: session open acct=root : exe="/usr/bin/sudo"
(hostname=?, addr=?, terminal=pts/6 res=success)'
----
time->Fri Dec  1 09:01:01 2006
type=USER_END msg=audit(1145249595.972:2484): user pid=2062 uid=0
auid=4294967295 msg='PAM: session close acct=root : exe="/usr/bin/sudo"
(hostname=?, addr=?, terminal=pts/6 res=success)'
```


Tracing a Process with Audit

The `autrace` utility can be used to generate audit records from a specific process. No other rules or watches can be enabled while `autrace` is running. As with the other audit utilities, `autrace` must be run as root. To audit trace a process, use the following steps:

1. Temporarily turn off all rules and watches:

   ```
   auditctl -D
   ```

2. (Optional) To isolate the audit records from the process, force a log file rotation:

   ```
   service auditd rotate
   ```

   The logs for the `autrace` will be in `/var/log/audit/audit.log`.

3. Execute `autrace` on the command:

   ```
   autrace <command to trace>
   ```

4. Wait until the process is complete. A message similar to the following will be displayed:

   ```
   Trace complete. You can locate the records with 'ausearch -i -p 10773'
   ```

5. Restart the audit daemon to re-enable the rules and watches:

   ```
   service auditd restart
   ```

6. Use `ausearch` to display details about the trace.

Summary

The Linux Auditing System and the audit daemon can be used to collect system call and file access information from the kernel. The audit daemon writes log messages about these events to a dedicated log file. Reports can then be generated with the `aureport` and `ausearch` utilities to find failed system calls, to determine who is accessing files and how often, successful and failed attempts at executing programs, and much more.

Appendixes

APPENDIX A
Installing Proprietary Kernel Modules

IN THIS APPENDIX

- Installing Proprietary Modules
- Installing the nVidia Display Driver
- Recognizing a Tainted Kernel

Red Hat Enterprise Linux includes support for a wide variety of hardware in the form of kernel modules. These kernel modules allow the hardware and the kernel to interact so that the rest of the operating system and applications can communicate with the hardware.

Ideally, all the kernel modules you need are included with Red Hat Enterprise Linux. However, if others are required, this appendix explains how they work with the kernel and how to identify them.

The Linux kernel is licensed under the GNU General Public License (GPL), meaning that its source code is available at kernel.org for anyone to download and read and that anyone can modify the code if the modified code is also available under the GPL. All the kernel modules distributed with Red Hat Enterprise Linux are licensed under the GPL or GPL-compatible licenses.

TIP

Chapter 6, "Analyzing Hardware," describes how to list and configure kernel module parameters.

How are kernel modules written? Sometimes open source developers have the cooperation of the hardware vendors to gain access to the hardware specifications necessary to write an open source kernel module for it. Because of the open source model, the module is improved over time as users find problems and report them to the developer or other developers tweak the code as they find problems.

Sometimes, hardware vendors write their own Linux kernel modules. Some even make the Linux modules they write open source. However, some choose not to release their kernel modules under the GPL or GPL-compatible license (called a proprietary module). If the open source community hasn't written an equivalent open source version of the module (usually because the hardware has just been released or because the open source community does not have enough information about the hardware to write an open source module), the proprietary module is an administrator's only option if he wants to use the hardware with the Linux operating system.

Installing Proprietary Modules

The process for installing third-party modules differs from module to module:

- Some modules are distributed in RPM format, which makes them easy to install. Refer to Chapter 5, "Working with RPM Software," for details on installing an RPM package.
- Some modules require the administrator to run a script (supplied with the module when downloaded) that guides you through the installation.
- Others might require that parts of the module to be compiled. However, most third-party modules come with detailed installation instructions.

Even the process of loading proprietary modules differs from module to module:

- Some use user-space applications to load them.
- Some use initialization scripts that can be run at boot time. Refer to Chapter 4, "Understanding Linux Concepts," for more information on initialization scripts.
- Some require the module be listed in `/etc/modprobe.conf` such as the following for a module named example for the first Ethernet card:

  ```
  alias eth0 example
  ```

After installing the module and following the instructions for loading it, use the `/sbin/lsmod` command to verify that it has been loaded.

Bottom line: Follow the instructions that are included with the proprietary module and contact the distributor of the module such as the hardware vendor if it does not load or work properly with the Red Hat Enterprise Linux kernel. It is difficult for the open source community or the Red Hat engineering team to troubleshoot and fix an issue if the source code is not available to debug.

Installing the nVidia Display Driver

This section shows the process of installing the nVidia Linux display driver for the x86_64 architecture. This example is based on version 1.0-9746 of the driver downloaded from http://www.nvidia.com/object/linux_display_amd64_1.0-9746.html. Instructions for installing a different version may differ.

CAUTION

The instructions in this section are specific to version 1.0-9746 of the nVidia display driver. Instructions for other kernel modules may differ. Be sure to carefully read the instructions for the driver you are downloading.

Use the following steps to install the display driver from http://www.nvidia.com/object/linux_display_amd64_1.0-9746.html:

NOTE

The driver does not currently work with the Virtualization kernel. Be sure you are not running the Virtualization kernel before continuing. Refer to Appendix B for details on Virtualization.

1. Read the NVIDIA software license and be sure you agree to it before proceeding. Note that it is not GPL-compatible. A link to the license is on the download page.
2. Before downloading the driver, install the `kernel-devel`, `xorg-x11-server-sdk`, and `gcc` RPM packages so that the precompiled kernel interface can be found or compiled. The `kernel-devel` package is specific to the kernel version running, so be sure to install the correct version. If you use the following command to download and install from RHN, the proper version is installed:

   ```
   yum install kernel-devel xorg-x11-server-sdk gcc
   ```

3. Download the installation script from the nVidia website, `NVIDIA-Linux-x86_64-1.0-9746-pkg2.run`.
4. You cannot be running the X server (the graphical desktop or login screen) when installing the driver. Log out of the graphical desktop if you are logged in so that you are at the graphical login screen. Press the key combination Ctrl+Alt+F1 to go to the first virtual terminal. Log in as the root user and execute the command `init 3` to completely stop the X server.
5. As root, run the installation script to start the installation process (specify the full path to the script if you are not in the same directory):

   ```
   sh  NVIDIA-Linux-x86_64-1.0-9746-pkg2.run
   ```

6. A simple text-based interface is used during the installation process. Accept the license to continue.
7. A message is displayed stating that no precompiled kernel interface was found to match the kernel. You can choose to download it from the nVidia FTP site.
8. If you choose to download it but it can't be found or you choose not to download it, the next step shows the kernel interface being compiled.
9. Answer Yes to the question asking whether to install the NVIDIA 32-bit compatibility OpenGL libraries. The interfaces shows the progress as it searches for conflicting OpenGL files and then installs the driver.
10. After driver installation is complete, you are asked whether you want the `nvidia-xconfig` utility run to configure the X server configuration file so that the nVidia driver is used the next time X is started. Choose Yes to this question to configure the `/etc/X11/xorg.conf` file. The old file is saved as `/etc/X11/xorg.conf.backup`.
11. Finally, select OK to exit the installation program.

12. Now, you can restart the X server and start using the nVidia display driver. Execute the `init 5` command as root to start the graphical login screen.

To verify that the driver is being used, execute the following command:

```
lsmod | grep nvidia
```

You should see a line similar to the following if the kernel module is loaded:

```
nvidia                5698648  22
```

Recognizing a Tainted Kernel

The license of a particular kernel module can be determined with the following command:

```
modinfo <module> | grep license
```

For example, the following output shows that the module is written under the GPL:

```
license:        GPL
```

The following shows the output from the `modinfo nvidia | grep license` for the nVidia display driver, which is distributed under the nVidia license:

```
license:        NVIDIA
```

If a proprietary kernel is loaded when a kernel crash occurs, it is very difficult to debug the problem because the source code is not available. For this reason, a mechanism was added to the kernel to allow developers and users to determine whether proprietary modules are loaded. When a kernel module is loaded, the kernel checks for a macro called MODULE_LICENSE. If the license is not an approved open source license such as the GPL, the kernel is flagged as "tainted."

How can you determine whether the kernel is tainted? The `/sbin/lsmod` command lists the currently loaded modules. If you pipe it through `less`, you can read the header:

```
/sbin/lsmod | less
```

If you see the phrase `Tainted: P` at the end of the header, proprietary kernel modules are loaded:

```
Module                  Size  Used by    Tainted: P
```

If the kernel crashes while a proprietary module is loaded, try reproducing the crash without the kernel module loaded. If the problem goes away, chances are that the module itself is causing the crash. If the problem still occurs with an untainted kernel, the problem is likely in either the kernel or another kernel module.

APPENDIX B
Creating Virtual Machines

IN THIS CHAPTER

- Virtualization System Requirements
- Installing Virtualization
- Setting Up the VM and Installing the Guest OS
- Introducing the `virsh` Command
- Starting and Stopping the Virtual Machine
- Modifying Dedicated Resources
- Performing Additional Actions
- Managing VMs with the `xm` Utility

Introduced in Fedora Core 4 as a technology preview, virtualization is now a supported feature of Red Hat Enterprise Linux 5. Virtualization allows multiple operating systems (OS) to run on the same physical hardware inside *virtual machines* (VM). The operating systems can be the same OS, different versions of the same OS, or different OSes.

The benefits of virtualization include the following:

- Better use of hardware. Instead of the system resources sitting idle, they can be used for multiple OS instances.
- Less hardware. It takes fewer systems to run multiple OS instances.
- Separation of services. Multiple services or applications do not have to work together in one OS environment. If different library versions or kernel versions are required, it is easily achieved with Virtualization.
- Separation of failures. If one VM goes down or needs to be taken offline for maintenance, the other VMs are not affected.
- Separation of data. The filesystems for each VM are not shared unless file sharing is explicitly configured. Users of one VM cannot view the data on a different VM, allowing an administrator to configure VMs for different groups who can share data among themselves. Also, if one VM is compromised, the data on the other VMs are safe from the security breach.
- Easier recovery. If a VM goes down, the host system and other VMs are still up and running so the failed VM can be recovered.

- Dedicated resource allocation. Each VM is allocated specific resources so one can't use 100% of the resources and cause the others to slow down or stop responding.
- Multiple OSes or OS versions. One system can run multiple OSes or different versions of the same OS, converting one test system into multiple test systems for software development.

This appendix guides the reader through the process of creating VMs, starting and stopping VMs, and managing them with the virtualization tools.

Virtualization System Requirements

The host system must use the GRUB boot loader, which is the default for Red Hat Enterprise Linux. It is required to be able to boot into the Virtualization guests.

CAUTION

The Virtualization feature of Red Hat Enterprise Linux will not work if SELinux is enabled. Refer to Chapter 23, "Protecting Against Intruders with Security-Enhanced Linux," for instructions on disabling it before continuing.

Before installing and configuring the Virtualization feature, be sure you have enough system resources for each virtual machine. The system resources for each VM must be in addition to the system resources needed for the host machine. The additional disk space requirements for each virtual machine are the same as those for a Red Hat Enterprise Linux install. The amount of disk space necessary depends on the type of system you are configuring. Approximately 4 GB is recommended as a minimum.

A disk partition or a disk image file can be used as the virtual disk space. The disk image is created during setup if it does not already exist, so the disk space for it just needs to be part of the existing mounted filesystem. To use a disk partition, create it first and then follow the steps for creating a VM. At least 500 MB of RAM is recommended for each virtual guest, possibly more depending on the desired function of the guest.

CAUTION

Red Hat Enterprise Linux 5 includes version 3 of the `xen` RPM package. It is not compatible with virtual guests set up with previous versions of this package.

Currently, Virtualization only runs as a supported feature on x86 and x86_64 systems. Virtualization for the Itanium2 is also available with Red Hat Enterprise Linux 5 but is only offered as a technology preview. To run Virtualization on an x86 system, the processor must have Physical Address Extension (PAE) support. To determine if your processor has PAE support, look for the `pae` flag in the list of flags for the processor in the `/proc/cpuinfo` virtual file. To only display the line of flags, use the command `cat /proc/cpuinfo | grep flags`, which shows a line similar to the following:

```
flags           : fpu vme de pse tsc msr pae mce cx8 apic mtrr pge mca \
cmov pat pse36 clflush dts acpi mmx fxsr sse sse2 ss ht tm up
```

There are two types of virtualization: para-virtualization and full virtualization. Para-virtualization creates a VM for the guest OS, but the virtual hardware is not exactly identical to the actual physical hardware. An OS run inside a para-virtualized VM must support para-virtualization so that the virtual hardware is recognized. For example, with Virtualization, the disk image used as the virtual hard drive has the device name xvda.

On a fully virtualized system, the hardware is simulated so that the guest OS does not have to support virtualization. For example, the virtual hard drive for a VM on a fully virtualized host uses the device name sda for the first SCSI hard drive so that the guest OS is unaware that it is running inside a VM. It is slower than para-virtualization.

Para-virtualization can be run on the x86_64 and Itanium2 architectures and x86 system with the PAE extension. To achieve full virtualization, the processor on the host system must be 64-bit (x86_64 or Itanium2) and must have a Hardware Virtual Machine (HVM) layer referred to as `vmx` for Intel processors and `svm` for AMD processors. Check the list of flags in `/proc/cpuinfo` for the flag corresponding to your 64-bit processor. If you do not find it, be sure this feature has been enabled in the BIOS.

Installing Virtualization

The Virtualization feature can be installed during the installation process or after it. To install it while installing the operating system, enter an installation code that includes virtualization support. This code should have been provided with your Red Hat Enterprise Linux subscription if you elected to purchase the virtualization feature. To verify that the installation will include the Virtualization packages, select to customize the software selection. On the next screen, the Virtualization software group should appear and should be selected as shown in Figure B.1. This software group is only shown if an installation code that includes virtualization is entered at the beginning of the installation program.

To install Virtualization after the initial installation process is complete, first subscribe the system to the Virtualization channel in Red Hat Network. It will be listed as a child channel of the Red Hat Enterprise Linux 5 channel for the system. Go to rhn.redhat.com to perform this action and for detailed instructions on subscribing to additional channels.

After the system has access to the Virtualization channel, use `yum` to install the necessary packages. As root, execute the following where `<packages>` is a space-separated list of package names:

```
yum install <packages>
```

Alternatively, schedule the package installation via the RHN website. The following packages are necessary to configure Virtualization (additional packages will be installed as dependencies):

- `kernel-xen`: Linux kernel with Virtualization support compiled into it.
- `xen`: Virtualization tools needed to set up and maintain the virtual machines.
- `xen-libs`: Libraries necessary for the Virtualization applications.

- `virt-manager`: Graphical application for Virtualization administration (not necessary if using the interactive command-line utility `virt-install` instead).
- `gnome-applet-vm`: Desktop panel applet to monitor virtual domains (not necessary for systems without a graphical desktop).
- `libvirt`: API for Virtualization and utility for managing virtual domains. Also includes the `virsh` utility used to manage VMs.

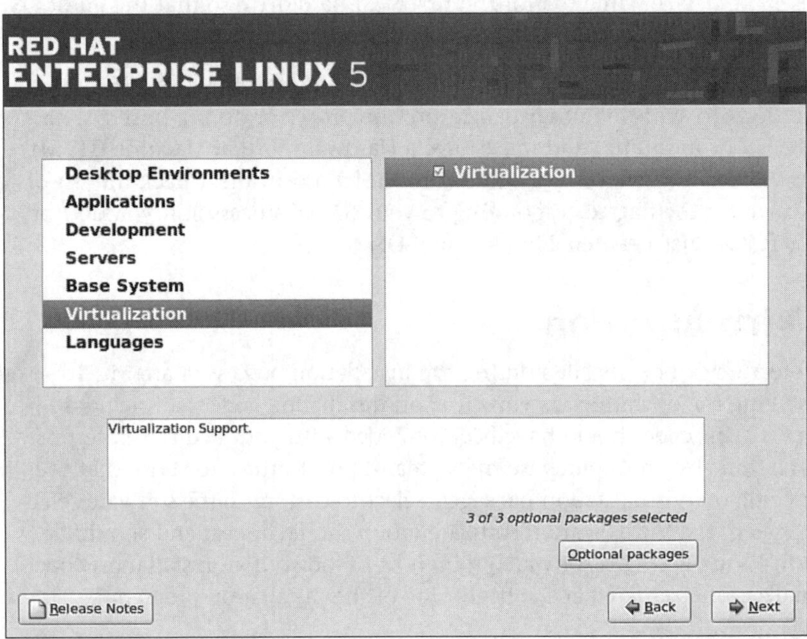

FIGURE B.1 Virtualization Software Group During Installation

The `kernel-xen` package installs the Linux kernel with Virtualization support compiled into it. It also adds a stanza for the Virtualization kernel to the GRUB configuration file `/etc/grub.conf` but does not set it to the default. To change it to the default, change the number following the `default` keyword with the stanza number for the Virtualization kernel (the kernel version for it ends with the keyword `xen`). The stanza count starts with the number 0 and goes from the top of the file to the bottom. After booting, the `uname -r` command can be used to determine which kernel is currently running.

Setting Up the VM and Installing the Guest OS

Before setting up a virtual machine, make sure you are running the Virtualization kernel as described in the last section. Execute the `uname -r` command and verify that the kernel version running ends with the `xen` keyword.

A virtual machine instance implemented with Virtualization is called a *domain*. Two programs are available for setting up a domain and installing the guest OS on the virtual machine: an interactive command-line utility `virt-install` and a graphical application named Virtual Machine Manager (`virt-manager`).

For a para-virtualized host, only network installation types (NFS, HTTP, and FTP) can be used for the installation of the guest OS. However, you can export the installation tree from the same system that is hosting the guest VM. Instructions for setting up for a network installation are provided in Chapter 1, "Installing Red Hat Enterprise Linux." For a fully virtualized host, an ISO image on the host filesystem, installation CD set, or DVD must be provided as the installation media.

TIP

Virtualization log files are located in the `/var/log/xen/` directory. Refer to these messages if an error occurs during creation or management of the virtual domains.

With the Virtual Machine Manager

To create the VM using a graphical interface, start the Virtual Machine Manager by executing the `virt-manager` command or selecting the **Applications** menu on the top panel of the desktop and then choosing **System Tools, Virtual Machine Manager**. If you are not the root user, you will be prompted for the root password before continuing. As shown in Figure B.2, select **Local Xen host** and click **Connect**. Even though it is seen as an option in the interface, connecting to a remote Virtualzation host is not yet implemented.

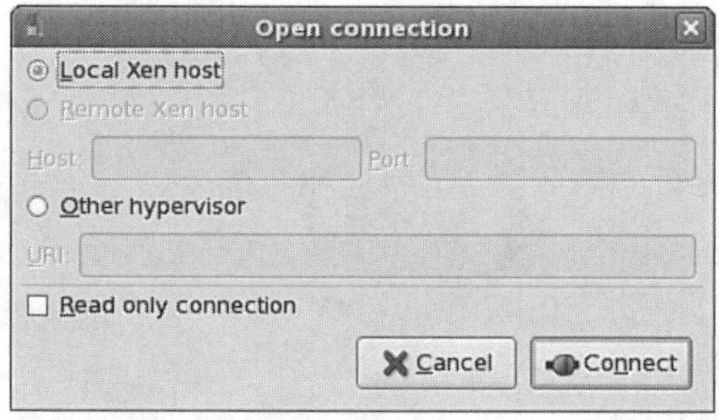

FIGURE B.2 Connecting to the Virtualization Host

To open the program without the ability to create new domains or modify existing domains, select the **Read only connection** option. In read-only mode, you can view the list of active domains and view the graphical and serial consoles for them, but you cannot modify their settings such as the amount of memory dedicated to them.

After connecting to the Virtualization host, all guest domains on the host are shown, with Domain-0 being the host OS running on the system. If no VMs are running (as is the case the first time you run the program to create the first VM), only Domain-0 is listed (see Figure B.3).

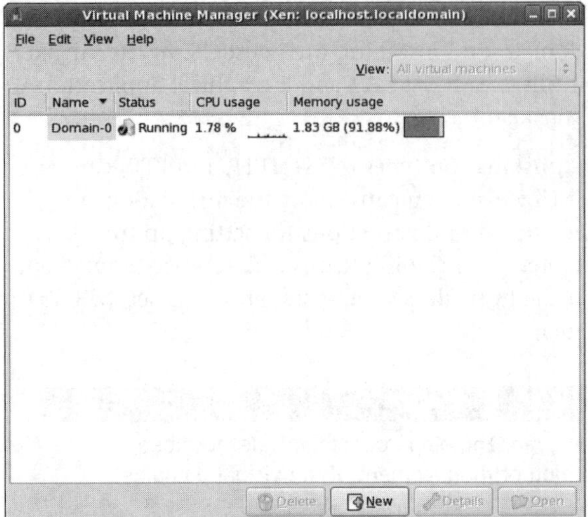

FIGURE B.3 Virtual Machine Manager

Click **New** on the bottom toolbar or select **File**, **New** to create a new domain. The wizard prompts you for the following information:

- *System name*: A unique descriptive name for the system. On the screen shown in Figure B.4, provide a name to use when managing VMs via the command line or the graphical program. It is also used as the configuration filename for the VM in the `/etc/xen/` directory.

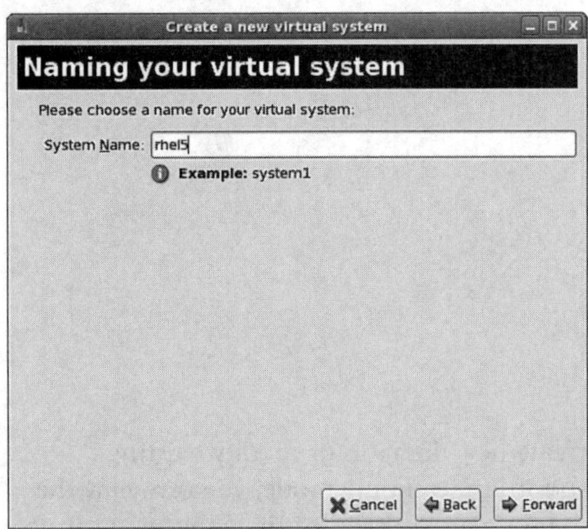

FIGURE B.4 Virtualization Domain Name

- *Virtualization method*: There are two types of virtualization: para-virtualization and full virtualization. If your hardware supports full virtualization as discussed earlier in this appendix, select one of the two methods as shown in Figure B.5. Otherwise, you are only allowed to select para-virtualization.

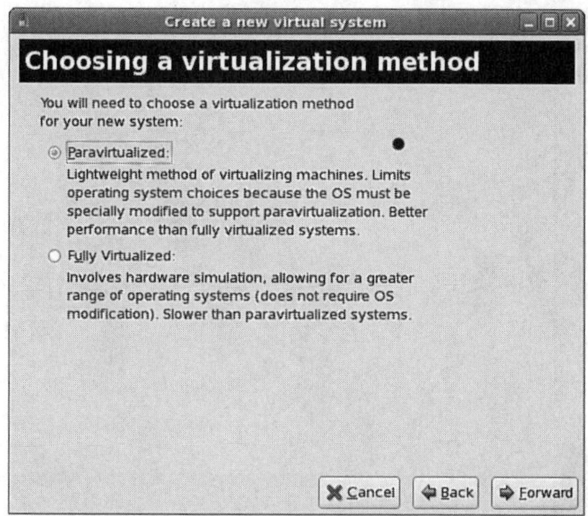

FIGURE B.5 Virtualization Method

- *Install media location*: For para-virtualization, provide the network location of the install media or the network location of the kickstart file to use for installation as shown in Figure B.6. The following formats are accepted (replace `<server>` with the hostname or IP address of the network file server and replace `location` with the directory containing the installation tree or the full path, including the filename, of the kickstart file):

```
nfs:<server>:/location
http://<server>/location
ftp://<server>/location
```

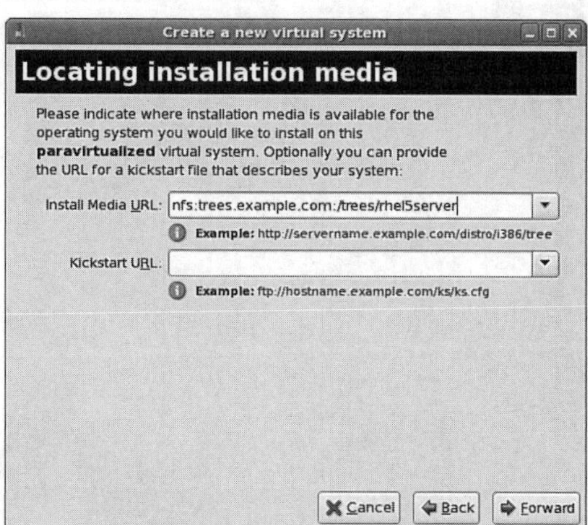

FIGURE B.6 Installation Media for Para-virtualization

For full virtualization, provide the location of the ISO image for the Red Hat Enterprise Linux version and variant to be installed on the VM or the full path to the installation CD or DVD as shown in Figure B.7.

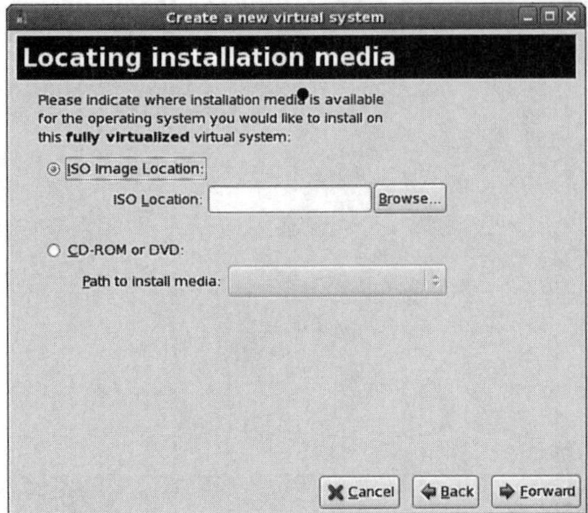

FIGURE B.7 Installation Media for Full Virtualization

- *Disk image location*: Provide the location of the disk image to use as the filesystem for the virtual machine as shown in Figure B.8. It can be either a disk partition or file on the host filesystem. If using a disk partition, it must already exist. If a file is specified and does not exist, a disk image file will be created using the size selected. Remember that the disk image size must be large enough to install the OS and store any files you might need on the local virtual filesystem for the VM. If you need more storage, the guest OS on the VM can access network storage using the same protocols as a normal Linux system such as NFS and Samba.

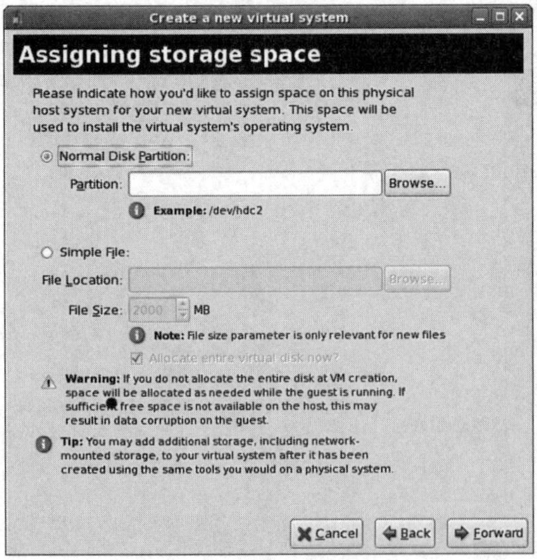

FIGURE B.8 Disk Image Location

- *Memory and CPU allocation*: Select the maximum amount of memory the VM has access to on the host system as shown in Figure B.9. If a smaller amount of startup memory is selected, the amount of startup memory is dedicated to the VM when it is started instead of the entire maximum amount of memory allowed. If more memory is needed by the VM later, the host system can allocate more memory to it up to the maximum amount configured.

  Select the number of virtual processors the VM should have as well. The VM cannot have more virtual processors than the host has physical processor cores. It is recommended that the VM have no more than one less virtual processor than the host has physical processor cores.

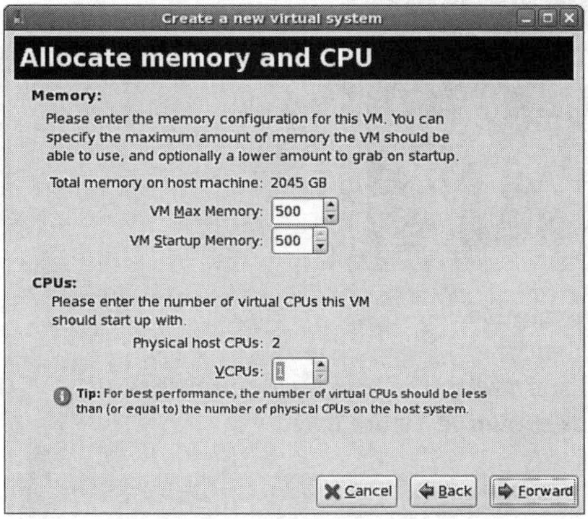

FIGURE B.9 System Resource Allocation

After reviewing the summary of the settings selected, click **Finish** to create the VM and show the virtual console through which the installation will occur. The configuration file `/etc/xen/<name>` is created. If the disk image doesn't exist, it is created as well. If you receive an error message that the domain can't be created, look in the `/var/log/xen/xend-debug.log` file for error messages or tracebacks. For example, the following message means that the host system does not have enough physical memory to allocate to the VM:

```
VmError: I need 262144 KiB, but dom0_min_mem is 262144 and shrinking to
262144 KiB would leave only 243968 KiB free.
```

If the host system is successful in creating the VM, a virtual console for the newly created VM appears. The new domain name appears in the domain list in the Virtual Machine Manager window. If you provided a kickstart file instead of a network installation tree, the contents of the Virtual Machine Manager window will show the OS being installed via kickstart instead. For a para-virtualized host, the installation starts with the language selection screen in Figure B.10.

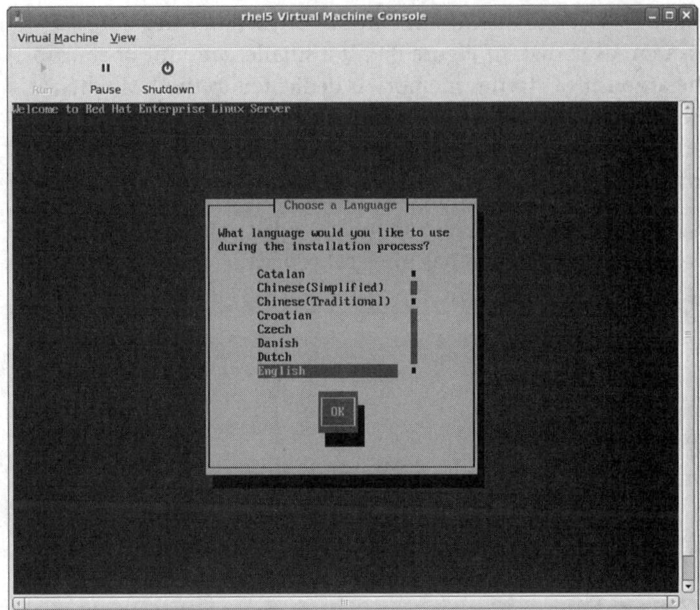

FIGURE B.10 Starting a Para-virtualization Installation

For a full virtualization host, the installation starts with the `boot:` prompt just as an installation would start on native hardware as shown in Figure B.11.

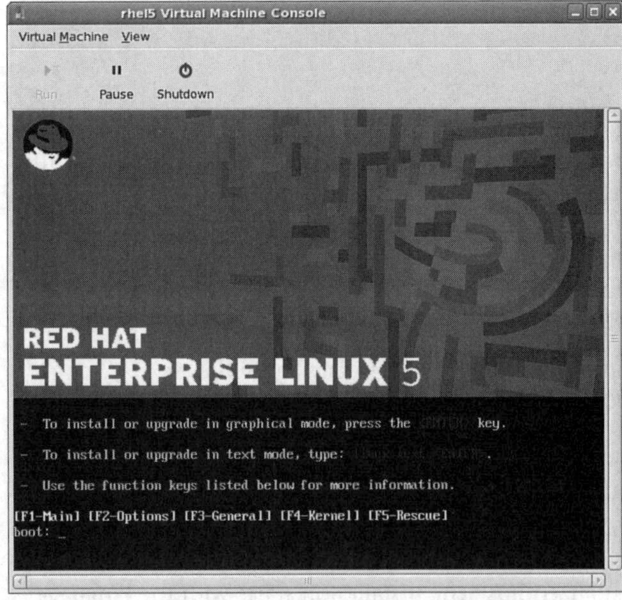

FIGURE B.11 Starting a Full Virtualization Installation

Follow the instructions from Chapter 1 to install the guest OS on the newly created VM.

The last step of the installation program is to click the **Reboot** button to reboot the system and complete the installation. After the VM shuts down for the reboot, the VM is not automatically restarted and the VM name disappears from the list of domains in the Virtual Machine Manager window. Refer to the section "Starting and Stopping the Virtual Machine" to learn how to start the VM and the guest OS.

With `virt-install`

The `virt-install` interactive command-line tool can be used to set up the domain and then start the installation program. Execute the `virt-install` command as root to begin. The same questions from the Virtual Machine Manager are asked along with whether the graphical or text-based installation program should be used. After the VM is successfully set up, the virtual machine window appears as with the graphical application. The command-line process should look similar to Listing B.1.

LISTING B.1 Creating a Virtualization Domain with `virt-install`

```
Would you like a fully virtualized guest (yes or no)?  This will allow you to run
unmodified operating systems. no
 What is the name of your virtual machine? rhel5
 How much RAM should be allocated (in megabytes)? 500
 What would you like to use as the disk (path)? /vm/rhel5
 How large would you like the disk to be (in gigabytes)? 4000
 Would you like to enable graphics support? (yes or no) yes
 What is the install location? nfs:installs.example.com:/trees/rhel5server


Starting install...
```

Just like with the Virtual Machine Manager, the system shuts down after the installation and will not automatically start up again. Refer to the section "Starting and Stopping the Virtual Machine" for detailed instructions.

Introducing the `virsh` Command

As of the initial release of Red Hat Enterprise Linux 5, the Virtual Machine Manager has limited functionality. A few VM management actions such as shutting down the guest OS and altering the amount of dedicated resources can be done with the Virtual Machine Manager. If you installed an updated version of Red Hat Enterprise Linux 5, refer to the *Release Notes* to determine if additional functionality has been added to the program.

To perform additional actions, the `virsh` and `xm` utilities are available to use from the command line of the host OS so that additional tasks can be performed.

CAUTION

All the `virsh` and `xm` commands given in this appendix must be executed on the host OS, *not* on the guest OS running inside the VM.

Development on the `virsh` utility started after `xm`, but it is rapidly developing. Its goal is to offer more functionality such as being able to maintain virtual machines from other programs such as VMWare instead of just from the Virtualization feature in Linux. Because it is projected that `virsh` is going to be the preferred utility, this appendix explains `virsh`. For a list of equivalent `xm` commands, refer to the "Managing VMs with the `xm` Utility" section at the end of this appendix.

The `virsh` commands can be executed in one of two ways. The `virsh` command can be executed as root from a shell prompt followed by a command and any options for the command:

```
virsh <command> <options>
```

It can also be started as an interactive so that just the commands and options need to be used. To start the interactive shell, type the `virsh` command at a shell prompt as root. The following prompt is then displayed:

```
virsh #
```

For example, the command to list the current domains (domains that are shut down are not shown) is `virsh list`. If you are in the interactive shell, the command would just be `list`.

Starting and Stopping the Virtual Machine

To start the VM again after installation or any time the VM is shut down, go to the shell prompt (such as starting a GNOME terminal) and execute the following command as root (where `<name>` is the unique name you gave the VM when setting it up earlier):

```
xm create -c <name>
```

NOTE

As of the initial release of Red Hat Enterprise Linux 5, the Virtual Machine Manager and the `virsh` utility do not include the ability to start a VM.

The pyGRUB menu is displayed as shown in Figure B.12. Select the OS to boot or let the default OS be selected and started.

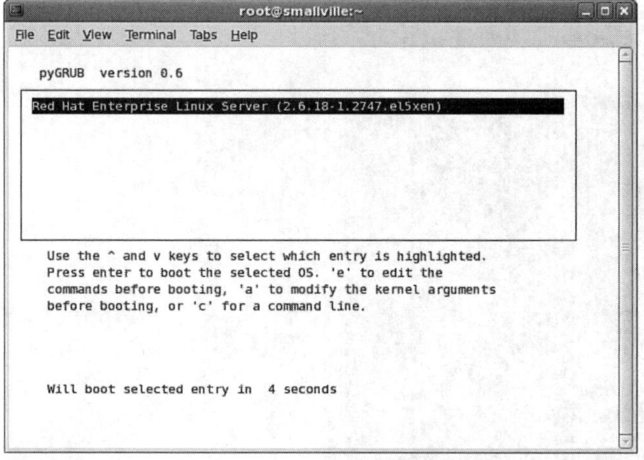

FIGURE B.12 Selecting OS to Boot

By default, the VM window (called the *console*) is not opened automatically to display the graphical bootup or the graphical desktop after the bootup. Start the Virtual Machine Manager if it is not already running, and go to the list of domains in the Virtual Machine Manager; the VM you just started should now appear in the list as shown in Figure B.13.

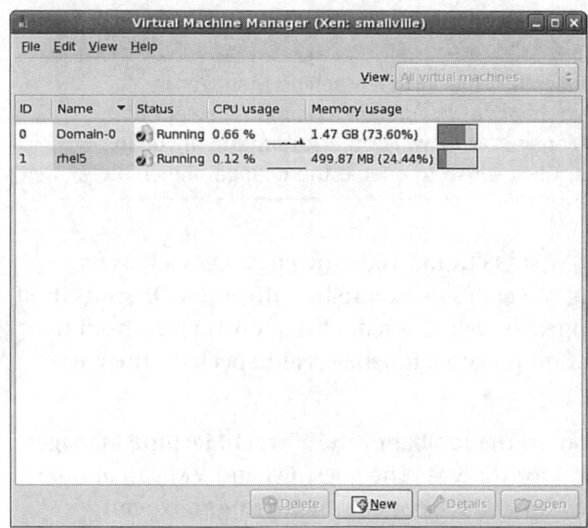

FIGURE B.13 Domain Running

Select it from the domain list, and double-click it to open the console for it. If this is the first time you have started the VM since the installation, the Setup Agent appears after the VM boots. Otherwise, the VM console shows the system booting up and then the login screen. After logging in to the system, the desktop appears as shown in Figure B.14 (unless the graphical desktop was not installed).

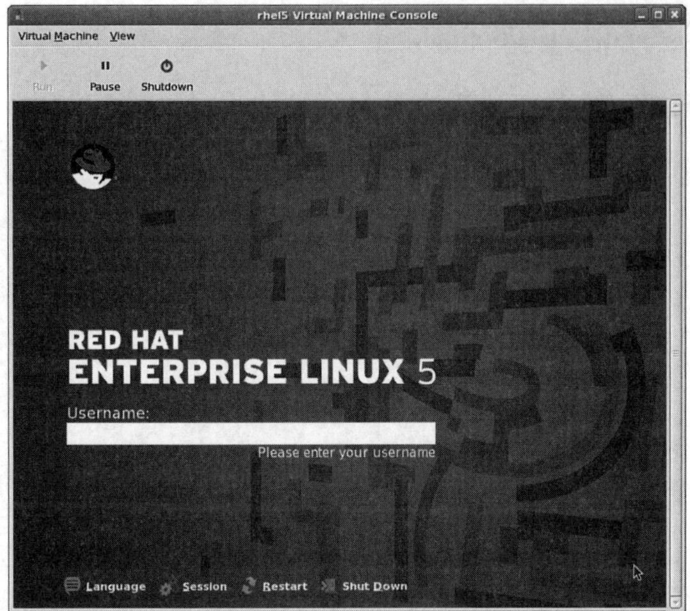

FIGURE B.14 Guest OS Running in the VM Console

TIP

To have the VM console opened automatically if the Virtual Machine Manager is already running when you execute the `xm create -c` <name> command, select **Edit**, **Preferences** from the Virtual Machine Manager window. For the **Automatically open consoles** option, select **For all domains**. Click **Close** to enable the change immediately.

If the shutdown request is given to the guest OS from inside the guest OS such as by selecting it from the menus or executing the `shutdown` command, the guest OS shuts itself down properly, and then the VM is stopped as well. If a reboot request is given from the guest OS (other than during the installation process), it behaves as expected—the guest OS reboots, keeping the VM active.

Alternatively, click the **Shutdown** button on the toolbar of the Virtual Machine Manager window containing the graphical desktop for the VM. The guest OS and VM can also be shut down by executing the following command as root at a shell prompt, where `<domain>` is the unique name for the domain:

```
virsh shutdown <domain>
```

The command returns after sending the shutdown action. To verify that the shutdown has been completed, either execute the `virsh list` command and make sure the domain is not in the list or watch the Virtual Machine Manager domain list until the domain is removed from the list.

To reboot the guest OS, execute the following as root from a shell prompt on the host OS:

```
virsh reboot <domain>
```

Just like the `shutdown` command for `virsh`, the command returns after sending the action, not after the reboot is complete.

TIP

An applet can be added to the desktop panel for quick monitoring of the guest domains. To add it to the panel, right-click on the panel, select **Add to Panel...**, and select **VM Applet.**

Modifying Dedicated Resources

To modify the settings for a guest domain using the Virtual Machine Manager, the domain must be running. Start the domain if necessary before continuing. From the domain list in the Virtual Machine Manager window, select the desired domain from the list, and select **Edit**, **Machine details** from the pull-down menu. The **Overview** tab on the **Details** window shows the VM name, the UUID for the virtual disk, the VM status such as Running or Paused, the CPU usage, and the memory usage. The **Hardware** tab as shown in Figure B.15 shows the virtual system resources assigned to the VM.

NOTE

If running the Virtual Machine Manager in read-only mode, you are not allowed to change hardware allocation for the VM.

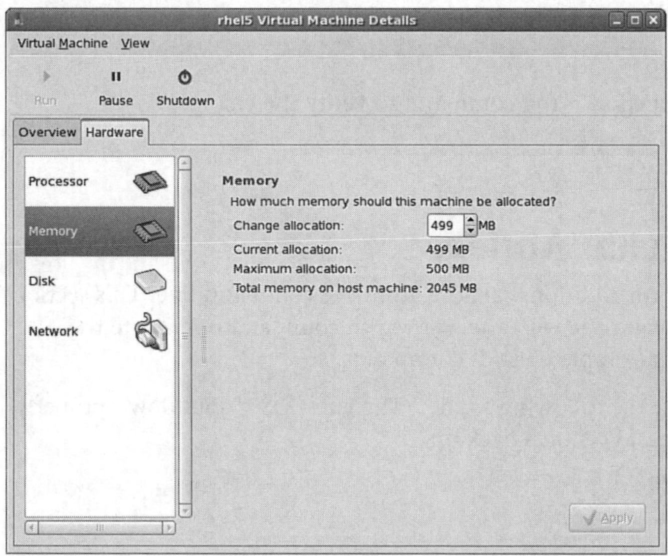

FIGURE B.15 Hardware Allocation for the VM

The number of virtual processors and amount of dedicated memory (both initial allocation and maximum allowed allocation) can be changed from the **Hardware** tab. Click **Apply** to enable the changes immediately.

To view information about a domain from the command line or verify hardware allocation changes, execute the following as root:

```
virsh dominfo <domain>
```

The output should look similar to Listing B.2.

LISTING B.2 Domain Information

```
Id:             2
Name:           rhel5
UUID:           b5c8ebec-dfe1-910e-26e9-80f2c7caccf0
OS Type:        linux
State:          blocked
CPU(s):         1
CPU time:       21.8s
Max memory:     512000 kB
Used memory:    511808 kB
```

The same hardware allocation changes can be made with the `virsh` command as the root user. To change the memory allocation, use `setmem` to set the amount of currently allocated memory, `setmaxmem` to set the maximum allowed memory allocation, and `setvcpus` to set the number of virtual CPUs for the domain:

```
virsh setmem <domain> <kb>
virsh setmaxmem <domain> <kb>
virsh setvcpus <num>
```

After setting each option, use the following command to verify the change:

```
virsh dominfo <domain>
```

Performing Additional Actions

The `virsh` command can perform additional actions from the command line. This section highlights a few. Refer to the man page with the `man virsh` command or execute the `virsh help` command to view a complete list of commands.

To reboot the guest OS, execute the following as root. The guest OS is shut down properly, the VM is restarted, and the guest OS boots back up.

```
virsh reboot <domain>
```

The command returns to the prompt as soon as the reboot command is sent to the guest OS and VM. Return of the prompt does not mean the reboot has been completed.

It is also possible to suspend the guest OS and VM. In the graphical console window, click **Pause** to suspend, and click it again to resume. Figure B.16 shows the paused state from the graphical console.

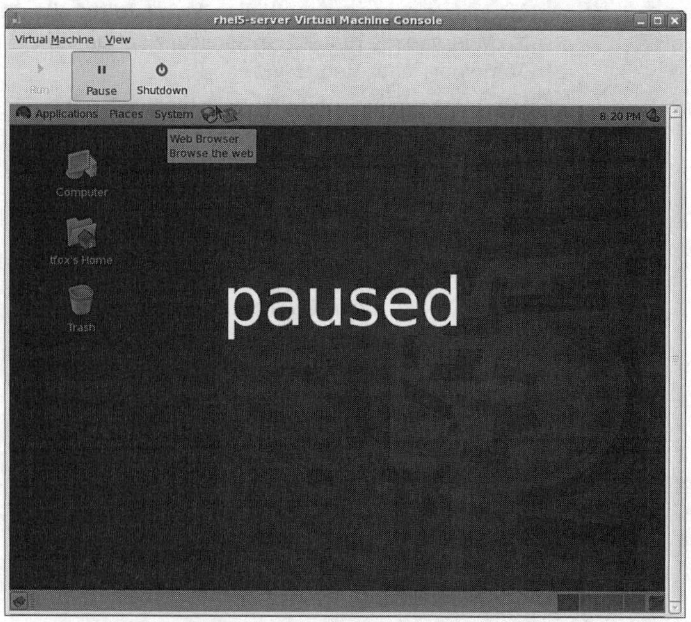

FIGURE B.16 Guest OS and VM Paused

From the command line, use the following two commands as root to pause and resume:

```
virsh suspend <domain>
virsh resume <domain>
```

Managing VMs with the xm Utility

The xm command can also be used to manage the VMs instead of virsh, or in addition to virsh. Because virsh has already been discussed, this section just gives a brief list of equivalent xm commands. It also includes a few additional commands not yet implemented for virsh.

Refer to the xm man page for a complete listing of command-line options. Table B.1 summarizes the most commonly used commands. Replace <domain> with the guest domain name configured during creation of the domain. All xm commands must be run as the root user.

TABLE B.1 Common xm Commands

Command	Description
`xm create -c <domain>`	Start an inactive domain.
`xm list`	List all running Virtualization domains along with information about them such as how much memory is allocated to each domain.
`xm mem-set <domain> <mb>`	Amount of memory to initially allocate to the VM. If VM is already running, dynamically set amount of memory allocated to VM.
`xm mem-max <domain> <mb>`	Maximum amount of memory in megabytes the domain is allowed to use.
`xm vcpu-set <domain> <num>`	Set number of virtual CPUs for the domain.
`xm vcpu-list <domain>`	List virtual CPU information for the domain.
`xm pause <domain>`	Pause the domain.
`xm unpause <domain>`	Unpause the domain.
`xm reboot <domain>`	Reboot the domain. The command will return before the reboot is finished. Use `xm list` to determine when the VM is back up and running.
`xm uptime <domain>`	Display uptime for domain. If no domain is given, all active domains and uptimes are shown.
`xm shutdown <domain>`	Shut down the domain.

APPENDIX C

Preventing Security Breaches with ExecShield

IN THIS APPENDIX

- How ExecShield Works
- Determining Status of ExecShield
- Disabling ExecShield

ExecShield is designed to prevent security breaches caused by software programs written to crawl through the Internet looking for systems with common vulnerabilities such as worms and viruses. It is enabled in the kernel and works in a way that is nonintrusive to the user. Its goal is not to defend against the expert hacker who has broken into your local network or an employee inside the company who already has access to parts of the network. Its goal is to prevent against intruders using scripts that look for vulnerabilities in the way a program running with root privileges is written.

You will still need to develop a security plan for keeping your systems secure while allowing authorized users to access them. However, ExecShield should help you avoid common exploits known to affect other operating systems.

ExecShield is enabled by default in Red Hat Enterprise Linux. This appendix gives a brief explanation of how ExecShield accomplishes this goal and how to disable it in Red Hat Enterprise Linux should it interfere with other programs.

How ExecShield Works

One of the ExecShield memory-management techniques is using random memory locations each time a program is started. Using random memory locations prevents worms or viruses from knowing which parts of memory to overwrite with executables that breach the security of the system. For example, if the same memory location is used by a program every time the program is run, a hacker can write a virus that waits until the program has written to memory and then overwrites that part of the memory. When the program goes to execute the instructions in memory at a later time, the virus has already overwritten it, and the code from the virus is executed instead. The virus code is executed with whatever permissions the program has. If the program is being run as the root user, significant damage can be done to the system or confidential data stored on the system can be sent to another computer over the network on the Internet.

ExecShield also marks memory locations that store program data as nonexecutable. If a virus or worm manages to overwrite parts of a program's memory for program data, the code cannot be executed with ExecShield enabled.

Worms and viruses look for common programming errors that allow for exploits such as the buffer overflow. If an application is not written properly, a buffer overflow operation overfills the memory buffer, which is a fixed size, until it overwrites the return address for the memory location so that the worm or virus can execute a different program with all the privileges of the application that was running in that memory location, including ones running as the root user.

Because the worm or virus must fill the buffer before overwriting the return address, the code to execute is often written to the buffer and then the return address is redirected to the code in the buffer, which is usually only filled with data. ExecShield works by separating executables and application data so that application data cannot be executed.

But what if the exploit points the return address to somewhere other than the buffer it overflowed to get to the return address? ExecShield combats this with two features:

- Ascii Zone
- Address Space Randomization

Functions that use string buffers stop when they reach zero. Ascii Zone tries to place as many string buffers as possible at memory locations that have a zero in the address so that an exploit that tries to overflow a string buffer fails. Address Space Randomization tries to use random memory locations for a program each time it starts so an exploit cannot predict where it is in memory.

Determining Status of ExecShield

ExecShield is enabled by default in the Red Hat Enterprise Linux kernel. To verify that ExecShield is enabled, execute the following command:

```
cat /proc/sys/kernel/exec-shield
```

If it returns the value of `1`, ExecShield is enabled. The value of `0` means it is disabled. You can also determine the status of ExecShield by executing the following command, but this command must be run as the root user:

```
sysctl -a | grep exec-shield
```

If it returns the following, ExecShield is enabled:

```
kernel.exec-shield = 1
```

Again, a value of 0 indicates that ExecShield is disabled.

Disabling ExecShield

ExecShield can be disabled by using `sysctl` or modifying the boot loader configuration file to set the `exec-shield` kernel parameter to `0`.

To disable ExecShield using `sysctl`, execute the following command:

```
sysctl -w kernel.exec-shield=0
```

ExecShield is disabled immediately. However, executing this command alone does not disable ExecShield on subsequent reboots. To disable ExecShield for all reboots, add the following line to `/etc/sysctl.conf` (as root):

```
kernel.exec-shield = 0
```

Changes made to this file are not enabled until a reboot occurs, because the file is only read once during system startup. To enable the change immediately, the `sysctl -w kernel.exec-shield=0` command still needs to be executed.

Another way to disable ExecShield at boot time is to add a boot parameter and value to the boot loader configuration file. For x86 and x86_64 systems that use GRUB as the boot loader, append the following line to the `kernel` line in `/etc/grub.conf` (as root):

```
exec-shield=0
```

Repeat this step for the kernel stanzas for which you want ExecShield disabled. Remember that this boot option and value must be added to any kernel stanzas added to the GRUB configuration file at a later time such as when a new kernel is installed.

C

CAUTION

If the same boot parameter is set in `/etc/grub.conf` and in `/etc/sysctl.conf`, the value from `sysctl.conf` takes precedence. If you add boot parameters to the GRUB configuration file, make sure there aren't any conflicting settings in `/etc/sysctl.conf`.

Changes to `grub.conf` do not go into effect immediately. The file is only read once during startup. The next time the system is booted, ExecShield will be disabled.

TIP

Adding a boot parameter to the boot loader for other architectures is described in Chapter 2, "Post-Installation Configuration."

To re-enable ExecShield, follow these same instructions, except set the value to `1` instead of `0`.

Refer to the "Determining the Status of ExecShield" section for instructions on how to verify that ExecShield has been disabled or enabled, depending on what value you have set.

APPENDIX D
Troubleshooting

IN THIS APPENDIX

- Installation and Configuration Troubleshooting
- OS Core Concepts Troubleshooting
- System Administration Troubleshooting
- Network Troubleshooting
- Monitoring and Tuning Troubleshooting
- Security Troubleshooting

When a failure or inadequate system performance occurs without an obvious solution, it can be quite frustrating. This appendix contains a list of common troubleshooting questions divided into six parts. The parts correspond to the six parts into which this book is divided to make it easier to find questions relevant to your problems. This appendix cannot address all possible issues, but hopefully it will provide a starting point for solving some of them.

Installation and Configuration Troubleshooting

Q. I have set up an FTP server with the ISO image files necessary for installation, but when I start the installation, I receive an error message that the installation media can't be found on the FTP server. How do I get the installation program to recognize the ISOs of the FTP server?

A. FTP and HTTP installations require the installation files from the ISO files be loopback mounted, one installation CD per directory. Refer to the "Using the ISO Files" section in Chapter 1, "Installing Red Hat Enterprise Linux," for details.

Q. How do I determine which repositories were enabled by the registration number entered during installation?

A. Look in the `/var/log/anaconda.log` file and search for the key word `regkey`. For example, the following lines show that Virtualization was enabled with the registration key by listing the VT repository:

```
03:14:17 INFO    : moving (1) to step regkey
03:14:44 INFO    : Adding ['VT'] repo
03:14:44 INFO    : Adding ['Server'] repo
03:14:44 INFO    : repopaths is {'virt': ['VT'],
➥'base': ['Server']}
```

Q. I didn't set my hostname during installation, and my DHCP server doesn't set it for me. How do I configure a hostname for my system?

A. As the root user, edit the `HOSTNAME` line in the `/etc/sysconfig/network` file. Sets its value to the desired hostname. This value is only read at boot time. To change the hostname immediately, execute the command `hostname <newhostname>` as the root user.

Q. I modified my boot parameters as described in Chapter 2, "Post-Installation Configuration." How do I verify that the boot parameter was used?

A. Use the command `cat /proc/cmdline` to view a list of options passed to the kernel at boot time.

Q. The first time my system booted after installation, the Setup Agent asked whether I wanted a firewall. I enabled it at the time. Now, I want to write my own custom firewall and need to disable the default firewall. How do I disable it?

A. Select the **System** menu from the top panel of the desktop and then select **Administration, Security Level and Firewall.** Enter the root password if prompted. The same interface used in the Setup Agent is displayed. Select **Disabled** from the pull-down menu, and then click **OK**. The changes take place immediately. Refer to Chapter 24, "Configuring a Firewall," if you need help writing custom firewall rules using IPTables.

Q. I received an email alert stating that some of the GFS packages have been updated. When I try to use Yum to update them, it says no updates are available. How do I download and install the updates?

A. Most likely, the system is not subscribed to the RHN software channel that provides the packages and updated packages for GFS. Log in to your RHN account at rhn.redhat.com, and make sure the system is subscribed to the correct channel. The channel containing the GFS packages will be a child channel of the Red Hat Enterprise Linux parent channel.

Q. After installing Red Hat Enterprise Linux as a guest OS in a VM using the Virtualization feature, the installation program says it is going to reboot, but the system shuts down and never comes back up. How do I start the VM again?

A. To start the VM after installation (and any time the VM is shutdown), execute the following command as root, where `<name>` is the unique name given to the VM during setup:

```
xm create -c <name>
```

Even if you are using the Virtual Machine Manager graphical program, this command must be performed on the command line. As of the initial release of Red Hat Enterprise Linux 5, the Virtual Machine Manager interface does not allow the VM to be started.

OS Core Concepts Troubleshooting

Q. I am trying to create a directory named data in my home directory, but every time I execute the `mkdir /data` command, I receive the error message `Permission denied`. Why am I not allowed to create a new directory?

A. If you are trying to create a directory in your home directory from the command line, be sure the current working directory is your home directory, and then execute the command `mkdir data`, without the slash (`/`) in front of `data`. The slash in front of the directory name means that you are providing the full path to the directory, and you don't have permission to create a directory on the top level of the filesystem.

Q. I want to update the RPM package for the Apache web server, but I have customized the configuration file already. If I update the package, will I lose my customized configuration file?

A. No. If you have a modified configuration file when updating the RPM that provides it, one of two actions occurs. If the default configuration file in the updated package hasn't changed between the package version you have installed and the version of the updated package, the configuration file is left alone because it still works with the updated package version.

If the configuration file has changed in the updated package version, the existing configuration file is renamed with a `.rpmsave` extension such as `httpd.conf.rpmsave`, and the new configuration file from the updated package is saved to the filesystem. If this occurs, the modifications must be redone in the new configuration file, but the old configuration file can be referenced because it is not lost.

Q. I need to remove some packages from my Red Hat Enterprise Linux server because they are not needed for the function of the server. Can I just use the `rpm -e <packages>` command to remove them or do I need to use the Yum utility to remove them?

A. You can use either the `rpm` or the `yum` command to delete the packages from the system, but using Yum has one major advantage. If the package being removed is required to be installed by other packages, the `rpm` command displays an error message listing the packages that require the one trying to be removed, and the package is not removed. Yum can provide this same list and also ask whether you want the additional packages removed at the same time. You can review the list of additional packages and decide whether it is safe to remove them as well.

Q. I modified the `/etc/modprobe.conf` file to change the kernel module used for the network card in my system. After rebooting to enable the changes, how do I verify that the different module is being used?

A. The `lsmod` command lists all the kernel modules currently loaded. Use the command `lsmod | grep <modulename>`, where `<modulename>` is the name of the new module to use. If the command outputs a line containing information about the module, it has been loaded.

Q. When trying to use the `setfacl` command to set the ACLs for a file, I receive the error message `Operation not supported`. I am using the syntax for the command from Chapter 4, "Understanding Linux Concepts." Why is it not working?

A. If you see this error message, most likely you have forgotten to enable ACLs for the filesystem in `/etc/fstab` or forgotten to reboot to enable the changes to `/etc/fstab`.

Refer to the section "Enabling ACLs" in Chapter 7, "Managing Storage," for details on modifying the `/etc/fstab` file.

Q. My system is running the 64-bit version of Red Hat Enterprise Linux. Most of the documentation I read refers to files in the `/lib/` and `/usr/lib/` directories, but I cannot find these files on my system. Where do I get these files?

A. Most likely, you are just looking in the wrong directory. Most of the packages and libraries for the 64-bit version of Red Hat Enterprise Linux are built specifically for the 64-bit architecture. Look in the `/lib64/` and `/usr/lib64/` directories instead.

System Administration Troubleshooting

Q. I am exporting the home directories of my organization to all workstations from a SAN using NFS. Because NFS does not perform any authentication, I need to make sure all the UIDs for each user are the same on all workstations. How do I do this?

A. This can be accomplished in a few different ways. If you are adding local users to each workstation, you can either specify the UID to use when creating each user with the `-u <uid>` option to the `useradd` command or select the **Specify user ID manually** option in the User Manager graphical application.

Or, you can configure all workstations to use a network authentication method for user login so that the user database comes from one location, meaning all the UIDs used on the workstations are the same. For more information about network authentication methods, refer to Chapter 12, "Identity Management."

Q. I am using the `tar` utility from Chapter 10, "Techniques for Backup and Recovery," in my backup process. However, when I recover the files, the ACLs for the files are not preserved. How do I back up the ACLs for the filesystem as well?

A. The `tar` and `dump` programs do not preserve ACLs. The `star` utility must be used instead. Installing the `star` RPM package will allow you to use the `star` program.

Q. The filesystem containing my `/boot` directory has failed, and I have installed a new hard drive with a new `/boot` partition, including files restored from backup. How do I configure the system to use the new `/boot` partition if I can start the operating system?

A. To boot the system without mounting any filesystems, boot in to rescue mode as described in the "Recovery and Repair" section of Chapter 10. Once the system is in rescue mode, mount the filesystem containing the `/etc/fstab` file. Modify the `/etc/fstab` file to use the new `/boot` partition.

Q. My system is configured to adjust the time and date for Daylights Savings Time. I have a cron task scheduled during the hour skipped for Daylights Savings time. Will the cron task get executed?

A. Cron is written such that any time change of less than three hours is compensated for by running any tasks scheduled for the missing time immediately. So, any jobs scheduled during the skipped hour is run immediately after the time change.

Network Troubleshooting

Q. I have an NIS server configured for my network for user authentication on all workstations. It recently had a disk failure and needed to be repaired. During the downtime, users could not log into their computers because the authentication server was down. Is there a way to allow users to log in when the NIS server goes down?

A. If your user database doesn't change that often, you can have a backup hard drive or hard drives ready to use should another disk failure occur. However, this solution still includes some downtime to change the disks. A better solution would be to set up a slave NIS server. Its user database is updated from the NIS master server, and it will answer NIS requests should the master go down or get overloaded. Users on the workstations will not even notice if the master NIS server goes down.

Q. I have a firewall that only allows traffic on specific ports. I know that NFS uses port 2049 by default, and I have not changed this. However, my NFS connections still aren't working. How do I allow NFS connections to my clients?

A. NFS does use port 2049. It also uses several other ports, some of which are not static by default. Refer to the "Assigning Static NFS Ports" section of Chapter 13, "Network File Sharing" for details.

Q. I have changed the default port of the Apache Web Server. I don't receive any errors when starting the daemon, but how do I connect to the server from a web browser now?

A. If you have modified the default port number of Apache, append the IP address, hostname of the server, or the registered domain name such as www.example.com with a colon and the port number:

http://www.example.com:<portnum>

Q. How do I know if my system is dropping network packets?

A. If you suspect packets are being dropped during network transfers, look at output of the `ifconfig` command. The stanza for each interface contains a line for RX and a line for TX packets. Read these lines and look for the number after `dropped`. If packets are being dropped, the number of dropped packets are listed as in the following:

```
RX packets:176430 errors:0 dropped:1567 overruns:0 frame:0
TX packets:160707 errors:0 dropped:5873 overruns:0 carrier:0
```

D

Q. I need to start a graphical program from a remote server. I used the SSH utility to log into it. But, when I run the command to start the graphical program, I see the following error:

```
Unable to initialize graphical environment. Most likely cause of failure
is that the tool was not run using a graphical environment. Please either
start your graphical user interface or set your DISPLAY variable.


Caught exception: could not open display
```

A. You need to enable X11 forwarding to be able to display a graphical interface on a remote system via SSH. Use the `-Y` option when executing the `ssh` command to connect to the server:

```
ssh -Y <servername>
```

Monitoring and Tuning Troubleshooting

Q. How do I limit the amount of memory each user is allowed to use so one user can't hog all the memory and slow down the other users?

A. The `/etc/security/limits.conf` file allows an administrator to limit the amount of memory locked in by an individual user or a user group. The file must be edited by the root user. Each line in the file contains four values:

```
<domain>        <type>  <item>          <value>
```

The `<domain>` value is a valid username or a group name preceded by the @ symbol such as `@legal`. The type must be either `soft` for enforcing as a soft limit or `hard` for enforcing as a hard limit. The item should be `memlock` for limiting locked in memory. The value is the value of the limit, which is an integer that represents the maximum amount of memory in kilobytes.

TIP

Read the comments in `/etc/security/limits.conf` and the `limits.conf` man page for details on how to limit other items such as maximum filesize allowed by a user and maximum number of users allowed to log into the system at the same time.

Q. The processors in my four-way server were being maxed out, so I installed two more processors. How do I tell whether Linux recognizes the new processors?

A. The kernel should automatically detect the new processors and balance the load between all processors. To verify the processors are recognized, use the `cat /proc/cpuinfo` command to view a list of all processors found by the kernel. You should see a processor stanza for each processor. If you have multi-core processors, each processor core is listed as a separate processor. Refer to Chapter 8, "64-Bit, Multi-Core, and Hyper-Threading Technology Processors" for details on reading the output for multi-core processors.

Q. Why does the syslog only report recent data?

A. If the syslog were allowed to grow indefinitely, it would eventually fill up the partition that it resides on. The logrotate daemon allows the syslog to be flushed out at a specified interval. By default, the logrotate daemon will keep up to four weeks of previous system logs. Once every week, the current `/var/log/messages` file will be renamed to `/var/log/messages.1` and a new `/var/log/messages` file will be created. If you need to keep syslogs for more than four weeks, this can be configured in the `/etc/logrotate.conf` file.

Q. Why is my system running slow?

A. Poor system performance can be caused by a number of factors. More often than not, performance problems are caused by excessive demand of the CPU, system memory, or the I/O subsystem.

Start troubleshooting by using the `sysstat` utilities as discussed in Chapter 20, "Monitoring System Resources" to determine if any of your resources are being 100% utilized for prolonged periods of time. Also consider writing scripts and scheduling them with cron so you can collect this data on a consistent basis as discussed in "Automating Tasks with Scripts," also in Chapter 20.

Q. Several times on my network file server a user has used all the free disk space in the `/home` partition, causing all users to receive failure to write to disc errors. How can I monitor the disk space on the partition and limit users to a specific amount of disk space?

A. Monitoring the amount of disk space free can be done easily with the audit daemon as discussed in Chapter 25, "Linux Auditing System." To limit the amount of disk space a user is allowed, try using disk quotas is discussed in Chapter 7, "Managing Storage."

Q. I suspect that the I/O transfer rates for my system are slower than they are supposed to be. How can I determine what the actual transfer rates are for my hard drives?

A. Try using `iostat` as discussed in Chapter 20 to monitor the transfer rates over a period of time. After gathering this information for a few weeks or even a month, calculate the averages to determine if your hard drives are performing adequately. Remember this task can be automated with cron as discussed in Chapter 11, "Automating Tasks with Scripts."

Q. I am seeing the message `kernel: CPU0: Temperature above threshold, cpu clock throttled` displayed at the console and virtual terminals. What is causing this and how can I prevent it?

A. This message is displayed when the processor has reached its maximum safe temperature. If the processor goes above this threshold, it might harm the processor. If you see this warning, check the processor fan to make sure it is running and seated properly. If it is not running or there is physical damage, replace the processor fan.

If the fan seems to be working properly, check the BIOS of your system for processor fan settings to make sure it is allowed to run at full capacity should it need to. If you still see the message, try replacing the processor with a known good processor or take the processor somewhere to be tested.

Security Troubleshooting

Q. I have stopped all unnecessary services on my servers with external IP addresses and blocked all unnecessary connection requests with IPTables. However, I would like to monitor which ports are open on each server to make sure someone hasn't compromised my system and opened up ports for other uses. How do I get a list of open ports?

A. Use the `nmap` program. If the system is registered with Red Hat Network, issue the `yum install nmap` command as root to install it. Then, use execute the `nmap <address>` command where `<address>` is the IP address or hostname of the system to scan. A list of open ports and the service associated with it are listed as in the following:

```
Starting Nmap 4.11 ( http://www.insecure.org/nmap/ ) at 2007-01-21 00:26 EST
Interesting ports on smallville (127.0.0.1):
Not shown: 1672 closed ports
PORT     STATE SERVICE
22/tcp   open  ssh
25/tcp   open  smtp
111/tcp  open  rpcbind
139/tcp  open  netbios-ssn
445/tcp  open  microsoft-ds
631/tcp  open  ipp
671/tcp  open  unknown
2049/tcp open  nfs
```

Q. I am using the default firewall from the Security Level tool. It is working for me except that I need to allow connections for an additional port for the corporate VPN. Can I continue to use the default security level and just add an IPTables rule for another port?

A. Yes. Start the Security Level tool by selecting the **System** menu from the top panel and then selecting **Administration, Security Level and Firewall.** You can also execute the `system-config-securitylevel` command to start the tool. At the bottom of the **Firewall Options** tab, there is an **Other ports** area. Click the triangle icon beside the **Other ports** label to show a table of ports. It should be empty since you haven't added any ports yet. Click the **Add** button to add your additional ports. When finished, click **OK** in the main window of the tool to enable the change immediately. Execute the `iptables -L` command to verify that the rule has been added.

Q. After modifying the `/etc/audit/audit.rules` file and restarting the daemon, I get the following error message:

```
There was an error in line 26 of /etc/audit/audit.rules
```

What does this mean and how do I fix it?

A. It means that there is a syntax error on line 26 of the rules file. Re-edit the file to fix the syntax error, and restart the deamon with the `service auditd restart` command. Then use the `auditctl -l` command to list all active audit rules and watches to verify.

Index

NUMBERS

A

How can we make this index more useful? Email us at indexes@samspublishing.com

D

E

F

G

H

I

J - K

L

M

N

O

P

Q

R

S

T

U

V

Z

THIS BOOK IS SAFARI ENABLED

INCLUDES FREE 45-DAY ACCESS TO THE ONLINE EDITION

The Safari® Enabled icon on the cover of your favorite technology book means the book is available through Safari Bookshelf. When you buy this book, you get free access to the online edition for 45 days.

Safari Bookshelf is an electronic reference library that lets you easily search thousands of technical books, find code samples, download chapters, and access technical information whenever and wherever you need it.

TO GAIN 45-DAY SAFARI ENABLED ACCESS TO THIS BOOK:

- Go to **http://www.samspublishing.com/safarienabled**
- Complete the brief registration form
- Enter the coupon code found in the front of this book on the "Copyright" page

If you have difficulty registering on Safari Bookshelf or accessing the online edition, please e-mail customer-service@safaribooksonline.com.